Praise for
Designing Software Product Lines with UML

"*Designing Software Product Lines with UML* is well-written, informative, and addresses a very important topic. It is a valuable contribution to the literature in this area, and offers practical guidance for software architects and engineers."

—Alan Brown
Distinguished Engineer,
Rational Software,
IBM Software Group

"Gomaa's process and UML extensions allow development teams to focus on feature-oriented development and provide a basis for improving the level of reuse across multiple software development efforts. This book will be valuable to any software development professional who needs to manage across projects and wants to focus on creating software that is consistent, reusable, and modular in nature."

—Jeffrey S Hammond
Group Marketing Manager,
Rational Software
IBM Software Group

"This book brings together a good range of concepts for understanding software product lines and provides an organized method for developing product lines using object-oriented techniques with the UML. Once again, Hassan has done an excellent job in balancing the needs of both experienced and novice software engineers."

—Robert G. Pettit IV, Ph.D.
Adjunct Professor of Software Engineering,
George Mason University

"This breakthrough book provides a comprehensive step-by-step approach on how to develop software product lines, which is of great strategic benefit to industry. The development of software product lines enables significant reuse of software architectures. Practitioners will benefit from the well-defined PLUS process and rich case studies."

—Hurley V. Blankenship II
Program Manager,
Justice and Public Safety,
Science Applications International Corporation

"The Product Line UML based Software engineering (PLUS) is leading edge. With the author's wide experience and deep knowledge, PLUS is well harmonized with architectural and design pattern technologies."

—Michael Shin
Assistant Professor,
Texas Tech University

Designing Software
Product Lines with UML

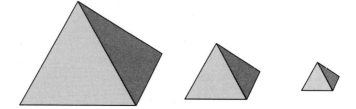

The Addison-Wesley Object Technology Series

Grady Booch, Ivar Jacobson, and James Rumbaugh, Series Editors
For more information, check out the series web site at www.awprofessional.com/otseries.

The Component Software Series

Clemens Szyperski, Series Editor
For more information, check out the series web site at www.awprofessional.com/csseries.

Designing Software Product Lines with UML

From Use Cases to Pattern-Based Software Architectures

Hassan Gomaa

George Mason University

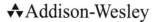 Addison-Wesley

Boston • San Francisco • New York • Toronto • Montreal
London • Munich • Paris • Madrid
Capetown • Sydney • Tokyo • Singapore • Mexico City

Many of the designations used by manufacturers and sellers to distinguish their products are claimed as trademarks. Where those designations appear in this book, and Addison-Wesley was aware of a trademark claim, the designations have been printed with initial capital letters or in all capitals.

The author and publisher have taken care in the preparation of this book, but make no expressed or implied warranty of any kind and assume no responsibility for errors or omissions. No liability is assumed for incidental or consequential damages in connection with or arising out of the use of the information or programs contained herein.

The publisher offers discounts on this book when ordered in quantity for bulk purchases and special sales. For more information, please contact:

U.S. Corporate and Government Sales
(800) 382-3419
corpsales@pearsontechgroup.com

For sales outside of the U.S., please contact:

International Sales
(317) 581-3793
international@pearsontechgroup.com

Visit Addison-Wesley on the Web: www.awprofessional.com

Library of Congress Cataloging-in-Publication Data

Gomaa, Hassan.
    Designing software product lines with UML : from use cases to
pattern-based software architectures / Hassan Gomaa.
        p. cm.
    Includes bibliographical references and index.
    ISBN 0-201-77595-6 (pbk. : alk. paper)
    1. Software engineering. 2. UML (Computer science) I. Title.

QA76.758.G64 2004
005.1—dc22

                                                2004005854

Text printed on recycled paper
1 2 3 4 5 6 7 8 9 10—CRW—0807060504
First printing, July 2004

To Gill, William, Alexander, Amanda,
Edward, and my mother Johanna

Contents

Foreword

This is a book about software product lines (known in Europe as software product families), which are families of software systems that have some commonality and some variability. The goal of developing software product lines is software reuse—from reuse of software requirements through reuse of software code. The promise of large scale software reuse has been a goal of the software industry since the dawn of software engineering in the late sixties. However, it has proved an elusive goal.

Software reuse is a subject that most of the larger corporations are facing. To reuse software is to improve productivity (less new software has to be built) and quality (presumably the existing software has been tested and errors have been corrected). Various technologies have been proclaimed as the solution to the software reuse problem, from subroutines to modular software to object-oriented programming to component-based programming. Each of these technologies made a contribution but the overall result in general has been much less than hoped. A major problem with these technologies is that the emphasis is on code reuse. Numerous studies have indicated that coding is only around 20% of the total cost of software development; hence improvements in coding will only be of limited value. Much greater payoff is likely from reuse of software requirements and architectures, which is the goal of software product lines.

I have long been an advocate of large scale software reuse. In a book I wrote together with Martin Griss and Patrik Jonsson on product line engineering in 1997, we addressed architecture, process and organization for software reuse. Product line engineering is about reuse of all artifacts, such as software requirements, analysis, designs including architectures, and test—not just code reuse.

Hassan Gomaa's book is taking a step forward. In particular, he follows the distinction between use cases and features made by Martin Griss in a 1998 paper: use cases are user oriented, with the objective of determining the functional requirements of the product line, whereas features are reuser oriented with the objective of organizing the results of a product line commonality and variability analysis. Following this distinction, Gomaa describes how features can be determined from the product line use case model, by analyzing kernel, optional, and alternative use cases, as well as use case variation points. He uses this analysis as a basis for describing product line commonality by means of common features, and product line variability by means of optional and alternative features, as well as feature groups that constrain how related features can be used by a product line member.

The book also describes how software architectural patterns for product lines can be used as a starting point for developing a reusable software architecture. In addition, it describes how commonality and variability can be modeled in component-based software architectures using the new UML 2.0 notation for composite structure diagrams.

Hassan clearly has a command of how to tie feature-based analysis and use case analysis together. I feel that this is the strongest part of the work, and is an area that is sorely lacking in most UML treatments.

Ivar Jacobson
April 2004

Preface

Overview

This book describes an evolutionary software engineering process for the development of software product lines, which uses the Unified Modeling Language (UML) notation. A software product line (or product family) consists of a family of software systems that have some common functionality and some variable functionality. The interest in software product lines emerged from the field of software reuse when developers and managers realized that they could obtain much greater reuse benefits by reusing software architectures instead of reusing individual software components. The field of software product lines is increasingly recognized in industry and government as being of great strategic importance for software development. Studies indicate that if three or more systems with a degree of common functionality are to be developed, then developing a product line is significantly more cost-effective than developing each system from scratch.

The traditional mode of software development is to develop single systems—that is, to develop each system individually. For software product lines, the development approach is broadened to consider a family of software systems. This approach involves analyzing what features (functional requirements) of the software family are common, what features are optional, and what features are alternatives. After the feature analysis, the goal is to design a software architecture for the product line, which has common components (required by all members of the family), optional components (required by only some members of the family), and variant components (different versions of which are required by different members of the family). Instead of starting from square one, the developer derives applications by adapting and tailoring the product line architecture.

To model and design families of systems, the analysis and design concepts for single product systems need to be extended to support software product lines. This book is intended to appeal to readers who are familiar with modeling and designing single systems but who wish to extend their knowledge to modeling and designing software product lines. It is also intended to appeal to readers who are familiar with applying UML to the modeling and design of single systems but not with developing software product lines.

What This Book Provides

Several textbooks on the market describe object-oriented concepts and methods, which are intended for single systems. Very few books address software families or product lines; and of those that do, even fewer use UML.

This book provides a comprehensive treatment of the application of UML-based object-oriented concepts to the analysis and design of software product lines. In particular, it does the following:

- Describes fundamental concepts and technologies in the design of software product lines.

- Describes, in considerable detail, a UML-based object-oriented analysis and design method for software product lines. It examines how each of the UML modeling views—use case modeling, static modeling, dynamic state machine modeling, and dynamic interaction modeling—is extended to address software product lines. Each UML modeling view is extended to reflect the commonality and variability of the product line. A new view, the feature modeling view, is added to explicitly model the commonality and variability of software requirements.

- Uses the Object Management Group (OMG) concept of model-driven architecture to develop a component-based software architecture for a product line. The product line architecture is expressed as a UML platform-independent model, which can then be mapped to a platform-specific model.

- Describes how architectures for software product lines are developed through the consideration of software architectural patterns in relation to the characteristics of the product line. The product line architecture is component-based and explicitly models the commonality and variability of the product line.

- Presents three case studies illustrating how a software product line architecture is developed, starting with use cases and feature modeling in the requirements modeling phase, static and dynamic modeling in the analysis modeling phase, and the development of the component-based software architecture in the design modeling phase. The case studies focus on a microwave oven product line, an electronic commerce product line, and a factory automation product line.

- Includes a glossary, a bibliography, and two appendices, which provide (1) an overview of UML 2 notation and (2) a catalog of software architectural patterns for product lines.

The PLUS Advantage

The UML-based software design method for software product lines described in this book is called PLUS (*Product Line UML-Based Software Engineering*). The PLUS method extends the UML-based modeling methods that are used for single systems to address software product lines. With PLUS, the objective is to explicitly model the commonality and variability in a software product line. PLUS provides a set of concepts and techniques to extend UML-based design methods and processes for single systems to handle software product lines. In particular, for modeling software product lines, PLUS provides the following additions to the process of modeling single systems:

Software Product Line Requirements Modeling

- **Use case modeling**. Model commonality and variability in the use case model. For this purpose, PLUS provides an approach to modeling kernel, optional, and alternative use cases, as well as an approach to modeling variation points in use cases.

- **Feature modeling**. Model product line features. Feature modeling is a key concept in software product lines. PLUS provides an approach for modeling common, optional, and alternative features, an approach for deriving the feature model from the use case model, and an approach for representing features with the UML notation.

Software Product Line Analysis Modeling

- **Static modeling**. Develop a product line context model for the product line boundary. Determine kernel, optional, and alternative external classes. Develop a product line information (entity class) model: determine kernel, optional, and alternative entity classes.

- **Dynamic interaction modeling**. Develop interaction diagrams to realize kernel, optional, and alternative use cases. Use evolutionary development: the kernel first approach is applied to determine product line commonality, followed by product line evolution to determine variability.
- **Dynamic state machine modeling**. Develop kernel, optional, and alternative statecharts. Manage state machine variability through inheritance and parameterization.
- **Feature/class dependency modeling**. Determine how the common, optional, and alternative features of the product lines depend on the kernel, optional, and variant classes.

Software Product Line Design Modeling

- **Software architectural patterns**. Determine the software architectural structure and communication patterns that are most appropriate for the product line given the catalog of architectural patterns.
- **Component-based software design**. Develop a component-based software design for the product line, which models kernel, optional, and variant components, as well as their ports and provided and required interfaces. Design the component-based architecture that explicitly models the components and their interconnections.

Software Application Engineering

Develop a software application that is a member of the product line by using the feature model to derive the application from the product line architecture and components.

Intended Audience

This book is intended for both professional and academic audiences. The professional audience includes analysts, software architects, software designers, programmers, project leaders, technical managers, program managers, and quality assurance specialists who are involved in the design and development of large-scale software product lines in industry and government. The academic audience includes senior undergraduate- and graduate-level students in computer science and software engineering, as well as researchers in the field.

Ways to Read This Book

This book may be read in various ways. It can be read in the order it is presented, in which case Chapters 1 and 2 provide introductory concepts, Chapter 3 provides an overview of product line engineering and the PLUS process, Chapters 4 through 12 provide an in-depth treatment of designing software product lines with PLUS, and Chapters 13, 14, and 15 provide detailed case studies.

Alternatively, some readers may wish to skip some chapters depending on their level of familiarity with the topics discussed. Chapters 1 and 2 are introductory and may be skipped by experienced readers. Readers familiar with software design concepts may skip Chapter 2. Readers particularly interested in product line development can proceed directly to the description of PLUS, starting in Chapter 3. Readers who are not familiar with UML, or who are interested in finding out about the changes introduced by UML 2.0, can read the appropriate sections in Appendix A in conjunction with reading Chapters 4 through 12.

Experienced product line designers may also use this book as a reference, referring to various chapters as their projects reach a particular stage of the requirements, analysis, or design process. Each chapter is relatively self-contained. For example, at different times you might refer to Chapter 4 for a description of use cases, Chapter 5 for developing the feature model, Chapter 7 for dynamic interaction modeling, Chapter 8 when designing statecharts (skip for non-state dependent product lines), Chapter 10 and Appendix B when referring to software architectural patterns, Chapter 11 for distributed component-based software design, and Chapter 12 for application engineering. You can also increase your understanding of how to use the PLUS method by reading the case studies, because each case study explains the decisions made at each step of the requirements, analysis, and design modeling processes.

Annotated Table of Contents

Chapter 1: Introduction

This chapter presents an introduction to software product lines, a discussion of software reuse issues, and an overview of object-oriented analysis and design with UML.

Chapter 2: Design Concepts for Software Product Lines

This chapter discusses and presents an overview of key design concepts and technologies for software product lines, including object-oriented technology, software architecture, and the software component technology.

Chapter 3: Software Product Line Engineering

This chapter introduces the software product line design method, which is described in much greater detail in subsequent chapters. One of the goals of this method is to be capable of extending other design methods, such as the author's COMET method (Concurrent Object Modeling and Architectural Design Method) to model and design software product lines. The acronym for the method is PLUS (Product Line UML-Based Software Engineering). However, the term *PLUS* is also intended to mean that other methods can be extended to support product lines such as COMET, ROPES, or RUP/USDP.

There are two main strategies for developing a software product line, referred to as *forward evolutionary engineering* and *reverse evolutionary engineering*. Forward evolutionary engineering is best used when a new product line is being developed with no previous systems to guide the development. Reverse evolutionary engineering is best used when the product line development begins with existing systems that are candidates for modernization and inclusion in a project to develop a product line.

Chapter 4: Use Case Modeling for Software Product Lines

This chapter describes how use case modeling concepts are extended to address software product lines—in particular, how the common and variable functionality of the product line is modeled with kernel, optional, and alternative use cases, and how variation points are used to model variability.

Chapter 5: Feature Modeling for Software Product Lines

This chapter describes feature modeling—a concept used widely in software product lines but not addressed by UML. The discussion covers how feature modeling concepts can be incorporated into the UML and how features can be determined from use cases.

Chapter 6: Static Modeling in Software Product Lines

This chapter describes how static modeling concepts are extended to address software product lines—in particular, to address modeling the boundary of the software product line and modeling entity classes, which are information-intensive classes. Also discussed is the categorization of application classes from two perspectives: the role the class plays in the application and the reuse characteristic of the class.

Chapter 7: Dynamic Interaction Modeling for Software Product Lines

This chapter describes how dynamic interaction modeling concepts are extended to address software product lines. Communication diagrams are developed for each kernel, optional, and alternative use case. Dynamic interaction modeling to address use case variation points is also covered. The kernel first approach is used for dynamic modeling, followed by the product line evolution approach.

Chapter 8: Finite State Machines and Statecharts for Software Product Lines

This chapter describes how finite state machine and statechart modeling concepts are extended to address software product lines. In particular, each state-dependent control class—whether kernel, optional, or variant—needs to be modeled with a finite state machine and depicted as a statechart. It is also possible to model variability using inherited state machines and parameterized state machines.

Chapter 9: Feature/Class Dependency Modeling for Software Product Lines

This chapter describes how to determine which classes from the analysis model are needed to support the features from the feature model. Product line classes are categorized as kernel, optional, and variant classes. Modeling class variability using both inheritance and parameterization is described. Feature-based dynamic modeling and static modeling are also covered.

Chapter 10: Architectural Patterns for Software Product Lines

This chapter describes a range of software architectural patterns that are particularly useful in the design of software product line architectures. Both architectural structure and communication patterns are described. Architectural structure patterns address the overall structure of the software architecture. Architectural communication patterns address the ways in which distributed components can communicate with each other. This chapter also describes how product line architectures can be built from these patterns.

Chapter 11: Software Product Line Architectural Design: Component-Based Design

This chapter describes how a product line architecture is designed as a component-based architecture. Separation of concerns in component design is an important issue. Components are categorized according to their roles in the software architecture. The design of component interfaces is described. The chapter also discusses how component-based software architectures can be depicted with the structured class and composite structure diagram notation introduced in UML 2, which allows components, ports, connectors, and provided and required interfaces to be depicted.

Chapter 12: Software Application Engineering

This chapter describes the process for deriving a member of the software product line from the product line architecture and components. This is a tailoring process involving selection of the appropriate components and setting of the parameter values for individual components to include in the product line member. The chapter covers how the feature model is used to help in this process.

Chapter 13: Microwave Oven Software Product Line Case Study

This chapter describes how the PLUS software product line method is applied to the design of a microwave oven software product line. Because this is a new product line, the forward evolutionary engineering product line development strategy is used, in which an iterative approach is used to determine the kernel functionality of the product line before the variable functionality is modeled.

Chapter 14: Electronic Commerce Software Product Line Case Study

This chapter describes how the PLUS software product line method is applied to the design of an e-commerce application product line. Because there are two main systems—business-to-business (B2B) and business-to-consumer (B2C)—in the electronic commerce product line, the reverse evolutionary engineering product line development strategy is applied first to each type of system, from which the product line commonality is determined first, followed by the product line variability.

Chapter 15: Factory Automation Software Product Line Case Study

This chapter describes how the PLUS software product line method is applied to the design of a factory automation product line. Because this product line starts with existing factory automation systems that are candidates for modernization and inclusion in the product line, the reverse evolutionary engineering product line development strategy is applied.

Appendix A: Overview of the UML Notation

This appendix provides an overview of the different UML 2.0 diagrams used by the PLUS method. The differences between the UML 2.0 notation and UML 1.x notation are also explained, as are the conventions used in this book.

Appendix B: Catalog of Software Architectural Patterns

In this appendix the software architectural structure and communication patterns, originally described in Chapter 10, are documented alphabetically in a common template for easy reference.

Contact

For questions or comments, please contact me at hgomaa@gmu.edu.

Hassan Gomaa
George Mason University,
June 2004
http://mason.gmu.edu/~hgomaa/index.htm

Acknowledgments

I gratefully acknowledge the reviewers of earlier drafts of the manuscript for their constructive comments—in particular, Alan W. Brown, Jeffrey Hammond, Stephen Mellor, James Dean Palmer, and Rob Pettit.

I am also grateful to the students in my software design and reusable software architecture courses at George Mason University for their enthusiasm, dedication, and valuable feedback. Thanks are also due to Hurley Blankenship, Michael Shin, Mohamed Hussein, and Erika Olimpiew for their hard work producing and reviewing the figures. Erika also carefully reviewed the manuscript and proofs, and provided many useful comments. I am also very grateful to Stephanie Hiebert for her meticulous copyediting of the manuscript. Thanks are also due to the Addison-Wesley editorial and production staff for all their efforts. I would also like to thank Bran Selic for his assistance in clarifying some of the intricate details of UML 2.0.

Last, but not least, I would like to thank my wife, Gill, for her encouragement, understanding, and support of this, my third textbook.

part

I

Overview

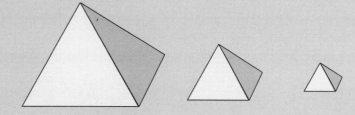

chapter

Introduction

A software product line consists of a family of software systems that have some common functionality and some variable functionality. To take advantage of the common functionality, reusable assets (such as requirements, designs, components, and so on) are developed, which can be reused by different members of the family. Clements and Northrop (2002) define a **software product line** as "a set of software intensive systems sharing a common, managed set of features that satisfy the specific needs of a particular market segment or mission and that are developed from a common set of core assets in a prescribed way" (p. 5).

The interest in software product lines emerged from the field of software reuse when developers realized that they could obtain much greater reuse benefits by reusing software architectures instead of reusing individual software components. The software industry is increasingly recognizing the strategic importance of software product lines (Clements and Northrop 2002).

The idea of a product line is not new. There are examples of product lines in ancient history; the pyramids of Egypt (Figure 1.1) might have been the first product line! A modern example of product lines comes from the airline industry, with the European Airbus A-318, A-319, A-320, and A-321 airplanes, which share common product features, including jet engines, navigation equipment, and communication equipment (Clements and Northrop 2002).

The traditional mode of software development is to develop single systems—that is, to develop each system individually. For software product lines, the development approach is broadened to consider a family of software systems. This approach involves analyzing what features (functional requirements) of the software family are common, what features are optional, and what features are alternatives. After the feature analysis, the goal is to design a software architecture

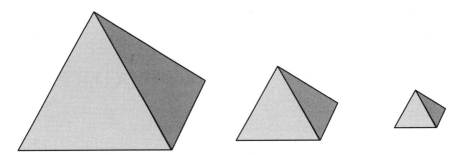

Figure 1.1   *A product line from ancient history: the pyramids of Egypt*

for the product line, which has **common components** (required by all members of the family), **optional components** (required by only some members of the family), and **variant components** (different versions of which are required by different members of the family). To model and design families of systems, the analysis and design concepts for single-product systems need to be extended to support software product lines.

This chapter presents an overview of software reuse and software product lines. It also gives an overview of using the Unified Modeling Language (UML) to develop component-based software product lines.

1.1   Software Reuse

Software reuse has been a goal in software engineering since 1968, when the term *software engineering* was first coined. This section briefly surveys different approaches to software reuse, starting with the most common form of software reuse (using reuse libraries) and leading up to software product lines.

1.1.1   Software Reuse Libraries

In traditional software reuse, a library of reusable code components is developed. This approach requires the establishment of a library of reusable components and of an approach for indexing, locating, and distinguishing between similar components (Prieto-Diaz and Freeman 1987). Problems with this approach include managing the large number of components that such a reuse library is likely to contain and distinguishing among similar though not identical components.

The reusable library components are the building blocks used in constructing the new system. Components are considered to be largely atomic and ideally unchanged when reused, although some adaptation may be required. Depending on the development approach, the library could contain functional or object-oriented components. This reuse approach has been used with both functional and object-oriented systems.

When a new design is being developed, the designer is responsible for designing the software architecture—that is, the overall structure of the program and the overall flow of control. Having located and selected a reusable component from the library, the designer must then determine how this component fits into the new architecture.

An example of this traditional reuse is a subroutine library, which consists of a collection of reusable subroutines in a given application area—for example, a statistical subroutine library. Another example is an object-oriented toolkit, which consists of a set of related and reusable classes designed to provide useful, general-purpose functionality. These reuse libraries and toolkits emphasize code reuse.

Apart from certain specific domains, such as mathematical libraries, the benefits of the traditional software reuse approach have been limited in general. With this approach, overall reuse is relatively low, and the emphasis is on code reuse.

1.1.2   Software Architecture and Design Reuse

Instead of reusing an individual component, it is much more advantageous to reuse a whole design or subsystem, consisting of the components and their interconnections. This means reuse of the control structure of the application. Architecture reuse has much greater potential than component reuse because it is large-grained reuse, which focuses on reuse of requirements and design.

1.2   Software Product Lines

The most promising approach for architecture reuse is to develop a product line architecture, which explicitly captures the commonality and variability in the family of systems that constitutes the product line. Various terms are used to refer to a software product line. A software product line is also referred to as a **software product family**, a **family of systems**, or an *application domain*. The terms used most often in the early days of this field were *domain analysis* (Prieto-Diaz 1987) and *domain modeling*. The architectures developed for application domains were referred to as *domain models* or *domain-specific software architectures* (Gomaa 1995).

Parnas referred to a collection of systems that share common characteristics as a *family of systems* (Parnas 1979). According to Parnas, it is worth considering the development of a family of systems when there is more to be gained by analyzing the systems collectively rather than separately—that is, when the systems have more features in common than features that distinguish them. A family of systems is now referred to as a *software product line* or a *software product family*. Some approaches attempt to differentiate between these two terms. This book, in common with other approaches, does not differentiate between the terms *software product line* and *software product family*, assuming that they both refer to a family of systems.

The architecture for a software product line is the architecture for a family of products. Some product line development approaches provide a **generic architecture**, or **reference model**, for the product line, which depicts the commonality of the product line but ignores all the variability. Each application starts with the generic architecture and adapts it manually as required. Although this approach provides a better starting point in comparison to developing a system without any reuse, it fails to capture any knowledge about the variability in the product family.

A more desirable approach is to explicitly model both what is common and what is different in the product family. A software product line architecture should therefore describe both the commonality and variability in the family. Depending on the development approach used (functional or object-oriented), the product line **commonality** is described in terms of common modules, classes, or components, and the product line **variability** is described in terms of optional or variant modules, classes, or components.

The term **application engineering** refers to the process of tailoring and configuring the product family architecture and components to create a specific application, which is a member of the product family.

1.2.1 Modeling Variability in Software Product Lines

Modeling commonality and variability is an important activity in developing software product lines. Early advocates of product line development included proponents of the FAST (Family-Oriented Abstraction, Specification, and Translation) approach and its predecessors (Coplien et al. 1998; Weiss and Lai 1999), work at the Software Engineering Institute (Clements and Northrop 2002; Cohen and Northrop 1998; Kang et al. 1990), work at the Software Productivity Consortium (Pyster 1990), and the EDLC (Evolutionary Domain Life Cycle) approach (Gomaa 1995; Gomaa and Farrukh 1999; Gomaa and O'Hara 1998; Gomaa, Kerschberg, et al. 1996). Jacobson et al. (1997) introduced the concept of variation points as a way to model variability in use cases and UML.

Variability in a software product line can be modeled at the software requirements level and at the software design level. The most widely used approach for modeling variability in requirements is through feature modeling, as described next.

1.3   Modeling Requirements Variability in Software Product Lines: Feature Modeling

Features are an important concept in software product lines because they represent reusable requirements or characteristics of a product line. The concept of a feature is quite intuitive and applies to all product lines, not just software product lines. Consider a vehicle product line. Several different models of cars might share common characteristics. For example, a vehicle product line (analogous to a software product line) might have a common chassis, which represents a *common* feature; a choice of engine size, where each engine represents an *alternative* feature; and optional cruise control, which represents an *optional* feature. For any individual car (analogous to a software member of the product line), a buyer would have no choice of chassis (there is no choice because this is a common feature), would have a choice of engine size (one of the alternative features), and could decide whether to have cruise control or not (the optional feature).

The FODA (feature-oriented domain analysis) method uses features, which are organized into a feature tree (Cohen and Northrop 1998; Kang et al. 1990). Features may be mandatory, optional, or mutually exclusive. The feature tree is a composition hierarchy of features, in which some branches are mandatory, some are optional, and others are mutually exclusive. In FODA, features may be functional features (hardware or software), nonfunctional features (e.g., relating to security or performance), or parameters (e.g., red, yellow, or green). Features higher up in the tree are composite features if they contain other lower-level features.

Other product line methods have used the FODA approach for modeling product line features (Dionisi et al. 1998; Griss et al. 1998). Feature modeling has also been prominent in other product line methods, such as the EDLC method (Gomaa 1995; Gomaa and Farrukh 1999; Gomaa, Kerschberg, et al. 1996). The feature concept is not an object-oriented concept, and it is not used in UML modeling of single systems. Chapter 5 describes an approach for modeling and describing features in UML.

1.4 Modeling Design Variability in Software Product Lines

Techniques for modeling variability in design include modeling variability using parameterization, modeling variability using information hiding, and modeling variability using inheritance (Gomaa and Webber 2004). The relative merits of each technique depend on the amount of flexibility needed in the product line. These approaches are described briefly in Sections 1.4.1 through 1.4.3.

1.4.1 Modeling Variability Using Parameterization

Parameters can be used to introduce variability into a software product line. The values of parameters defined in the product line components are where the variation comes in. Different members of the product line would have different values assigned to the parameters.

Parameterization approaches use four different types of parameters:

1. **Compilation parameters**. Values are set at compile time. This approach is sometimes used to conditionally compile code depending on the parameter setting.

2. **Configuration parameters**. Values are set at system configuration time, which is sometimes referred to as system generation (sysgen) time or system installation time.

3. **Runtime initialization parameters**. Values are set at system initialization time. The component could provide operations that are called at system initialization to initialize or change the values of parameterized attributes.

4. **Table-driven parameters**. Some reusable applications are configured with parameters that are stored in tables. This can be an effective way of allowing users to configure the application.

Several product line analysis methods use parameterization. The FODA method developed at the Software Engineering Institute (SEI) uses features to characterize the domain (Kang et al. 1990). In FODA, one kind of feature is the parameter. In the Domain-Specific Software Architecture (DSSA) program, generic components were parameterized to simplify customization for particular applications (Hayes-Roth 1995). The FAST product line method (Weiss and Lai 1999), which emphasizes analyzing commonality and variability in a product line, uses parameterization extensively as one of the approaches to achieve variability. The EDLC model for software product lines uses parameterization at configuration time to define the values of component parameters (Gomaa and Farrukh 1999).

A well-documented case study of a product line that used parameterization is CelsiusTech (Bass et al. 2003). CelsiusTech's Ship System 2000 (SS2000) is a product line for command and control of naval systems. The SS2000 consisted of parameterized components for which the application engineers supplied the parameter values. The SS2000 features 3,000 to 5,000 parameters that must be individually set for each member system of the product line. Managing such a large number of parameters could be a problem because little or no guidance is given on how to ensure that parameters are not in conflict with each other.

1.4.2 Modeling Variability Using Information Hiding

Information hiding can also be used to introduce variability into a software product line. Different versions of a component have the same interface but different implementations for different members of the product line. Thus the variability is hidden inside each version of the component. In this case the variants are the different versions of the same component but must adhere to the same interface. This approach works well as long as changes can be limited to individual components and no changes to the interface or assumptions about how the interface will be used are required. From a reuse perspective, the application engineer selects a component from a limited set of choices and uses it in the application.

Most product line methods use information hiding. In addition to parameterization, the FODA, DSSA, FAST, and EDLC methods already described all use information hiding.

1.4.3 Modeling Variability Using Inheritance

A third way of introducing variability into a software product line is to use inheritance. In this case, different versions of a class use inheritance to inherit operations from a superclass, and then operations specified in the superclass interface are redefined and/or the interface is extended by the addition of new operations. For a given member of the product line, the application engineer selects the version of the component.

With the widespread use of object-oriented techniques, variability using inheritance has become increasingly common in software product lines. The KobrA approach (Atkinson et al. 2002), which is an object-oriented customization of the Product Line Software Engineering (PuLSE) method (Bayer et al., 1999; DeBaud and Schmid 1999), uses inheritance to model component variability. In the EDLC product line method (Gomaa and Farrukh 1999), inheritance is used to model different variant subclasses of an abstract class, such that the variants are used by different members of the product line.

1.4.4 Comparison of Approaches for Modeling Design Variability

Modeling variability using parameterization allows application engineers to define the values of product line attributes, which are maintained by various product line components. If all the variability in a product line can be defined in terms of parameters, then this can be a simple way to provide variability. However, the variability is limited in that no functionality can change. In some product lines parameterization is used to select among functionality alternatives, although it is a complicated and error-prone approach and needs to be used with care.

Modeling variability using information hiding allows application engineers to choose variants from a limited set of choices in which the interface is common but the implementations are variable. Information hiding allows a higher degree of variability than parameterization does because both functionality and parameters can be varied.

Modeling variability using inheritance allows application engineers to choose variants whose functionality can vary. Because of the nature of inheritance, this approach also allows a wider range of variants by extending the superclass interface in variant subclasses.

In most product lines, a combination of all three approaches is needed. The object-oriented approach to software development helps by supporting all three of these approaches to modeling variability. However, other approaches are also needed, as explained next.

1.5 Reusable Design Patterns

A different approach for providing design reuse is through design patterns. A **design pattern** describes a recurring design problem to be solved, a solution to the problem, and the context in which that solution works (Buschmann et al.

1996; Gamma et al. 1995). The description specifies objects and classes that are customized to solve a general design problem in a particular context. A design pattern is a larger-grained form of reuse than a class because it involves more than one class and the interconnection among objects from different classes. A design pattern is sometimes referred to as a *microarchitecture*.

After the original success of the design pattern concept, other kinds of patterns were developed. The main kinds of reusable patterns are

- **Design patterns**. In a widely cited book (Gamma et al. 1995), design patterns were described by four software designers—Erich Gamma, Richard Helm, Ralph Johnson, and John Vlissides—who were named in some quarters as the "gang of four." A design pattern is a small group of collaborating objects.

- **Architectural patterns**. This work was described by Buschmann et al. (1996) at Siemens. Architectural patterns are larger-grained than design patterns, addressing the structure of major subsystems of a system.

- **Analysis patterns**. Analysis patterns were described by Fowler (2002), who found similarities during analysis of different application domains. He described recurring patterns found in object-oriented analysis and described them with static models, expressed in class diagrams.

- **Product line–specific patterns**. These are patterns used in specific application areas, such as factory automation (Gomaa 1998) or electronic commerce.

- **Idioms**. Idioms are low-level patterns specific to a programming language—for example, Java or C++. These patterns are closest to code, but they can be used only by applications that are coded in the same programming language.

From the perspective of software product lines, the biggest benefit can usually be obtained through the reuse of software architectural patterns, which is described in more detail in Chapter 10.

1.6   Modeling Single Systems with UML

Object-oriented concepts are considered important in software reuse and evolution because they address fundamental issues of adaptation and evolution. Object-oriented methods are based on the concepts of information hiding, classes, and inheritance. Information hiding can lead to systems that are more self-contained and hence are more modifiable and maintainable. Inheritance provides an approach for adapting a class in a systematic way.

With the proliferation of notations and methods for the object-oriented analysis and design of software applications, the Unified Modeling Language (UML) was developed to provide a standardized notation for describing object-oriented models. For the UML notation to be applied effectively, however, it needs to be used together with an object-oriented analysis and design method.

Modern object-oriented analysis and design methods are model-based and use a combination of use case modeling, static modeling, state machine modeling, and object interaction modeling. Almost all modern object-oriented methods use the UML notation for describing software requirements, analysis, and design models (Booch et al. 2005; Fowler 2004; Rumbaugh et al. 2005).

In **use case modeling**, the functional requirements of the system are defined in terms of use cases and actors. **Static modeling** provides a structural view of the system. Classes are defined in terms of their attributes, as well as their relationships with other classes. **Dynamic modeling** provides a behavioral view of the system. The use cases are realized to show the interaction among participating objects. Object interaction diagrams are developed to show how objects communicate with each other to realize the use case. The state-dependent aspects of the system are defined with statecharts.

1.7   COMET: A UML-Based Software Design Method for Single Systems

An example of a UML-based software design method for single systems is COMET (*C*oncurrent *O*bject *M*odeling and Architectural Design *Me*thod), which is described in Gomaa 2000. COMET is a highly iterative object-oriented software development method that addresses the requirements, analysis, and design modeling phases of the object-oriented development life cycle. The functional requirements of the system are defined in terms of actors and use cases. Each use case defines a sequence of interactions between one or more actors and the system. A use case can be viewed at various levels of detail. In a *requirements* model, the functional requirements of the system are defined in terms of actors and use cases. In an *analysis* model, the use case is realized to describe the objects that participate in the use case, and their interactions. In the *design* model, the software architecture is developed, addressing issues of distribution, concurrency, and information hiding. Sections 1.7.1 through 1.7.3 discuss each of these phases of object-oriented development.

1.7.1   Requirements Modeling

During the **requirements modeling** phase, a requirements model is developed in which the functional requirements of the system are defined in terms of actors and use cases. A narrative description of each use case is developed. User inputs and active participation are essential to this effort. If the requirements are not well understood, a throwaway prototype can be developed to help clarify the requirements.

1.7.2   Analysis Modeling

In the **analysis modeling** phase, static and dynamic models of the system are developed. The *static model* defines the structural relationships among problem domain classes. The classes and their relationships are depicted on class diagrams. Object-structuring criteria are used to determine which objects should be considered for the analysis model. A *dynamic model* is then developed in which the use cases from the requirements model are realized to show the objects that participate in each use case and how they interact with each other. Objects and their interactions are depicted on either communication diagrams or sequence diagrams. In the dynamic model, state-dependent objects are defined with statecharts. A **statechart** is a graphical representation of a finite state machine in the form of a hierarchical state transition diagram.

1.7.3   Design Modeling

In the **design modeling** phase, the software architecture of the system is designed; that is, the analysis model is mapped to an operational environment. The analysis model (which emphasizes the problem domain) is mapped to the design model (which emphasizes the solution domain). Subsystem structuring criteria are provided to structure the system into subsystems, which are considered as aggregate or composite objects. Special consideration is given to designing distributed subsystems as configurable components that communicate with each other using messages.

Each subsystem is then designed. For sequential systems, the emphasis is on the object-oriented concepts of information hiding, classes, and inheritance. For the design of concurrent systems, such as real-time, client/server, and distributed applications, it is necessary to consider concurrent tasking concepts in addition to object-oriented concepts.

1.8 Modeling Software Product Lines with UML

The field of software reuse has evolved from reuse of individual components toward large-scale reuse with software product lines. Software modeling approaches are now widely used in software development and have an important role to play in software product lines. Modern software modeling approaches, such as UML, provide greater insights into understanding and managing commonality and variability by modeling product lines from different perspectives.

The UML-based software design method for software product lines described in this book is called PLUS (*Product Line U*ML-Based *S*oftware Engineering). The PLUS method extends the UML-based modeling methods that are used for single systems to address software product lines. With PLUS, the objective is to explicitly model the commonality and variability in a software product line. PLUS provides a set of concepts and techniques to extend UML-based design methods and processes for single systems to handle software product lines.

The PLUS method is similar to other UML-based object-oriented methods when used for analyzing and modeling a single system. Its novelty, and where it differs from other methods, is the way it extends object-oriented methods to model product families. In particular, PLUS allows explicit modeling of the similarities and variations in a product line.

In order to understand the product line and develop a model of it, an analyst needs to consider several different perspectives of the product line. A product line model is therefore a multiple-viewpoint representation of the product family, such that each viewpoint presents a different perspective on the family. The different viewpoints are developed iteratively. By analyzing the different viewpoints of the family, an analyst can get a better understanding of the product line. For product line analysis and modeling, the object-oriented analysis and design method used for individual systems is extended to product lines. Requirements, analysis, and design models of the product line are developed.

1.9 UML as a Standard

This section briefly reviews the evolution of UML into a standard. The history of UML's evolution is described in detail by Kobryn (1999). UML 0.9 unified the modeling notations of Booch (1994), Jacobson (1992), and Rumbaugh et al. (1991). This version formed the basis of a standardization effort, with the additional involvement of a diverse mix of vendors and system integrators. The standardization effort culminated in submission of the initial UML 1.0 proposal to the Object Management Group (OMG) in January 1997. After some revisions, the final UML 1.1 proposal was submitted later that year and adopted as an object modeling standard in November 1997.

The first widely used version of the standard was UML 1.3. There were minor revisions with UML 1.4 and 1.5. A major revision to the notation was made in 2003 with UML 2.0. Many books on UML, including the revised editions of the major UML references—*The Unified Modeling Language User Guide* by Booch et al. (2005) and *The Unified Modeling Language Reference Manual* by Rumbaugh et al. (2005)—conform to UML 2.0. Other books describing the UML 2.0 standard include the revised edition of *UML Distilled* by Fowler (2004), *UML 2 Toolkit* by Eriksson et al. (2004), and the revised edition of *Real-Time UML* by Douglass (2004).

1.9.1   Model-Driven Architecture with UML for Software Product Lines

The OMG maintains UML as a standard. In the OMG's view, "modeling is the designing of software applications before coding." The OMG promotes model-driven architecture as the approach in which UML models of the software architecture are developed prior to implementation. According to the OMG, UML is methodology-independent; UML is a notation for describing the results of an object-oriented analysis and design developed via the methodology of choice.

A UML model can be either a platform-independent model (PIM) or a platform-specific model (PSM). The platform-independent model is a precise model of the software architecture before a commitment is made to a specific platform. Developing the PIM first is particularly useful because the same PIM can be mapped to different middleware platforms, such as COM, CORBA, .NET, J2EE, Web Services, or another platform. The approach in this book is to use the concept of model-driven architecture to develop a component-based software architecture for a product line, which is expressed as a UML platform-independent model.

An object-oriented analysis and design method for software product lines needs to extend single-system analysis and design concepts to model product lines, in particular to model the commonality and variability in the product line, and to extend the UML notation to describe this commonality and variability. The goal is to extend UML for software product lines using the standard UML extension mechanisms of stereotypes, constraints, and tagged values (Rumbaugh et al. 2005) (see Appendix A, Section A.10).

1.10 Related Texts

This book presents a comprehensive UML-based object-oriented method addressing requirements modeling, analysis modeling, and design modeling for software product lines. This book complements books in other areas.

There are several books on UML-based object-oriented analysis and design for single systems. These include the set of three books by Booch, Jacobson, and Rumbaugh (Booch et al. 2005; Jacobson et al. 1999; Rumbaugh et al. 2005), as well as other UML books, such as Eriksson et al. 2004 and Fowler 2004, books on tool usage with UML (Quatrani 2003), books on real-time design with UML (Douglass 2004; Gomaa 2000), and books on using patterns with UML (Douglass 2002; Larman 2002).

There are few books on software reuse and software product lines. The Jacobson book on software reuse (Jacobson et al. 1997) addresses object-oriented software reuse in general and introduces the topic of variability in use cases and classes using the variation point concept. Weiss's book on software product lines (Weiss and Lai 1999) is a comprehensive treatment of this topic, with particular emphasis on how information hiding can be used effectively in product line design. The book on software product lines (Jazayeri et al. 2000) consists of a collection of papers published as a result of a European industry/university collaborative project. The book provides interesting research-oriented perspectives on product lines, including some papers on software architecture. Bosch also addresses software architecture and product lines in an interesting book (Bosch 2000) that covers a range of topics on software architecture and addresses both technical and management issues in software product lines. Clements and Northrop (2002) provide a very good introduction to the field of software product lines and coverage of the major management issues (in particular the practice areas of technical management and organizational management for product lines), as well as detailed case studies of organizations that have successfully developed software product lines.

There are a growing number of books on component technology, which describe the design of individual components (Brown 2000; Szyperski 2003) or UML components (Cheesman and Daniels 2001). These books complement this book but do not address how to design components so that they can be incorporated into software product lines.

There are several books on software architecture, including Shaw and Garlan 1996 and Bass et al. 2003, and also a UML-based book (Hofmeister et al. 2000). Bass et al. 2003 has some chapters on software product lines, a topic that is not addressed by the other two books. Finally, there are several books on architecture and design patterns, most notably Buschmann et al. 1996, Gamma et al. 1995, Larman 2002, and Schmidt et al. 2000. However, none of these books describe patterns in terms of how they could be incorporated into software product lines.

This book places an emphasis on object orientation, UML, designing software architectures for product lines, and addressing how to incorporate component and pattern technology into software product lines.

1.11 Summary

This chapter discussed software reuse and the reason for developing software product lines, which are also referred to as software product families, as well as modeling variability in software product lines. It also introduced the UML notation, which is used throughout this book, and described the concept of model-driven architecture. Chapter 2 will describe important design and architecture concepts for software product lines. Chapter 3 will describe the software product line engineering process. Appendix A provides an overview of the UML notation.

Design Concepts for Software Product Lines

This chapter describes key concepts in the software design of software product lines, as well as important concepts for developing the architecture of these systems. First, object-oriented concepts are introduced, including a description of objects and classes, as well as a discussion of the role of information hiding in object-oriented design and an introduction to the concept of inheritance. Next the concurrent processing concept is introduced, as well as the concept of concurrent objects in concurrent applications. The chapter also describes the underlying technologies for designing software product lines, including component-based systems and technologies. Examples in this chapter are described in UML. An overview of the UML notation is given in Appendix A.

Section 2.1 provides an overview of object-oriented concepts. Section 2.2 describes information hiding. Section 2.3 describes the relationships between classes, including associations, whole/part relationships, and generalization/specialization relationships. Section 2.4 provides an overview of dynamic modeling. Section 2.5 discusses the differences between sequential and concurrent applications and provides an overview of concurrent objects. Finally, Section 2.6 gives an overview of software architecture and the main characteristics of component-based systems.

2.1 Object-Oriented Concepts

The term **object-oriented** was first introduced in connection to object-oriented programming and Smalltalk (Goldberg and Robson 1983), although the object-oriented concepts of information hiding and inheritance have earlier origins. Information hiding and its use in software design date back to Parnas (1972), who advocated using information hiding as a way to design modules that were more self-contained and hence could be changed with little or no impact on other modules. The concepts of classes and inheritance were first used in Simula 67 (Dahl and Hoare 1972), but only with the introduction of Smalltalk did they start gaining widespread acceptance.

Object-oriented concepts are considered important in product line development because they address fundamental issues of adaptation and evolution. Because the object-oriented model of software development is considered especially conducive to evolution and change, the product line modeling approach takes an object-oriented perspective. The goal is to apply object-oriented concepts and extend them to modeling software product lines.

2.1.1   Objects and Classes

An **object** is a real-world physical or conceptual entity that provides an understanding of the real world and hence forms the basis for a software solution. A real-world object can have physical properties (they can be seen or touched); examples are a door, motor, or lamp. A conceptual object is a more abstract concept, such as an account or transaction.

Object-oriented applications consist of objects. From a design perspective, an object groups both data and procedures that operate on the data. The procedures are usually called operations or methods. Some approaches, including the UML notation, refer to the operation as the specification of a function performed by an object and the method as the implementation of the function (Rumbaugh et al. 2005). In this book the term **operation** refers to both the specification and the implementation, in common with Gamma et al. 1995, Meyer 1997, and others.

The **signature** of an operation specifies the operation's name, the operation's parameters, and the operation's return value. An object's **interface** is the set of operations it provides, as defined by the signatures of the operations. An object's type is defined by its interface. An object's implementation is defined by its class. Thus, Meyer refers to a class as an implementation of an **abstract data type** (Meyer 1997).

An **object** (also referred to as an *object instance*) is a single "thing"—for example, John's car or Mary's account. A **class** (also referred to as an *object class*) is a collection of objects with the same characteristics; for example, Account, Employee, Car, or Customer. Figure 2.1 depicts a class Customer and two

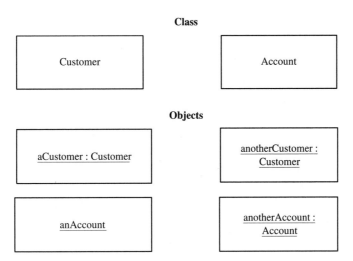

Figure 2.1 *Examples of classes and objects*

objects: a Customer and another Customer,[1] which are instances of the class Customer. The objects an Account and another Account are instances of the class Account.

An **attribute** is a data value held by an object in a class. Each object has a specific value of an attribute. Figure 2.2 shows a class with attributes. The class Account has two attributes: account Number and balance. Two objects of the Account class are shown: an Account and another Account. Each account has specific values of the attributes. For example, the value of account Number of the object an Account is 1234, and the value of account Number of the object another Account is 5678. The value of balance of the former object is $525.36, and the value of balance of the latter is $1,897.44.

An **operation** is the specification of a function performed by an object. An object has one or more operations. The operations manipulate the values of the attributes maintained by the object. Operations may have input and output parameters. All objects in the same class have the same operations. For exam-

---

1. See Appendix A for an overview of the UML notation. To improve readability, spaces are inserted in multiword names of classes, objects, and other design elements when they appear in the text itself. See Section A.11 in Appendix A for a complete explanation of the naming conventions used in this book.

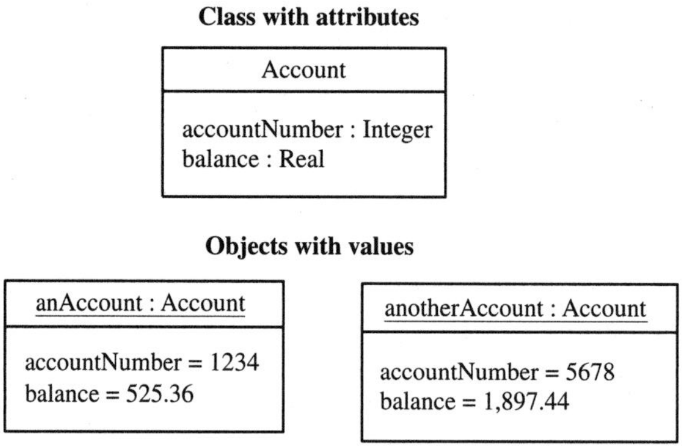

Class with attributes

Account
accountNumber : Integer balance : Real

Objects with values

anAccount : Account
accountNumber = 1234 balance = 525.36

anotherAccount : Account
accountNumber = 5678 balance = 1,897.44

Figure 2.2   *Example of a class with attributes*

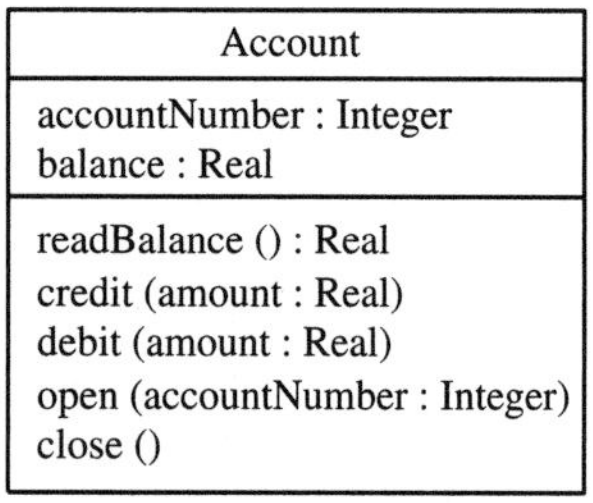

Account
accountNumber : Integer balance : Real
readBalance () : Real credit (amount : Real) debit (amount : Real) open (accountNumber : Integer) close ()

Figure 2.3   *Class with attributes and operations*

ple, the class `Account` has the operations `read Balance`, `credit`, `debit`, `open`, and `close`. Figure 2.3 shows the `Account` class with its operations.

An object is an instance of a class. Individual objects are instantiated as required at execution time. Each object has a unique identity, which is the characteristic that distinguishes it from other objects. In some cases, this identity may be an attribute (e.g., an account number or a customer name), but it does not need to be an attribute. Consider two blue balls: They are identical in every respect; however, they have different identities.

2.2   Information Hiding

Information hiding is a fundamental software design concept relevant to the design of all software systems. Early systems were frequently error-prone and difficult to modify because they made widespread use of global data. Parnas (1972, 1979) showed that by using information hiding, developers could design software systems to be substantially more modifiable by greatly reducing or—ideally—eliminating global data. Parnas advocated information hiding as a criterion for decomposing a software system into modules. Each information hiding module should hide a design decision that is considered likely to change. Each changeable decision is called the *secret* of the module. With this approach, the goal of *design for change* could be achieved.

Information hiding is a basic concept of object-oriented design. Information hiding is used in designing the object, in particular when deciding what information should be visible and what information should be hidden. Aspects of an object that need not be visible to other objects are hidden. Hence, if the internals of the object change, only this object is affected. The term **encapsulation** is also used to describe information hiding by an object.

With information hiding, the information that could potentially change is encapsulated (i.e., hidden) inside an object. The information can be externally accessed only indirectly by the invocation of operations—access procedures or functions—that are also part of the object. Only these operations can access the information directly. Thus the hidden information and the operations that access it are bound together to form an **information hiding object**. The specification of the operations (i.e., the name and the parameters of the operations) is called the *interface* of the object. The object's interface is also referred to as the *abstract interface*, *virtual interface*, or *external interface*. The interface represents the visible part of the object—that is, the part that is revealed to users of the object. Other objects access the hidden information indirectly by calling the operations provided by the object.

A potential problem in application software development is that an important data structure, one that is accessed by several objects, might need to be changed. Without information hiding, any change to the data structure is likely to require changes to all the objects that access that data structure. Information hiding can be used to hide the design decision concerning the data structure, its internal linkage, and the details of the operations that manipulate it. The information hiding solution is to encapsulate the data structure in an object. The data structure is accessed only directly by the operations provided by the object.

Other objects may only indirectly access the encapsulated data structure by calling the operations of the object. Thus, if the data structure changes, the only object affected is the one containing the data structure. The external interface supported by the object does not change; hence the objects that indirectly access the data structure are not affected by the change. This form of information hiding is called **data abstraction**.

Example of Information Hiding

An example of information hiding is a stack object. The information hiding solution is to hide the representation of the stack—for example, an array—from the objects needing to access it. An information hiding object—the stack object—is designed as follows (see Figure 2.4):

- A set of operations is defined to manipulate the data structure. In the case of the stack, typical operations are `push`, `pop`, `full`, and `empty`.

- The data structure is defined. In the case of the stack, for example, a one-dimensional array is defined. A variable is defined to refer to the top of the stack, and another variable has the value of the size of the array.

- Other objects are not permitted to access the data structure directly. They can access the data structure only indirectly by calling the object's operations.

Now assume that the design of the stack is changed from an array to a linked list. In the information hiding solution, in addition to the internal stack data structure changing drastically, the internals of the information hiding object's operations have to change because they now access a linked list instead of an array (see Figure 2.5). However, the external interface of the object, which is what is visible to the other objects, does not change. Thus the objects that use the stack are not affected by the change; they continue to call the object's operations without even needing to be aware of the change.

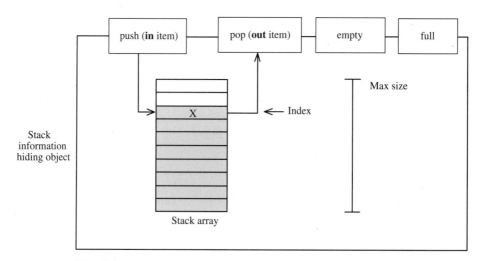

Note: This diagram does not use the UML notation.

Figure 2.4 *Example of a stack information hiding object implemented as an array*

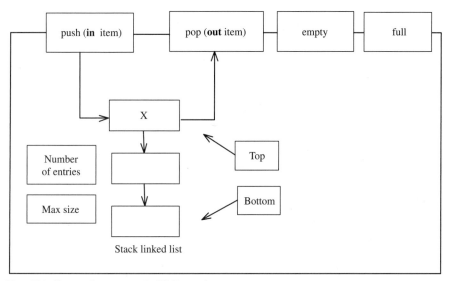

Note: This diagram does not use the UML notation.

Figure 2.5   *Example of a stack information hiding object implemented as a linked list*

The same concepts can be applied to designing a stack class, which is a template for creating stack objects. A stack class is defined as containing the data structure to be used for the stack and the operations that manipulate it, as shown in Figure 2.6. Individual stack objects are instantiated as required by the application. Each stack object has its own identity. It also has its own local copy of the stack data structure, as well as a local copy of any other instance variables required by the stack's operations.

Stack
push (**in** item) pop (**out** item) empty () : Boolean full () : Boolean

Figure 2.6   *Example of a stack information hiding class*

2.3   Relationships between Classes

There are three main types of relationships between classes: associations, whole/part relationships, and generalization/specialization relationships. Sections 2.3.1 through 2.3.3 describe each type in turn.

2.3.1   Associations

An **association** is a static, structural relationship between two or more classes. The **multiplicity** of an association specifies how many instances of one class may relate to a single instance of another class. The multiplicity of an association may be

- **One-to-one (1..1)**. In a one-to-one association between two classes, the association is one-to-one in both directions.

- **One-to-many (1..*)**. In a one-to-many association, two classes have a one-to-many association in one direction and a one-to-one association in the opposite direction.

- **Numerically specified (m..n)**. A numerically specified association is an association that refers to a specific range of numbers.

- **Optional (0..1)**. In an optional association, two classes have a zero-to-one association in one direction and a one-to-one association in the opposite direction. This means that there might not always be a link from an object in one class to an object in the other class.

- **Many-to-many (*)**. In a many-to-many association, two classes have a one-to-many association in each direction.

An example of classes and their associations in a banking application is given in Figure 2.7. The Bank class has a one-to-many relationship with the Customer class and the Debit Card class. Customer has a many-to-many relationship with Account; so a customer might have more than one account, and an account could be a joint account belonging to more than one customer. Customer has an optional association with Debit Card; so a given customer might or might not own a debit card, but a debit card must belong to a customer. Bank has a one-to-one relationship with President; so a bank can have only one president, and a president can be president of only one bank. The attributes of these classes are shown in Figure 2.8.

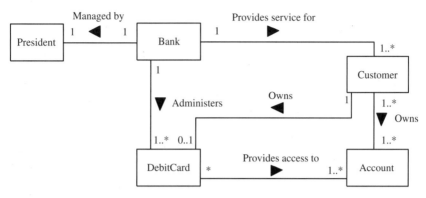

Figure 2.7   *Example of associations on a class diagram*

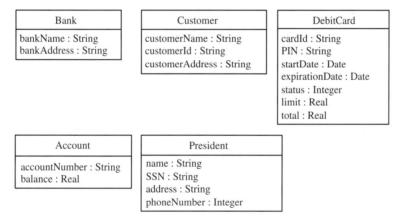

Figure 2.8   *Example of class attributes on a class diagram*

2.3.2   Composition and Aggregation Hierarchies

Composition and aggregation are special forms of relationships in which the classes are tightly bound by the **whole/part** relationship. Both composition and aggregation hierarchies address a class that is made up of other classes.

Composition is a stronger form of aggregation, and an aggregation is stronger than an association. In particular, the **composition** relationship demonstrates a stronger relationship between the parts and the whole than does the aggregation relationship. A composition is also a relationship among instances.

Thus the part objects are created, live, and die together with the whole. The part object can belong to only one whole.

An example of a composition hierarchy is the class `Microwave Oven`, which represents the whole and is composed of several part classes: `Door Sensor`, `Heating Element`, `Display`, `Weight Sensor`, and `Turntable`. There is a one-to-one association between the `Microwave Oven` composite class and each of the part classes, as shown in Figure 2.9.

The **aggregation** hierarchy is a weaker form of whole/part relationship. In an aggregation, part instances can be added to and removed from the aggregate whole. For this reason, aggregations are likely to be used to model conceptual classes rather than physical classes. In addition, a part may belong to more than one aggregation.

An example of an aggregation hierarchy is the `Automated Storage & Retrieval System` (`ASRS`), which consists of one-to-many relationships with `ASRS Bin`, `ASRS Stand`, and `Forklift Truck` (see Figure 2.10). The reason that the ASRS is modeled as an aggregation is that it could be expanded to add more bins, stands, and trucks after it has been created.

2.3.3   Inheritance and Generalization/Specialization

Inheritance is a useful abstraction mechanism in analysis and design. Inheritance naturally models objects that are similar in some but not all respects, thus having some common properties but other unique properties that distinguish them. Inheritance is a classification mechanism that has been widely used in other fields. An example is the taxonomy of the animal kingdom, in which animals are classified as mammals, fish, reptiles, and so on. Cats and dogs have common properties that are generalized into the properties of mammals. However, they also have unique properties: A dog barks and a cat mews.

Inheritance is a mechanism for sharing and reusing code between classes. A child class inherits the properties (encapsulated data and operations) of a parent class. It can then adapt the structure (i.e., encapsulated data) and behavior (i.e., operations) of its parent class. The parent class is referred to as a **superclass** or *base class*. The child class is referred to as a **subclass** or *derived class*. The adaptation of a parent class to form a child class is referred to as *specialization*. Child classes may be further specialized, allowing the creation of class hierarchies, also referred to as **generalization/specialization** hierarchies.

Class inheritance is a mechanism for extending an application's functionality by reusing the functionality specified in parent classes. Thus a new class can be incrementally defined in terms of an existing class. A child class can adapt

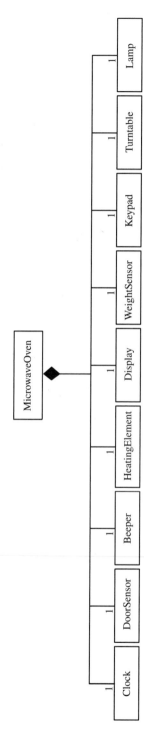

Figure 2.9 *Example of a composition hierarchy*

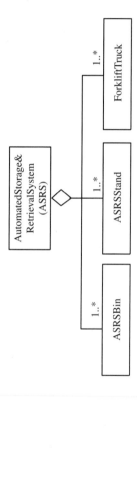

Figure 2.10 *Example of an aggregation hierarchy*

the encapsulated data (referred to as instance variables) and operations of its parent class. It adapts the encapsulated data by adding new instance variables. It adapts the operations by adding new operations or by redefining existing operations. It is also possible for a child class to suppress an operation of the parent; however, such suppression is not recommended, because in that case the subclass no longer shares the interface of the superclass.

Consider the example of bank accounts given in Figure 2.11. Checking accounts and savings accounts have some attributes in common and others that are different. The attributes that are common to all accounts—namely, account Number and balance—are made attributes of an Account superclass. Attributes specific to a savings account, such as cumulative Interest (in this bank, checking accounts do not accumulate any interest), are made attributes of the subclass Savings Account. Attributes specific to a checking account, such as last Deposit Amount, are made attributes of the subclass Checking Account.

For each of the subclasses, new operations are added. For the Savings Account subclass, the new operations are read Cumulative Interest to read cumulative Interest, and add Interest to add the daily interest. For the Checking Account subclass, the new operation is read Last Deposit Amount. This example is treated in more detail in Chapter 9.

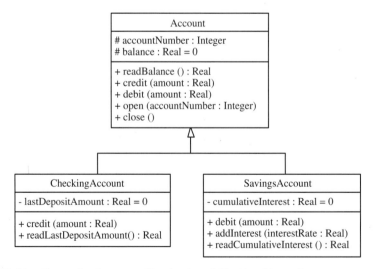

Figure 2.11 *Example of a generalization/specialization hierarchy*

2.4 Dynamic Modeling

Whereas static modeling provides insight into the static structure of a system, dynamic modeling provides a view of a system in which control and sequencing are considered, either within an object (by means of a finite state machine) or among objects (by consideration of the sequence of interactions among them).

To model the sequence of interaction among objects for a particular scenario, it is necessary to define the objects that participate in the scenario, the external object and external event that trigger the scenario, and the subsequent sequence of interactions among the internal objects. If an object's actions are state-dependent, then its sequence of internal states, events, and actions can be modeled with a finite state machine.

An example of dynamic modeling is given in Figure 2.12, in which a user makes a request to view some account information. The object named a User Interface sends the read request to the object an Account, which responds with the account data. The user interface object then formats and displays the response to the user. The messages are numbered to depict the sequence of message interactions, as shown in the UML communication diagram in Figure 2.12.

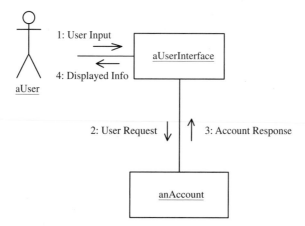

Figure 2.12 *Example of dynamic modeling*

2.5 Sequential and Concurrent Applications

An object may be active or passive. Whereas objects are often passive—that is, they wait for another object to invoke an operation and never initiate any actions—some object-oriented methods and languages, such as Ada and Java, support active objects. Active (concurrent) objects execute independently of other active objects.

A **sequential application** is a sequential program that consists of passive objects and has only one thread of control. When an object invokes an operation in another object, control is passed from the calling operation to the called operation. When the called operation finishes executing, control is passed back to the calling operation. In a sequential application, only synchronous message communication (i.e. procedure call or method invocation) is supported.

In a **concurrent application**, there are typically several concurrent objects, each with its own thread of control. Asynchronous message communication is supported, so a concurrent source object can send an asynchronous message to a concurrent destination object and then continue executing, regardless of when the destination object receives the message. If the destination object is busy when the message arrives, the message is buffered for the object.

2.5.1 Concurrent Objects

Concurrent objects are also referred to as *active objects*, *concurrent tasks*, or *threads* (Gomaa 2000). A **concurrent object** (**active object**) has its own thread of control and can initiate actions that affect other objects. **Passive objects** have operations that are invoked by concurrent objects. Passive objects can invoke operations in other passive objects. A passive object has no thread of control; thus, passive objects are instances of passive classes. An operation of a passive object, once invoked by a concurrent object, executes within the thread of control of the concurrent object.

A concurrent object represents the execution of a sequential program or a sequential component in a concurrent program. Each concurrent object deals with one sequential thread of execution; thus, no concurrency is allowed within a concurrent object. However, overall system concurrency is achieved by the execution of multiple concurrent objects in parallel. Concurrent objects often execute asynchronously (i.e., at different speeds) and are relatively independent of each other for significant periods of time. From time to time, concurrent objects need to communicate and synchronize their actions.

2.5.2   Cooperation between Concurrent Objects

In the design of concurrent systems, several problems need to be considered that do not arise in the design of sequential systems. In most concurrent applications, concurrent objects must cooperate with each other in order to perform the services required by the application. The following three problems commonly arise when concurrent objects cooperate with each other:

1. The **mutual exclusion problem** occurs when concurrent objects need to have exclusive access to a resource, such as shared data or a physical device. A variation on this problem, in which the mutual exclusion constraint can sometimes be relaxed, is the *multiple readers and writers* problem.

2. The **synchronization problem** occurs when two concurrent objects need to synchronize their operations with each other.

3. The **producer/consumer problem** occurs when concurrent objects need to communicate with each other in order to pass data from one concurrent object to another. Communication between concurrent objects is often referred to as interprocess communication (IPC).

Example of Cooperation between Concurrent Objects

Consider an example of event synchronization from concurrent robot systems. Each robot system is designed as a concurrent object and controls a moving robot arm. A pick-and-place robot brings a part to the work location so that a drilling robot can drill four holes in the part. On completion of the drilling operation, the pick-and-place robot moves the part away.

Several synchronization problems need to be solved here. First, there is a collision zone where the pick-and-place and drilling robot arms could potentially collide. Second, the pick-and-place robot must deposit the part before the drilling robot can start drilling the holes. Third, the drilling robot must finish drilling before the pick-and-place robot can remove the part. The solution is to use event synchronization, as described next.

The pick-and-place robot moves the part to the work location, moves out of the collision zone, and then signals the event `part Ready`. This signal awakens the drilling robot, which moves to the work location and drills the holes. After completing the drilling operation, the drilling robot moves out of the collision zone and then signals a second event, `part Completed`, which the pick-and-place robot is waiting to receive. After being awakened, the pick-and-place robot removes the part. Each robot task executes a loop, because the robots repetitively perform their operations. The solution is as follows (see also Figure 2.13):

Figure 2.13   *Example of synchronization between concurrent objects*

Pick-and-Place Robot:

```
while workAvailable do
    Pick up part
    Move part to work location
    Release part
    Move to safe position
    signal (partReady)
    wait (partCompleted)
    Pick up part
    Remove from work location
    Place part
end while;
```

Drilling Robot:

```
while workAvailable do
    wait (partReady)
    Move to work location
    Drill four holes
    Move to safe position
    signal (partCompleted)
end while;
```

2.6 Software Architecture and Components

A **software architecture** (Bass et al. 2003; Shaw and Garlan 1996) separates the overall structure of the system, in terms of components and their interconnections, from the internal details of the individual components. The emphasis on components and their interconnections is sometimes referred to as *programming-in-the-large*, and the detailed design of individual components is referred to as *programming-in-the-small*.

Component-based systems need an infrastructure that is specifically intended to accommodate preexisting components. Previously developed components are integrated with other components. For such integration to be possible, components must conform to a particular software architecture standard.

This section describes the main characteristics of component-based systems that make them a vehicle for building flexible and extensible software product lines. Component technology provides an environment for software product lines to evolve more easily and to be more easily integrated with legacy systems.

The concepts listed here, which are fundamental to software components and component-based systems regardless of the specific technology used, are described in Sections 2.6.1 through 2.6.8:

1. Components and component interfaces

2. Connectors

3. Middleware

4. Distributed component communication protocols

5. Application services

6. Registration services

7. Brokering and discovery services

8. Wrapper components

2.6.1 Components and Component Interfaces

A **component** is a self-contained, usually concurrent, object with a well-defined interface, capable of being used in different applications from that for which it was originally designed. To fully specify a component, it is necessary to define it in terms of the operations it *provides* and the operations it *requires* (Magee et al. 1994; Shaw and Garlan 1996). Such a definition is in contrast to conventional object-oriented approaches, which describe an object only in terms of the operations it provides. However, if a preexisting component is to be integrated into a component-based system, it is just as important to understand—and therefore to represent explicitly—both the operations that the component requires and those that it provides.

2.6.2 Connectors

In addition to defining the components, a software architecture must define the connectors that join the components. A **connector** encapsulates the interconnection protocol between two or more components. Different kinds of message communication between components include **asynchronous** (loosely coupled) and **synchronous** (tightly coupled). The interaction protocols for each of these types of communication can be encapsulated in a connector. For example, although asynchronous message communication between components on the same node is logically the same as between components on different nodes, different connectors would be used in the two cases. In the former case, the connector could use a shared memory buffer; the latter case would use a different connector that sends messages over a network.

2.6.3 Middleware

Middleware is a layer of software that sits above the heterogeneous operating system to provide a uniform platform above which distributed applications, such as client/server systems (Figure 2.14), can run (Bacon 1997). An early form of middleware was the remote procedure call (RPC). Other examples of middleware technology are DCE (Distributed Computing Environment) that uses RPC technology, Java remote method invocation (RMI), Component Object Model (COM) (Box 1998), Jini (Arnold et al. 1999), J2EE (Java 2 Platform Enterprise Edition) (Szyperski 2003), and CORBA (Common Object Request Broker Architecture) (Mowbray and Ruh 1997).

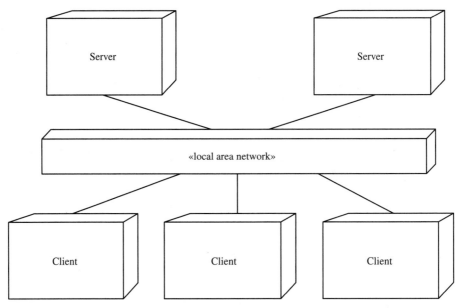

Figure 2.14 *Distributed processing configuration*

By providing a uniform way of interconnecting and reusing objects, middleware technologies such as CORBA, COM, and JavaBeans promote component reuse, and hence are also referred to as component technologies (Szyperski 2003). Distributed component technologies include CORBA, which is an OMG standard, COM and .NET from Microsoft, and JavaBeans and Jini connection technology from Sun Microsystems.

An example of middleware in a client/server configuration is shown in Figure 2.15. On the client node is the client application, which uses a graphical user interface (GUI). There is a standard operating system, such as Windows XP, and network communication software, such as TCP/IP (Transmission Control Protocol/Internet Protocol), which is the most widely used protocol on the Internet. A middleware layer sits above the operating system and the network communication software. On the server node is the server application software, which makes use of the middleware services that reside on top of the operating system (e.g., UNIX or Windows XP), and the network communication software. A file or database management system, usually relational, is used for long-term information storage.

2.6.4   Distributed Component Communication Protocols

Application components need to have a communication protocol for intercomponent communication—for example, between clients and servers. Distributed components communicate over a network using a network protocol, such as

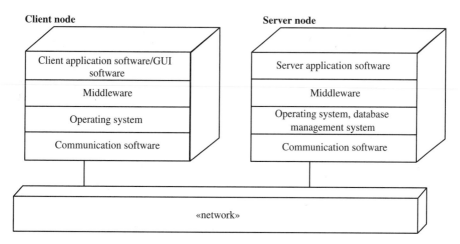

Figure 2.15   *Example of middleware in distributed component-based applications*

TCP/IP. Applications communicate using an application layer protocol that sits above TCP/IP, such as FTP (File Transfer Protocol), electronic mail, and HTTP (HyperText Transfer Protocol) on the World Wide Web.

XML (Extensible Markup Language) is a technology that allows different systems to interoperate through exchange of data and text. The Simple Object Access Protocol (SOAP) is a lightweight protocol, developed by the World Wide Web Consortium (W3C), that builds on XML and HTTP to permit exchange of information in a distributed environment. SOAP defines a unified approach for sending XML-encoded data consisting of three parts: an envelope that defines a framework for describing what is in a message and how to process it, a set of encoding rules for expressing instances of application-defined data types, and a convention for representing remote procedure calls and responses.

2.6.5   Application Services

Applications provide services for clients. One example of application services is **Web services**, which use the World Wide Web for application-to-application communication. From a software perspective, Web services are the application programming interfaces (APIs) made available to provide a standard means of communication among different software applications on the World Wide Web. From a business application perspective, a Web service is business functionality provided by a company in the form of an explicit service over the Internet for other companies or programs to use. A Web service is provided by a service provider and may be composed of other services to form new services and applications. An example of a Web client invoking a Web service is given in Figure 2.16.

Several component technologies exist to support the building of applications by means of component technology and Web services, including .NET, J2EE, WebSphere, and WebLogic.

2.6.6   Registration Services

A registration service is provided for servers to make their services available to clients. Servers register their services with a registration service—a process referred to as *publishing* or *registering* the service. Most brokers, such as CORBA and Web service brokers, provide a registration service. For Web services, a **service registry** is provided to allow services to be published and located via the World Wide Web. Service providers register their services together with service descriptions in a service registry. Clients searching for a service can look up the

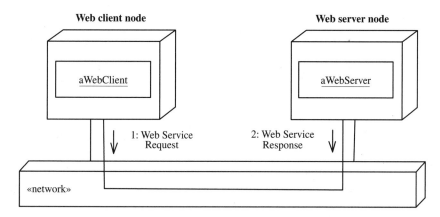

Figure 2.16 *Web client and Web server in a World Wide Web services application*

service registry to find a suitable service. The Web Services Description Language (WSDL) is an XML-based language used to describe what a service does, where it resides, and how to invoke it.

2.6.7 Brokering and Discovery Services

In a distributed environment, an **object broker** is an intermediary in interactions between clients and servers. Servers register the services that they provide with the broker. Clients can then request these services via the broker. The broker provides location transparency and platform transparency. Sophisticated object brokers provide white pages (naming services) and yellow pages (trader services) to help clients locate services more easily. Broker patterns are described in Chapter 10.

An example of brokering technology is the Common Object Request Broker Architecture (CORBA), which is an open systems standard, developed by the Object Management Group, that allows communication between objects on heterogeneous platforms (Mowbray and Ruh 1997). The Object Request Broker (ORB) middleware allows client/server relationships between distributed objects. Server objects provide services that can be invoked from client objects by means of the ORB. Using an ORB, a client object can invoke an operation on a server object without having to know where the object is located, what platform (hardware and operating system) it is running on, what communication protocol is required to reach it, or what programming language it is implemented in.

Another example of brokering technology is a Web services broker. Information about a Web service can be defined by the Universal Description, Discovery, and Integration (UDDI) framework for Web services integration. A UDDI specification consists of several related documents and an XML schema that defines a SOAP-based protocol for registering and discovering Web services. A Web services broker can use the UDDI framework to provide a mechanism for clients to dynamically find services on the Web.

Figure 2.17 shows an example of a Web client making a Web services discovery request to a Web services broker and getting a response from the broker identifying a particular Web service. The Web client then sends a request to the Web server for the discovered service.

2.6.8 Wrapper Components

Although many legacy applications cannot be easily integrated into a software product line, one approach is to develop wrapper components. A **wrapper component** is a distributed application component that handles the communication and management of client requests to legacy applications (Mowbray and Ruh 1997). A wrapper registers its service with the naming service so that it can receive client service requests.

Most legacy applications were developed as stand-alone applications. In some cases the legacy code is modified so that the wrapper component can access it. However, such modification is often impractical because there is often little or no documentation and the original developers are no longer present.

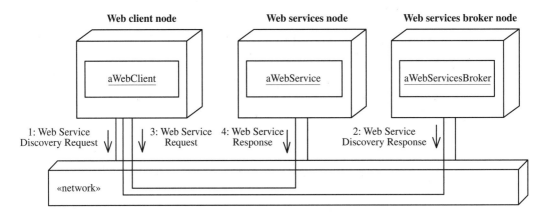

Figure 2.17 *Example of a Web services broker*

Consequently, wrapper components often interface to legacy code through crude mechanisms such as files, which might be purely sequential or indexed sequential files. The wrapper component reads or updates files maintained by the legacy application. If the legacy application uses a database, the database could be accessed directly through the use of database wrapper components that would hide the details of how to access the database. For example, with a relational database, the database wrapper would use Structured Query Language (SQL) statements to access the database.

Developers can integrate legacy code into a component-based application by placing a wrapper around the legacy code and providing an interface to it. The wrapper maps external requests from components into calls in the legacy code. The wrapper also maps outputs from the legacy code into responses to the component.

2.7   Summary

This chapter described key concepts in the design of software product lines, as well as important concepts for developing the component-based architecture of these systems. The object-oriented concepts introduced here form the basis of several of the forthcoming chapters. Chapter 6 will describe how static modeling is applied to modeling software product lines. Chapters 7 and 8 will describe how dynamic modeling is applied to modeling software product lines—Chapter 7 focusing on dynamic modeling between objects using object interaction modeling, and Chapter 8 focusing on dynamic modeling within an object using finite state machines.

This chapter also described the concepts of components and component-based systems, emphasizing component fundamentals rather than technologies, which tend to change frequently. The development of component-based software architectures will be described further in Chapter 11. All three case studies in Chapters 13, 14, and 15 will develop component-based software solutions.

chapter

Software Product Line Engineering

This chapter introduces the UML-based software product line design method, which is described in much greater detail in subsequent chapters of the book. One of the goals of this method is to be capable of extending other design methods, such as the author's COMET method (Concurrent Object Modeling and Architectural Design Method) (Gomaa 2000), to model and design software product lines. The acronym for the method is PLUS (*Product Line UML-Based Software Engineering*). However, PLUS is also intended to be capable of integration with other software methods and processes to give them the capability of supporting product line development.

This chapter considers the PLUS method from a software process perspective. The development process for the PLUS method is an iterative object-oriented software process that is compatible with the Unified Software Development Process (USDP) (Jacobson et al. 1999) and the spiral process model (Boehm 1988). This chapter presents an evolutionary software process for product lines and describes how the PLUS method may be used with the USDP or the spiral model. It then outlines the main activities of the PLUS method and concludes with a description of the steps in using PLUS.

Section 3.1 introduces the Evolutionary Software Product Line Engineering Process (ESPLEP), the process by which the PLUS method is used. Section 3.2 describes phases of the software product line engineering process. Section 3.3 describes the two main strategies for developing a software product line: forward evolutionary engineering and reverse evolutionary engineering. Section 3.4 describes the integration of the PLUS method with the spiral model. Section 3.5 describes the integration of the PLUS method with the Unified Software Development Process. Section 3.6 describes the requirements, analysis, and design models in software product lines. Finally, the important topic of product line scoping is discussed in Section 3.7.

3.1 Evolutionary Software Product Line Engineering Process

The Evolutionary Software Product Line Engineering Process (ESPLEP) model is a software process model that eliminates the traditional distinction between software development and maintenance. Instead, systems evolve through several iterations. Hence, systems developed with this approach need to be capable of adapting to changes in requirements during each iteration. Furthermore, because new software systems are often outgrowths of existing ones, the ESPLEP model takes a software product line perspective, allowing the development of software product families.

When considering the development of a family of products that constitute a product line, it is necessary to replace the model-based software development activities for single systems of requirements modeling, analysis modeling, and design modeling by development activities that span the product family.

The ESPLEP process model consists of two major processes or life cycles, as depicted in Figure 3.1:

1. **Software product line engineering**. During this process, the commonality and variability in the product line are analyzed in light of the overall requirements of the product line. This activity consists of developing a product line use case model, product line analysis model, software product line architecture, and reusable components. Testing is carried out on the components, as well as on some application configurations of the product line. Artifacts produced during product line engineering are stored in a software product line repository.

2. **Software application engineering**. During this process, an individual application that is a member of the software product line is developed. Instead of starting from scratch, as is usually done with single systems, the application developers make full use of all the artifacts developed during the software product line engineering life cycle. Given the overall requirements of the individual application, the product line use case model is adapted to derive the application use case model, the product line analysis model is adapted to derive the application analysis model, and the software

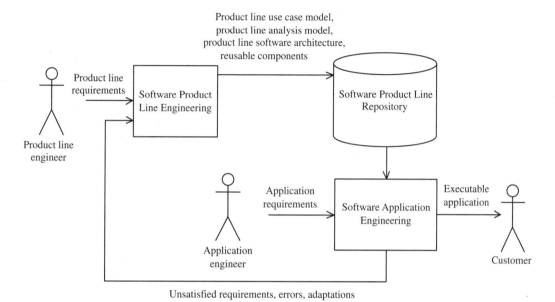

Figure 3.1 *Evolutionary Software Product Line Engineering Process*

product line architecture is adapted to derive the architecture of the software application. Given the application architecture and the appropriate components from the product line repository, the executable application is deployed. Software application engineering will be described in Chapter 12.

3.2 Software Product Line Engineering Phases

The ESPLEP model is a highly iterative software development process based on the use case concept. During requirements modeling, the functional requirements of the product line are defined in terms of actors and use cases. During analysis modeling, each product line use case is realized to describe the objects that participate in the use case, and their interactions. During design modeling, the component-based software architecture for the product line is developed. The phases of ESPLEP for the Software Product Line Engineering process are described in Sections 3.2.1 through 3.2.5 and depicted in Figure 3.2. All artifacts produced during each phase are stored in the software product line repository.

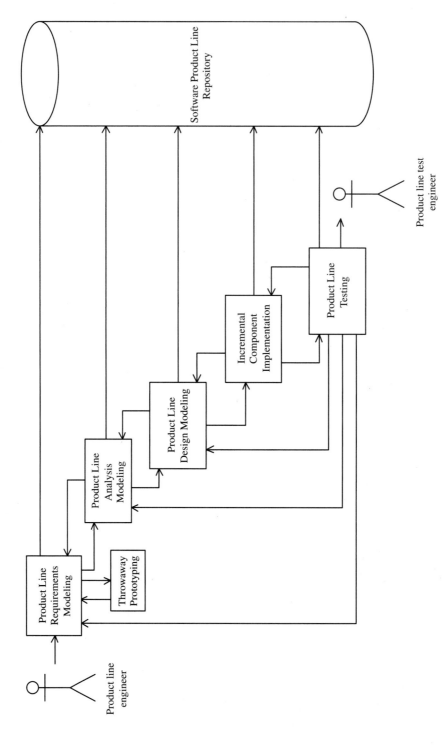

Figure 3.2 *Software Product Line Engineering with ESPLEP*

3.2.1   Software Product Line Requirements Modeling

During the software product line requirements modeling phase, a requirements model consisting of a use case model and a feature model is developed. As with single systems, the use case model defines the functional requirements of the product line in terms of actors and use cases. However, the use case model for a product line needs to be extended to model the commonality and variability in the product line through the development of kernel, optional, and alternative use cases. A narrative description of each use case is also developed. User inputs and active participation are essential to this effort. If the application requirements are not well understood, a throwaway prototype can be developed to help clarify the requirements.

For software product lines, a feature model also needs to be developed. A **feature** is a requirement or characteristic that is provided by one or more members of the product line. In particular, features are characteristics that are used to differentiate among members of the product line and hence to determine and define the common and variable functionality of a software product line. Features can be either functional or parameterized.

3.2.2   Software Product Line Analysis Modeling

In the software product line analysis modeling phase, static and dynamic models are developed. The *static model* defines the structural relationships among problem domain classes. The classes and their relationships are depicted on class diagrams. Object structuring criteria are used to determine the objects to be considered for the analysis model. A *dynamic model* is then developed in which the use cases from the requirements model are realized to show the objects that participate in each use case and how they interact. Objects and their interactions are depicted on object interaction diagrams, which are either communication diagrams or sequence diagrams. In the dynamic model, state-dependent objects are defined by means of statecharts.

For software product lines, the *static model* addresses the commonality and variability among the members of the product line by categorizing classes as kernel, optional, or variant. The *dynamic model* addresses commonality and variability by developing interaction diagrams for each use case from the requirements model—namely, kernel, optional, and alternative use cases—and providing an impact analysis approach for analyzing changes to use cases. The approach starts with development of the dynamic model for the kernel use cases and then evolves that model to address the optional and alternative use cases.

A special consideration for product lines is the development of **feature/ class dependencies**. For each functional feature, the classes that realize the product line feature's functionality are determined. For each parameterized feature, the values that can be given to each product line parameter are determined.

3.2.3   Software Product Line Design Modeling

In the software product line design modeling phase, the component-based software architecture of the product line is designed; that is, the analysis model is mapped to an operational environment. The analysis model (which emphasizes the problem domain) is mapped to the design model (which emphasizes the solution domain). Component structuring criteria are provided to structure the system into component-based subsystems, which are considered as composite objects. The architectural design starts by considering software architectural patterns, which address both the structure of the architecture (in particular, addressing component dependencies) and the dynamics of the architecture (in terms of how components communicate with each other).

3.2.4   Incremental Component Implementation

After the software architecture has been designed, the next step is incremental component implementation. In this phase, a subset of the product line is selected to be implemented for each increment. The product line developers determine the subset by choosing the use cases to be included in this increment, as well as the components that participate in those use cases. Incremental software implementation starts with the kernel use cases followed by the optional and alternative use cases, according to the sequence established during dynamic modeling.

Incremental component implementation consists of the detailed design, coding, and unit testing of the components in the subset. This is a phased approach by which the product line components supporting each use case are gradually implemented.

3.2.5   Product Line Testing

Product line testing includes both the integration testing and the functional testing of the product line.

During integration testing, the components in each increment are tested. The integration test for the increment is based on the use cases selected for that increment. Integration test cases are developed for each use case. Integration testing is a form of white box testing in which the interfaces between the components that participate in each use case are tested.

Functional testing involves testing the system against its functional requirements. This testing is black box testing and is based on the use cases. Thus, functional test cases are built for each use case. Any software increment released to the customer needs to go through the product line testing phase.

After the software increment is judged to be satisfactory, the next increment is constructed and integrated by iteration through the incremental component implementation and product line testing phases. However, if significant problems are detected in the software increment, iteration through the requirements, analysis, and design modeling phases might be necessary.

With the product line approach, integration and functional testing can be carried out for the **kernel system**, which is a minimal subset of the product line consisting of the kernel components and any default components. Some testing with optional and variant components could be carried out, although this is more likely to be deferred to the software application engineering process, as described in Chapter 12.

3.3   Forward and Reverse Evolutionary Engineering

There are two main strategies for developing a software product line: forward engineering and reverse engineering. In both cases the development is incremental and evolutionary; hence the strategies can be further named *forward evolutionary engineering* and *reverse evolutionary engineering*. Forward evolutionary engineering is best used when a new product line is being developed with no previous systems to guide the development. Reverse evolutionary engineering is best used when the product line development begins with existing systems that are candidates for modernization and inclusion in a project to develop a product line.

3.3.1   Forward Evolutionary Engineering

The initial emphasis of the **forward evolutionary engineering** strategy is development of the kernel of the product line. The product line functionality is analyzed with the goal of determining the common functionality of the product line. Usually this analysis starts with development of the kernel use cases, so that the common use cases that are used by all members of the product line are the first to be developed. This approach is also used for static modeling, in which the kernel product line context model and the kernel entity class model are developed.

During dynamic modeling, the communication diagrams depicting the interaction among the objects that realize the kernel use cases are developed. The designers develop the software architecture for the product line kernel by considering the most appropriate architectural patterns for the product line and mapping the classes from the analysis model to components in the architecture.

During product line evolution, the use case model evolves with additional optional and alternative use cases, which are determined iteratively. During evolution of the static models, the context class diagram and entity class model are expanded to include optional and variant classes. The dynamic model evolves to incorporate optional and alternative communication diagrams. The product line architecture evolves with the addition of optional and variant components.

This strategy has the advantage that evolution is built into the development process, so later the product line can be evolved further. The forward evolutionary engineering strategy works best when a new product line is being developed and the kernel functionality can be determined before the variable functionality.

3.3.2 Reverse Evolutionary Engineering

The **reverse evolutionary engineering** strategy is most applicable when there are existing systems to analyze and model. With this strategy, the use case model of each individual system is analyzed and documented first. The different use case models are then integrated into a product line use case model. Kernel use cases—that is, use cases that are common to all members of the product line—constitute the kernel of the application domain. Use cases that are used by only an individual system or a subset of the product line members constitute optional or alternative use cases.

The reverse evolutionary engineering strategy is also used for the static models. The product line context class model and entity class model are developed through integration of the static models of the individual systems. Classes used by all systems become kernel classes of the product line. Classes used by only some members become optional or variant classes of the product line.

Dynamic modeling takes advantage of the reverse engineering and subsequent model integration by starting with the dynamic modeling based on the kernel use cases, called the *kernel first approach*. The next step is dynamic modeling for the optional and alternative use cases, referred to as *evolutionary product line development*. In this respect, dynamic modeling proceeds in a similar way for both the reverse evolutionary and the forward evolutionary engineering strategies, because the evolutionary engineering stage of the two strategies is being addressed.

3.4   Integration of PLUS with the Spiral Model

3.4.1   Spiral Model

The **spiral model** is a risk-driven process model originally developed by Boehm (1988) to address known problems with earlier process models of the software life cycle—in particular, the waterfall model. The spiral model is intended to encompass other life cycle models, such as the waterfall model, the incremental development model, and the throwaway prototyping model.

In the spiral model, the radial coordinate represents cost, and the angular coordinate represents progress in completion of a cycle of the model. The spiral model consists of the following four quadrants, as shown in Figure 3.3:

1. Define objectives, alternatives, and constraints

2. Analyze risks

3. Develop product

4. Plan next cycle

Each cycle of the spiral model iterates through these four quadrants, although the number of cycles is project-specific. The descriptions of the activities in each quadrant are intended to be general enough that they can be included in any cycle.

The goal of the spiral model is to be risk-driven, so the risks in a given cycle are determined in the "Analyze risks" quadrant. To manage these risks, certain additional project-specific activities may be planned to address the risks, such as requirements prototyping if the risk analysis indicates that the software

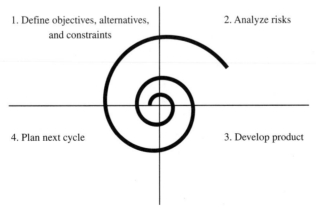

Note: This diagram does not use the UML notation.

Figure 3.3   *Spiral process model*

requirements are not clearly understood. These project-specific risks are termed *process drivers*. For any process driver, one or more project-specific activities need to be performed to manage the risk (Boehm and Belz 1990).

3.4.2   Double Spiral Model for Software Product Line Engineering

The spiral model can be applied to the development of a software product line, as well as the development of individual products that are members of the product line. This dual capability leads to the concept of a double spiral model for software product line engineering: one spiral for product line development and one for each of the product line members (see Figure 3.4). In effect, there are

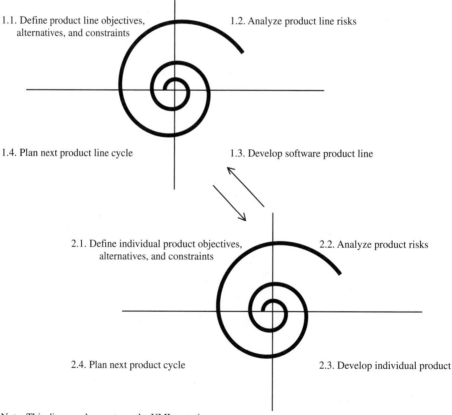

Note: This diagram does not use the UML notation.

Figure 3.4   *Double spiral process model for software product lines*

multiple spiral instances, but the activities for product line engineering and application engineering are sufficiently different that considering the development as being double spirals is warranted. In particular, sometimes the two spirals need to execute in parallel and feed information back and forth, especially when both the product line spiral and the individual product spiral are evolving at the same time.

The PLUS method is used with the spiral model as follows. During the project planning for a given cycle of the spiral model, the project manager decides what specific technical activity should be performed in the third quadrant, which is the product development quadrant. The selected technical activity, such as software product line requirements modeling, software product line analysis modeling, or software product line design modeling, is then performed in the third quadrant. The risk analysis activity (performed in the second quadrant) and cycle planning (performed in the fourth quadrant) determine how many iterations are required through each of the technical activities.

3.5   Integration of PLUS with Unified Software Development Process

3.5.1   Unified Software Development Process

The Unified Software Development Process (USDP), as described in Jacobson et al. 1999, is a use case–driven software process that uses the UML notation. The USDP is also known as the *Rational Unified Process* (*RUP*) (Kroll and Kruchten 2003; Kruchten 2003). USDP/RUP is a popular process for UML-based software development. This section describes how the PLUS method can be used with the USDP/RUP process.

The USDP consists of five core workflows and four phases and is iterative, as shown in Figure 3.5. An **artifact** is defined as a piece of information that is produced, modified, or used by a process (Kruchten 2003). A **workflow** is defined as a sequence of activities that produces a result of observable value (Kruchten 2003). A **phase** is defined as the time between two major milestones during which a well-defined set of objectives is met, artifacts are completed, and decisions about whether to move on to the next phase are made (Kruchten 2003). There is usually more than one iteration in a phase. Thus a phase iteration in USDP corresponds to a cycle in the spiral model.

Each cycle goes through all four phases and addresses the development of a core workflow. The workflows and products of each workflow are as follows:

Phases

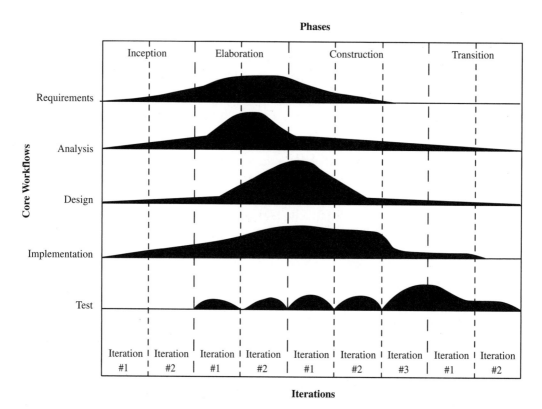

Figure 3.5 *Unified Software Development Process* (I. Jacobson, G. Booch, J. Rumbaugh, *The Unified Software Development Process*, [Figure 1.5, p. 11], © 1999 Addison-Wesley Longman, Inc. Reprinted with permission.)

1. **Requirements**. The product of the Requirements workflow is the use case model.
2. **Analysis**. The product of the Analysis workflow is the analysis model.
3. **Design**. The products of the Design workflow are the design model and the deployment model.
4. **Implementation**. The product of the Implementation workflow is the implementation model.
5. **Test**. The product of the Test workflow is the test model.

Like the spiral model, the USDP is a risk-driven process. The life cycle phases of the USDP are as follows (Jacobson et al. 1999; Kruchten 2003):

1. **Inception**. During the inception phase, the seed idea is developed to a sufficient level to justify entering the elaboration phase.

2. **Elaboration**. During the elaboration phase, the software architecture is defined.

3. **Construction**. During the construction phase, the software is built to the point at which it is ready for release to the user community.

4. **Transition**. During the transition phase, the software is turned over to the user community.

3.5.2   How PLUS Relates to USDP

The USDP, as described in Jacobson et al. 1999, emphasizes process and—to a lesser extent—method. The USDP provides considerable detail about the life cycle aspects and some detail about the method to be used. The PLUS method is compatible with the USDP. As explained in Section 3.5.1, the workflows of the USDP are Requirements, Analysis, Design, Implementation, and Test.

PLUS and USDP are related like this: Each phase of the PLUS life cycle corresponds to a workflow of the USDP. The phases of PLUS have the same names as the workflows of the USDP—not surprisingly, because the PLUS life cycle was strongly influenced by Jacobson's work on object-oriented software engineering (Jacobson 1992) and USDP (Jacobson et al. 1999).

Sections 3.5.3 through 3.5.8 will discuss, step-by-step, how the PLUS method is integrated with the USDP. All of the phases, each involving several workflows, are iterative; and the number of iterations is project-specific.

3.5.3   Inception

The first PLUS iteration, inception, involves a feasibility study to determine whether the product line is viable and what its scope is—namely, what its size, functionality, degree of commonality and variability, and estimated number of product line members are. This iteration yields sufficient information about the product line to allow a decision to be made about whether to proceed with further development. Product line scoping is described in more detail in Section 3.7.

During inception, initial use cases are identified for each potential member of the product line. Using the use case model integration approach, the developers determine the kernel use cases of the product line. Sufficient static modeling at the analysis level is carried out to determine the initial product line context class diagram. An initial feature model is developed to determine the common, optional, and alternative features. This iteration helps establish the size, functionality, and degree of commonality and variability in the product line.

3.5.4   Elaboration—Iteration #1: Kernel First

During the first iteration of the elaboration phase, the use case model is reviewed and developed in greater detail. Kernel, optional, and alternative use cases are determined. Variation points are analyzed.

This use case analysis leads into feature analysis. In fact, use case analysis and feature analysis can proceed in tandem because the commonality and variability analysis needs to be done for both use cases and features. The relationship between the use case model and the feature model for the product line needs to be clearly analyzed and documented. Once the feature model has been completed, it becomes the primary driver in the product line for describing common and variable requirements.

Once the kernel of the product line has been determined, it is necessary to develop the analysis and design models around that kernel. For the analysis model, the communication diagrams for the kernel use cases are determined, and the statecharts for the state-dependent control objects are designed. During initial design modeling, the relevant architectural patterns for the product line are analyzed, and an initial high-level kernel software architecture is developed.

If a new product line is being developed with the forward evolutionary engineering approach, this iteration addresses development of the kernel use case model, kernel static model, and kernel dynamic model of the product line. If the product line is being developed with the reverse evolutionary engineering approach, this iteration starts with analysis of the existing systems and the subsequent model integration, to determine the kernel use case model, kernel static model, and kernel dynamic model of the product line.

3.5.5   Elaboration—Iteration #2: Product Line Evolution

During the second iteration of the elaboration phase, developers address product line evolution by considering the optional and alternative use cases and features, and examining the details of the variation points.

In the corresponding analysis modeling, communication diagrams for the optional and alternative use cases are developed, along with statecharts for the optional and variant state-dependent control classes. In addition, the expanded versions of the parameterized statecharts (where additional events, transitions, and actions are needed) address the variability introduced by the optional and alternative features and variation points.

For design modeling, the product line architecture is expanded to include the optional and variant components.

This iteration proceeds in a similar way for both the forward evolutionary engineering and reverse evolutionary engineering approaches because it addresses the evolutionary engineering stages of the two approaches.

3.5.6 Construction—Iteration #1: Construction of the Kernel Components

During the first construction iteration, detailed design, coding, and unit testing of the kernel components are carried out. Integration testing of the kernel components is also performed.

3.5.7 Transition—Iteration #1: Testing of the Kernel System

During the first transition iteration, the integration and functional testing of the kernel system, a minimal executable product line system consisting of the kernel components and any default components, is carried out. The kernel system is a member of the product line and can be released to users for further testing and usage.

3.5.8 Further Iterations of Product Line Engineering

Further iterations could be carried out to develop additional optional and variant components. The project manager(s) must decide whether any additional components should be implemented or whether any further implementation should instead be part of the software application engineering process. Further iterations would involve the construction and testing of the evolved architecture consisting of optional and variant components.

3.5.9 The Unified Process with Software Application Engineering

The USDP can also be applied to software application engineering. For each member application of the product line, the USDP process is applied in full, from inception to transition. The software application engineering process is described further in Chapter 12.

3.6 Requirements, Analysis, and Design Modeling in Software Product Lines

The UML notation supports requirements, analysis, and design concepts. The PLUS method described in this book separates requirements activities, analysis activities, and design activities for software product lines.

Requirements modeling addresses the functional requirements of the product line—in particular, defining commonality and variability. PLUS differentiates analysis from design as follows: *Analysis* is breaking down or decomposing the problem so that it is understood better; *design* is synthesizing or composing (putting together) the solution. These activities are described in more detail in Sections 3.6.1 through 3.6.3.

3.6.1 Activities in Requirements Modeling for Software Product Lines

Requirements modeling for software product lines consists of three main activities:

1. **Product line scoping**. At a high level, the following aspects of the product line are determined: its functionality, the degree of commonality and variability, and the likely number of product line members. Product line scoping is described in Section 3.7.

2. **Use case modeling**. Actors and use cases are defined, and the functional requirements of the product line are specified in terms of those use cases and actors. Product line commonality is determined by the development of kernel use cases. Product line variability is determined by the development of optional and alternative use cases, and by the identification of variation points within use cases. Use case modeling is described in Chapter 4.

3. **Feature modeling**. Features are the primary vehicle for describing commonality and variability in software product lines. A **feature** is a requirement or characteristic that is provided by one or more members of the software product line. Software product line commonality is characterized by kernel features; product line variability is characterized by optional and alternative features. Features can also be organized into sets—for example, a set of mutually exclusive features. Features can be identified from the use cases determined during use case modeling. Feature modeling is described in Chapter 5.

3.6.2 Activities in Analysis Modeling for Software Product Lines

The analysis model for software product lines emphasizes understanding the problem. An important objective is to identify the problem domain objects and the information passed between them. Issues such as whether an object is active or passive, whether a message sent is asynchronous or synchronous, and what operation is invoked at a receiving object are deferred until design time.

The activities in analysis modeling for software product lines are as follows:

- **Static modeling**. A problem-specific static model is defined. This model is a structural view of the information aspects of the system. Classes are defined in terms of their attributes, as well as their relationships with other classes. For information-intensive systems, this view is of great importance. The emphasis is on the information modeling of real-world classes in the problem domain—in particular, entity classes and external classes. Static modeling is described in Chapter 6.

- **Object structuring**. The objects—kernel, optional, and alternative—that participate in each use case are determined. Object structuring criteria are provided to help determine the objects, which can be entity objects, interface objects, control objects, and application logic objects. Object structuring is described in Chapter 6. After the objects have been determined, the dynamic relationships between objects are depicted in the dynamic model.

- **Dynamic modeling**. The use cases from the use case model are realized to show the interaction among the objects participating in each kernel, optional, and alternative use case. Communication diagrams or sequence diagrams are developed to show how objects interact to execute the use case. Chapter 7 describes dynamic modeling, including the kernel first and product line evolution approaches, which are used to help determine how objects interact with each other to support the use cases.

- **Finite state machine modeling**. The state-dependent aspects of the product line are defined by means of hierarchical statecharts. Each state-dependent control object is defined in terms of its constituent statechart. For state-dependent object interactions, the interactions among the state-dependent control objects and the statecharts they execute need to be modeled explicitly. Finite state machines are described in Chapter 8.

- **Feature/class dependency analysis**. This step is used to determine what classes from the analysis model are needed to realize the features from the feature model. Product line classes are categorized as kernel, optional, or variant. Feature/class dependency analysis is described in Chapter 9.

3.6.3   Activities in Design Modeling for Software Product Lines

In the design model for software product lines, the solution domain is considered. The goal is to develop a component-based software architecture for the product line. To create the product line architecture, developers consider what software architectural patterns should provide its foundation.

The activities in design modeling for software product lines are as follows:

- **Software architectural pattern–based design**. It is necessary to understand both the structural and communication patterns that can be used for designing the product line software architecture. Structural patterns address the overall structure of the software architecture. Communication patterns address the ways in which distributed components can communicate with each other. Software architectural patterns for product lines are described in Chapter 10.

- **Software product line architectural design**. The design of the product line architecture is approached from the viewpoint of structuring a distributed application into software components and their interconnections. Separation of concerns in component design is an important issue. Components are categorized according to their roles in the software architecture. Software product line architectural design is described in Chapter 11.

3.7   Software Product Line Scoping

Software product line scoping involves assessing what functionality—in particular, what degree of commonality and variability—should be provided by the product line. Having variability in a product line adds another dimension of complexity. Managing variability is an important concern in a product line because it adds another dimension to version and configuration control. The goal of product line scoping is to provide a preliminary estimate of the size of the product line, the degree of common functionality with respect to total product line functionality, and the degree of variable functionality in the product line, as well as a preliminary identification of the potential members of the product line.

The product line needs to be in a well-understood application domain. Having one or more domain experts is important to an understanding of the product line's requirements. The application domain needs to be relatively stable to avoid unexpected volatility. It is necessary to be able to identify several potential systems that could be members of the product line. The additional analysis and design effort required for a software product line needs to be justified through cost savings from having multiple product line members whose development costs can be shared. The members of the product line must have both a significant degree of common functionality and significant differences. If the differences completely outweigh the commonality, however, these systems may not constitute an adequate product line, and in that case it is better not to pursue development of a product line.

The analysis starts with a single system or existing systems that have sufficient similarity to warrant forming the basis of a product line. Both the commonality and the variability in the product line need to be explored. The analysis must not abstract away the differences between systems and create a generic architecture. Rather, differences between systems need to be actively investigated. It is helpful to describe each system using a common notation, such as UML, even though that notation may not have originally been used to describe the system. If there is little or no existing documentation for legacy systems, it may be necessary to analyze the original code used in those systems. It is essential to extract the requirements of existing systems, and to do so, it may be necessary to reverse-engineer the requirements from the code. In such cases, care must be taken to avoid incorporating design and coding decisions in the reverse-engineered requirements model. It is also useful to anticipate future requirements in these systems where possible and to include those in the requirements model.

Product line scoping is the first attempt at analyzing the requirements of the product line. It involves identifying the boundary of the product line—that is, what functionality is inside the product line and what is outside the product line. An initial feature analysis of each potential member of the product line is carried out to provide a preliminary assessment of what the common features are, and what the scope of the optional and alternative features is.

3.8 Summary

This chapter described an evolutionary software process model for product lines that incorporates the PLUS design method, before describing how the PLUS method could be integrated with existing software engineering process models—in particular, the spiral model and the Unified Software Development Process. The process model for developing software product lines consists of two main processes. One process is software product line engineering, which was described in this chapter. There are two main strategies for software product line engineering: forward evolutionary engineering and reverse evolutionary engineering. The other process is software application engineering, which involves adapting the software product line architecture to derive a software application, which is a member of the product line. Software application engineering will be described in more detail in Chapter 12.

The evolutionary software product line engineering process, as described in this book, consists of three iterative phases. The first phase is requirements modeling, which consists of use case modeling (described in Chapter 4) and feature modeling (described in Chapter 5). The second phase is analysis modeling, which consists of static modeling (described in Chapter 6), dynamic modeling (described in Chapters 7 and 8), and feature/class dependency modeling (described in Chapter 9). The third phase is design modeling, which consists of analyzing the product line architectural patterns (described in Chapter 10) and developing the component-based software architecture (described in Chapter 11).

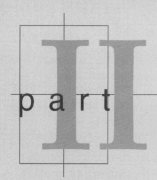

part

II

Requirements, Analysis, and Design Modeling for Software Product Lines

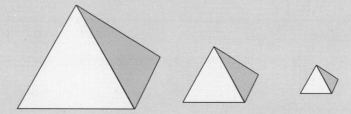

Use Case Modeling for Software Product Lines

The use case approach has been very successful for modeling the functional requirements of single systems. This chapter describes how the use case approach can be extended to model software product lines.

All of the software requirements specified for a single system need to be provided by the system. For a software product line, which consists of a family of systems, only some requirements are common to all family members. To specify the functional requirements of a software product line, it is important to capture the common requirements of the product line—that is, the requirements that are common to all members of the family—as well as the optional and alternative requirements. Optional requirements are needed by only some members of the product line. Alternative requirements are handled differently by different members of the product line.

In extending the use case modeling approach to specify the functional requirements of software product lines, it is necessary to define different kinds of use cases: kernel use cases, which are needed by all members of the product line; optional use cases, which are needed by only some members of the product line; and alternative use cases, where different use cases are needed by different members of the product line.

This chapter starts with a description in Section 4.1 of use case modeling in single systems. Section 4.2 then gives an overview of use case modeling in software product lines. The important topic of how to identify use cases is covered in Section 4.3. Section 4.4 describes how to document use cases. Section 4.5 gives an example of a use case description. The key topic of modeling variability in use cases is introduced in Section 4.6. Section 4.7 then describes how to model small variations. Modeling variability with the extend relationship is described in Section 4.8; modeling variability with the include relationship is described in Section 4.9. Finally, Section 4.10 describes use case modeling from the perspective of the software product line engineering process.

4.1   The Use Case Model in Single Systems

This section briefly describes use case modeling in single systems, as a prelude to the discussion in Section 4.2 of how these concepts are extended to software product lines.

4.1.1   Use Cases

In the use case approach, functional requirements are defined in terms of actors, which are users of the system, and use cases. An actor participates in a use case. A **use case** defines a sequence of interactions between one or more actors and the system. In the requirements phase, the use case model considers the system as a black box and describes the interactions between the actor(s) and the system in a narrative form consisting of user inputs and system responses. The **use case model** describes the functional requirements of the system in terms of the actors and use cases. The use cases in the use case model define the external requirements of the system. Each use case defines the functional behavior of one part of the system without revealing its internal structure. During subsequent analysis modeling, the objects that participate in each use case are determined.

An example of a simple use case model is given in Figure 4.1, which consists of two use cases (View Alarms and View Factory Status) and one

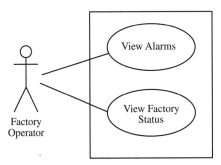

Figure 4.1   *Example of an actor and use cases*

actor (Factory Operator). Factory Operator is the actor for both use cases. In View Alarms, factory alarms are displayed to the operator. In View Factory Status, the operator requests the system to display the current status of the different factory workstations.

4.1.2   Actors

An **actor** characterizes an outside user or related set of users that interact with the system (Rumbaugh et al. 2005). In the use case model, actors are the only external entities that interact with the system.

There are several variations on how actors are modeled (Fowler 2004). An actor is very often a human user. In many information systems, humans are the only actors. It is also possible in information systems for an actor to be an external system. In some applications, an actor can also be an external I/O device or a timer. External I/O device and timer actors are particularly prevalent in real-time embedded systems, in which the system interacts with the external environment through sensors and actuators.

A **primary actor** initiates a use case. Thus the use case starts with an input from the primary actor to which the system has to respond. Other actors, referred to as **secondary actors**, may participate in the use case later. A primary actor in one use case can be a secondary actor in another use case. At least one actor must gain value from the use case; usually this is the primary actor. In real-time embedded systems, however, where the primary actor can be an external I/O device or timer, the primary beneficiary of the use case can be a human secondary actor who receives some information from the system.

A human actor may use various I/O devices to physically interact with the system. For example, the human actor in Figure 4.1, Factory Operator, interacts with the system via standard I/O devices, such as a keyboard, display, or mouse. In some cases, however, an actor can be the I/O device itself—in particular, when a use case does not involve a human, such as in real-time applications. An example of an I/O actor is Factory Sensor, which provides sensor input to the Monitor Factory Sensors use case shown in Figure 4.2.

An actor can also be a timer that periodically sends timer events to the system. Periodic use cases are needed when certain information needs to be output by the system on a regular basis. This capability is particularly important in real-time systems, but it can also be useful in information systems. In the microwave product line, for example, a timer actor either initiates or participates in several use cases. An example is given in Figure 4.3. The Timer actor initiates the Display Time of Day use case, which periodically (every minute) computes

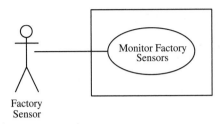

Figure 4.2   *Example of an input device actor*

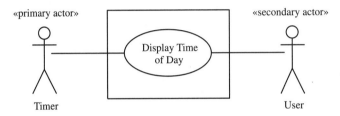

Figure 4.3   *Example of a timer actor*

and updates the time-of-day clock and displays its value to the user. In this case the timer is the primary actor, and the user is the secondary actor. This is an example of the secondary actor gaining value from the use case.

An actor can also be an external system that either initiates (as primary actor) or participates (as secondary actor) in the use case. An example of an external system actor is Factory Robot in the factory automation software product line. Factory Robot initiates the Generate Alarm and Notify use case, as shown in Figure 4.4. The robot generates alarm conditions that are sent to interested factory operators who have subscribed to receive alarms. In this

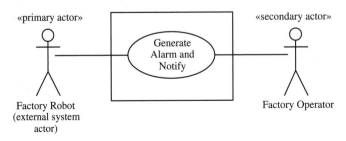

Figure 4.4   *Example of an external system actor*

use case, `Factory Robot` is the primary actor that initiates the use case, and `Factory Operator` is a secondary actor who receives the alarms.

An actor represents a role played in the application domain, typically by a user. Whereas a user is an individual, an actor represents the role played by all users of the same type. For example, a factory automation software product line has three human actors: `Factory Operator`, `Workflow Engineer`, and `Production Manager`. If it is possible for a human user to play two or more independent roles, then each role can be represented by a different actor. For example, the same user might play, at different times, both a `Production Manager` role and a `Factory Operator` role and thus be modeled by two actors.

It is also possible to have multiple users playing the same role; for example, the factory automation system may have several operators. Thus an actor models a user type, and individual users are instances of the actor.

4.2   The Use Case Model for Software Product Lines

For a single system, all use cases and actors are required. When a product line is being modeled, however, usually only some of the use cases and actors are required by a given member of the product line. Use cases that are required by all members of the product line are referred to as **kernel use cases**. **Optional use cases** are required by some but not all members of the product line. Some use cases may be alternatives; that is, different versions of the use case are required by different members of the product line. These **alternative use cases** are usually mutually exclusive.

UML **stereotypes** are a standard extension mechanism provided by UML and used to distinguish among the different kinds of modeling elements (Rumbaugh et al. 2005). For product line use cases, the stereotypes «kernel», «optional», and «alternative» are used, respectively, to distinguish among use cases that are always required, use cases that are sometimes required, and use cases in which a choice must be made.

In the use case model for the microwave oven software product line (Figure 4.5), the `Cook Food` use case is kernel because a microwave oven cannot function without the capability of cooking food. On the other hand, the `Set Time of Day` and `Display Time of Day` use cases are optional because in this product line, a time-of-day clock is not provided on basic microwave ovens. Similarly, the `Cook Food with Recipe` use case is also optional because only upscale microwave ovens have the recipe capability.

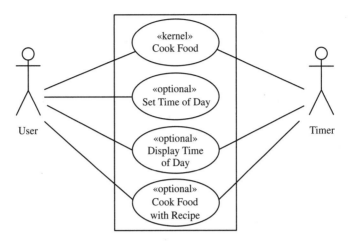

Figure 4.5 *Example of kernel and optional use cases*

In this example, User is a primary actor for the Cook Food, Cook Food with Recipe, and Set Time of Day use cases because the user is the actor who initiates these use cases. However, User is a secondary actor for the Display Time of Day use case because Timer is the primary actor that initiates this use case. On the other hand, Timer is a secondary actor for the Cook Food and Cook Food with Recipe use cases because it participates in the use cases by providing timer events but does not initiate them.

In the electronic commerce product line, in addition to kernel and optional use cases, there are alternative use cases. Figure 4.6 gives an example of three use cases and one actor, Supplier. The Confirm Shipment use case is kernel

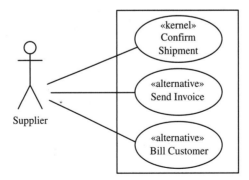

Figure 4.6 *Example of kernel and alternative use cases*

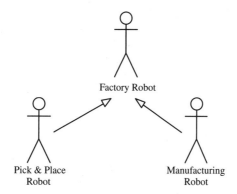

Figure 4.7   *Generalization and specialization of actors*

because the supplier always confirms a shipment after the customer's order has been handled. However, there are also two alternative use cases for billing customers. For home customers, Supplier executes the Bill Customer use case because the customer is billed as soon as the purchased item has been shipped. For corporate customers, Supplier executes the Send Invoice use case because an invoice is sent to the customer after the item has been shipped. The use cases Bill Customer and Send Invoice are alternative use cases because they represent mutually exclusive functionality provided in business-to-consumer (B2C) systems and business-to-business (B2B) systems, respectively.

In a software product line, just as some use cases can be optional, some actors might also be optional. In the same way that there can be alternative use cases, there might also be alternative actors. Sometimes different actors might have some roles in common but other roles that are different. In this situation, the actors can be generalized so that the common part of their roles is captured as a generalized actor. An example is provided by the factory automation product line in Figure 4.7. The Factory Robot actor (see Figure 4.4) captures the generalized role played by all factory robots. However, the Pick & Place Robot and Manufacturing Robot actors are modeled as specialized roles.

4.3   Identifying Use Cases

A use case starts with input from the primary actor. The use case is a complete sequence of interactions initiated by an actor, specifying the interaction between the actor and the product line system. **Product line system** is the name given to a software system that is a member of the software product family. Simple use cases might involve only one interaction with an actor, whereas more-complicated use cases involve several interactions with the actor and might also involve more than one actor.

To determine the use cases in a system, it is useful to start by considering the actors and the actions they initiate in the system. Each use case describes a sequence of interactions between the actor(s) and the system. A use case should provide some value to an actor.

Thus the functional requirements of the system are defined in terms of the use cases, which constitute an external specification of a system. When developing use cases, however, it is important to avoid a functional decomposition in which several small use cases describe individual functions of the system rather than describing a sequence of interactions that provides a useful result to the actor.

The main sequence of the use case describes the most common sequence of interactions between the actor and the system. There may also be branches off the main sequence of the use case that address less-frequent interactions between the actor and the system. These deviations from the main sequence are executed only under certain circumstances—for example, if the actor makes an incorrect input to the system. Depending on the application requirements, these alternative branches through the use case sometimes join up later with the main sequence. The alternative branches are also described in the use case.

Consider the microwave oven software product line. This product line has one kernel use case: the Cook Food use case (see Figure 4.5). The primary actor is the user who wishes to cook some food. A secondary actor, the timer, counts down the time when the oven is cooking the food. In the main sequence, the user opens the door, places the food in the oven, closes the door, selects the cooking time, and presses **Start**. The oven starts cooking the food. When the cooking time elapses, the oven stops cooking. The user opens the door and removes the food.

There are various alternatives. For example, the customer might open the door before cooking is finished, in which case cooking is stopped. In other cases the user might press **Cancel** or might press **Start** when the door is open.

4.4 Documenting Product Line Use Cases

Product line use cases are documented as follows:

- **Use case name**. Each use case is given a name.
- **Reuse category**. This section specifies whether the use case is kernel, optional, or alternative.

- **Summary**. This section briefly describes the use case, typically in one or two sentences.

- **Actors**. This section names the actors in the use case. There is always a primary actor that initiates the use case. In addition, secondary actors may participate in the use case.

- **Dependency**. This optional section describes whether the use case depends on other use cases—that is, whether it includes or extends another use case.

- **Preconditions**. This section specifies one or more conditions that must be true at the start of the use case.

- **Description**. The bulk of the use case is a narrative description of the main sequence of the use case, which is the most usual sequence of interactions between the actor(s) and the system. The description is in the form of the input from the actor, followed by the response of the system. The system is treated as a black box—that is, dealing with *what* the system does in response to the actor's inputs, not the internals of *how* it does it.

- **Alternatives**. This section provides a narrative description of alternative branches off the main sequence. There may be several alternative branches.

- **Variation points**. This section defines the places in the use case description where different functionality can be introduced for the different members of the product line. Variation points are described in more detail in Section 4.6.

- **Postcondition**. This section identifies the condition that is always true at the end of the use case if the main sequence has been followed.

- **Outstanding questions**. This section documents questions about the use case for discussions with users.

4.5   Example of a Use Case Description

This section contains a use case description for the Cook Food use case (see Figure 4.5) from the microwave oven software product line. The use case description is given for the main sequence of the kernel use case, followed by a description of the alternative paths. In Section 4.6, a description of the variation points is added. In this use case the main sequence is numbered. Each alternative sequence identifies the line number at which the alternative applies. The same approach is used later for describing the variation points.

Use case name: Cook Food.

Reuse category: Kernel.

Summary: User puts food in oven, and microwave oven cooks food.

Actors: User (primary), Timer (secondary).

Precondition: Microwave oven is idle.

Description:

1. User opens the door, puts food in the oven, and closes the door.
2. User presses the **Cooking Time** button.
3. System prompts for cooking time.
4. User enters cooking time on the numeric keypad and presses **Start**.
5. System starts cooking the food.
6. System continually displays the cooking time remaining.
7. Timer elapses and notifies the system.
8. System stops cooking the food and displays the end message.
9. User opens the door, removes the food from the oven, and closes the door.
10. System clears the display.

Alternatives:

Line 1: User presses **Start** when the door is open. System does not start cooking.

Line 4: User presses **Start** when the door is closed and the oven is empty. System does not start cooking.

Line 4: User presses **Start** when the door is closed and the cooking time is equal to zero. System does not start cooking.

Line 6: User opens door during cooking. System stops cooking. User removes food and presses **Cancel**, or user closes door and presses **Start** to resume cooking.

Line 6: User presses **Cancel**. System stops cooking. User may press **Start** to resume cooking. Alternatively, user may press **Cancel** again; system then cancels timer and clears display.

Postcondition: Microwave oven has cooked the food.

4.6 Modeling Variability in Use Cases

In a software product line it is necessary to describe variations that are handled differently by different members of the product line. One way of handling use case variability in software product lines is through variation points. A **variation point** is a location in a use case where a change can take place (Jacobson et al. 1997). The term *variation* in this context means a situation that is handled differently by different members of the product line.

Variation points in use cases can be handled in one of two ways. For small variations, the variation point is described in the use case itself, identifying the place in the use case where the change can occur. This could be stated as a line number in a use case description or in an alternative branch. Modeling small variations is described in Section 4.7.

When a use case becomes too complex because modeling the alternatives or variation points within the use case is very intricate, dependencies between use cases can be defined by include and extend relationships. The objective is to maximize the extensibility and reuse of use cases. Abstract use cases are determined to identify common patterns in several use cases, which can then be extracted and reused. Use case relationships are a powerful modeling tool in single systems. In software product lines, variation points can also be effectively modeled with the include and extend relationships. Modeling variability with the extend relationship is described in Section 4.8; modeling variability with the include relationship is described in Section 4.9.

4.7 Modeling Small Variations

Using extension and inclusion use cases to handle variations in a product line works best when the use case contains a block of functionality that can be described as a sequence of interactions between an actor and the system. In some situations, however, a small variation affects only one or two lines in the use case descriptions. Trying to address those situations in separate use cases is liable to fragment the use case model, leading to several small use cases. A different approach for handling small variations is to identify them as variation points within the use case itself. Variation points within a use case are used to specify optional functionality or alternative functionality within the product line.

To document a small variation, the following information should be provided:

- **Name** of the variation point.
- **Type of functionality** to be inserted at the variation point: optional, mandatory alternative, optional alternative.
- **Line in the use case** description where the variability can be introduced.

- **Description of functionality** inserted at the variation point. Either optional functionality or alternative functionality can be introduced at the variation point.

4.7.1 Modeling Optional Functionality with Variation Points

A variation point that specifies optional functionality in the use case describes functionality that might be, but does not have to be, provided by a given member of the product line. If the option identified by the variation point is selected for a given member of the product line, then that functionality will be inserted in the use case at the location(s) specified by the variation point.

Consider the following two examples of optional functionality from a use case for a microwave oven: a light and a turntable. The first variation point is for a lighting option, in which the light is turned on when the door is opened and turned off when the door is closed. The light is also turned on when the oven starts cooking the food and turned off when the oven stops cooking. The second variation point is for an optional turntable, where the turntable starts rotating when the oven starts cooking and stops rotating when the oven stops cooking. This optional functionality is identified through the variation points `Light` and `Turntable` in the use case, as shown in the following examples:

Name: Light.

Type of functionality: Optional.

Line number(s): 1, 5, 8, 9.

Description of functionality: If `Light` option is selected, light is switched on for duration of cooking and when the door is open. Light is switched off when the door is closed and when cooking stops.

Name: Turntable.

Type of functionality: Optional.

Line number(s): 5, 8.

Description of functionality: If `Turntable` option is selected, turntable rotates for duration of cooking.

4.7.2 Modeling Alternative Functionality with Variation Points

A variation point that specifies alternative functionality in the use case describes several possible alternative functions, one of which could be inserted at the location in the use case specified by the variation point. One of the alternatives may be a default. Depending on the variation point, one of the alternatives must always be selected; this alternative is referred to as a *mandatory* (also *required* or *necessary*) *alternative*. With the other kind of alternative functionality variation point, one possibility is not to select any of the alternatives; this alternative is referred to as an *optional alternative*.

As an example of alternative functionality, assume that the manufacturer of the oven is an original equipment manufacturer with an international market, where the microwave oven will form the basis of a product line from basic to top-of-the-line. The microwave oven displays messages to the user such as prompts and warning messages. Because the oven is to be sold around the world, it is necessary to be able to vary the display language. The default language is English; other possible languages are French, Spanish, German, and Italian. In this case the display language is a variation point. Every microwave oven must incorporate a display language, but there is a choice of which language. This is defined as a variation point called `Display Language`, as described next.

Name: Display Language.

Type of functionality: Mandatory alternative.

Line number(s): 3, 8.

Description of functionality: There is a choice of language for displaying messages. The default is English. Alternative mutually exclusive languages are French, Spanish, German, and Italian.

4.8   Modeling Variability with the Extend Relationship

In certain situations, a use case can become very complex, with many alternative branches. The extend relationship is used to model alternative paths that a basic use case might take. This section describes the extend relationship in single systems and then goes on to describe how it may be used to model variability in software product lines.

4.8.1   The Extend Relationship in Single Systems

A use case can become too complex if it has too many alternative, optional, and exceptional sequences of interactions. A solution to this problem is to split off an alternative or optional sequence of interactions into a separate use case. The purpose of this new use case is to extend the old use case, if the appropriate conditions hold. The use case that is extended is referred to as the **base use case**, and the use case that does the extending is referred to as the **extension use case**.

Under certain conditions, a base use case can be extended by a description given in the extension use case. A base use case can be extended in different ways, depending on whether certain conditions are true. The extend relationship can be used as follows:

- To show a conditional part of the base use case that is executed only under certain circumstances

- To model complex or alternative paths

It is important to note that the base use case does not depend on the extension use case and can function independently. The extension use case, on the other hand, executes only if the condition in the base use case that causes it to execute is true. The extension use case cannot function without the presence of a base use case. Although an extension use case usually extends only one base use case, it is possible for it to extend more than one. A base use case can be extended by more than one extension use case.

An example of the extend relationship is provided by the factory automation product line case study. A workflow engineer defines several manufacturing operations and then defines a workflow plan describing a sequence of operations to manufacture a part. All of this could be modeled as one use case. Adding an extension use case, however, offers more flexibility, as shown in Figure 4.8. Create/Update Operation is a base use case that is executed once for each operation created. The Create/Update Workflow Plan use case extends the Create/Update Operation use case. The alternatives section of

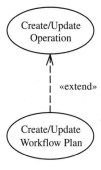

Figure 4.8 *Example of an extend relationship*

the `Create/Update Operation` use case description states that the workflow engineer may choose to create a workflow plan defining a sequence of operations that have previously been created. Thus a workflow engineer can create several operations with the `Create/Update Operation` use case and then optionally create a workflow plan with the `Create/Update Workflow Plan` use case.

4.8.2   Extension Points in Software Product Lines

Extension points are used to specify the precise locations in the base use case at which extensions can be added. An extension use case may extend the base use case only at these extension points (Fowler 2004; Rumbaugh et al. 2005).

Each extension point is given a name. The extension use case may have one or more insertion segments—one segment for each extension point. Each segment is inserted at the location of its extension point in the base use case. The extend relationship is given a list of extension point names, which must be equal to the number of segments in the extension use case. The extend relationship can be conditional, meaning that a condition is defined that must be true for the extension use case to be invoked. Thus it is possible to have more than one extension use case for the same extension point, but with each extension use case satisfying a different condition.

A segment defines a behavior sequence to be executed when the extension point is reached. When an instance of the use case is executed and reaches the extension point in the base use case, if the condition is satisfied, then execution of the use case is transferred to the corresponding segment in the extension use case. Execution transfers back to the base use case after completion of the segment. If more than one extension use case exists for the same extension point, then execution is transferred to the extension use case whose condition is true.

In software product lines, an extension point with one extension use case can be used to model an optional variation in which the extension use case specifies the optional functionality. If the extension condition is true for a given member of the product line, then the optional functionality is provided by that member.

In software product lines, an extension point with multiple extension use cases can be used to model several alternative variations in which each extension use case specifies a different alternative. The extension conditions are designed such that only one condition can be true, and hence only one extension use case selected, for any given member of the product line.

There are different kinds of extension conditions. A *selection condition* can be used in either single systems or product lines. It is used to identify which extension condition is selected during runtime execution of the use case because at any one time, one extension use case could be chosen, and at a different time an alternative extension use case could be chosen. In other words, the selection condition is set and changes during runtime of the use case. Selection conditions for alternative extension use cases are mutually exclusive, so at any one time only one of these conditions can be true.

On the other hand, a *product line condition* identifies whether the functionality described by a particular extension use case is provided by a given member of the product line. If the product line condition is true, then the functionality is provided; whereas if the condition is false, the functionality is not provided. The product line condition is set during configuration of the product line member and does not change at runtime. Product line conditions for alternative extension use cases are not usually mutually exclusive, because it is possible for a given product line member to provide more than one alternative. If an extension use case is kernel, then it is not necessary to allocate it a product line condition, because it will always be available. However, if the extension use case is an optional or alternative use case, it will need to have a product line condition.

Example of Extension Points in Software Product Lines

Consider the following example for a supermarket product line (Figure 4.9). An extension point called `payment` is declared in a base use case called `Check Out Customer`. The base use case deals with checking out customer purchases. Three extension use cases deal with the type of payment made: `Pay by Cash`, `Pay by Credit Card`, and `Pay by Debit Card`. Consider two different prod-

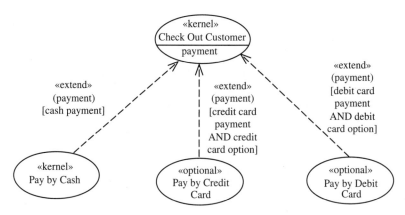

Figure 4.9   *Example of an extend relationship and extension use cases*

uct line situations. If the three extension use cases are kernel—that is, if every member of the product line provides these three types of payment—then it is only necessary to provide a selection condition for each extension use case. The mutually exclusive selection conditions are [cash payment], [credit card payment], and [debit card payment], respectively. During execution of the use case, depending on how the customer chooses to pay, the appropriate selection condition is set to true.

On the other hand, consider the situation in which payment by cash is kernel—that is, every member of the product line provides this feature. In this situation, payment by credit card and payment by debit card are optional use cases, provided by some systems but not others. Hence, Pay by Cash is a kernel use case, while Pay by Credit Card and Pay by Debit Card are optional use cases. The mutually exclusive selection conditions are as before: [cash payment], [credit card payment], and [debit card payment]. For each of the optional alternative use cases, however, there also needs to be a product line condition. These conditions are called [credit card option] and [debit card option], respectively. Note that although the credit card and debit card selection conditions are mutually exclusive, the product line conditions are not, because both credit card and debit card options could be selected for a given member of the product line.

At the location in the base use case where payment is required, the use case description is as follows:

Check Out Customer base use case:

Use case name: Check Out Customer.

Reuse category: Kernel.

Summary: System checks out customer.

Actor: Customer.

Precondition: Checkout station is idle, displaying a "Welcome" message.

Description:

1. Customer scans selected item.

2. System displays the item name, price, and cumulative total.

3. Customer repeats steps 1 and 2 for each item being purchased.

4. Customer selects payment.

5. System prompts for payment by cash, credit card, or debit card.

6. <payment>

7. System displays thank-you screen.

In this base use case description, at step 6 <payment> is a placeholder that identifies the location at which the appropriate extension use case is executed. For the `Pay by Cash` extension use case, the extension condition is a selection condition called [cash payment]. This extension use case is executed if the condition [cash payment] is true.

Pay by Cash extension use case:

Use case name: Pay by Cash.

Reuse category: Kernel.

Summary: Customer pays by cash for items purchased.

Actor: Customer.

Dependency: Extends `Check Out Customer`.

Precondition: Customer has scanned items but not yet paid for them.

Description:

1. Customer selects payment by cash.
2. System prompts customer to deposit cash in bills and/or coins.
3. Cashier enters cash amount.
4. System computes change.
5. System displays total amount due, cash payment, and change.
6. System prints total amount due, cash payment, and change on receipt.

For the `Pay by Credit Card` extension use case, the selection condition is called [credit card payment]. There is also a product line condition, which is called [credit card option]. The extension condition is the logical AND of the selection condition and product line condition—namely, [credit card payment AND credit card option] (see Figure 4.9). This extension use case is executed if the extension condition is true, meaning that the credit card option is provided by this member of the product line *and* the user chose to pay by credit card. Of course, if the user chose instead to pay by cash, then the `Pay by Cash` use case would be executed instead.

Pay by Credit Card extension use case:

Use case name: Pay by Credit Card.

Reuse category: Optional.

Summary: Customer pays by credit card for items purchased.

Actor: Customer.

Dependency: Extends `Check Out Customer`.

Precondition: Customer has scanned items but not yet paid for them.

Description:

1. Customer selects payment by credit card.
2. System prompts customer to swipe card.
3. Customer swipes card.
4. System reads card ID and expiration date.
5. System sends transaction to authorization center containing card ID, expiration date, and payment amount.
6. If transaction is approved, authorization center returns positive confirmation.
7. System displays payment amount and confirmation.
8. System prints payment amount and confirmation on receipt.

The use case description for the `Pay by Debit Card` extension use case is handled in a similar way, except that the customer also needs to enter a PIN. `Pay by Debit Card` has a selection condition called [debit card payment] and a product line condition called [debit card option].

4.8.3   Modeling Product Line Variability with Extension Points

Extension points can be used to model software product line variability in the following ways:

- **Alternative variability**. Alternative extension use cases are mutually exclusive. Each extension use case has a product line condition in the extend relationship, which must be true for the alternative use case to be provided. For a variation point providing mandatory alternative functionality, at least one of the product line conditions must be true. For a variation point providing optional alternative functionality, it is possible for none of the product line conditions to be true.

- **Optional variability**. An optional use case is provided by a product line system only if the product line condition is true.

- **Future product line evolution**. An extension point can also allow future evolution of the software product line because other extension use cases could be added later, with different conditions to represent new functionality. With this approach, the extension point is used as a placeholder for future extensions to the product line. For example, someday supermarkets may allow payment by electronic cash cards. In that case a `Pay by Electronic Cash` extension use case would need to be written. There would also need to be a product line condition called [electronic cash option] and a selection condition called [electronic cash payment].

4.9 Modeling Variability with the Include Relationship

The use case include relationship is used in situations where, after the initial use cases for an application have been developed, common sequences of interactions between the actor and the system are determined that span several use cases.

This section describes the include relationship in single systems before describing how it may be used to model variability in software product lines.

4.9.1 The Include Relationship in Single Systems

These common sequences of interactions reflect functionality that is common to more than one use case. A common sequence of interactions can be extracted from several of the original use cases and made into a new use case, which is called an **inclusion use case**. An inclusion use case is usually abstract; that is, it cannot be executed on its own. An abstract use case must be executed as part of a concrete—that is, executable—use case.

When this common functionality is separated into an inclusion use case, this abstract use case can now be reused by several other use cases. It is then possible to define a more concise version of the old use case, with the common pattern removed. This concise version of the old use case is referred to as a **concrete use case** (or *base use case*), which includes the abstract use case.

Abstract use cases always reflect functionality that is common to more than one use case. When this common functionality is separated into an abstract use case, the abstract use case can be reused by several concrete (executable) use cases. Abstract use cases can often be developed only after an initial iteration in which several use cases have been developed. Only then can repeated sequences of interactions be observed that form the basis for the abstract use cases.

An abstract use case is never executed alone. It is executed in conjunction with a concrete use case, which includes, and hence executes, the abstract use case. In programming terms, an abstract use case is analogous to a library routine, and a concrete use case is analogous to a program that calls the library routine.

An abstract use case might not have a specific actor. The actor is in fact the actor of the concrete use case that includes the abstract use case. Because different concrete use cases use the abstract use case, it is possible for the abstract use case to be used by different actors.

As an example of an abstract use case, consider the Withdraw Funds, Query Account, and Transfer Funds use cases in a banking application. Analysis reveals that the first part of each use case—namely, validating the customer's personal identification number (PIN)—is identical. There is no advantage to repeating the PIN validation process in each use case, so instead, the PIN validation sequence is split off into a separate abstract use case called Validate PIN, which is used by the (revised) Withdraw Funds, Query Account, and Transfer Funds use cases. The use case diagram for this example is shown in Figure 4.10. The relationship between the two types of use cases is an include relationship; the Withdraw Funds, Query Account, and Transfer Funds use cases include the Validate PIN use case.

The include relationship can also be used to structure a lengthy use case. The concrete use case provides the high-level sequence of interactions between actor(s) and system. Abstract use cases provide lower-level sequences of interactions between actor(s) and system. An example of this is the Manufacture High-Volume Part use case (see Figure 4.11), which describes the sequence of interactions in manufacturing a part. This process involves receiving the raw material for the part to be manufactured (described in the Receive Part use case), executing a manufacturing step at each factory workstation (described in the Process Part at High-Volume Workstation use case), and shipping the manufactured part (described in the Ship Part use case).

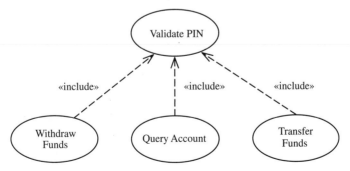

Figure 4.10   *Example of an abstract use case and include relationships*

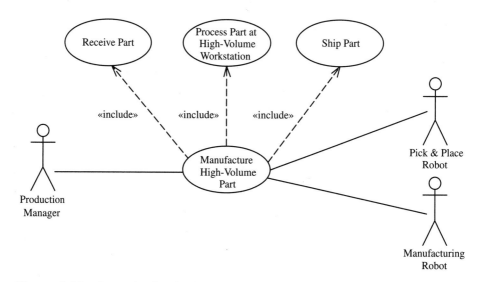

Figure 4.11   *Example of multiple abstract use cases and include relationships*

4.9.2   The Include Relationship in Software Product Lines

The include relationship can be used to support optional use cases. The abstract inclusion use case could be a kernel use case. Some of the concrete use cases, which include the abstract use case, could be kernel; others could be optional. The optional use cases are guarded by an inclusion condition. For a given member of the product line, if the inclusion condition is true, then the optional use case is available for that member.

Example of the Include Relationship in Software Product Lines

Consider the banking example described in Section 4.9.1, which has a kernel abstract use case (Validate PIN) and three kernel concrete use cases (Withdraw Funds, Query Account, and Transfer Funds). Other optional concrete use cases, such as Deposit Funds and Print Statement could also include the kernel Validate PIN use case. The revised use case diagram is shown in Figure 4.12. The optional use cases have to be guarded by inclusion conditions. Hence these optional use cases would be available only if the inclusion condition were true. Thus, if the inclusion condition [deposit option] is true, then the Deposit Funds use case is provided by that member of the product line. Note that optional base use cases could be added later, representing another way of evolving the use case model.

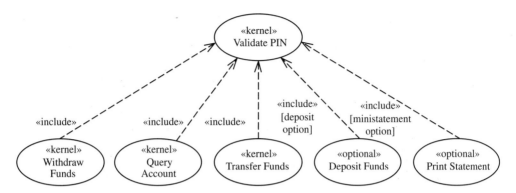

Figure 4.12 *Example of kernel and optional use cases with include relationships*

The main parts of the use case descriptions are given for the kernel abstract use case, a kernel concrete use case, and an optional concrete use case:

Validate PIN abstract use case

Use case name: Validate PIN.

Reuse category: Kernel.

Summary: System validates customer PIN.

Actor: ATM Customer.

Precondition: ATM is idle, displaying a "Welcome" message.

Description:

1. Customer inserts the ATM card into the card reader.
2. If system recognizes the card, it reads the card number.
3. System prompts customer for PIN.
4. Customer enters PIN.
5. System checks the card's expiration date and whether the card has been reported as lost or stolen.
6. If card is valid, system then checks whether the user-entered PIN matches the card PIN maintained by the system.
7. If PIN numbers match, system checks what accounts are accessible with the ATM card.
8. System displays customer accounts and prompts customer for transaction type: withdrawal, query, or transfer.

Alternatives: {Description of alternatives}.

Withdraw Funds concrete use case

Use case name: Withdraw Funds.

Reuse category: Kernel.

Summary: Customer withdraws a specific amount of funds from a valid bank account.

Actor: ATM Customer.

Dependency: Include `Validate PIN` abstract use case.

Precondition: ATM is idle, displaying a "Welcome" message.

Description:

    1. Include `Validate PIN` abstract use case.

    2. Customer selects **Withdrawal**.

    3. {Continue with withdrawal description}.

Deposit Funds concrete use case

Use case name: Deposit Funds.

Reuse category: Optional.

Summary: Customer deposits a specific amount of funds into a valid bank account.

Actor: ATM Customer.

Dependency: Include `Validate PIN` abstract use case.

Inclusion condition: [deposit option].

Precondition: ATM is idle, displaying a "Welcome" message.

Description:

    1. Include `Validate PIN` abstract use case.

    2. Customer selects **Deposit**.

    3. {Continue with deposit description}.

4.9.3   Some Guidelines on Using Abstract Use Cases

Careful application of use case relationships can help with the overall organization of the use case model; however, use case relationships should be employed judiciously. It should be noted that small abstract use cases corresponding to individual functions (such as `Dispense Cash`, `Print Receipt`, and `Eject Card`) should not be considered. These functions are too small, and making them separate use cases would result in a functional decomposition with fragmented use cases in which the use case descriptions would be only a sentence each and not a description of a sequence of interactions. The result would be a use case model that is overly complex and difficult to understand—in other words, a problem of not being able to see the forest (the overall sequence of interactions) for the trees (the individual functions)!

4.10   Use Case Development Strategies

A major challenge in developing use case models for software product lines is distinguishing among the kernel, optional, and alternative use cases. This process is often referred to as **commonality/variability analysis**. As described in Chapter 3, there are two main strategies for developing a software product line: forward evolutionary engineering and reverse evolutionary engineering. The forward evolutionary engineering strategy is best used when a new product line is being developed and the kernel functionality can be determined before the variable functionality. The reverse evolutionary engineering strategy is most applicable when existing systems that are candidates for modernization and inclusion in the product line are available to be analyzed and modeled.

4.10.1   Forward Evolutionary Engineering

The **forward evolutionary engineering** strategy initially emphasizes development of the kernel use case model. The product line functionality is analyzed with the goal of determining the common functionality of the product line and describing this functionality in the kernel use cases. In other words, the kernel use cases (those common to all members of the product line) are developed initially. During product line evolution, additional optional and alternative use cases are determined iteratively. During each iteration, some adjustments can be made as to which use cases are kernel and which use cases are optional. This strategy has the advantage that evolution is built into the development process, so that later the product line can be evolved further.

An example in which the forward evolutionary engineering strategy is used is the banking software product line shown in Figures 4.10 and 4.12. The kernel of the product line consists of the abstract use case `Validate PIN` and the concrete use cases `Withdraw Funds`, `Query Account`, and `Transfer Funds`, as shown in Figure 4.10. During product line evolution, the optional use cases `Deposit Funds` and `Print Statement` are then added (Figure 4.12); these use cases are needed by some but not all ATM systems. Later, additional functionality could be added, such as an optional use case `Download Electronic Funds to Cash Card`.

Another example in which the forward evolutionary engineering strategy is used is the microwave oven product line. The kernel of the product line consists of the `Cook Food` use case. During product line evolution, the optional use cases `Set Time of Day` and `Display Time of Day` are added to provide an optional time-of-day functionality. The `Cook Food with Recipe` use case is also added, to provide an optional recipe functionality (see Figure 4.5).

4.10.2   Reverse Evolutionary Engineering

With the **reverse evolutionary engineering** strategy, the use case model of each individual system is analyzed and documented first. The different use case models are then integrated into a product line use case model. This means that the use cases for each member of the product line are specified first. If the use cases for a given system do not exist, then it is necessary to develop them; in effect, this is an exercise in reverse engineering. After the use cases for each member of the product line have been developed, the use cases from the different systems are compared. Use cases that are needed by all members of the product line constitute the kernel use cases. Use cases that are needed by only an individual system or a subset of the product line members constitute the optional use cases. If some functionality exists that is handled differently by different product line members, then alternative use cases are developed. If only part of the functionality described in an individual system use case is common, then this common functionality can be split off into a kernel use case, with the remaining functionality allocated to an optional or alternative use case. A kernel or optional use case may also have variation points.

An example in which the reverse evolutionary engineering strategy is used is the factory automation product line, which encompasses high-volume low-flexibility manufacturing systems, flexible manufacturing systems, and factory monitoring systems. During the analysis of the use cases for these different members of the product line, it is determined that use cases involving the factory operator for viewing and updating alarms and workstation status are common to all members of the product line. However, use cases for workflow management and production management are optional, because they are used by only some factory systems. Yet other use cases are alternatives; for example, the use case for manufacturing a high-volume part is an alternative to the use case for flexibly manufacturing a part. This case study will be described in detail in Chapter 15.

Another example in which the reverse evolutionary engineering strategy is used is the electronic commerce product line, as described in the full case study that will be presented in Chapter 14. There are two main kinds of e-commerce systems handled by the product line: B2C systems and B2B systems. In B2C systems, in which the home customer sends order requests to the supplier, the `Supplier` actor needs to interact with the use cases `Process Delivery Order`, `Confirm Shipment`, and then `Bill Customer`, as shown in Figure 4.13.

In B2B systems, in which the business customer sends order requests to the supplier, the `Supplier` actor needs to interact with the use cases `Process Delivery Order`, `Confirm Shipment`, and then `Send Invoice`, as shown in Figure 4.14.

When integrating a product line use case model from the two application use case models, we need to consider the use cases of the applications. Because

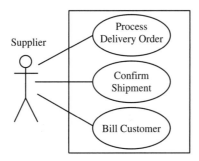

Figure 4.13   *Example of reverse evolutionary engineering: supplier use cases in B2C systems*

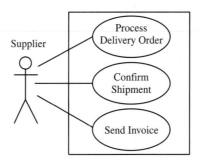

Figure 4.14   *Example of the reverse evolutionary engineering: supplier use cases in B2B systems*

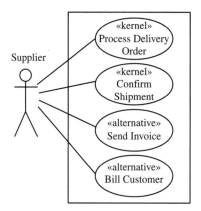

Figure 4.15 *Example of reverse evolutionary engineering: supplier use cases in an e-commerce product line*

the `Process Delivery Order` and `Confirm Shipment` use cases are needed for both B2C and B2B systems, they become kernel use cases in the e-commerce product line. On the other hand, `Bill Customer` is needed only for B2C systems, and `Send Invoice` is needed only for B2B systems. Because these two use cases represent alternative ways of billing the customer, they become alternative use cases in the product line use case model. Figure 4.15 depicts the supplier use cases for the e-commerce product line.

4.11 Summary

This chapter described the use case approach to defining the functional requirements of a software product line. It covered the concepts of actor and use cases, as well as how use cases in product lines can be modeled as kernel, optional, or alternative use cases. The concept of a variation point was introduced, explaining how variation points can be used to model variability within use cases. Use case relationships were also described—in particular, the extend and include relationships, and how they can be used to model variability in software product lines. In addition, two different strategies for developing product line use case models were presented: forward evolutionary engineering and reverse evolutionary engineering.

The use case model has a strong influence on subsequent software development. The object structuring criteria that will be described in Chapter 6 are used to determine the objects that participate in each use case. The sequence of interactions between the objects that participate in the use case is determined during dynamic modeling, as will be described in Chapter 7. Software can be incrementally developed by the selection of use cases to be developed in each phase of the project, as was described in Chapter 3. Integration and system test cases should also be based on use cases.

c h a p t e r

Feature Modeling for Software Product Lines

This chapter describes feature modeling, a concept used widely in software product lines to model variability, but not specifically addressed by UML. The characteristics of software product line requirements and features are described, and the discussion continues with a description of how feature modeling concepts can be incorporated into the UML—in particular, how they relate to use cases. The chapter also describes how features can be determined from use cases.

Davis (1993) points out that a software requirements specification is frequently referred to as a "complete description of *what* the software will do without describing *how* it will do it." Because there are several ways of viewing requirements, we choose to consider software product line requirements from the perspective of the end user, who thinks in terms of functional requirements—namely, what requirements the product line needs to support. As with use case modeling, this perspective is a black box perspective of the software product line in that it considers only the external behavior of the system.

During the requirements modeling phase, the scope of the software product line is determined, and the functional requirements of the software product line are identified, analyzed, and then categorized. The term *requirement* is used to mean a need that a software product line, and hence at least one of the members of the product line, must be capable of satisfying. Once the software product line has captured this requirement, the requirement is referred to as a *feature* provided by the software product line.

Section 5.1 introduces feature analysis, which is a new topic for those who are not familiar with product lines, although it is considered crucial by product line developers. Section 5.2 describes commonality/variability feature analysis, in which common, optional, and alternative features are determined. Section 5.3

describes how features relate to use cases and can be determined from use cases. Section 5.4 describes how features can be depicted with the UML notation. Related features can be put into feature groups, as described in Section 5.5. Finally, Section 5.6 describes some advanced feature modeling issues and how they can be depicted in UML.

5.1 Introduction to Feature Analysis

Marketing product planners often use the term *feature* to describe a significant distinguishing function provided by a product. For example, the term *feature* is widely used in the telephone industry, where a telephone is said to provide features such as call waiting or voice mail.

In software product lines, a **feature** is a requirement or characteristic that is provided by one or more members of the product line. In particular, features are characteristics that are used to differentiate among members of the product line and hence to determine and define the common and variable functionality of a software product line. Feature analysis is an important aspect of product line analysis and has been used widely for the requirements analysis of software product lines in methods such as FODA (Feature-Oriented Domain Analysis) (Cohen and Northrop 1998; Kang et al. 1990) and other feature-based methods (Dionisi et al. 1998; Gomaa 1995; Griss et al. 1998).

In specifying a single system, a system is not considered complete unless all the requirements have been satisfied; hence the system must provide all the features. If a system is being developed in phases, the order in which features are introduced must be considered. When certain features depend on others, features need to be introduced in a specific sequence to ensure that prerequisite features are introduced prior to the features that depend on them.

When it comes to specifying the requirements of a software product line, the product line requirements (and hence features) are the aggregate requirements of all the members of the software product line. Any given member of the product line typically provides only some of the product line features. Unlike a single system, in which all features must be provided, a given feature might not be provided by a particular member of the product line. It is necessary to analyze the commonality and variability of the product line features and to categorize them according to their reuse characteristics. Because of the added difficulty in analyzing variability, feature analysis for a software product line is usually significantly more complex than for a single system.

5.1.1   Modeling Product Line Variability with Features

In analyzing and categorizing the features of a software product line, an important distinction is made among common features, optional features, and alternative features. The common features are the subset of the product line features that must be provided by every member of the product line. Optional features are those that need to be provided by only some members of the product line. Alternative features are needed when there is a choice of features to select for a given member of the product line. The optional and alternative features describe the variability in the product line and determine the characteristics of a given member of the product line. Thus, in product line feature analysis, the emphasis is on analyzing the optional and alternative features.

Consider a vehicle product line. There can be several vehicle models. For example, the hypothetical car manufacturer Variable Vehicles Venture has a Volcano model with sedan, sports, and station wagon versions. All versions share the same chassis, which can be considered a common feature. There are optional features, such as the sports package, automatic transmission, and sliding roof. The station wagon version comes with an automatic transmission only (feature prerequisite). There are also alternative features, such as the engine size and color of the vehicle. Obviously every vehicle must have an engine. The engine size feature has a default 2-liter engine, with alternative 2.5-liter and 3-liter V6 engines. However, there is no default color feature, so a color must always be picked for a new member of the product line. Alternative features are often mutually exclusive, meaning that only one of the features can be picked. In some cases, not picking a feature is also an option. Consider a vehicle roof rack. There can be alternative roof rack features (basic rack, ski rack, or bicycle rack), although not having a roof rack is also possible. The roof rack features are all mutually exclusive.

5.2   Commonality/Variability Feature Analysis

During **commonality/variability feature analysis**, product line features are analyzed and categorized as common, optional, or alternative, as described in Sections 5.2.1 through 5.2.3. The common features determine the degree of commonality in the product line. The optional and alternative features determine the degree of variability in the product line.

5.2.1 Common Features

Common features are those features that must be provided by every member of the software product line. Common features are sometimes referred to as *mandatory, necessary,* or *kernel* features of the product line.

It is possible to group all the common requirements into one common feature or to identify them separately as several common features. The approach of grouping all the common requirements into one common feature is used when the common requirements of the product line are well understood and the goal is to concentrate on the variability in the product line. The approach of identifying common features separately is used when the commonality is not well understood and individual requirements need to be analyzed before it can be determined which of these are common and which are variable. This approach can also be used when it is considered possible that an apparently common feature might become optional as the product line evolves.

A common feature is depicted in UML with the stereotype «common feature» followed by the feature name:

«common feature» Feature Name

In the factory automation product line, for example, the common requirements are all grouped together into one common feature as follows:

«common feature» Factory Kernel

5.2.2 Optional Features

Optional features are those features that need to be provided by only some members of the product line. Optional features can assume that the common features are provided and so can depend on the presence of the common features.

An optional feature is depicted in UML with the stereotype «optional feature» followed by the feature name:

«optional feature» Feature Name

In the factory automation product line, for example, an optional feature is `Workflow Management`, which is provided in high-volume factory systems and flexible manufacturing systems but not in factory monitoring systems:

«optional feature» Workflow Management

5.2.3 Alternative Features

Two or more features may be alternatives to each other, where only one of them can be provided in any given member of the software product line. Thus the features are mutually exclusive. The relationship among such **alternative features** is specified in a feature group, as described in Section 5.5.

An alternative feature is depicted in UML with the stereotype «alternative feature» followed by the feature name:

«alternative feature» Feature Name

An example of an alternative feature is `Display Language` in the microwave oven product line, where alternative languages for displaying prompts on the LCD display are provided:

«alternative feature» French, «alternative feature» Spanish

With a group of alternative features, one of them may be a **default feature**. In the microwave oven product line, for example, the default display language is English:

«default feature» English

5.2.4   Parameterized Features

A **parameterized feature** is a feature that defines a product line parameter whose value needs to be defined at system configuration time. A parameterized feature needs to specify the type of the parameter, the range or permitted values of the parameter, and optionally a default value for the parameter. These characteristics of a parameterized feature are described by UML tagged values. The following reserved words are used for tags: `type`, `permitted value`, and `default value`. A parameterized feature is depicted as follows:

«parameterized feature» Feature Name {type = parameter type, permitted value = parameter value range or enumerated parameter values, default value = parameter value}

Three examples are provided by the banking system product line: (1) the maximum number of allowable prompts for the ATM password, (2) the length of the ATM password, and (3) the value of the ATM password:

1. «parameterized feature» Max # Prompts {type = integer, permitted value = 1..5, default value = 3}

2. «parameterized feature» ATM Password Length {type = integer, permitted value = 4..8, default value = 4}

3. «parameterized feature» ATM Password Value {type = string, permitted value = alphabetic, numeric, alphanumeric}

Note that having a default value for a parameterized feature is optional. The first two examples, `Max # Prompts` and `ATM Password Length`, do have a default value for the parameterized feature; the third example, ATM Password Value, does not. In the cases of Max # Prompts and ATM Password Length, if a value for the parameter is not specified at system configuration time, then the default value is used. In the case of ATM Password Value, where there is no default value, it is necessary to specify a parameter value at system configuration time.

5.2.5 Prerequisite Features

A feature may depend on another feature; the feature it depends on is called a **prerequisite feature**. It is not necessary to explicitly specify common features as prerequisite features, because every member of the product line provides them. However, it is essential to explicitly specify any optional or alternative features that are prerequisites.

A feature prerequisite is depicted as a UML tagged value with the reserved word prerequisite as the tag and the prerequisite feature name as the value. It is possible for a feature to have more than one prerequisite feature. The two cases are depicted here:

{prerequisite = Prerequisite Feature Name}

{prerequisite = First Prerequisite Feature Name, ..., Nth Prerequisite Feature Name}

If an optional feature, alternative feature, or parameterized feature has a prerequisite, then the prerequisite feature tagged value is depicted after the feature name:

«optional feature» Feature Name {prerequisite = Prerequisite Feature Name}

«alternative feature» Feature Name {prerequisite = Prerequisite Feature Name}

For example, the optional feature Workflow Planning User has the optional Workflow Management feature as a prerequisite feature:

«optional feature» Workflow Planning User {prerequisite = Workflow Management}

An example from the microwave oven product line is TOD Clock (TOD stands for *time of day*). If this optional feature is provided, the time of day is displayed. A prerequisite feature is Multi-line Display.

«optional feature» TOD Clock {prerequisite = Multi-line Display}

5.2.6   Mutually Inclusive Features

If two features are always needed together, then the features are considered **mutually inclusive features**. Although this kind of dependency might seem to be redundant because it could be handled by feature prerequisites, in some situations it is useful.

A mutually inclusive feature is depicted as a UML tagged value with the reserved word `mutually includes` as the tag and the mutually inclusive feature name as the value:

{mutually includes = Mutually Inclusive Feature Name}

An optional feature with a mutually inclusive feature is expressed as follows:

«optional feature» Feature Name {mutually includes = Mutually Inclusive Feature Name}

In the microwave oven product line, for example, `Boolean Weight` (a sensor that indicates whether an item is in the oven) and `Analog Weight` (a sensor that measures the actual weight of an item in the oven) are mutually exclusive features. In addition, `Boolean Weight` is the default feature. The `Analog Weight` feature is provided only in microwave ovens that have the `Recipe` feature, because recipes need the item's weight to compute the cooking time. Hence, `Analog Weight` and `Recipe` are mutually inclusive features.

«optional feature» Recipe {mutually includes = Analog Weight}

Note that with mutually inclusive features, it is not permitted to use one of the features by itself. A feature that is not allowed to be selected individually is termed an **implicit feature**; a feature that can be selected individually is termed an **explicit feature**. Thus, `Analog Weight` is an implicit feature because it cannot be selected without the `Recipe` feature also being selected. It is possible for a feature to both mutually include an implicit feature and have a different explicit feature as a prerequisite; an example of this is given in Chapter 13. When two or more features could be used together but could also be used individually, either the at-least-one-of feature group (see Section 5.5.3) or the zero-or-more-of feature group (see Section 5.5.4) should be used.

5.3   Features and Use Cases

In the object-oriented analysis of single systems, use cases are used to determine the functionality of a system. Use cases can also serve this purpose in software product lines. Griss et al. (1998) have pointed out that the goal of use case analysis is to get a clear understanding of the functional requirements, whereas the goal of feature analysis is to enable reuse. The emphasis in feature analysis is on modeling the variability provided by the optional and alternative features, because these features are what differentiate one member of the software product line from the others. Use cases and features may be used to complement each other. In particular, use cases can be mapped to features on the basis of their reuse properties.

The relationship between use cases and features is a many-to-many association, such that one feature could encompass many use cases, whereas a different use case could encompass many features. The reason is that it is possible to group use cases that are reused together into a feature; in this situation, one feature encompasses several use cases. However, a use case may also have several variation points within it, where the variation points are mapped to features. In this case, one use case encompasses several features.

Functional requirements that are required by all members of the product line are packaged into common features. From a use case perspective, this means that the kernel use cases, which are required by all members of the family, constitute common features. Optional use cases, which are always used together, can be packaged into optional features. Section 5.3.1 describes these issues in greater detail.

Features can be determined from use cases in several different ways, as described in this section. These features can be functional features or parameterized features. A feature can correspond to a single use case, a group of use cases, or a variation point within a use case.

5.3.1 Modeling Functional Features as Groups of Use Cases

A functional feature can be modeled as a group of use cases that are reused together. When a group of use cases are always reused together, they can be mapped to a feature and depicted as a use case package. Such is the case when the reusable functionality described by the feature is captured by the functionality described in a group of related use cases. When a feature is depicted as a use case package, containing one or more use cases, the package is given the name of the feature and a stereotype name corresponding to the type of feature.

Consider an example from the microwave oven product line: The `Set Time of Day` and `Display Time of Day` optional use cases are always used together, so they are combined into a use case package that corresponds to the `TOD Clock` optional feature, as depicted in Figure 5.1. The feature is given the stereotype «optional feature».

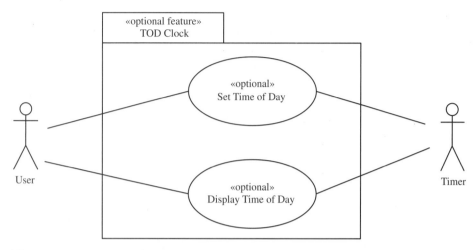

Figure 5.1 *Example of a feature as a use case package*

Another example is the `High-Volume Manufacturing` alternative feature in the factory automation product line, which is captured as a group of four related use cases: `Manufacture High-Volume Part` and the three use cases it includes—`Receive Part`, `Process Part at High-Volume Workstation`, and `Ship Part`. In this situation the use cases can be combined into a use case package that corresponds to the `High-Volume Manufacturing` alternative feature (see Figure 5.2), which is given the stereotype «alternative feature».

The reusable functionality described by a functional feature can exactly match the functionality described in one use case. When a feature and a use case match, the feature could be represented as a use case package consisting of one use case. Such representations should, however, be used sparingly because a package is intended for grouping several modeling elements, not just one.

5.3.2 Modeling Feature Dependencies as Use Case Dependencies

Feature dependencies can be depicted in terms of the dependencies between the use cases. If one use case depends on another use case through the include or extend relationship, and the two use cases have been allocated to different features, then the two features are also interdependent. Thus, if a use case in use case package A depends on another use case in use case package B, this means that the feature represented by use case package A depends on the prerequisite feature represented by use case package B. Dependencies between use cases

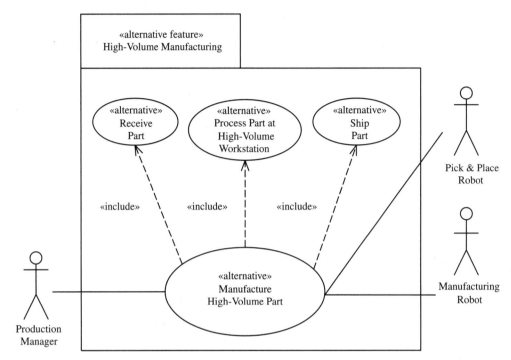

Figure 5.2   High-Volume Manufacturing *use cases and feature*

illustrate feature dependencies at a fine degree of resolution; dependencies between use case packages (i.e., between the features themselves) show feature dependencies at a larger degree of resolution.

An example from the factory automation product line is shown in Figure 5.3, which depicts two features: the Storage & Retrieval optional feature, which depends on the Flexible Manufacturing alternative feature. Both features are depicted as use case packages. The Flexible Manufacturing alternative feature consists of five use cases, and the Storage & Retrieval optional feature encompasses two use cases. The dependency between the features is shown as a dependency between the packages. Furthermore, the feature dependency corresponds to the dependency between the use cases within the packages, as Figure 5.3 shows. Thus the Store Part and Retrieve Part optional use cases, which are in the use case package for the Storage & Retrieval optional feature, depend on the Flexibly Manufacture Part use case, which is in the use case package for the Flexible Manufacturing alternative feature.

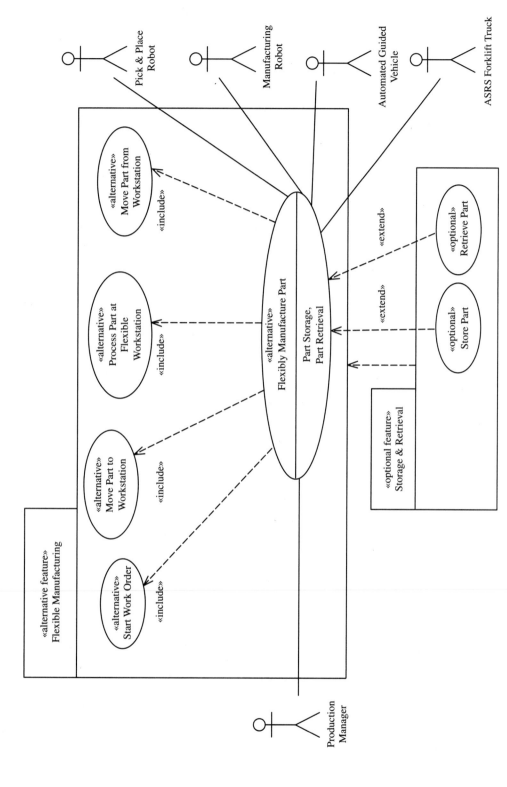

Figure 5.3 Flexible Manufacturing *use case and feature dependencies*

5.3.3   Modeling Functional Features with Variation Points

Small features can be modeled by means of variation points within use cases. There are two cases to consider: optional features and alternative features. The **variation point** identifies the location within the use case where the optional or alternative functionality is inserted.

An optional feature can be modeled as an optional functional requirement, which is inserted at a location within the use case identified by the variation point. In the microwave oven product line, for example, the light, turntable, and beeper are all optional functional requirements in a microwave oven, which are captured by variation points in the Cook Food use case. Each of these variation points maps directly to a feature, for example:

«optional feature» Turntable

«optional feature» Beeper

An alternative feature can be modeled as an alternative functional require-ment, which is inserted at a location within the use case identified by the varia-tion point. For example, in the Cook Food use case from the microwave oven product line, the one-line display unit and the multi-line display unit are two alternative features. Furthermore, a default alternative can be specified. If a choice is not made, the default option is automatically selected. For example, the default display unit is a one-line display:

«default feature» One-line Display

«alternative feature» Multi-line Display

5.3.4   Modeling Parameterized Features as Variation Points

A parameterized feature can also be modeled by means of a variation point in the use case. The variation point identifies the location within the use case where the parameterized functionality is inserted. In the banking product line, for example, the number of alphanumeric characters in the ATM password is a use case parameter in the Validate PIN use case, which is mapped to a parameterized feature. Another example of a use case parameter from this use case is the maximum number of times the user is prompted for the password. In the former case there is no default value, so a value must be specified at config-uration time. In the latter case, the default value is to prompt the user for the password a maximum of three times. If a maximum number of prompts is not chosen at configuration time, then the default is used:

«parameterized feature» ATM Password Length {type = integer, permitted value = 4..8} «parameterized feature» Max # Prompts {type = integer, permitted value = 1..5, default value = 3}

5.4   Feature Modeling with UML

There are various ways in which features can be modeled in UML, as described in this section. It is often useful to use more than one approach to provide greater insight into feature modeling.

5.4.1   Modeling Features as a Use Case Package

When a group of use cases are always reused together, they can be mapped to a feature and depicted as a use case package. In the factory automation product line described earlier, for instance, because four related use cases are always used together, they can be depicted as a use case package (see Figure 5.2). Feature dependencies can be depicted as dependencies between use case packages, as shown in Figure 5.3.

Although the full feature model of a product line could be depicted with features as use case packages and feature dependencies as use case package dependencies, two other approaches—namely, modeling features as metaclasses and using feature tables—are generally more effective, as described next.

5.4.2   Modeling Features as Metaclasses

The UML static modeling capability, which was introduced in Chapter 2, can be used to model metaclasses. With metaclass modeling, a class is used to represent a modeling element. For feature modeling, features and feature groups are represented as metaclasses so that the full power of static modeling can be used to depict features, feature groups, and their relationships.

As described earlier in this chapter, there are stereotypes for the different kinds of features, such as «optional feature» and «alternative feature». In metaclass modeling, the feature stereotypes are used as the stereotypes of the metaclasses, which represent the features. The classification of the different categories (types) of features according to stereotypes is depicted in Figure 5.4 on a metaclass diagram.

Figure 5.5 shows examples of metaclasses representing features from the microwave oven product line. It depicts a metaclass representing a common feature (`Microwave Oven Kernel`), an optional feature (`Light`), a parameterized

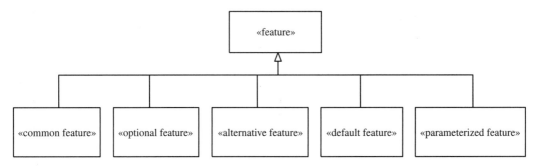

Figure 5.4 *Classification of product line feature categories using UML stereotypes*

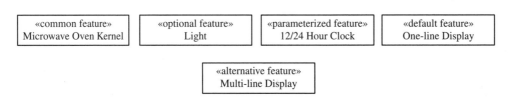

Figure 5.5 *Examples of software product line features*

feature (`12/24 Hour Clock`), a default feature (`One-line Display`), and an alternative feature (`Multi-line Display`).

Dependencies between features are depicted as associations, such as `requires` or `mutually includes`, and constraints are also shown, such as `mutually exclusive`. Note that a greater modeling capability is possible with class relationships than with package dependencies. Figure 5.6 shows examples of feature dependencies from the microwave oven product line. `Recipe` is an optional feature that requires the `Multi-line Display` feature and mutually includes the `Analog Weight` feature. The different association names used to model these relationships are used to show that `Multi-line Display` is an explicit feature that can be selected independently for a product line member, whereas `Analog Weight` is an implicit mutually inclusive feature that can be selected only in conjunction with the `Recipe` feature (see Section 5.2.6).

5.4.3 Representing Features in Tables

Features can be concisely described in a tabular representation. Each row of the table identifies a feature. The columns are the feature name, the feature category (depicted by its stereotype), the use case from which the feature is derived, the

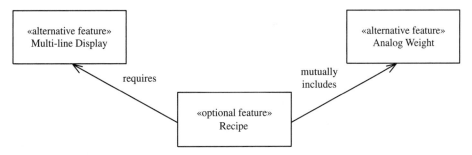

Figure 5.6 *Examples of software product line feature dependencies*

use case category or variation point, and if applicable, the variation point within the use case to which it relates. This approach is used in the microwave oven product line to concisely depict the feature/use case relationships, as shown in Table 5.1.

Table 5.1 *Tabular representation of feature/use case relationships: microwave oven software product line*

Feature Name	Feature Category	Use Case Name	Use Case Category/ Variation Point (vp)	Variation Point Name
Microwave Oven Kernel	common	Cook Food	kernel	
Light	optional	Cook Food	vp	Light
Turntable	optional	Cook Food	vp	Turntable
Beeper	optional	Cook Food	vp	Beeper
Minute Plus	optional	Cook Food	vp	Minute Plus
One-line Display	default	Cook Food	vp	Display Unit
Multi-line Display	alternative	Cook Food	vp	Display Unit
English	default	Cook Food	vp	Display Language
French	alternative	Cook Food	vp	Display Language
Spanish	alternative	Cook Food	vp	Display Language
German	alternative	Cook Food	vp	Display Language
Italian	alternative	Cook Food	vp	Display Language
Boolean Weight	default	Cook Food	vp	Weight Sensor
Analog Weight	alternative	Cook Food	vp	Weight Sensor

(continues)

Table 5.1 *Tabular representation of feature/use case relationships: microwave oven software product line (continued)*

Feature Name	Feature Category	Use Case Name	Use Case Category/ Variation Point (vp)	Variation Point Name
One-level Heating	default	Cook Food	vp	Heating Element
Multi-level Heating	alternative	Cook Food	vp	Heating Element
Power Level	optional	Cook Food	vp	Power Level
TOD Clock	optional	Set Time of Day	optional	
		Display Time of Day	optional	
12/24 Hour Clock	parameterized	Set Time of Day	vp	12/24 Hour Clock
		Display Time of Day		
Recipe	optional	Cook Food with Recipe	optional	

The common feature `Microwave Oven Kernel` consists of the `Cook Food` kernel use case. However, this use case has several variation points, at which the functionality specified by optional, default, or alternative features is inserted. For example, `Light` is an optional feature determined from the `Cook Food` use case; it represents a variation point in the use case, which has the same name, `Light`. `TOD Clock` is an optional feature that groups the two optional time-of-day use cases, and `Recipe` is an optional feature that corresponds to one use case: `Cook Food with Recipe`.

5.5 Feature Groups

Related features can be grouped into **feature groups**, which place a constraint on how the features are used by a given member of the software product line. Feature groups are described in Sections 5.5.1 through 5.5.5.

Feature groups can also be depicted as metaclasses, in the same way that features can. Each kind of feature group metaclass is identified by means of a stereotype. There are stereotypes for the different categories of feature groups, such as «exactly-one-of feature group» and «zero-or-one-of feature group».

Feature groups can be depicted by means of the textual notation consisting of stereotypes and tagged values that was used earlier in this chapter. Feature

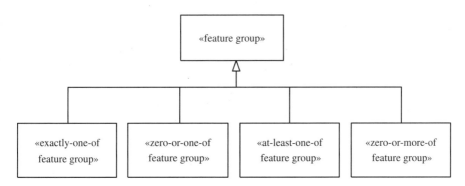

Figure 5.7   *Classification of product line feature group categories using UML stereotypes*

groups can also be depicted with the UML metaclass and static modeling notation originally used for features, as depicted in Figure 5.7.

5.5.1   Mutually Exclusive Features

A feature can be an alternative—that is, one of a group of mutually exclusive features. In some product families, one of the alternatives must always be chosen for a given product family member. In other cases, however, selecting one of the alternatives is optional for a given family member. A **zero-or-one-of feature group** handles the case in which selecting one of the alternatives is optional.

This feature group is given the name and stereotype «zero-or-one-of feature group». It is possible for such a feature group to have a prerequisite. There must be at least two features in a feature group. Alternative and prerequisite features are depicted as tagged values. The general format is

«zero-or-one-of feature group» Feature Group Name {alternative = First Alternative Feature Name, …, Nth Alternative Feature Name, prerequisite = Prerequisite Feature Name}

An example from the vehicle product line is a group of roof rack features. The choices are one of the alternative roof racks or no roof rack:

«zero-or-one-of feature group» Roof Rack {alternative = Basic Rack, Ski Rack, Bicycle Rack}

The «zero-or-one-of feature group» `Roof Rack` can be depicted as a metaclass, as shown in Figure 5.8a. The alternative features `Basic Rack`, `Ski Rack`, and `Bicycle Rack`, which are members of the `Roof Rack` group, can also be depicted as metaclasses, as shown in Figure 5.8. Each individual feature is

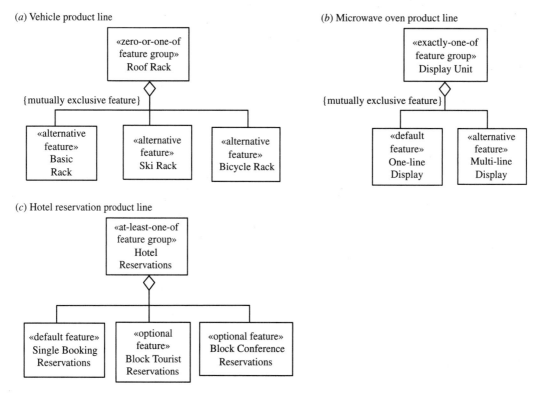

Figure 5.8 *Examples of software product line feature groups*

shown as part of the feature group by means of the aggregation relationship. Aggregation means that the features are part of the feature group. There is a {mutually exclusive feature} constraint among the features of the Roof Rack feature group.

5.5.2   Exactly-One-Of Feature Group

In an **exactly-one-of feature group** (also referred to as a *one-and-only-one-of feature group*), a feature must always be selected from the group. Unlike the mutually exclusive case, the option of not selecting a feature does not exist. This feature group is given the name and stereotype «exactly-one-of feature group». It is possible for such a feature group to have a default feature and to have a prerequisite. The feature group must contain at least two features, one of which could be a default feature. The default, alternative, and prerequisite features are depicted as tagged values. The general format is

«exactly-one-of feature group» Feature Group Name {default = Default
Feature Name, alternative = First Alternative Feature Name, …,
Nth Alternative Feature Name, prerequisite = Prerequisite Feature Name}

An example of an exactly-one-of feature group from the microwave oven
product line is the `Display Unit` feature group (see Figure 5.8*b*), whose members are the default `One-line Display` feature and the alternative `Multi-
line Display` feature, as specified here:

«exactly-one-of feature group» Display Unit {default = One-line Display,
alternative = Multi-line Display}

The `One-line Display` and `Multi-line Display` features are shown as
part of the feature group by means of the aggregation relationship. There is a
{mutually exclusive feature} constraint between the two features in the `Display
Unit` feature group.

Another example from the microwave oven product line is the `Display
Language` feature group, which specifies the language in which microwave
prompts are to be displayed. Because one of these alternatives must always be
selected for a given oven, these features are grouped into an exactly-one-of feature group. Thus the display language features—namely, the choice of `English`,
`French`, `Spanish`, `German`, or `Italian`—are alternative features, exactly one
of which must be chosen. Furthermore, a default alternative can be specified. If
a choice is not made, the default option is automatically selected. For example,
the default display language is English. In the following example, the default
and alternative features are defined first, followed by the feature group:

«default feature» English, «alternative feature» French, «alternative
feature» Spanish, «alternative feature» German, «alternative feature» Italian

«exactly-one-of feature group» Display Language {default = English,
alternative = French, Spanish, German, Italian}

5.5.3   At-Least-One-Of Feature Group

In an **at-least-one-of feature group**, one or more optional features can be
selected from the group, but at least one feature must be selected. It is also possible for such a feature group to have a default feature and to have a prerequisite. The feature group must contain at least two features, one of which could be
a default feature. The general format is

«at-least-one-of feature group» Feature Group Name {default = Default
Feature Name, feature = Second Optional Feature Name, …, Nth Optional
Feature Name, prerequisite = Prerequisite Feature Name}

In an example from a hotel reservation product line (see Figure 5.8c), one or more reservation types are provided—single booking reservations, block tourist reservations, block conference reservations—and the default is single booking reservations. Once again the feature group is shown as an aggregation of the features that are part of the group:

«at-least-one-of feature group» Hotel Reservations {default = Single Booking Reservations, feature = Block Tourist Reservations, Block Conference Reservations}

An example from the vehicle product line is an `Entertainment` feature group that consists of the features `AM/FM Radio`, `Tape Cassette Player`, and `CD Player`. The user can select one or more of the features in the `Entertainment` feature group:

«at-least-one-of feature group» Entertainment {default = AM/FM Radio, feature = Tape Cassette Player, CD Player}

5.5.4 Zero-or-More-of Feature Group

At first, a **zero-or-more-of feature group** might seem unnecessary, since *zero or more of* means that all features in the group are optional and there are no constraints on feature selection from within the group. However, sometimes it is useful to group optional features together because of a dependency. For example, all features in the group depend on another feature or feature group. There is usually no default feature in this case:

«zero-or-more-of feature group» Feature Group Name {feature = First Optional Feature Name, …, Nth Optional Feature Name, prerequisite = Prerequisite Feature Name}

An example from the vehicle product line is a group of features that all depend on automatic transmission, such as cruise control and automatic traction:

«zero-or-more-of feature group» Automated Drive Control {feature = Cruise Control, Automatic Traction, prerequisite = Automatic Transmission}

5.5.5 Representing Feature Groups in Tables

Feature group information can also be summarized in a table. For each feature group, the table depicts the feature group name, feature group category, features in the feature group, and feature category of each feature. A tabular representation of the three feature groups depicted in Figure 5.8 is given in Table 5.2. They are shown in the same table for convenience, although they would normally be in separate tables because they are from different product lines.

Table 5.2 *Example of a tabular representation of feature groups*

Feature Group Name	Feature Group Category	Features in Feature Group	Feature Category
Roof Rack	zero-or-one-of	Basic Rack	alternative
		Ski Rack	alternative
		Bicycle Rack	alternative
Display Unit	exactly-one-of	One-line Display	default
		Multi-line Display	alternative
Hotel Reservations	at-least-one-of	Single Booking Reservations	default
		Block Tourist Reservations	optional
		Block Conference Reservations	optional

5.6   Advanced Feature Modeling with UML

In some product lines it is desirable to have feature groups consisting of other feature groups. For example, two feature groups may themselves be mutually exclusive. In residential hotels where bookings are made in one-month blocks, the optional features are different from those in conventional hotels, where rooms are booked for one or more nights. The two groups of optional features for the residential hotel and the conventional hotel could be allocated to two mutually exclusive zero-or-more-of feature groups. At configuration time, either the residential or the conventional hotel feature group is selected, and then zero or more features are available for selection from that feature group.

Hence, in the feature relationships described in the previous sections, the term *feature* could be replaced by the term *feature group*, as shown here:

- «zero-or-one-of feature group» Feature Group Name {alternative = First Alternative Feature Group Name, …, Nth Alternative Feature Group Name, prerequisite = Prerequisite Feature Name}

- «exactly-one-of feature group» Feature Group Name {default = Default Feature Group Name, alternative = First Alternative Feature Group Name, …, Nth Alternative Feature Group Name, prerequisite = Prerequisite Feature Name}

- «at-least-one-of feature group» Feature Group Name {default = Default Feature Group Name, feature = Second Optional Feature Group Name, …, Nth Optional Feature Group Name, prerequisite = Prerequisite Feature Name}

- «zero-or-more-of feature group» Feature Group Name {feature = First Optional Feature Group Name, …, Nth Optional Feature Group Name, prerequisite = Prerequisite Feature Name}

It is also possible for a feature group to have another feature group as a prerequisite.

5.6.1 Example of Advanced Feature Modeling

Consider the case of the hotel product line illustrated in metaclass notation in Figure 5.9. There is one common feature, `Hotel Kernel`:

«common feature» Hotel Kernel

There is one feature group of optional features for conventional hotels, including features for block bookings, automated cancellation after 6:00 PM for nonguaranteed reservations, and automated no-show billing for guaranteed reservations. These features are modeled as a zero-or-more-of feature group called `Conventional Hotel`, as follows:

«zero-or-more-of feature group» Conventional Hotel {feature = Automated Cancellation, Automated No-Show Billing, Block Booking, prerequisite = Hotel Kernel}

There is another feature group of optional features for residential hotels, including features for a meal plan (where all meals are provided) and maid service (where beds are made and the room is cleaned daily). These features are similarly modeled as a second zero-or-more-of feature group called `Residential Hotel`, as follows:

«zero-or-more-of feature group» Residential Hotel {feature = Meal Plan, Maid Service, prerequisite = Hotel Kernel}

A third group of optional features, which can be used with either residential or conventional hotels, includes room service, laundry service, and restaurant service. These features are provided in full-service hotels but not necessarily in budget hotels, and they are modeled as a third zero-or-more-of feature group called `Hotel Options`, as follows:

«zero-or-more-of feature group» Hotel Options {feature = Room Service, Laundry Service, Restaurant Service, prerequisite = Hotel Kernel}

Because the two feature groups for conventional hotel options and residential hotel options are alternatives, they are related by an exactly-one-of feature group called `Hotel Alternatives`. Furthermore, because there are typically

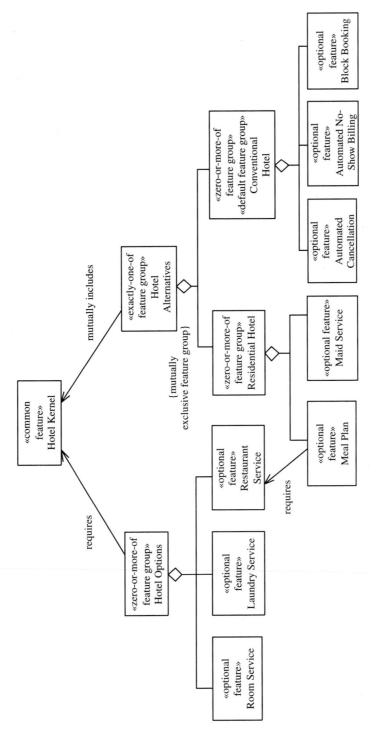

Figure 5.9   *Example of hotel product line feature modeling*

more conventional hotels than residential hotels in the hotel product line, the conventional hotel options are made the default feature group:

«exactly-one-of feature group» Hotel Alternatives {default = Conventional Hotel, alternative = Residential Hotel}

To summarize, the hotel product line has the following features and feature groups:

- One common feature: `Hotel Kernel`.

- A zero-or-more-of feature group, `Hotel Options`, that depends on `Hotel Kernel`.

- An exactly-one-of feature group, `Hotel Alternatives`, that consists of two alternative feature groups—for conventional and residential hotels, respectively—one of which must be chosen.

- Two alternative zero-or-more-of feature groups: `Conventional Hotel` and `Residential Hotel`, are available for selection depending on whether a conventional hotel or residential hotel, respectively, is being selected.

5.7 Summary

This chapter described feature modeling, a concept used widely in software product lines to model variability, but not specifically addressed by UML. The features are used to distinguish between the different characteristics of the members of a product line. This chapter described the characteristics of software product line requirements and features. It also described how feature modeling concepts can be incorporated into the UML—in particular, how features relate to use cases, how features can be determined from use cases, and how features can be modeled in the UML. Finally, feature groups were described in which related features are grouped together on the basis of constraints on how they are used in product line members. Chapter 9 will describe feature/class dependencies, in which the classes required to realize the functionality of each feature are determined. Examples of feature modeling are given in the three case studies presented in Chapters 13, 14, and 15.

Static Modeling in Software Product Lines

Static modeling has an important role to play in modeling software product lines because it is a powerful notation for capturing the commonality and variability in a product family. A static model describes the static structure of the product line being modeled. The static modeling notation can be used for modeling the associations between classes (as is done for single systems), as well as for modeling the hierarchies used in product line models for families of systems—namely, composition/aggregation hierarchies and generalization/specialization hierarchies.

This chapter describes how static modeling concepts are applied to software product lines. The approach starts by modeling real-world classes, which are determined from the problem domain, before modeling the software classes within the software product line. Static modeling of the real-world physical classes leads to analysis of the product line boundary and development of the product line context model. Static modeling is also used to analyze product line entity classes, which are information-intensive classes. This chapter also describes the categorization of product line classes from two perspectives: the role the class plays in the application, and the reuse characteristic of the class.

Static modeling concepts, including classes and relationships between classes, were introduced in Chapter 2. Appendix A provides an overview of the UML static modeling notation. Section 6.1 provides an introduction to how static modeling is used to model commonality and variability in software product lines. Section 6.2 describes static modeling of the product line problem domain, where the initial emphasis is on modeling the physical classes and entity classes. The next topic, covered in Section 6.3, is static modeling of the scope of the product line in order to determine the boundary between the software product

line and the external environment. Static modeling of the entity classes, which
are data-intensive classes, is described in Section 6.4. Section 6.5 describes modeling and categorizing software application classes on the basis of their roles in
the product line.

6.1   Modeling Commonality and Variability in Product Lines

A crucial issue in modeling software product lines is how to analyze and model
the commonality and variability in the product family. In a static model of a single system, all classes are required. In a software product line, however, a class
is required by at least one member of the product line but may not be required
by all members of the product line. A class that is required by all members of
the product line is referred to as a **kernel class**. An **optional class** is a class provided by some members of the family but not all. Sometimes different members
of the product family require alternative versions of a class. These classes are
referred to as **variant classes**. Among a group of variant classes, one may be
designated as the default class. Depending on the characteristics of the product
line, some of the variants may be able to coexist in the same product line member. In other product lines, on the other hand, the variants are mutually exclusive in a given family member. A generalization/specialization hierarchy can be
used to model the different variants of a class, which are used by different family members.

6.1.1   Categorization and UML Stereotypes

The dictionary definition of *category* is "a specifically defined division in a system of classification." In class structuring, we categorize objects in order to
group together objects with similar characteristics. In UML, stereotypes are
used to distinguish among the various kinds of application classes. A **stereotype**
is a subclass of an existing modeling element (in this case a product line class),
which is used to represent a usage distinction (in this case the kind of class). In
the UML notation, a stereotype is enclosed by guillemets, like this: «kernel».

In single systems, a class is categorized by the role it plays. External classes
are classified on the basis of characteristics such as «external system» or «external user», as will be described in Section 6.3. Application classes are classified
according to their role in the application, such as «entity class» or «interface
class», as will be described in Sections 6.4 and 6.5.

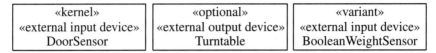

Figure 6.1 *Example of UML classes and their stereotypes*

In the modeling of software product lines, each class can be categorized according to its reuse characteristic. The stereotypes «kernel», «optional», and «variant» are used to distinguish among the reuse characteristics of the product line classes.

In UML 2.0, a modeling element can be described with more than one stereotype. Thus one stereotype can be used to represent the reuse characteristic while a different stereotype is used to represent a different characteristic—in particular, the role played by the modeling element, such as whether it is an interface or entity class. This capability is very useful, and the PLUS method takes full advantage of it.

It is important to realize that the role a class plays in the application and the reuse characteristic are orthogonal—that is, independent of each other. Thus a class designated as «entity» could also be specified as «kernel», «optional», or «variant» in a product line. During development, if the role of a class is identified, but not yet its reuse category, then the class can be depicted with only its role stereotype. Later the reuse category can be added.

Examples shown in Figure 6.1 from the microwave oven product line are the kernel external input device `Door Sensor`, the optional external output device `Turntable`, and the variant external input device `Boolean Weight Sensor`.

6.2   Static Modeling of the Software Product Line Problem Domain

In static modeling of the problem domain, the initial emphasis is on modeling physical classes and entity classes. **Physical classes** are classes that have physical characteristics; that is, they can be seen and touched. Such classes include physical devices (which are often part of the problem domain in embedded applications), users, external systems, and timers. **Entity classes** are conceptual data-intensive classes that are often persistent—that is, long-living. Entity classes are particularly prevalent in information systems; in banking applications, examples include debit cards, accounts, and transactions.

In embedded system product lines, which have several sensors and actuators, class diagrams help with modeling these real-world devices. In the microwave oven product line, for example, it is useful to model real-world devices (such as the door, heating element, weight sensor, turntable, beeper, display, keypad, lamp, and clock), their associations, and the multiplicity of the associations. Composite classes are often used to show how a real-world class is composed of other classes. Thus the microwave oven is a composite class that consists of a clock, a door sensor, a heating element, a beeper, a turntable, a weight sensor, a keypad, a display, and a lamp. The conceptual static model for a single microwave oven system is depicted in Figure 6.2.

In contrast to the static model for a single system (in which all classes are required), in a software product line it is possible for some of the real-world classes to be kernel, while others are optional and yet others are alternatives. Figure 6.3 depicts the conceptual static model of the problem domain for a microwave oven product line. It shows kernel classes such as `Clock` and `Door Sensor`; and it shows three optional classes: `Beeper`, `Turntable`, and `Lamp`. Kernel classes, such as `Keypad` and `Door Sensor`, have a one-to-one association with the composite `Microwave Oven` class. Optional classes such as `Beeper` and `Lamp`, however, have an optional (zero-or-one) association with the composite `Microwave Oven` class.

The static model of the problem domain also depicts variant classes such as `Boolean Weight Sensor` and `Analog Weight Sensor`. These real-world classes are modeled as a generalization/specialization hierarchy. The variants are depicted as subclasses of a `Weight Sensor` class, which is a kernel class because it captures the common properties of a weight sensor. If one of the variant classes is the default class, such as `Boolean Weight Sensor`, it is given the stereotype «default». The other variant class(es) are given the stereotype «variant», such as `Analog Weight Sensor`. A {mutually exclusive} constraint is also depicted to indicate that the subclasses can never coexist in the same microwave oven.

6.3 Static Modeling of the Software Product Line Scope

It is very important to understand the scope of a software product line—in particular, what is to be included within the product line and what is outside the product line. The boundary between the software product line and the external environment is referred to as the **software product line context**. In structured

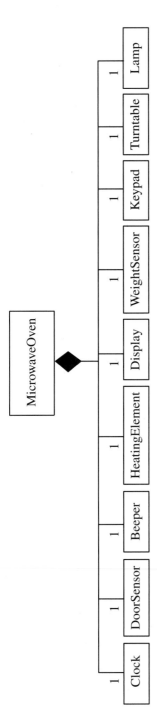

Figure 6.2 *Conceptual static model for a microwave oven system*

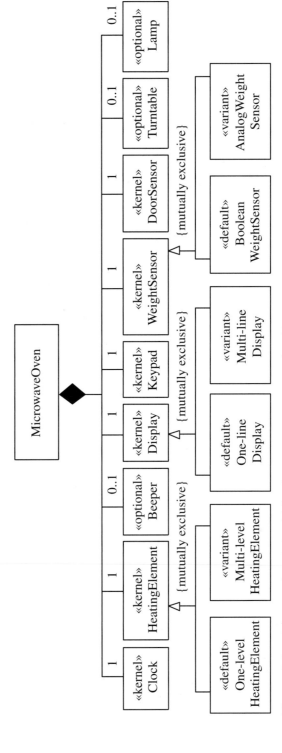

Figure 6.3 *Conceptual static model for the microwave oven product line*

analysis, the boundary between a system and the external environment is called the *system context* and is shown on a **system context diagram**. The UML notation does not explicitly support a system context diagram; instead, the system context is depicted by a static model (Douglass 2004; Gomaa 2000). When the problem domain for a single system is being modeled, it is instructive to understand the boundary of the system by developing a **system context class diagram**. This is a more detailed view of the system boundary than that provided by a use case diagram.

When the context of a software product line is being modeled, the **product line context class diagram** defines the hardware/software boundary of a member of the product family, referred to as a **product line system**. Unlike a single system, where the boundary is fixed, the product line context class diagram has to capture the variability in the boundary. In particular, some of the external classes may only be optional, meaning that they are present in only some members of the family. In some cases, variants of the external class may be used in different family members. For this case, the external class is modeled as a generalization/specialization hierarchy. The superclass, which captures the common aspects of the variant classes, is depicted on the product line context class diagram. Subclasses are depicted on the conceptual static model of the problem domain, as shown in Figure 6.3.

6.3.1 Product Line External Classes

The product line context model uses UML stereotypes to represent the product line boundary with a UML class diagram. The product line context is depicted showing a product line system (member of the product line) as an aggregate class with the stereotype «product line system», and the external environment is depicted as external classes to which the system has to interface.

External classes are categorized by stereotype. As depicted in Figure 6.4, an external class is classified as an external user, an external device, an external system, or an external timer. An external device is classified further as follows:

- **External input device**. A device that only provides input to the system—for example, a sensor

- **External output device**. A device that only receives output from the system—for example, an actuator

- **External input/output device**. A device that both provides input to the system and receives output from the system—for example, an ATM card reader

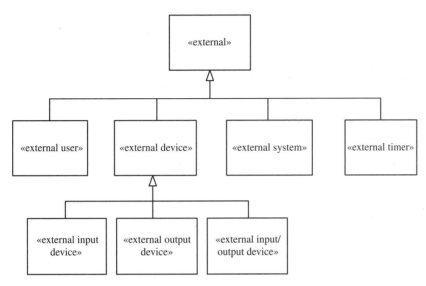

Figure 6.4   *Classification of external classes by stereotype*

For a real-time embedded system, it is desirable to identify low-level external classes that correspond to the physical I/O devices to which the system must interface. These external classes are depicted with the stereotypes «external input device», «external output device», and «external input/output device». Examples are the Door Sensor external input device and the Heating Element external output device in the microwave oven product line (see Figure 6.5).

A human user often interacts with the system by means of standard I/O devices such as a keyboard/display and mouse. The characteristics of these standard I/O devices are of no interest because they are handled by the operating system. The interface to the user is of much greater interest in terms of what information is being output to the user and what information is being input from the user. For this reason, an external user interacting with the system via standard I/O devices is depicted with the stereotype «external user». An example is the Factory Operator in the factory automation product line.

A general guideline is that a human user should be represented as an external user class only if the user interacts with the system via standard I/O devices. On the other hand, if the user interacts with the system via application-specific I/O devices, these I/O devices should be represented as external I/O device classes.

An «external system» class is needed when the members of the product line interface to other systems to either send data or receive data. Thus, in the factory automation product line, members interface to two external systems: `Pick & Place Robot` and `Manufacturing Robot`.

An «external timer» class is used if the application needs to keep track of time and/or if it needs external timer events to initiate certain actions in the system. External timer classes are most frequently needed in real-time systems. An example from the microwave oven product line is `Clock`. It is needed because the system needs to keep track of elapsed time to determine the cooking time. Sometimes the need for periodic activities becomes apparent only during design.

The associations between the product line system class and the external classes are depicted on the product line context class diagram, showing in particular the multiplicity of the associations. The standard association names on product line context class diagrams are *Inputs to, Outputs to, Interfaces to, Interacts with*, and *Awakens*. These associations are used as follows:

«external input device» *Inputs to* «product line system»

«product line system» *Outputs to* «external output device»

«external user» *Interacts with* «product line system»

«external system» *Interfaces to* «product line system»

«external timer» *Awakens* «product line system»

Examples of associations on product line context class diagram taken from the discussion in Section 6.3.2 (Figures 6.6 and 6.7) are

`Door Sensor` *Inputs to* `Microwave Oven Product Line System`

`Microwave Oven Product Line System` *Outputs to* `Heating Element`

`Factory Operator` *Interacts with* `Factory Automation Product Line System`

`Pick & Place Robot` *Interfaces to* `Factory Automation Product Line System`

`Clock` *Awakens* `Microwave Oven Product Line System`

6.3.2 Development Stategies for the Software Product Line Context Model

The way the software product line context model is developed depends on the strategy used for developing the product line. With the reverse evolutionary engineering strategy, a separate context model is developed for each member of the product line. Each context model is reverse-engineered from an existing system that is considered to be a potential member of the product line. The software product line context model is produced by integration of the individual context models. If the forward evolutionary engineering strategy is used, then the context model for the kernel system is developed first and evolved as variations are considered for inclusion in the product line context model. The kernel of the software product line system is referred to as the *kernel system*.

When static models for the different members of the product line are integrated, external classes that are common to all members of the family are considered kernel classes of the integrated context model, which is referred to as the software product line context model. External classes that are used by one product line member but not others are considered optional classes of the product line context model. External classes that have some common properties but also some differences are generalized. The superclass is shown on the product line context model.

Kernel external classes have a one-to-one or one-to-many association with the product line system class because they are included in every member of the product line. However, optional external classes have a zero-or-one or zero-to-many association with the product line system class to indicate that they are included in only some members of the product line.

Examples of Developing Software Product Line Context Models

Two examples of developing software product line context models are described here. The first applies the forward evolutionary engineering strategy to the microwave oven product line, and the second applies the reverse evolutionary engineering strategy to the factory automation product line.

In the first example, a software product line context class model is developed first for the kernel system as illustrated in Figure 6.5, which shows the external classes to which `Microwave Oven Product Line Kernel System` has to interface. The external classes are determined directly from the conceptual static model of the problem domain described previously (see Figure 6.3). Figure 6.5 depicts each external class with two stereotypes: the first depicting the reuse category (such as «kernel» or «optional»), the second representing the category of external class (such as «external input device»).

From the *total system perspective*—that is, both hardware and software—the microwave oven user is external to the system, whereas the physical devices (which include the door, heating element, keypad, and display) are part of the system. From a *software perspective*, the physical devices are external to the software product line and hence are modeled as external classes.

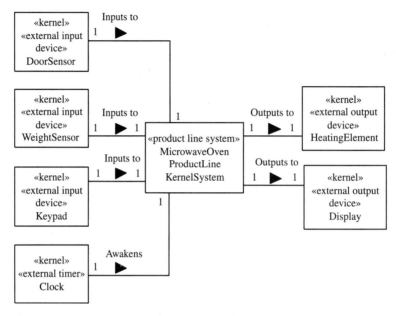

Figure 6.5 *Microwave oven product line kernel context class diagram*

Figure 6.5 shows the product line kernel context class model, which considers only the kernel external classes, which are in every member of the product line. The kernel context class model is similar to that for a single system because it depicts only those classes that always interface to the product line kernel system. Variability is introduced into the product line context model through evolutionary development (the evolutionary part of the forward evolutionary engineering strategy) by consideration of the optional external classes, as shown in Figure 6.6. As a result, the product line context model is developed more fully as additional optional external classes are added to it.

The microwave oven product line example shows several kernel external device classes, including `Door Sensor`, `Heating Element`, and `Display`. It also includes an external timer: `Clock`. Optional external device classes include `Lamp`, `Beeper`, and `Turntable`. The kernel classes have a one-to-one association with the product line system because they are always present; the optional classes have a zero-or-one association because they are present in only some product line systems.

In both Figures 6.5 and 6.6, each external class is depicted with two stereotypes: The first one identifies the reuse category; for example, `Door Sensor` is a kernel class and `Turntable` is an optional class. The second one represents the

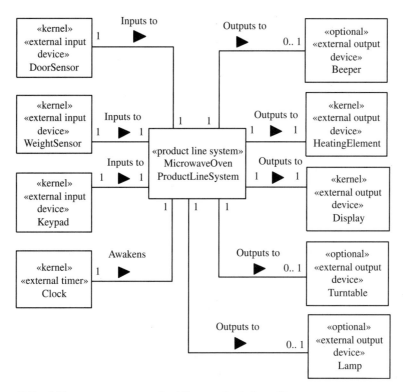

Figure 6.6   *Microwave oven product line context class diagram*

category of external class; for example, Door Sensor is an external input device class and Turntable is an external output device class.

As an example of the reverse evolutionary engineering strategy, consider the factory automation product line, which is shown in Figure 6.7. This product line encompasses high-volume low-flexibility manufacturing systems, flexible manufacturing systems, and factory monitoring systems. Factory monitoring systems have three external classes; two are external systems (Manufacturing Robot and the Pick & Place Robot), and the third is an external user (Factory Operator). High-volume manufacturing systems have the same three external classes as factory monitoring systems; in addition, they have two other external users: Production Manager and Workflow Engineer. Flexible manufacturing systems have the same five external classes as high-volume manufacturing systems have, as well as two additional external systems: Automated Guided Vehicle and Automated Storage & Retrieval System. When the different context models are being integrated, the external classes that are common to

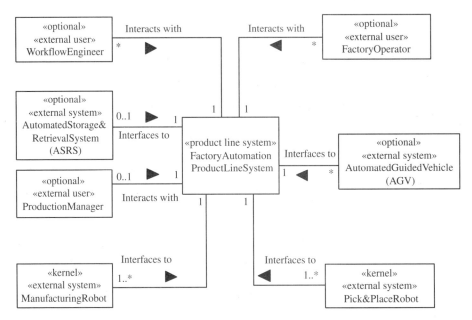

Figure 6.7   *Factory automation product line context class diagram*

all factory automation systems are categorized as kernel classes—namely, `Manufacturing Robot` and `Pick & Place Robot`. The other external classes are all categorized as optional.

6.4 Static Modeling of Entity Classes

Entity classes are conceptual data-intensive classes that store persistent (i.e., long-living) data. Whereas some approaches advocate static modeling of all software classes during analysis, the PLUS approach emphasizes static modeling of entity classes in order to take advantage of the strengths of the static modeling notation for expressing classes, attributes, and relationships among classes. Entity classes are particularly prevalent in information system product lines; however, many real-time and distributed system product lines have significant data-intensive aspects. Concentrating on modeling entity classes is similar to modeling a logical database schema (Booch et al. 2005). Entity classes are often mapped to a database in the design phase.

The main difference between static modeling in UML and entity relationship modeling, which is frequently used for logical database design, is that whereas both approaches allow classes, attributes of each class, and relationships among classes to be modeled, UML also allows class operations to be specified. During static modeling of the problem domain, the emphasis is on determining the entity classes that are defined in the problem, their attributes, and their relationships. Specifying operations is deferred until product line design modeling. Static modeling of entity classes is referred to as *entity class modeling*.

One example of entity class modeling comes from the e-commerce product line, in which bank accounts, customers, invoices, and catalogs are all mentioned in the problem description. Each of these real-world conceptual entities is modeled as an entity class and depicted with the stereotype «entity». The attributes of each entity class are determined, and the relationships among the entity classes are defined.

An example of an entity class model for a B2C e-commerce application is shown in Figure 6.8. Because this static model depicts only entity classes, all the classes have the «entity» stereotype to depict the role they play in the application. Figure 6.8 shows the Customer entity class, which has a one-to-one association with the Customer Account class, which in turn has a one-to-many association with the Delivery Order class. The latter class is an aggregation of the Selected Item class.

6.4.1   Developing Entity Class Models in Software Product Lines

The way the entity class model for the product line is developed depends on the strategy used. With the reverse evolutionary engineering strategy, a separate entity class model is developed for each member of the product line. The entity class model for the product line is then produced by integration of the individual entity class models. With the forward evolutionary engineering strategy, the entity class model for the kernel system is developed first and then evolves as variations are considered for inclusion in the entity class model.

When entity class models for the different members of the product line are integrated, classes that are common to all members of the product line become kernel classes of the integrated product line entity class model. Classes that are in one view but not others become optional classes in the product line entity class model. Classes that have some common attributes and operations, but also some differences, are generalized. The common attributes and operations are captured in the superclass; the differences are captured in the variant subclasses of the superclass.

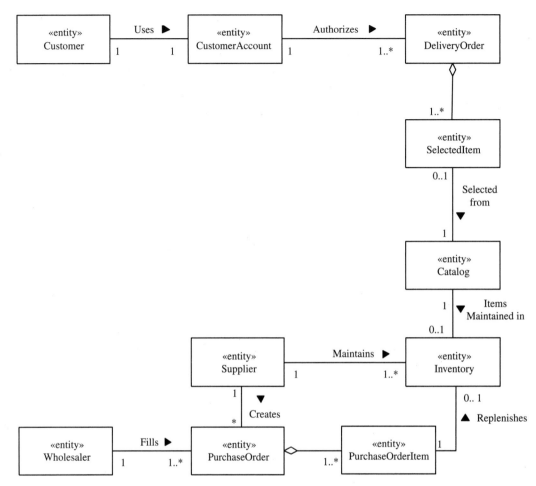

Figure 6.8 *Entity class model for e-commerce B2C entity classes*

Example of Entity Class Modeling in Software Product Lines

One example of applying the reverse evolutionary engineering strategy for entity class modeling comes from the e-commerce product line. There are two main groups of applications in this product line: business-to-consumer (B2C) applications and business-to-business (B2B) applications. The entity class model for B2C applications just described is illustrated in Figure 6.8. The entity class model for B2B applications is shown in Figure 6.9. The integrated entity class model for the product line is shown in Figure 6.10.

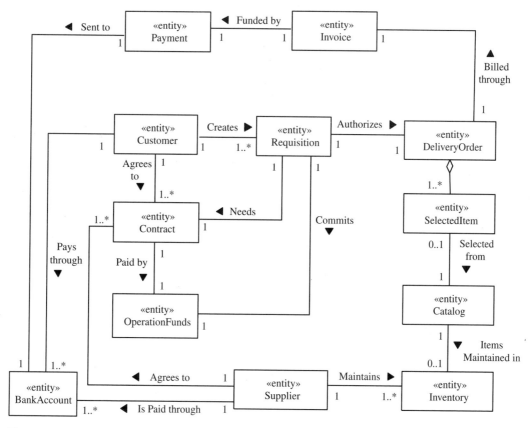

Figure 6.9 *Entity class model for e-commerce B2B entity classes*

In the product line entity class model, classes have a second stereotype to depict the reuse category of each class, either «kernel» or «optional». Classes such as Customer and Catalog, which exist in the entity class models of both B2C and B2B applications, become kernel classes in the product line entity class model. Classes that appear in only one of the entity class models, such as Contract (which appears only in the B2B entity class model) and Customer Account (which appears only in the B2C entity class model), become optional classes in the software product line entity class model. Entity classes that might exist in either a B2B or a B2C application, such as Purchase Order, also become optional classes in the software product line entity class model.

Figure 6.10 shows the kernel Customer entity class, which has a one-to-many association with the optional Bank Account class and the optional

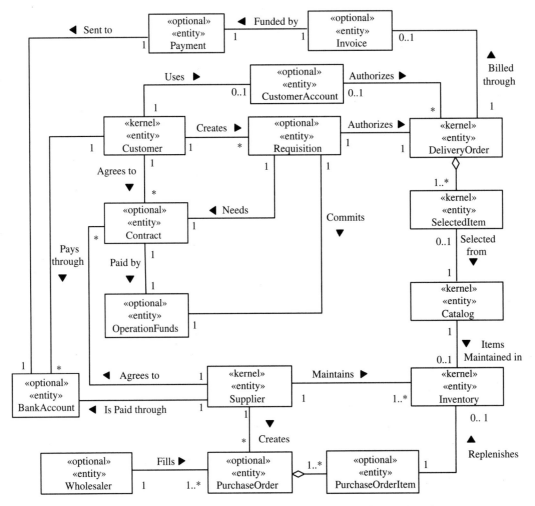

Figure 6.10 *Integrated entity class model for e-commerce product line entity classes*

`Contract` class. The `Requisition` class has a one-to-one association with the `Contract` class. Another entity class is the `Delivery Order` class, which is an aggregation of the `Selected Item` class. The attributes of the kernel classes are shown in Figure 6.11, and the attributes of the optional classes are shown in Figure 6.12. This example is described in more detail in the e-commerce product line case study (Chapter 14).

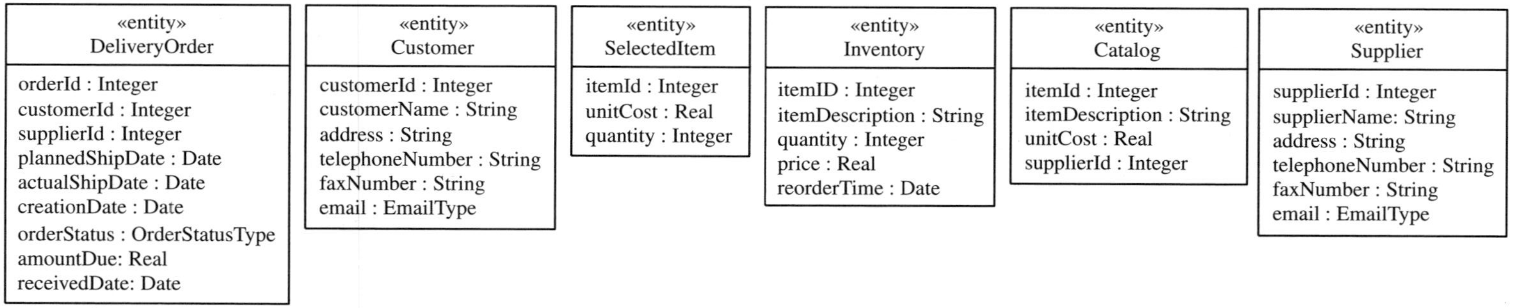

Figure 6.11 *Entity class model for e-commerce product line: kernel class attributes*

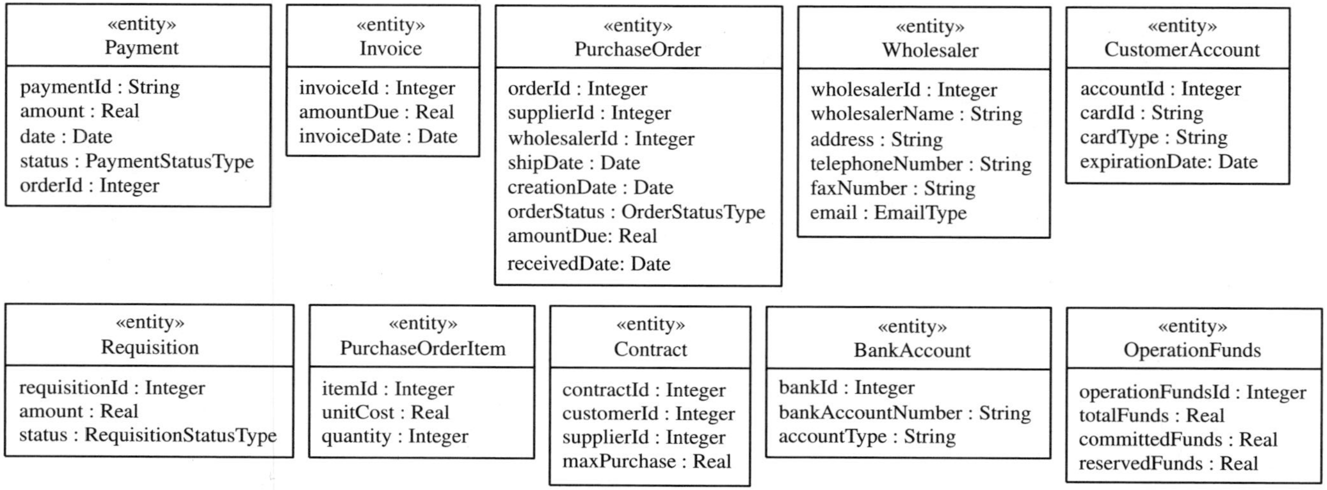

«entity» DeliveryOrder
- orderId : Integer
- customerId : Integer
- supplierId : Integer
- plannedShipDate : Date
- actualShipDate : Date
- creationDate : Date
- orderStatus : OrderStatusType
- amountDue: Real
- receivedDate: Date

«entity» Customer
- customerId : Integer
- customerName : String
- address : String
- telephoneNumber : String
- faxNumber : String
- email : EmailType

«entity» SelectedItem
- itemId : Integer
- unitCost : Real
- quantity : Integer

«entity» Inventory
- itemID : Integer
- itemDescription : String
- quantity : Integer
- price : Real
- reorderTime : Date

«entity» Catalog
- itemId : Integer
- itemDescription : String
- unitCost : Real
- supplierId : Integer

«entity» Supplier
- supplierId : Integer
- supplierName: String
- address : String
- telephoneNumber : String
- faxNumber : String
- email : EmailType

Figure 6.12 *Entity class model for e-commerce product line: optional class attributes*

«entity» Payment
- paymentId : String
- amount : Real
- date : Date
- status : PaymentStatusType
- orderId : Integer

«entity» Invoice
- invoiceId : Integer
- amountDue : Real
- invoiceDate : Date

«entity» PurchaseOrder
- orderId : Integer
- supplierId : Integer
- wholesalerId : Integer
- shipDate : Date
- creationDate : Date
- orderStatus : OrderStatusType
- amountDue: Real
- receivedDate: Date

«entity» Wholesaler
- wholesalerId : Integer
- wholesalerName : String
- address : String
- telephoneNumber : String
- faxNumber : String
- email : EmailType

«entity» CustomerAccount
- accountId : Integer
- cardId : String
- cardType : String
- expirationDate: Date

«entity» Requisition
- requisitionId : Integer
- amount : Real
- status : RequisitionStatusType

«entity» PurchaseOrderItem
- itemId : Integer
- unitCost : Real
- quantity : Integer

«entity» Contract
- contractId : Integer
- customerId : Integer
- supplierId : Integer
- maxPurchase : Real

«entity» BankAccount
- bankId : Integer
- bankAccountNumber : String
- accountType : String

«entity» OperationFunds
- operationFundsId : Integer
- totalFunds : Real
- committedFunds : Real
- reservedFunds : Real

6.5 Modeling Application Classes and Objects

Section 6.4 described static modeling of entity classes, which benefit most from static modeling in the analysis phase because they are information-intensive. Entity classes, however, are only one kind of software class within the product line. Before dynamic modeling can be undertaken, as described in Chapters 7 and 8, it is necessary to determine what software classes and objects are needed to realize each use case. Identification of software objects can be greatly assisted by object structuring criteria, which provide guidance on structuring an application into objects. The approach categorizes software classes and objects by the roles they play in the application.

In this step, classes are categorized in order to group together classes with similar characteristics. Figure 6.13 shows the categorization of application classes. Stereotypes (Section 6.1.1) are used to distinguish among the various kinds of application classes. Because an object is an instance of a class, an object has the same stereotype as the class from which it is instantiated. Thus the categorization described in this section applies equally to classes and objects.

In Figure 6.13, each box represents a different category of application class, and the relationships between them are inheritance relationships. Thus an application class is classified as an entity class, an interface class, a control class, or an application logic class. These stereotypes are classified further, as shown in Figure 6.13 and described here. An instance of a stereotype class is a stereotype object, which can also be shown in guillemets, like this: the stereotype «entity» object.

This classification process is analogous to classifying books in a library, with major classes such as fiction and nonfiction, and further classification of fiction into classics, mysteries, adventure, and so on, and nonfiction into biography, autobiography, travel, cooking, history, and other categories. It is also analogous to the taxonomy of the animal kingdom, which is divided into major categories (mammal, bird, fish, reptile, and so on) that are further divided into subclasses (e.g., cat, dog, and monkey in the mammals).

Objects and classes are categorized according to the roles they play in the application. There are four main object and class structuring categories, as shown in Figure 6.13: interface objects, entity objects, control objects, and application logic objects. Most applications will have objects from each of the four categories. These object structuring categories are described in Sections 6.5.1 through 6.5.4.

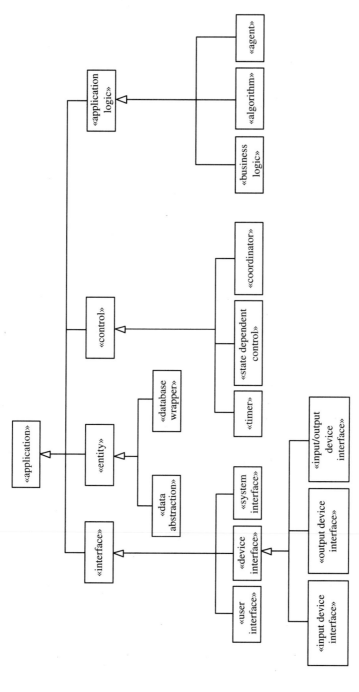

Figure 6.13 *Classification of application classes by stereotype*

6.5.1 Interface Objects

An **interface object** is an object that interfaces to and communicates with the external environment. For every external class in the product line context model, there is a corresponding interface class within the software product line. Interface objects are sometimes also referred to as *boundary objects*. They can be further categorized as follows:

- **Device interface object**, which interfaces to a hardware I/O device. A device interface object is further categorized as an **input device interface object**, which interfaces to an input device, an **output device interface object**, which interfaces to an output device, or an **input/output device interface object**, which interfaces to an input/output device.
- **User interface object**, which provides an interface to a human user
- **System interface object**, which interfaces to an external system or subsystem

6.5.2 Entity Objects

An **entity object** is a long-living object that stores information. Entity objects are instantiated from the classes that would typically be modeled as entities in entity relationship models. Entity class modeling was described in Section 6.4. Entity objects may be further categorized into data abstraction and database wrapper classes.

For information systems, it is likely that, in some cases, the encapsulated data will need to be stored in a database. In this situation, the entity class will actually provide an interface to the database rather than encapsulating the data. Thus, entity classes are further categorized as **data abstraction classes** (which encapsulate data structures) and **database wrapper classes**. A database wrapper class hides the details of how to access an existing database management system or (less frequently) file management system from which data needs to be retrieved. Typically, this existing system is a legacy system.

6.5.3 Control Objects

A **control object** provides the overall coordination for a collection of objects in a use case. Control objects may be any of the following:

- **Coordinator object**. A decision-making object that determines the overall sequencing for a collection of related objects and is not state-dependent.

- **State-dependent control object**. A control object that hides the details of a finite state machine; that is, the object encapsulates a statechart, a state transition diagram, or the contents of a state transition table.
- **Timer object**. A control object that executes at regular intervals and is activated by an external timer.

Because control objects coordinate the interaction among several objects, they are usually considered only at the time of developing the dynamic model and not the initial conceptual static model.

6.5.4 Application Logic Objects

An **application logic object** contains the details of the application logic. Such an object is needed when it is desirable to hide the application logic separately from the data being manipulated because it is considered likely that the application logic will change independently of the data.

For information systems, application logic objects are usually **business logic objects**; whereas for real-time, scientific, or engineering applications, they are usually **algorithm objects**. In intelligent or knowledge-based systems, it is also possible to have **agent objects**, which encapsulate some knowledge of the application domain. As with control objects, application logic objects are more likely to be considered when the dynamic model, not the initial conceptual static model, is being developed.

6.5.5 Applying Object and Class Structuring Criteria

The object and class structuring categories are also referred to as *structuring criteria* because they provide guidelines for deciding what software objects are needed in a given application. Object structuring is necessary before dynamic interaction models are developed, as described in Chapter 7. For each use case, the object structuring criteria are applied to determine the objects that participate in realizing the use case. Object and class structuring is described in more detail in Gomaa 2000.

Figure 6.14 shows an example of the classes in the ATM client subsystem of a banking application. There are device interface classes, user interface classes, entity classes, and a state-dependent control class. Additional examples are given in the case studies in Chapters 13, 14, and 15.

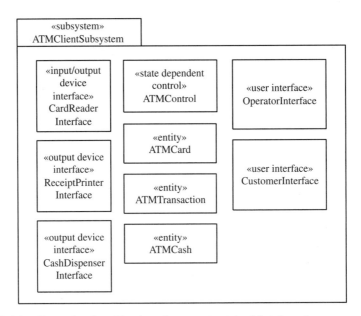

Figure 6.14   *Example of application classes categorized by stereotype*

6.6 Summary

This chapter described how static modeling can be used in modeling software product lines. During the analysis modeling phase, static modeling is used for analyzing the real-world classes in the problem domain, from which the boundary of the software product line can be determined in the product line context model. Static modeling is also used for modeling the entity classes in the problem domain, which is similar to developing a logical database schema. Stereotypes are used to distinguish among two orthogonal characteristics of classes: the role of the class in the application (such as «entity» or «control») and the reuse category (such as «kernel» or «optional».) Finally, the chapter described the categorization of application classes using the object and class structuring criteria. These criteria are used to determine the objects that participate in each use case. During dynamic modeling, as will be described in Chapter 7, the sequence of interaction among these objects is determined. Chapter 9 will describe how variability can be introduced into class design through specialization of abstract classes and through parameterized classes.

Dynamic Interaction Modeling for Software Product Lines

Dynamic modeling provides a view of a product line in which control and sequencing is considered, either within an object (by means of a finite state machine) or between objects (by analysis of object interactions). The state-dependent aspect of dynamic modeling involving finite state machines and statecharts is described in Chapter 8. This chapter addresses dynamic interaction between objects. The discussion focuses briefly on dynamic modeling in single systems before moving on to dynamic modeling for software product lines.

Dynamic modeling is based on the use cases developed during use case modeling. For each use case, the objects that participate in the use case are determined, and the ways in which the objects interact are shown in order to satisfy the requirements described in the use case. To determine the objects in each use case, the object structuring criteria that were described in Chapter 6 are applied. For each use case, an interaction diagram is developed to show the objects that participate in the use case and the sequence of messages passed between them. The interaction is depicted either on a communication diagram (which was called a *collaboration diagram* in UML 1.x) or a sequence diagram. A narrative description of the object interaction is provided in a message sequence description.

Dynamic modeling was introduced in Chapter 2. An overview of the UML dynamic modeling notation is given in Appendix A. Section 7.1 provides a brief introduction to the basics of dynamic modeling in single systems and can be skipped by those who are already familiar with the topic. Section 7.2 introduces evolutionary dynamic modeling in software product lines, which is then described in more detail in Sections 7.3 and 7.4. Section 7.3 describes the kernel first approach to dynamic analysis, which is used to determine the interaction among kernel objects. Section 7.4 describes the product line evolution approach, which is used to determine the interaction among kernel, optional, and variant objects. Section 7.5 describes conventions for message sequence numbering. Section 7.6 gives an example of evolutionary dynamic modeling for the microwave oven product line.

7.1 Dynamic Modeling in Single Systems

For each use case, the objects are determined by use of the object structuring criteria described in Chapter 6. The way objects dynamically cooperate with each other can then be depicted on communication diagrams or sequence diagrams, as described in this section.

7.1.1 Object Interaction Modeling with Communication Diagrams

A **communication diagram** is developed for each use case; only objects that participate in the use case are depicted. On a communication diagram, the sequence in which the objects participate in each use case is described and depicted by means of message sequence numbers. The message sequencing on the communication diagram should correspond to the sequence of interactions between the actor and the system already described in the use case.

A **message sequence description** is developed as part of the dynamic model and describes how the analysis model objects participate in each use case. The message sequence description is a narrative description, describing what happens when each message arrives at a destination object depicted on a communication diagram or sequence diagram. The message sequence description uses the message sequence numbers that appear on the communication diagram. It describes the sequence of messages sent from source objects to destination objects and describes what each destination object does with a message it receives. The message sequence description usually provides additional information that is not depicted on the object interaction diagram. For example, every time an entity object is accessed, the message sequence description can provide additional information, such as which attributes of the object are referenced.

In the analysis model, messages represent the information passed between objects. Communication diagrams help in determining the operations of the objects because the arrival of a message at an object usually invokes an operation. In PLUS, however, the emphasis during analysis modeling is on capturing the information passed between objects, rather than on the operations invoked. During design, we might decide that two different messages arriving at an object invoke different operations—or alternatively, the same operation, with the message name being a parameter of the operation. However, these decisions should be postponed until the design phase. The kind of message passed between objects—synchronous or asynchronous—is a design decision that is also postponed until the design phase. At the analysis stage, all messages passed between objects are shown as simple messages.

As an example of using a communication diagram to depict the objects that participate in a use case, consider the View Workstation Status use case shown in Figure 7.1, in which a factory operator views the status of one or more factory workstations (Figure 7.1*a*). The communication diagram for this simple use case consists of only two objects: a client object and a server object. The

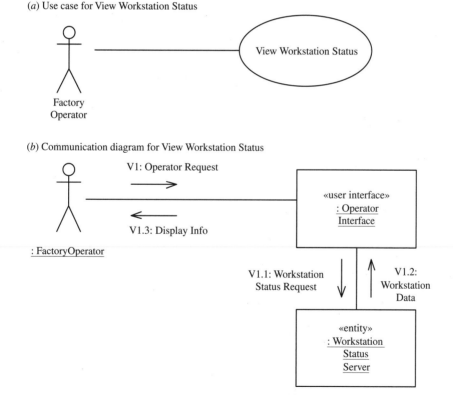

Figure 7.1   *Communication diagram for the* View Workstation Status *use case*

client object is a user interface object: `Operator Interface`. The server object is an entity object: `Workstation Status Server`.

The communication diagram for this use case depicts the client object, `Operator Interface`, making a request to the server object, `Workstation Status Server` (see Figure 7.1*b*). The message sequence description is as follows (see Section 7.5 for an explanation of message numbering):

V1: The operator requests a workstation status service—for example, to view the status of a factory workstation.

V1.1: The `Operator Interface` object sends a workstation status request to the `Workstation Status Server` object.

V1.2: `Workstation Status Server` responds—for example, with the requested workstation status data.

V1.3: `Operator Interface` displays the workstation status information to the operator.

7.1.2 Sequence Diagrams

The interaction among objects can also be shown on a sequence diagram, which shows object interactions arranged in time sequence. A **sequence diagram** shows the objects participating in the interaction and the sequence in which messages are sent. Sequence diagrams and communication diagrams depict similar (although not identical) information, but in different ways. Usually either communication diagrams or sequence diagrams are used to describe a system, but not both. Sequence diagrams have been substantially enhanced in UML 2.0, although only the UML 1.x subset is used in this chapter.

Because the sequence diagram shows the order of messages sent sequentially from the top to the bottom of the diagram, numbering the messages is not necessary. In the following example, however, the messages on the sequence diagram are numbered to show their correspondence to the communication diagram.

An example of a sequence diagram for the `View Workstation Status` use case is shown in Figure 7.2. This sequence diagram conveys the same information as the communication diagram shown in Figure 7.1. The messages are numbered on this diagram to show the correspondence with the communication diagram. In fact, the message sequence description given in the previous section is applicable to both the sequence diagram and the communication diagram.

Note that in the analysis phase, no decision is made about whether an object is active or passive, so no assumptions should be made about object activation. Consequently, the object lifeline is always shown as a dashed line in the

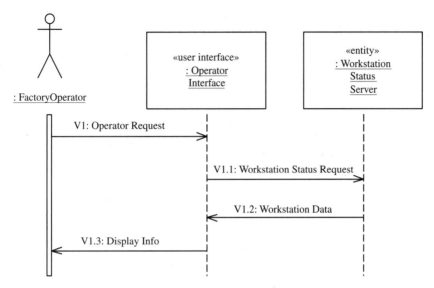

Figure 7.2   *Sequence diagram for the* View Workstation Status *use case*

analysis model. On the other hand, the lifeline for the actor is always shown as an activation (double line), because it is assumed that the actor is active.

7.1.3   Sequence Diagram versus Communication Diagram

Either a sequence diagram or a communication diagram can be used to depict the object interaction and sequence of messages passed among objects. The sequence diagram clearly shows the order in which messages are passed between objects, but seeing how the objects are connected to each other is difficult. The communication diagram shows the layout of the objects—in particular, how the objects are connected to each other. The message sequence is shown on both diagrams. Because the message sequence depicted on the communication diagram is less readily visible than on the sequence diagram, the message sequence is numbered. However, even with the message numbering on the communication diagram, it sometimes takes longer to see the sequence of messages. On the other hand, if an interaction involves many objects, a sequence diagram also becomes difficult to read. The diagram might have to be shrunk to fit on a page, or it might span several pages.

In the PLUS method, communication diagrams are generally preferred over sequence diagrams—for several reasons. First, an impact analysis of the effect of features on the object interactions can be clearly depicted on communication diagrams. Second, an important step in the transition from analysis to design is the integration of the communication diagrams to create feature-based communication diagrams (as described in Chapter 9) and the software architecture of the system (as described in Chapter 11). This integration is much easier with communication diagrams than with sequence diagrams. If the analysis started with sequence diagrams, it would be necessary to convert each sequence diagram to a communication diagram before the integration could be done. Sometimes, however, the sequence diagram is very helpful—in particular, for very complex interactions and for timing diagrams in real-time applications (Gomaa 2000).

7.1.4   Use Cases and Scenarios

A **scenario** is one specific path through a use case. Thus a particular message sequence depicted on an interaction diagram actually depicts a scenario and not a use case. To show all the alternatives through a use case, development of more than one interaction diagram is often necessary.

By using conditions, it is possible to depict alternatives on an interaction diagram and hence to depict the whole use case on a single interaction diagram. However, such comprehensive interaction diagrams are usually more difficult to read. In practice, depicting an individual scenario on an interaction diagram is usually clearer.

7.1.5   Generic and Instance Forms of Interaction Diagrams

The two forms of an interaction (sequence or communication) diagram are the generic form (also referred to as *descriptor form*) and the instance form. The **instance form** describes a specific scenario in detail, depicting one possible sequence of interactions among object instances. The **generic form** describes all possible interactions in which the objects might participate, so it can include loops, branches, and conditions. The generic form of an interaction diagram can be used to describe both the main sequence and the alternatives of a use case. The instance form is used to depict a specific scenario, which is one instance of the use case. Using the instance form might require several interaction diagrams to depict a given use case, depending on how many alternatives are described in the use case.

For all but the simplest use cases, an interaction diagram is usually much clearer when it depicts an instance form rather than a generic form of interaction. It can rapidly become too complicated if several alternatives are depicted on the same diagram.

In the instance form of the sequence diagram, time moves down the page. In the generic form—with loops, branches, and conditions—this is no longer the case. Thus, with the generic form one of the main benefits of using sequence diagrams is lost.

The sequence and communication diagrams shown in this chapter all use the instance form of interaction diagram. The generic form of communication diagram is used for feature-based communication diagrams in Chapter 9 and to depict the software architecture in Chapter 11. There are some differences in notation for the generic form, which will be pointed out in Chapter 9.

7.2   Evolutionary Dynamic Modeling in Software Product Lines

In single systems, every use case is required. In software product lines, however, use cases are categorized as kernel, optional, or alternative. A given member of the product line needs all the kernel use cases but only some of the optional and/or alternative use cases. For software product lines, it is necessary to perform dynamic modeling on all the use cases—whatever their reuse category—in order to determine what objects are needed for each use case and how they interact with each other.

As one would do for single systems, develop at least one communication diagram for each use case. Communication diagrams are categorized as kernel, optional, or alternative, corresponding to the reuse category of the use cases for which they are developed. Variant communication diagrams can also be developed to show the impact of use case variation points.

In addition, it is possible to develop feature-based communication diagrams—that is, a communication diagram for each functional feature. This approach is useful when use cases are reused together and hence combined into a feature, for which a feature-based communication diagram is developed, as described in Chapter 9.

7.2.1   Evolutionary Dynamic Analysis for Software Product Lines

Evolutionary dynamic analysis is an iterative strategy to help determine how the analysis model objects interact with each other to support the use cases. Dynamic analysis is carried out for each use case. A first attempt is made to determine the objects that participate in a use case, using the object structuring criteria described in Chapter 6. Then the way in which these objects collaborate to execute the use case is analyzed. This analysis might show a need for additional objects and/or additional interactions to be defined.

Given that the use cases have been categorized as kernel, optional, or alternative, the evolutionary dynamic analysis strategy starts with the kernel first approach (described in Section 7.3), followed by the product line evolution approach (described in Section 7.4). In other words, the strategy starts with the kernel use cases followed by the optional and alternative use cases. Furthermore, the order of developing the object communication diagrams follows the feature dependency hierarchy, as described in Chapter 5. This means that when a communication diagram is developed, it can assume the existence of objects supporting prerequisite features and use cases.

Dynamic analysis can be either state-dependent or non-state-dependent, depending on whether the object communication is state-dependent. This chapter describes non-state-dependent dynamic analysis. State-dependent dynamic analysis is described in Chapter 8.

7.3   Kernel First Approach

With the **kernel first approach**, the dynamic analysis is carried out for the kernel use cases, which are the use cases that are needed by every member of the software product line. The kernel use cases define the kernel of the product line, which is also referred to as the *kernel system*. Dynamic analysis for the kernel system is similar to dynamic analysis for a single system. Thus communication diagrams for the kernel system, referred to as *kernel communication diagrams*, are similar to communication diagrams for a single system. Only kernel objects participate in kernel communication diagrams, except when default objects are also needed, as will be described here.

The **kernel system** is a minimal member of the product line. In some product lines the kernel system consists of only the kernel objects. For other product lines, some objects may be needed in addition to the kernel objects. This can happen when there are alternative use cases, one of which must be selected. In that case, some product line members consist of the kernel system plus objects from one or other of the use cases, but not the kernel system by itself. Objects other than the kernel objects may also be needed when there is a variation point in a kernel use case that necessitates the inclusion of an alternative object. For the kernel system to be a complete system, it might be necessary to include certain default objects or to select one (or more) objects from a group(s) of alternatives. In this situation, the kernel system consists of the kernel objects together with the default objects.

7.3.1 Kernel First Approach: Non-State-Dependent Dynamic Analysis

The main steps in the non-state-dependent **kernel first approach** are as follows: Start with a kernel use case and consider each interaction between the primary actor and the kernel system. Start by developing the communication for the scenario described in the main path of the use case. (The actor starts the interaction with the kernel system through an external event. The sequence of external events generated by the actor is described in the use case.) Consider each interaction in sequence, as follows:

1. **Determine interface object(s)**. Consider the actor (or actors) that participates in the use case; determine the external objects (external to the system) through which the actor interfaces with the system and the software internal objects that receive the actor's inputs.

    Start by considering the events generated by the external objects that interface to the system and participate in the use case. For each external event, consider the software objects required to process the event. An interface object is needed to receive the external event from the external environment. On receipt of the external input, the interface object does some processing and typically sends a message to an internal object.

2. **Determine internal objects**. Start with the main sequence of the use case. Using the object structuring criteria, make a first attempt at determining the internal objects that participate in the use case, such as control or entity objects.

3. **Determine object communication**. For each external event generated by an actor, consider the communication required between the interface object that receives the event and the subsequent objects—entity or control objects—that cooperate in processing this event. Draw a communication diagram or sequence diagram showing the objects participating in the use case and the sequence of messages passing between them. Repeat this process for each subsequent interaction between the actor(s) and the system. As a result, additional objects may be required to participate, and additional message communication, along with message sequence numbering, will need to be specified.

4. **Consider alternative sequences**. Consider the different alternatives, such as error handling, that the use case needs to address. Then consider what objects need to be involved in executing the alternative branches.

5. **Consider the variation points**. Consider what objects are needed and what message sequences are needed to address each variation point. Variant communication diagrams are developed as described in Section 7.4.3.

7.3.2 Examples of the Kernel First Approach

As an example of the non-state-dependent kernel first approach, consider the Factory Operator use cases from the factory automation product line. These use cases are kernel use cases. Kernel objects depicted include Workstation Status Server, Alarm Handling Server, and Workstation Controller. For each kernel use case, a kernel communication diagram is developed, such as the one for View Workstation Status shown in Figure 7.1*b*.

As another example of the non-state-dependent kernel first approach, consider a kernel use case from the electronic commerce software product line. The Process Delivery Order use case is kernel because it is used in all member electronic commerce systems. In this use case, the supplier starts working on a customer's delivery order.

First the supplier must check that sufficient inventory exists to satisfy the order. From an object structuring point of view, there is a user interface object (Supplier Interface), and there are two entity objects (Inventory Server and Order Server). In addition, this case study adopts a software agent solution, so there are two agent objects: Supplier Agent (which acts on behalf of the supplier) and Delivery Order Agent (which acts on behalf of the delivery order server, interacting with other software agents, including Supplier Agent).

Because these objects participate in a kernel use case, they will later be categorized as kernel objects from a reuse perspective, as described in Chapter 9. Note that although a first cut at object reuse categorization might determine an object as kernel, subsequent dynamic modeling might determine that the object is really a default or optional object. For this reason, object reuse categorization is deferred until all dynamic modeling has been completed.

In the communication diagram for the Process Delivery Order use case (Figure 7.3), Supplier Agent queries Delivery Order Agent for a new delivery order from Order Server; the agent selects a delivery order. The Supplier Agent checks the inventory maintained by Inventory Server and then displays the order and inventory information to the supplier via Supplier Interface.

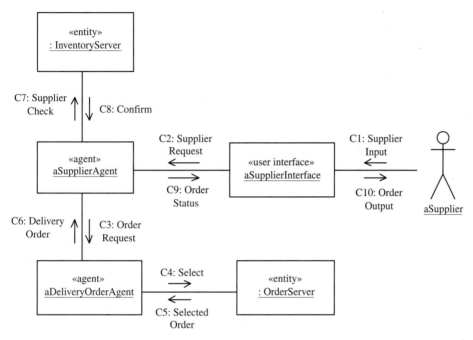

Figure 7.3 *Communication diagram for a kernel use case:* Process Delivery Order

7.4 Software Product Line Evolution Approach

The **software product line evolution approach** starts with the kernel communication diagrams developed with the kernel first approach, as described in Section 7.3. The product line evolves with the addition of the optional and alternative use cases. With the software product line evolution approach, optional and alternative communication diagrams are developed to depict the objects that participate in the optional and alternative use cases, as well as the sequence of object interactions.

The approach for developing individual optional or alternative communication diagrams is similar to that used for the kernel communication diagrams. It is to be expected that new objects will appear on these additional communication diagrams, which are then categorized as optional or variant objects.

There are two main types of evolution to consider. In the first case, one or more variation points within a use case need to be considered. In that situation, the communication diagram that needs to be developed is a modified version of the original communication diagram, which is referred to as a variant communication diagram. In the second case, there are separate optional and/or alternative use cases, for which separate optional and/or alternative communication diagrams need to be developed. This section describes the development of the optional and alternative communication diagrams for the separate use cases before describing the variant communication diagrams.

7.4.1 Optional Communication Diagrams

For optional use cases, product line evolution consists of developing optional communication diagrams in which optional and possibly variant objects participate. The approach is to develop a separate optional communication diagram for each optional use case, depicting the optional and variant objects that participate in that use case. In some cases these optional and variant objects might interact with kernel objects in order to execute the use case. In such cases, the kernel objects involved are also depicted on the optional communication diagram.

Consider the optional communication diagram (Figure 7.4) for an optional use case, `Prepare Purchase Order`, which is also from the electronic commerce software product line. This use case is optional because for some members, purchase orders are handled by the product line system, whereas for other members, purchase orders are handled by an external system. The objects required for this communication include `Supplier Interface`, `Inventory Server`, and `Supplier Agent`. These objects were previously categorized as kernel objects because they participate in the kernel use case `Process Delivery Order`.

Three additional objects are needed to handle a purchase order: (1) an entity object, `Purchase Order Server`; (2) another software agent, `Purchase Order Agent`; and (3) a system interface object, `Wholesaler Interface`. These objects will be categorized as optional objects from a reuse perspective (as described in Chapter 9) because they participate only in optional use cases. The role of `Purchase Order Agent` is to make sure that the purchase order is created and sent to the wholesaler, to handle the purchase order when it is delivered by updating inventory and updating the purchase order, and to send an electronic payment request to the supplier's bank, as described in Chapter 14.

7.4.2 Alternative Communication Diagrams

Alternative communication diagrams are developed for alternative use cases that occur in different members of the product line. Because alternative use

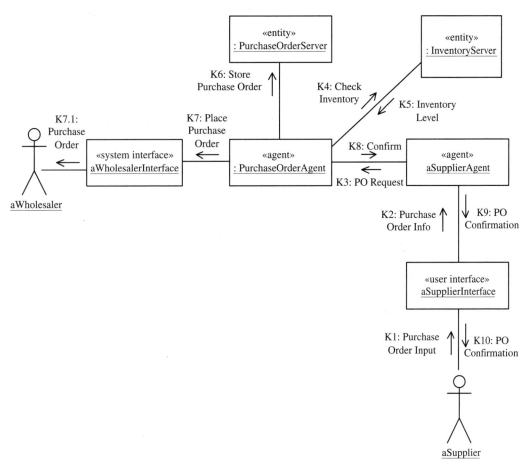

Figure 7.4 *Communication diagram for an optional use case:* `Prepare Purchase Order`

cases are mutually exclusive, the alternative communication diagrams are also mutually exclusive. This means that the alternative communication diagrams can never be part of the same product line member. However, they will be in different product line members.

For each alternative use case, a separate alternative communication diagram is developed to depict the variant objects and/or optional objects that participate in that use case, and possibly some kernel objects. Consider also an example from the electronic commerce software product line in which alternative use cases support two mutually exclusive member systems: business-to-consumer (B2C) applications and business-to-business (B2B) applications.

The Bill Customer use case is an example of a B2C use case in which the home customer is billed directly for a purchase. The alternative is the Send Invoice B2B use case for business customers who receive invoices for their purchases. The communication diagram for Bill Customer (Figure 7.5) involves three kernel objects from the kernel use case: Supplier Interface, Delivery Order Agent, and Supplier Agent. In addition, three other objects are required: (1) Customer Account Server, to encapsulate home customer accounts, and (2) Billing Agent, which is responsible for making sure that customer accounts are first validated and later billed by sending payment requests to (3) Authorization Center Interface. These new objects will be categorized as optional objects from a reuse perspective. Although these objects participate in an alternative use case, they are categorized as optional (and not variant) because their roles are unique in the product line and there are

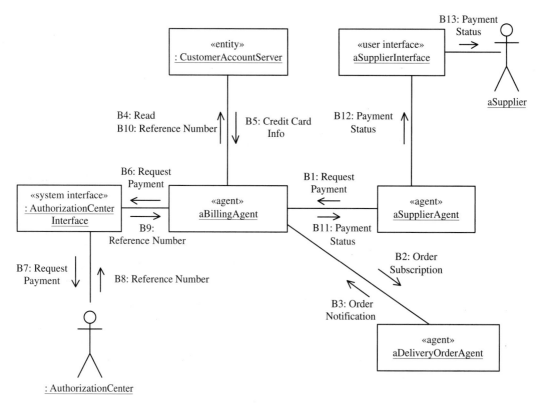

Figure 7.5 *Communication diagram for an alternative use case:* Bill Customer

no other variant objects. Chapter 9 will provide more details on object categorization for reuse.

7.4.3   Variant Communication Diagrams

For a use case that has one or more variation points (which correspond to features) specified within it, a different approach is used. Instead of developing a different communication diagram for each use case, the approach is to consider the impact of each variation point on the original communication diagram for the use case and develop optional branches on that diagram. This section describes the approach in terms of variation points to a kernel use case. However, the approach is the same regardless of whether the use case is kernel, optional, or alternative.

Consider a kernel use case with variation points. First the kernel communication diagram is developed as described in Section 7.3. Next the impact of each variation point on the kernel communication diagram is analyzed by the development of optional branches on the kernel communication diagrams corresponding to optional interactions. The optional branches depict optional and/or variant objects and the interaction between these objects. These optional and variant objects can also interact with kernel objects. For this reason the variant communication diagram also depicts the interaction of the objects in the optional branch with the kernel objects.

There are two ways to depict a variant communication diagram. The first is to show the optional branches added to the kernel communication diagram. The other approach is just to show the changes to the communication diagram—in other words, just to depict the newly added optional and/or variant objects, as well as the objects affected by the variation point.

7.5   Message Sequence Numbering on Interaction Diagrams

Messages on a communication diagram or sequence diagram are given message sequence numbers. This section provides some guidelines for numbering message sequences. These guidelines follow the general UML conventions; however, they have been extended to address concurrency, alternatives, and large message sequences better. These conventions are followed in the example of evolutionary dynamic modeling for the microwave oven product line given in Section 7.6 and in the case studies in Chapters 13, 14, and 15. This section can be skipped at first reading.

7.5.1 Message Labels on Interaction Diagrams

A message label on a communication or sequence diagram has the following syntax (only those parts of the message label that are relevant in the analysis phase are described here):

[sequence expression]: Message Name (argument list)

where the sequence expression consists of the message sequence number and an indicator of recurrence.

- **Message sequence number**. The message sequence number is described as follows: The first message sequence number represents the event that initiates the message sequence depicted on the communication diagram. Typical message sequences are 1, 2, 3, …; A1, A2, A3, …

  A more elaborate message sequence can be depicted with the Dewey classification system, such that A1.1 precedes A1.1.1, which in turn precedes A1.2. In the Dewey system, the a typical message numbering sequence would be A1, A1.1, A1.1.1, A1.2.

- **Recurrence**. The recurrence term is optional and represents conditional or iterative execution only on communication diagrams. It is no longer used on UML 2.0 sequence diagrams, because UML 2.0 uses a different notation for iterative and conditional execution. The recurrence term represents zero or more messages that are sent, depending on the conditions being met. There are two choices:

  1. *** [iteration-clause]**. An asterisk (*) is added after the message sequence number to indicate that more than one message is sent. The optional iteration clause is used to specify repeated execution, such as [j := 1,n]. An example of an iteration by putting an asterisk after the message sequence number is 3*.

  2. **[condition-clause]**. A condition is specified in square brackets to indicate a branch condition. The optional condition clause is used for specifying branches—for example, [x < n]—meaning that the message is sent only if the condition is true. Examples of conditional message passing by showing a condition after the message sequence number are 4[x < n] and 5[Normal]. In each case, the message is sent only if the condition is true.

- **Message name**. The message name is specified.

- **Argument list**. The argument list of the message is optional and specifies any parameters sent as part of the message.

There can also be optional return values from the message sent. However, it is recommended to use only simple messages during the analysis phase, in which case there are no return values, and to postpone to the design phase the decision about which kind of message to use.

7.5.2   Message Sequence Numbering on Interaction Diagrams

On a communication diagram supporting a use case, the sequence in which the objects participate in each use case is described and depicted by message sequence numbers. A message sequence number for a use case takes the following form:

[first optional letter sequence] [numeric sequence] [second optional letter sequence]

The first optional letter sequence is an optional use case ID and identifies a specific concrete use case or abstract use case. The first letter is an uppercase letter and might be followed by one or more upper- or lowercase letters if a more descriptive use case ID is desired.

In an interactive system with several external inputs from the actor, it is often helpful to include a numeric sequence—that is, to number the external events as whole numbers followed by decimal numbers for the ensuing internal events. For example, if the actor's inputs were designated as A1, A2, and A3, the full message sequence depicted on the communication diagram would be A1, A1.1, A1.2, A1.3, …, A2, A2.1, A2.2, …, and A3, A3.1, A3.2, ….

An example is V1, where the letter *V* identifies the use case and the number identifies the message sequence within the communication diagram supporting the use case. The object sending the first message—V1—is the initiator of the use case–based communication. In a concrete use case, the initiator should be an actor; in an abstract use case, however, the initiator can be an object. Thus, in the communication and sequence diagram examples in Figures 7.1 and 7.2, respectively, the input from the actor is V1. Subsequent message numbers following this input message are V1.1, V1.2, and V1.3. If the dialog were to continue, the next input from the actor would be V2.

7.5.3   Concurrent and Alternative Message Sequences

The second optional letter sequence is used to depict special cases of branches—either concurrent or alternative—in the message sequence numbering.

Concurrent message sequences may also be depicted on a communication diagram. A lowercase letter represents a concurrent sequence; in other words, sequences designated as A3 and A3a would be concurrent sequences. For example, the arrival of message A2 at an object X might result in the sending of two messages from object X to two objects Y and Z, which could then execute in parallel. To indicate the concurrency in this case, the message sent to object Y would be designated as A3; and the one to object Z, as A3a. Subsequent messages in the A3 sequence would be A4, A5, A6, …, and subsequent messages in the independent A3a sequence would be A3a.1, A3a.2, A3a.3, and so on. Because the sequence numbering is more cumbersome for the A3a sequence, use A3 for the main message sequence and A3a and A3b for the supporting message sequences. An alternative way to show two concurrent sequences is to avoid A3 altogether and use the sequence numbers A3a and A3b; however, this can lead to a more cumbersome numbering scheme if A3a initiates another concurrent sequence, so the former approach is preferred.

Alternative message sequences are depicted with the condition indicated after the message. An uppercase letter is used to name the alternative branch. For example, the main branch may be labeled 1.4[Normal], and the other, less frequently used branch could be named 1.4A[Error]. The message sequence numbers for the normal branch would be 1.4[Normal], 1.5, 1.6, and so on. The message sequence numbers for the alternative branch would be 1.4A[Error], 1.4A.1, 1.4A.2, and so on.

Examples of concurrent and alternative message sequences are given in the following example and in the case studies.

7.6 Example of Evolutionary Dynamic Analysis for the Microwave Oven Product Line

This section gives an example of evolutionary dynamic analysis, which starts with the kernel first approach and continues with the product line evolution approach. Evolutionary dynamic analysis is used in the microwave oven product line (see Chapter 13), where several scenarios involving optional objects are depicted. The communication diagrams for these scenarios depict variations on the kernel communication diagram resulting from the presence of variation points in the kernel use case Cook Food.

7.6.1 Example of the Kernel First Approach

With the kernel first approach, the objective is first to determine objects in the kernel use case. These objects consist of kernel objects—that is, objects used by every member of a product line—and default objects. A default object is one of a group of variant objects in the product line. The default object is the variant object that is automatically selected for a given member of the product line unless an alternative user selection is made.

Several kernel objects are required for the `Cook Food` use case, as depicted on the kernel communication diagram (Figure 7.6) for the use case. These include `Door Sensor Interface`, `Weight Sensor Interface`, and `Keypad Interface`, which are kernel input device interface objects. `Heating Element Interface` and `Display Interface` are kernel output device interface objects. `Oven Timer` is the software timer object. There is an entity object to store microwave oven data, such as the cooking time, which is called `Oven Data`. Finally, because of the complex sequencing and control required for the oven, a state-dependent control object is required, `Microwave Oven Control`, which executes the statechart for the oven.

On the basis of the object structuring criteria described in Chapter 6, the kernel objects are categorized as follows:

Input device interface objects:

- `Door Sensor Interface`
- `Weight Sensor Interface`
- `Keypad Interface`

Output device interface objects:

- `Heating Element Interface`
- `Display Interface`

Control objects:

- `Microwave Oven Control`
- `Oven Timer`

Entity objects:

- `Oven Data`
- `Display Prompts`

In addition, the following default objects are determined from the kernel use case and variation points:

- `Boolean Weight Sensor Interface`
- `One-level Heating Element Interface`
- `One-line Display Interface`
- `English Display Prompts`

The kernel objects, together with the default objects already named, constitute the kernel system.

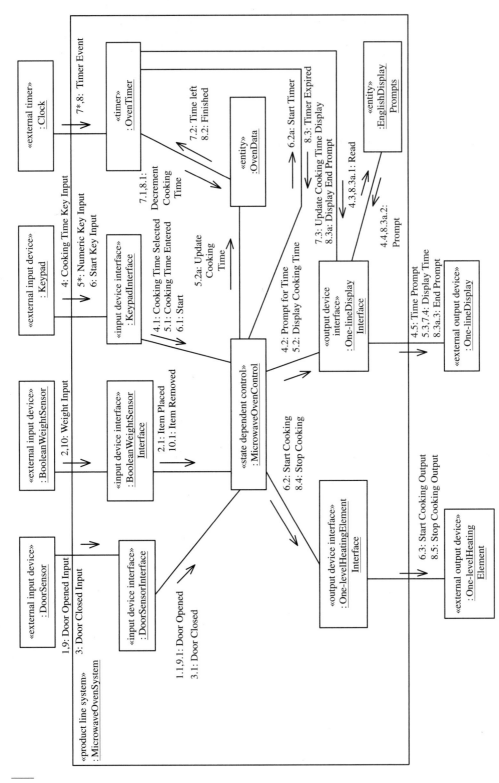

Figure 7.6 *Communication diagram for a kernel use case:* Cook Food

7.6.2   Example of the Product Line Evolution Approach

After the kernel first approach is applied, the product line evolution approach is applied to determine the impact of optional and alternative features on the kernel communication diagram. The approach, which is called **feature-based impact analysis**, systematically analyzes the impact of each feature and variation point on the kernel communication diagram

Consider the impact of the use case variation points. First consider a variation point, which represents an optional feature—for example, the Beeper variation point. This optional feature requires the addition of the Beeper Interface optional object to the Microwave Oven Kernel communication diagram, as shown in Figure 7.7. This variant communication diagram shows the addition of the optional Beeper Interface object and the optional Beeper external hardware object, as well as the modified Microwave Oven Control object, which has to send the Beep message (message 8.4a) to the Beeper Interface object, which in turns sends Beep Output (message 8.4a.1) to the Beeper external output device. Because this is a conditional message, it is guarded by a Boolean feature condition [beeper], which is true only if the feature is provided. This means that the Beep message is sent only if the [beeper] condition is true— that is, if the microwave oven system provides this feature. Note that, by convention, the first letter of a feature condition is lowercase to distinguish it from other types of conditions.

Another way of depicting the same information is to show only the branch that has changed on the communication diagram. This branch consists of the Microwave Oven Control, Beeper Interface, and Beeper objects, starting with the Beep message, as depicted in Figure 7.8. Because this diagram shows the impact of the variation point much more clearly than Figure 7.7 does, it is the preferred approach and will be used in future. An alternative, however, is to use color coding—that is, to show the complete communication diagram, with the affected objects in a different color.

Now consider the situation in which the use case variation point represents an alternative feature; for example, Display Language is French instead of English. In this case, a variant object, French Display Prompts, replaces a default object, English Display Prompts, as shown in Figure 7.9. The impact of another alternative feature, Display Unit = Multi-line Display (also shown in Figure 7.9), results in the variant output device interface object Multi-line Display Interface replacing the default One-line Display Interface object. More-complicated alternatives might lead to the development of alternative branches on kernel communication diagrams, showing how the variant and optional objects interact with kernel objects.

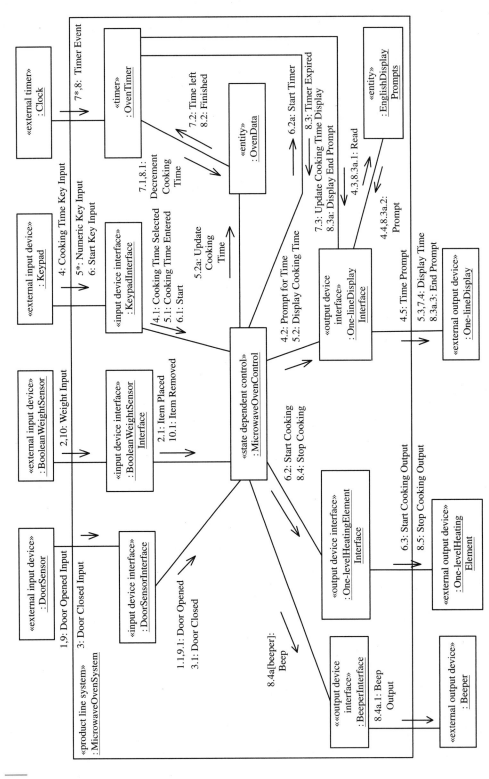

Figure 7.7 *Variant communication diagram depicting the impact of the* Beeper *variation point and optional feature*

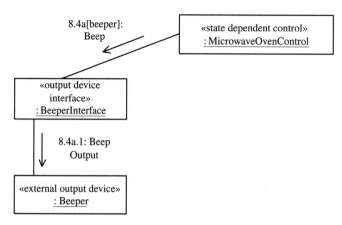

Figure 7.8 *Variant* `Beeper` *branch depicting the impact of the* `Beeper` *variation point and optional feature*

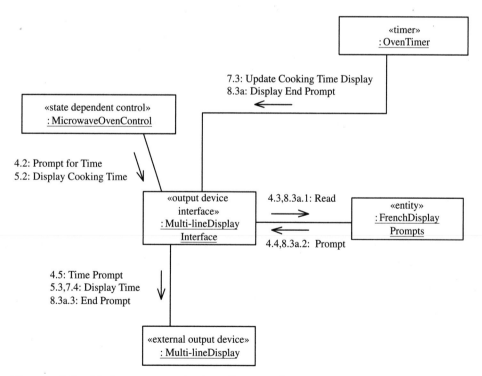

Figure 7.9 *Variant communication diagram depicting the impact of* `Display Language` *and* `Display Unit` *variation points and alternative features*

7.6.3   Analyzing the Impact of Variation Points and Features

Variation points and features can affect the kernel system in different ways. Consider the impact of variation points and features through the following examples:

- **Impact of variation points that lead to new concurrent actions**. The impact of the `Beeper` feature described in the preceding section is to result in the new `Beeper Interface` object and `Beeper` external object (see Figures 7.7 and 7.8), a new `Beeper` branch on the communication diagram, and a change to `Microwave Oven Control`, which has to send a `Beep` message to `Beeper Interface`. Because `Microwave Oven Control` sends the `Beep` message at the same time as it sends the `Stop Cooking` message, the convention for concurrent message sequences (see Section 7.5.3) is used. Thus the `Beep` message, depicted as 8.4a: `Beep`, is sent to `Beeper Interface` at the same time as the message 8.4: `Stop Cooking` is sent to `Heating Element Interface`. The `Beep` message has a ripple effect because 8.4a: `Beep` is followed by `Beeper Interface` sending the 8.4.a.1: `Beep Output` message to the external `Beeper` object.

- **Impact of variation points that lead to additional sequential actions**. Some variation points lead to optional sequential actions that need to be inserted into the message sequence depicted on the kernel communication diagrams. The `Minute Plus` feature allows the user to press a **Minute Plus** key either before or during cooking. In the latter case, a minute is added to the cooking time and cooking continues without interruption. On the kernel communication diagram, message 6 is the `Start Key Input` message from the external `Keypad` object to start cooking, which leads to a sequence ending in 6.3: `Start Cooking Output` to the external `Heating Element` object (see Figure 7.6). The next message on the kernel communication diagram is 7*: `Timer Event`. Because the effect of the `Minute Plus` feature is that the external `Keypad` object sends `Keypad Interface` a message between messages 6.3 and 7, the convention is to show the additional key press as 6.10[minuteplus]: `Minute Plus Input`, as shown in Figure 7.10. The "6.10" indicates that this message is sent between 6.3 and 7. The message sequence number 6.10 is preferred over 6.4 to delineate between the 6: `Start Key Input` sequence and the 6.10: `Minute Plus Input` sequence. The 6.10 sequence is followed by 6.11, 6.12, and so on. The [minuteplus] condition is a feature condition, which indicates that the 6.10[minuteplus] sequence is a conditional sequence, taking place only when the Boolean feature condition [minuteplus] is true.

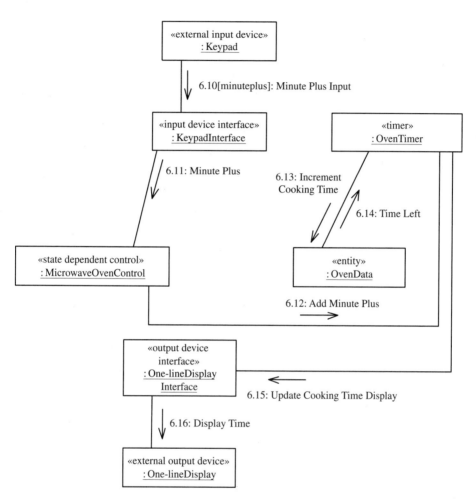

Figure 7.10 *Variant communication diagram depicting the impact of the* Minute Plus *variation point and optional feature: pressing* **Minute Plus** *after* **Start**

- **Impact of variation points that lead to alternative actions.** Continuing with the Minute Plus feature, a second option is for the **Minute Plus** key to be pressed before cooking has started, as shown in Figure 7.11. In this case, cooking is started and will stop after a minute (unless another external event takes place first). Pressing **Minute Plus** in this situation takes the place of pressing three other types of keys shown in Figure 7.6: the **Cooking Time** key (message 4: Cooking Time Key Input), the numeric keys (message 5*:

Numeric Key Input), and the **Start** key (message 6: Start Key Input). Because pressing **Minute Plus** in this situation is an alternative sequence, the message sequence numbering starts with 4M[minuteplus]: Minute Plus Input. The 4M indicates that this is an alternative sequence. As in the previous example, the [minuteplus] condition is a feature condition indicating that this is a conditional sequence.

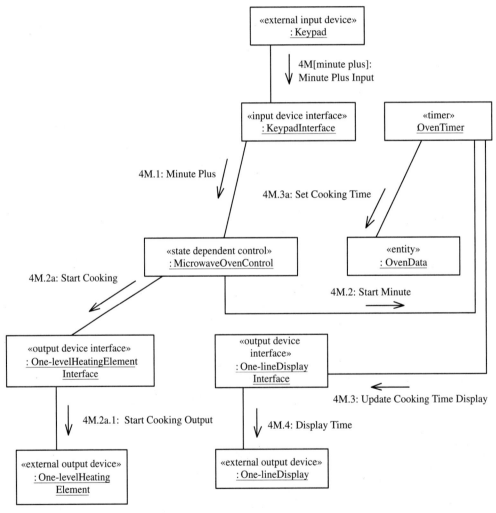

Figure 7.11 *Variant communication diagram depicting the impact of the* Minute Plus *variation point and optional feature: pressing **Minute Plus** in place of **Start***

- **Impact of new features resulting from optional use cases**. The TOD Clock feature is captured by two use cases—Set Time of Day and Display Time of Day—as described in Chapter 5. Each of these use cases is realized as depicted on a communication diagram. In this situation, it is more concise to show the impact of both use cases on the same communication diagram, as Figure 7.12 does. However, it is important to clearly distinguish

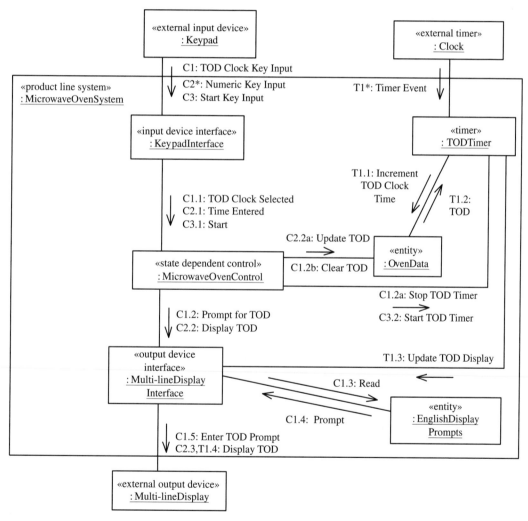

Figure 7.12   *Communication diagram for the* TOD Clock *feature*

between the message sequences depicting the realization of each use case. The following measures help make this distinction:

- The message sequence for the Set Time of Day communication is prefixed by the letter C, starting with C1: TOD Clock Key Input sent by Keypad to Keypad Interface.

- The message sequence for the Display Time of Day communication is prefixed by the letter T, starting with T1*: Timer Event sent by the external Clock object to TOD Timer.

7.7 Summary

This chapter described dynamic modeling for software product lines. The dynamic model addresses interaction between objects, describing how objects interact with each other; as well as within objects, describing how an active state-dependent object is defined by means of a finite state machine and depicted as a statechart. The state-dependent aspect of dynamic modeling involving finite state machines and statecharts is described in Chapter 8.

This chapter briefly described dynamic modeling in single systems before describing dynamic modeling for software product lines. It then described how the kernel first approach is used to determine the interaction among kernel objects, which realize the kernel use cases. The discussion continued with an explanation of how the product line evolution approach is subsequently used to determine the interaction among optional and variant objects. Optional communication diagrams are developed to realize the optional use cases, while alternative communication diagrams are developed to realize the alternative use cases; variant communication diagrams are developed to depict the impact of variation points in use cases.

Chapter 9 will describe how communication diagrams are integrated to form feature-based communication diagrams. Chapter 10 will describe software architectural communication patterns using communication diagrams. Chapter 11 will describe how communication diagrams can be used to depict software architectures.

Finite State Machines and Statecharts for Software Product Lines

Finite state machines are used for modeling the control and sequencing view of a system. Many systems, such as real-time systems, are highly state-dependent. That is, their actions depend not only on their inputs but also on what has previously happened in the system. Notations used to define finite state machines are the state transition diagram, statechart, and state transition table. In highly state-dependent systems, these notations can help substantially by providing a means of understanding the complexity of these systems.

In the UML notation, a state transition diagram is referred to as a *statechart diagram*. The UML statechart diagram notation is based on Harel's statechart notation (Harel 1988; Harel and Politi 1998). In this book the terms **statechart** and **statechart diagram** are used interchangeably. We refer to a traditional state transition diagram, which is not hierarchical, as a *flat statechart* and use the term *hierarchical statechart* to refer to the concept of hierarchical state decomposition. A brief overview of the statechart notation is given in Appendix A (Section A.6).

This chapter describes how to develop finite state machines (also referred to as just *state machines*) and statecharts for software product lines. Although statecharts can be used to model different perspectives of a system, such as the different states of a state-dependent use case (Gomaa 2000), the best use of statecharts in software product lines is for modeling state-dependent classes and objects. In particular, each state-dependent control class—whether kernel, optional, or variant—needs to be modeled with a finite state machine and depicted as a statechart. It is also possible to model variability in a software product line by using inherited state machines and parameterized state machines.

In dynamic interaction modeling, as described in Chapter 7, if the object interaction is state-dependent, then a state-dependent control object is needed, which executes a statechart. The state-dependent interactions are much clearer to understand if the corresponding events are depicted on both the statechart and the interaction diagram.

This chapter starts in Section 8.1 with a description of the finite state machines for the kernel system of software product lines, which is similar to the design of finite state machines for single systems. Section 8.2 then describes the hierarchical decomposition of statecharts, a unique capability that distinguishes statecharts from state transition diagrams. Section 8.3 considers developing finite state machines for software product lines. Two approaches to modeling variability are described: Section 8.4 describes inherited state machines in software product lines, Section 8.5 describes parameterized state machines in software product lines, and Section 8.6 compares the two approaches. The discussion then returns to a theme first introduced in Chapter 7—namely, dynamic analysis using interaction models—except that the treatment in this chapter is of state-dependent dynamic analysis, in which both statecharts and interaction diagrams are depicted. The kernel first approach to state-dependent dynamic analysis is described in Section 8.7, and the product line evolution approach is described in Section 8.8. Finally, Section 8.9 describes dynamic analysis with communicating state-dependent objects.

8.1 Finite State Machines for Kernel and Single Systems

A **finite state machine** (also referred to as just *state machine*) is a conceptual machine with a finite number of states. It can be in only one of the states at any specific time. A **state transition** is a change in state that is caused by an input event. In response to an input event, the finite state machine might transition to a different state. Alternatively, the event may have no effect, in which case the finite state machine remains in the same state. The next state depends on the current state, as well as on the input event. Optionally, an output action may result from the state transition.

Although a whole system can be modeled by means of a finite state machine, in object-oriented analysis and design a finite state machine is encapsulated inside one object. In other words, the object is state-dependent and is always in one of the states of the finite state machine. The object's finite state machine is depicted by means of a statechart. In an object-oriented model, the state-dependent aspects of a system are defined by means of one or more finite state machines, where each finite state machine is encapsulated inside its own object. This section briefly reviews the basic concepts of events and states before giving some examples of statecharts.

8.1.1   Events

An **event** is an occurrence at a point in time; it is also known as a *discrete signal* or *stimulus*. An event is an atomic occurrence (not interruptible) and conceptually has zero duration. Examples of events are ATM Card Inserted, Part Removed, Part Placed, Brake Pressed, and Elevator Departed.

A **timer event** is a special event, specified by the keyword after, which indicates that an event occurs after an elapsed time identified by an expression in parentheses, such as after (10 seconds) or after (elapsed time). On a statechart, the timer event causes a transition out of a given state. The elapsed time is measured from the time of entry into that state until exit from the state, which is caused by the timer event.

8.1.2   States

A **state** represents a recognizable situation that exists over an interval of time. Whereas an event occurs at a point in time, a finite state machine is in a given state over an interval of time. The arrival of an event at the finite state machine usually causes a transition from one state to another. Alternatively, an event can have a null effect, in which case the finite state machine remains in the same state. In theory, a state transition is meant to take zero time to occur. In practice, the time for a state transition to occur is negligible compared to the time spent in the state.

The initial state of a statechart is the state that is entered when the statechart is activated.

8.1.3   Examples of Statecharts

As an example of a statechart, consider the Microwave Oven Control kernel statechart, which is taken from the microwave oven product line case study and shown in Figure 8.1. The statechart follows the sequencing described in the Cook Food use case (see Chapter 13) and shows the different states for cooking food. The initial state is Door Shut. When the user opens the door, the statechart transitions into the Door Open state. The user places an item in the oven, causing the statechart to transition into the Door Open with Item state. When the user closes the door, the statechart then transitions into the Door Shut with Item state. After the user inputs the cooking time, the Ready to Cook state is entered. When the user presses the **Start** button, the statechart transitions into the Cooking state. When the timer expires, the Door Shut with Item state is reentered. If instead the door were opened during cooking, the Door Open with Item state would be entered. Another possibility is for the user to press the **Cancel** button during cooking, in which case the Ready to Cook state is entered.

In the microwave oven product line, the Microwave Oven Control kernel object executes the statechart shown in Figure 8.1. The sequence numbers in Figure 8.1 correspond to the main sequence of events and actions for the Cook Food kernel communication diagram, as explained in Section 8.7.

8.1.4   Events and Guard Conditions

Events and guard conditions may be combined in defining a state transition. The notation used is *Event [Condition]*. Thus an event is allowed to cause a state transition, provided that the guard condition given in parentheses is true. Conditions are optional.

In some cases an event does not cause an immediate state transition, but its impact needs to be remembered because it will affect a future state transition. The fact that an event has occurred can be stored as a condition that can be checked later.

Examples of guard conditions in Figure 8.1 are Zero Time and Time Remaining. The two transitions out of the Door Open with Item state are Door Closed [Zero Time] and Door Closed [Time Remaining]. Thus the transition taken depends on whether the user has entered the time or not. If the condition Zero Time is true, the statechart transitions to Door Shut with Item, waiting for the user to enter the time. If the condition Time Remaining is true, the statechart transitions to the Ready to Cook state.

8.1.5   Actions

Associated with a state transition is an optional output **action**. An action is a computation that executes as a result of a state transition. An action is triggered at a state transition. It executes and then terminates itself. The action executes instantaneously at the state transition; thus, conceptually an action is of zero duration. In practice, the duration of an action is very small compared to the duration of a state.

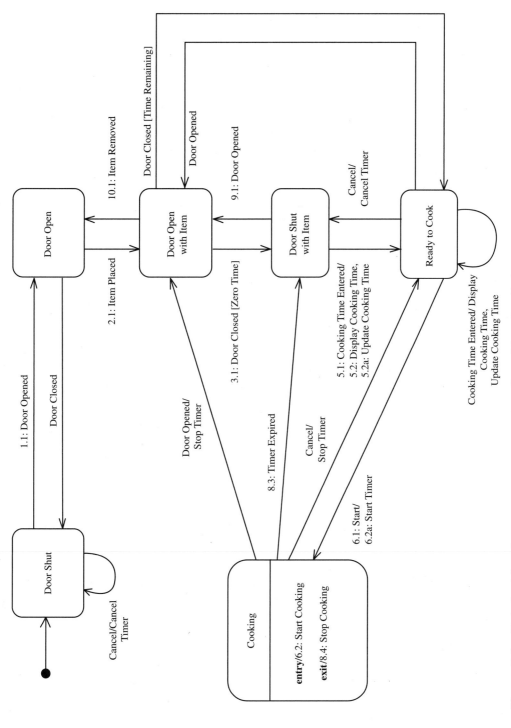

Figure 8.1 *Statechart for* Microwave Oven Control *(kernel functionality)*

173

To show an action on a statechart, the state transition is labeled *Event/Action* or *Event [Condition]/Action*. For example, when the microwave oven transitions from `Ready to Cook` state back to `Door Shut with Item` state as a result of the `Cancel` input event (because the user pressed the **Cancel** button), the action `Cancel Timer` is executed (see Figure 8.1). This state transition is labeled `Cancel/Cancel Timer`. More than one action may be associated with a transition. The actions all execute simultaneously; consequently, they must not have any interdependencies.

8.1.6 Entry and Exit Actions

Certain actions may also be depicted more concisely as being associated with the state rather than with the transition into or out of the state. These are entry and exit actions, which are represented by the reserved words **entry** and **exit**. An **entry action** is depicted as **entry**/*Action* and is an instantaneous action that is performed on entry to the state. An **exit action** is depicted as **exit**/*Action* and is an instantaneous action that is performed on exit from the state.

Examples of entry and exit actions are given in Figure 8.1. If the **Start** button is pressed (resulting in the `Start` event) while the microwave oven is in the `Ready to Cook` state, the statechart transitions to the `Cooking` state. One transition action, `Start Timer`, is executed; and one entry action, `Start Cooking`, is also executed. If the timer expires, or the **Cancel** button is pressed, or the door is opened, the oven will transition out of the `Cooking` state. In all these cases, the exit action is `Stop Cooking`. Having the action as an exit action instead of an action on the state transition is more concise. The alternative of having transition actions would require the action to be explicitly depicted on each of the state transitions out of the `Cooking` state.

8.1.7 Activities

In addition to actions, it is possible to have an activity executed as a result of a state transition. An **activity** is a computation that executes for the duration of a state. Thus, unlike an action, an activity executes for a finite amount of time. An activity is enabled on entry into the state and disabled on exit from the state. Enable and disable actions always come in pairs. The cause of the state change, which results in disabling the activity, is usually an input event from a source that is not related to the activity. In some cases, however, the activity itself generates the event that causes the state change.

One way to depict an activity on the statechart is to label the transition into the state in which the activity executes as *Event*/**enable** *Activity* and the transition out of the state as *Event*/**disable** *Activity*. However, it is more concise not to show the enable and disable actions on the transitions and instead to show the activity as being associated with the state, by depicting the activity in the state box with a dividing line between the state name and the activity name. The activity is shown as **do**/*Activity*, where **do** is a reserved word. This means that the activity is enabled on entry into the state and disabled on exit from the state.

For examples of activities, consider the Cruise Control statechart shown in Figure 8.2. Initially the statechart is in the Idle state. When the driver switches the ignition switch on, the Engine On event occurs and the Cruise Control statechart transitions to the Initial state. When the driver engages the cruise control lever in the **ACCEL** position, the Accel event occurs and the statechart transitions to the Accelerating state. During this state, the statechart executes the Increase Speed activity shown on Figure 8.2 as **do**/Increase Speed. In the Accelerating state, when the driver releases the cruise control

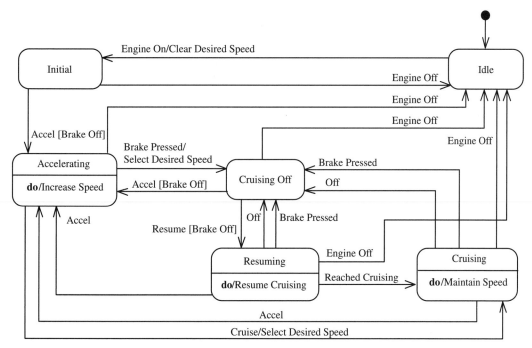

Figure 8.2   *Statechart for* Cruise Control *(with activities)*

lever, the `Cruise` event occurs, and the statechart transitions to the `Cruising` state, disabling the `Increase Speed` activity and enabling the `Maintain Speed` activity. The statechart executes the `Maintain Speed` activity for the duration of the `Cruising` state. If the driver places his/her foot on the brake, the `Brake Pressed` event occurs, and the statechart transitions to the `Cruising Off` state, disabling `Maintain Speed`. If the driver later engages the cruise control lever in the **RESUME** position, the `Resume` event occurs and the statechart transitions to the `Resuming` state. During this state, the statechart executes the `Resume Cruising` activity. When the car reaches the cruising speed, the statechart reenters the `Cruising` state, disabling the `Resume Cruising` activity and enabling the `Maintain Speed` activity.

8.2   Hierarchical Statecharts

One of the potential problems of flat statecharts is the proliferation of states and transitions, which makes the statechart very cluttered and difficult to read. A very important way of simplifying statecharts and increasing their modeling power is to introduce superstates and the hierarchical decomposition of statecharts. With this approach, a superstate (also known as a composite state) at one level of a statechart is decomposed into several substates on a lower-level statechart.

The objective of hierarchical statecharts is to exploit the basic concepts and visual advantages of state transition diagrams while overcoming the disadvantages of overly complex and cluttered diagrams through hierarchical structuring. Note that any hierarchical statechart can be mapped to a flat statechart, so for every hierarchical statechart there is a semantically equivalent flat statechart.

Hierarchical state machines are useful for modeling variability in software product lines. This section describes hierarchical state machine concepts before describing the two main approaches to introducing state machine variability into product lines: inheritance and parameterization.

8.2.1   Hierarchical State Decomposition

Statecharts can often be significantly simplified by the hierarchical decomposition of states, in which a superstate is decomposed into two or more interconnected sequential substates. This kind of decomposition is referred to as *sequential state decomposition*. The notation for state decomposition also allows both the superstate and the substates to be shown on the same diagram or, alternatively, on separate diagrams, depending on the complexity of the decomposition.

An example of hierarchical state decomposition is given in Figure 8.3, where the `Door Shut with Item` superstate is decomposed into the `Waiting for User` and `Waiting for Cooking Time` substates. (On the hierarchical statechart, the superstate is the outer rounded box, which contains the name of the superstate at the top left. The substates are shown as inner rounded boxes.) When the system is in the `Door Shut with Item` superstate, it is in one (and only one)

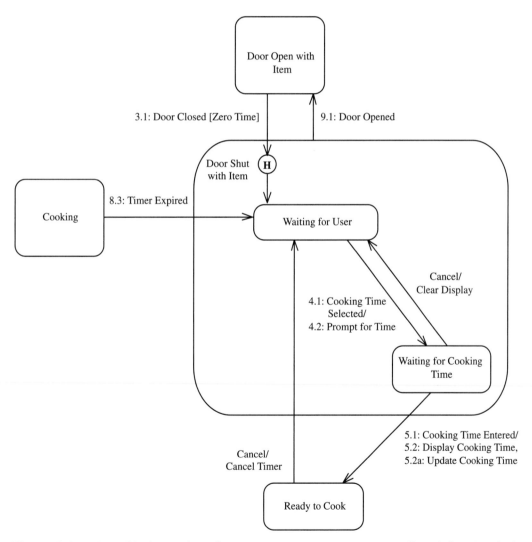

Figure 8.3   *Hierarchical statechart for* `Microwave Oven Control` *(kernel functionality): decomposition of the* `Door Shut with Item` *state*

of the substates. Because the states are executed sequentially, this kind of hierarchical state decomposition is referred to as resulting in a *sequential statechart*.

Note that each transition into the superstate is a transition into one (and only one) of the substates on the lower-level statechart. Each transition out of the superstate has to originate from one (and only one) of the substates on the lower-level statechart.

The hierarchical statechart notation also allows a transition out of every one of the substates on a statechart to be aggregated into a transition out of the superstate. Careful use of this feature can significantly reduce the number of state transitions on a statechart. In Figure 8.3, for example, the `Door Opened` event may occur in either the `Waiting for User` or the `Waiting for Cooking Time` substate, in which case the statechart transitions to the `Door Open with Item` state. Instead of depicting the `Door Opened` event as causing a transition out of each substate, it is more concise to show this event causing the transition out of the superstate `Door Shut with Item`.

8.2.2   History State

The history state is another useful characteristic in hierarchical statecharts. Indicated by an *H* inside a small circle, a **history state** is a pseudostate within a sequential superstate, which means that the superstate remembers its previously active substate after it exits. Thus, when the superstate is reentered, the previously active substate is entered.

Consider how the history state is used within the `Door Shut with Item` superstate shown in Figure 8.3. The history state is used to remember which of the two substates the superstate `Door Shut with Item` is in when an event transitions the statechart out of the superstate. Thus the previous substate is reentered when the `Door Shut with Item` superstate is reentered. For example, if the superstate is in the `Waiting for User` substate when the door is opened, the statechart will transition to `Door Open with Item`. When the door is closed (and assuming zero time), the `Door Shut with Item` superstate is reentered, and in particular the `Waiting for User` substate is reentered. On the other hand, if the superstate is in the `Waiting for Cooking Time` substate when the door is opened, then that substate is reentered when the door is closed. Without the history state, this behavior would be much more difficult to model.

8.2.3   Orthogonal Statecharts

Another kind of hierarchical state decomposition is concurrent state decomposition. That is, a state on one statechart can be decomposed into two or more concurrent statecharts. The two concurrent statecharts are shown separated by a dashed line. Consider the case of a superstate on a statechart that is decomposed into two lower-level concurrent statecharts. When the higher-level statechart is in the superstate, it is simultaneously in one of the substates on the first lower-level concurrent statechart *and* in one of the substates on the second lower-level concurrent statechart.

The most effective use of a concurrent statechart is for modeling the orthogonal aspects of the same object. Although the name *concurrent statechart* implies that there is concurrent activity within the object containing the statechart, this kind of decomposition can also be used to show different aspects of the same object that are not concurrent. Designing objects with only one thread of control is much simpler and is strongly recommended. Where true concurrency is required, use multiple concurrent objects and define each object with its own statechart, as described in more detail in Section 8.9.

The term *orthogonal statechart* describes a concurrent statechart used to depict the states of different aspects of an object. An example of using orthogonal statecharts to depict guard conditions is given in Figure 8.4 for the microwave oven statechart. The Microwave Oven Control statechart is now decomposed into two orthogonal statecharts: one for sequencing the events and actions in the oven (Microwave Oven Sequencing), and the other for Cooking Time Condition. The two statecharts are depicted on a high-level statechart, with a dashed line separating them.

At any one time, the Microwave Oven Control superstate is in one of the substates of the Microwave Oven Sequencing statechart and one of the substates of the Cooking Time Condition statechart. Cooking Time Condition is a simple statechart consisting of two states—Zero Time and Time Remaining—with Zero Time as the initial state. The Update Cooking Time event causes a transition from Zero Time to Time Remaining. Either the Timer Expired event or the Cancel Timer event can cause a transition back to Zero Time. The Microwave Oven Sequencing statechart depicts the sequence of states the oven goes through while handling a user request to cook food, as shown in Figure 8.1. The Microwave Oven Control statechart is the union of the Microwave Oven Sequencing and the Cooking Time Condition statecharts.

The Zero Time and Time Remaining states of the Cooking Time Condition statechart (see Figure 8.4) are the guard conditions checked on the Microwave Oven Sequencing statechart when the Door Closed event is received while in the Door Open with Item state (see Figure 8.1). Cancel Timer is an action (cause) on the Microwave Oven Sequencing statechart and an event (effect) on the Cooking Time Condition statechart, which causes a transition to the

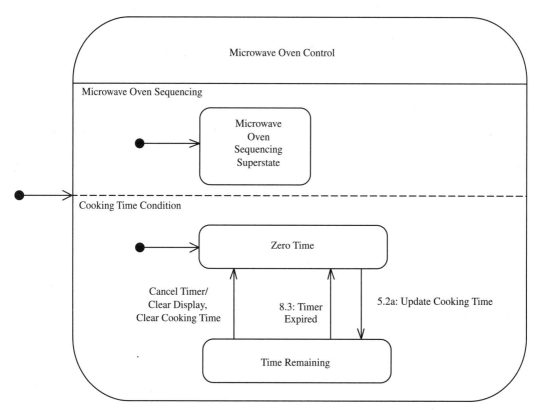

Note: Microwave Oven Sequencing superstate is decomposed into Microwave Oven Control Statechart in Figure 8.1.

Figure 8.4 *Orthogonal statecharts for* `Microwave Oven Control`

`Zero Time` **state.** `Update Cooking Time` is also an action on the former statechart and an event on the latter. `Timer Expired` is an event on both statecharts.

8.3 Finite State Machines and Statecharts for Software Product Lines

State-dependent control classes are depicted by means of statecharts. Because there can be product line variants of a control class, each variant can be modeled with its own statechart. If the variants are all mutually exclusive, then the statecharts are also mutually exclusive, because they model alternative variants.

For example, a given microwave oven system can come with or without a recipe feature. The product line would need to have (at least) two mutually exclusive variants of the `Microwave Oven Control` class, each with its own different statechart. The recipe version of the statechart would need to have additional states and transitions to handle cooking food with a recipe.

However, it is possible in some applications for the variant features to coexist in the same system; that is, they are not mutually exclusive. Consider an elevator control system with multiple elevators, only some of which have a high-speed feature for bypassing the first 20 floors. This case would again be represented by two different features, where each type of elevator is modeled with a different statechart. Because the two elevators can coexist in the same system, however, it is possible to select both features (for different elevators) and hence to have coexisting variant statecharts.

There are two choices for modeling variants of a software product line. Each variant can be modeled with its own finite state machine. This approach has the advantage of encapsulating each change in a separate class, hence encouraging the separation of concerns. If there are potentially many variants and combinations of variants, however, configuration management becomes a major problem—in particular, keeping track of the variants. In addition, if statechart variability is introduced through inheritance, a change in a superclass could have an impact on all its subclasses. An alternative is to use parameterized statecharts and feature conditions, which act as guards preventing a branch of the statechart to be entered if the feature has not been selected. The two approaches for managing state machine variability in product lines—inheritance and parameterization—are described and compared next. Section 8.4 describes inherited state machines in software product lines, and Section 8.5 describes parameterized state machines in software product lines. The two approaches are compared in Section 8.6.

8.4   Inherited State Machines in Software Product Lines

Inheritance is one of the two main approaches of introducing state machine variability into software product lines. When a state machine is specialized, the child state machine inherits the properties of the parent state machine; that is, it inherits the states, events, transitions, actions, and activities depicted in the parent state machine model. The child state machine can then modify the inherited state machine as follows:

1. **Add new states**. The new states can be at the same level of the statechart hierarchy as the inherited states. Furthermore, new substates can be defined for either the new or the inherited states. In other words, a state in the parent state machine can be decomposed further in the child state machine. It is also possible to add new orthogonal states—that is, new states that execute concurrently with the inherited states.

2. **Add new events and transitions**. These events cause new transitions to new or inherited states.

3. **Add or remove actions and activities**. New actions can be defined that are executed on transitions into and out of new or inherited states. Exit and entry actions, as well as new activities, can be defined for new or inherited states. It is also possible to remove predefined actions and activities, although this should be done with care and is generally not recommended.

The child state machine must not delete states or events defined in the parent. It must not change any superstate/substate dependency defined in the parent state machine.

Examples of Inherited State Machines

As an example of an inherited state machine, consider the `Microwave Oven Control` class from the microwave oven software product line, which specifies the state machine of the same name. The `Microwave Oven Control` kernel state machine, which captures the kernel functionality of the product line, is depicted in Figures 8.1, 8.3, and 8.4. The `Microwave Oven Control` state machine is then specialized to provide the additional features for the `Enhanced Microwave Oven Control` child state machine. The specialization of the `Microwave Oven Control` state-dependent control superclass to produce the `Enhanced Microwave Oven Control` subclass is depicted in the class diagram of Figure 8.5.

The statechart for the `Enhanced Microwave Oven Control` class is shown in Figures 8.6 and 8.7. Only parts of the solution are given in this chapter; for the full solution, refer to Chapter 13. Consider the impact of the following features incorporated into the specialized state machine:

- `Power Level`
- `Recipe`
- `TOD Clock`
- `Turntable`

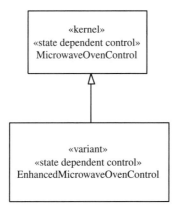

Figure 8.5   *Example of inheritance of a state-dependent control class*

- Light
- Beeper
- Minute Plus

  Example of new states added (see Figure 8.7). To support the Power Level feature, a new state is introduced called Waiting for User after Power Level. To support the Recipe feature, a new superstate is introduced called Recipe (see Figure 8.6), which has three recipe-related substates (see Chapter 13). To support the TOD (time-of-day) Clock feature, the inherited Door Shut state is specialized to create three new substates (see Chapter 13).

  Example of new transitions added (see Figure 8.7). To support the Power Level feature, a new transition is introduced into the new Waiting for User after Power Level state, which is triggered by the new event Power Level Selected. To support the Recipe feature, several new transitions are introduced, including the Recipe Entered event, which transitions the statechart into the Recipe superstate (see Chapter 13).

  Example of new actions added (see Figure 8.6). There are several examples. To support the Turntable feature, two new actions are provided: Start Turning (which is executed on entry into the inherited Cooking state) and Stop Turning (which is executed on exit from the Cooking state). To support the Light feature, two new actions are provided: the Switch On entry action and the Switch Off transition action. To support the Beeper feature, the Beep action is added, which is also executed on exit from the inherited Cooking state.

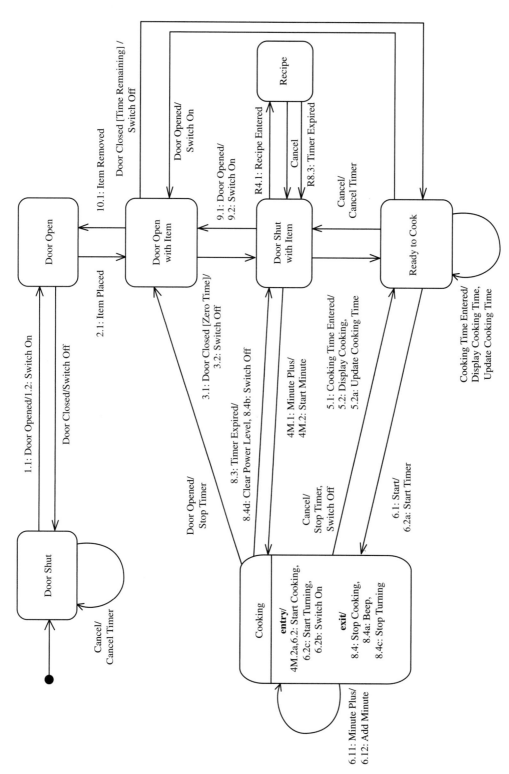

Figure 8.6 *Inherited statechart for* Enhanced Microwave Oven Control *(with all features)*

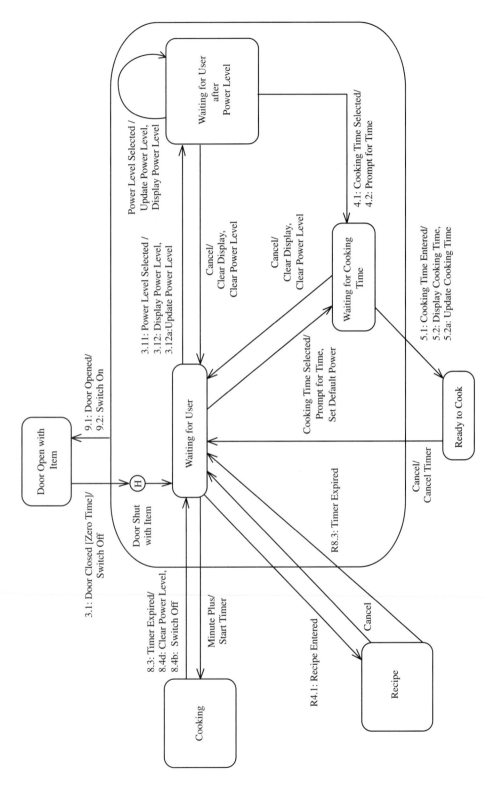

Figure 8.7 *Inherited statechart for* Enhanced Microwave Oven Control *(with all features): decomposition of the* Door Shut with Item *state*

As a second example, consider the Oven Timer state machine. The kernel Oven Timer (Figure 8.8) has three states: Cooking Time Idle, Cooking Food, and Updating Cooking Time. Oven Timer & Minute Plus is a variant state machine that supports the Minute Plus optional feature (Figure 8.9). It inherits the Oven Timer state machine and adds two new transitions to address two new events when the **Minute Plus** key is pressed: Start Minute and Add Minute. Another inherited state machine is Oven & Recipe Timer (Figure 8.10), which also inherits from the kernel Oven Timer statechart and adds an orthogonal state machine for Recipe Timer, which consists of four sequential states: Recipe Idle, Cooking with Recipe, Updating Recipe Time, and Ending Recipe Step (see Chapter 13).

Although this approach works quite well when the effects of individual features are considered, feature interactions become a major problem when combinations of features are considered. Each feature combination could require a new state machine. Consider the state machine for Oven & Recipe Timer & Minute Plus, which combines the Recipe and Minute Plus features. This is an example of feature interaction because the two previous state machines—the Oven & Recipe Timer statechart and the Oven Timer & Minute Plus statechart—have to be replaced by one state machine that combines the effects of the Minute Plus and Recipe features. Oven & Recipe Timer & Minute Plus inherits from Oven Timer, and then one orthogonal state machine is added for Recipe Timer (see Figure 8.10), as well as two new transitions for Minute

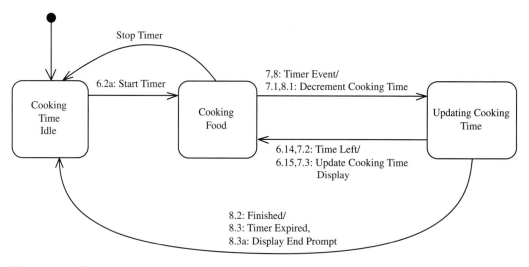

Figure 8.8 *Kernel statechart for* Oven Timer

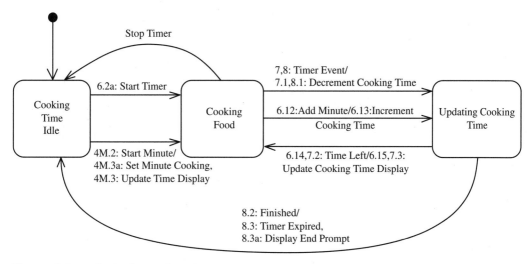

Figure 8.9   *Inherited statechart for* Oven Timer & Minute Plus

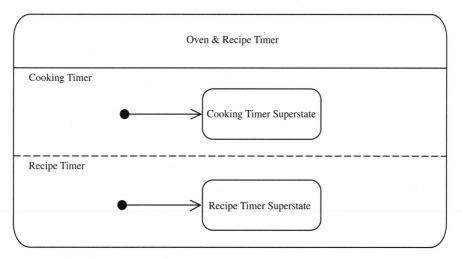

Figure 8.10   *Inherited statechart for* Oven & Recipe Timer

Plus (see Figure 8.9). Note that Cooking Timer Superstate on Figure 8.10 is decomposed into the three substates on Figure 8.9.

There is a state-dependent control class for each of these statecharts. The generalization/specialization hierarchy for these classes is depicted in Figure 8.11, which shows that the kernel Oven Timer state-dependent control class

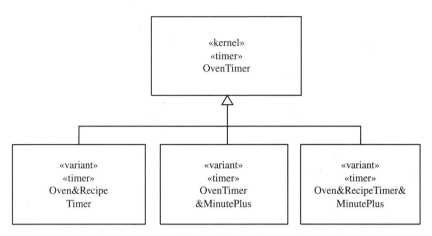

Figure 8.11   Oven Timer *generalization/specialization hierarchy*

is specialized into the Oven & Recipe Timer, Oven Timer & Minute Plus, and Oven & Recipe Timer & Minute Plus state-dependent control classes. The combinatorial problem is exacerbated if one more feature is added, affecting the statechart as described further in Section 8.6.

8.5 Parameterized State Machines in Software Product Lines

An alternative approach to inheritance for introducing state machine variability into software product lines is to use parameterization and parameterized state machines. With this approach, there is one parameterized state machine and one state-dependent control class, which contains the state machine. This state machine should be designed with all the states, transitions, events, actions, and activities corresponding to all the features. The state machine is tailored to the needs of an individual system by the setting of appropriate values for the parameters. In particular, parameters are used for feature conditions, as described next.

Each feature that affects a state machine is given a Boolean guard condition, which is called a *feature condition* and depicted in square brackets: [feature condition]. If the feature condition is true, then the feature is selected; if the feature condition is false, then the feature is not selected. In the case of several alternatives of which only one feature must be selected, only one of the alternatives must be true; all the others must be false. Feature conditions are used as guard conditions on the new state transitions that are introduced because of the optional and alternative features. For a state transition to take place, the event must arrive *and* the feature guard condition must be true, meaning that the feature is provided. If a feature results in a sequence of new states and transitions, then only the transition into the first state in the sequence needs to have a guard condition, because the subsequent states can be reached only if the first state is entered. The values of the feature conditions are set either at system configuration or at runtime initialization of the application, and subsequently they remain unchanged for the duration of the application. Note that, by convention, the first letter of a feature condition is lowercase to distinguish it from other types of guard conditions.

Consider the Enhanced Microwave Oven Control state machine, which incorporates all the features of the microwave oven. For the Power Level feature (Figure 8.13), the feature condition [power] is defined, which is used to guard the transition Power Level Selected [power]. Thus this transition can be taken only if the feature is selected, in which case the feature condition [power] is true. The same approach is used for the Recipe feature which has a transition Recipe Entered [recipe], guarded by the [recipe] feature condition (Figure 8.12).

It is also possible to have feature-dependent actions and activities. If a state transition that occurs has an action or activity guarded by a feature condition, then the action or activity is feature-dependent and will execute only if the feature condition is true.

To support the Turntable feature, two new actions are provided: Start Turning (which is executed on entry into the inherited Cooking state) and Stop Turning (which is executed on exit from the Cooking state) (see Figure 8.12). Both actions are given the feature guard condition [turn] to indicate that their execution is conditional on the condition being true. To support the Light feature, two new actions are provided—Switch On and Switch Off—which are guarded by the feature condition [light]. To support the Beeper feature, the Beep action is added, which is also executed on exit from the inherited Cooking state and is guarded by the feature condition [beeper]. If the transition is taken, the action is executed only if the feature condition is true.

Finally, a state that is dependent on a feature for its existence is referred to as a feature-dependent state and is identified by a UML constraint. For example, the notation {feature = recipe} Recipe is used to indicate that the Recipe superstate is provided only if the Recipe feature has been selected (see Figure 8.12).

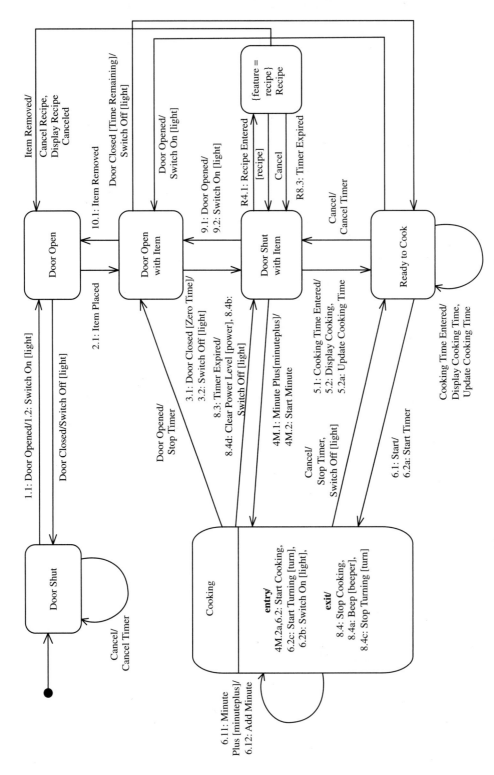

Figure 8.12 *Parameterized statechart for* Microwave Oven Control *(with all features)*

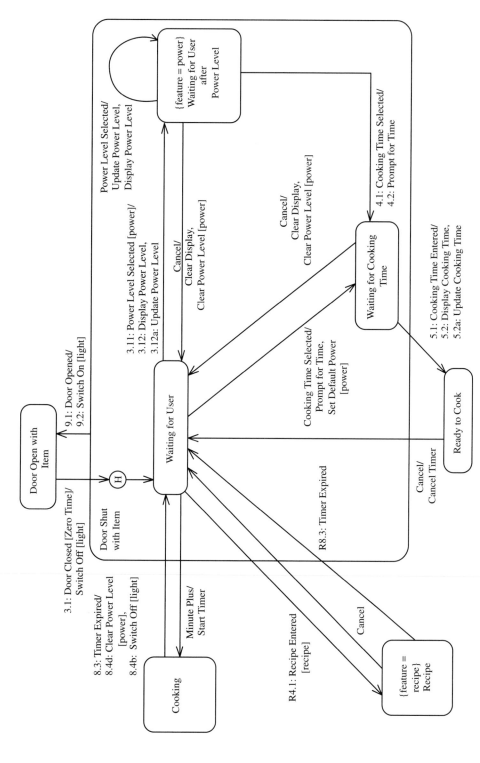

Figure 8.13 *Parameterized statechart for* Microwave Oven Control *(with all features): decomposition of the* Door Shut with Item *state*

191

8.6   Comparison of Approaches

As described in Sections 8.4 and 8.5, there are two different approaches to providing software product line variability for state-dependent control classes: One is to design inherited state machines, and the other is to design parameterized state machines. This section compares the two approaches.

Consider the approach of designing an inherited state machine for each variation. The main advantage of this approach is that it isolates each variation in one variant state machine model. It is also means that each variant state machine is affected by only one feature or feature combination. However, the main disadvantage of this approach is that a large number of variations can lead to a combinatorial explosion of variant state machines. One approach to help manage this problem is to reduce the number of combinations by permitting only certain prespecified packaged feature and variant combinations, as illustrated in Section 8.6.

An alternative approach to designing inherited state machines is to design one parameterized state machine that captures the states, events, transitions, actions, and activities needed by all the different features. The main advantage of this approach is that there is only one parameterized state machine instead of many variant state machines, so the configuration management problem is simplified. Furthermore, the addition of a new state-dependent feature affects only one state machine instead of several. The main disadvantage is that a parameterized state machine is affected by more than one feature.

Although it is possible to use a combination of inherited and parameterized state machines in order to take advantage of both approaches, the recommendation is to use only inherited state machines if there are a small number of variants. If there are many state-dependent features, as in the `Microwave Oven Control` example, the parameterized state machine approach is strongly recommended.

Examples of Inherited and Parameterized State Machines

Now consider some examples of both inherited and parameterized state machines from the microwave oven product line. Consider the features that affect the `Microwave Oven Control` state-dependent control class. These include `Power Level`, `Recipe`, `TOD Clock`, `Minute Plus`, `Light`, `Turntable`, and `Beeper`. If an inherited state machine were designed for each feature and feature combination, the result would be a large number of possible combinations. Each feature and feature combination would need its own inherited state machine and subclass. With a parameterized state machine, there would be only one parameterized state machine and class, so parameterization is the preferred approach.

Consider another example from the microwave oven product line—namely, `Oven Timer`. Two features affect this state machine: `Recipe` and `Minute Plus`. The result is four variants, as described in Section 8.4. However, consider the impact of another feature, `Delayed Timer`. Even with this small number of variations, the effects of the combinatorial explosion are obvious. Designing an inherited state machine for each feature and feature combination would result in eight variants to support each of the possible combinations: `Timer`, `Timer & Minute Plus`, `Timer & Delayed Timer`, `Timer & Recipe`, `Timer & Minute Plus & Delayed Timer`, `Timer & Minute Plus & Recipe`, `Timer & Delayed Timer & Recipe`, and `Timer & Minute Plus & Delayed Timer & Recipe`. It is possible to reduce the number of combinations by restricting the number of combinations—for example, by specifying beforehand certain permitted packaged feature combinations for the product line. For example, the number of variants could be reduced from eight to four if the following kernel plus three feature combinations were chosen: `Timer`, `Timer & Minute Plus`, `Timer & Minute Plus & Recipe`, `Timer & Minute Plus & Recipe & Delayed Timer`.

Because of the potential combinatorial explosion with inheritance, parameterization is the preferred approach and is used in the statecharts for the microwave oven product line case study in Chapter 13.

8.7 Kernel First Approach: State-Dependent Dynamic Analysis

During object structuring, the objects that participate in the realization of a use case are determined. If at least one of the objects is a state-dependent control object, then the interaction is defined as state-dependent. **State-dependent dynamic analysis** is a strategy to help determine how objects interact with each other in state-dependent interactions. A state-dependent interaction involves at least one state-dependent control object, which executes a statechart that provides the overall control and sequencing of the interactions. In more-complex interactions, it is possible to have more than one state-dependent control object. Each state-dependent control object is defined by a statechart.

With the kernel first approach, state-dependent dynamic analysis for the kernel system is similar to dynamic analysis for a single system. This is followed with the software product line evolution approach, which analyzes the impact of each feature on the kernel statechart(s) and kernel object interactions.

8.7.1 Determining Objects and Interactions

In state-dependent dynamic analysis, the objective is to determine the interactions among the following objects:

- The state-dependent control object, which executes the statechart
- The objects, usually interface objects, that send the events to the control object that cause the state transitions
- The objects that provide the actions and activities, which are triggered by the control object as a result of the state transitions
- Any other objects that participate in the use case

The interaction among these objects is depicted on a communication diagram or sequence diagram.

The main steps in the state-dependent dynamic analysis strategy are as follows:

1. **Determine the interface object(s)**. Consider the objects that receive the inputs sent by the actor.
2. **Determine the state-dependent control object**. There is at least one control object, which executes the statechart. Others might also be required.
3. **Determine the other internal objects**. These are internal objects that interact with the control object or interface objects.
4. **Determine object interactions**. Carry out this step in conjunction with step 5 because the interaction between the state-dependent control object and the statechart it executes needs to be determined in detail.
5. **Determine the execution of the statechart**. See Section 8.7.2.
6. **Consider alternative sequences**. Perform the state-dependent dynamic analysis on the alternative sequences of the use case.

8.7.2 Modeling Interaction Scenarios on Communication Diagrams and Statecharts

This section describes how interaction diagrams—in particular, communication diagrams and statecharts—can be used together to model state-dependent interaction scenarios.

A message on an interaction diagram consists of an event and the data that accompanies the event. Consider the relationship between messages and events in the case of a state-dependent control object that executes a statechart. When a message arrives at the control object on a communication diagram, the event part of the message causes the state transition on the statechart. The action on the statechart is the result of the state transition and corresponds to the output event depicted on the communication diagram. In general, a *message* on an interaction diagram (communication or sequence diagram) is referred to as an *event* on a statechart; in descriptions of state-dependent dynamic scenarios, however, for conciseness only the term *event* is used.

A source object sends an event to the state-dependent control object. The arrival of this input event causes a state transition on the statechart. The effect of the state transition is one or more output events. The state-dependent control object sends each output event to a destination object. An output event is depicted on the statechart as an action (which can be a state transition action, an entry action, or an exit action), an enable activity, or a disable activity.

The statechart needs to be considered in conjunction with the communication diagram. In particular, it is necessary to consider the messages that are received and sent by the control object, which executes the statechart. An input event into the control object on the communication diagram must be consistent with the same event depicted on the statechart. The output event (which causes an action, enables an activity, or disables an activity) on the statechart must be consistent with the output event shown on the communication diagram.

To ensure that the communication diagram and statechart are consistent with each other, the equivalent communication diagram *message* and statechart *event* must be given the same name. Furthermore, for a given state-dependent scenario it is necessary to use the same message numbering sequence on both diagrams. Using the same sequence ensures that the scenario is represented accurately on both diagrams and can be reviewed for consistency. These issues will be illustrated in the following example.

8.7.3   Example of the Kernel First Approach

As an example of the kernel first approach to state-dependent dynamic modeling, consider the kernel communication diagram for the Cook Food use case. Several objects support this use case, as depicted in Figure 8.14. The state-dependent control object, Microwave Oven Control, executes the Microwave Oven Control statechart and thereby controls the execution of several objects. To fully understand and design the state-dependent interactions, it is necessary to analyze how the communication diagram and statechart work together. A message on the communication diagram and its equivalent event on the statechart

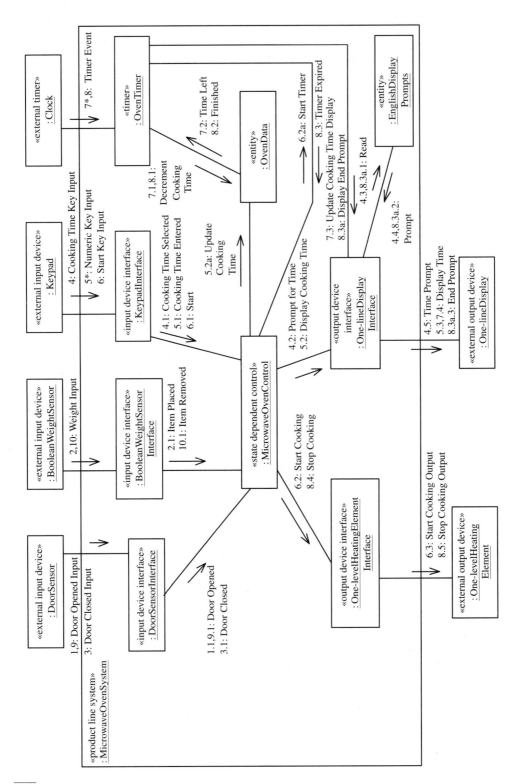

Figure 8.14 *Communication diagram for a kernel use case:* Cook Food

196

are given the same name and sequence number to emphasize how the diagrams work together.

Consider one event sequence initiated by an external object—namely, `Keypad`. At the start of this scenario, the statechart is in the `Ready to Cook` state (see Figure 8.1). When the user presses the **Start** key, the external `Keypad` object sends the `Start Key Input` message (message 6 on Figure 8.14) to the software `Keypad Interface` object, which in turn sends a `Start` message (message 6.1) to the `Microwave Oven Control` object. The arrival of the message triggers the `Start` event on the `Microwave Oven Control` statechart (event 6.1 on Figure 8.1), which in turn causes the state transition from the `Ready to Cook` state to the `Cooking` state. The resulting actions are the transition action `Start Timer` and the entry action `Start Cooking`. The effect of the `Start Timer` action (event 6.2a on Figure 8.1) is that the `Microwave Oven Control` object sends the `Start Timer` message (message 6.2a on Figure 8.14) to the `Oven Timer` object. The arrival of this event at `Oven Timer` triggers a state transition from `Cooking Time Idle` to `Cooking Food` (event 6.2a on Figure 8.8). The effect of the `Start Cooking` action (event 6.2 on Figure 8.1) is that the `Microwave Oven Control` object sends the `Start Cooking` message (message 6.2 on Figure 8.14) to the `One-level Heating Element Interface` object, which then sends `Start Cooking Output` (message 6.3) to the external `One-level Heating Element` object. Switching on this actuator physically initiates the cooking.

When the timer counts down to zero, the `Oven Timer` object sends the `Timer Expired` message (event 8.3 on Figures 8.1, 8.8, and 8.14) to `Microwave Oven Control`, resulting in the transition to `Door Shut with Item` and the execution of the exit action `Stop Cooking`. The effect of the `Stop Cooking` action (event 8.4 on Figures 8.1 and 8.14) is that the `Microwave Oven Control` object sends the `Stop Cooking` message to the `One-level Heating Element Interface` object, which then sends `Stop Cooking Output` to the external `One-level Heating Element` object. Switching off this actuator physically stops the cooking.

8.8   Software Product Line Evolution Approach

To model state-dependent variability with the software product line evolution approach, start with kernel state-dependent communication diagrams developed with the kernel first approach, and then consider the impact of those features that affect the state-dependent control object and statechart. On the statechart, this analysis is likely to result in new states and new transitions, requiring new events and actions or activities. On the communication diagram, the analysis is likely to result in additional objects, which are then categorized as optional or alternative objects, which replace objects in the kernel system, as well as additional messages.

Consider the impact of adding optional features to the kernel system for the microwave oven product line. As an example, consider the Light, Turntable, and Beeper optional features; each feature needs an optional output device interface object added, as well as state-dependent actions to control it. The new objects are Lamp Interface, Turntable Interface, and Beeper Interface, which in turn communicate with the external output device objects Lamp, Turntable, and Beeper, respectively. However, these features also affect the state-dependent control object, Microwave Oven Control, because this object has to trigger the actions that control the output device interface objects. Thus the actions have to be added to the statechart for Microwave Oven Control, as shown in Figure 8.12.

For example, the Turntable feature affects the Cooking state, which needs the entry action Start Turning (action 6.2c on Figure 8.12) on entering the state and the exit action Stop Turning (action 8.4c) on leaving the state. The Beeper feature requires the exit action Beep (action 8.4a) on leaving the state. For the Light feature, other transitions are affected as the light is switched on (such as actions 1.2 and 9.2) whenever the door is opened and switched off when the door is closed (such as action 3.2). Thus the Light feature necessitates the additional transition actions Switch On and Switch Off.

The impact of these three features on the Cook Food communication diagram is shown in Figure 8.15, which shows only the affected and new objects compared to Figure 8.14. Microwave Oven Control is affected by the new features and sends messages—which correspond to the new statechart actions—to the new objects as follows:

1. Start Turning (message 6.2c) and Stop Turning (message 8.4c)— which correspond to the actions with the same names on the statechart— to Turntable Interface, the output device interface object

2. Switch On (messages 1.2, 6.2b, 9.2) and Switch Off (messages 3.2, 8.4b)— which correspond to the actions with the same names on the statechart—to Lamp Interface

3. Beep (message 8.4a)—which corresponds to the action with the same name on the statechart—to Beeper Interface

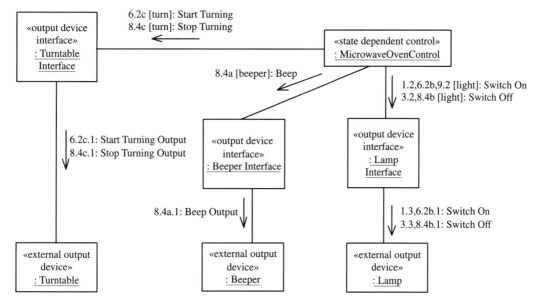

Figure 8.15 *Impact of features on the microwave oven communication diagram*

Other features result in the design of new transitions. An example is the `Minute Plus` feature, which has a state-dependent impact. **Minute Plus** can be pressed either when the oven is in the state `Door Shut with Item` (see Figure 8.12), in which case the `Cooking` state is entered, or during the `Cooking` state, in which case the state does not change but the cooking time is incremented.

Other features (e.g., `Recipe`) result in the design of new states. In fact, the impact of the `Recipe` feature is to add a `Recipe` superstate (see Figure 8.12), which is decomposed into the substates `Ready to Cook with Recipe`, `Door Open with Recipe`, and `Cooking with Recipe`. The transitions between these states also need to be defined. This is described in more detail in Chapter 13.

8.9   Dynamic Analysis with Communicating State-Dependent Objects

This section describes how scenarios involving communicating state-dependent control objects are developed. Each state-dependent control object executes a finite state machine, which is depicted as a statechart. If the finite state machines need to communicate with each other, they do so indirectly. The objects that contain these state machines send messages to each other as described in this section.

Consider the following. As a result of transitioning from one state to another, the action of a finite state machine is to send a message. This message is actually sent by the object that executes the finite state machine, referred to as the *source object*. A *destination object* receives the message. The message causes a state transition in the finite state machine executed by the destination object. Thus the action of a source finite state machine causes a state change on a destination finite state machine.

An example can be extracted from the factory automation product line case study, which is described in detail in Chapter 15. Three instances of the Line Workstation Controller class communicate with each other. These three objects—predecessor Line Workstation Controller, a Line Workstation Controller, and successor Line Workstation Controller—are connected in series as depicted on the communication diagram in Figure 8.16. The factory uses a just-in-time algorithm, which is fully explained in Chapter 15. Briefly, a workstation sends a physical part to the next workstation in sequence (its successor) after it receives a Part Request message from the successor. After sending the part, the workstation sends a Part Coming message to its successor and a Part Request message to its predecessor, as depicted in Figure 8.16. Each Line Workstation Controller object executes a statechart. The statecharts are identical, but the objects are usually in different states on their statecharts. The instances of the statecharts for the three objects are depicted in Figures 8.17, 8.18, and 8.19.

The high-level statechart for each Line Workstation Controller is depicted in Figure 8.20 and consists of two orthogonal superstates: Part Processing Superstate (which is decomposed into the sequential statecharts shown in Figures 8.17 through 8.19) and Part Requesting Superstate (which is decomposed into the sequential statechart shown in Figure 8.21). The latter statechart has two substates, Part Not Requested and Part Has Been Requested. These two substates correspond to the guard conditions with the same names on the Part Processing statecharts, as depicted in Figures 8.17 through 8.19.

Consider the communication diagram in Figure 8.16 and the statechart for a Line Workstation Controller shown in Figure 8.18. Figure 8.18 shows that when this object transitions from the Robot Placing state to Awaiting Part from Predecessor Workstation, the transition triggers two actions: Part Coming (B15) and Part Request (B15a). These actions result in corresponding

Figure 8.16 *Communicating state-dependent control objects: communication diagram for three instances of* Line Workstation Controller

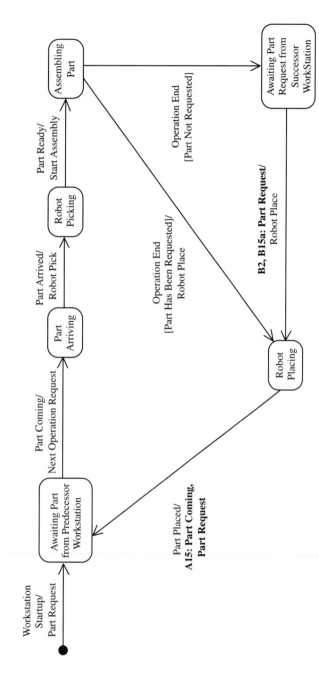

Figure 8.17 *Communicating state-dependent control objects: statechart for* Predecessor Line Workstation Controller

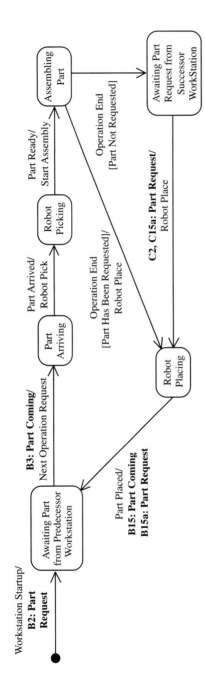

Figure 8.18 *Communicating state-dependent control objects: statechart for* a Line Workstation Controller

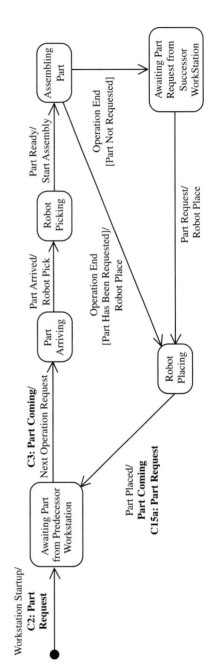

Figure 8.19 *Communicating state-dependent control objects: statechart for* Successor Line Workstation Controller

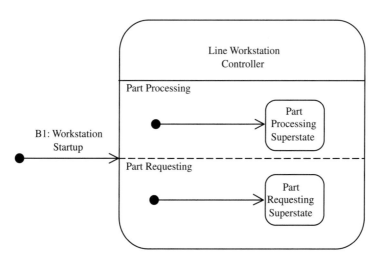

Figure 8.20   `Line Workstation Controller` *statechart: superstates for* `Line Workstation Controller`

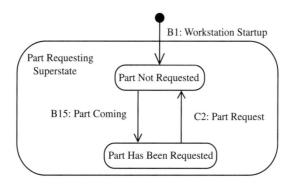

Figure 8.21   `Line Workstation Controller` *statechart: statechart for* `Part Requesting Superstate`

messages being sent to the neighbor workstations. Figure 8.16 shows that the `Part Request` message is sent to the `predecessor Line Workstation Controller` object, causing it to transition from the `Awaiting Part Request from Successor Workstation` state to the `Robot Placing` state (see Figure 8.17). Figure 8.16 also shows that the `Part Coming` message is sent to the `successor Line Workstation Controller` object, causing it to transition from the `Awaiting Part from Predecessor Workstation` state to the `Part Arriving` state (see Figure 8.19). The reason that some messages have two sequence numbers—for example, A15 and B3 for `Part Coming` on Figure 8.16—is that the same message occurs at different places in the message sequencing scenarios for the sender (A15) and receiver (B3) objects.

8.10 Summary

This chapter described how to develop finite state machines and statecharts for software product lines. The most effective use of statecharts in software product lines is for modeling state-dependent control classes and objects, taking advantage of hierarchical statechart decomposition. In particular, each state-dependent control class—whether kernel, optional, or variant—needs to be modeled with a finite state machine and depicted as a statechart. It is also possible to model variations in software product lines using inherited state machines and parameterized state machines; the two approaches were described and compared in this chapter. The integration of statecharts and interaction diagrams—in particular, communication diagrams—during state-dependent object interactions was also described.

Chapter 10 will describe several software architectural control patterns in which finite state machines and state-dependent control objects play an important role. These patterns include the centralized control architectural pattern, the distributed control architectural pattern, and the hierarchical control architectural pattern. Examples of finite state machines, state-dependent control objects, and software architectural control patterns will be given in the case studies in Chapters 13 and 15.

chapter

9

Feature/Class Dependency Modeling for Software Product Lines

Chapter 5 described feature modeling in software product lines in which the common, optional, and alternative features are determined. Chapter 6 described static modeling in software product lines, in which kernel, optional, and variant classes are determined. This chapter describes feature/class dependency modeling, in which the relationship between features and classes in the software product line are developed. In particular, the discussion covers how the features that address the functional requirements of the product line relate to the software classes that realize the product line's functionality.

In software product lines, feature/class dependency modeling shows the classes required to support each product line feature. During feature modeling, features are analyzed and categorized as common features (required by all members of the product line), optional features (required by only some members of the product line), and alternative features (a choice of features exists). Feature/ class dependency modeling emphasizes optional and alternative features because the selection of these features, and the classes required to realize them, are what determine the nature of the specific members of the product line.

Section 9.1 focuses on classes and variation points, describing how variability can be introduced in two ways—first, through abstract classes and subclasses; and second, through parameterization. Section 9.2 describes class reuse categorization for software product lines and how this is depicted with stereotypes. Section 9.3 discusses feature/class dependencies, and Section 9.4 continues the discussion by describing how these dependencies can be determined by means of feature-based impact analysis. Section 9.5 describes feature/object and feature/class modeling in UML using feature-based communication diagrams and feature-based class diagrams, respectively.

9.1   Classes and Variation Points

In modeling software product lines, it is very important to anticipate where change can be introduced into the product line, thereby permitting evolution of the product line after initial deployment. Variation point modeling provides a systematic approach for addressing change.

A **variation point** identifies a location at which change will occur in a software product line. The variation point also identifies the mechanism by which changes can be made (Webber and Gomaa 2002, Gomaa and Webber 2004). In Chapter 4, variation points were described with respect to use cases. In this chapter, variation points are described in regard to classes. The two main variation point mechanisms provided are abstract classes and parameterization. With an abstract superclass, the inheritance mechanism is used to specialize the superclass differently for various members of the software product line. With parameterization, a product line class has configuration parameters, which are assigned different values for different members of the product line.

9.1.1   Abstract Classes

An **abstract class** is a class with no instances. Because an abstract class has no instances, it is used as a template for creating subclasses instead of as a template for creating objects. Thus, it is used only as a superclass and defines a common interface for its subclasses. An **abstract operation** is an operation that is declared in an abstract class but not implemented. An abstract class must have at least one abstract operation.

An abstract class defers all or some of its operation implementations to operations defined in subclasses. Given the interface provided by the abstract operation, a subclass can define the implementation of the operation. Different subclasses of the same abstract class can define different implementations of the same abstract operation. An abstract class can thus define an interface in the form of abstract operations. The subclasses define the implementation of the abstract operations and may extend the interface by adding other operations.

Some of the operations may be implemented in the abstract class, especially in cases where some or all of the subclasses need to use the same implementation. Thus the abstract class may define a default implementation of an operation. A subclass may choose to override an operation defined by a parent class by providing a different implementation for the same operation. This approach can be used when a particular subclass has to deal with a special case that requires a different implementation of the operation.

9.1.2   Abstract Classes in Software Product Lines

The abstract class captures common properties for all related classes in the superclass. Although abstract classes are often used to represent kernel classes of the product line, they can also represent optional classes. A subclass inherits the common properties from the abstract class and then extends it with variant properties, which could be in the form of new attributes, new operations, or alternative implementations of abstract operations. Thus the subclasses are variant classes.

Variability can be introduced at the abstract class level or at the abstract operation level. At the abstract class level, a class can be specified consisting entirely of abstract operations. The variant subclass must therefore provide the implementation of all the operations. In such a case, the variation point applies at the class level—that is, to the entire class. At the abstract operation level, an abstract class can be designed such that only one of its operations is abstract and variability is introduced through implementation of this operation. In that case, the variation point applies at the abstract operation level.

With the abstract class approach, a variant subclass is used for each variation to the abstract class. This approach has the advantage of isolating each variation in one variant class. It provides separation of concerns by ensuring that a variant class is affected by only one feature. However, a potential disadvantage in product lines with a large degree of variability is that isolating each variation in one variant class could lead to a combinatorial explosion of variant classes.

Example of Abstract Classes and Subclasses

The software product line example of abstract classes and subclasses is for a banking product line, in which different banks provide different kinds of accounts. Initially checking accounts and saving accounts are provided, although later other types of accounts, such as money market accounts, could be added.

An abstract class is designed called `Account`, which represents a variation point because variability is introduced by specialization of the class. `Account` is designed to have two generalized attributes that are needed by all accounts: `account Number` and `balance`. Because it is necessary to be able to open and close accounts, read the account balance, and credit and debit the account, the following generalized operations are specified for the `Account` class:

- `open (accountNumber : Integer)`
- `close ()`
- `read Balance () : Real`

- credit (amount : Real)
- debit (amount : Real)

Initially the banking product line handles two types of accounts: checking accounts and savings accounts. Account is a good candidate for using inheritance, with a generalized account superclass and specialized subclasses for checking account and savings account. Questions we need to ask at this stage are: What should be the generalized operations and attributes of the account superclass? What are the specialized operations and attributes of the checking account and savings account subclasses? Should the account class be an abstract class; that is, which of the operations should be abstract, if any?

Before we can answer these questions, we need to understand in what ways checking and savings accounts are similar and in what ways they differ. First consider the attributes. It is clear that both checking and saving accounts need account Number and balance attributes, so these attributes can be generalized and made attributes of the Account class, to be inherited by both the Checking Account and Savings Account subclasses. One requirement for checking accounts is that it is desirable to know the last amount deposited in the account. Checking Account thus needs a specialized attribute called last Deposit Amount. On the other hand, in this bank, savings accounts accrue interest but checking accounts do not. We need to know the accumulated interest on a savings account, so the attribute cumulative Interest is declared as an attribute of the Savings Account subclass. In addition, only three debits are allowed per month from a savings account without a bank charge, so the attribute debit Count is also declared as an attribute of the Savings Account subclass.

Two additional static class attributes are declared for Savings Account; these are attributes for which only one value exists for the whole class, which is accessible to all objects of the class. The static attributes are max Free Debits (the maximum number of free debits, which is initialized to 3) and bank Charge (the amount the bank charges for every debit over the maximum number of free debits, which is initialized to $2.50).

Both Checking Account and Savings Account will need the same operations as the Account class—namely, open, close, read Balance, credit, and debit. The interface of these operations is defined in the Account superclass, so the two subclasses will inherit the same interface from Account. The open and close operations are done in the same way on checking and savings accounts, so the implementation of these operations can also be defined in Account and then inherited. The credit and debit operations are handled differently for checking and savings accounts. For this reason, the `credit` and `debit` operations are designed as abstract operations with the interface for the operations specified in the superclass but the implementations of the operations deferred to the subclasses.

In the case of the `Checking Account` subclass, the implementation of the `debit` operation needs to deduct `amount` from `balance`. The implementation of the `credit` operation needs to increment `balance` by `amount` and then set `last Deposit Amount` equal to `amount`. For `Savings Account`, the implementation of the `credit` operation needs to increment `balance` by `amount`. The implementation of the `debit` operation must, in addition to debiting the `balance` of the savings account, increment `debit Count` and deduct `bank Charge` for every debit in excess of `max Free Debits`. There is also a need for an additional `clear Debit Count` operation, which reinitializes `debit Count` to zero at the end of each month.

At first glance, the `read` operations for checking and savings accounts appear to be identical; however, a more careful examination reveals that this is not the case. When we read a checking account, we wish to read the balance and the last deposit amount. When we read a savings account, we wish to read the balance and the accumulated interest. The solution is to have more than one read operation. The generalized read operation is the `read Balance` operation, which is inherited by both `Checking Account` and `Savings Account`. A specialized read operation, `read Cumulative Interest`, is then added in the `Savings Account` subclass; and a specialized read operation, `read Last Deposit Amount`, is added to the `Checking Account` subclass.

The design of the `Account` generalization/specialization hierarchy is depicted in Figure 9.1 and described here. This figure uses the UML convention of depicting abstract class names in italics.

Design of the Checking Account subclass

- **Attributes**:
  - Inherits the attributes `account Number` and `balance`. Both attributes are declared as protected in the `Account` superclass; hence they are visible to the subclasses.
  - Adds the attribute `last Deposit Amount`.
- **Operations**:
  - Inherits the specification and implementation of the operations `open`, `close`, and `read Balance`.

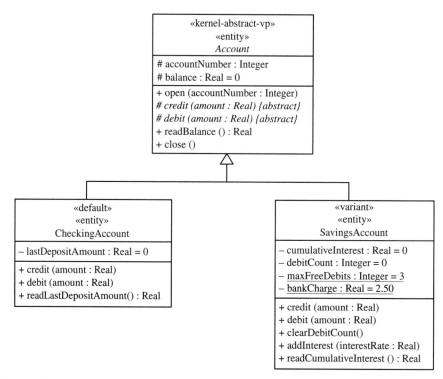

Figure 9.1 *Example of an abstract superclass and subclasses*

- Inherits the specification of the abstract operation credit; defines the implementation to add amount to balance as well as to set last Deposit Amount equal to amount.

- Inherits the specification of the abstract operation debit; defines the implementation to deduct amount from balance.

- Adds the operation read Last Deposit Amount () : Real.

Design of the Savings Account subclass

- **Attributes**:

  - Inherits the attributes account Number and balance.

  - Adds the attributes cumulative Interest and debit Count.

  - Adds the static class attributes max Free Debits and bank Charge. Static attributes are underlined in UML, as shown in Figure 9.1.

- **Operations**:
  - Inherits both the specification and implementation of the operations open, close, and read Balance.
  - Inherits the specification of the abstract operation debit; defines the implementation to deduct amount from balance, increment debit Count, and deduct bank Charge from balance if max Free Debits is greater than debit Count.
  - Inherits the specification of the abstract operation credit; defines the implementation to add amount to balance.
  - Adds the following operations:
    - add Interest (interest Rate : Real), which adds interest on a daily basis
    - read Cumulative Interest () : Real
    - clear Debit Count (), which reinitializes debit Count to zero at the end of each month

9.1.3   Parameterized Classes in Software Product Lines

One way to avoid the potential problem of a combinatorial explosion, caused by a large number of variant classes, is to use parameterized classes instead of specialized subclasses.

With parameterized classes, a product line class has configuration parameters, which are assigned different values for different members of the product line. In a parameterized class with multiple parameters, different parameters can be associated with different features. The main advantage of this approach is simplification in that there is one parameterized class instead of many variant classes. The disadvantage is the potential loss of separation of concerns in that a parameterized class can be affected by more than one feature.

Parameterized classes can be kernel, optional, variant, or default classes. In each case, the configuration parameters need to be set by the product line member. This is done either at configuration time or at runtime during system initialization.

Example of a Parameterized Class

One example of a parameterized class comes from the microwave oven product line. The class is an entity class called Oven Data, which contains all the parameters that need to be set for cooking food. Several parameterized variables are maintained for the microwave oven, many of which relate to optional features.

The Oven Data class can be designed as one class with several attributes or as a composite class with an internal class for each parameterized attribute. The class is designed as a parameterized kernel class because it is easier to manage than having one class for each parameter. For each optional attribute of the class, a constraint defines the feature that applies to this attribute. The attribute is relevant for a given product line member only if the feature is selected as indicated by the feature constraint.

«kernel-param-vp» «entity» Oven Data

- **Kernel attribute**:
  - cookingTime. Remaining time to cook food.
- **Optional attributes**, which are relevant only if the named feature is selected:
  - selectedPowerLevel {feature = Multi-level Heating}. Possible values of this variable are: High, Medium, and Low; the initial value is High. If this feature is not selected, the power level is a constant set to High.
  - itemWeight {feature = Analog Weight}. This *Real* variable is used only with analog weight and records the actual weight of the item.
  - selectedRecipe {feature = Recipe}. Initialized to "none selected".
  - TODvalue {feature = TOD Clock}. Time variable initialized to 12:00.
  - TODmaxHour {feature = TOD Clock}. Parameterized constant set at system configuration to 12:00 or 24:00 to indicate maximum hour on clock.

The attributes held by the parameterized Oven Data class are depicted in Figure 9.2, which shows the variable name, the type of variable, the range for

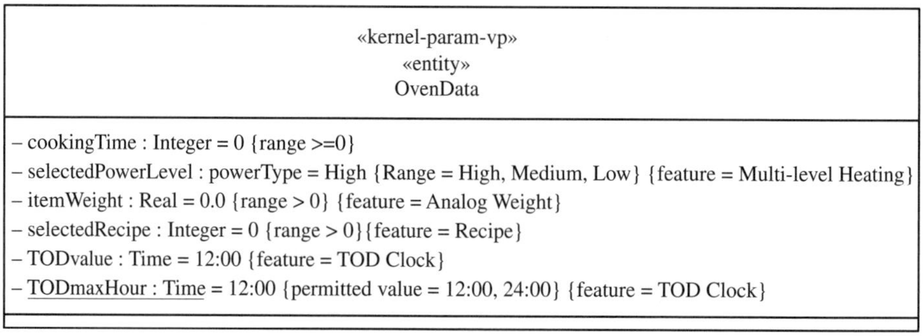

«kernel-param-vp» «entity» OvenData
– cookingTime : Integer = 0 {range >=0} – selectedPowerLevel : powerType = High {Range = High, Medium, Low} {feature = Multi-level Heating} – itemWeight : Real = 0.0 {range > 0} {feature = Analog Weight} – selectedRecipe : Integer = 0 {range > 0}{feature = Recipe} – TODvalue : Time = 12:00 {feature = TOD Clock} – TODmaxHour : Time = 12:00 {permitted value = 12:00, 24:00} {feature = TOD Clock}

Figure 9.2 *Example of a parameterized class*

the variable, permitted values for configuration parameters, and the feature constraint if the attribute is optional. Configuration parameters, such as TOD max Hour, are depicted as static variables because once the value of the parameter is set at configuration time, it cannot be changed and is the same for all object instances.

9.2   Class Reuse Categorization for Software Product Lines

As pointed out in Chapter 6, multiple UML stereotypes may be used to depict different aspects of the modeler's problem. For software product lines, two different kinds of stereotypes are used, depicting two orthogonal (i.e., independent) ways of categorizing a class: categorization by role and categorization by reuse. A stereotype is used to identify the role played by the class in the product line. Class **role stereotypes** are used for the same purpose as in single systems (Gomaa 2000). Examples of class role stereotypes are «entity», «interface», «control», and «application logic»; these are described in more detail in Chapter 6.

A second stereotype is used to identify the reuse category for the class in the software product line. A class **reuse category** is used to identify how the class is to be reused in a specific member of the product line. Chapter 6 described the main kinds of class reuse categories—namely, kernel, optional, and variant classes. This section describes the full set of class reuse categories, which are depicted in UML with the stereotype notation. In particular, some product line classes are always used without change, some provide variation points through abstract classes, and some provide variation points through parameterized classes. When an abstract or parameterized class is designed to be a source of variability, it defines a variation point, which is explicitly identified in the name of the stereotype, abbreviated vp.

The class reuse categories are described in the list that follows and depicted as class reuse stereotypes in Figure 9.3. Examples of class reuse categorization from the microwave oven software product line are given in Figure 9.4.

Main class reuse categories:

- «kernel» (*kernel class*). A class provided by every member of the product line and used without change by every member. An example of a kernel class with no variants is the input device interface class Door Sensor Interface, as shown in Figure 9.4:

  «kernel» «input device interface» Door Sensor Interface

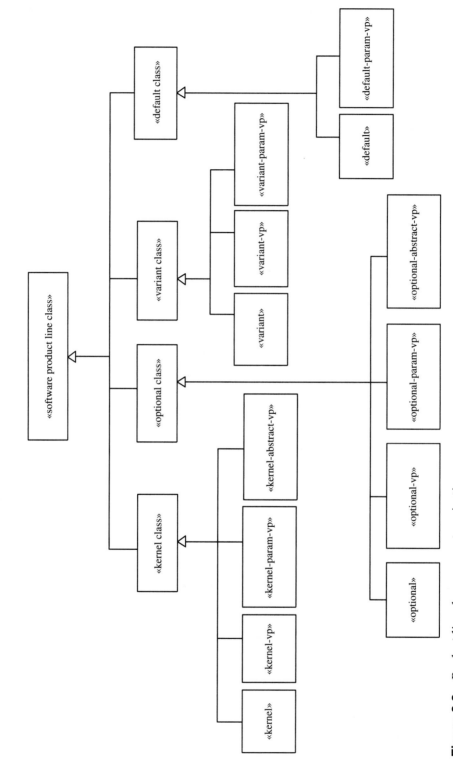

Figure 9.3 *Product line class reuse categorization*

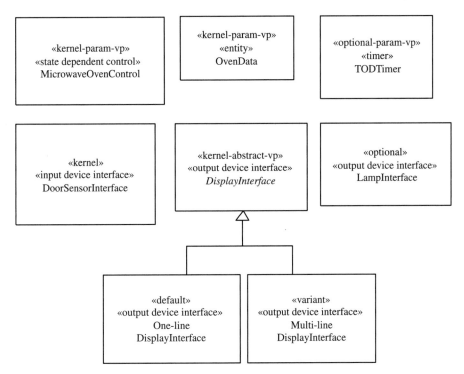

Figure 9.4 *Examples of class reuse categorization in the microwave oven software product line*

- **«optional»** (*optional class*). A class provided by some members of the product line but not all. When used, it is used without change. An example of an optional class is the output device interface class `Lamp Interface`, as shown in Figure 9.4:

  «optional» «output device interface» Lamp Interface

- **«variant»** (*variant class*). One of a set of similar classes, which have some identical properties but others that are different. Different variant classes are used by different members of the product line. An example of a variant class is the output device interface class `Multi-line Display Interface`, as shown in Figure 9.4:

  «variant» «output device interface» Multi-line Display Interface

- **«default»** (*default class*). The default class among a set of variant classes, which is provided by some members of the product line. An example of a default class is the output device interface class `One-line Display Interface`, as shown in Figure 9.4:

«default» «output device interface» One-line Display Interface

Parameterized class reuse categories:

- **«kernel-param-vp»** (*kernel parameterized class*). A parameterized class that is provided by every member of the product line. The values of the configuration parameters need to be set by the individual product line member. This class represents a variation point, as explicitly identified by "vp" in the stereotype name, because product line variability is introduced at this point through parameterization. An example of a kernel parameterized class is the state-dependent control class `Microwave Oven Control`, as shown in Figure 9.4:

  «kernel-param-vp» «state dependent control» Microwave Oven Control

- **«optional-param-vp»** (*optional parameterized class*). A parameterized class provided by some members of the product line but not all. The values of the configuration parameters need to be set by the individual product line member, making this class a variation point. An example of an optional parameterized class is the timer class `TOD Timer`, as shown in Figure 9.4:

  «optional-param-vp» «timer» TOD Timer

- **«variant-param-vp»** (*variant parameterized class*). One of a set of variant parameterized classes, which is provided by some members of the product line. The values of the configuration parameters need to be set by the individual product line member, making this class a variation point.

- **«default-param-vp»** (*default parameterized class*). The default class among a set of variant parameterized classes, which is provided by some members of the product line. The values of the configuration parameters need to be set by the individual product line member, making this class a variation point.

Abstract class reuse categories:

- **«kernel-abstract-vp»** (*abstract kernel class*). An abstract class provided by every member of the product line. The abstract class cannot be instantiated; instead it provides a standard interface for its subclasses. This class represents a variation point, as explicitly identified by "vp" in the stereotype name, because product line variability is introduced at this point through specialization. An example of an abstract kernel class is the output device interface class `Display Interface`, as shown in Figure 9.4:

  «kernel-abstract-vp» «output device interface» Display Interface

- **«optional-abstract-vp»** (*abstract optional class*). An abstract class provided by some members of the product line but not all. The abstract class provides a standard interface for its subclasses and represents a variation point because product line variability is introduced at this point through specialization.

Concrete class reuse categories:

- **«kernel-vp»** (*concrete kernel class*). A concrete class provided by every member of the product line. The class provides a standard interface for its subclasses. This class represents a variation point, as explicitly identified by "vp" in the stereotype name, because product line variability is introduced at this point through specialization. This category is different from the abstract kernel class in that the class can be instantiated.

- **«optional-vp»** (*concrete optional class*). A concrete class provided by some members of the product line but not all. This class provides a standard interface for its subclasses and represents a variation point because product line variability is introduced at this point through specialization. This category is different from the abstract optional class in that the class can be instantiated.

- **«variant-vp»** (*concrete variant class*). One of a set of concrete variant classes. This class provides a standard interface for its subclasses, which are also variant. It also represents a variation point because product line variability is introduced at this point through specialization.

9.3   Feature/Class Dependencies

For every feature in the software product line, certain classes realize the functionality specified by the feature. Because a common feature is provided by every member of the product line, the classes that support or realize a common feature are always kernel classes. Because common features, by definition, are provided by every member of the product line, it follows that kernel classes are always present in all product line members. If an optional or alternative feature is selected for a given member of the product line, then the optional or variant classes that realize this feature are also selected.

Depending on the feature analysis, different variants of the same abstract class might or might not be permitted to coexist in the same product line member. Figure 9.5 depicts the variant subclasses of the kernel abstract `Workstation Controller` class from the factory automation product line. To see whether

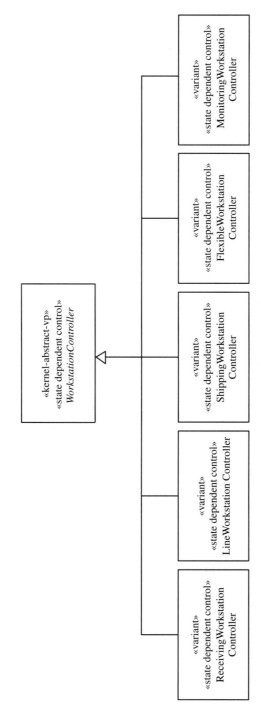

Figure 9.5 *Example of variant classes in the factory automation product line*

these variants can coexist or not, it is necessary to understand the feature analysis. In the case of an exactly-one-of feature group or a mutually exclusive feature group, the variants are not permitted to coexist in the same product line member. The `Line Workstation Controller`, `Receiving Workstation Controller`, and `Shipping Workstation Controller` variant classes all support the `High-Volume Manufacturing` feature and can therefore coexist. However, `Flexible Workstation Controller` supports the `Flexible Manufacturing` feature, and `Factory Monitoring Workstation Controller` supports the `Factory Monitoring` feature. The `High-Volume Manufacturing`, `Flexible Manufacturing`, and `Factory Monitoring` features are members of an exactly-one-of feature group. Hence the subclasses that support these features are mutually exclusive state-dependent control classes that exist in different kinds of factories, as described in detail in Chapter 15.

In the case of a common or optional feature, variant classes are permitted to coexist in the same product line system. For example, `Receiving Workstation Controller`, `Line Workstation Controller`, and `Shipping Workstation Controller` all coexist in `High-Volume Manufacturing` members of the factory automation product line.

9.4 Feature-Based Impact Analysis

An effective approach to determining the feature/class dependencies is to perform an impact analysis of each feature. The goal of **feature-based impact analysis** is to determine what optional, parameterized, or variant classes depend on each new feature. Feature-based impact analysis is best addressed through object interaction modeling, as a step on the way to determining the feature/class dependencies.

As described in Chapter 7, the analysis begins with the kernel first approach and continues with the product line evolution approach. Applying the kernel first approach to the microwave oven product line results in the kernel classes being identified as described in Chapter 7 and depicted in Figure 9.6.

After feature-based impact analysis is applied as described in Section 9.4.1 for optional features and Section 9.4.2 for alternative features, feature/class dependencies can be depicted on feature-based class diagrams (as described in Section 9.5.2) or feature/class dependency tables (as described in Section 9.5.3).

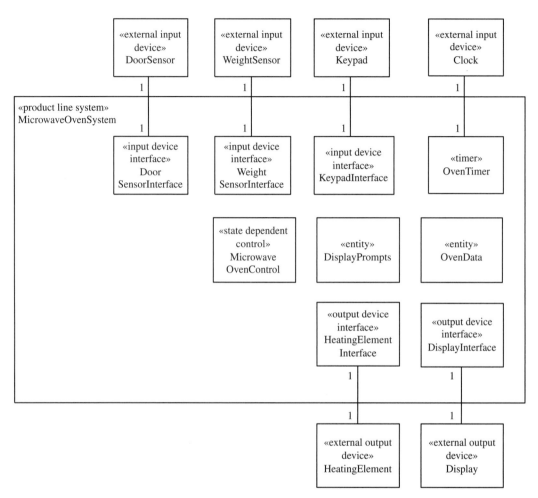

Figure 9.6   *Kernel classes in the microwave oven product line*

9.4.1   Feature-Based Impact Analysis of Optional Features

After the kernel first approach has been applied, the product line evolution approach (see Chapter 7) is applied to determine the impact of optional and alternative features on the kernel communication diagram. This overall approach, called *feature-based impact analysis*, systematically analyzes the impact of each feature on the kernel communication diagram. If there are cascading feature dependencies (e.g., feature B depends on feature A), then the order of feature analysis is to

1. Analyze the impact of feature A on the kernel communication diagram and create a modified communication diagram depicting this impact

2. Analyze the impact of feature B on the kernel communication diagram modified by feature A

For optional features, analyze the impact of each feature on the kernel communication diagram. Determine what optional objects need to be added to provide the functionality needed by the feature. Also determine what objects are affected by the feature—that is, objects whose behavior needs to change as a result of the impact. When a new optional object is added, often an existing object needs to be modified to communicate with the new object. It is then necessary to decide whether the affected object should be designed as an instance of a parameterized class or an instance of a specialized class. In the latter case, it will be necessary to replace a default class with a variant class, both of which could be subclasses of an abstract class.

As an example, consider the optional features from the microwave oven software product line. In the case of the `Light`, `Turntable`, and `Beeper` optional features, each feature needs to have an optional output device interface object added. These are `Lamp Interface`, `Turntable Interface`, and `Beeper Interface`, respectively. However, these features also affect the state-dependent control object, `Microwave Oven Control`, because this object has to trigger the actions, which are executed by the output device interface objects. The decision is made to design `Microwave Oven Control` as a parameterized class because the alternative of introducing a variant class for each feature would result in a combinatorial explosion of variant classes to keep track of. The classes are defined as follows:

- «optional» «output device interface» Beeper Interface
- «optional» «output device interface» Light Interface
- «optional» «output device interface» Turntable Interface
- «kernel-param-vp» « state dependent control» Microwave Oven Control

On the other hand, the `Minute Plus` optional feature does not require any optional object to be added, but it does affect three kernel objects: `Keypad Interface` (because it needs to read the input from the extra input key for `Minute Plus`), `Microwave Oven Control` (because it needs additional capability to deal with the `Minute Plus` feature), and `Oven Timer` (which has to increment the cooking time by 60 seconds when the **Minute Plus** key is pressed). For the same reasons as for `Microwave Oven Control`, the decision is made to design the `Keypad Interface` and `Oven Timer` classes as parameterized classes:

- «kernel-param-vp» «input device interface» Keypad Interface
- «kernel-param-vp» «timer» Oven Timer

In short, the goal of feature-based impact analysis is to determine what optional, parameterized, or variant objects depend on the new feature. From this information, the classes from which the objects are instantiated can easily be determined.

9.4.2 Feature-Based Impact Analysis of Alternative Features

For alternative features, it is necessary to analyze the impact of each alternative feature on the kernel communication diagram. For each of the alternatives, consider whether any additional optional objects are needed to satisfy the feature, whether any replacement of default object with variant objects resulting from the feature is needed, and whether there is any impact on existing kernel objects that communicate with the new objects.

As an example, consider the alternative features from the microwave oven software product line. Consider the «exactly-one-of feature group» for `Display Language`. Because one of the software product line requirements is to be able to display prompts in different languages, a separate `Display Prompts` abstract class is designed that is specialized to support the prompts for the specific language. The default language is English. The alternative languages are French, Spanish, German, and Italian. The default class is `English Display Prompts`, and an instance of this class is depicted on the kernel communication diagram. If a different language is required—for example, French—only this class is affected, and the `French Display Prompts` variant class replaces the `English Display Prompts` default class:

Abstract kernel class:
- «kernel-abstract-vp» «entity» Display Prompts

Default variant class:
- «default» «entity» English Display Prompts

Alternative variant classes:
- «variant» «entity» French Display Prompts
- «variant» «entity» Spanish Display Prompts

- «variant» «entity» German Display Prompts
- «variant» «entity» Italian Display Prompts

9.5   Feature/Object and Feature/Class Dependency Modeling in UML

Feature/class dependencies and feature/object dependencies can be modeled in UML with the package notation, where a **package** is a grouping of model elements (Booch et al. 2005). A UML package is used to depict the modeling elements that are grouped into a feature. During requirements modeling, the package notation is used to depict the use cases that are reused together in a feature. During feature-based interaction modeling, a UML package is used to depict the objects that are reused together in a feature. Finally, the feature package can be used to depict the classes that support the feature, and from which the objects in the feature-based communication diagram are instantiated.

Examples of the different usage of feature packages to depict reusable use cases, objects, and classes are given in the factory automation software product line. For example, the `High-Volume Manufacturing` feature is depicted as a package with the stereotype «feature», which groups the three variant classes that support this feature: `Receiving Workstation Controller`, `Line Workstation Controller`, and `Shipping Workstation Controller`.

9.5.1   Feature-Based Communication Diagrams

Whereas a communication diagram depicts the objects required to support a use case, a feature-based communication diagram depicts the objects required to support a feature. Because a feature can support one or more use cases, a feature-based communication diagram can also support one or more use cases. When a feature supports one use case, it might seem that the feature-based communication diagram and use case–based communication diagram should be identical. In fact, however, a feature-based communication diagram must clearly delineate the objects that provide the functionality specified by the feature.

A feature-based communication diagram shows the objects required to realize that feature. In particular, it assumes the presence of objects in other prerequisite features, including common features. Thus, if one of the objects in the use case–based communication diagram already appears in a prerequisite feature, that object needs to be depicted as belonging to the prerequisite feature. A feature-based communication diagram can be drawn in one of two ways: The first approach is to show only the objects that support the feature. The second approach is to show one or more feature packages in which each package depicts the objects that support the feature. Note that for parameterized objects that support more than one feature, only the former approach can be used.

For a feature supported by more than one use case, the objects required by the feature are determined by analysis of the objects from each use case that supports the feature. Thus the feature-based communication diagram is the synthesis of the use case–based communication diagrams for the use cases that support the feature. As before, any object in the use case–based communication diagram that already supports a prerequisite feature is shown inside the package of the prerequisite feature on the feature-based communication diagram. The interconnected objects that support one feature depend on objects in prerequisite feature packages. They can communicate with those objects in the prerequisite feature-based communication diagrams.

A feature-based communication diagram is a generic UML communication diagram, which means that it depicts all possible interactions between the objects (see Section 7.1.5). Because it does not depict a specific scenario, message sequence numbers are not used. Furthermore, because generic communication diagrams depict generic instances (which means that they depict potential instances rather than actual instances), they use the UML 2.0 convention of not underlining the object names.

As an example, consider the communication diagrams for the factory automation product line. The common feature `Factory Kernel` consists of four use cases. During dynamic modeling, the objects supporting each use case are depicted on a communication diagram, as follows:

1. **View Alarms.** This use case is realized by the `Operator Interface` and `Alarm Handling Server` objects.

2. **View Workstation Status.** This use case is realized by the `Operator Interface` and `Workstation Status Server` objects

3. **Generate Alarm and Notify.** This use case is realized by the `Workstation Controller`, `Alarm Handling Server`, and `Operator Interface` objects.

4. **Generate Workstation Status and Notify.** This use case is realized by the `Workstation Controller`, `Workstation Status Server`, and `Operator Interface` objects.

On the basis of these four use cases, a first attempt at modeling the objects supporting the `Factory Kernel` common feature identifies the `Alarm Handling`

Server, Workstation Status Server, Workstation Controller, and Operator Interface objects. However, another consideration is that there is a need for the product line to support automated factories without a user interface. This means that only the first three objects are needed to support the Factory Kernel feature, and the Operator Interface object should be assigned to an optional feature called Factory Operations User. Another issue is that each factory automation system supports a different type of Workstation Controller object and must be represented by an alternative feature. For example, factory monitoring systems need the Monitoring Workstation Controller object. Thus a factory monitoring system would need at least the following features, as depicted here in the feature notation:

- «common feature» Factory Kernel
- «optional feature» Factory Operations User{prerequisite = Factory Kernel}
- «alternative feature» Factory Monitoring{prerequisite = Factory Kernel}

Figure 9.7 shows the feature-based communication diagram in which these three features from the factory automation product line are depicted as packages, with the objects supporting the features depicted inside the packages. The optional Operator Interface object in the Factory Operations User optional feature communicates with the Alarm Handling Server and Workstation Status Server kernel objects in the Factory Kernel feature package. The variant Monitoring Workstation Controller object is depicted inside the Factory Monitoring alternative feature package and also communicates with the kernel objects.

9.5.2 Feature-Based Class Diagrams

Once the feature-based communication diagrams have been developed, it should be relatively straightforward to develop feature-based class diagrams. For each object on the feature-based communication diagram, the class from which it is instantiated is depicted on the feature-based class diagram. If more than one feature is depicted on the feature-based class diagram, then the features are depicted as packages with the classes that support the feature depicted inside the package.

For each communication link between objects on the feature-based communication diagram, an association is depicted between the corresponding classes on the feature-based class diagram. The direction of navigability is depicted on the association. It is determined by consideration of which class provides the operation and which class uses the operation. The direction of navigability on

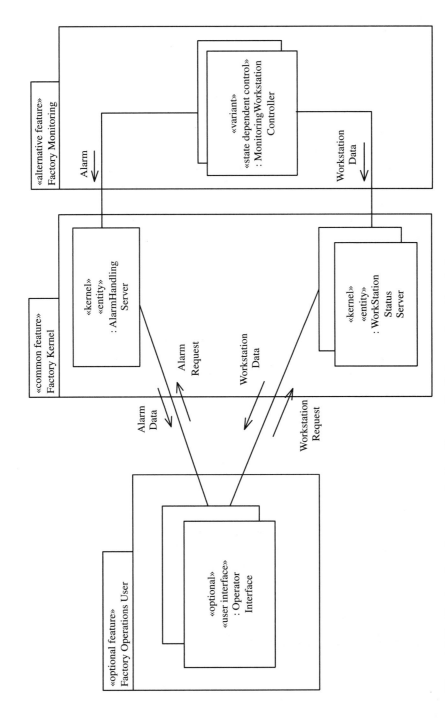

Figure 9.7 *Feature-based communication diagram for factory automation features*

the class diagram should correspond to the direction of the messages sent between objects on the communication diagram. Because the direction of navigability shows the direction of the dependency, the class dependencies should correspond to the feature dependencies. The direction of the association is from the dependent class to the class that it *requires the presence* of (i.e., depends on). Thus if feature X depends on feature Y, then a class supporting feature X *requires the presence* of a class supporting feature Y.

When the decision is made to use variant classes, the generalization/specialization hierarchy depicting the abstract superclass and the subclasses is depicted on the feature-based class diagram. A superclass can support one feature while the subclass supports a different feature. The feature supported by the subclass should depend on the feature supported by the superclass.

An example of a feature-based class diagram is given in Figure 9.8. This class diagram depicts the same features shown in the feature-based communication diagram of Figure 9.7. Thus the `Operator Interface` class in the `Factory Operations User` optional feature package uses the `Alarm Handling Server` and `Workstation Status Server` classes in the `Factory Kernel` feature package. Because this is a class diagram, abstract superclasses can also be depicted. The abstract `Workstation Controller` superclass, originally depicted in Figure 9.5, is a kernel superclass and is therefore allocated to the `Factory Kernel` feature package, while its subclass `Monitoring Workstation Controller` belongs to the alternative `Factory Monitoring` feature package. Because there are never any instances of the `Workstation Controller` superclass, it can never be depicted on a communication diagram.

Note in Figure 9.8 that the dependency of the optional feature `Factory Operations User` on the common feature `Factory Kernel` corresponds to the optional `Operator Interface` class being a client of, and hence depending on, the kernel `Alarm Handling Server` and `Workstation Status Server` classes. Similarly, the dependency of the alternative feature `Factory Monitoring` on the common feature `Factory Kernel` corresponds to the dependency due to the specialization of the variant `Monitoring Workstation Controller` subclass from the kernel abstract `Workstation Controller` superclass.

9.5.3   Feature/Class Dependency Tables

A concise way of depicting feature/class dependencies is to use a table to show the features and classes that realize the functionality described by the feature. The feature/class dependency table is particularly useful for depicting the relationship between features and parameterized classes because the individual

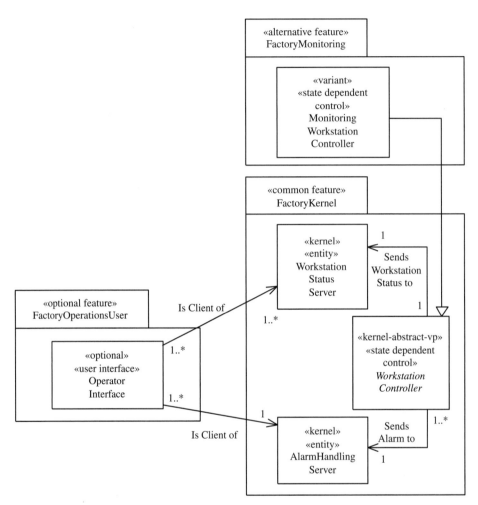

Figure 9.8 *Feature-based class diagram for factory automation features*

parameters can be explicitly shown. Such a feature/class dependency table has
the following columns:

- Feature name
- Feature category
- Class name
- Class reuse category
- Class parameter (the parameter of the class that is affected by the feature)

An example of a feature/class dependency table is given for a subset of the microwave oven product line in Table 9.1. For example, `Light` is an optional feature. It is supported by two classes: `Lamp Interface` and `Microwave Oven Control`. `Lamp Interface` is an optional class. `Microwave Oven Control` is a kernel parameterized class. The feature condition is stored as a Boolean class attribute of `Microwave Oven Control` called `light`, which is set to true or false, depending on whether the feature is selected (light = True) or not selected (light = False).

Table 9.1 *Example of feature/class dependencies: microwave oven software product line*

Feature Name	Feature Category	Class Name	Class Reuse Category	Class Parameter
Microwave Oven Kernel	common	Door Sensor Interface	kernel	
		Weight Sensor Interface	kernel-abstract-vp	
		Keypad Interface	kernel-param-vp	
		Heating Element Interface	kernel-abstract-vp	
		Display Interface	kernel-abstract-vp	
		Microwave Oven Control	kernel-param-vp	
		Oven Timer	kernel-param-vp	
		Oven Data	kernel-param-vp	
		Display Prompts	kernel-abstract-vp	
Light	optional	Lamp Interface	optional	
		Microwave Oven Control	kernel-param-vp	light : Boolean
Turntable	optional	Turntable Interface	optional	
		Microwave Oven Control	kernel-param-vp	turntable : Boolean
Beeper	optional	Beeper Interface	optional	
		Microwave Oven Control	kernel-param-vp	beeper : Boolean
Minute Plus	optional	Keypad Interface	kernel-param-vp	minuteplus : Boolean
		Microwave Oven Control	kernel-param-vp	minuteplus : Boolean
		Oven Timer	kernel-param-vp	minuteplus : Boolean
One-line Display	default	One-line Display Interface	default	

(continues)

Table 9.1   *Example of feature/class dependencies: microwave oven software product line (Continued)*

Feature Name	Feature Category	Class Name	Class Reuse Category	Class Parameter
Multi-line Display	alternative	Multi-line Display Interface	variant	
English	default	English Display Prompts	default	
French	alternative	French Display Prompts	variant	
Spanish	alternative	Spanish Display Prompts	variant	
German	alternative	German Display Prompts	variant	
Italian	alternative	Italian Display Prompts	variant	

9.6 Summary

This chapter described feature/class dependency modeling, in which the relationships between features and software classes in the software product line are developed. In particular, the discussion covered how the features that address the functional requirements of the product line relate to the software classes that realize the product line's functionality.

In the software product line method, for each feature, feature/class dependency modeling shows the classes required to support each product line feature. This approach emphasizes optional and alternative features because it is the selection of these features, and the classes required to realize them, that determines the nature of the specific members of the product line.

This chapter described classes and variation points, discussing how variability can be introduced in two ways—first, through abstract classes and subclasses; and second, through parameterization. The chapter also described how product line classes are categorized according to their reuse characteristics and how this categorization is depicted with stereotypes. The discussion included a description of feature/class dependencies and how they can be determined by feature-based impact analysis. Feature/object and feature/class modeling in UML using feature-based communication diagrams and feature-based class diagrams, respectively, was introduced.

chapter

Architectural Patterns for Software Product Lines

In software design, one frequently encounters a problem that one has solved before on a different project. Often the context of the problem is different; it might be a different application, a different platform, or a different programming language. Because of the different context, one usually ends up redesigning and reimplementing the solution, thereby falling into the "reinventing the wheel" trap. The field of software patterns, including architectural and design patterns, is helping developers avoid unnecessary redesign and reimplementation.

The concept of a pattern was first conceived by Christopher Alexander in the architecture of buildings and described in his book *The Timeless Way of Building* (Alexander 1979). In software, the field of design patterns was popularized by Gamma, Helms, Johnson, and Vlissides in their book *Design Patterns* (1995), in which they described 23 design patterns. Later, Buschmann et al. (1996) described patterns that span different levels of abstraction, from high-level architectural patterns through design patterns to low-level idioms (see Chapter 1).

This chapter describes several software architectural structure patterns and software architectural communication patterns. It also explains how to document a software architectural pattern using a standard template. Finally, it describes how a software architecture can be designed starting from the software architectural patterns. Section 10.1 provides an overview of the different kinds of software patterns. Sections 10.2 through 10.4 describe the different software architectural patterns, with Section 10.2 focusing on patterns that address the structure of the software architecture, Section 10.3 discussing patterns that address the message communication among distributed components of the software architecture, and Section 10.4 covering patterns that address transaction management in client/server architectures. Section 10.5 describes how to document software architectural patterns. Section 10.6 discusses how to use software architectural patterns.

10.1 Categorization of Software Patterns

Architectural patterns, which are the highest-level patterns, provide the skeleton or template for the overall software architecture or high-level design of an application. Shaw and Garlan (1996) referred to *architectural styles* or patterns of software architecture, which are recurring architectures used in a variety of software applications (see also Bass 2003). These include such widely used architectures as client/server and layered architectures.

Design patterns (Gamma et al. 1995) address smaller reusable designs than architectural patterns, such as the structure of subsystems within a system. The description is in terms of communicating objects and classes customized to solve a general design problem in a particular context. A design pattern is a larger-grained form of reuse than a class because it involves more than one class and the interconnection among objects from different classes. A design pattern is sometimes referred to as a *microarchitecture*. It can have a strong influence on the structure of a subsystem, although it does not affect the fundamental structure of the application.

Idioms are low-level patterns that are specific to a given programming language and describe implementation solutions to a problem that use the features of the language.

This chapter groups software architectural patterns into two main categories: architectural structure patterns (which address the static structure of the architecture) and architectural communication patterns (which address the dynamic communication among distributed components of the architecture).

10.2 Software Architectural Structure Patterns

This section describes the architectural structure patterns, which address the static structure of the architecture.

10.2.1 Layers of Abstraction Architectural Pattern

The layers of a hierarchy are sometimes referred to as *levels* or *layers of abstraction*. The **Layers of Abstraction** pattern (also known as the *Hierarchical Layers* or

Levels of Abstraction pattern) is a common architectural pattern in many different software domains (Buschmann et al. 1996). Operating systems, database management systems, and network communication software are examples of software systems often structured as hierarchies.

One of the first hierarchically structured software systems was the T.H.E. operating system developed by Dijkstra and his team (Dijkstra 1968). Dijkstra's goals were to provide a systematic approach for designing, coding, and testing a hierarchical system. The T.H.E system was structured into several layers, with modules at one layer providing services for modules at higher layers. In this system a module can invoke a module in a lower layer but not one in a higher layer. Each layer provides a distinct class of service, such as processor management, memory management, or file management.

In his seminal paper on design for ease of extension and contraction, Parnas (1979) pointed out that the layered architecture lends itself to incremental design and design of product families, such that later increments are layered on top of earlier increments, and optional increments are layered above required increments.

With a *strict hierarchy*, each layer uses services in the layer immediately below it. With a *flexible hierarchy*, a layer does not have to invoke a service at the layer immediately below it but can directly invoke services at lower layers.

The Layers of Abstraction architectural pattern is used in the International Organization for Standardization's Open Systems Interconnection (ISO/OSI) reference model, which is a standard seven-layered architecture for networked communication between open systems (see Figure 10.1). Each layer deals with a specific aspect of network communications and provides an interface, as a set of operations, to the layer above it. For each layer on the sender node, there is an equivalent layer on the receiver node. The seven layers of the OSI reference model (Comer 2004) are as follows:

Layer 1: Physical layer. Corresponds to the basic network hardware, including electrical and mechanical interfaces, and the physical transmission medium.

Layer 2: Data link layer. Specifies how data is organized into frames and how frames are transmitted over the network.

Layer 3: Network layer. Specifies how packets are routed over the network from a source node to a destination node, including details of how addresses are assigned.

Layer 4: Transport layer. Specifies how to provide reliable data transfer.

Layer 5: Session layer. Specifies how to establish a communication session with a remote node.

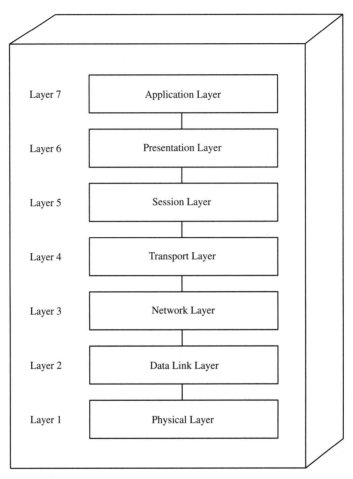

Figure 10.1   *Example of the Layers of Abstraction architectural pattern: ISO/OSI reference model*

Layer 6: Presentation layer. Specifies how to represent data in a standard way, which can then be translated to the internal representation on a given computer.

Layer 7: Application layer. Supports various network applications, such as file transfer and electronic mail.

An interesting characteristic of the layered architecture is that it is straightforward to replace the upper layers of the architecture with different layers that use the unchanged services provided by the lower layers. Thus, TCP/IP, which is the most widely used protocol on the Internet (Comer 2004), has the same two lower layers—layers 1 and 2—as the OSI reference model but different upper layers. TCP/IP is organized into five conceptual layers, as shown in Figure 10.2:

Layer 1: Physical layer. Corresponds to the basic network hardware.

Layer 2: Network interface layer. Specifies how data is organized into frames and how frames are transmitted over the network.

Layer 3: Internet layer (IP). Specifies the format of packets sent over the Internet and the mechanisms for forwarding packets through one or more routers from a source to a destination (see Figure 10.3). The router node in Figure 10.3 is a gateway that interconnects a local area network to a wide area network.

Layer 4: Transport layer (TCP). Assembles packets into messages in the order they were originally sent. TCP is the Transmission Control Protocol,

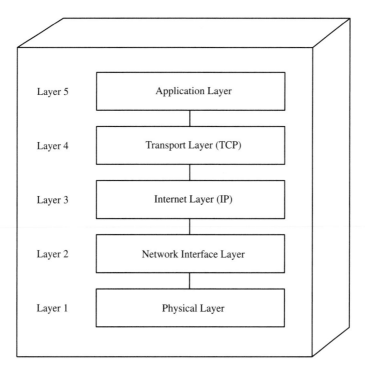

Figure 10.2 *Example of the Layers of Abstraction architectural pattern: Internet (TCP/IP) reference model*

which uses the IP network protocol to carry messages. It provides a virtual connection from an application on one node to an application on a remote node, hence providing what is termed an *end-to-end protocol* (see Figure 10.3).

Layer 5: Application layer. Supports various network applications, such as file transfer (FTP), electronic mail, and the World Wide Web.

Layers 1 and 2 of TCP/IP—the physical and network interface layers—correspond to the ISO reference model. Layer 3 of TCP/IP has no equivalent in the ISO model, which does not have a layer for Internet protocols. Layer 4 of TCP/IP corresponds to layer 4 in the ISO model, and layer 5 in TCP/IP corresponds to layer 7 of the ISO model. The ISO model's layers 5 and 6 (the session and presentation layers) are not supported in TCP/IP.

Another interesting characteristic of the layered architecture is shown in Figure 10.3. The router node uses the lower three layers of the TCP/IP protocol, while the application nodes use all five layers. Thus the OSI protocol, TCP/IP application node protocol, and TCP/IP router node protocol can all be considered members of a communication protocol product line in which layers 1 and 2 are kernel. Alternatively, the TCP/IP application node protocol and TCP/IP router node protocol could be considered members of a TCP/IP application protocol product line in which layers 1, 2, and 3 are kernel.

Another example of the Layers of Abstraction architectural pattern comes from the cruise control and monitoring system, in which the lower layers (Shaft Layer, Calibration Layer, and Distance & Speed Layer) compute essential data values—in particular, the distance traveled by the vehicle and the current speed of the vehicle. These values are used by the upper layers: Auto Control Layer, Trip Averages Layer, and Maintenance Layer (see Figure 10.4). Each layer depends on the services provided by the lower layers, but no layer depends on services provided by layers above it. This example uses the flexible Layers of Abstraction pattern; for example, Distance & Speed Layer uses services provided by Shaft Layer, which is two layers below it.

Software Product Line Implications of the Layers of Abstraction Pattern

Where possible, the Layers of Abstraction pattern should be applied when one is designing a software product line because a layered architecture fits in very well with the software product line concept. As Parnas (1979) pointed out in his seminal paper on designing for ease of extension and contraction (see also Hoffman and Weiss 2001), if software is designed in the form of layers, it can be contracted by the removal of upper layers and extended by the addition of upper layers that use services provided by lower layers. In the context of a software

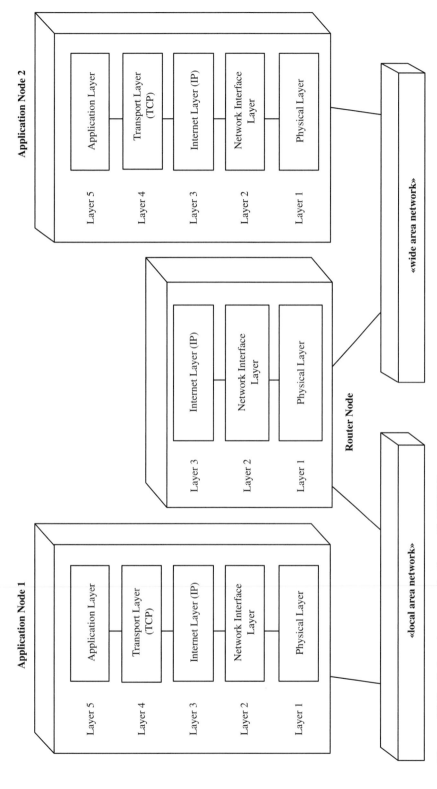

Figure 10.3 *Internet communication with TCP/IP*

237

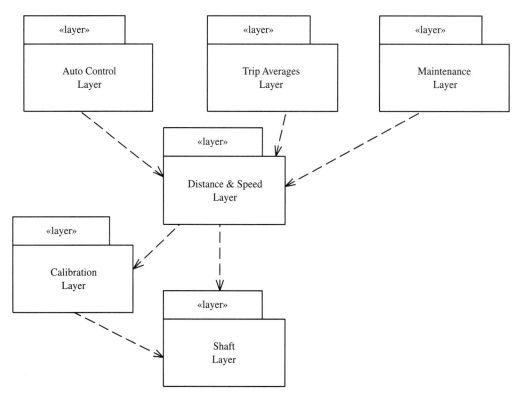

Figure 10.4 *Example of the Layers of Abstraction architectural pattern: cruise control and monitoring system*

product line, *contracting* the software means designing the kernel of the product line—that is, those essential components that are needed by all members of the product line. *Extending* the software means designing optional and variant components that use the kernel components. In a software product line, an additional restriction in the use of the Layers of Abstraction pattern is that an optional or variant component can depend on a kernel component. However, a kernel component must never depend on an optional or variant component.

In multiorganization applications, such as business-to-business (B2B) applications, a layered architecture can be developed for each organization, with each organization's software architecture loosely coupled with other organizations' software architectures. The result is a federation of cooperating layered architectures, as illustrated by the e-commerce product line in Chapter 14.

10.2.2   Kernel Architectural Pattern

With the **Kernel** pattern, the core of a software system is encapsulated inside the kernel. If the kernel is very small, then this pattern is sometimes called the *Microkernel* pattern (Buschmann et al. 1996). The kernel provides a well-defined interface consisting of operations, in the form of procedures and/or functions, that can be called by other parts of the software system. This pattern is frequently used in operating systems where the kernel or microkernel provides the minimal essential functionality that is needed for the operating system. Other services provided by the operating system use the core services provided by the kernel. The UNIX operating system and the Windows NT operating system have kernels. The kernel of an application can also be the lowest layer of a hierarchical architecture developed with the Layers of Abstraction pattern (described in Section 10.2.1), as shown in Figure 10.5.

The following list names the typical services provided by an operating system kernel, which provides core services to allow multiple tasks (also known as *lightweight processes* or *threads*) to execute concurrently, synchronize their actions, and communicate with each other:

- **Priority preemption scheduling**. The highest-priority task executes as soon as it is ready—for example, after being activated by an I/O interrupt.

- **Intertask communication using messages**.

- **Mutual exclusion using semaphores**.

- **Event synchronization using signals**. Alternatively, messages may be used for synchronization purposes.

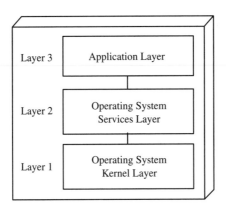

Figure 10.5   *Example of the Kernel architectural pattern*

- **Interrupt handling and basic I/O services**.
- **Memory management**. Each task's virtual memory is mapped onto physical memory.

Examples of widely used operating systems with kernels that support concurrent processing are several versions of UNIX (including Linux, Solaris, and AIX) and MS Windows NT. For more details on operating system kernels, refer to Bacon 1997, Silberschatz and Galvin 1998, and Tanenbaum 2003.

Figure 10.5 shows the operating system kernel layer as the lowest layer in the layered architecture. Above this is the operating system services layer, which provides additional services, such as file management and user account management. The third layer is the application layer, where applications consist of concurrent tasks that take advantage of the services of the lower layers.

Software Product Line Implications of the Kernel Pattern

The design of the software architecture should start with consideration of the kernel of the product line. Within the Layers of Abstraction pattern (see Section 10.2.1), it is possible to apply the Kernel pattern, where the kernel classes could be structured at the lowest layer of the hierarchy. In fact, the Layers of Abstraction and Kernel patterns are a natural fit for software product lines.

It is possible to have kernel and optional classes in the same layer provided that they do not depend on each other. All systems will have the kernel classes in the lowest layer. Only some systems will have the optional classes in that layer. What this means is that within the layered architecture of a software product line, any layer can contain variability. The kernel system is a minimal member of the software product line, which consists of the kernel components plus any default components that are needed to create a viable product line system. The kernel system is the system with the thinnest layers because it has the fewest components at any layer. Other members of the product line can have thicker layers if more components are provided at any given layer.

10.2.3 Client/Server Architectural Pattern

The **Client/Server** architectural pattern consists of two logical components: a client that requests services and a server that provides services. The **server** is a provider of services, and the **client** is a consumer of services. The simplest client/server architecture has one server and many clients, and for this reason the Client/Server architectural pattern is also known as the *Multiple-Client/Single-Server* pattern. An example of this pattern is an ATM application for a single bank, in which automated teller machines (ATMs) distributed around the country communicate with the bank's central server. The basic Client/Server architectural pattern can be depicted on a deployment diagram, as in Figure 10.6, which shows multiple clients connected to a server via a local area network.

An example of this pattern comes from the banking system, as depicted on the class diagram in Figure 10.7. This system contains multiple ATMs and one bank server. For each ATM there is one ATM Client Subsystem, which handles customer requests by reading the ATM card and prompting for transaction details at the keyboard/display. For an approved withdrawal request, the ATM dispenses cash, prints a receipt, and ejects the ATM card. The bank server maintains a database of customer accounts and customer ATM cards. It validates ATM transactions and either approves or rejects customer requests, depending on the status of the customer accounts.

More-complex client/server systems might have multiple servers. A client might communicate with several servers, and servers might communicate with each other. A banking consortium consisting of multiple interconnected banks is an example of a *Multiple-Client/Multiple-Server* pattern, as shown in Figure 10.8. Continuing with the ATM example, besides several ATM clients accessing the

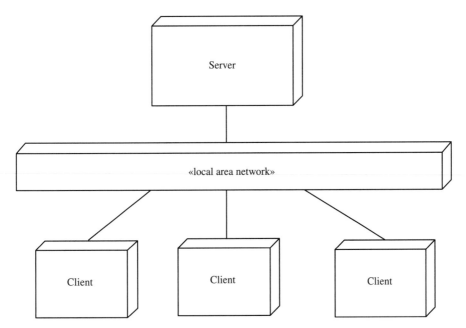

Figure 10.6   *Basic Client/Server architectural pattern: deployment diagram*

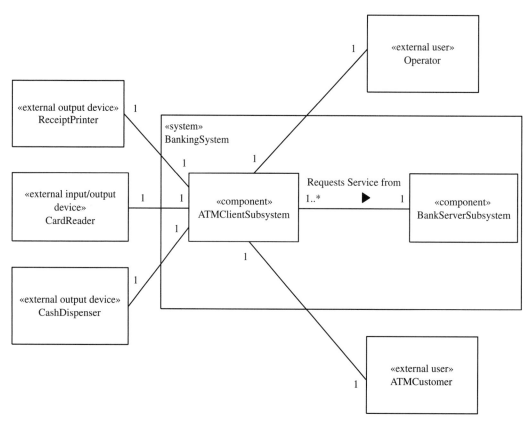

Figure 10.7 *Example of the basic Client/Server architectural pattern: banking system class diagram*

same bank server, it is possible for one ATM client to access multiple bank servers. This feature allows customers to access their own bank server from a different bank's ATM client.

Another variation on the Client/Server pattern is the *Multitier Client/Server* pattern. In a multitier pattern, each intermediate tier provides both a client and a server role. The intermediate tier is a client of its server tier and provides services for its clients. An example of a three-tier client/server pattern for the banking system is given in Figure 10.9. The Bank Server tier provides banking services to the ATM Client tier but is itself a client of the Database Server tier. Because the third tier is provided by a database management system, it is not part of the application software, so it is not explicitly depicted in the application-level class diagram shown in Figure 10.7.

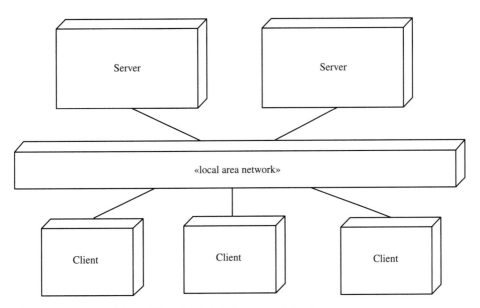

Figure 10.8   *Multiple-Client/Multiple-Server architectural pattern*

Figure 10.9   *Example of the Multitier Client/Server architectural pattern: a three-tier banking system*

Most distributed applications are based either entirely or partially on the Client/Server architectural pattern. The banking system is based entirely on the Client/Server architectural pattern (see Figure 10.7). In Chapter 15, the factory automation product line case study incorporates several instances of the Client/Server architectural pattern. Some of these are depicted in the static model for the factory automation software product line shown in Figure 10.10.

The factory automation software product line contains two instances of the basic Client/Server pattern, in which a single server—Workflow Planning Server and Alarm Handling Server, respectively—has multiple clients. Clients of Workflow Planning Server are the Workflow Engineer Interface components. Alarm Handling Server has two sets of clients: Operator

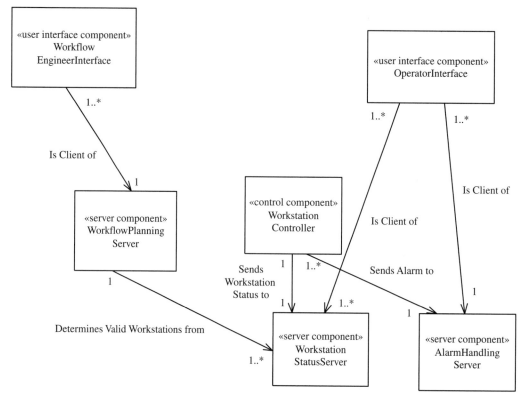

Figure 10.10   *Examples of the Client/Server architectural pattern: factory automation software product line*

`Interface` components and `Workstation Controller` components. There is one instance of the Multiple-Client/Multiple-Server pattern, in which each of the multiple instances of the distributed `Workstation Status Server` (one instance per workstation) has multiple instances of `Operator Interface` as its clients. A given `Operator Interface` client can request services from any instance of `Workstation Status Server`, and a given instance of `Workstation Status Server` can receive service requests from any `Operator Interface` client. Thus there is a many-to-many association between `Operator Interface` and `Workstation Status Server`. However, a given client `Workstation Controller` sends workstation status to only one instance of `Workstation Status Server` because there is one instance of each per workstation and hence there is a one-to-one association between them.

Software Product Line Implications of the Client/Server Pattern

Client/server patterns are widely used in software architectures for product lines. Within the Layers of Abstraction pattern (see Section 10.2.1), it is possible to use the Multiple-Client/Single-Server and the Multiple-Client/Multiple-Server patterns. Because servers do not need to know their clients but clients depend on servers, clients should be at higher layers of the architecture than servers.

Multiple servers that do not depend on each other can all be at the same layer. It is possible to have multiple independent instances of the Client/Server pattern within the Layers of Abstraction pattern. On the other hand, servers that depend on each other need to be at different layers of the architecture.

10.2.4   Broker Architectural Pattern

In a distributed component-based environment, clients and servers are designed as distributed components. More-complex client/server architectures often involve object brokers that act as intermediaries between the clients and servers. The broker frees clients from having to maintain information about where a particular service is provided and how to obtain that service. The broker also provides location transparency and platform transparency. Sophisticated brokers provide white pages (naming services) and yellow pages (trader services) so that clients can locate services more easily.

In the **Broker** pattern (which is also known as the *Object Broker* or *Object Request Broker* pattern), the **broker** acts as an intermediary between the clients and server, as depicted in the static model in Figure 10.11. Servers register their services with the broker. Clients locate services through the broker. After the broker has brokered the connection between client and server, the client can request services from the server. The communication between client and server may be direct or via the broker, as described by the Broker Forwarding and Broker Handle communication patterns (see Section 10.3.6).

Both the electronic commerce and the factory automation product lines (discussed in Chapters 14 and 15, respectively) use broker technology to enable communication between components on heterogeneous platforms, and wrappers to enable access to legacy databases.

Software Product Line Implications of the Broker Pattern

The Broker pattern is widely used in software product lines to provide greater decoupling between clients and servers, thereby permitting greater software

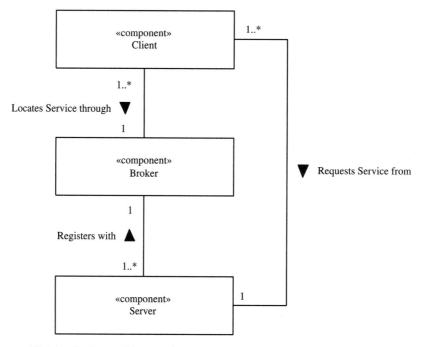

Figure 10.11 *Broker architectural pattern*

adaptability and evolution. The decoupling provided by brokers is described in greater detail in Section 10.3.6.

10.2.5   Client/Agent/Server Architectural Pattern

In another variation on the Client/Server pattern (described in Section 10.2.3), communicating software agents act as intermediaries between clients and servers. In particular, the agents negotiate with servers on behalf of their clients. The server might itself have an agent act on its behalf, in which case a client agent acts on behalf of the client and a server agent acts on behalf of the server. This situation is analogous to a house buyer using one real estate agent to search for a house and the house seller using a different real estate agent.

The **Client/Agent/Server** architectural pattern (which is also known as the *Distributed Agents* or *Multi-Agent* pattern) is depicted in Figure 10.12. In this example of the pattern, a client is assisted by one agent, so there is a one-to-one association between `Client` and `Agent`. A given agent locates services provided by several servers and negotiates with them. A server is also contacted by

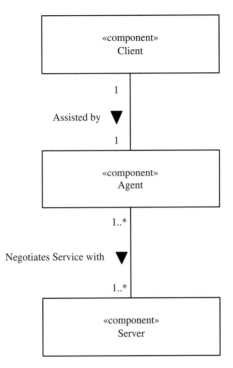

Figure 10.12   *Client/Agent/Server architectural pattern*

several agents, so there is a many-to-many association between `Agent` and `Server`. The agent-based electronic commerce product line uses this pattern with several clients, servers, client agents, and server agents, as described in Chapter 14.

10.2.6   Centralized Control Architectural Pattern

In the **Centralized Control** architectural pattern, there is one control component, which conceptually executes a statechart and provides the overall control and sequencing of the system or subsystem. The control component receives events from other components with which it interacts. These include events from various input components and user interface components that interact with the external environment, for example, through sensors that detect changes in the environment. An input event to a control component usually causes a state transition on its statechart, which results in one or more state-dependent actions. The control component uses these actions to control other components, such as output components, which output to the external environment—for example, to switch actuators on and off. Entity objects are also used to store any temporary data needed by the other objects.

Examples of this pattern can be found in the cruise control system (Gomaa 2000) and the microwave oven control product line case study (see Chapter 13). Figure 10.13 gives an example of the Centralized Control architectural pattern from the latter case study, in which the concurrent components are depicted on a generic communication diagram. The `Microwave Control` component is a centralized control component, which executes the statechart that provides the overall control and sequencing for the microwave oven. `Microwave Control` receives messages from three input components—`Door Component`, `Weight Component`, and `Keypad Component`—when they detect inputs from the external environment. `Microwave Control` actions are sent to five output components—for example, `Heating Element Component` (to switch the heating element on or off) and `Microwave Display` (to display information and prompts to the user).

10.2.7 Distributed Control Architectural Pattern

The **Distributed Control** pattern contains several control components. Each of these components controls a given part of the system by conceptually executing a statechart. Control is distributed among the various control components, with no single component in overall control. To notify each other of important events, the components communicate through peer-to-peer communication. They also interact with the external environment as in the Centralized Control pattern (see Section 10.2.6).

An example of the Distributed Control pattern can be found in the high-volume manufacturing system case study, in which the control is distributed among the various workstation controller components, as shown in Figure 10.14. There are three different types of workstation controllers. Each workstation controller executes its own statechart. The statecharts for `Receiving Workstation Controller` and `Shipping Workstation Controller` are different from the statecharts for the multiple instances of the `Line Workstation Controller` component. The workstation controller components communicate by means of messages. The application of the Distributed Control pattern to the factory automation product line is described in more detail in Chapter 15.

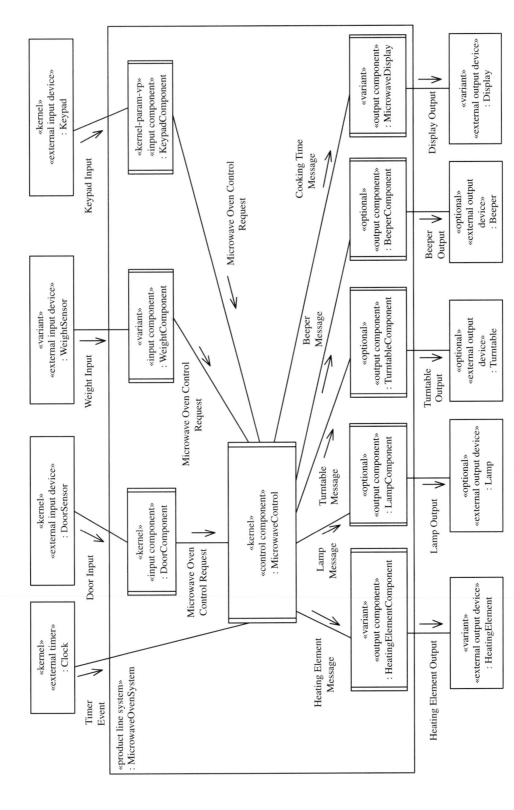

Figure 10.13 *Example of the Centralized Control architectural pattern: microwave oven control system*

249

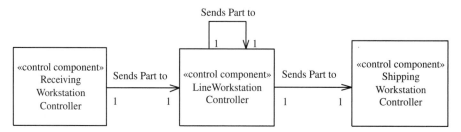

Figure 10.14 *Example of the Distributed Control architectural pattern: high-volume manufacturing system*

10.2.8   Hierarchical Control Architectural Pattern

The **Hierarchical Control** pattern (also known as the *Multilevel Control* pattern) contains several control components. Each component controls a given part of a system by conceptually executing a statechart. In addition, a coordinator component provides the overall system control by coordinating several control components. The coordinator provides high-level control by deciding the next job for each control component and communicating that information directly to the control component. The coordinator also receives status information from the control components.

One example of the Hierarchical Control pattern is the elevator control system (Gomaa 2000); another comes from the flexible manufacturing system case study that is described in Chapter 15. In the latter case study, `Part Agent`, assisted by `Scheduler`, sends operational commands to the `Flexible Workstation Controller` component, move commands to the `AGV Dispatcher` component, and store/retrieve commands to the `ASRS Handler` component, as shown in Figure 10.15.

10.2.9   Implications of Control Patterns

For an application with an important real-time or distributed control component, the Centralized Control, Distributed Control, and Hierarchical Control patterns are all patterns that could potentially be applied. In the microwave oven product line, the Centralized Control pattern is the main architectural structure pattern because the `Microwave Oven Control` component is at the heart of the application controlling input and output components.

In the factory automation product line, which is highly distributed, both the Distributed Control and the Hierarchical Control patterns are used as substructures within the Layers of Abstraction pattern. High-volume manufacturing systems

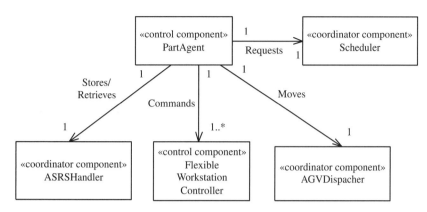

Figure 10.15 *Example of the Hierarchical Control architectural pattern: flexible manufacturing system*

use the Distributed Control pattern, in which workstation controller components are connected to each other and pass work from one control component to the next, with each control component communicating with its neighboring components. Hierarchical Control is used in both the flexible manufacturing system and the elevator control system, in which one control component provides high-level control and makes overall decisions, sending commands to subordinate components to execute the commands and provide the low-level control.

10.2.10 Communicating Components Architectural Pattern

A widely used software architectural pattern is that of a network of concurrent components with a separate thread of control for each component. The two variations of this pattern are communicating components with shared memory and communicating components without shared memory. Concurrent components that share memory must reside on the same computational node. Greater flexibility is achieved with concurrent components that have no shared memory, because components can then be allocated to different nodes in a distributed environment. Components communicate through discrete messages. If components have shared memory, they can also communicate and synchronize their operations by using monitors (Gomaa 2000).

The **Communicating Components** architectural pattern is very common in real-time and distributed applications because concurrency is a characteristic of the problem domain. An example of the distributed Communicating Components architectural pattern is depicted on a communication diagram in Figure 10.16. Concurrent components communicate with each other in many different ways.

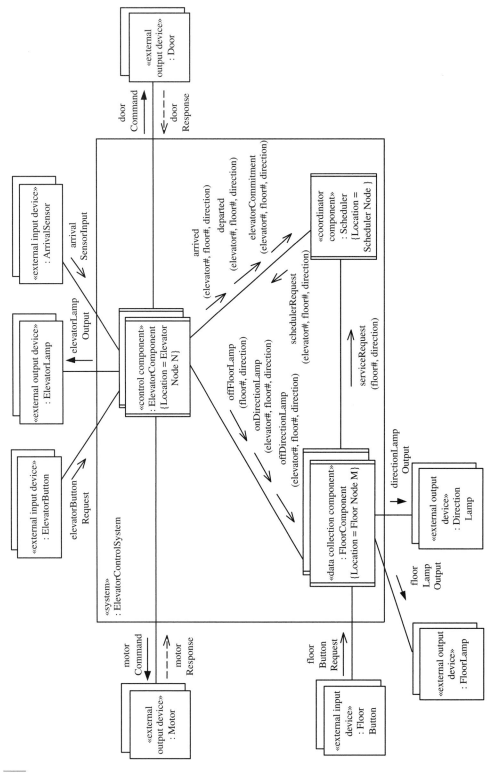

Figure 10.16 *Example of the distributed Communicating Components pattern*

To help in the process of deciding on the precise type of message communication to use among components, software architectural communication patterns are provided as described in Section 10.3.

10.3   Software Architectural Communication Patterns

This section describes the architectural communication patterns, which address the dynamic communication among distributed components of the architecture. Because distributed components reside on different nodes in a geographically distributed environment, all communication between components must be restricted to message communication. Concurrent and distributed components communicate with each other using several patterns of message communication, as described in this section. Communication patterns are frequently used protocols by which distributed components communicate with each other. Concurrent communication diagrams are the most effective way to depict patterns that address message communication between concurrent components (see Appendix A, Section A-8).

10.3.1   Asynchronous Message Communication Pattern

With the **Asynchronous** (also referred to as *Loosely Coupled*) **Message Communication** pattern, the producer component sends a message to the consumer component (Figure 10.17) and does not wait for a reply. The producer continues because it either does not need a response or has other functions to perform before receiving a response (see the discussion of bidirectional asynchronous communication in Section 10.3.2). The consumer receives the message; if the consumer is busy when the message arrives, the message is queued. Because the producer and consumer components proceed asynchronously (i.e., at different speeds), a first-in, first-out (FIFO) message queue can build up between producer and consumer. If no message is available when the consumer requests one, the consumer is suspended. The consumer is then reawakened when a

Figure 10.17 *Asynchronous Message Communication pattern*

message arrives. In distributed environments, Asynchronous Message Communication is used wherever possible for greater flexibility. This approach can be used if the sender does not need a response from the receiver.

In a distributed environment, an additional requirement is that the producer needs to receive a positive or negative acknowledgment indicating whether or not the message has arrived at its destination. This is not an indication that the message has been received by the destination component—merely that it has safely arrived at the destination node. Thus a significant additional amount of time might elapse before the message is actually received by the destination component. A timeout is associated with sending a message, so that a failure in message transmission will result in a negative acknowledgement being returned to the source component. It is up to the source component to decide how to handle this failure.

An example of the Asynchronous Message Communication pattern in a distributed environment is given in Figure 10.18 for the elevator control system, in which all communication between the components is asynchronous. `Elevator Subsystem` sends an `off Floor Lamp` message to `Floor Subsystem` to switch off the appropriate floor lamp (up or down) when an elevator arrives at the floor. `Elevator Subsystem` also sends `on Direction Lamp` and `off Direction Lamp` messages to `Floor Subsystem` to switch on and off the appropriate up or down direction lamp when the elevator arrives at and leaves the floor, respectively.

10.3.2 Bidirectional Asynchronous Message Communication Pattern

The **Bidirectional Asynchronous Message Communication** pattern is used in situations where the producer sends a message asynchronously to the consumer and does not need an immediate reply but does need a reply later, as shown in Figure 10.19. This pattern is similar but not identical to the Asynchronous Message Communication with Callback pattern (see Section 10.3.4). The Bidirectional Asynchronous Message Communication pattern is used when the producer needs to send a burst of messages before receiving the response to the first message. Producer messages are queued up at the consumer. Consumer responses are queued up at the producer, which receives them when it needs to.

An example of the Bidirectional Asynchronous Message Communication pattern in a distributed environment is given in Figure 10.20 for the elevator control system, where all communication between the components is asynchronous. The `Scheduler` component sends `scheduler Request` messages to the

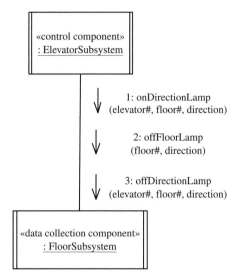

Figure 10.18 *Example of the Asynchronous Message Communication pattern: elevator control system*

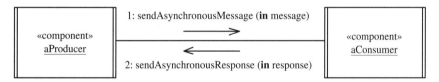

Figure 10.19 *Bidirectional Asynchronous Message Communication pattern*

`Elevator Subsystem` component, requesting it to visit specific floors. `Elevator Subsystem` sends `arrived` and `departed` messages (indicating the floor that the elevator is on and the direction it is taking) and `elevator Commitment` messages (indicating what floors it is planning to visit) to the `Scheduler` component. In this example, `Scheduler` could send several requests to a given elevator to visit various floors. The elevator gradually services these requests as it moves up or down, acknowledging the floors it is visiting.

10.3.3 Synchronous Message Communication with Reply Pattern

With the **Synchronous** (also referred to as *Tightly Coupled*) **Message Communication with Reply** pattern, the client component sends a message to the server

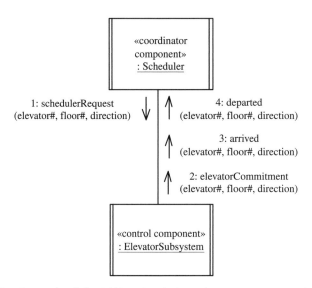

Figure 10.20 *Example of the Bidirectional Asynchronous Message Communication pattern: elevator control system*

component and then waits for a reply from the server (Figure 10.21). When the message arrives, the server accepts it, processes it, generates a reply, and then sends the reply. The client and server then both continue. The server is suspended if no message is available. For a given client/server pair, no message queue develops between the client and the server. There may be only one client and one server. More often, however, synchronous message communication involves multiple clients and one server. In distributed environments, this form of communication is typically provided by middleware technology such as the remote procedure call or remote method invocation.

In the typical client/server situation, several clients request services from a server by sending messages to it. In this pattern, a message queue can build up at the server. The client uses synchronous message communication and waits

Figure 10.21 *Synchronous Message Communication with Reply pattern*

for a response from the server. Alternatively, the client can use asynchronous message communication as described in Section 10.3.4.

Whether the client uses synchronous or asynchronous message communication with the server depends on the application and does not affect the design of the server. Indeed, some of a server's clients may communicate with it via synchronous message communication and others via asynchronous message communication. An example of Multiple-Client/Single-Server message communication using synchronous communication is shown in Figure 10.22, where the server is Bank Server, which responds to service requests from multiple clients. Bank Server has a message queue of incoming requests from the multiple clients (ATMs), together with a synchronous response. The server processes each incoming ATM Transaction message on a FIFO basis and then sends the response message to the client. Each ATM Client component sends a message to Bank Server and then waits for the response.

If the client and server are to have a dialog that involves several messages and responses, a connection can be established between them. Messages are then sent and received over the connection.

10.3.4 Asynchronous Message Communication with Callback Pattern

The **Asynchronous Message Communication with Callback** pattern is used between a client and a server when the client does not need to wait for the server response but does need the server response later (Figure 10.23). The callback is an asynchronous response to a message sent previously. This pattern allows the client to execute asynchronously but still follows the client/server paradigm in which a client sends only one message at a time to the server.

With the callback pattern, the client sends a remote reference or handle, which is then used by the server to respond to the client. A variation on the callback pattern is for the server to delegate the response to another component by forwarding to it the callback handle.

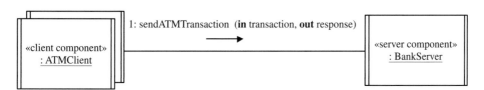

Figure 10.22 *Example of the Synchronous Message Communication with Reply pattern: ATM application*

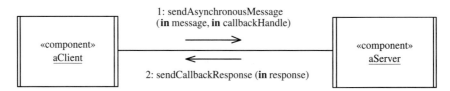

Figure 10.23   *Asynchronous Message Communication with Callback pattern*

10.3.5   Synchronous Message Communication without Reply Pattern

In the **Synchronous** (also referred to as *Tightly Coupled*) **Message Communication without Reply** pattern, the producer sends a message to the consumer and then waits for acceptance of the message by the consumer (Figure 10.24). When the message arrives, the consumer accepts it, thereby releasing the producer. The producer and the consumer then both continue. The consumer is suspended if no message is available. For a given producer/consumer pair, no message queue develops between the producer and the consumer. The best time to use this pattern is when the producer is faster than the consumer and it is necessary to slow down the producer so that it does not get ahead of the consumer.

An example of the Synchronous Message Communication without Reply pattern is shown in Figure 10.25. Sensor Statistics Display Interface is a concurrent output component that accepts a message to display from the Sensor Statistics Algorithm component. It displays the sensor statistics while the Sensor Statistics Algorithm component is computing the next set of values to display. Thus the computation is overlapped with the output.

The producer component, Sensor Statistics Algorithm, sends temperature and pressure statistics to the consumer component, Sensor Statistics Display Interface, which then displays the information. In this example, the decision is made that there is no point in having the Sensor Statistics Algorithm component compute temperature and pressure statistics if the

Figure 10.24   *Synchronous Message Communication without Reply pattern*

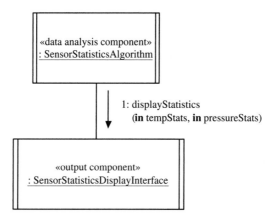

Figure 10.25 *Example of the Synchronous Message Communication without Reply pattern*

`Sensor Statistics Display Interface` component cannot keep up with displaying them. Consequently, the communication between the two components uses the Synchronous Message Communication without Reply pattern, as depicted on the concurrent communication diagram in Figure 10.25.

The `Sensor Statistics Algorithm` component computes the statistics, sends the message, and then waits for the message to be accepted by `Sensor Statistics Display Interface` before resuming execution. `Sensor Statistics Algorithm` is held up until `Sensor Statistics Display Interface` finishes displaying the previous message. As soon as `Sensor Statistics Display Interface` accepts the new message, `Sensor Statistics Algorithm` is released from its wait and computes the next set of statistics while `Sensor Statistics Display Interface` displays the previous set. This approach allows computation of the statistics (a compute-bound activity) to be overlapped with displaying of the statistics (an I/O-bound activity), while preventing an unnecessary message queue buildup of statistics at the display component. Thus the tightly coupled interface between the two components acts as a brake on the producer component.

In distributed communication, synchronous message communication without reply is usually not necessary and should be used only in situations such as those described in this section. Communication between components should be loosely coupled whenever possible; synchronous message communication should be used primarily when a response is required.

10.3.6   Broker Communication Patterns

A *broker* is an intermediary in interactions between clients and servers. Servers register the services they provide with the broker. Clients can then request these services via the broker. The broker also provides **location transparency**, meaning that if the server component is moved to a different location, clients are unaware of the move and only the broker needs to be notified.

Servers register the services they provide and the location of these services with the broker. This type of brokering service is referred to as a *name service*. Instead of a client having to know the locations of services provided by servers, the client queries the broker for services provided. This pattern of communication, in which the client knows the service required but not the location, is referred to as **white page brokering**, analogous to the white pages of the telephone directory. (Yellow page brokering will be described in Section 10.3.7.)

Broker Forwarding

There is more than one way for a broker to handle a request. With the **Broker Forwarding** pattern, a client sends a message identifying the service required—for example, to withdraw cash (service) from a given bank (server). The broker receives the client request, determines the location of the server (the node the server resides on), and forwards the message to the server at the specific location. The message arrives at the server, and the requested service is invoked. The broker receives the server response and forwards it back to the client. The pattern is depicted in Figure 10.26 and consists of the following message sequence:

1: The client sends a request to the broker.

2: The broker looks up the location of the server and forwards the request to the appropriate server.

3: The server services the request and sends the reply to the broker.

4: The broker forwards the reply to the client.

The Broker Forwarding pattern provides an intermediary for every message sent between clients and servers. It thus provides a high level of security because each message can be vetted. However, this security comes at the cost of performance compared with the Client/Server pattern (see Section 10.2.3) because the message traffic is doubled.

Broker Handle

The **Broker Handle** pattern keeps the benefit of location transparency while adding the advantage of reducing message traffic. It is particularly useful when

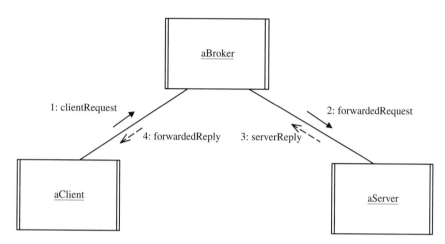

Figure 10.26   *Broker Forwarding (white pages) pattern*

the client and server are likely to have a dialog and exchange several messages. The pattern is depicted in Figure 10.27 and consists of the following message sequence:

B1: The client sends a request to the broker.

B2: The broker looks up the location of the server and returns a service handle to the client.

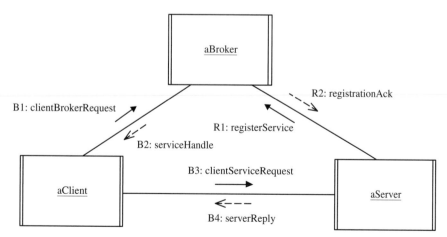

Figure 10.27   *Broker Handle (white pages) pattern*

B3: The client uses the service handle to request the service from the appropriate server.

B4: The server services the request and sends the reply directly to the client.

This approach is more efficient than Broker Forwarding if the client and server are likely to have a dialog that results in the exchange of several messages. Most commercial object brokers use a Broker Handle design. With this approach, it is the responsibility of the client to discard the handle after the dialog is over. Using an old handle is liable to fail because the server might have moved in the interval. If the server does move, it needs to inform the broker so that the broker can update the name table.

In both broker patterns—Broker Forwarding and Broker Handle—the server needs to register its services with the broker, providing the service name, a description of the service, and the location at which the service is provided. The registration is carried out the first time the server joins the brokering exchange (analogous to the stock exchange). On subsequent occasions, if the server relocates, it needs to inform the broker of its new location. The server registration and reregistration pattern is illustrated in Figure 10.27, which also depicts the server registering a service with the broker in the following sequence:

R1: The server sends a `register Service` request to the broker.

R2: The broker registers the service in the name table and sends a registration acknowledgment to the server.

10.3.7 Discovery Pattern

The brokered patterns of communication described in Section 10.3.6, in which the client knows the service required but not the location, are referred to as *white page brokering*. A different brokering pattern is **yellow page brokering**, analogous to the yellow pages of the telephone directory, in which the client knows the type of service required but not the specific service. This pattern, which is shown in Figure 10.28, is also known as the **Discovery** pattern because it allows the client to discover new services. The client sends a query request to the broker, requesting all services of a given type. The broker responds with a list of all services that match the client's request. The client, typically after consultation with the user, selects a specific service. The broker returns the service handle, which the client uses for communicating directly with the service provider. The pattern interactions, in which a yellow pages request is followed by a white pages request, are described in more detail as follows:

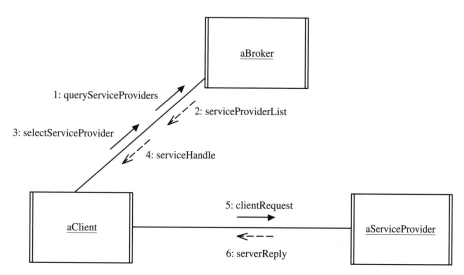

Figure 10.28   *Discovery (yellow pages) pattern*

1: The client sends a "yellow pages" request to the broker requesting information about all service providers.

2: The broker looks up this information and returns a list of all service providers registered with it.

3: The client selects one of the service providers and sends a "white pages" request to the broker.

4: The broker looks up the location of the service provider and returns a service handle to the client.

5: The client uses the service handle to request the service from the appropriate service provider.

6: The service provider services the request and sends the response directly to the client.

10.3.8   Group Message Communication Patterns

The message communication patterns described so far have involved one source and one destination component. A desirable property in some distributed applications is group communication. This is a form of one-to-many message communication in which a sender sends one message to many recipients. Two kinds of group message communication (sometimes referred to as *groupcast communication*) supported in distributed applications are broadcast and multicast communication.

With the **Broadcast** (or *Broadcast Communication*) pattern, an unsolicited message is sent to all recipients, perhaps informing them of a pending shutdown. Each recipient must then decide whether it wishes to process the message or discard it. An example of the Broadcast pattern is given in Figure 10.29. Alarm Handling Server sends alarm Broadcast messages to all instances of the Operator Interface component. Each recipient must decide whether it wishes to take action in response to the alarm or to ignore the message. The pattern interactions are described in more detail as follows:

B1: Event Monitor sends an alarm message to Alarm Handling Server.

B2a, B2b, B2c: Alarm Handling Server broadcasts the alarm as an alarm Broadcast message to all the Operator Interface components. Each recipient decides whether to take action or discard the message.

Multicast communication provides a more selective form of group communication, in which the same message is sent to all members of a group. The

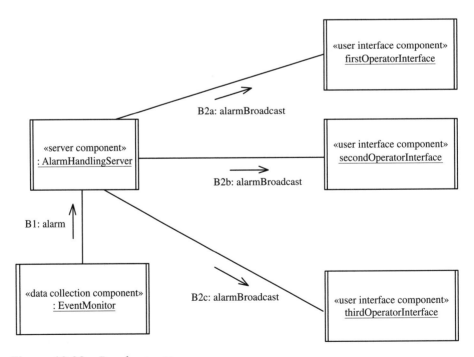

Figure 10.29   *Broadcast pattern*

Subscription/Notification pattern uses a form of multicast communication in which components subscribe to a group and receive messages destined for all members of the group. A component can subscribe to (request to join) or unsubscribe from (leave) a group and can be a member of more than one group. A sender, also referred to as a *publisher*, sends a message to the group without having to know who all the individual members are. The message is then sent to all members of the group. Sending the same message to all members of a group is referred to as *multicast communication*. A message sent to a subscriber is also referred to as an *event notification*. While on a subscription list, a member can receive several event notification messages. The Subscription/Notification pattern is popular on the Internet.

An example of the Subscription/Notification pattern is shown in Figure 10.30. First, three instances of the `Operator Interface` component send a `subscribe` message to `Alarm Handling Server` to receive alarms of a certain type. Every time the `Alarm Handling Server` component receives a new `alarm` message of this type, it multicasts the `alarm Notification` message to all subscriber `Operator Interface` components. The pattern interactions are described in more detail as follows:

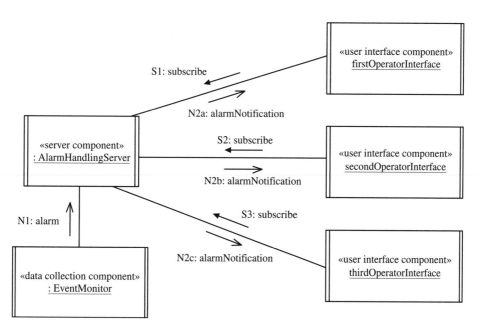

Figure 10.30   *Example of the Subscription/Notification pattern*

S1, S2, S3: `Operator Interface` components subscribe to receive alarm notifications.

N1: `Event Monitor` sends an `alarm` message to `Alarm Handling Server`.

N2a, N2b, N2c: `Alarm Handling Server` looks up the list of subscribers who have requested to be notified of alarms of this type. The server multicasts the `alarm Notification` message to the appropriate subscriber `Operator Interface` components. Each recipient takes appropriate action in response to the alarm notification.

A variation on the Subscription/Notification pattern is to have only one subscriber. This arrangement is useful in peer-to-peer situations where the producer does not know who the consumer is and the consumer might be optional. The consumer can subscribe to the producer, sending it a handle, which the producer then uses for sending messages to the consumer. This is useful for reversing a dependency because, by virtue of the subscription, the consumer is dependent on the producer rather than vice versa.

10.3.9 Negotiated Communication Patterns

In multi-agent systems, it is necessary to allow software agents to negotiate with each other so that they can cooperatively make decisions. In the **Negotiation** pattern (also known as the *Agent-Based Negotiation* or *Multi-Agent Negotiation* pattern), a client agent acts on behalf of the user and makes a proposal to a server agent. The server agent attempts to satisfy the client's proposal, which might involve communication with other servers. Having determined the available options, the server agent then offers the client agent one or more options that come closest to matching the original client agent proposal. The client agent may then request one of the options, propose further options, or reject the offer. If the server agent can satisfy the client agent request, it accepts the request; otherwise, it rejects the request.

To allow software agents to negotiate with each other, the following communication services are provided (Pitt et al. 1996):

The client agent, who acts on behalf of the client, may do any of the following:

- **Propose a service**. The client agent proposes a service to the server agent. This proposed service is *negotiable*, meaning that the client agent is willing to consider counteroffers.

- **Request a service**. The client agent requests a service from the server agent. This requested service is *nonnegotiable*, meaning that the client agent is not willing to consider counteroffers.

- **Reject a server offer.** The client agent rejects an offer made by the server agent.

The server agent, who acts on behalf of the server, may do any of the following:

- **Offer a service.** In response to a client proposal, a server agent offers a counterproposal.

- **Reject a client request/proposal.** The server agent rejects the client agent's proposed or requested service.

- **Accept a client request/proposal.** The server agent accepts the client agent's proposed or requested service.

Consider the following detailed example involving negotiation among agents. The example addresses intelligent agent-based negotiation to find the best telecommunication service from among the services provided by various telecommunication service providers. In this example, the server agent is a videoconference agent who negotiates with various telecommunication service providers that provide a videoconference service.

The videoconference agent communicates with various service provider agents in order to find the most appropriate videoconference service. Assume that the client would like to set up a videoconference for a specific date at a specific time for a price of less than $700. The Negotiation pattern for this example is depicted on the communication diagram in Figure 10.31 and described in detail as follows:

1: A client agent sends a proposal to the videoconference agent for a videoconference at the specified date, time, and price.

2a, 2b, 2c: The videoconference agent sends the client agent's proposal to three service provider agents that provide a videoconferencing service: `AA&T Service Provider Agent`, `NCI Service Provider Agent`, and `RUN Service Provider Agent`.

2a.1, 2b.1, 2c.1: The videoconference agent receives offers from all three service provider agents with the times and prices of the available slots for a videoconference.

3: The videoconference agent sends to the client agent an `offer` message consisting of the available videoconference slots at the proposed price. If only more-expensive videoconference slots are available, the videoconference agent offers the cheapest it can find based on a metric combining low cost and quality of service. In this case, it determines that the two best offers for the proposed dates are from AA&T for $750 and NCI for $775. There are

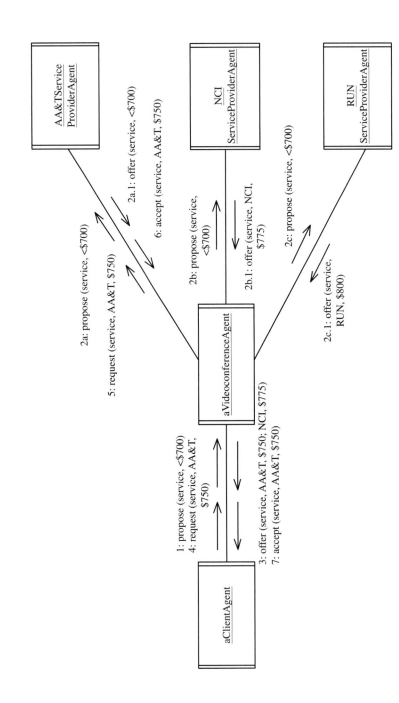

Figure 10.31 *Example of the Negotiation pattern*

no videoconference slots below $700, so it offers the two available video-conference slots that come closest to the proposed price.

4: The client agent displays the choice to the user, who selects the AA&T offer. The client agent may either request a service (one of the choices offered by the videoconference agent) or reject the videoconference agent's offer if the user does not like any of the options and propose a service on a different date. In this example, the client agent requests the AA&T video-conference slot.

5: The videoconference agent sends a reservation request to `AA&T Service Provider Agent`.

6: Assuming that the videoconference slot is still available, `AA&T Service Provider Agent` accepts the reservation request.

7: The videoconference agent responds to the client agent's `request` message with an `accept` message. If the videoconference slot were no longer available, the videoconference agent would send a `reject` message.

10.3.10 Product Line Implications of Communication Patterns

Whereas client/server communication often requires synchronous communication, peer-to-peer communication can take advantage of asynchronous communication. In software product lines, it is often desirable to decouple components. The Broker Forwarding, Broker Handle, Discovery, and Subscription/Notification patterns encourage such decoupling. With the broker patterns, servers register with brokers, and clients can then discover new servers. Thus a product line can evolve with the addition of new clients and servers. A new version of a server can replace an older version and register itself with the broker. Clients communicating via the broker would automatically be connected to the new version of the server. The Subscription/Notification pattern also decouples the original sender of the message from the recipients of the message.

10.4 Software Architectural Transaction Patterns

A **transaction** is a request from a client to a server that consists of two or more operations that perform a single logical function, and that must be completed in its entirety or not at all. Transactions are generated at the client and sent to the server for processing. For transactions that need to be atomic (i.e., indivisible), services are needed to begin the transaction, commit the transaction, or abort the transaction. Transactions are typically used for updates to a distributed database that need to be atomic—for example, transferring funds from an account at one bank to an account at a different bank. With this approach, updates to the distributed database are coordinated such that they are either all performed (commit) or all rolled back (abort).

10.4.1 Two-Phase Commit Protocol Pattern

The **Two-Phase Commit Protocol** pattern addresses the problem of managing atomic transactions in distributed systems. Consider two examples of banking transactions:

1. **Withdrawal transaction**. A withdrawal transaction can be handled in one operation. A semaphore is needed for synchronization to ensure that access to the customer account record is mutually exclusive. The transaction processor locks the account record for this customer, performs the update, and then unlocks the record.

2. **Transfer transaction**. Consider a transfer transaction between two accounts—for example, from a savings account to a checking account—in which the accounts are maintained at two separate banks (servers). In this case, it is necessary to debit the savings account and credit the checking account. Therefore, the transfer transaction consists of two operations that must be atomic—a debit operation and a credit operation—and the transfer transaction must be either committed or aborted:

    • **Committed**. Both credit and debit operations occur.

    • **Aborted**. Neither the credit nor the debit operation occurs.

    One way to achieve this result is to use the Two-Phase Commit Protocol, which synchronizes updates on different nodes in distributed applications. The result of the Two-Phase Commit Protocol is that either the transaction is committed (in which case all updates succeed) or the transaction is aborted (in which case all updates fail).

    One server is designated `Commit Server`. There is one participant server for each node. There are two participants in the bank transfer transaction: `first Bank Server`, which maintains the account *from* which money is being transferred (`from Account`); and `second Bank Server`, which maintains the account *to* which money is being transferred (`to Account`). In the first phase of the Two-Phase Commit Protocol (shown in Figure 10.32), `Commit Server` sends a `prepare To Commit` message (1a, 1b) to each participant server. Each partici-

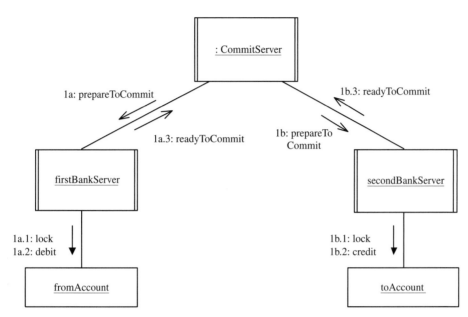

Figure 10.32 *Example of the first phase of the Two-Phase Commit Protocol: bank transfer*

pant server locks the record (1a.1, 1b.1), performs the update (1a.2, 1b.2), and then sends a `ready To Commit` message (1a.3, 1b.3) to `Commit Server`. If a participant server is unable to perform the update, it sends a `refuse To Commit` message. `Commit Server` waits to receive responses from all participants.

When all participant servers have responded, `Commit Server` proceeds to the second phase of the Two-Phase Commit Protocol (shown in Figure 10.33). If all participants have sent `ready To Commit` messages, `Commit Server` sends the `commit` message (2a, 2b) to each participant server. Each participant server makes the update permanent (2a.1, 2b.1), unlocks the record (2a.2, 2b.2), and sends a `commit Completed` message (2a.3, 2b.3) to `Commit Server`. `Commit Server` waits for all `commit Completed` messages.

If a participant server responds to the `prepare To Commit` message with a `ready To Commit` message, it is committed to completing the transaction. The participant server must then complete the transaction even if a delay occurs (e.g., even if it goes down after it has sent the `ready To Commit` message). If, on the other hand, any participant server responds to the `prepare To Commit` message with a `refuse To Commit` message, the `Commit Server` sends an `abort` message to all participants. The participants then roll back the update.

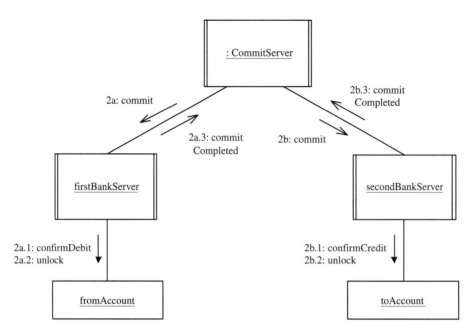

Figure 10.33   *Example of the second phase of the Two-Phase Commit Protocol: bank transfer*

10.4.2   Compound Transaction Pattern

The previous bank transfer transaction is an example of a flat transaction, which has an "all-or-nothing" characteristic. A compound transaction, in contrast, might need only a partial rollback. The **Compound Transaction** pattern can be used when the client's transaction requirement can be broken down into smaller flat atomic transactions, in which each atomic transaction can be performed separately and rolled back separately. For example, if a travel agent makes an airplane reservation, followed by a hotel reservation and a rental car reservation, it is more flexible to treat this reservation as consisting of three flat transactions. Treating the transaction as a compound transaction allows part of a reservation to be changed or canceled without the other parts of the reservation being affected.

The example of the travel agent, which is depicted in Figure 10.34, illustrates the Compound Transaction pattern. The travel agent plans a trip for a client consisting of separate reservations for an airline (1, 2), a hotel (3, 4), and a rental car (5, 6). If the three parts of the trip are treated as separate flat transactions, each transaction can be handled independently. Thus the hotel reservation

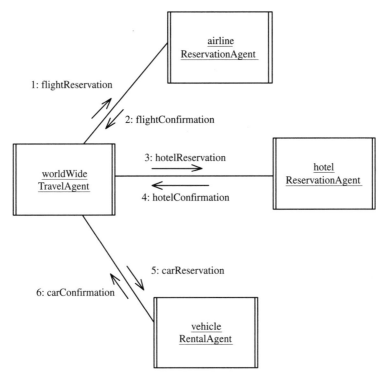

Figure 10.34 *Example of the Compound Transaction pattern*

could be changed from one hotel to another independently of the airline and car rental reservations. In certain cases, of course—for example, if the trip is postponed or canceled—all three reservations have to be changed.

10.4.3 Long-Living Transaction Pattern

A **long-living transaction** is a transaction that has a human in the loop and that could take a long and possibly indefinite time to execute, because individual human behavior is unpredictable. With transactions involving human interaction, it is undesirable to keep records locked while the human is considering various options. For example, in an airline reservation using a flat transaction, the record would be locked for the duration of the transaction. With human involvement in the transaction, the record could be locked for several minutes. In this case, it is better to use the **Long-Living Transaction** pattern, which splits a long-living transaction into two or more separate transactions (usually two) so that human decision making takes place between the successive pairs (such as first and second) of transactions.

For the airline reservation example, first a `query` transaction displays the available seats. The `query` transaction is followed by a `reserve` transaction. With this approach, it is necessary to recheck seat availability before the reservation is updated. A seat available at query time might no longer be available at reservation time because several agents might be querying the same flight at the same time. If only one seat is available, the first agent will get the seat but not the others. Note that this problem still applies even if the airline allows seat overbooking, although the upper limit would then be the number of actual seats on the aircraft plus the number of seats allowed to be overbooked on the flight.

This approach is illustrated in the travel agent example depicted in Figure 10.35. The travel agent first queries the airline server agents (1a, 1b, 1c) to determine available flights. The three airline server agents all respond positively with seat availability (1a.1, 1b.1, 1c.1). After considering the options and consulting the client, the travel agent makes a `reserve` request (2) to the Unified Airlines reservation agent. Because no lock was placed on the record, however,

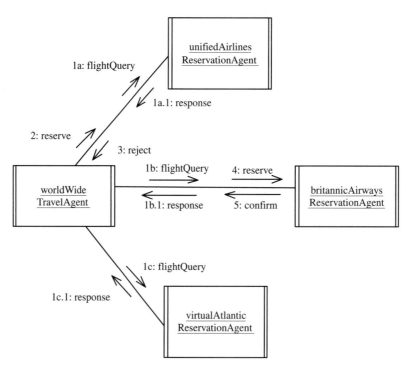

Figure 10.35 *Example of the Long-Living Transaction pattern*

the reservation is no longer available, so the reservation agent responds with a `reject` response (3). The reservation agent then reserves a flight with the second choice: Britannic Airways (4). This time the reservation agent responds with a confirmation that the reservation was accepted (5).

10.5   Documenting Software Architectural Patterns

Whatever the category of pattern, it is very useful to have a standard way of describing and documenting a pattern so that it can be easily referenced, compared with other patterns, and reused. Three important aspects of a pattern that need to be captured (Buschmann et al. 1996) are the context, problem, and solution. The *context* is the situation that gives rise to a problem. The *problem* refers to a recurring problem that arises in this context. The *solution* is a proven resolution to the problem. A template for describing a pattern usually also addresses its strengths, weaknesses, and related patterns. A typical template looks like this:

- **Pattern name**.
- **Aliases**. Other names by which this pattern is known.
- **Context**. The situation that gives rise to this problem.
- **Problem**. Brief description of the problem.
- **Summary of solution**. Brief description of the solution.
- **Strengths of solution**.
- **Weaknesses of solution**.
- **Applicability**. When you can use the pattern.
- **Related patterns**.
- **Reference**. Where you can find more information about the pattern.

The patterns described in this chapter are documented with this standard template in Appendix B.

10.6   Applying Software Architectural Patterns

This section describes how to develop a software architecture starting from software architectural patterns. A very important decision is to determine which architectural patterns—in particular, which structure and communication patterns—are required. Architectural structure patterns can initially be identified during dynamic modeling (see Chapter 7) because patterns can be recognized during development of the communication diagrams. For example, Client/Server and any of the control patterns can first be used during dynamic modeling. Although architectural structure patterns can be identified during dynamic modeling, the real decisions are made during software architectural design. It is necessary to decide the architectural structure patterns first and then the architectural communication patterns.

The different architectural structure and communication patterns described in this chapter can be used together. For example, a Layers of Abstraction architecture may incorporate the Kernel and Client/Server patterns. The factory automation product line incorporates various control patterns and client/server patterns within a layered pattern, as shown in Figure 10.36.

For example, the high-volume manufacturing system, one of the members of this product line, incorporates both the Distributed Control pattern and the Client/Server pattern within the Layers of Abstraction architectural pattern. The control components are all at one layer, and the client components are always at higher layers than the server components because they have to use the services provided by the servers, as shown in Figure 10.36. The `Receiving Workstation Controller`, `Line Workstation Controller`, and `Shipping Workstation Controller` components participate in the Distributed Control pattern, as described in Section 10.2.7. All workstation controller components also participate in a Multiple-Client/Multiple-Server pattern with both `Alarm Handling Server` and `Workstation Status Server`, as described in Section 10.2.3. `Line Workstation Controller` also participates in a Multiple-Client/Single-Server pattern with `Workflow Planning Server`. `Operator Interface` participates in a Multiple-Client/Single-Server pattern with `Alarm Handling Server` and a Multiple-Client/Multiple-Server pattern with `Workstation Status Server`.

The factory automation product line also incorporates several architectural communication patterns, including Synchronous Message Communication with/without Reply, Asynchronous Message Communication, and Subscription/Notification. An example is shown in Figure 10.37, which is a concurrent communication diagram for a factory monitoring system, one of the members of this product line. `Monitoring Workstation Controller` uses the Asynchronous Message Communication pattern for communicating with `Alarm Handling Server` and `Workstation Status Server`. The `Operator Interface` component uses both the Synchronous Message Communication with Reply pattern and the Subscription/Notification pattern in its communication with `Alarm Handling Server` and `Workstation Status Server`.

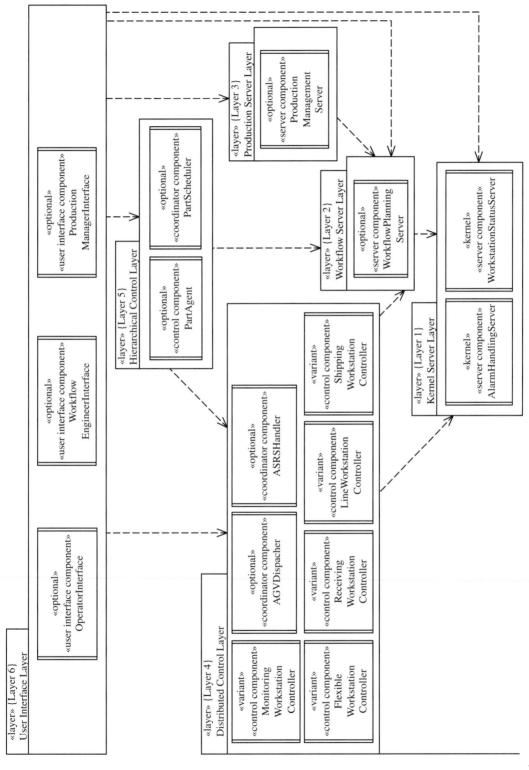

Figure 10.36 *Layered architectural pattern for the factory automation product line. (Note: Layers are compressed due to page size.)*

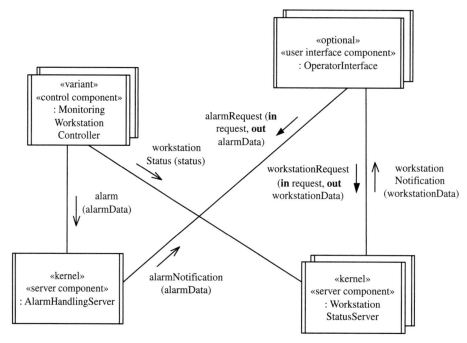

Figure 10.37 *Architectural communication patterns in a factory monitoring system*

10.7 Summary

This chapter described several software architectural patterns. Architectural structure patterns are used to address the structure of a software architecture. Architectural communication patterns address how distributed components of the software architecture communicate with each other.

This chapter also described how to document software architectural patterns using a standard template. The software architectural patterns described in this chapter are documented with the standard template in Appendix B. Finally, the discussion covered how a software architecture can be designed, starting from software architectural patterns. Chapter 11 will discuss several important topics in designing component-based software architectures. The case studies in Chapters 13 through 15 will give examples of applying the software architectural structure and communication patterns.

c h a p t e r

Software Product Line Architectural Design: Component-Based Design

In the component-based distributed design phase, the component-based software architecture for the product line is developed. The software product line is structured into components, and the interfaces between the components are defined. The architecture of a product line contains kernel, optional, and variant components. To assist with this process, guidelines are provided for determining the components. Components are designed to be configurable so that each component instance can be assigned to a node in a geographically distributed environment.

In designing the overall software architecture, it helps to consider applying the software architectural patterns described in Chapter 10, both architectural structure patterns and architectural communication patterns. Architectural structure patterns are applied to design of the overall structure of the software architecture, which addresses how the product line is structured into components. Architectural communication patterns address the ways in which components communicate with each other. Each component is designed such that its interface is explicitly defined in terms of the operations it provides as well as the operations it uses. Communication between distributed components can be synchronous or asynchronous.

Section 11.1 describes issues in software architecture. Section 11.2 provides an overview of configurable architectures and software components. Section 11.3 outlines the steps in designing distributed applications. Section 11.4 outlines the overall design of the software architecture and describes the design decisions that need to be made in the transition from analysis modeling to design modeling. Section 11.5 gives an overview of the design of the component-based software architecture. Section 11.6 addresses the separation of concerns in component design. Section 11.7 discusses and compares aggregate and composite subsystems. Section 11.8 describes criteria for structuring components. Section 11.9 describes the design of server components. Section 11.10 describes issues in the distribution of data. Section 11.11 describes the design of component interfaces, including provided and required interfaces, ports, and connectors that interconnect components. Section 11.12 describes considerations and tradeoffs in component design.

11.1 Software Architecture Issues

A system is structured into subsystems, which contain objects that are functionally dependent on each other. A subsystem should be relatively independent of other subsystems and should therefore have low coupling with other subsystems. On the other hand, the coupling between the components of the system should be high. A subsystem can be considered a composite or aggregate object that contains the simple objects that compose that subsystem. There can be many subsystems of the same type.

In analyzing the problem domain and structuring a system into subsystems, the emphasis is on separation of concerns (as discussed in Section 11.6). Each subsystem performs a major function, which is relatively independent of the functionality provided by other subsystems. A subsystem can be structured further into smaller subsystems consisting of a subset of the functionality provided by the parent subsystem. After the interface between subsystems has been defined, subsystem design can proceed independently.

A subsystem provides a larger-grained information hiding solution than an object. To structure the system into subsystems, start with the use cases. The object interaction model for a use case forms the basis of a subsystem because the objects in it are all related. Objects in the same use case have higher coupling because they communicate with each other and have lower (or no) coupling with objects in other use cases. An object that participates in more than one use case needs to be allocated to a single subsystem—usually the subsystem with which it is most highly coupled. In some cases, a subsystem might incorporate the objects from more than one use case—most probably when the use cases share common objects because they are functionally related.

11.2   Configurable Architectures and Software Components

An important goal of software architecture for a distributed application is to provide a concurrent message-based design that is highly configurable. In other words, the objective is that the same software product line architecture should be capable of being mapped to many different system configurations. Thus a given product line application could be configured to have each component-based subsystem allocated to its own separate physical node or, alternatively, to have all or some of its subsystems allocated to the same physical node. To achieve this flexibility, it is necessary to design the product line architecture in such a way that the decision about how subsystems will be mapped to physical nodes is not made at design time but is made later, at system deployment time.

A component-based development approach, in which each subsystem is designed as a distributed self-contained component, helps achieve the goal of a distributed, highly configurable, message-based design. A **distributed component** is a concurrent object with a well-defined interface, which is a logical unit of distribution and deployment. A component is usually a composite object composed of other objects. A component is self-contained and thus can be compiled separately, stored in a library, and then subsequently instantiated and linked into an application. A well-designed component is capable of being reused in applications other than the one for which it was originally developed. A component can be either a composite component or a simple component. A **composite component** is composed of other part components. A **simple component** has no part components within it.

Because components can be allocated to different nodes in a geographically distributed environment, all communication between components must be restricted to message communication. Thus a source component on one node sends a message over the network to a destination component on a different node.

11.3   Steps in Designing Distributed Applications

A **distributed application** consists of distributed components that can be configured to execute on distributed physical nodes. The three main steps in designing a distributed application are

1. **Design software architecture**. Structure the distributed application into constituent components that potentially could execute on separate nodes in a distributed environment. Because components can reside on separate nodes, all communication between components must be restricted to message communication. The interfaces between components are defined. The component structuring criteria, as described in Section 11.8, are used to determine the components. To design a configurable distributed application, it is necessary to ensure that the components are designed as configurable components that can be effectively mapped to physical nodes.

2. **Design constituent components**. Structure components into concurrent objects and passive information hiding objects. Because, by definition, a component can execute on only one node, each component can be designed by means of a design method for nondistributed concurrent systems; for example, the COMET method can be used for subsystem design (Gomaa 2000).

3. **Deploy the application**. After a distributed application has been designed, instances of it can be defined and deployed. During this stage the component instances of the application (a member of the product line) are defined, interconnected, and mapped onto a hardware configuration consisting of distributed physical nodes, as described in Chapter 12.

11.4   Design of Software Architecture

To design the software architecture, it is necessary to start with the product line analysis model. Several decisions need to be made in the transition from the product line analysis model to the product line design model:

*   Because the objective is to develop a component-based software architecture, the structure of the components needs to be determined. Component design is described in Sections 11.5 through 11.12.

*   The precise type of message communication among the components needs to be determined, as described in Section 11.4.1. The software architectural communication patterns described in Chapter 10 are applied here.

*   The use case–based interaction models must be integrated into a component-based software architecture, as described in Section 11.4.2.

11.4.1   Decisions about Message Communication between Components

In the transition from the product line analysis model to the product line design model, one of the most important decisions relates to what type of message communication is needed between the components. A second related decision is to determine more precisely the name and parameters of each message. In the analysis model, no decisions are made about the type of message communication. In addition, the emphasis is on the information passed between objects, rather than on precise message names and parameters. In design modeling, after the component structure is determined (as described in Section 11.8), a decision has to be made about the precise semantics of message communication, such as whether message communication will be synchronous or asynchronous.

Message communication between two components can be unidirectional or bidirectional. Figure 11.1a gives an analysis model example of unidirectional message communication between a producer and a consumer, as well as an example of bidirectional message communication between a client and a server. All messages in the analysis model are depicted with one notation (the stick arrowhead) because no decision has yet been made about the type of message communication. This decision is made during design, so the designer now needs to decide what type of message communication is required in both of these examples. (In UML 2.0, the stick arrowhead means asynchronous communication. For an overview of the UML notation for message communication, see Appendix A, Section A.8.1.)

Figure 11.1b shows the result of two design decisions. First, the four analysis model objects in Figure 11.1a are designed as concurrent components in Figure 11.1b. Second, the design decision is made about the type of message communication between the components. Figure 11.1b depicts the decision to use asynchronous message communication between the producer and consumer, and synchronous message communication between the client and server. In addition, the precise name and parameters of each message are determined. Thus the Asynchronous Message Communication pattern is applied to the unidirectional message between the producer and consumer; the asynchronous message has the name `send Asynchronous Message` and content called `message`. The Synchronous Message Communication with Reply pattern is applied to the message and response between the client and server; the synchronous message has the name `send Synchronous Message With Reply`, with the input content called `message` and the server's reply called `response`.

(*a*) Analysis model: before decisions about concurrency and message communication

(1) Unidirectional message communication between producer and consumer

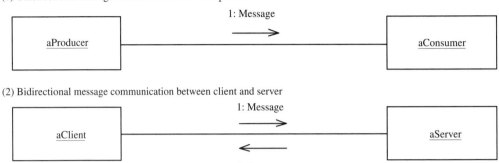

(*b*) Design model: after decisions about concurrency and message communication

(3) Asynchronous message communication between concurrent producer and consumer

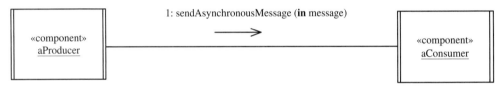

(4) Synchronous message communication between concurrent client and server

Figure 11.1 *Transition from analysis to design: decisions about concurrency and message communication*

11.4.2   Decisions about Integrating Communication Models

The integration of use case–based communication diagrams to form feature-based communication diagrams was described in Chapter 9. The same approach can be used to integrate feature-based communication diagrams to create system communication diagrams, which depict all the objects in the system and the message communication between them. It is often necessary to introduce high-level communication diagrams (e.g., system communication diagrams to depict high-level communication between subsystems) and then lower-level communication diagrams for each subsystem.

The example in Figure 11.2 illustrates the integration of communication diagrams to form a system communication diagram from the factory automation product line case study. Two communication diagrams from the analysis model (Figure 11.2*a*), which realize use cases for `View Alarms` and `Generate Alarm and Notify`, are integrated during design modeling (Figure 11.2*b*). Two other communication diagrams, which are not shown but depict similar interactions with a `Workstation Status Server` object, are also integrated into the design model for the factory monitoring system. The decisions to be made are

- How to integrate the various analysis model communication diagrams into one design model communication diagram. Two of the objects—`Operator Interface` and `Alarm Handling Server`—participate in different scenarios in the analysis model, and therefore appear on both communication diagrams in Figure 11.2*a*. The integrated communication diagram in Figure 11.2*b* shows the four components, which are determined from the analysis model communication diagrams.

- Whether the objects from the analysis model should be designed as distributed (and hence concurrent) components. Applying the component structuring criteria described in Section 11.8 leads to a decision to design the four objects from the analysis model (`Operator Interface`, `Monitoring Workstation Controller`, `Alarm Handling Server`, and `Workstation Status Server` in Figure 11.2*a*) as distributed components (Figure 11.2*b*).

- What types of message communication are to be used between the components. The software architectural patterns from Chapter 10 are applied to help with these decisions. The patterns applied in Figure 11.2*b* are Asynchronous Message Communication (e.g., message M2), Synchronous Message Communication with Reply (e.g., synchronous message S1.1 depicts both the message and the response), and Subscription/Notification (e.g., subscription in S1.1 and notification in M3).

11.5   Design of Component-Based Software Architecture

To successfully manage the inherent complexity of large-scale distributed applications, it is necessary to provide an approach for structuring the application into components in which each component can potentially execute on its own node. Because they communicate with each other by means of messages, components can be mapped to different nodes. After this design is performed and the interfaces

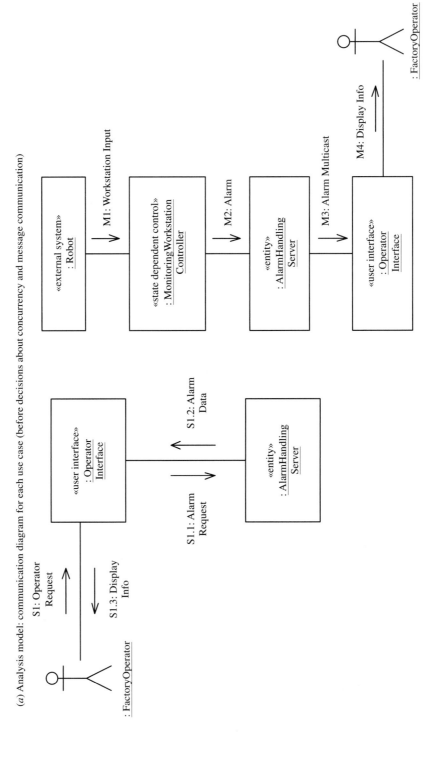

(a) Analysis model: communication diagram for each use case (before decisions about concurrency and message communication)

(b) Design model: integrated communication diagram for entire system (after decisions about concurrency and message communication)

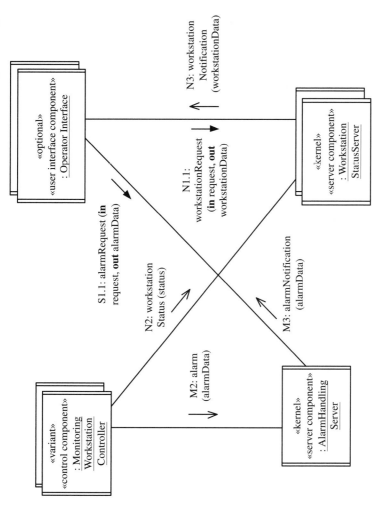

Figure 11.2 *Dynamic modeling: transition from analysis model to design model*

between the components are carefully defined, each component can be designed independently.

11.5.1 Designing Distributed Components

Some distributed components can be determined relatively easily because of geographical distribution or server responsibility. To give a simple example, if one object is located at a geographically remote location from another object, the two objects should be in different components. One of the most common forms of geographical distribution involves clients and servers, which are always allocated to different components: a client component and a server component. Thus the banking system illustrated in Figure 11.3 has a client component called ATM Client, which is located at each ATM machine, and a central server component called Bank Server. This is an example of geographical component structuring, in which the geographical distribution of the system is given in the problem description. Geographical distribution is a very strong reason for component structuring.

It is also possible for peer components (i.e., those that have a peer-to-peer relationship and not a client/server relationship) to be geographically distributed. For example, Elevator Component and Floor Component in Figure 11.4 are peer components that are geographically distributed.

An example of asynchronous message communication in a distributed environment is given in Figure 11.4, where all communication between the components is asynchronous. The Elevator Component subsystem sends arrived and departed messages (indicating the floor that the elevator is on and the direction it is taking) and elevator Commitment messages (indicating what floors it is planning to visit) to the Scheduler component. Elevator Component also sends lamp command messages to the Floor Component subsystem to switch on and off the floor and direction lamps. Floor Component sends service Request messages (requests for an elevator to come to a specific floor) to Scheduler. Scheduler sends scheduler Request messages to Elevator Component requesting that the elevator visit specific floors.

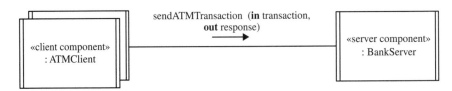

Figure 11.3   *Example of geographical distribution: client/server banking system*

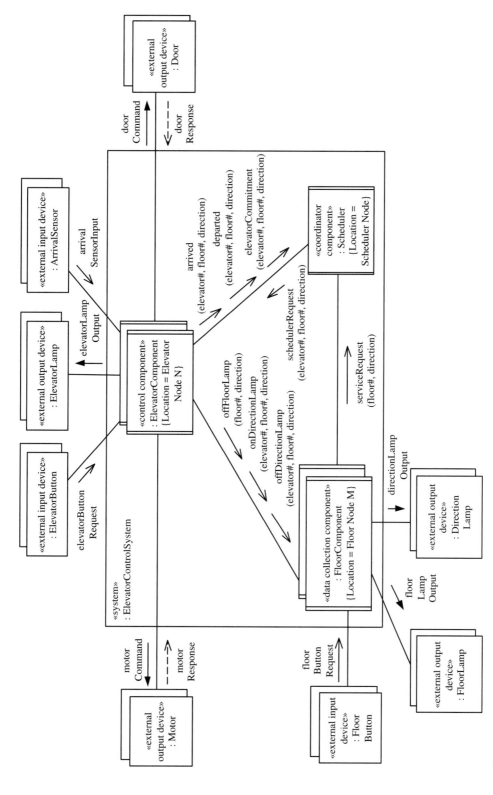

Figure 11.4 *Example of geographical distribution: elevator control system*

289

11.6   Separation of Concerns in Component Design

To ensure high coupling within a component and low coupling between components, the following guidelines addressing **separation of concerns** should be observed in structuring the system into components. The goal is to make components more self-contained so that individual concerns are addressed by different components.

11.6.1   Composite Object

Objects that are part of the same composite object should be in the same component and separate from objects that are not part of the same composite object. As described in Chapter 2, both aggregation and composition are whole/part relationships; however, composition is a stronger form of aggregation. With composition, the composite object (the whole) and its constituent objects (the parts) are created together, live together, and die together. Thus a subsystem consisting of a composite object and its constituent objects is more strongly coupled than one consisting of an aggregate object and its constituent objects.

A subsystem supports information hiding at a more abstract level than an individual object does. A software object can be used to model a real-world object in the problem domain. A composite object models a composite real-world object in the problem domain. A composite object is typically composed of a group of related objects that work together in a coordinated fashion. This arrangement is analogous to the assembly structure in manufacturing. Often, multiple instances of a composite object (and hence multiple instances of each of its constituent objects) are needed in an application. The relationship between a composite class and its constituent classes is best depicted in the static model because the class diagram depicts the multiplicity of the association between each constituent class and the composite class. It is possible for an aggregate subsystem to be a higher-level subsystem that contains composite subsystems (components), as described in more detail in Section 11.7.

An example of a composite class is the Elevator class (see Figure 11.5). Each Elevator composite object is composed of n Elevator Button objects, n Elevator Lamp objects, one Motor object, and one Door object. There are several instances of the Elevator composite class—one for each elevator. Another example of a composite class is Floor (also shown in Figure 11.5). A Floor composite object consists of two Floor Button objects (covering both up and down requests), and two Floor Lamp objects, except for Floor composite objects representing the top and bottom floors, which have only one

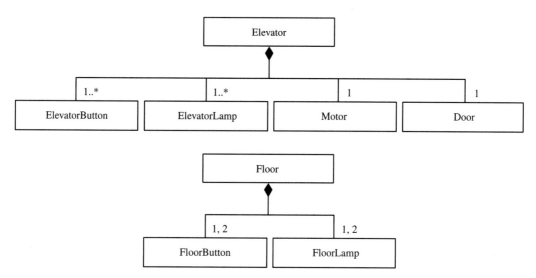

Figure 11.5   *Example of composite classes:* `Elevator` *and* `Floor`

of each. There are several instances of the `Floor` composite class—one for each floor.

11.6.2   Geographical Location

If two objects could potentially be physically separated in different locations, they should be in different components. In a distributed environment, components communicate only by means of messages that can be sent from one component to another. In the elevator control system shown in Figure 11.4, each instance of the `Elevator Component` subsystem could physically reside on a separate microprocessor located in the real-world elevator, and each instance of the `Floor Component` subsystem could reside on a separate microprocessor located at the specific floor.

11.6.3   Clients and Servers

Clients and servers must be in separate components. This guideline can be viewed as a special case of the geographical location rule because clients and servers are usually at different locations. For example, the banking system shown in Figure 11.3 has many `ATM Client` components of the same type, which reside at physical ATMs distributed around the country. `Bank Server` is located at a centralized location, perhaps in New York City.

11.6.4 User Interface

Users often use their own PCs as part of a larger distributed configuration, so the most flexible option is to keep user interface objects in separate components. Because user interface objects are usually clients, this guideline can be viewed as a special case of the client/server guideline. Furthermore, a user interface object may be a composite graphical user interface object composed of several simpler user interface objects.

11.6.5 Proximity to the Source of Physical Data

In a distributed environment, the sources of data might be physically distant from each other. Designing the component so that it is close to the source of physical data ensures fast access to the data, which is particularly important if data access rates are high.

11.6.6 Localized Autonomy

A distributed component often performs a specific site-related service, where the same service is performed at multiple sites. Each instance of the component resides on a separate node, thereby providing greater local autonomy. Assuming that a component on a given node operates relatively independently of other nodes, it can be operational even if the other nodes are temporarily unavailable. Examples of local autonomy components are ATM Client in Figure 11.3, Elevator Component in Figure 11.4, and Monitoring Workstation Controller in Figure 11.2.

11.6.7 Performance

If a time-critical function is provided within a node, better and more-predictable component performance can often be achieved. In a given distributed application, a real-time component can perform a time-critical service at a given node, with non-real-time or less-time-critical services performed elsewhere. Examples of time-critical components are all three components of the elevator control system shown in Figure 11.4 (Elevator Component, Floor Component, and Scheduler) and the Monitoring Workstation Controller component in Figure 11.2.

11.6.8 Specialized Hardware

A component might need to reside on a particular node because it supports special-purpose hardware, such as a vector processor, or because it has to interface to special-purpose peripherals, sensors, or actuators that are connected to a specific node. In the elevator control system illustrated in Figure 11.4, both `Elevator Component` and `Floor Component` interface to sensors and actuators.

11.6.9 Interface to External Objects

A component deals with a subset of the actors shown in the use case model and a subset of the external real-world objects shown on the context diagram. An external real-world object should interface to only one component. Examples are given for the `Elevator Component` and `Floor Component` in Figure 11.4.

11.6.10 Scope of Control

A control object and all the entity and interface objects it directly controls should all be part of one component and not split among components. An example is the `Elevator Control` object within the `Elevator Component`, which controls several internal interface and entity objects.

11.7 Aggregate and Composite Subsystems

A composite subsystem is a component and adheres to the principle of geographical distribution. Thus, objects that are part of a composite subsystem must reside at the same location, but objects in different geographical locations are never in the same composite subsystem. An aggregate subsystem has a broader arrangement, as described next.

An **aggregate subsystem** contains objects grouped by functional similarity, which might span geographical boundaries. These objects, which might be composite objects, are grouped together because they are functionally similar or because they interact with each other in the same use case(s). Aggregate subsystems can be used as a convenient higher-level abstraction than composite subsystems, particularly when there are many components in a highly distributed application. In a software product line that spans multiple organizations, it can be useful to depict each organization as an aggregate subsystem, which itself consists of multiple components that are geographically distributed. The electronic commerce case study is an example of a product line with customer and supplier organizations, each of which is depicted as an aggregate subsystem, as described in Chapter 14.

A **composite subsystem** is a component that encapsulates the internal components (objects) it contains. The component is both a logical and a physical container; however, it adds no further functionality. Thus, a component's functionality is provided entirely by the part components it contains. Incoming messages to a component are passed through to the appropriate internal destination component, and outgoing messages from an internal component are passed through to the appropriate external destination component. The exact pass-through mechanisms are implementation-dependent. This is a view of whole/part relationships (Buschmann et al. 1996) that is shared by many component-based systems (Bass et al. 2003; Magee et al. 1989, 1994; Selic et al. 1994; Shaw and Garlan 1996; Szyperski 2003). An example of a product line with composite components is the microwave oven product line, as described in Section 11.12.1 and Chapter 13.

11.8 Component Structuring Criteria

A distributed application needs to be designed with an understanding of the distributed environments in which it is likely to operate. The component structuring criteria provide guidelines on how to structure a distributed application into configurable distributed components, which can be mapped to geographically distributed nodes in a distributed environment. The actual mapping of components to physical nodes is done later when an individual target system is instantiated and deployed. However, it is necessary to design the components as configurable components, which are indeed capable of later being effectively mapped to distributed physical nodes. Consequently, the component structuring criteria need to consider the characteristics of distributed environments.

In a distributed environment, a service provided by a component might be associated with a particular physical location or constrained to execute on a given hardware resource. In such a case, a component is constrained to execute on the node at that location or on the given hardware.

The distributed component structuring criteria are provided to help ensure that components are designed effectively as configurable distributed components. A component can satisfy more than one of the criteria, which are described in Sections 11.8.1 through 11.8.8.

11.8.1 Client Component

A client component is a requester of services in a client/server system. There are many different types of clients, some of which may be wholly dependent on a server, while others are partially dependent. Client components include user interface components, control components, and data collection components, which are described in more detail in Sections 11.8.2, 11.8.4, and 11.8.6, respectively. In some applications a client component combines more than one role. For example, the ATM Client component depicted in Figure 11.3, which is a client of Bank Server, has both user interface and control aspects.

11.8.2   User Interface Component

A user interface component provides the user interface and performs the role of a client in a client/server system, providing user access to services provided by one or more servers. There may be more than one user interface component—one for each category of user. A user interface component is usually a composite object that is composed of several simpler user interface objects. It may also contain one or more entity objects for local storage and/or caching, as well as control objects for overall sequencing of I/O.

With the proliferation of graphical workstations and personal computers, a component providing a user interface might run on a separate node, interacting with components on other nodes. This kind of component can provide rapid responses to simple requests supported completely by the node and relatively slower responses to requests requiring the cooperation of other nodes. This kind of component usually needs to interface to specific user I/O devices, such as graphical displays and line printers. The ATM Client component in Figure 11.3 and the Operator Interface component in Figure 11.2 satisfy this criterion.

Figure 11.6 gives an example of a user interface component, Operator Interface, several instances of which send requests to the Sensor Data Server component. In the factory monitoring system depicted in Figure 11.2, the Operator Interface component has one internal user interface object to display factory alarms, requested from the Alarm Handling Server component, and a different internal user interface object to display factory workstation status, requested from the Workstation Status Server component.

11.8.3   Server Component

A server component provides a service for other components. It responds to requests from client components; however, it does not initiate any requests. A server component is any component that acts in a server capacity, servicing client requests. In the simplest case, a server component could consist of a single entity object. More-complex server components are composite objects composed of two or more objects. These include entity objects, coordinator objects

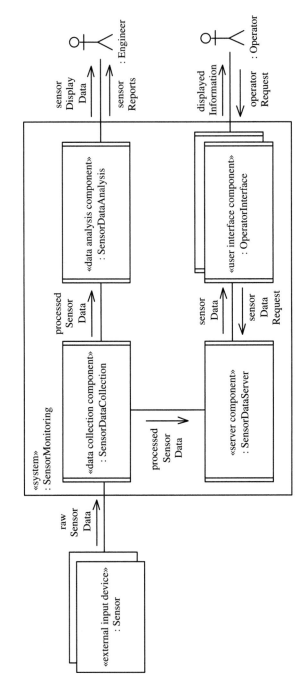

Figure 11.6 *Example of client and server component structuring*

that service client requests and determine what object should be assigned to handle them, and business logic objects that encapsulate application logic. Frequently the server provides services that are associated with a data repository or a set of related data repositories, or it might provide access to a database or to some relations in a database. Alternatively, the server might be associated with an I/O device or a set of related I/O devices. Examples of servers are file servers and line printer servers.

A server component is often allocated its own node. A data server supports remote access to a centralized database or file store. An I/O server services requests for a physical resource that resides at that node. An example of a data server is the `Sensor Data Server` component shown in Figure 11.6, which stores current and historical sensor data. `Sensor Data Server` receives new sensor data from the `Sensor Data Collection` component. Sensor data is requested by other components, such as the `Operator Interface` component, which displays the data. Another example of a server component is `Bank Server` in the banking system depicted in Figure 11.3, which services `ATM Client` requests. Server components are frequently used in distributed applications. The design of server components is described in Section 11.9.

11.8.4 Control Component

A control component controls a given part of the system. The component receives its inputs from the external environment and generates outputs to the external environment, usually without any human intervention. A control component is often state-dependent, in which case it includes at least one state-dependent control object. In some cases, some input data might be gathered by some other component(s) and used by this component. Alternatively, this component might provide some data for use by other components.

A control component might receive some high-level commands from another component giving it overall direction, after which it provides the lower-level control, sending status information to other nodes, either on an ongoing basis or on demand.

An example of a control component is `Elevator Component` in Figure 11.4. This component receives its inputs from the elevator buttons and arrival sensors, as well as from the `Scheduler` component. Its outputs control the elevator motor and door, as well as the elevator lamps. Decisions about starting and stopping the motor, as well as opening and closing the door, are state-dependent and made without human intervention. Another example of a control component is the `Microwave Control` component in Figure 11.7, which receives inputs from several input components and controls two output components.

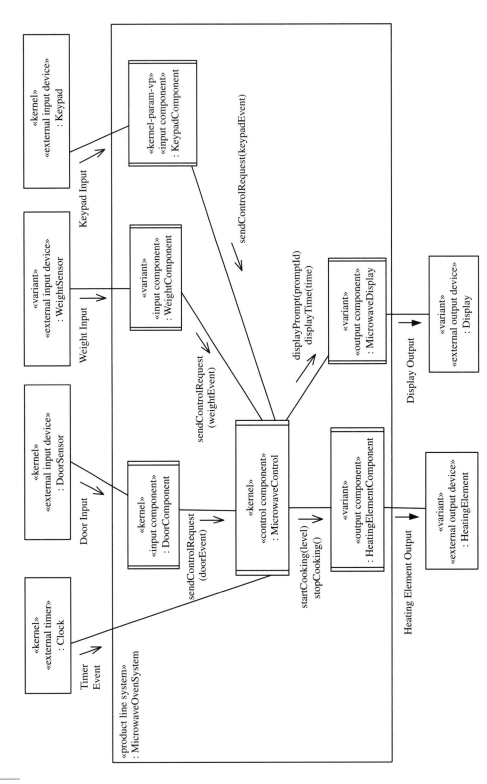

Figure 11.7 *Example of control and I/O components: microwave oven system*

298

11.8.5   Coordinator Component

In cases with multiple control components, it is sometimes necessary to have a coordinator component that coordinates them. If the multiple control components are completely independent of each other, no coordination is required. Another possibility is for the control components to coordinate activities among themselves. Such distributed coordination is usually possible if the coordination is relatively simple, as between the workstation controllers in the high-volume manufacturing system described in Chapter 15. If the coordination activity is relatively complex, however, it is usually more advantageous to have a separate coordinator component. For example, the coordinator component might decide what item of work a control component should do next.

An example of a coordinator component is the `Scheduler` component in the elevator control system (see Figure 11.4). In this system, any service request made by a passenger in a given elevator has to be handled by that elevator. But when a service request is made by a prospective passenger at a floor, a decision has to be made concerning which elevator should service that request. If an elevator is already on its way to this floor and moving in the desired direction, no special action is required. If this is not the case, however, an elevator needs to be dispatched to this floor. The decision of which elevator should respond to the request usually takes into account the proximity of the elevators to this floor and the direction in which they are heading. This decision can be handled by a `Scheduler` component, as shown in Figure 11.4. When `Scheduler` receives a `service Request` message from `Floor Component`, it has to decide whether an elevator should be dispatched to the requested floor; and if so, it sends a `scheduler Request` message to the selected `Elevator Component`.

11.8.6   Data Collection Component

A data collection component collects data from the external environment. In some cases it stores the data, possibly after collecting, converting, and reducing the data. Depending on the application, the component responds to requests for values of the data. Alternatively, the component passes on the data in reduced form; for example, it might collect several raw sensor readings and pass on the average value, converted to engineering units. In other cases it might output results directly to the external environment. A combination of these options is also possible.

An example of a data collection component is the `Sensor Data Collection` component in Figure 11.6, which collects raw data from a variety of digital and analog sensors in real time. The frequency with which the data is collected depends on the characteristics of the sensors. Data collected from analog sensors is converted to engineering units. Processed sensor data is sent to consumer components such as the `Sensor Data Analysis` component.

11.8.7 Data Analysis Component

A data analysis component analyzes data and provides reports and/or displays for data collected by another component. A component can provide both data collection and data analysis. In some cases data is collected in real time, but data analysis is a non-real-time activity.

An example of a data analysis component is the `Sensor Data Analysis` component shown in Figure 11.6, which receives sensor data from the `Sensor Data Collection` component. The `Sensor Data Analysis` component analyzes current and historical sensor data, performs statistical analysis (such as computing the means and standard deviations), produces trend reports, and generates alarms if disturbing trends are detected.

11.8.8 I/O Component

An I/O component can be designed to be relatively autonomous and in close proximity to the source of physical data. In particular, "smart" devices are given greater local autonomy and consist of the hardware plus the software that interfaces to and controls the device. An I/O component typically consists of one or more device interface objects, and it may also contain control objects to provide localized control and entity objects to store local data.

I/O component is a general name given to components that interact with the external environment; they include input components, output components, I/O components (which provide both input and output), network interface components, and system interface components.

In the microwave oven example illustrated in Figure 11.7, `Door Component`, `Weight Component`, and `Keypad Component` are examples of input components; and `Heating Element` and `Microwave Display` are examples of output components.

11.9 Design of Server Components

Server components play an important role in the design of distributed applications. A server component provides a service for client components. Typical server components are file servers, database servers, and line printer servers.

In a nondistributed application, a data structure is encapsulated in a data abstraction object. Components that need to access the data maintained by the object invoke operations provided by the object. In a distributed application, components on separate nodes cannot directly access a passive data abstraction object. It is therefore necessary for the passive data abstraction object to be encapsulated in a server component. In this case a concurrent object (i.e., a thread provided by the distributed component) accesses the passive object.

The server component responds to client requests to read or update the data maintained by the passive object. A server component may also encapsulate a set of related passive data abstraction objects and provide services for all of them. A simple server component does not initiate any requests for services from other components. There are two kinds of server components: sequential and concurrent.

11.9.1   Sequential Server Component

A sequential server component services client requests sequentially; that is, it completes one request before it starts servicing the next. A **sequential server** is designed as one concurrent object (thread of control) that provides one or more services and responds to requests from client components to access the service. For example, a simple sequential server component responds to requests from client components to update or read data from a passive data abstraction object. When the server component receives a message from a client component, it invokes the appropriate service provided by the passive data abstraction object—for example, to credit or debit an account object in a banking system.

The server component typically has a message queue of incoming service request messages. There is one message type for each service provided by the server. The server coordinator unpacks the client's message and, depending on the message type, invokes the appropriate operation provided by a server object. The parameters of the message are used as the parameters of the operation. The server object services the client's request and returns the appropriate response to the server coordinator, which packs the response into a service response message and sends it to the client. The server coordinator is equivalent to the server stub used in remote procedure calls or the server proxy used in remote method invocations.

An example of a sequential server is shown in Figure 11.3. The `Bank Server` component sequentially services ATM transactions requesting withdrawals, transfers, and queries. `Bank Server` receives the transaction, invokes the service, returns a `response` message to the client, and then receives the next transaction. Each transaction is executed to completion before the next transaction is started. The sequential server design can be used only if the server can adequately handle the transaction rate.

11.9.2 Concurrent Server Component with Multiple Readers and Writers

If the client demand for services is high enough that the sequential server component could potentially become a bottleneck in the system, an alternative approach is for the services to be provided by a concurrent server component and hence shared among several concurrent objects. This approach assumes that improved throughput can be obtained by objects providing concurrent access to the data—for example, if the data is stored on secondary storage. In this case, while one concurrent object is blocked, waiting for a disk I/O operation to be completed, another concurrent object is allocated the CPU.

In a concurrent server component, several concurrent objects might wish to access the data repository at the same time, so access needs to be synchronized. The most appropriate synchronization algorithm to use is typically application-dependent. Possible algorithms include the **mutual exclusion** algorithm and the **multiple readers and writers** algorithm. In the latter case, multiple readers are allowed to access a shared data repository concurrently; however, only one writer is allowed to update the data repository at any one time, and only after the readers have finished.

In the multiple readers and writers solution shown in Figure 11.8, each read and write service is performed by a concurrent object, either a reader or a writer. The `Server Coordinator` object keeps track of all service requests—those currently being serviced and those waiting to be serviced. When it receives a request from a client, `Server Coordinator` allocates the request to an appropriate reader or writer concurrent object to perform the service. For example, if the coordinator receives a read request from a client, it instantiates a `Reader` object and increments its count of the number of readers. The reader notifies the coordinator when it finishes, so that the coordinator can decrement the reader count. If a write request is received from a client, the coordinator allocates the request to a `Writer` object only when all readers have finished. This delay ensures that writers have mutually exclusive access to the data. The coordinator does not allocate any new read requests until the writer has finished. If the overhead of instantiating new concurrent objects is too high, the coordinator can maintain a pool of concurrent `Reader` objects and one concurrent `Writer` object, and allocate new requests to concurrent objects that are free.

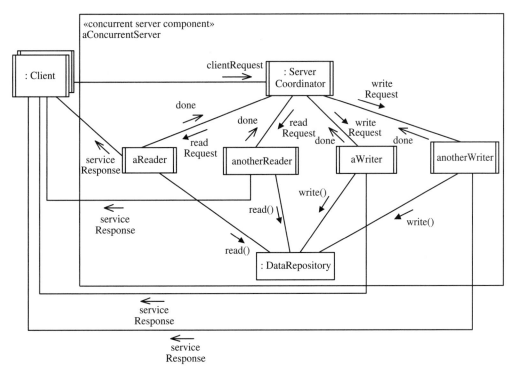

Figure 11.8   *Example of a concurrent server component: multiple readers and writers*

If new readers keep coming and are permitted to read, a writer could be indefinitely prevented from writing; this problem is referred to as *writer starvation*. The coordinator avoids writer starvation by queuing up new reader requests after receiving a writer request. After the current readers have finished reading, the waiting writer is then allowed to write before any new readers are permitted to read.

In this example, the clients communicate with the server by using the Asynchronous Message Communication with Callback pattern (see Section 10.3.4). This means that the clients do not wait and can do other things before receiving the server response. In this case the server response is handled as a **callback**. With the callback approach, the client sends an operation handle with the original request. The server uses the handle to remotely call the client operation (the callback) when it finishes servicing the client request. In the example illustrated in Figure 11.8, `Server Coordinator` passes the client's callback handle to the reader (or writer). On completion, the `Reader` concurrent object remotely invokes the callback, which is depicted on as the `service Response` message sent to the client.

11.9.3 Concurrent Server Component with Subscription and Notification

Another example of a concurrent server is shown in Figure 11.9, which uses the Subscription/Notification Pattern (see Section 10.3.8). This server maintains an event archive and also provides a subscription/notification service to its clients. An example is given of a `Real-Time Event Monitor` concurrent component that monitors external events. The `Subscription Server` component maintains a subscription list of clients that wish to be notified of these events. When an external event occurs, `Real-Time Event Monitor` updates an event archive and informs `Event Distributor` of the event arrival. `Event Distributor` queries `Subscription Server` to determine the clients who have subscribed to receive events of this type, and then notifies those clients of the new event.

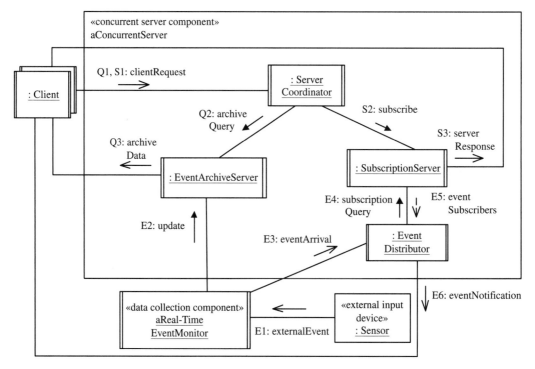

Figure 11.9 *Example of a concurrent server component: subscription/notification*

The concurrent communication diagram in Figure 11.9 shows three separate interactions: a simple query interaction, an event subscription interaction, and an event notification interaction. In the query interaction (which does not involve a subscription) a client makes a request to `Server Coordinator`, which queries `Event Archive Server` and sends the response directly to `Client`. The three event sequences are given different prefixes to differentiate them:

Query interaction (Q prefix):

Q1: A client sends a query to `Server Coordinator`—for example, requesting events over the past 24 hours.

Q2: `Server Coordinator` forwards the query to `Event Archive Server`.

Q3: `Event Archive Server` sends the appropriate archive data—for example, events over the past 24 hours—to the client.

Event subscription interaction (S prefix):

S1: `Server Coordinator` receives a subscription request from a client.

S2: `Server Coordinator` sends a `subscribe` message to `Subscription Server`.

S3: `Subscription Server` confirms the subscription by sending a `server Response` message to the client.

Event notification interaction (E prefix):

E1: An external event arrives at `Real-Time Event Monitor`.

E2: `Real-Time Event Monitor` determines that this is a significant event and sends an `update` message to `Event Archive Server`.

E3: `Real-Time Event Monitor` sends an `event Arrival` message to `Event Distributor`.

E4, E5: `Event Distributor` queries `Subscription Server` to get the list of event subscribers (i.e., client agents that have subscribed to receive events of this type).

E6: `Event Distributor` multicasts an `event Notification` message to all clients that have subscribed for this event.

11.10   Distribution of Data

Both sequential and concurrent server subsystems are single-server subsystems; thus the data repositories they encapsulate are centralized. In distributed applications, the potential disadvantages of centralized servers are that the server could become a bottleneck and that it is liable to be a single point of failure. A solution to these problems is data distribution. Two approaches to data distribution are the distributed server and data replication.

11.10.1   Distributed Server

With the **distributed server**, data that is collected at several locations is stored at those locations. Each location has a local server, which responds to client requests for that location's data. This approach is used in the distributed factory automation product line case study (see Figure 11.2), where manufacturing workstation status data is maintained at each location by a local `Workstation Status Server` component, which responds to client requests from factory operators.

11.10.2   Data Replication

With **data replication**, the same data is duplicated in more than one location to speed up access to it. Ensuring that procedures exist for updating the local copies of the replicated data is, of course, important so that the data does not become outdated. This approach is used in the distributed elevator control system example in Figure 11.4. Each instance of `Elevator Component` (one per elevator) maintains its own `Local Status & Plan` data abstraction object to keep track of where the elevator is and what floors it is committed to visit. In order for `Scheduler` to select an elevator when a floor request is made, it needs to have access to the status and plan data for all the elevators. To expedite its access to this information, `Scheduler` maintains its own copy of each elevator's status and plan in an `Overall Status & Plan` data abstraction object. This data is updated by elevator status and commitment messages sent to `Scheduler` by each instance of `Elevator Component`.

11.11   Design of Component Interfaces

This section describes the design of component interfaces, an important issue in software architecture. It describes how interfaces are specified before describing provided and required interfaces, ports (and how they are specified in terms of provided and required interfaces), connectors that interconnect components, and guidelines on designing components for software product lines.

11.11.1   Modeling Components in UML 2.0

UML 2.0 has added new concepts for depicting software architectures and components. Components can be effectively modeled with structured classes and depicted on composite structure diagrams. Structured classes have ports with provided and required interfaces. Structured classes can be interconnected through their ports via connectors that join the ports of communicating classes. Sections 11.11.2 and 11.11.3 describe how component-based software architectures can be designed with the UML 2.0 notation. Components are usually concurrent, so they are also depicted with the UML active class notation.

11.11.2   Component Interfaces in UML

An **interface** is a collection of operations that are used to specify a service of a class or component (Booch et al. 2005). It is similar but not identical to an abstract class. Unlike an abstract class, an interface cannot have attributes. An interface has a different name from the class or component that provides (realizes) it. By convention, the name starts with the letter *I*. In UML, an interface can be modeled separately from a component. There are two ways to depict an interface: simple and expanded.

A component provides one or more interfaces. Many components are designed with one interface. If different clients use a server component differently, however, it is possible to design a separate interface for each client component that requires a different service.

Similarly, it is possible to design the interfaces provided by a component such that one interface is a kernel interface that is used by all members of the product line, while other interfaces are optional or variant (i.e., used by only some members of the product line). In the latter situation, different interfaces are used by different variant clients.

An example of a component that provides more than one interface is `Alarm Handling Server`. Three interfaces from the factory automation software product line will be used in the examples that follow. Each interface consists of one or more operations, as follows:

1. **Interface**: IAlarmServer
   Operations provided:
   - alarmRequest (**in** request, **out** alarmData)
   - alarmSubscribe (**in** request, **in** notificationHandle, **out** ack)

2. **Interface**: IAlarmStatus
   Operation provided: postAlarm (**in** alarmData)

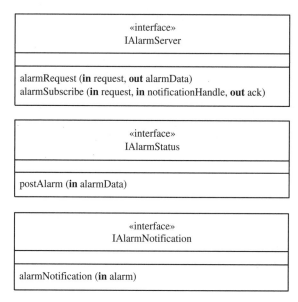

Figure 11.10 *Component interfaces for* `Alarm Handling Server`

3. **Interface**: IAlarmNotification
   Operation provided: alarmNotification (**in** alarm)

The interface of a component can be depicted with the static modeling notation, as shown in Figure 11.10, with the stereotype «interface».

11.11.3 Component Interfaces: Provided and Required Interfaces

To provide a complete definition of the component-based software architecture for a software product line, it is necessary to specify the interface(s) provided by each component and the interface(s) required by each component. A **provided interface** is a collection of operations that specify the services that a component must fulfill. A **required interface** describes the services that other components provide for this component to operate properly in a particular environment.

A component has one or more ports through which it interacts with other components. Each component port is defined in terms of provided and/or required interfaces. A *provided* interface of a port specifies the requests that other components can make of this component. A *required* interface of a port specifies the requests that this component can make of other components. A provided port supports a provided interface. A required port supports a required interface. A complex port supports both a provided interface and a required interface. A component can have more than one port. In particular, if a component communicates with more than one component, it can use a different port for each component with which it communicates. Figure 11.11 shows an example of components with ports, as well as provided and required interfaces.

In the PLUS method, by convention the name of a component's required port starts with the letter *R* to emphasize that the component has a *required* port. The name of a component's provided port starts with the letter *P* to emphasize that the component has a *provided* port. A connector joins the required port of one component to the provided port of another component. The connected ports must be compatible with each other. This means that if two ports are connected, the required interface of one port must be compatible with the provided interface of the other port; that is, the operations required in one component's required interface must be the same as the operations provided in the other component's provided interface. In the case of a connector joining two complex ports (each with one provided interface and one required interface), the required interface of the first port must be compatible with the provided interface of the second port, and the required interface of the second port must be compatible with the provided interface of the first port.

In Figure 11.11, the `Workstation Controller` component has one required port, called `RAlarmStatus`, which supports a required interface

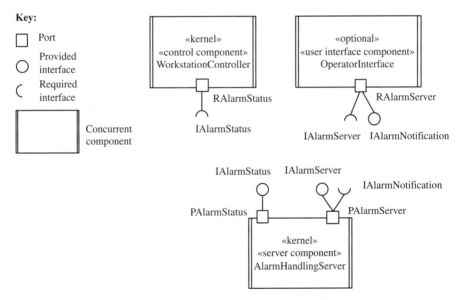

Figure 11.11 *Examples of component ports, with provided and required interfaces*

called IAlarmStatus, which was defined in Section 11.11.2 (see Figure 11.10). The Operator Interface component has a complex port with both a required interface (IAlarmServer) and a provided interface (IAlarmNotification). Because this component is a client using a subscription/notification protocol, the port is considered primarily a required port and is therefore called RAlarm-Server because it needs to connect to an alarm server. The Alarm Handling Server component has two ports: a provided port called PAlarmStatus and a complex port called PAlarmServer. The port PAlarmStatus provides an interface called IAlarmStatus, through which alarm status messages are sent. The port PAlarmServer provides the main interface through which clients request alarm services (provided interface IAlarmServer) and receive alarm notifications (required interface IAlarmNotification).

Figure 11.12 shows how the three components (Workstation Controller, Operator Interface, and Alarm Handling Server) are interconnected. The first connector is unidirectional (as shown by the direction of the arrow representing the connector) and joins Workstation Controller's RAlarmStatus required port to Alarm Handling Server's PAlarmStatus provided port. Figure 11.11 shows that these ports are compatible because it results in the IAlarmStatus required interface being connected to the IAlarmStatus provided interface. The second connector is bidirectional and joins Operator Interface's complex port RAlarmServer to Alarm Handling Server's complex port PAlarmServer. Examination of the port design in Figure 11.11

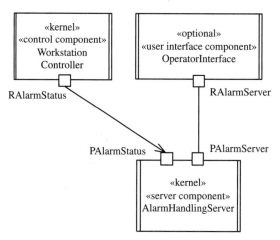

Figure 11.12 *Example of components, ports, and connectors in a software architecture*

shows that these ports are also compatible, with the required interface connected to the provided interface, respectively, for both the `IAlarmServer` and `IAlarmNotification` interfaces.

11.12   Design of Components

There are several considerations in designing components. This section describes the considerations and tradeoffs involved in component design.

11.12.1   Designing Composite Components

A composite component is structured into part components, which are also depicted as UML 2.0 structured classes. A component with no internal components is referred to as a *simple component*. The part components within a composite component are depicted as instances because it is possible to have more than one instance of the same part within the composite component.

   Figure 11.13 shows an example of a composite component, the `Microwave Display` component, which contains two simple components: a concurrent component called `Display Interface` and a passive component called `Display Prompts`. The provided port of the composite `Microwave Display` component is connected directly to the provided port of the internal `Display Interface` component. The connector joining the two ports is called a **delegation connector**, which means that the outer delegating port provided by `Microwave Display` forwards each message it receives from `Microwave Control` to the inner port provided by `Display Interface`. By convention, the two ports are given the same name, `PDisplay`, because they provide the same interface.

   Only distributed components can be deployed to the physical nodes of a distributed configuration. Passive components cannot be independently deployed, nor can any component that directly invokes the operations of a passive component; in that situation, only the composite component (which contains the passive component) can be deployed. Thus, in Figure 11.13, only the `Microwave Display` composite component can be deployed. By a PLUS convention, only the deployable components are depicted with the component stereotype.

11.12.2   Designing "Plug-Compatible" Components

There are various ways to design components. It is highly desirable, where possible, to design components that are *plug-compatible*, so that the required port of

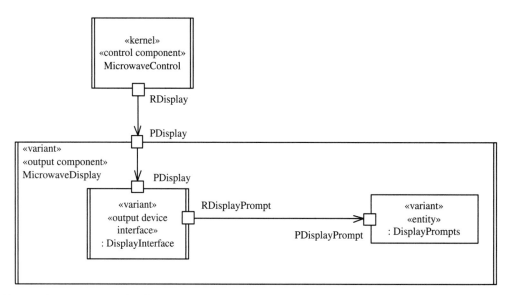

Figure 11.13   *Example of composite component design*

one component is compatible with the provided ports of alternative components to which it needs to connect. Consider the case in which a producer component needs to be able to connect to different alternative consumer components in different product line members. The most desirable approach, if possible, is to design all the consumer components with the same provided interface, so that the producer can be connected to any consumer without changing its required interface.

An example of plug-compatible component design comes from the microwave oven product line, as shown in Figure 11.14. The `Microwave Display` component has a provided port called `PDisplay`, and the interface it provides is called `IDisplay`. The specification of the interface is shown in Figure 11.14*b*. There are two variants of the `Microwave Display` component—the default `One-line Microwave Display` component and the variant `Multi-line Microwave Display` component—such that the two variants realize the same provided interface. One of the operations provided by the `IDisplay` interface, `display TOD`, is implemented in full only by the multi-line display; it results in an exception in the one-line display. This means that `Microwave Control` must be designed so that it invokes the `display TOD` operation only if the `TOD` feature is selected.

An alternative design would give each `Microwave Display` variant component a different interface: one with the `display TOD` operation and one without. However, two different interfaces would need two different provided ports

(*a*) Distributed component architecture

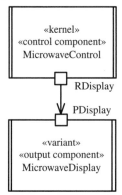

(*b*) Design of individual components

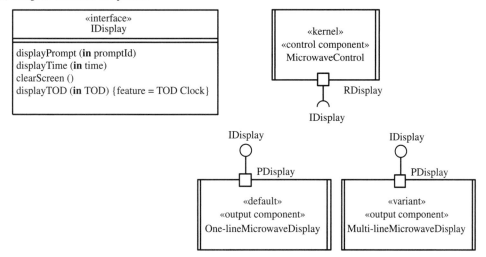

Figure 11.14 *Example of plug-compatible component design*

for the two display variants and two different required ports for the `Microwave Control` component to interface to the two alternative provided ports. This alternative is rejected because it results in a much more complicated design.

11.12.3 Design of Variable Component Architectures

It is possible for a component to connect to different components and have different interconnections such that in one case it communicates with one component and in a different case it communicates with two different components.

One such example, illustrated in Figure 11.15, comes from the factory automation product line case study described in Chapter 15. New parts start being manufactured as a result of a `start Part` message sent by the `Production Manager Interface` component through its `RStartPart` port. In a flexible manufacturing system (illustrated in Figure 11.15a)—a product line member that uses a hierarchical control pattern—the `Production Manager Interface` component communicates only with the `Part Agent` component, which receives the `start Part` message through its `PStartPart` port. `Part Agent` then initiates and controls the part manufacturing by interacting with several other components until the part is completed. The `start Part` message has a callback handle that is used to identify the operation in the provided interface of the `PCallback` port to which the `part Completed` message is sent by `Part Agent`.

In a high-volume manufacturing system (illustrated in Figure 11.15b)—a product line member that uses a distributed control pattern—the `Production Manager Interface` component uses the same ports and interfaces. However, it sends the `start Part` message to the `Receiving Workstation Controller` component, which provides the same `PStartPart` port. In this system the workstation controllers are connected in series, and the part information with the callback handle is sent from each workstation controller component to its neighbor as the part is being manufactured. Eventually the part information arrives at the `Shipping Workstation Controller` component, which uses the callback handle to send the `part Completed` message to the `Production Manager Interface`'s `PPartCallback` port. The `Production Manager Interface` component is completely unaware that the part was manufactured in an entirely different way.

The design of the individual components is depicted in Figure 11.15c. Using the callback mechanism decouples the `Part Agent` and `Shipping Workstation Controller` components, respectively, from the `Production Manager Interface` component so that the former components are not dependent on the latter.

11.12.4 Design of Component Interface Inheritance

When plug-compatible components are not practical, an alternative component design approach is *component interface inheritance*. Consider a component architecture in which the interface through which the two components communicate is specialized to allow for additional functionality. In that case, both the component that provides the interface and the component that requires the interface have to be modified—the former to realize the new functionality and the latter to request it.

(*a*) Distributed component architecture of flexible manufacturing system

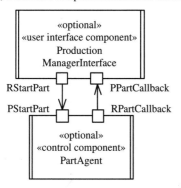

(*b*) Distributed component architecture of high-volume manufacturing system

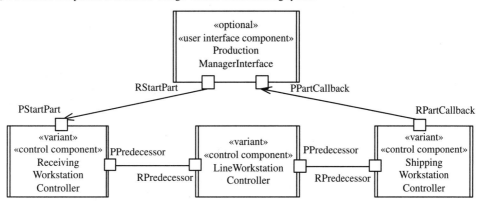

(*c*) Design of individual components

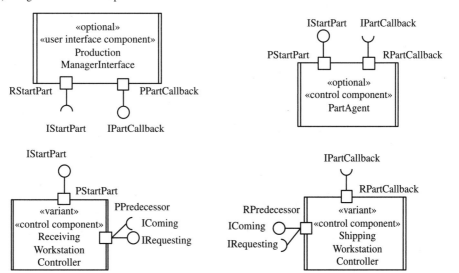

Figure 11.15 *Examples of variable component architecture design*

Consider the following example from the e-commerce product line, illustrated in Figure 11.16. In the kernel design (Figure 11.16a), the `Supplier Interface` component has a port `RSupplierAgent` that requires the `ISupplierAgent` interface. This port is connected to `Supplier Agent`'s `PSupplierAgent` port, which provides the `ISupplierAgent` interface. To support optional purchase order (PO) functionality, the interface through which the two components communicate is specialized to create an interface called `IPOSupplierAgent` (Figure 11.16c), which provides two additional purchase order operations. As a result, both the required and provided ports have to be modified to `RPOSupplierAgent` and `PPOSupplierAgent`, respectively. Furthermore, the components themselves have to be modified to realize the PO functionality—`PO Supplier Agent` to implement the new operations, and `PO Supplier Interface` to invoke them and use the response (Figure 11.16b).

11.13 Summary

This chapter described the component-based software architectural design of product lines. The overall design of the software architecture was described, including the design decisions that need to be made when in the transition from analysis modeling to design modeling. Components are categorized according to the roles they play in the software architecture. Issues regarding the separation of concerns and the design of server components are considered in the design of the architecture. Finally, the design of component interfaces was described, with component ports that have provided and required interfaces, and connectors that join compatible ports. The component-based software architecture was depicted with the new UML 2.0 notation for composite structure diagrams. Considerations and tradeoffs in component design were also discussed. Several examples of such architectures will be given in the product line case studies described in Chapters 13, 14, and 15.

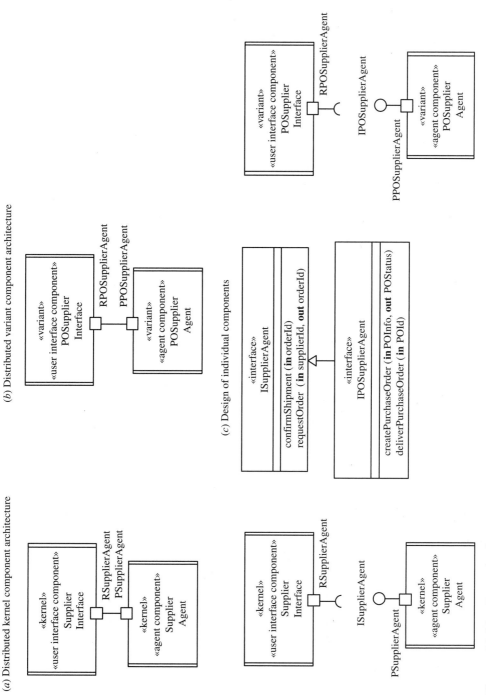

(a) Distributed kernel component architecture

(b) Distributed variant component architecture

(c) Design of individual components

Figure 11.16 *Example of component interface inheritance design*

c h a p t e r

Software Application Engineering

During software application engineering, the software product line architecture is adapted and tailored to derive a given software application, which is a member of the software product line. Application derivation involves considering the overall requirements of the individual application; selecting the application features by matching them against the product line features; and using the selected features to tailor the product line use case model to derive the application use case model, to tailor the product line analysis model to derive the application analysis model, and to tailor the product line architecture to derive the architecture of the application. Given the application architecture, the appropriate components from the product line repository are instantiated, interconnected, and deployed. A high-level view of software application engineering is shown in Figure 12.1.

The steps in software application engineering are described in more detail in Section 12.1. Section 12.2 describes how software application engineering can be carried out in conjunction with the Unified Software Development Process (USDP). Section 12.3 describes how an application is deployed. Section 12.4 discusses some typical tradeoffs that need to be made in the development of an application from a product line architecture. Section 12.5 gives an example of software application engineering for the microwave oven case study.

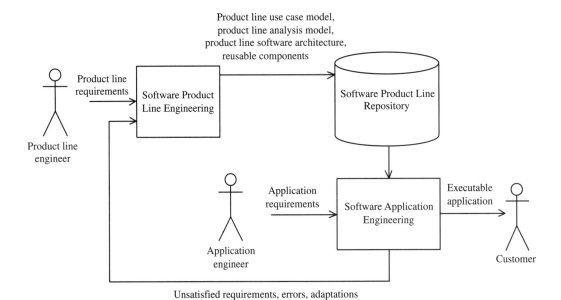

Product line use case model,
product line analysis model,
product line software architecture,
reusable components

Product line
requirements

Product line
engineer

Software Product
Line Engineering

Software Product Line
Repository

Application
requirements

Application
engineer

Software Application
Engineering

Executable
application

Customer

Unsatisfied requirements, errors, adaptations

Figure 12.1 *Evolutionary software process for product lines*

12.1   Phases in Software Application Engineering

During software application engineering, an individual application that is a
member of the software product line is developed. Instead of starting from
scratch, as is usually done, in a software product line process, the application
development makes full use of all the artifacts developed during the product
line engineering process. The phases of the software application engineering
process are shown in Figure 12.2.

12.1.1   Application Requirements Modeling

During the application requirements modeling phase, a requirements model is
developed in which the functional requirements of the application are defined
in terms of actors and use cases. The application requirements are matched
against the product line feature model to determine what features are to be
incorporated in the application. A typical application consists of all kernel features and some optional and alternative features. Based on the application features, the feature/use case dependency table is then analyzed to determine

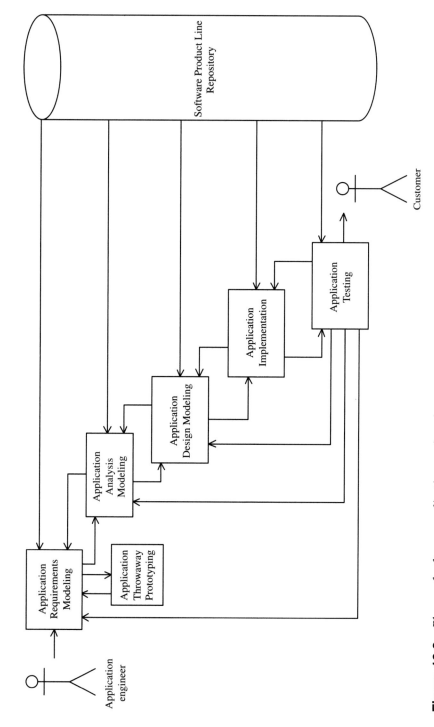

Figure 12.2 *Phases of software application engineering*

what use cases are needed for the application and what variability is to be inserted at the variation points. The application use cases will consist of all of the product line kernel use cases and a selection of optional and alternative use cases. User inputs and active participation are essential to this effort. If the application requirements are not well understood, a throw-away prototype can be developed to help clarify the requirements.

12.1.2   Application Analysis Modeling

In the application analysis modeling phase, static and dynamic models of the application are developed. The static models of the entity classes and system context are tailored to the selected feature/class dependencies. Only the classes and relationships relevant to this application member of the product line are selected. For the dynamic model, the communication diagrams corresponding to the selected features and use cases are selected for the application member. In addition, any default or variant objects corresponding to a variation point need to be included in the application's communication diagrams. The statecharts must correspond to the selected state-dependent control classes. If the statechart is parameterized with feature-dependent transitions and actions, the feature conditions need to be set to true so that those transitions and actions are enabled.

12.1.3   Application Design Modeling

In the application design modeling phase the software architecture of the application is adapted from the software product line architecture. The application features dictate which components are selected for the application architecture. For any parameterized features, the appropriate parameters are set.

12.1.4   Incremental Application Implementation

After completion of the software architectural design, an incremental application implementation approach is taken. This approach is based on selection of a subset of the application to be implemented for each increment. The subset consists of the use cases to be included in this increment and the components that realize these use cases. Some components will already exist in the product line repository. Other components will need to be constructed. Component implementation consists of the detailed design, coding, and unit testing of the new classes in the subset. This is a phased approach by which the software is gradually implemented and integrated until the whole system is built.

12.1.5   Application Testing

Application testing includes the integration and functional testing of the system. During integration testing, each software increment is tested. The integration test for the increment is based on the use cases selected for the increment. Integration test cases are developed for each use case. Integration testing is a form of **white box testing,** in which the interfaces between the components that participate in each use case are tested.

Each software increment forms an *incremental prototype*. After the software increment is judged to be satisfactory, the next increment is constructed and integrated by iteration through the incremental software construction and incremental software integration phases. However, if significant problems are detected in the software increment, iteration through the requirements modeling, analysis modeling, and design modeling phases might be necessary. In turn, changes might be required at the product line level and hence relate back to the software product line engineering process.

In functional testing, the system is tested against its functional requirements. This testing is **black box testing** and is based on the use cases. Thus, functional test cases are built for each use case. Any software increment released to the customer needs to go through the system testing phase.

12.2   Software Application Engineering with the USDP

Just as the software product line engineering process can be integrated with the Unified Software Development Process, so, too, can software application engineering, as shown in Figure 12.3. Instead of starting with use case modeling, software application engineering starts with the software product line artifacts stored in the software product line repository. Software application engineering is feature-driven because the product line features are key to modeling the product line variability.

12.2.1   Inception

During the inception phase of the software application, the requirements of the application need to be determined and categorized as features. The key assessment is to determine whether the application is indeed a viable member of the product line—that is, whether the application features are indeed matched by the

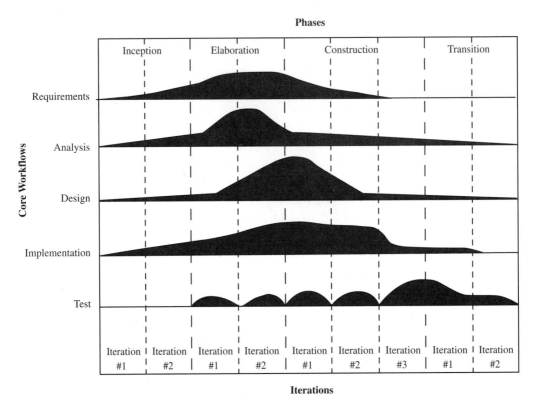

Figure 12.3 *Software application engineering with the USDP* (I. Jacobson, G. Booch, J. Rumbaugh, *The Unified Software Development Process*, [Figure 1.5, p. 11], © 1999 Addison-Wesley Longman, Inc. Reprinted with permission.)

product line features. If there is a mismatch, then two alternatives are possible: (1) There is sufficient diversity that it is better to develop the application separately. (2) The product line can be evolved so that any missing requirements are addressed by the incremental evolution.

12.2.2 Elaboration—Iteration 1: Evolution

If product line evolution is required, this phase is similar to the elaboration phase in product line engineering, in which the product line model is evolved by the consideration of optional and alternative features. If product line evolution is not required for this application, this phase can be skipped.

12.2.3   Elaboration—Iteration 2: Adaptation

In this phase the application features drive the adaptation of the product line architecture to create the software architecture for the application. On the basis of these features, the use case model, analysis model, and design model are all tailored to suit the application's needs.

12.2.4   Construction

The construction phase involves selecting the kernel components from the product line repository, selecting optional and variant components that have previously been implemented, and implementing any component whose interfaces have previously been specified but that have not yet been implemented. The implementation of new components involves the detailed design, coding, and unit testing of the components. Integration testing of the new components with the existing components is also performed.

12.2.5   Transition

During the transition phase the software application system is thoroughly tested. System test cases are developed on the basis of the functional requirements specified in the use cases selected for this application.

12.3   Application Deployment

After a distributed application has been designed and implemented, instances of it can be defined and deployed. During system deployment, an instance of the distributed application—referred to as a *target application*—is defined and mapped to a distributed configuration consisting of multiple geographically distributed physical nodes connected by a network.

12.3.1   Application Deployment Issues

During application deployment, a decision is made about what component instances are required. In addition, it is necessary to determine how the component instances should be interconnected and how the component instances should be allocated to nodes. Specifically, the following activities need to be performed:

- **Define instances of the component**. For each component that can have multiple instances, it is necessary to define the instances desired. For example, in a distributed elevator control system, it is necessary to define the number of elevators and the number of floors required in the target application. It is also necessary to define one `Elevator Component` instance for each elevator and one `Floor Component` instance for each floor. Each `Elevator Component` and `Floor Component` instance must have a unique name so that it can be uniquely identified. For components that are parameterized, the parameters for each instance need to be defined. Examples of component parameters are instance name (such as elevator ID or floor ID), sensor names, sensor limits, and alarm names.

- **Interconnect component instances**. The application architecture defines how components communicate with one another. At this stage the component instances are connected. In the distributed elevator control system in Figure 12.4, for example, each instance of the `Floor Component` sends a `service Request` message to `Scheduler`. `Scheduler` sends `scheduler Request` messages to individual instances of `Elevator Component`, so it must identify the elevator to which it is sending the message. Similarly, when an `Elevator Component` instance sends a message to a `Floor Component` instance, it must identify the floor to which it is sending the message.

- **Map the component instances to physical nodes**. For example, two components could be deployed such that each one could run on a separate physical node. Alternatively, they could both run on the same physical node. The physical configuration of the target application is depicted on a deployment diagram.

12.3.2 Example of Application Deployment

As an example of application deployment, consider the distributed elevator control system. The application configuration is depicted on a deployment diagram as shown in Figure 12.5. Each instance of `Elevator Component` (one per elevator) is allocated to a node to achieve localized autonomy and adequate performance. Thus the failure of one elevator node will not affect other elevator nodes. Each instance of `Floor Component` (one per floor) is allocated to a node because of proximity to the source of physical data. Loss of a floor node means that the specific floor will not be serviced, but service to other floors is not affected. `Scheduler` is allocated to a separate node for performance reasons so that it can rapidly respond to elevator requests. Loss of the scheduler node

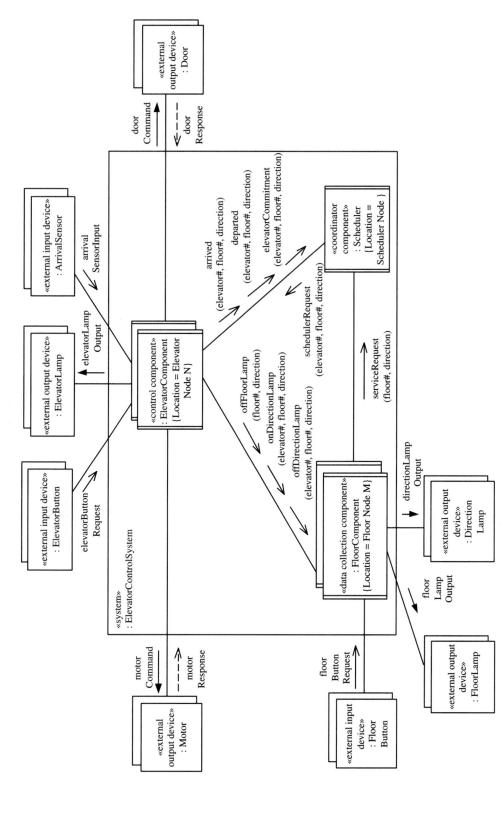

Figure 12.4 Example of a distributed elevator control system

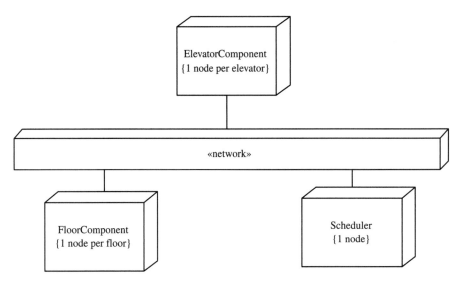

Figure 12.5   *Example of a distributed application deployment: elevator control system*

(preferably temporarily) means that no new floor requests will be assigned to elevators, but current passengers on elevators will continue to be serviced until they arrive at their destinations.

12.4   Tradeoffs in Software Application Engineering

Software application engineering starts with the product line artifacts and adapts them for the application. The application may have a requirement that is not addressed by the product line use case model and feature model, or it may need a component that is not quite compatible with the product line architecture. There are two main approaches to address this problem: the systematic approach and the pragmatic approach.

The *systematic* approach is to address this problem by iterating through one more cycle in the evolutionary product line engineering process and incorporating the change in the product line requirements, analysis, and design models. The new iteration starts with the addition of a new use case or the adaptation of an existing use case, and any new variation points are identified. Next, the new features are determined and related to the use case model. The static and dynamic models are adapted, followed by the change to the product line architecture. Thus the needs of the new application are incorporated into enhanced product line requirements, analysis, and design models.

The *pragmatic* approach is to adapt the application models without changing the product line models. In this case the application models, initially derived from the product line models, are enhanced independently. The application developers provide their updates to the product line developers, who then need to decide whether these changes should be retroactively applied to the product line models. If the changes are not incorporated into the product line architecture, the application architecture is no longer compatible with the product line architecture.

12.5   Example of Software Application Engineering

This section discusses an example of software application engineering from the microwave oven product line case study, which is described in detail in Chapter 13. First the feature model, and then the use case model, analysis model, and design model, are adapted to derive the architecture for the software application.

12.5.1   Feature Model for the Microwave Oven Application

Given the product line feature model, the features selected for the application are depicted in Figure 12.6, where the selected features are shown in bold and the features not selected are shown in gray.

The selected features, as well as the use cases that relate to them, are shown in Table 12.1, which uses the tabular notation introduced in Chapter 5.

12.5.2   Use Case Model for the Microwave Oven Application

Three use cases—Cook Food, Set Time of Day, and Display Time of Day—are selected for the software application, and certain variation points are set. The use case model for the microwave oven application is depicted in Figure 12.7, which shows the selected use cases in bold and the unselected use case in gray.

12.5.3   Static Model for the Microwave Oven Application

During development of the static model for the microwave oven application, the context class diagram shown in Figure 12.8 is created. The kernel external

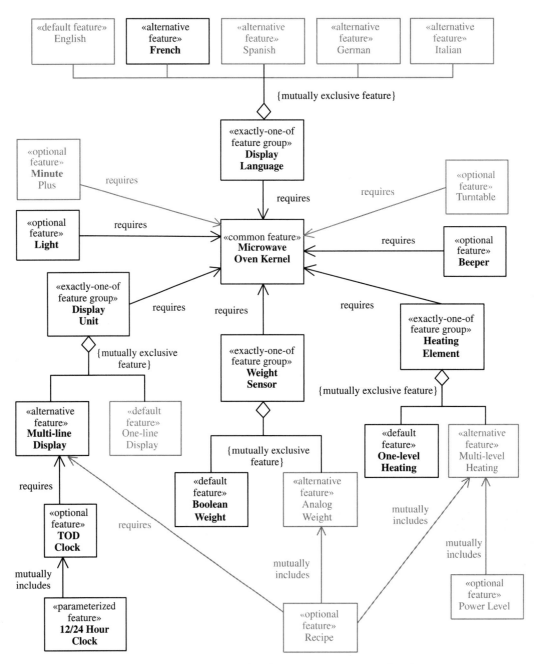

Figure 12.6 *Feature dependency diagram for the microwave oven application*

Table 12.1 *Microwave oven application: feature/use case dependencies*

Feature Name	Feature Category	Use Case Name	Use Case Category/ Variation Point (vp)	Variation Point
Microwave Oven Kernel	common	Cook Food	kernel	
Light	optional	Cook Food	vp	Light
Beeper	optional	Cook Food	vp	Beeper
Multi-line Display	alternative	Cook Food	vp	Display Unit
French	alternative	Cook Food	vp	Display Language
Boolean Weight	default	Cook Food	vp	Weight Sensor
One-level Heating	default	Cook Food	vp	Heating Element
TOD Clock	optional	Set Time of Day Display Time of Day	optional optional	
12/24 Hour Clock	parameterized	Set Time of Day Display Time of Day	optional optional	12/24 Hour Clock

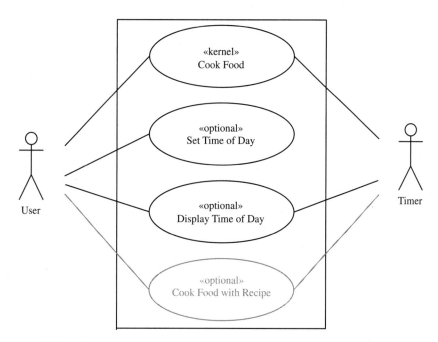

Figure 12.7 *Use case model for the microwave oven application*

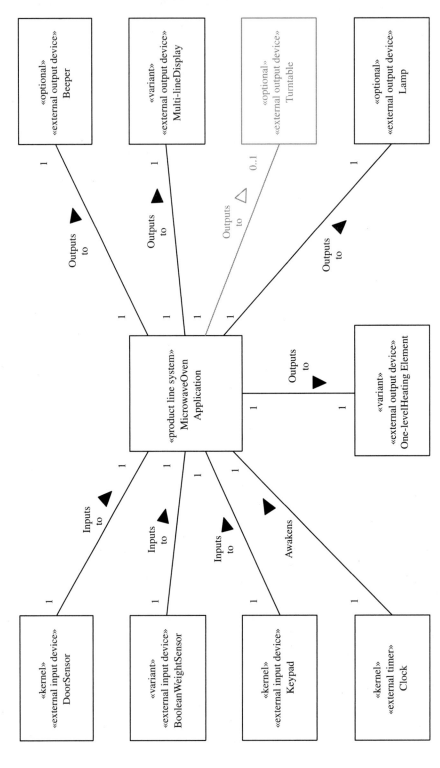

Figure 12.8 *Context class diagram for the microwave oven application*

332

devices (Door Sensor and Keypad) and the external timer (Clock) are automatically included. Given the features selected for the application, two optional
external devices (Beeper and Lamp) are also included, as are three variant
external devices: one external input device (Boolean Weight Sensor) and
two external output devices (One-level Heating Element and Multi-
line Display).

12.5.4   Dynamic Model for the Microwave Oven Application

For dynamic modeling, the communication diagram for the Cook Food use
case consists of the kernel communication diagram that was originally shown
in Figure 7.6, with the following changes, as Figure 12.9 illustrates:

- Branches for the Lamp Interface and Beeper Interface output device
  interface objects have been added to address the Light and Beeper
  optional features (and use case variant points), respectively.

- The Multi-line Display Interface and French Display Prompts
  variants have been substituted for the default objects to address the selection of the Multi-line Display and French alternative features,
  respectively.

In addition, the two optional use cases (Set Time of Day and Display
Time of Day) are captured by one optional feature (TOD Clock). The objects
that realize this feature are depicted on the communication diagram in Figure 12.10.

12.5.5   Feature/Class Dependency for the Microwave Oven
Application

Next the feature/class dependency for the microwave oven application is considered. The product line feature/class dependency table is adapted on the
basis of the features selected for the application, as shown in Table 12.2.

The class hierarchy for the microwave oven application can now be developed. The classes selected are all the kernel classes and those optional and alternative classes that are required because of the selected optional and alternative
features, as indicated in Table 12.2. The classes in the microwave oven application are shown in Figures 12.11 and 12.12.

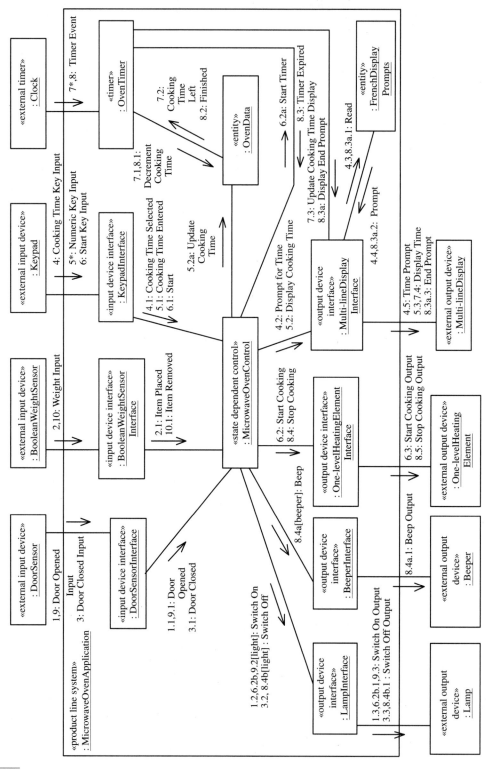

Figure 12.9 *Communication diagram for the microwave oven application: the* Cook Food *use case*

334

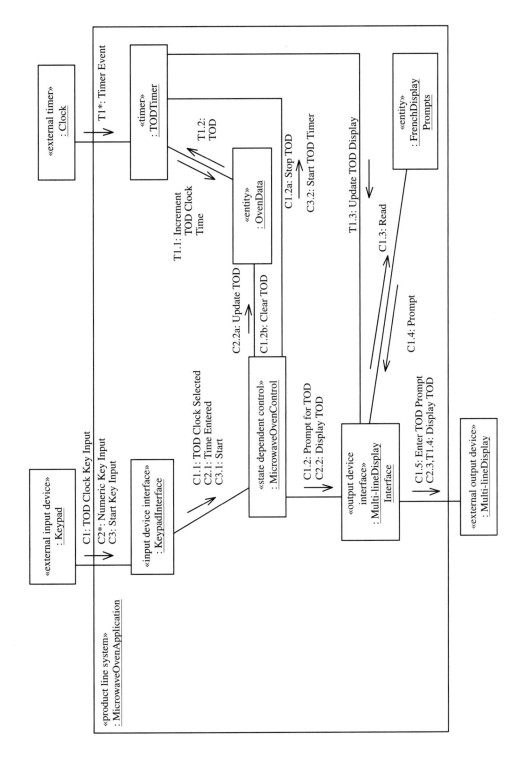

Figure 12.10 *Communication diagram for microwave oven application:* TOD Clock

335

Table 12.2 *Microwave oven application: feature/class dependencies*

Feature Name	Feature Category	Class Name	Class Reuse Category	Class Parameter
Microwave Oven Kernel	common	Door Sensor Interface	kernel	
		Weight Sensor Interface	kernel-abstract-vp	
		Keypad Interface	kernel-param-vp	
		Heating Element Interface	kernel-abstract-vp	
		Display Interface	kernel-abstract-vp	
		Microwave Oven Control	kernel-param-vp	
		Oven Timer	kernel-param-vp	
		Oven Data	kernel-param-vp	
		Display Prompts	kernel-abstract-vp	
Light	optional	Lamp Interface	optional	
		Microwave Oven Control	kernel-param-vp	light : Boolean
Beeper	optional	Beeper Interface	optional	
		Microwave Oven Control	kernel-param-vp	beeper : Boolean
Multi-line Display	alternative	Multi-line Display Interface	variant	
French	alternative	French Display Prompts	variant	
Boolean Weight	default	Boolean Weight Sensor Interface	default	
One-level Heating	default	One-level Heating Element Interface	default	
TOD Clock	optional	TOD Timer	optional	
		Keypad Interface	kernel-param-vp	TODClock : Boolean
		Microwave Oven Control	kernel-param-vp	TODClock : Boolean
		Oven Data	kernel-param-vp	TODvalue : Real
12/24 Hour Clock	Parameterized	Oven Data	kernel-param-vp	TODmaxHour : Integer

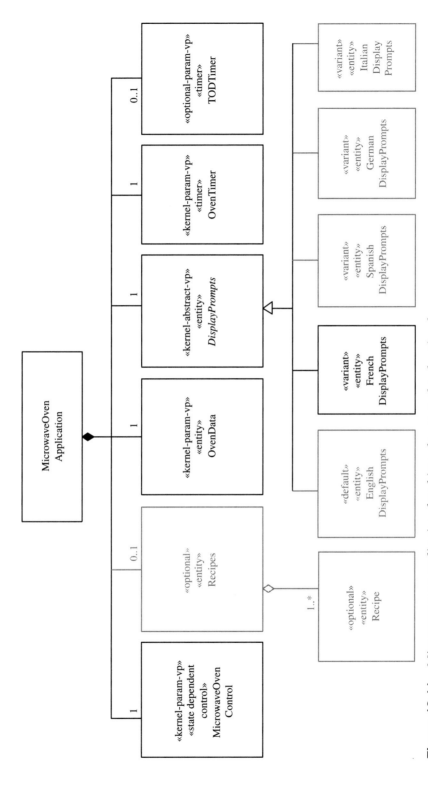

Figure 12.11 *Microwave oven application class hierarchy: control and entity classes*

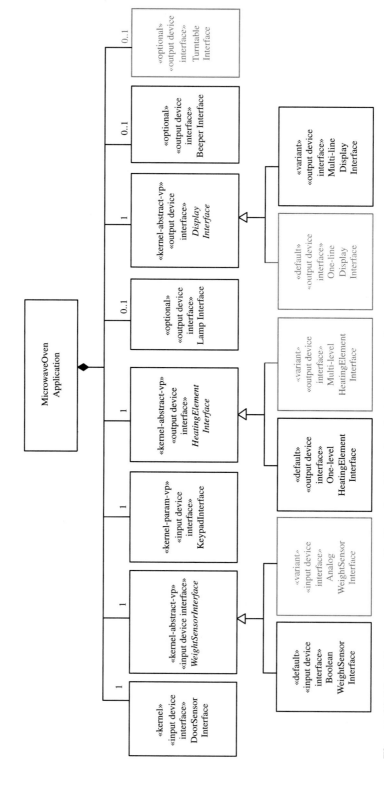

Figure 12.12 *Microwave oven application class hierarchy: device interface classes*

12.5.6   Software Architecture for the Microwave Oven Application

The software architecture for the microwave oven application is depicted in Figure 12.13, which shows all the components selected for this application:

- All the kernel components: `Door Component`, `Keypad Component`, and the composite `Microwave Control` component.

- Two default components—`Boolean Weight Component` and `One-level Heating Element Component`—because no alternative was selected.

- Two optional components—`Lamp Component` and `Beeper Component`—because the optional `Light` and `Beeper` features, respectively, were selected.

- A variant component—`Multi-line Display Interface`—which is an alternative to the default `One-line Display Interface` component and was selected because the `Multi-line Display` alternative feature was required as a prerequisite feature by the `TOD Clock` optional feature. Another variant component—`French Display Prompts`—is an alternative to the default `English Display Prompts` and was selected because of the `French` alternative feature. Because these two simple components are variant, the composite component that contains them (`Microwave Display`) is also variant.

- Within the composite `Microwave Control` component, the kernel `Microwave Oven Control`, `Oven Data`, and `Oven Timer` components. In addition, the optional `TOD Timer` component is included because the `TOD Clock` feature was selected.

The dynamic message communication between components in the microwave oven application is shown in Figure 12.14. All communication between components is asynchronous and is based on the Asynchronous Message Communication pattern (see Chapter 10).

The architecture diagram depicting the port and component interfaces for the components in the microwave oven application is shown in Figure 12.15. Note that the port `RTurntable` is not connected to any other port because the `Turntable` feature was not selected. This is not a problem, because the turntable feature condition in `Microwave Oven Control` is set to false for this application, meaning that the turntable actions are disabled, and hence the port will be idle.

Finally, the deployment diagram for the microwave oven application is shown in Figure 12.16, which shows the components that have been deployed for this application connected via a high-speed bus.

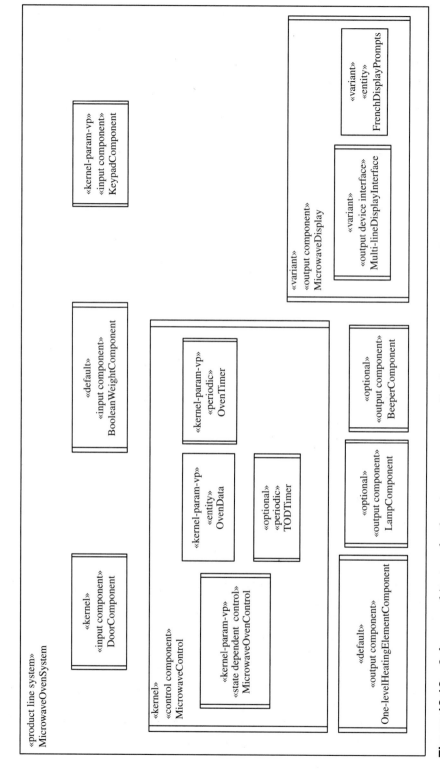

Figure 12.13 *Software architecture for the microwave oven application: component structuring*

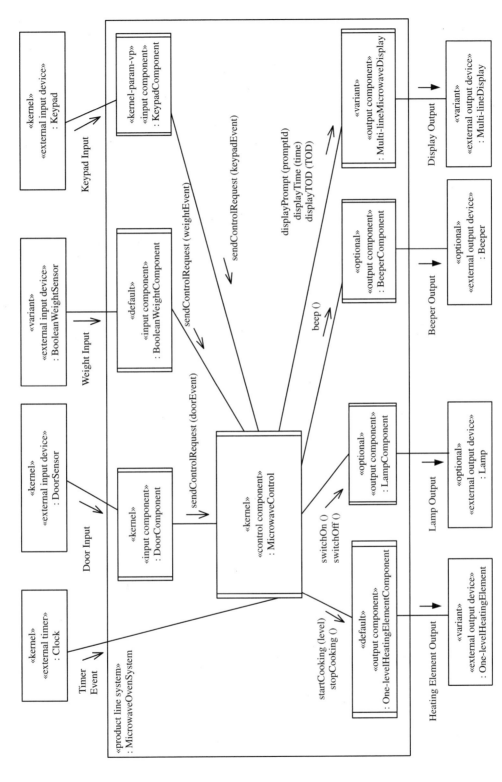

Figure 12.14 *Software architecture for the microwave oven application: message interfaces*

341

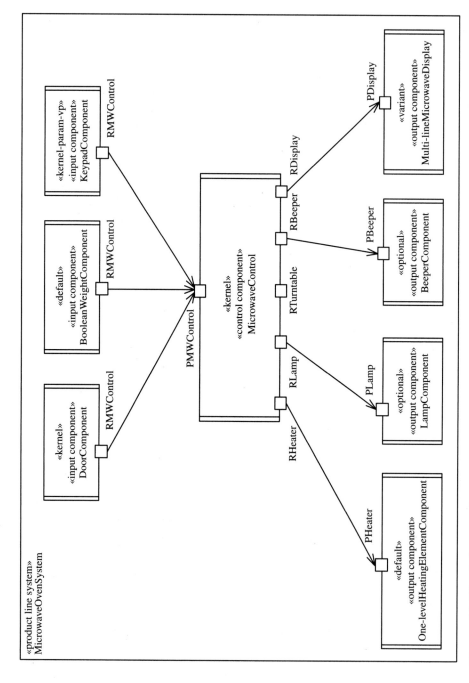

Figure 12.15 *Software architecture for the microwave oven application: component ports and interfaces*

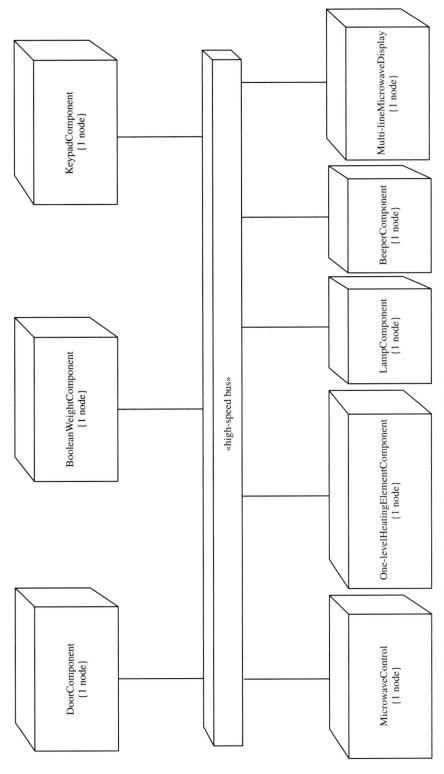

Figure 12.16 *Deployment diagram for the microwave oven application*

12.6 Summary

A software application is a member of a software product line. This chapter described how software application engineering is carried out via adaptation and tailoring of the software product line architecture, previously developed through the evolutionary software product line development process described in Chapter 3, to derive a given software application. During application derivation, the selected application features are used to tailor the product line use case model to derive the application use case model, to tailor the product line analysis model to derive the application analysis model, and to tailor the product line architecture to derive the application architecture. Given the application architecture, the appropriate components from the product line repository are instantiated, interconnected, and deployed.

This chapter also described how software application engineering can be carried out in conjunction with the Unified Software Development Process. In addition, an example of software application engineering for the microwave oven case study was given.

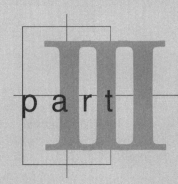

part III

Case Studies

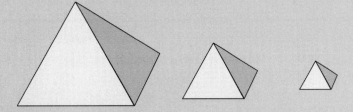

c h a p t e r

Microwave Oven Software Product Line Case Study

This chapter describes a case study for a product line of microwave oven systems. Because this is a new product line, the *forward evolutionary engineering* strategy is used, in which an iterative approach is used to determine the kernel functionality of the product line before the variable functionality is modeled.

The problem is described in Section 13.1. Section 13.2 describes the use case model for the microwave oven product line, starting by modeling the commonality with the kernel use cases and then progressing to modeling the variability with optional use cases and use case variation points. Section 13.3 proceeds to describe the microwave oven product line feature model, in which common, optional, and alternative features are determined from the use case model. Section 13.4 describes static modeling, in which the product line context class diagram is developed depicting the boundary between a product line member and the external environment. Section 13.5 describes dynamic modeling in which the kernel first approach is initially used to develop communication diagrams and statecharts for the kernel use cases. In Section 13.6 the software product line evolution approach is applied to analyze the impact of the variable features on the communication diagrams and statecharts. Then Section 13.7 describes the feature/class dependencies and discusses a categorization of the optional and variant classes. Section 13.8 describes the design model for the microwave oven software product line, which is designed as a component-based software architecture based on the Centralized Control pattern. The design also takes an iterative approach in which the kernel software architecture is developed first, followed by the optional and variant components. Section 13.9, on software application engineering, cross-references Chapter 12, Section 12.5, which describes this process for a given microwave oven application.

13.1   Problem Description

The manufacturer of the microwave oven product line is an original equipment manufacturer with an international market. The microwave oven will form the basis of this product line, which will offer options from basic to top-of-the-line.

The basic microwave oven system has input buttons for selecting **Cooking Time**, **Start**, and **Cancel**, as well as a numeric keypad. It also has a display to show the cooking time left. In addition, the oven has a microwave heating element for cooking the food, a door sensor to sense when the door is open, and a weight sensor to detect if there is an object in the oven. Cooking is possible only when the door is closed and when there is something in the oven.

Options available for more-advanced ovens are a beeper to indicate when cooking is finished, a light that is switched on when the door is open and when food is being cooked, and a turntable that turns during cooking. The microwave oven displays messages to the user such as prompts and warning messages. Because the oven is to be sold around the world, it must be able to vary the display language. The default language is English, but other possible languages are French, Spanish, German, and Italian. The basic oven has a one-line display; more-advanced ovens can have multi-line displays. Other options include a time-of-day clock, which needs the multi-line display option.

The top-of-the-line oven has a recipe cooking feature, which needs an analog weight sensor in place of the basic Boolean weight sensor, the multi-line display feature, and a multi-level power feature (high, medium, low) in place of the basic on/off power feature. Vendors can configure their microwave oven systems of choice from a wealth of optional and alternative features, although feature dependency constraints must be obeyed.

13.2   Use Case Modeling

Analyzing the commonality and variability in the functionality of the microwave oven product line indicates that commonality can be captured by one kernel use case, `Cook Food`, which all members of the product line must provide. Some of the variability in the product line can be captured by variation points in the kernel use case, reflecting small variations. However, the large variations need to be addressed by different use cases, which are the three optional use cases `Set Time of Day`, `Display Time of Day`, and `Cook Food with Recipe`. Only some members of the product line provide these use cases. The use case model is depicted on the use case diagram in Figure 13.1.

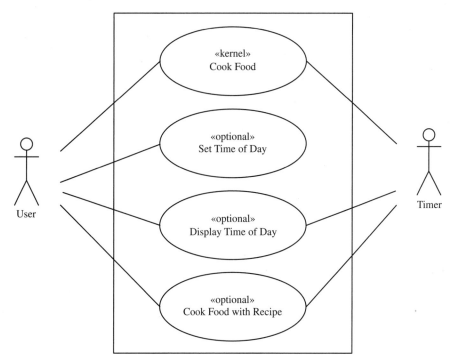

Figure 13.1   *Use case model for the microwave oven software product line*

The product line *commonality* is given by the `Cook Food` kernel use case, as described in Section 13.2.1. The product line *variability* is given by the variation points in the `Cook Food` kernel use case (Section 13.2.2), as well as by the optional use cases and the variation points in these optional use cases (Sections 13.2.3 through 13.2.5). Thus, part of the `Cook Food` use case description captures product line commonality (the use case main sequence and alternatives), and part of it captures product line variability (the description of the variation points). This is different from the optional use cases, where the description is entirely of product line variability.

13.2.1   Cook Food Kernel Use Case

The `Cook Food` use case captures the *common functionality* of this product line, in particular through the description of the main sequence and alternatives. The user is the primary actor, and the timer is the secondary actor.

Use case name: Cook Food.

Reuse category: Kernel.

Summary: User puts food in oven, and microwave oven cooks food.

Actors: User (primary), Timer (secondary).

Precondition: Microwave oven is idle.

Description:
1. User opens the door, puts food in the oven, and closes the door.
2. User presses the **Cooking Time** button.
3. System prompts for cooking time.
4. User enters the cooking time on the numeric keypad and presses **Start**.
5. System starts cooking the food.
6. System continually displays the cooking time remaining.
7. Timer elapses and notifies the system.
8. System stops cooking the food and displays the end message.
9. User opens the door, removes the food from the oven, and closes the door.
10. System clears the display.

Alternatives:

Line 1: User presses **Start** when the door is open. System does not start cooking.

Line 4: User presses **Start** when the door is closed and the oven is empty. System does not start cooking.

Line 4: User presses **Start** when the door is closed and the cooking time is equal to zero. System does not start cooking.

Line 6: User opens door during cooking. System stops cooking. User removes food and presses **Cancel**, or user closes door and presses **Start** to resume cooking.

Line 6: User presses **Cancel**. System stops cooking. User may press **Start** to resume cooking. Alternatively, user may press **Cancel** again; system then cancels timer and clears display.

Postcondition: Microwave oven has cooked the food.

13.2.2 Variation Points in the Cook Food Use Case

After modeling the common functionality in the main sequence of the use case and the alternatives, small *variability* can be addressed by means of *variation points* in the kernel use case. The variation points represent optional or alternative requirements that are present in only some members of the product line. Each line number refers to the location in the main use case description where the variation point is inserted. These variation points would normally appear directly after the alternatives in the use case description in the previous section, but they are shown separately in this section to emphasize that describing variation points is part of the *variability analysis*.

Name: Display Language.

Type of functionality: Mandatory alternative.

Line number(s): 3, 8.

Description of functionality: There is a choice of language for displaying messages. The default is English. Alternative mutually exclusive languages are French, Spanish, German, or Italian.

Name: Weight Sensor.

Type of functionality: Mandatory alternative.

Line number(s): 1.

Description of functionality: Cooking is prohibited if no item is present. The default is Boolean weight sensor, which indicates if item is present. Alternative mutually exclusive variation is analog weight sensor. Analog weight sensor provides weight of item.

Name: Heating Element.

Type of functionality: Mandatory alternative.

Line number(s): 5.

Description of functionality: Default is a one-level heating element: high power level. Alternative is a multi-level heating element, with high, medium, and low power levels.

Name: Power Level.

Type of functionality: Optional.

Line number(s): 2.

Description of functionality: Microwave oven has power level buttons for high power (default), medium, and low. User may select the power level. Requires multi-level heating element as prerequisite.

Name: Display Unit.

Type of functionality: Mandatory alternative.

Line number(s): 3, 4, 6, 8, 10.

Description of functionality: Default is one-line display unit. Alternative is multi-line display unit.

Name: Minute Plus.

Type of functionality: Optional.

Line number(s): 2, 6.

Description of functionality: User may press **Minute Plus**, which results in one minute being added to the cooking time. If the cooking time was previously zero, cooking is started.

Name: Light.

Type of functionality: Optional.

Line number(s): 1, 5, 8, 9.

Description of functionality: If light option is selected, lamp is switched on for duration of cooking and when the door is open. Light is switched off when door is closed and when cooking stops.

Name: Turntable.

Type of functionality: Optional.

Line number(s): 5, 8.

Description of functionality: If turntable option is selected, turntable rotates for duration of cooking.

Name: Beeper.

Type of functionality: Optional.

Line number(s): 8.

Description of functionality: If beeper option is selected, system activates the beeper when cooking stops.

13.2.3 Set Time of Day Use Case

Modeling *variability* in the product line can now focus on modeling the optional use cases, in particular the Time of Day and Cook Food with Recipe use cases. Set Time of Day and Display Time of Day are separate use cases because they have different primary actors and represent separate sequences of interactions. The user is the only actor for the `Set Time of Day` use case. This use case has the following dependency: In order to display the time of day, in addition to the prompts and messages needed by the `Cook Food` use case, it is necessary to have a multi-line display. Therefore, at the `Display Unit` variation point in the `Cook Food` use case, the `Multi-line Display` alternative must be selected. In addition, the `Set Time of Day` use case has its own variation point dealing with the type of clock: 12 hour or 24 hour.

Use case name: Set Time of Day.

Reuse category: Optional.

Dependency: Variation point in `Cook Food` use case: at `Display Unit` variation point, select `Multi-line Display`.

Summary: User sets time-of-day clock.

Actor: User.

Precondition: Microwave oven is idle.

Description:
1. User presses **Time of Day (TOD)** button.
2. System prompts for time of day.
3. User enters the time of day (in hours and minutes) on the numeric keypad.
4. System stores and displays the entered time of day.
5. User presses **Start**.
6. System starts the time-of-day timer.

Alternatives:

Lines 1, 3: If the oven is busy, the system will not accept the user input.

Line 5: The user may press **Cancel** if the incorrect time was entered. The system clears the display.

Variation Points in the Set Time of Day Use Case

Name: 12/24 Hour Clock.

Type of functionality: Mandatory alternative.

Line number(s): 4.

Description of functionality: TOD display is either 12-hour clock (default) or 24-hour clock.

Postcondition: TOD clock has been set.

13.2.4   Display Time of Day Use Case

The timer is the primary actor for the `Display Time of Day` use case, and the user is the secondary actor. This use case executes periodically, every second, when triggered by the timer actor. This use case has the same dependency on the multi-line display unit and the same variation point, 12/24 hour clock, that `Set Time of Day` has.

Use case name: Display Time of Day.

Reuse category: Optional.

Dependency: Variation point in `Cook Food` use case: at `Display Unit` variation point, select `Multi-line Display`.

Summary: System displays time of day.

Actors: Timer (primary actor), User (secondary actor).

Precondition: TOD clock has been set (by `Set Time of Day` use case).

Description:

1. Timer notifies system that one second has elapsed.

2. System increments TOD clock every second, adjusting for minutes and hours.

3. System updates the display with time of day every minute.

Variation Points in the Display Time of Day Use Case

Name: 12/24 Hour Clock.

Type of functionality: Mandatory alternative.

Line number(s): 2.

Description of functionality: TOD display is either 12-hour clock (default) or 24-hour clock.

Postcondition: TOD clock has been updated (every second) and time of day displayed (every minute).

13.2.5   Cook Food with Recipe Use Case

The requirement to support recipes in a microwave oven is a significant increase in functionality, which justifies a separate use case rather than a variation point in the kernel `Cook Food` use case.

Use case name: Cook Food with Recipe.

Reuse category: Optional.

Dependency: Variation points in `Cook Food` use case: at `Display Unit` variation point, select `Multi-line Display`; at `Heating Element` variation point, select `Multi-level Heater`; at `Weight Sensor` variation point, select `Analog Weight Sensor`.

Summary: User puts food in microwave oven and cooks food, using recipe.

Actors: User (primary), Timer (secondary).

Precondition: Microwave oven is idle.

Description:

1. User opens the door, puts food in the oven, and closes the door.
2. User presses the desired recipe button from the recipe buttons on the keypad.
3. System displays the recipe name. Recipe has name, power level (p), fixed time (t_1), and time per unit weight (t_2).
4. User presses the **Start** button.
5. System starts cooking the food for a time given by the following equation: Cooking Time = t_1 + w * t_2, where t_1 and t_2 are times specified in the recipe and w is the weight of the item, and the power level p is specified in the recipe.
6. System continually displays the cooking time remaining.
7. Timer elapses and notifies the system.
8. System stops cooking the food and displays the end message.
9. User opens the door, removes the food from the oven, and closes the door.
10. System clears the display.

Alternatives:

Line 1: User presses **Start** when the door is open. System does not start cooking.

Line 4: User presses **Start** when the door is closed and the oven is empty. System does not start cooking.

Line 4: User presses **Start** when the door is closed and a recipe has not been chosen. System does not start cooking.

Line 4: User presses **Cancel**. System cancels recipe and clears display.

Line 6: User opens the door during cooking. System stops cooking. User removes food and presses **Cancel**, or user closes the door and presses **Start** to resume cooking.

Line 6: User presses **Cancel**. System stops cooking. User may press **Start** to resume cooking. Alternatively, user may press **Cancel** again; system then cancels the recipe and clears the display.

Line 7: If the recipe has more than one step, system completes one step, cooking food for the computed time and specified power level, and then proceeds to the next step.

Variation Points in the Cook Food with Recipe Use Case

This use case also needs variation points, which in this case study are the same as those provided by the `Cook Food` use case; thus, no new functionality is introduced by these variation points. As before, the description of the variation points comes immediately after the description of the alternatives. The postcondition description comes after the variation points.

Name: Display Language.

Type of functionality: Mandatory alternative.

Line number(s): 3, 8.

Description of functionality: There is a choice of language for displaying messages. The default is English. Alternative mutually exclusive languages are French, Spanish, German, or Italian.

Name: Light.

Type of functionality: Optional.

Line number(s): 1, 5, 8, 9.

Description of functionality: If light option is selected, lamp is switched on for duration of cooking and when the door is open. Light is switched off when the door is closed and when cooking stops.

Name: Turntable.

Type of functionality: Optional.

Line number(s): 5, 8.

Description of functionality: If turntable option is selected, turntable rotates for duration of cooking.

Name: Beeper.

Type of functionality: Optional.

Line number(s): 8.

Description of functionality: If beeper option is selected, system activates the beeper when cooking stops.

Postcondition: Microwave oven has cooked the food using the recipe.

13.3   Feature Modeling

After the use case model, the next step is to address is the feature model and to determine how the use cases and use case variation points correspond to features. The feature model is developed as a result of a commonality/variability analysis in which the common, optional, and alternative features are determined. The common features identify the common functionality in the product line, as specified by the kernel use case; the optional and alternative features represent the variability in the product line as specified by the optional use cases and the variation points.

The variable features correspond to optional or alternative functional requirements, which are determined from the use case model. A number of features are determined from the kernel use case, Cook Food. Some of these (e.g., Light, Turntable, and Beeper) are optional features that can be added to the kernel functionality. Others (such as Display Unit and Heating Element) are alternative features, where one feature out of a group must be chosen. Two features correspond to the optional use cases. The TOD Clock feature corresponds to a use case package containing the Set Time of Day and Display Time of Day use cases. The Recipe feature corresponds to the Cook Food with Recipe use case.

Some features are alternative features; that is, one out of a group of alternatives must be chosen. If an alternative is not chosen, then the default is used. Some features have prerequisite features, meaning that for the feature to be selected, the prerequisite feature must also be selected.

This section describes a commonality/variability analysis in which features are categorized as common, optional, or alternative. Feature groups are also determined. The relationships between the features and the use cases are depicted in Table 13.1. Three features correspond to use cases, and the remaining features correspond to variation points in the use cases. For example, Microwave Oven Kernel is a common feature determined from the kernel use case, Cook Food. Light is an optional feature determined from the Cook Food use case; however, it represents a use case variation point also called Light. TOD Clock is an optional feature that corresponds to the two optional time-of-day use cases.

13.3.1   Commonality Analysis

The common requirements are all determined from the problem description and the Cook Food kernel use case; they describe the functionality that every microwave oven must have:

Table 13.1 *Feature/use case dependencies in the microwave oven software product line*

Feature Name	Feature Category	Use Case Name	Use Case Category/ Variation Point (vp)	Variation Point Name
Microwave Oven Kernel	common	Cook Food	kernel	
Light	optional	Cook Food	vp	Light
Turntable	optional	Cook Food	vp	Turntable
Beeper	optional	Cook Food	vp	Beeper
Minute Plus	optional	Cook Food	vp	Minute Plus
One-line Display	default	Cook Food	vp	Display Unit
Multi-line Display	alternative	Cook Food	vp	Display Unit
English	default	Cook Food	vp	Display Language
French	alternative	Cook Food	vp	Display Language
Spanish	alternative	Cook Food	vp	Display Language
German	alternative	Cook Food	vp	Display Language
Italian	alternative	Cook Food	vp	Display Language
Boolean Weight	default	Cook Food	vp	Weight Sensor
Analog Weight	alternative	Cook Food	vp	Weight Sensor
One-level Heating	default	Cook Food	vp	Heating Element
Multi-level Heating	alternative	Cook Food	vp	Heating Element
Power Level	optional	Cook Food	vp	Power Level
TOD Clock	optional	Set Time of Day	optional	
		Display Time of Day	optional	
12/24 Hour Clock	parameterized	Set Time of Day	vp	12/24 Hour Clock
		Display Time of Day		
Recipe	optional	Cook Food with Recipe	optional	

- **Door.** Every microwave oven has a door. Cooking is permitted only when the door is closed.

- **Weight sensor.** Every microwave oven has a weight sensor. Cooking is permitted only when there is an item in the oven, as detected by the weight sensor.

- **Keypad.** The basic keypad consists of a numeric keypad for entering the time, a **Cooking Time** button, a **Start** button, and a **Stop/Cancel** button.

- **Display**. Every microwave oven has a display to show the time remaining, as well as any prompts or warning messages.
- **Heating element**. This is the power source for cooking food.
- **Timer**. A timer is needed to count down the cooking time remaining and to determine when cooking must be stopped.

From a reuse perspective, these common requirements are grouped into one common feature called `Microwave Oven Kernel`.

13.3.2 Optional Features

For the variability analysis, it is necessary to analyze the variation points in the `Cook Food` use case, and to analyze the optional use cases. The variability analysis determines the optional and alternative features. Some features depend on other prerequisite features. In the following analysis, first the optional features are analyzed, followed by the alternative features (Section 13.3.3), and finally those optional features that have prerequisites (Section 13.3.4). The features are also depicted with the feature notation introduced in Chapter 5.

The optional functional features all correspond to optional variability described in the variation points of the `Cook Food` use case, as follows:

- «optional feature» `Light`. This optional feature is determined from the variation point in the `Cook Food` use case. If the light option is selected, the lamp is switched on for the duration of cooking and when the door is open.
- «optional feature» `Turntable`. If the turntable option is selected, the turntable rotates for the duration of cooking.
- «optional feature» `Beeper`. If the beeper option is selected, the system activates the beeper when cooking stops.
- «optional feature» `Minute plus`. The **Minute Plus** button is selected from the keypad. If the oven is already cooking food, pressing **Minute Plus** adds one minute to the cooking time. If the oven is not cooking food and the cooking time is set to zero, the cooking time is set to 60 seconds and cooking is started. If the door is open, a press of the **Minute Plus** button is ignored. If the oven is not cooking food but the cooking time is greater than zero, a press of the **Minute Plus** button is ignored.

13.3.3 Alternative Features and Feature Groups

The alternative features and the feature groups in which they participate correspond to variation points in the `Cook Food` use case, as follows (both the alternative features and the feature groups are described):

- «exactly-one-of feature group» Display Unit {default = One-line Display, alternative = Multi-line Display}. The default display unit is a one-line display; the alternative is a multi-line display. The large display provides more information. This alternative can be selected by itself. However, it is required by other features, including the TOD Clock and Recipe features.

- «exactly-one-of feature group» Display Language {default = English, alternative = French, Spanish, German, Italian}. The default language for displaying information is English. Alternative languages are French, Spanish, German, and Italian.

- «exactly-one-of feature group» Weight {default = Boolean Weight, alternative = Analog Weight}. The default weight sensor is Boolean weight; the alternative is analog weight. The analog weight feature is used only with the Recipe option, so these are mutually inclusive features.

- «exactly-one-of feature group» Heating Element {default = One-level Heating, alternative = Multi-level Heating}. The default heating element mode is one level: high. The alternative is multi-level, with high, medium, and low power levels. Multi-level heating is an implicit feature, so it cannot be selected on its own. It must be selected mutually inclusively with either the Power Level explicit feature or the Recipe explicit feature, or both.

Feature group information can also be presented in tabular format, as shown in Table 13.2.

Table 13.2 *Feature groups of the microwave oven software product line*

Feature Group Name	Feature Group Category	Features in Feature Group	Feature Category
Display Unit	exactly-one-of	One-line Display	default
		Multi-line Display	alternative
Display Language	exactly-one-of	English	default
		French	alternative
		Spanish	alternative
		German	alternative
		Italian	alternative
Weight	exactly-one-of	Boolean Weight	default
		Analog Weight	alternative
Heating Element	exactly-one-of	One-level Heating	default
		Multi-level Heating	alternative

13.3.4   Optional Features with Prerequisite and Mutually Inclusive Features

The following optional features have other features as prerequisites or as mutually inclusive features.

- **Power Level**. With this optional feature, a **Power Level** button is provided on the keypad. The power level can be set to high, medium, or low. One consideration is whether this functionality should be part of the `Multi-level Heating` feature. However, multi-level heating can be provided for cooking with recipes, in which case it can be used without a **Power Level** button. For this reason, `Power Level` and `Multi-level Heating` are kept as separate but mutually inclusive features:

  «optional feature» Power Level {mutually includes = Multi-level Heating}

  This feature corresponds to the variation point called `Power Level` in the `Cook Food` use case.

- **Recipe**. With this optional feature, a **Recipe** button is provided on the keypad. Food is cooked as prescribed in the selected recipe. There is one prerequisite feature: `Multi-line Display`. There are two mutually inclusive features: `Analog Weight` (which is used only for cooking with recipes) and `Multi-level Heating` (as described above):

  «optional feature» Recipe {prerequisite = Multi-line Display, mutually includes = Analog Weight, Multi-level Heating }

  This feature corresponds to the `Cook Food with Recipe` use case.

- **TOD Clock**. If this optional feature is provided, the oven has a time-of-day clock and the time of day is displayed. A prerequisite feature is `Multi-line Display`:

  «optional feature» TOD Clock {prerequisite = Multi-line Display}

  This feature corresponds to the use case package consisting of the `Set Time of Day` and `Display Time of Day` use cases.

13.3.5   Parameterized Features

There is one parameterized feature: `12/24 Hour Clock`. The value of this feature determines whether the TOD clock display is either a 12-hour clock (U.S. civilian style) or a 24-hour clock (U.S. military and European style). The default of these two alternatives is the 12-hour clock. Furthermore, a mutually inclusive feature is TOD Clock. The 12/24 Hour Clock feature can be specified as a parameterized feature as follows:

```
«parameterized feature» 12/24 Hour Clock {type = Time,
permitted value = 12:00, 24:00, default value = 12:00,
mutually includes = TOD Clock}
```

13.3.6 Feature Dependency Diagram

The way the features depend on each other is shown in Figure 13.2, which uses the UML metaclass and stereotype notation described in Chapter 5. The root of the feature dependency hierarchy is the common feature Microwave Oven Kernel, which every microwave oven system needs. Several optional features require Microwave Oven Kernel, including Beeper, Light, Turntable, and Minute Plus. Four exactly-one-of feature groups also depend on Microwave Oven Kernel: Weight Sensor, Heating Element, Display Unit, and Display Language. Each of these groups has two or more features, with one default feature. For example, the Display Unit feature group has the default One-line Display feature and the alternative Multi-line Display feature. The default and alternative features are all mutually exclusive.

Other features have mutually inclusive relationships: The parameterized 12/24 Hour Clock feature mutually includes the optional TOD Clock feature. The optional Recipe feature also mutually includes the Analog Weight alternative feature because the only time analog weight is needed is to weigh items used in a recipe.

13.4 Static Modeling

After developing the use case and feature models, the next step is to develop a static model of the problem domain, from which the product line context class diagram is developed.

13.4.1 Static Modeling of the Problem Domain

An important step in product line modeling is to determine the boundary of the product line. First the real-world classes are determined by modeling of the static aspects of the problem domain. The microwave oven is a composition of

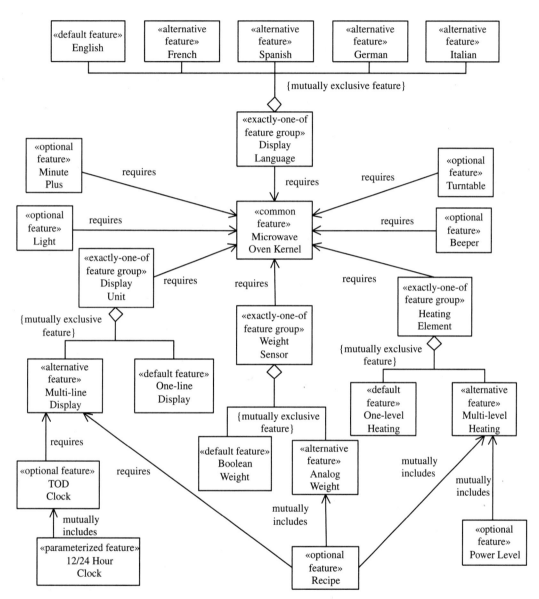

Figure 13.2 *Feature dependency diagram for the microwave oven software product line*

several physical I/O devices, including several sensors and actuators, which the actor uses to interact with the system. The real-world classes are depicted in the class diagram in Figure 13.3.

As determined from the common features, the kernel external classes are Door Sensor, Weight Sensor, Keypad, Display, Heating Element, and Clock. The variability analysis reveals that there are several optional external classes: Beeper, Turntable, and Lamp. Furthermore, variability is also captured in the following variant classes, which are designed as mutually exclusive subclasses of previously determined kernel classes:

- One-level Heating Element and Multi-level Heating Element, which are mutually exclusive subclasses of the Heating Element superclass. The default is One-level Heating Element.

- Boolean Weight Sensor and Analog Weight Sensor, which are mutually exclusive subclasses of the Weight Sensor superclass. The default is Boolean Weight Sensor.

- One-line Display and Multi-line Display, which are mutually exclusive subclasses of the Display superclass. The default is One-line Display.

13.4.2 Software Product Line Context Model

The product line context model is determined from the static model of the problem domain. The product line context class diagram defines the boundary between a product line system (i.e., any member of the product line) and the external environment (i.e., the external classes to which members of the product line have to interface). The product line context model is depicted on a class diagram (Figure 13.4) and shows the multiplicity of the associations between the external classes and the product line system, which is depicted as one aggregate class. With the forward evolutionary engineering strategy, the product line context class diagram is developed in two stages: first for the kernel external classes, and then for the kernel and optional external classes.

Each external class is depicted with two stereotypes: One represents the role of the external class; for example, Door Sensor is an external input device. The second stereotype represents the reuse category, whether the external class is a kernel or optional class in the product line. In this case study, Door Sensor, Weight Sensor, and Keypad are all external input devices; they are also kernel classes. Heating Element and Display are external output devices that are also kernel. Clock is an external timer that is kernel. On the other hand,

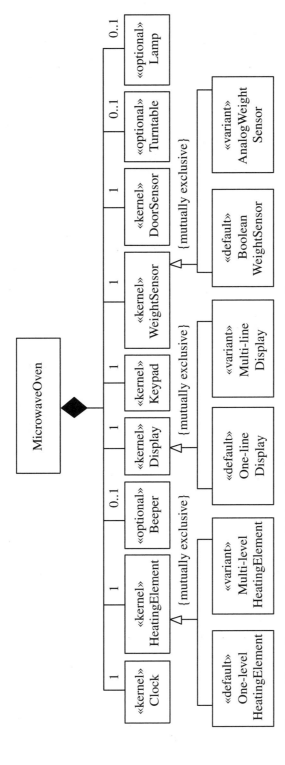

Figure 13.3 *Conceptual static model for the microwave oven software product line*

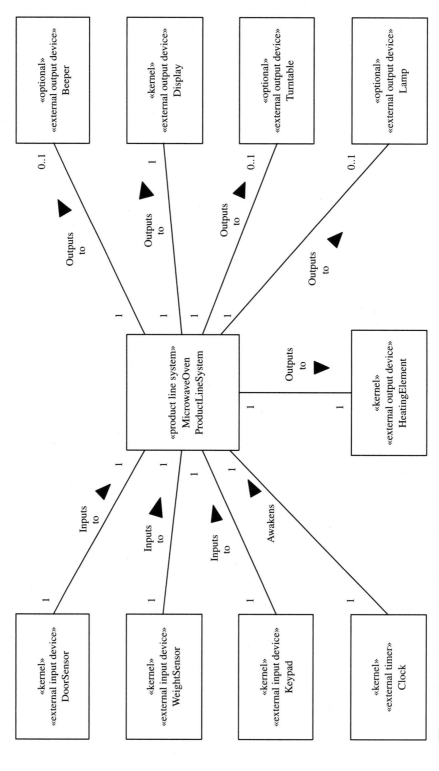

Figure 13.4 *Context class diagram for the microwave oven software product line*

Beeper, Turntable, and Lamp are external output devices that are optional. Kernel external classes have a one-to-one association with the product line system aggregate class; optional external classes have a zero-or-one association with the product line system aggregate class.

13.5 Dynamic Modeling

After the external classes have been determined in the system context model, the next step is to develop a dynamic model of the product line. With the forward evolutionary engineering strategy, the kernel of the product line is analyzed first. Initially the kernel classes are determined by consideration of the kernel use cases and the interactions among those objects on communication diagrams and statecharts. After that, the optional and variant classes are determined by consideration of the variation points (as determined from the use case and feature models) and the optional use cases. Additional communication diagrams and statecharts are developed. Because object/class structuring and dynamic modeling are iterative activities, they are both described in this section.

13.5.1 Object and Class Structuring: Kernel Classes

The first step is to determine what the kernel classes are. How these classes interact with each other will be determined during dynamic modeling. During design modeling, decisions are made about whether a given class is active or passive, and what the operations of each class are.

The kernel classes are all determined by consideration of the Cook Food use case because this is the only kernel use case. The kernel classes are categorized according to the object and class structuring criteria.

The kernel input device interface classes are determined by consideration of the kernel external device classes on the product line context diagram. In this case study, Door Sensor Interface, Weight Sensor Interface, and Keypad Interface are all kernel input device interface classes that communicate with the corresponding kernel external device classes. Heating Element Interface and Display Interface are kernel output device interface classes that communicate with the corresponding kernel external output devices. Clock is a kernel external timer that appears on the context diagram. Oven Timer is the software timer object that communicates with the external Clock object.

There is also a need for an entity class to store microwave oven data, such as the cooking time, which is called Oven Data. In addition, because there is a need to provide display prompts to the user in different languages, the decision is made to separate the textual prompts from the `Display Interface` object. The prompts are stored in an entity class called `Display Prompts`. Finally, because of the complex sequencing and control required for the oven, a state-dependent control class is required—`Microwave Oven Control`—which executes the statechart for the oven. The kernel classes are therefore categorized as follows:

- **Input device interface classes:**
  - `Door Sensor Interface`
  - `Weight Sensor Interface`
  - `Keypad Interface`
- **Output device interface classes:**
  - `Heating Element Interface`
  - `Display Interface`
- **Control classes:**
  - `Microwave Oven Control`
- **Timer classes:**
  - `Oven Timer`
- **Entity classes:**
  - `Oven Data`
  - `Display Prompts`

The kernel classes are depicted on a class diagram as shown in Figure 13.5. These kernel classes by themselves do not constitute an executable system. In order to have a minimally functional system—a kernel system—it is necessary to consider situations in which there is a choice of classes. In each case, the default class is chosen to constitute a kernel system. Given the defaults described in the kernel use case and kernel features, the following default classes are chosen for inclusion in the kernel system:

- `Boolean Weight Sensor Interface`
- `One-level Heating Element Interface`
- `One-line Display Interface`
- `English Display Prompts`

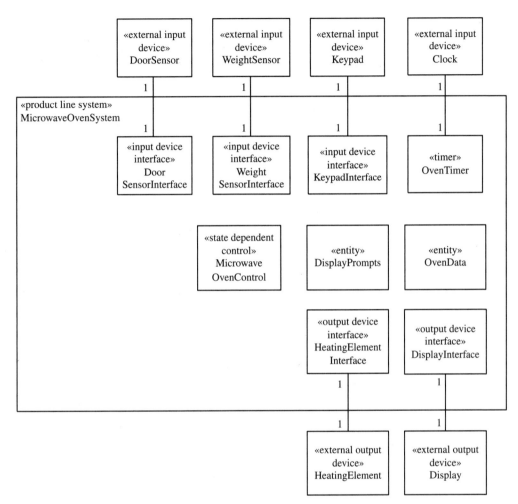

Figure 13.5   *Kernel classes in the microwave oven software product line*

13.5.2   Dynamic Modeling: Kernel First Approach

With the kernel first approach, the kernel communication diagram is developed on the basis of the Cook Food kernel use case. Instances of the kernel classes are depicted in Figure 13.6, with the default object chosen where such a choice is required. Because this interaction is state-dependent, the scenario is also shown on the statecharts for the state-dependent objects: Microwave Oven Control and Oven Timer (Figures 13.7 and 13.8, respectively).

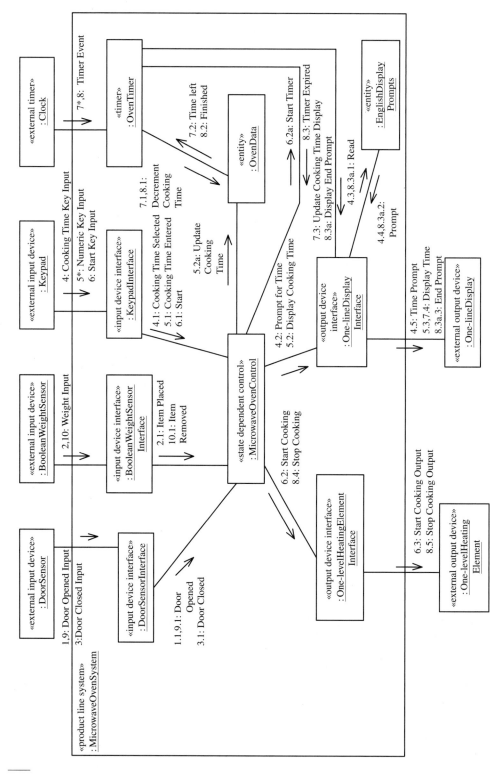

Figure 13.6 *Communication diagram for kernel use case:* Cook Food *use case*

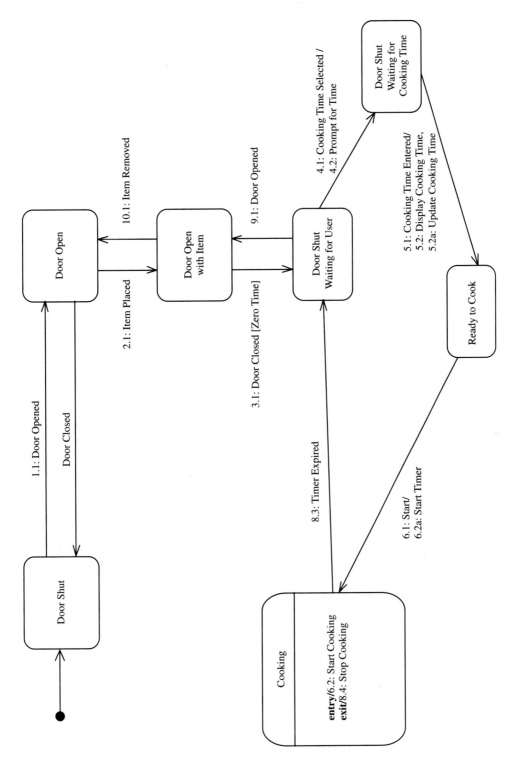

Figure 13.7 *Statechart for* Microwave Oven Control: Cook Food *use case*

371

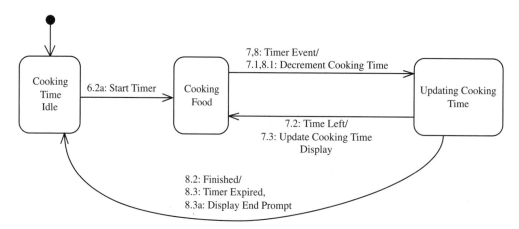

Figure 13.8 *Statechart for* Oven Timer: Cook Food *use case*

The following is the sequence of messages for the kernel communication diagram and statecharts based on the main sequence through the Cook Food kernel use case, as described in Section 13.2.1. The sequence numbers correspond to the messages on the communication diagram depicted in Figure 13.6 and to the events and actions depicted on the statecharts in Figures 13.7 and 13.8.

1: Door Opened Input. The user opens the door. The external Door Sensor object sends this input to the Door Sensor Interface object.

1.1: Door Opened. Door Sensor Interface sends the Door Opened message to the Microwave Oven Control object, which changes state.

2: Weight Input. The user places an item to be cooked into the oven. The external Boolean Weight Sensor object sends this input to the Boolean Weight Sensor Interface object.

2.1: Item Placed. Boolean Weight Sensor Interface sends the Item Placed message to the Microwave Oven Control object, which changes state.

3: Door Closed Input. The user closes the door. The external Door Sensor object sends this input to the Door Sensor Interface object.

3.1: Door Closed. Door Sensor Interface sends the Door Closed message to the Microwave Oven Control object, which changes state.

4: Cooking Time Key Input. The user presses the **Cooking Time** button on the keypad. The external Keypad object sends this input to the Keypad Interface object.

4.1: Cooking Time Selected. `Keypad Interface` sends the `Cooking Time Selected` message to the `Microwave Oven Control` object, which changes state.

4.2: Prompt for Time. As a result of changing state, `Microwave Oven Control` sends the `Prompt for Time` message to the `One-line Display Interface` object.

4.3: Read. The message arriving at `One-line Display Interface` contains a prompt ID, so `One-line Display Interface` sends a `Read` message to `English Display Prompts` to get the corresponding prompt message.

4.4: Prompt. `English Display Prompts` returns the text for the `Time Prompt` message.

4.5: Time Prompt. `One-line Display Interface` sends the `Time Prompt` output to the external `One-line Display` object.

5*: Numeric Key Input. The user enters the numeric value of the time on the keypad, pushing one or more keys. `Keypad` sends the value of the numeric key(s) input to `Keypad Interface`.

5.1: Cooking Time Entered. `Keypad Interface` sends the internal value of each numeric key to `Microwave Oven Control`.

5.2: Display Cooking Time. `Microwave Oven Control` sends the value of each numeric key to `One-line Display Interface`, to ensure that these values are sent only in the appropriate state.

5.2a: Update Cooking Time. `Microwave Oven Control` concurrently sends the numeric value of each numeric key to `Oven Data` to update the cooking time.

5.3: Display Time. `One-line Display Interface` shifts the previous digit to the left and adds the new digit. It then sends the new value of cooking time to the external `One-line Display` object.

6: Start Key Input. The user presses the **Start** button. The external `Keypad` object sends this input to the `Keypad Interface` object.

6.1: Start. `Keypad Interface` sends the `Start` message to `Microwave Oven Control`, which changes state.

6.2: Start Cooking. As a result of changing state, `Microwave Oven Control` sends the `Start Cooking` message to the `One-level Heating Element Interface` object.

6.2a: Start Timer. Microwave Oven Control concurrently notifies the Oven Timer to start the oven timer.

6.3: Start Cooking Output. One-level Heating Element Interface sends this output to One-level Heating Element to start cooking the food.

7*: Timer Event. The external Clock object sends a timer event every second to Oven Timer.

7.1: Decrement Cooking Time. As Oven Timer is counting, it sends this message to the Oven Data object, which maintains the cooking time.

7.2: Time Left. After decrementing the cooking time, which is assumed to be greater than zero at this step of the scenario, Oven Data sends the Time Left message to Oven Timer.

7.3: Update Cooking Time Display. Oven Timer sends the cooking time left to One-line Display Interface.

7.4: Display Time. One-line Display Interface outputs the new cooking time value to the external One-line Display object.

8: Timer Event. The external Clock object sends a timer event every second to Oven Timer.

8.1: Decrement Cooking Time. As Oven Timer is counting, it sends this message to the Oven Data object, which maintains the cooking time.

8.2: Finished. After decrementing the cooking time, which is assumed to be equal to zero at this step of the scenario, Oven Data sends the Finished message to Oven Timer.

8.3: Timer Expired. Oven Timer sends the Timer Expired message to Microwave Oven Control, which changes state.

8.3a: Display End Prompt. Oven Timer concurrently sends the Display End Prompt message to One-line Display Interface.

8.3a.1: Read. The message arriving at One-line Display Interface contains a prompt ID, so One-line Display Interface sends a Read message to English Display Prompts to get the corresponding prompt message.

8.3a.2: Prompt. English Display Prompts returns the text for the End Prompt message.

8.3a.3: End Prompt. One-line Display Interface outputs the End Prompt message to the external One-line Display object.

8.4: Stop Cooking. As a result of changing state (in step 8.3), `Microwave Oven Control` sends the `Stop Cooking` message to `One-level Heating Element Interface` object.

8.5: Stop Cooking Output. `One-level Heating Element Interface` sends this output to the `One-level Heating Element` object to stop cooking the food.

9: Door Opened Input. The user opens the door. The external `Door Sensor` object sends this input to the `Door Sensor Interface` object.

9.1: Door Opened. `Door Sensor Interface` sends the `Door Opened` message to the `Microwave Oven Control` object, which changes state.

10: Weight Input. The user removes the cooked item from the oven. The external `Boolean Weight Sensor` object sends this input to the `Boolean Weight Sensor Interface` object.

10.1: Item Removed. `Boolean Weight Sensor Interface` sends the `Item Removed` message to the `Microwave Oven Control` object, which changes state.

13.5.3 Kernel Statechart for Microwave Oven Control

Whereas the statechart in Figure 13.7 models the states and transitions for one scenario representing the main sequence through the `Cook Food` use case, the next step in state machine modeling is to develop the kernel statechart, which has states and transitions to represent all possible sequences through the use case. The kernel statechart for `Microwave Oven Control` (Figure 13.9) is composed of two orthogonal finite state machines. One is `Microwave Oven Sequencing` (which is decomposed into substates as shown in Figure 13.10); the other is `Cooking Time Condition`, which consists of two sequential substates: `Zero Time` and `Time Remaining`. The reason for this design is to explicitly model the time condition, without which `Microwave Oven Control` would be a lot more complicated. Thus the `Zero Time` and `Time Remaining` substates of `Cooking Time Condition` are guard conditions on the `Microwave Oven Sequencing` statechart (Figure 13.10). The sequence numbers for the main `Cook Food` scenario are also shown on the figures. This statechart is also used as an example in Chapter 8.

`Microwave Oven Sequencing` is hierarchically structured and consists of the following substates (see Figure 13.10):

- **Door Shut**. This is the initial state, in which the oven is idle with the door shut and there is no food in the oven.

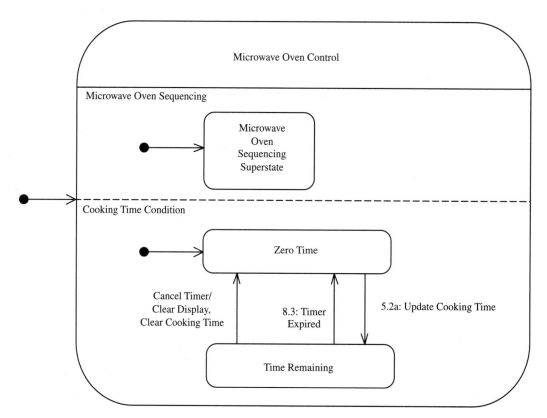

Figure 13.9 *Statechart for* Microwave Oven Control: *kernel top-level statechart*

- **Door Open**. In this state the door is open and there is no food in the oven.
- **Door Open with Item**. This state is entered after an item has been placed in the oven.
- **Door Shut with Item**. This state is entered after the door has been closed with an item in the oven. This state is a superstate consisting of the following substates (see Figure 13.11):
  - **Waiting for User**. Waiting for user to press the **Cooking Time** button.
  - **Waiting for Cooking Time**. Waiting for user to enter the cooking time.

  These substates are entered via a history state H. Entry via a history state allows a superstate that has sequential substates to remember the last substate entered and to return to it when the superstate is reentered. This

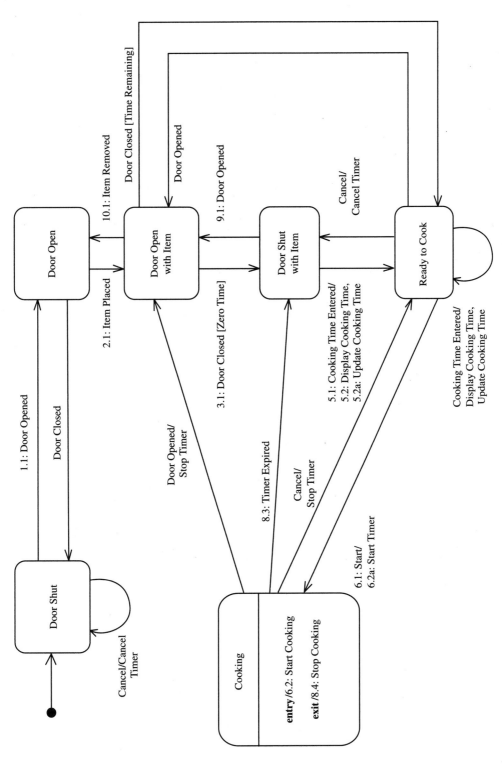

Figure 13.10 *Kernel statechart for* Microwave Oven Control: *decomposition of the* Microwave Oven Sequencing *superstate*

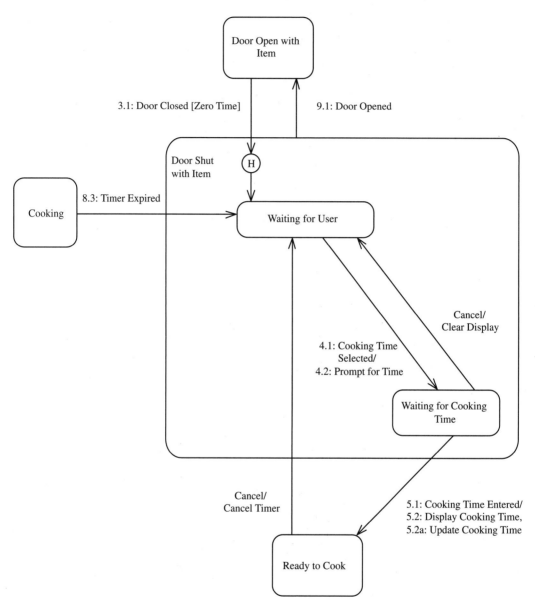

Figure 13.11 *Kernel statechart for* Microwave Oven Control: *decomposition of the* Door Shut with Item *superstate*

mechanism is used in the `Door Shut with Item` superstate so that when the door is opened (e.g., while in the `Waiting for Cooking Time` substate) and then closed again, the previously active substate (in this case `Waiting for Cooking Time`) is reentered.

- **Ready to Cook.** The oven is ready to start cooking food.
- **Cooking.** The food is cooking. This state is entered from the `Ready to Cook` state when the **Start** button is pressed. This state is exited if the timer expires, the door is opened, or **Cancel** is pressed.

13.5.4 Kernel Statechart for Oven Timer

The kernel statechart for `Oven Timer` has the following states for cooking food (Figure 13.12):

- **Cooking Time Idle.** This is the initial state, in which the oven is idle.
- **Cooking Food.** The timer is keeping track of the cooking time. This state is entered when the timer is started.
- **Updating Cooking Time.** This state is entered every time a timer event is received, which is every second. It is an interim state from which either `Cooking Food` is reentered if the timer has not yet expired, or `Cooking Time Idle` is entered if the timer has expired.

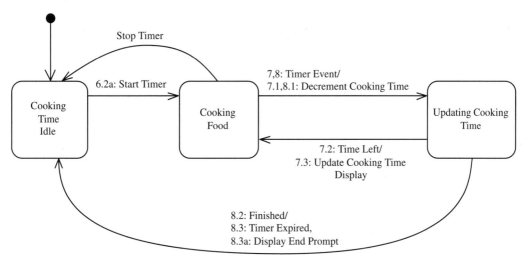

Figure 13.12 *Kernel statechart for* Oven Timer

13.6   Software Product Line Evolution

After the kernel communication diagram for the Cook Food use case and the kernel statecharts have been determined, the product line evolution approach is used to analyze the impact of the variable features. First consider the variation points of the Cook Food use case, which represent optional and alternative features. Product line evolution consists of analyzing the impact of these features on the kernel communication diagram, as described next. In each case the impact of the feature is to modify the communication diagram to a lesser or greater extent. The impact of many of these features is to add new objects and messages, as described in Sections 13.6.1 through 13.6.9. The impact on the statecharts is described in Sections 13.6.10 and 13.6.11.

13.6.1   Impact Analysis of the Beeper Feature

The impact of the Beeper feature is that the beeper is switched on when cooking has finished. The first impact is the need for the Beeper external output device and the Beeper Interface output device interface object, as shown in Figure 13.13. The second impact is on Microwave Oven Control, which is the state-dependent control object that sends the Beep command to Beeper Interface when cooking is stopped (message 8.4a). Beeper Interface in turn sends the Beep Output command (message 8.4a.1) to the Beeper external output device. On the communication diagram, Beep messages are guarded by the feature condition. The impact on the Microwave Oven Control statechart

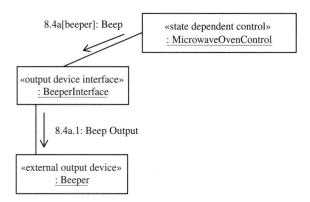

Figure 13.13   *Communication diagram for the* Cook Food *use case: impact of the* Beeper *feature*

is that it needs to have an optional `Beep` action, which is also guarded by the [beeper] feature condition, as described in Section 13.6.10.

«optional feature» Beeper

Optional object: `Beeper Interface`, to interface to external `Beeper`.

Affected object: `Microwave Oven Control`, because it controls when to start the beeper.

13.6.2   Impact Analysis of the Multi-Line Display Feature

The `Multi-Line Display` feature affects only one object: `Display Interface`. The `Multi-line Display Interface` object replaces the `One-line Display Interface` object:

```
«exactly-one-of feature group» Display Unit {default = One-line
Display, alternative = Multi-line Display}
```

No other objects are affected, and there is no change in the message sequence. The impact is depicted in Figure 13.14.

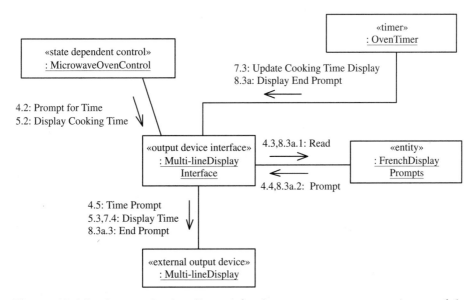

Figure 13.14 *Communication diagram for the* Cook Food *use case: impact of the* Multi-line Display *and French* Display Language *features*

«alternative feature» Multi-line Display

Variant object: `Multi-line Display Interface`, to interface to the external `Multi-line Display` instead of `One-line Display`.

13.6.3 Impact Analysis of the Display Language Feature

The `Display Language` feature affects only one object: `Display Prompts`. The `English Display Prompts` object is replaced by one of the alternative `Display Prompts` objects, such as `Spanish Display Prompts` or `French Display Prompts`:

```
«exactly-one-of feature group» Display Language {default = English,
alternative = French, Spanish, German, Italian}
```

No other objects are affected, and there is no change in the message sequence shown in Figure 13.14.

«alternative feature» French

Variant object: `FrenchDisplayPrompts`, to store display prompts in French instead of the default language, English.

«alternative feature» Spanish

Variant object: `SpanishDisplayPrompts`, to store display prompts in Spanish.

«alternative feature» German

Variant object: `GermanDisplayPrompts`, to store display prompts in German.

«alternative feature» Italian

Variant object: `ItalianDisplayPrompts`, to store display prompts in Italian.

13.6.4 Impact Analysis of the Light Feature

The impact of the `Light` feature is that the lamp is switched on whenever the door is opened or whenever food is cooking. The lamp is switched off whenever the door is closed or whenever cooking is stopped. The first impact is the need for the `Lamp` external output device and the `Lamp Interface` output device interface object, as shown in Figure 13.15. Although `Door Sensor Interface` plays an important role, this object is not modified by the `Light` feature. It is the job of the `Microwave Oven Control` object to send the `Switch On` and `Switch Off` commands to the `Lamp Interface` object, as depicted in Figure 13.15. `Microwave Oven Control` sends the `Switch On`

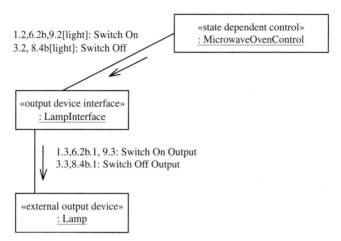

Figure 13.15 *Communication diagram for the* Cook Food *use case: impact of the* Light *feature*

command when the door is opened (messages 1.2 and 9.2) and when cooking is started (message 6.2b). It sends the Switch Off command when the door is closed (message 3.2) and when cooking is stopped (message 8.4b).

Lamp Interface in turn sends the Switch On Output command (messages 1.3, 6.2b.1, and 9.3) and Switch Off Output command (3.3 and 8.4b.1) to the Lamp external output device. On the communication diagram, Switch On and Switch Off messages are guarded by the [light] feature condition. The impact on the Microwave Oven Control statechart is the addition of the optional Switch On and Switch Off actions, which are also guarded by the [light] feature condition, as described in Section 13.6.10.

«optional feature» Light

Optional object: Lamp Interface, to interface to external Lamp.

Affected object: Microwave Oven Control, which controls when to switch the lamp on and off.

13.6.5   Impact Analysis of the Turntable Feature

The impact of the Turntable feature is that the turntable needs to turn when food is cooking and to be stationary when food is not cooking. The first impact is the need for the Turntable external output device and the Turntable Interface output device interface object, as shown in Figure 13.16.

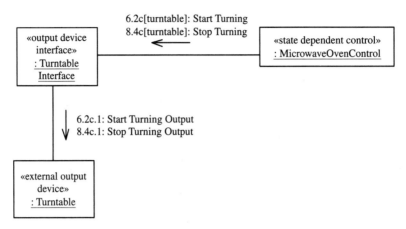

Figure 13.16 *Communication diagram for the* Cook Food *use case: impact of the* Turntable *feature*

The second impact is on Microwave Oven Control, which is the state-dependent control object that sends the Start Turning command (message 6.2c) to Turntable Interface when cooking is started and the Stop Turning command (message 8.4c) when cooking is stopped. Turntable Interface in turn sends the Start Turning Output command (message 6.2c.1) and the Stop Turning Output command (message 8.4c.1) to the Turntable external output device. On the communication diagram, the Start Turning and Stop Turning messages are guarded by the [turntable] feature condition. The impact on the Microwave Oven Control statechart is the addition of the optional Start Turning and Stop Turning actions, which are also guarded by the [turntable] feature condition, as described in Section 13.6.10.

«optional feature» Turntable

Optional object: Turntable Interface, to interface to external Turntable.

Affected object: Microwave Oven Control, which controls when to start and stop the turntable.

13.6.6   Impact Analysis of the Minute Plus Feature

The Minute Plus feature requires the addition of a **Minute Plus** button on the keypad. This feature affects the Cook Food kernel communication diagram in two ways, which are depicted on two separate communication diagrams. If

Minute Plus is pressed after cooking has started, then the cooking time is updated. If **Minute Plus** is pressed before cooking has started, then the cooking time is updated and cooking is started (assuming that the oven is ready to start cooking).

The impact of pressing **Minute Plus** after cooking has started is depicted in Figure 13.17: The user presses the **Minute Plus** button on the keypad after pressing the **Start** button (message 6). This is depicted on Figure 13.17 as the Keypad external input device sending the Minute Plus Input message guarded by the [minuteplus] feature condition (6.10 [minuteplus]). Keypad Interface

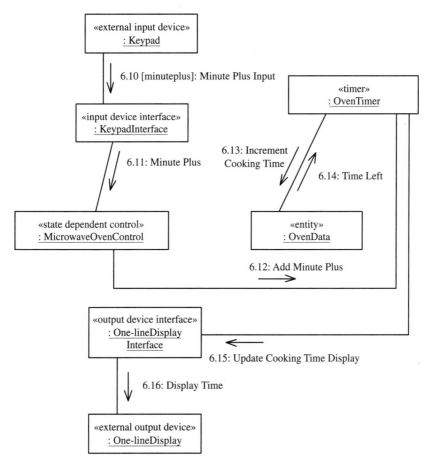

Figure 13.17 *Communication diagram for the* Cook Food *use case: impact of the* Minute Plus *feature after* **Start** *is pressed*

sends the `Minute Plus` message (shown as message 6.11) to `Microwave Oven Control`. What follows is state-dependent. If cooking is in progress, `Microwave Oven Control` sends an `Add Minute Plus` message (6.12) to `Oven Timer`, which adds 60 seconds to the cooking time in `Oven Data` (messages 6.13 and 6.14) and then sends the new time to `One-line Display Interface` (6.15).

The impact of pressing **Minute Plus** when cooking is not in progress is depicted in Figure 13.18. Because this scenario represents an alternative way of

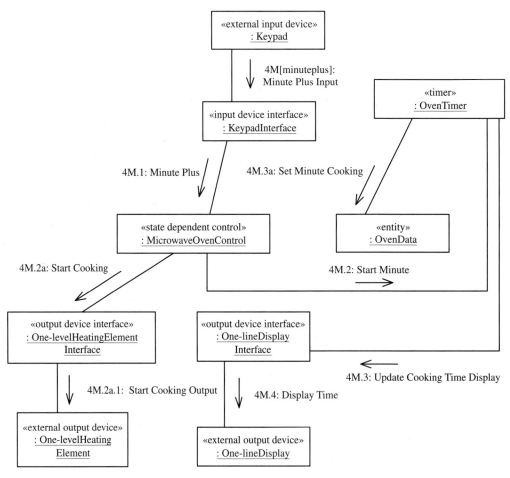

Figure 13.18 *Communication diagram for the* Cook Food *use case: impact of the* Minute Plus *feature in place of* **Start** *being pressed*

starting cooking, it is depicted with an alternative message sequence and a feature condition: 4M [minuteplus]. `Keypad Interface` sends the `Minute Plus` message (4M.1) to `Microwave Oven Control`. `Microwave Oven Control` behaves differently in this situation, sending a `Start Minute` message (4M.2) to `Oven Timer` and a `Start Cooking` message (4M.2a) to `One-level Heating Element Interface`. `Oven Timer` then sets the cooking time to 60 seconds in `Oven Data` (message 4M.3a) and sends the new time to `One-line Display Interface` (message 4M.3), which in turn outputs the `Display Time` message (4M.4) to the external display.

«optional feature» Minute Plus

Affected objects:

> `Keypad Interface`, because a **Minute Plus** button is needed on the keypad.
>
> `Microwave Oven Control`, which, depending on the current state, decides whether to set the timer and start cooking or just increment the timer.
>
> `Oven Timer`, which needs to adjust the cooking time.

13.6.7   Impact Analysis of the Power Level and Multi-level Heating Features

Because the `Power Level` feature has a prerequisite feature—`Multi-level Heating`—the impact of both these features is considered together. The objects affected are `Keypad Interface` (to provide additional **Power** buttons), `Microwave Oven Control` (for new states and transitions), `Oven Data` (to store the selected power level), and `Multi-level Heating Element Interface` (to provide a heater with multiple levels).

The communication diagram for the `Power Level` feature is shown in Figure 13.19, which illustrates what happens when the user presses the selected power level button via the `Keypad` external input device. The effect is depicted as an additional sequence started by message 3.10 [power] `Power Level Input` sent by `Keypad` to `Keypad Interface`. `Keypad Interface` sends the `Power Level Selected` message (3.11) to `Microwave Oven Control`, which in turn sends the selected power level to `One-Line Display Interface` (message 3.12) and to be stored in `Oven Data` (message 3.12a). After **Start** is pressed, prompting the `Start` message (6.1) to be sent, there is an additional sequence in which `Multi-level Heating Element Interface` reads the power level from `Oven Data` (messages 6.2.1 and 6.2.2).

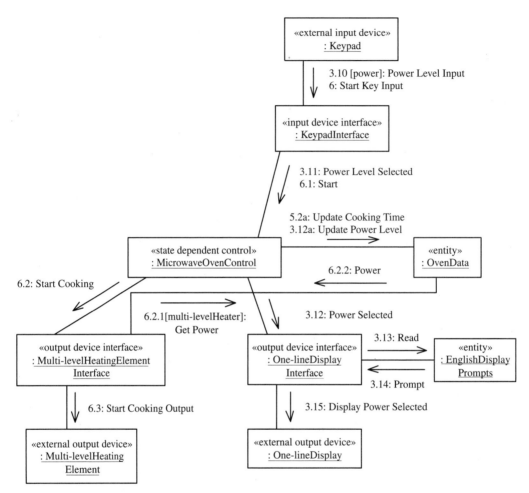

Figure 13.19 *Communication diagram for the* Cook Food *use case: impact of the* Power Level *feature*

«alternative feature» Multi-level Heating

Variant object: Multi-level Heating Interface, to interface to the external Multi-level Heating Element **instead of** One-level Heating Element, (which is required by the mutually exclusive One-level Heating default feature):

```
«exactly-one-of feature group» Heating Element {default = One-level
Heating, alternative = Multi-level Heating}
```

Affected objects:

- `Microwave Oven Control`, which must provide different actions for multi-level heating.
- `Oven Data`, to store the selected power level.

«optional feature» Power Level {prerequisite = Multi-level Heating}
Affected objects:

- `Keypad Interface`, to provide user buttons for high, medium, and low power levels.
- `Microwave Oven Control`, which needs additional states and transitions for user input of power level.
- `Oven Data`, to update and store selected power level.

Prerequisite object from prerequisite feature: `Multi-level Heating Interface`.

13.6.8   Impact Analysis of the TOD Clock Feature

The `TOD` (time of day) `Clock` feature corresponds to the two optional use cases that deal with time of day: `Set Time of Day` and `Display Time of Day`. Because these are different use cases, it is necessary to determine the objects needed to support each of them and to develop new communication diagrams to depict the dynamic execution of the objects for these use cases.

For the `Set Time of Day` use case, the objects needed are `Keypad Interface` (because the keypad will need a new **TOD Clock** button), `Microwave Oven Control` (because the time of day can be set only when the oven is idle), `Oven Data` (to store the current time of day), and `Multi-line Display Interface` (a prerequisite requirement for the `TOD Clock` feature). In addition to these affected objects, one new object—`TOD Timer`—needs to be activated.

For the `TOD Clock` feature in the `Display Time of Day` use case, the objects needed are `TOD Timer` (to receive timer events), `Oven Data` (to store the time of day that needs to be incremented), and `Multi-line Display Interface` (to display the new time). In other words, no new objects are needed.

Figure 13.20 shows the communication diagram for both the `Set Time of Day` and the `Display Time of Day` use cases. Note that the related feature (`12/24 Hour Clock`) does not affect this communication diagram, because it is a parameter, which is stored with `TOD value` in `Oven Data`. When `TOD value` is incremented every minute, this parameter is checked to determine whether after 12:59, the clock should be set to 1:00 or 13:00.

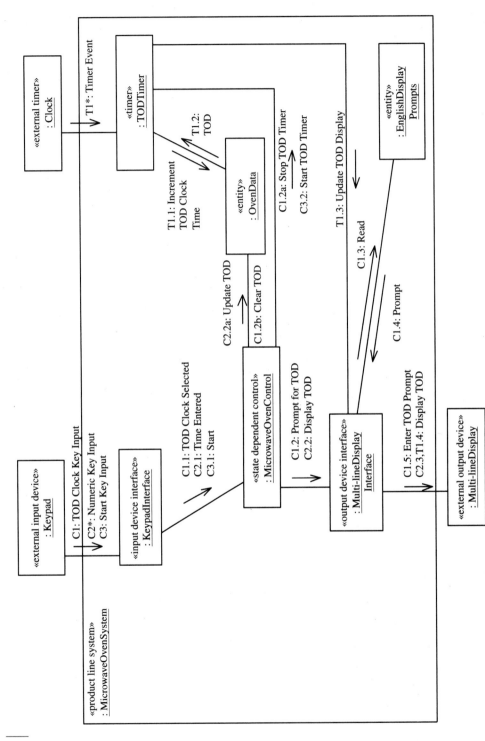

Figure 13.20 *Communication diagram for optional* Set Time of Day *and* Display Time of Day *use cases*

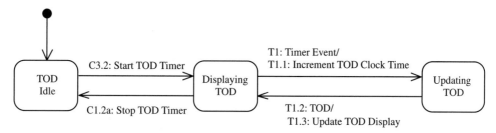

Figure 13.21   *Statechart for* TOD Timer

The statechart for the state-dependent TOD Timer object is shown in Figure 13.21.

The following is the sequence of messages for the communication diagram and statecharts based on the Set Time of Day and Display Time of Day optional use cases. Because the TOD Clock feature captures both of these use cases, its impact is shown on the same communication diagram for both use cases. The sequence numbers correspond to the messages on the communication diagram depicted in Figure 13.20 and to the events and actions depicted on the statechart for TOD Timer in Figure 13.21. The impact on the Microwave Oven Control statechart is described in Section 13.6.10.

The message sequence for the Set Time of Day use case is as follows:

C1: TOD Clock Key Input. The user presses the **TOD Clock** button on the keypad. The external Keypad object sends this input to the Keypad Interface object.

C1.1: TOD Clock Selected. Keypad Interface sends the TOD Clock Selected message to the Microwave Oven Control object, which changes state.

C1.2: Prompt for TOD. As a result of changing state, one action is for Microwave Oven Control to send the Prompt for TOD message to the Multi-line Display Interface object.

C1.2a: Stop TOD Timer. As a result of changing state, a second concurrent action is for Microwave Oven Control to send the Stop TOD Timer message to the TOD Timer object.

C1.2b: Clear TOD. As a result of changing state, a third concurrent action is for Microwave Oven Control to send the Clear TOD message to the Oven Data object.

C1.3: Read. The message arriving at Multi-Line Display Interface contains a prompt ID, so Multi-Line Display Interface sends a Read message to `English Display Prompts` to get the corresponding prompt message.

C1.4: Prompt. `English Display Prompts` returns the text for the `Enter TOD Prompt` message.

C1.5: Enter TOD Prompt. `Multi-Line Display Interface` sends the `Enter TOD Prompt` output to the external `Multi-Line Display` object.

C2*: Numeric Key Input. The user enters the numeric value of the time on the keypad, pushing one or more keys. `Keypad` sends the value of the numeric key(s) input to `Keypad Interface`.

C2.1: Time Entered. `Keypad Interface` sends the internal value of each numeric key to `Microwave Oven Control`.

C2.2: Display TOD. `Microwave Oven Control` sends the value of each numeric key to `Multi-Line Display Interface` to ensure that these values are sent only in the appropriate state.

C2.2a: Update TOD. `Microwave Oven Control` concurrently sends the numeric value of each numeric key to `Oven Data` to update the time of day.

C2.3: Display TOD. `Multi-Line Display Interface` shifts the previous digit to the left and adds the new digit. It then sends the new time of day to the external `Multi-line Display`.

C3: Start Key Input. User presses the **Start** button. The external `Keypad` object sends this input to the `Keypad Interface` object.

C3.1: Start. `Keypad Interface` sends the `Start` message to `Microwave Oven Control`, which changes state.

C3.2: Start TOD Timer. As a result of changing state, `Microwave Oven Control` notifies `TOD Timer` to start the TOD timer.

The message sequence for the `Display Time of Day` use case is as follows:

T1*: Timer Event. The external `Clock` sends a timer event every second to `TOD Timer`.

T1.1: Increment TOD Clock Time. `Oven Timer` sends this message to the `Oven Data` object, which adds one second to the time of day.

T1.2: TOD. After incrementing the time of day, `Oven Data` sends the `TOD` message to `TOD Timer`.

T1.3: Update TOD Display. `TOD Timer` sends the current time of day to `Multi-line Display Interface`.

T1.4: Display TOD. `Multi-line Display Interface` outputs the new `TOD value` to the external `Multi-line Display`.

The affected objects are as follows:

«optional feature» TOD Clock {prerequisite = Multi-line Display}

Optional object: TOD Timer, to control updating and displaying the time-of-day clock.

Affected objects:

Keypad Interface, because a **TOD Clock** button is needed.

Microwave Oven Control, to handle setting the time of day.

Oven Data, to store the TOD value.

Prerequisite object from prerequisite features: Multi-line Display Interface, to display the time of day.

The parameterized 12/24 Hour Clock feature affects the Oven Data object:

«parameterized feature» 12/24 Hour Clock {type = Time, permitted value = 12:00, 24:00, default value = 12:00, prerequisite = TOD Clock}

Affected object: Oven Data, to store configuration parameter TOD max Hour identifying either a 12-hour or a 24-hour clock.

13.6.9   Impact Analysis of the Recipe Feature

The Recipe feature has a major impact. It is a separate use case, so it warrants its own communication diagram, which is depicted in Figure 13.22. Many of the objects, however, are shared with the Cook Food communication diagram. Because of prerequisite features, the Analog Weight Interface, Multi-level Heating Element Interface, and Multi-line Display Interface objects are all needed. Furthermore, Keypad Interface (recipe buttons), Microwave Oven Control (new states and transitions), Oven Data (recipe data), and Oven Timer (new states and transitions) are all affected. In addition, two new entity objects are required: Recipe and Recipes. The parameters for the selected recipe are stored in Recipe; the parameters for all the recipes as a group are stored in Recipes.

The following is the sequence of messages for the communication diagram and statecharts based on the Cook Food with Recipe optional use case. The sequence numbers correspond to the messages on the communication diagram depicted in Figure 13.22 and to the events and actions depicted on the statecharts in Figures 13.23 through 13.26.

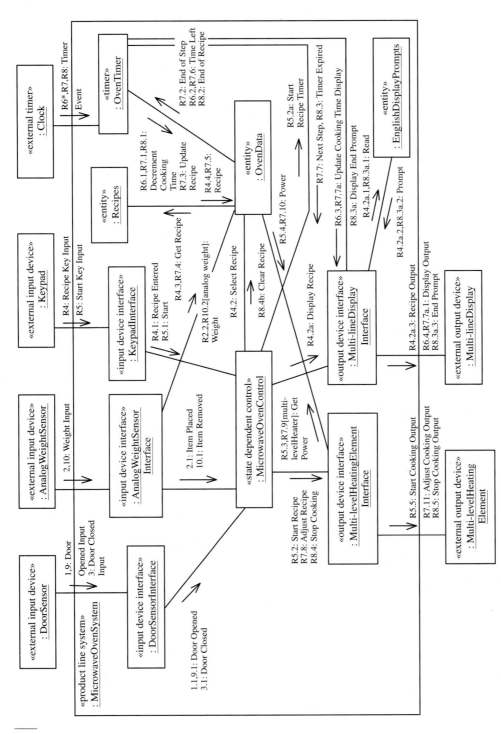

Figure 13.22 *Communication diagram for the optional* Cook Food with Recipe *use case*

1: Door Opened Input. The user opens the door. The external `Door Sensor` object sends this input to the `Door Sensor Interface` object.

1.1: Door Opened. `Door Sensor Interface` sends the `Door Opened` message to the `Microwave Oven Control` object, which changes state.

2: Weight Input. The user places an item to be cooked into the oven. The external `Analog Weight Sensor` object sends this input to the `Analog Weight Sensor Interface` object.

2.1: Item Placed. `Analog Weight Sensor Interface` sends the `Item Placed` message to the `Microwave Oven Control` object, which changes state.

R2.2: [analog weight] Weight. `Analog Weight Sensor Interface` sends the weight of the food to `Oven Data` for storage.

3: Door Closed Input. The user closes the door. The external `Door Sensor` object sends this input to the `Door Sensor Interface` object.

3.1: Door Closed. `Door Sensor Interface` sends the `Door Closed` message to the `Microwave Oven Control` object, which changes state.

R4: Recipe Key Input. The user presses the **Recipe** button on the keypad. The external `Keypad` object sends this input to the `Keypad Interface` object.

R4.1: Recipe Entered. `Keypad Interface` sends the `Recipe Entered` message to the `Microwave Oven Control` object, which changes state.

R4.2: Select Recipe. As a result of changing state, one action is for `Microwave Oven Control` to send the `Select Recipe` message to `Oven Data`.

R4.2a: Display Recipe. As a result of changing state, a second concurrent action is for `Microwave Oven Control` to send the `Display Recipe` message to the `Multi-line Display Interface` object.

R4.2a.1: Read. The message arriving at `Multi-line Display Interface` contains a prompt ID, so `Multi-line Display Interface` sends a `Read` message to `English Display Prompts` to get the corresponding prompt message.

R4.2a.2: Prompt. `English Display Prompts` returns the text for the `Recipe Output` message.

R4.2a.3: Recipe Output. `Multi-line Display Interface` sends the `Recipe Output` message to the external `Multi-line Display` object.

R4.3: Get Recipe, R4.4: Recipe. `Oven Data` requests the `Recipes` object to return the parameters of the selected recipe.

R5: Start Key Input. The user presses the **Start** button. The external `Keypad` object sends this input to the `Keypad Interface` object.

R5.1: Start. `Keypad Interface` sends the `Start` message to `Microwave Oven Control`, which changes state.

R5.2: Start Recipe. As a result of changing state, `Microwave Oven Control` sends the `Start Recipe` message to the `Multi-level Heating Element Interface` object.

R5.2a: Start Recipe Timer. `Microwave Oven Control` concurrently notifies `Oven Timer` to start the recipe timer.

R5.3: Get Power, R5.4: Power. `Multi-level Heating Element Interface` requests `Oven Data` to return the selected power level.

R5.5: Start Cooking Output. `Multi-level Heating Element Interface` sends this output to `Multi-level Heating Element` to start cooking the food.

R6*: Timer Event. The external `Clock` object sends a timer event every second to `Oven Timer`.

R6.1: Decrement Cooking Time. `Oven Timer` sends this message to the `Oven Data` object, which subtracts one second from the cooking time.

R6.2: Time Left. After decrementing the cooking time, which is assumed to be greater than zero at this step of the scenario, `Oven Data` sends the `Time Left` message to `Oven Timer`.

R6.3: Update Cooking Time Display. `Oven Timer` sends the cooking time left to `Multi-line Display Interface`.

R6.4: Display Output. `Multi-line Display Interface` outputs the new cooking time value to the external `Multi-line Display`.

R7: Timer Event. The external `Clock` object sends a timer event every second to `Oven Timer`.

R7.1: Decrement Cooking Time. `Oven Timer` sends this message to the `Oven Data` object, which subtracts one second from the cooking time.

R7.2: End of Step. After decrementing the cooking time, which is assumed to be equal to zero at this step of the scenario, `Oven Data` sends the `End of Step` message to `Oven Timer`.

R7.3: Update Recipe. `Oven Timer` sends the `Update Recipe` message to `Oven Data`.

R7.4: Get Recipe, R7.5: Recipe. `Oven Data` requests the `Recipes` object to return the parameters of the next step of the selected recipe.

R7.6: Time Left. Oven Timer sends the Time Left message to Oven Timer.

R7.7: Next Step. Oven Timer sends the Next Step message to Microwave Oven Control, which changes state.

R7.7a: Update Cooking Time Display. Oven Timer sends the cooking time left to Multi-line Display Interface.

R7.7a.1: Display Output. Multi-line Display Interface outputs the new cooking time value to the external Multi-line Display.

R7.8: Adjust Recipe. As a result of changing state, Microwave Oven Control sends the Adjust Recipe message to the Multi-level Heating Element Interface object.

R7.9 [multi-levelHeater]: Get Power, R7.10: Power. Multi-level Heating Element Interface requests Oven Data to return the selected power level.

R7.11: Adjust Cooking Output. Multi-level Heating Element Interface sends this output to Multi-level Heating Element to continue cooking the food at a different power level.

R8: Timer Event. The external Clock object sends a timer event every second to Oven Timer.

R8.1: Decrement Cooking Time. Oven Timer sends this message to the Oven Data object, which subtracts one second from the cooking time.

R8.2: End of Recipe. After decrementing the cooking time, which is assumed to be equal to zero at this step of the scenario, Oven Data sends the End of Recipe message to Oven Timer.

R8.3: Timer Expired. Oven Timer sends the Timer Expired message to Microwave Oven Control, which changes state.

R8.3a: Display End Prompt. Oven Timer concurrently sends the Display End Prompt message to Multi-line Display Interface.

R8.3a.1: Read. The message arriving at Multi-line Display Interface contains a prompt ID, so Multi-line Display Interface sends a Read message to English Display Prompts to get the corresponding prompt message.

R8.3a.2: Prompt. English Display Prompts returns the text for the End Prompt message.

R8.3a.3: End Prompt. Multi-line Display Interface outputs the End Prompt message to the external Multi-line Display object.

R8.4: Stop Cooking. As a result of changing state (in step 8.3), `Microwave Oven Control` sends the `Stop Cooking` message to `Multi-level Heating Element Interface` object.

R8.4b: Clear Recipe. As a result of changing state, a second concurrent action is for `Microwave Oven Control` to send this message to `Oven Data`.

R8.5: Stop Cooking Output. `Multi-level Heating Element Interface` sends this output to `Multi-level Heating Element` to stop cooking the food.

9: Door Opened Input. The user opens the door. The external `Door Sensor` object sends this input to the `Door Sensor Interface` object.

9.1: Door Opened. `Door Sensor Interface` sends the `Door Opened` message to the `Microwave Oven Control` object, which changes state.

10: Weight Input. The user removes the cooked item from the oven. The external `Analog Weight Sensor` object sends this input to the `Analog Weight Sensor Interface` object.

10.1: Item Removed. `Analog Weight Sensor Interface` sends the `Item Removed` message to the `Microwave Oven Control` object, which changes state.

For the `Recipe` feature, the weight of the item is needed; this means that the alternative `Analog Weight` feature is needed in place of the default `Boolean Weight` feature:

```
«exactly-one-of feature group» Weight Sensor {default = Boolean
Weight, alternative = Analog Weight}
```

The affected objects are as follows:

« alternative feature» Analog Weight

Variant object: `Analog Weight Sensor Interface`, to interface to the external `Analog Weight Sensor` instead of `Boolean Weight Sensor`.

Affected object: `Oven Data`, to store the weight of the item.

«optional feature» Recipe {prerequisite = Multi-line Display, mutually includes = Analog Weight, Multi-level Heating}

Optional objects:

- `Recipes`, a container class that provides access to individual recipes.
- `Recipe`, which holds information about an individual recipe.

Affected objects:

- `Keypad Interface`, to provide a user button for each recipe.
- `Microwave Oven Control`, which needs additional states and transitions for cooking with recipes.
- `Oven Data`, to store information about the selected recipe.
- `Oven Timer`, to control the recipe timer.

Prerequisite objects from prerequisite features:

- `Multi-level Heating Interface`
- `Multi-line Display Interface`
- `Analog Weight Sensor Interface`

13.6.10   Impact Analysis of the Statechart for Microwave Oven Control

Consider the impact of various features on the `Microwave Oven Control` statechart (Figures 13.23–13.27). The impact of the optional and alternative features on the objects was described previously, so the features that affect `Microwave Oven Control` have already been determined.

Each feature is given a Boolean guard condition, which is called a *feature condition* and depicted in square brackets: [*feature*]. If the feature condition is *true*, then the feature is selected; if it is *false*, then the feature is not selected. Feature conditions are used as guard conditions on the new state transitions that are introduced because of the optional and alternative features. For a state transition to take place, the event must arrive *and* the feature guard condition must be true, meaning that the feature is provided. If a state transition has an action guarded by a feature condition, then the action is feature-dependent and will execute only if the feature condition is *true*. The top-level statechart for the feature-laden `Microwave Oven Control` is shown in Figure 13.23.

The features that affect `Microwave Oven Control`, illustrated in Figures 13.24 through 13.27, are as follows:

- **`Light`, `Turntable`, and `Beeper` optional features** (see Figure 13.24). Each feature needs an optional output device interface object added, as well as state-dependent actions to control it. The objects are `Lamp Interface`, `Turntable Interface`, and `Beeper Interface`, respectively. These features also affect the state-dependent control object—`Microwave Oven Control`—because this object has to trigger the actions, which are executed by the output device interface objects. Thus the `Turntable` feature affects

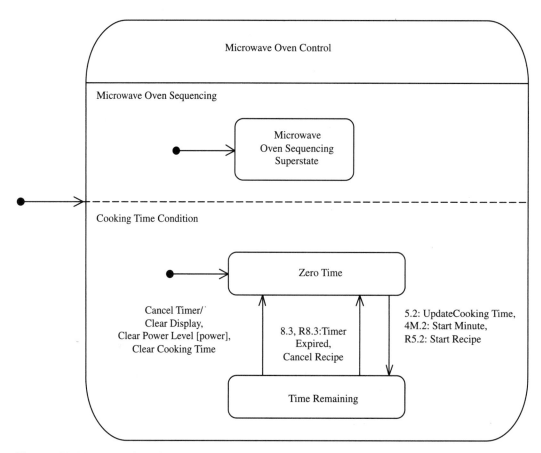

Figure 13.23 *Statechart for* Microwave Oven Control *with all features: top-level statechart*

the Cooking state, which needs a Start Turning entry action on entering the state and a Stop Turning exit action on leaving the state. The Beeper feature requires a Beep exit action on leaving the state. For the Light feature, other transitions are affected because the light is switched on whenever the door is opened and switched off when the door is closed, so this feature necessitates the additional transition actions Switch On and Switch Off.

- **Minute Plus optional feature** (see Figure 13.24). The impact of this feature is state-dependent and results in additional transitions. **Minute Plus** can be pressed when the oven is in the state Door Shut with Item, in which case the Cooking state is entered and the output action is Start Minute.

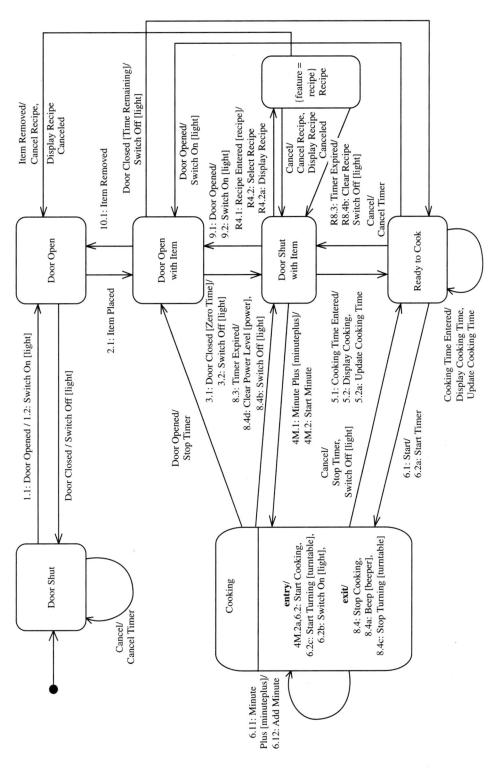

Figure 13.24 *Statechart for* Microwave Oven Control *with all features: decomposition of the* Microwave Oven Sequencing *superstate*

401

Minute Plus can also be pressed while the oven is in the `Cooking` state, in which case the state is not changed and an internal transition causes the `Add Minute` action. These output actions are sent to `Oven Timer`, as described in Section 13.6.11.

- **`Power Level` feature** (see Figure 13.25). This feature allows the user to select the power level. The impact of this feature is to add a new substate in the `Door Shut with Item` superstate called `Waiting for User after Power Level`. The new substate is entered when the `Power Level Selected` event is received during the `Waiting for User` state. The actions are `Update Power Level` and `Display Power Level`. These actions are repeated if `Power Level Selected` is reentered during this substate.

- **`Recipe` optional feature** (see Figure 13.26). The impact of the `Recipe` feature is to add a `Recipe` superstate, which is decomposed into the following substates:

  - `Ready to Cook with Recipe`. This state is entered when a recipe is selected, as given by the `Recipe Entered` event, when the `recipe` feature condition is true

  - `Door Open with Recipe`.

  - `Cooking with Recipe`.

The *R* prefix on the sequence numbers in Figures 13.24 through 13.26 (starting with R4.1: `Recipe Entered [ recipe]`) indicates that this is a recipe-specific sequence.

- **`TOD Clock` feature** (see Figure 13.27). This feature allows the time-of-day clock to be set and updated. Setting the TOD clock is allowed when the door is shut and the oven is idle—that is, in the `Door Shut` state. Because of the effect of opening and closing the door, the same approach is used as with the `Door Shut with Item` state—namely, to make the `Door Shut` state a superstate with various substates, which are entered via a history state H. The substates are `Idle`, `Waiting for TOD`, and `Setting TOD`.

13.6.11 Impact Analysis of the Statechart for Oven Timer

Two features—`Minute Plus` and `Recipe`—affect the `Oven Timer` statechart as described here and depicted in Figures 13.28 through 13.30. `Oven Timer` is a concurrent statechart with two orthogonal superstates: `Cooking Timer` and `Recipe Timer`.

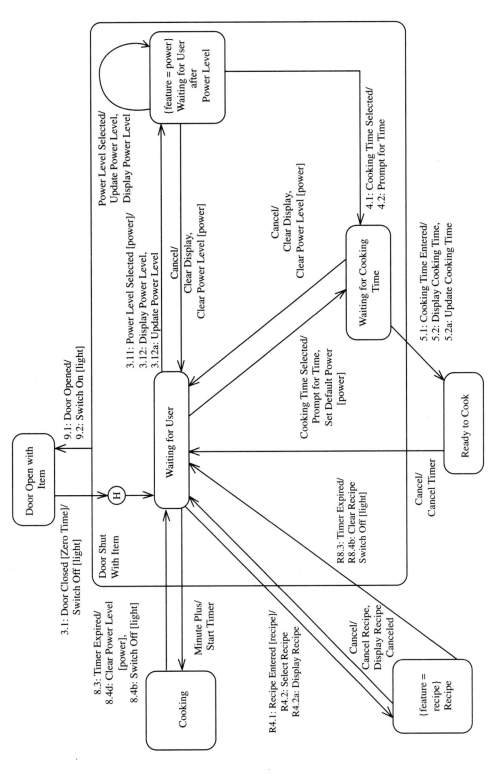

Figure 13.25 *Statechart for* Microwave Oven Control *with all features: decomposition of the* Door Shut with Item *superstate*

403

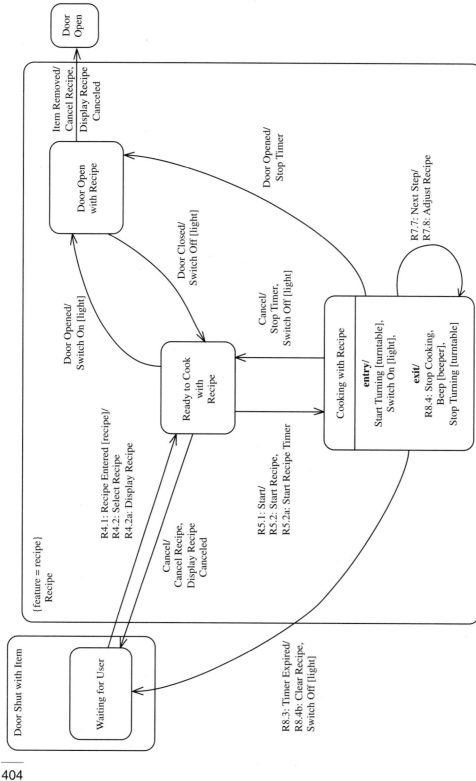

Figure 13.26 *Statechart for* Microwave Oven Control *with all features: decomposition of the* Recipe *superstate*

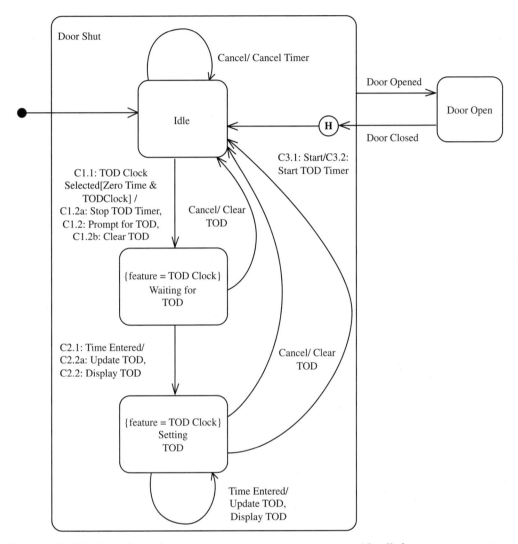

Figure 13.27 *Statechart for* Microwave Oven Control *with all features:* Door Shut *superstate showing impact of* TOD Clock *feature*

1. **Minute Plus feature** (see Figure 13.29). The impact of this feature is state-dependent and results in two additional transitions on the Cooking Timer statechart. If the timer is in the Cooking Time Idle state when **Minute Plus** is pressed, the input event is Start Minute and the timer transitions to the Cooking Food state. On the other hand, if the statechart is in the

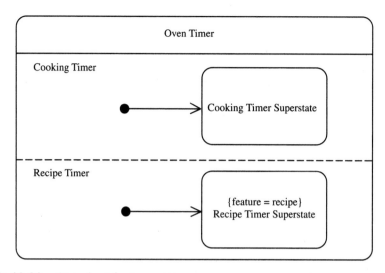

Figure 13.28 *Statechart for* Oven Timer

Cooking Food state when Minute Plus is pressed, the input event is Add Minute and the timer transitions to the Updating Cooking Time state.

2. **Recipe feature** (see Figure 13.30). This feature results in the addition of an orthogonal state machine for Recipe Timer, which consists of four sequential states:

    a. **Recipe Idle**. No recipe is being used.

    b. **Cooking with Recipe**. Cooking is in progress and is using a recipe.

    c. **Updating Recipe Time**. This state is entered when there is a timer event; the action is to decrement the recipe time. There are three possible transitions out of this state. If there is time left, the state machine returns to the Cooking with Recipe state and the cooking time is displayed. If the recipe time is zero and this is the end of the recipe step, the state Ending Recipe Step is entered. Otherwise, if the recipe time is zero and this is the end of the recipe, the statechart transitions back to the Recipe Idle state.

    d. **Ending Recipe Step**. This is an interim state, entered when the recipe step has ended, during which the system determines the time remaining for the next recipe step.

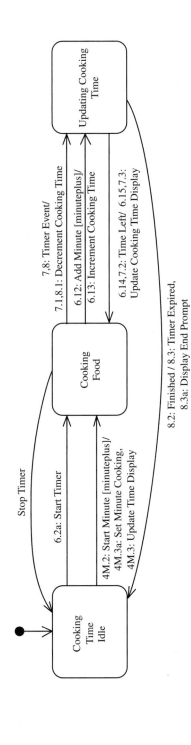

Figure 13.29 *Statechart for* Cooking Timer

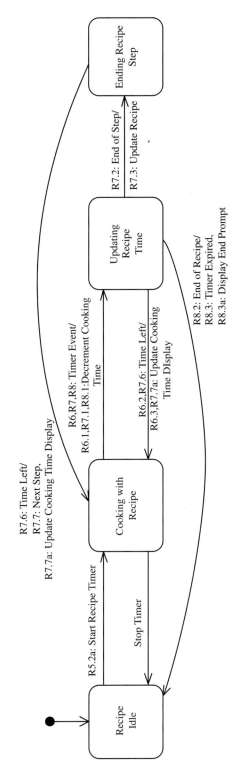

Figure 13.30 *Statechart for* Recipe Timer

13.7   Feature/Class Dependency Analysis

The impact analyses described in Section 13.6 identified both the optional objects and the affected objects. *Optional objects* are new objects that were not used in the kernel communication diagrams but are needed to support an optional or alternative feature. *Affected objects* are objects that must behave differently to support an optional or alternative feature. For the affected objects, an important decision is whether to handle the change by using inheritance or by parameterization.

The feature/class dependencies for the microwave oven software product line are summarized in Table 13.3. In this section, each of the classes is considered from a product line reuse perspective.

Table 13.3   *Feature/class dependencies of the microwave oven software product line*

Feature Name	Feature Category	Class Name	Class Category	Class Parameter
Microwave Oven Kernel	common	Door Sensor Interface	kernel	
		Weight Sensor Interface	kernel-abstract-vp	
		Keypad Interface	kernel-param-vp	
		Heating Element Interface	kernel-abstract-vp	
		Display Interface	kernel-abstract-vp	
		Microwave Oven Control	kernel-param-vp	
		Oven Timer	kernel-param-vp	
		Oven Data	kernel-param-vp	
		Display Prompts	kernel-abstract-vp	
Light	optional	Lamp Interface	optional	
		Microwave Oven Control	kernel-param-vp	light : Boolean
Turntable	optional	Turntable Interface	optional	

Feature Name	Feature Category	Class Name	Class Category	Class Parameter
		Microwave Oven Control	kernel-param-vp	turntable : Boolean
Beeper	optional	Beeper Interface	optional	
		Microwave Oven Control	kernel-param-vp	beeper : Boolean
Minute Plus	optional	Keypad Interface	kernel-param-vp	minuteplus : Boolean
		Microwave Oven Control	kernel-param-vp	minuteplus : Boolean
		Oven Timer	kernel-param-vp	minuteplus : Boolean
		Oven Data	kernel-param-vp	minuteplus : Boolean
One-line Display	default	One-line Display Interface	default	
Multi-line Display	alternative	Multi-line Display Interface	variant	
English	default	English Display Prompts	default	
French	alternative	French Display Prompts	variant	
Spanish	alternative	Spanish Display Prompts	variant	
German	alternative	German Display Prompts	variant	
Italian	alternative	Italian Display Prompts	variant	
Boolean Weight	default	Boolean Weight Sensor Interface	default	
Analog Weight	alternative	Analog Weight Sensor Interface	variant	
		Oven Data	kernel-param-vp	itemWeight : Real

(continues)

Table 13.4   *Feature/class dependencies of the microwave oven software product line (Continued)*

Feature Name	Feature Category	Class Name	Class Category	Class Parameter
One-level Heating	default	One-level Heating Element Interface	default	
Multi-level Heating	alternative	Multi-level Heating Element Interface	variant	
		Microwave Oven Control	kernel-param-vp	multi-levelHeater : Boolean
		Oven Data	kernel-param-vp	selectedPowerLevel : Integer
Power Level	optional	Keypad Interface	kernel-param-vp	power : Boolean
		Microwave Oven Control	kernel-param-vp	power : Boolean
TOD Clock	optional	TOD Timer	optional	
		Keypad Interface	kernel-param-vp	TODClock : Boolean
		Microwave Oven Control	kernel-param-vp	TODClock : Boolean
		Oven Data	kernel-param-vp	TODvalue : Real
12/24 Hour Clock	parameterized	Oven Data	kernel-param-vp	TODmaxHour : Integer
Recipe	optional	Recipes	optional	
		Recipe	optional	
		Keypad Interface	kernel-param-vp	recipe : Boolean
		Microwave Oven Control	kernel-param-vp	recipe : Boolean
		Oven Data	kernel-param-vp	selectedRecipe : Integer
		Oven Timer	kernel-param-vp	recipe : Boolean

13.7.1   Input Device Interface Classes

The input device interface classes are categorized as kernel, abstract, variant, default, or parameterized as follows:

- **Door Sensor Interface**. This is a kernel class for which there are no variants; hence it is used unchanged by all members of the product line:
  - **Kernel class**: «kernel» «input device interface» Door Sensor Interface
- **Weight Sensor Interface**. There are two versions of this class. The default is Boolean Weight Sensor Interface. However, there is also an optional alternative class: Analog Weight Sensor Interface. Weight Sensor Interface is designed as an abstract superclass. It is further categorized as kernel and a variation point. Boolean Weight Sensor Interface and Analog Weight Sensor Interface are designed as subclasses; the former is the default class, and the latter is a variant class:
  - **Abstract kernel class**: «kernel-abstract-vp» «input device interface» Weight Sensor Interface
  - **Variant subclasses**:
    - «default» «input device interface» Boolean Weight Sensor Interface
    - «variant» «input device interface» Analog Weight Sensor Interface
- **Keypad Interface.** This class has several potential variations because four different features, if selected, are accessed from the keypad. These features are Power Level, Recipe, TOD Clock, and Minute Plus. If each of these variations is handled as a subclass, then there is a combinatorial problem with all the different variants. Therefore, it is better to handle Keypad Interface as one parameterized class. Essentially, the buttons that are not selected are marked as unavailable. Hence the class is a parameterized class:
  - **Parameterized kernel class**: «kernel-param-vp» «input device interface» Keypad Interface
    All four class parameters are Boolean feature conditions. If the value of the feature condition is true, then the feature is provided, meaning that the appropriate keypad buttons are provided, otherwise not: [power], [recipe], [TODClock], [minuteplus].

13.7.2   Output Device Interface Classes

The output device interface classes are categorized as kernel, optional, abstract, default, or variant as follows:

- **Beeper Interface**. This is an optional class:

  «optional» « output device interface» Beeper Interface

- **Lamp Interface**. This is an optional class:

  «optional» « output device interface» Lamp Interface

- **Turntable Interface**. This is an optional class:

  «optional» « output device interface» Turntable Interface

- **Heating Element Interface**. There are two versions of this class. The default class interfaces to One-level Heating Element, which has only one power level and can be switched on or off. An alternative is a high-grade Multi-level Heating Element with multiple power levels as options:

  - **Abstract kernel class**: «kernel-abstract-vp» «output device interface» Heating Element Interface

  - **Variant subclasses**:

    - «default» «output device interface» One-level Heating Element Interface

    - «variant» «output device interface» Multi-level Heating Element Interface

- **Display Interface**. There are two versions of this class. The default class interfaces to a simple One-line Display. An alternative class interfaces to an advanced Multi-line Display:

  - **Abstract kernel class**: «kernel-abstract-vp» «output device interface» Display Interface

  - **Variant subclasses**:

    - «default» «output device interface» One-line Display Interface

    - «variant» «output device interface» Multi-line Display Interface

13.7.3 Control Classes

The control classes are categorized as state-dependent control or timer classes from a role category perspective and parameterized kernel classes from a reuse category perspective, as follows:

- **Microwave Oven Control**. Many possible versions and combinations of features are possible for this class. The choices are to design several variants or to parameterize the class so that it can be tailored to the individual member of the product line by having the appropriate parameters set. Because

of the combinatorial explosion problem, the decision is made to parameterize the class with the introduction of several Boolean feature conditions.
The feature condition is *true* if the feature is provided, otherwise not. A
feature condition that is *true* enables a state transition branch or state transition action on the `Microwave Oven Control` statechart, as shown in Figures 13.23 through 13.27:

- **Parameterized kernel class**: «kernel-param-vp» «state dependent control» Microwave Oven Control

  The seven class parameters are all Boolean feature conditions: [power],
  [recipe], [TODClock], [minuteplus] [light], [turntable], [beeper].

- **`Oven Timer`**. Again, the choice is between multiple versions of the class
  with a basic timer class as default or a single parameterized version of the
  class. Consider the inheritance option. There is a kernel `Oven Timer` class
  for the basic microwave oven. There needs to be a specialized version to
  deal with the `Recipe` feature called `Oven & Recipe Timer`; then there is
  the specialized version that deals with the `Minute Plus` feature called
  `Oven Timer & Minute Plus`. Finally, because it is possible to have both
  `Recipe` and `Minute Plus` features in an oven, there is a need for a third
  specialized version: `Oven & Recipe Timer & Minute Plus`. The design
  decision with inheritance is depicted in Figure 13.31.

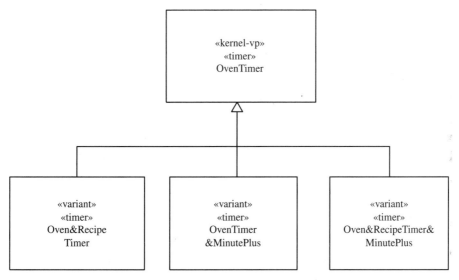

Figure 13.31 `Oven Timer` *generalization/specialization hierarchy (alternative design)*

This design seems overly complicated, so the decision is made to design a parameterized version of Oven Timer, which uses feature conditions. A feature condition that is true enables a state transition branch on the Oven Timer statechart, as shown in Figures 13.28 through 13.30:

- **Parameterized kernel class**: «kernel-param-vp» «timer» Oven Timer
  The two class parameters are Boolean feature conditions: [recipe], [minuteplus].

- **TOD Timer.** This class is optional and needs to be available only in those microwave ovens that are fitted with a time-of-day clock:

  - **Optional class**: «optional» TOD Timer

13.7.4 Entity Classes

The entity classes are categorized as kernel, optional, abstract, variant, default, or parameterized as follows:

- **Oven Data**. This entity class contains all the attributes that need to be set for cooking food. This class could be designed as one superclass with kernel attributes and one optional subclass for each combination of optional attributes. The class is instead designed as a parameterized kernel class to avoid the combinatorial explosion of too many subclasses. For each optional attribute of the class, there is a feature that must be selected for the variable to be provided by a product line member:

  - **Parameterized kernel class**: «kernel-param-vp» «entity» Oven Data

  - **Kernel attribute**: cookingTime (remaining time to cook food).

  - **Optional attributes**, which are relevant only if the named feature is selected as indicated by the feature constraint:

    - **selectedPowerLevel {feature = Multi-level Heating}**. Possible values of this variable are: High, Medium, Low; initial value = High. If this feature is not selected, the power level is a constant set to High.

    - **itemWeight {feature = Analog Weight}**. This *Real* variable is used only with analog weight and records the actual weight of the item.

    - **selectedRecipe {feature = Recipe}**. This variable is initialized to "none selected".

    - **TODvalue {feature = TOD Clock}**. This is a time variable initialized to 12:00.

- **TODmaxHour {feature = TOD Clock}**. This is a parameterized constant set at system configuration to 12:00 or 24:00 to indicate the maximum hour on the clock.

  The attributes held by the parameterized `Oven Data` class are depicted in Figure 13.32, which shows the variable name, the feature constraint if the attribute is optional, the type of variable, the range for the variable, and permitted values for configuration parameters. Configuration parameters, such as `TOD max Hour`, are depicted as static variables because once the value of the parameter is set at configuration time, it cannot be changed.

- **Recipes**. This optional entity container class provides access to individual recipes:
  - **Optional class**: «optional» «entity» Recipes

- **Recipe**. This optional class stores information about an individual recipe. In particular, the number of steps for each recipe needs to be stored, along with three values for each step: constant t_1, time per unit weight t_2, and power level p. This feature needs the analog weight sensor to measure the weight (w), which is then substituted into the equation for cooking time as follows: Cooking Time = t_1 + w*t_2, where t_1 and t_2 are constant times specified in the recipe and w is the weight of the item, and the power level p is specified in the recipe:
  - **Optional class**: «optional» «entity» Recipe

- **Display Prompts**. Each set of language prompts is stored in a separate subclass:
  - **Abstract kernel class**: «kernel-abstract-vp» «entity» Display Prompts
  - **Default variant class**: «default» «entity» English Display Prompts

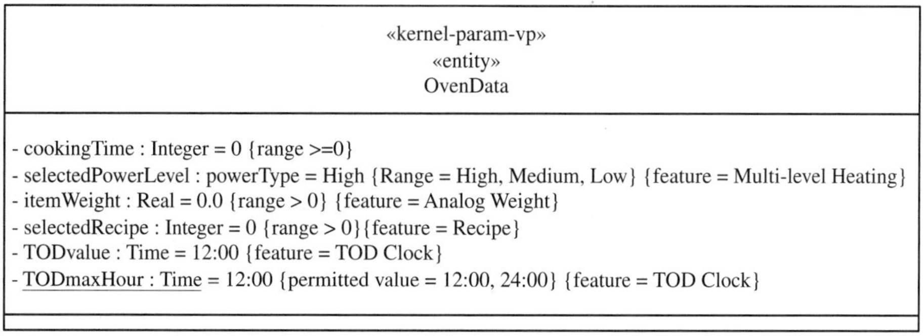

«kernel-param-vp» «entity» OvenData
- cookingTime : Integer = 0 {range >=0} - selectedPowerLevel : powerType = High {Range = High, Medium, Low} {feature = Multi-level Heating} - itemWeight : Real = 0.0 {range > 0} {feature = Analog Weight} - selectedRecipe : Integer = 0 {range > 0}{feature = Recipe} - TODvalue : Time = 12:00 {feature = TOD Clock} - TODmaxHour : Time = 12:00 {permitted value = 12:00, 24:00} {feature = TOD Clock}

Figure 13.32 Oven Data *parameterized class*

- **Alternative variant classes**:
  - «variant» «entity» French Display Prompts
  - «variant» «entity» Spanish Display Prompts
  - «variant» «entity» German Display Prompts
  - «variant» «entity» Italian Display Prompts

There is another variability factor in the `Display Prompts` class. Several features need feature-specific prompts, such as prompting for recipe or power level. Each prompt is identified by an ID, which is an index into a prompt table maintained by the `Display Prompts` class. Either this table can be configured specifically for the feature selected, or the table contains all possible prompts, including prompts for features not selected. Prompts for features not selected will never be displayed. This is a simpler solution from a variability management perspective, but it consumes more memory.

13.7.5 Product Line Composition Hierarchy

The classes described in Section 13.7.4 are now organized into the class hierarchy for a microwave oven system, which is a member of the microwave oven product line, as shown in Figure 13.33. This is a composition hierarchy, which shows all the classes that can be selected for a given member of the product line, including kernel, optional, default, and variant classes. Each class is depicted with two orthogonal stereotypes: the reuse category and role of the class in the product line.

The following classes are depicted in Figure 13.33:

- **Unchanged classes**. Unchanged classes have no variation points. When selected, these kernel or optional classes are reused without change. There is one unchanged kernel class: `Door Sensor Interface`. There are six unchanged optional classes: `Beeper Interface`, `Lamp Interface`, `Turntable Interface`, `TOD Timer`, `Recipes`, and `Recipe`.

- **Abstract classes with variant subclasses**. The abstract superclass is considered a variation point because variant subclasses are designed as specializations of the abstract class. The specific variant subclass provided by a product line member depends on which feature is selected. For alternative features, the features and hence the variant subclasses are mutually exclusive. An example of a kernel abstract class with a variation point is `Weight Sensor Interface`. The default subclass is `Boolean Weight Sensor Interface`. The alternative subclass is `Analog Weight Sensor Interface`.

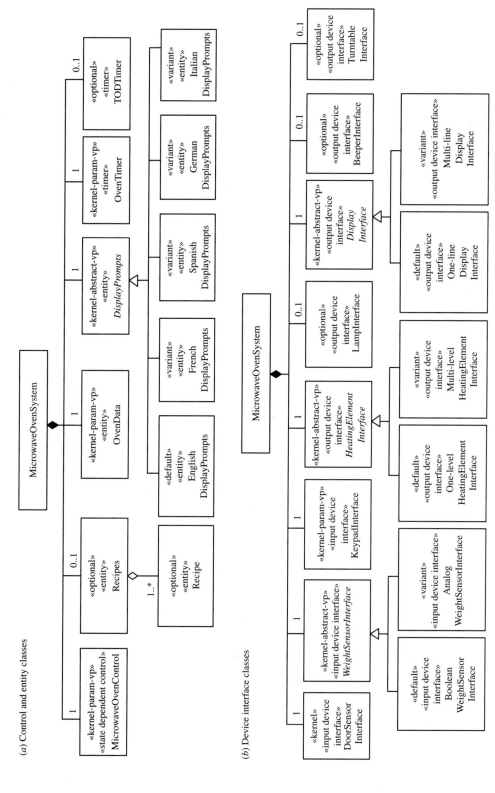

(a) Control and entity classes

(b) Device interface classes

Figure 13.33   *Class hierarchy of the microwave oven system, a member of the microwave oven software product line*

417

- **Parameterized classes**. A variation point is realized in a parameterized class through the value assigned to a configuration parameter. The features that affect each parameterized class are also shown. The parameterized classes are all kernel classes: `Keypad Interface`, `Microwave Oven Control`, `Oven Timer`, and `Oven Data`.

13.8 Design Modeling

The microwave oven software product line is designed as a component-based software architecture based on the Centralized Control pattern (see Chapter 10). One control component provides the overall control of the system, receiving messages from other components that contain events causing the control component to change state and send action messages to other components. The product line is designed as a distributed component-based software architecture, allowing the option for input and output components to reside on separate nodes connected by a high-speed bus. At system deployment time, the type of configuration required—centralized or distributed—is determined.

The component architecture is developed gradually in this section, starting with the design of the kernel system, which contains the kernel and default components. Next, the message communication between components is designed. With the evolutionary design approach, this process is repeated for the full product line, at which point the optional and variant components are added. On the basis of the design of the overall product line component and communication architecture, the component ports and connectors are designed with the goal of maximizing component reuse in the different product line member configurations. Finally, the provided and required interfaces of each component are described. Each component port is defined in terms of its provided and/or required interfaces.

13.8.1 Component-Based Software Architecture

With the kernel first approach, the component structuring criteria are applied to determine the components in the kernel system. The following list describes the mapping from the kernel analysis model of Figure 13.5 to the kernel component model depicted in Figure 13.34. This figure depicts the components in the microwave oven system, which is the kernel member of the microwave oven product line.

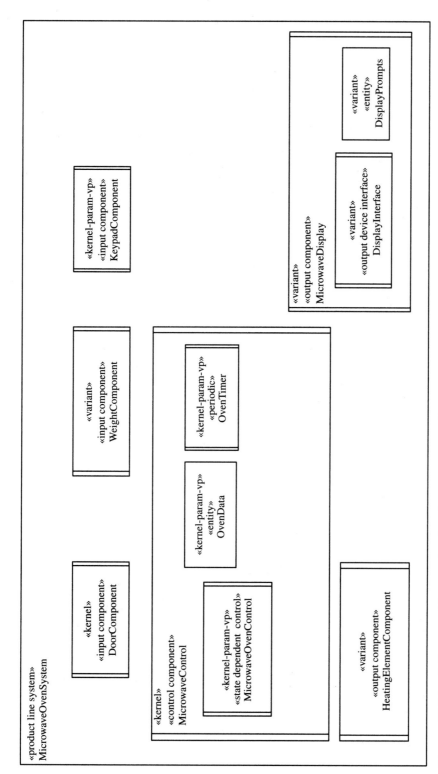

Figure 13.34 Software architecture for the microwave oven software product line kernel: component structuring

- **Input components**. Input components are concurrent components that receive inputs from the external environment and send corresponding messages to the control component. Door Component, Weight Component, and Keypad Component (see Figure 13.34) are simple components determined from the analysis model. These input components consist of the individual input device interface classes depicted in the analysis model (see Figure 13.5): Door Sensor Interface, Weight Sensor Interface, and Keypad Interface, respectively. Door Component and Keypad Component are both kernel components. Weight Component is a variant component but is always needed by a member of the microwave oven product line—either the default Boolean Weight component or the variant Analog Weight component.

- **Control component**. The Microwave Control component is the centralized control component for the product line. It is a composite concurrent component composed of the Microwave Oven Control component, the Oven Timer component, and the Oven Data component, as shown in Figure 13.34. Microwave Oven Control and Oven Timer are both concurrent components with their own threads of control. Oven Data is a passive entity object that provides operations that execute in the threads of control of the two active components. All three internal components are kernel classes determined in the analysis model (see Figure 13.5). These three components are grouped into the Microwave Control component because the overall control of the microwave oven needs both the state-dependent control class Microwave Oven Control and the timer class Oven Timer, as well as the entity class Oven Data, which stores essential data. In the kernel system, cooking Time is the only attribute of Oven Data.

- **Output components**. The Heating Element Component interfaces to the external Heating Element. The Heating Element Interface class from the analysis model is mapped to this simple component (see Figure 13.5). Heating Element Component is a variant component because in any member of the product line, either the default One-level Heating Element component or the variant Multi-level Heating Element component is needed.

The Microwave Display component is a composite component composed of the Display Interface component and the Display Prompts component. As Figure 13.34 shows, Display Interface is a concurrent component with its own thread of control, and Display Prompts is a passive entity object. These two components are grouped together because they must always be used together. `Display Interface` receives commands to display prompts, in which each prompt is identified by a prompt ID. The text for the prompts is maintained by the `Display Prompts` entity object. This separation of concerns means that the prompt language and prompt text can be changed independently of the display interface.

13.8.2 Architectural Communication Patterns

The messages to be sent between the components in the microwave oven system are determined from the communication diagrams of the analysis model. The communication diagram for the kernel of the product line (the `Cook Food` use case) is depicted in Figure 13.6. The actual type of message communication—synchronous or asynchronous—still needs to be determined. To handle the variety of communication between the components in the software product line architecture, four communication patterns are applied:

1. **Asynchronous Message Communication**. The Asynchronous Message Communication pattern is widely used in the microwave oven software product line because most communication is one-way, and this pattern has the advantage of not letting the consumers hold up the producers. The order in which messages are sent by the three input components to the `Microwave Control` component (see Figures 13.35 and 13.36) is nondeterministic, because it is based on the user's actions. The `Microwave Control` component (which contains the `Microwave Oven Control` and `Oven Timer` components) needs to be able to receive a message from any of its three producers in any order. The best way to handle this requirement for flexibility is through asynchronous message communication, with one input message queue for the `Microwave Oven Control` component. The `Microwave Oven Control` component may also receive a message from the `Oven Timer` component (see Figure 13.36), which arrives on the same message queue.

   The `Microwave Display` component also receives messages from two producers: the `Microwave Oven Control` component and the `Oven Timer` component (see Figure 13.36). To avoid race conditions, the two producer components are designed to send display messages in different states. The `Microwave Oven Control` component sends display messages only when the oven is not cooking. The `Oven Timer` component sends messages when the oven is cooking. The `Display Interface` component receives these messages on a message queue.

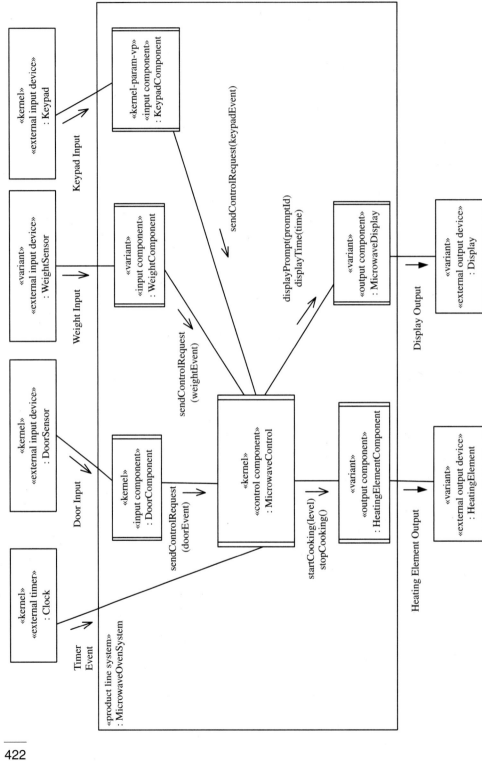

Figure 13.35 *Distributed software architecture for the microwave oven software product line kernel: message interfaces*

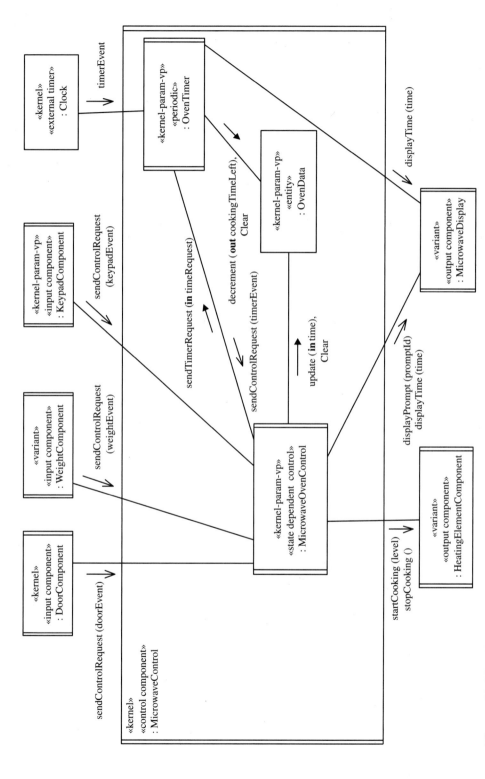

Figure 13.36 *Concurrent communication diagram for the* Microwave Control *component:* kernel

423

2. **Synchronous Message Communication without Reply**. This pattern is used when the producer needs to make sure that the consumer has accepted the message before it continues. This pattern is used between the `Microwave Oven Control` and `Oven Timer` components (see Figure 13.36), both of which are within the `Microwave Control` component. The `Microwave Oven Control` component sends `Start Timer` and `Cancel Timer` messages to the `Oven Timer` component. In both cases, the `Microwave Oven Control` component is suspended until `Oven Timer` accepts the message because in these situations `Oven Timer` is the most important (highest-priority) concurrent component. The `Microwave Oven Control` component defers to `Oven Timer` because it is more important for `Oven Timer` to react to these messages than for the `Microwave Oven Control` component to continue executing. `Oven Timer` has a very short execution cycle, so the `Microwave Oven Control` component will be suspended for only a very short time.

3. **Synchronous Message Communication with Reply**. The version of this pattern used for the microwave oven system is the invocation of operations on the passive entity objects—in particular, for accessing `Oven Data` (see Figure 13.36) and `Display Prompts` (see Figure 13.37) entity objects.

4. **Broker Handle**. The broker patterns can be used during system initialization. The Broker Handle pattern can be used to allow producers to query the broker to determine the consumers to which they should be connected. Before this brokering can be done, the consumers must register their services and location with the broker. For example, because there is a choice of heating element component and display component, after the components for a given member of the product line have been deployed (see Section 13.8.3), the selected components register with the broker during initialization so that the control component can query the broker to find out which of the heating element and display components it is to communicate with.

13.8.3 System Deployment

At system deployment time, the type of configuration required—centralized or distributed—is determined. Figure 13.38 shows one possible configuration, in which each of the components of the kernel system is allocated to a separate node in a distributed configuration. The nodes are physically connected by means of a high-speed bus.

Only distributed components can be deployed to the physical nodes of a distributed configuration. Passive components (such as `Oven Data` in Figure 13.36)

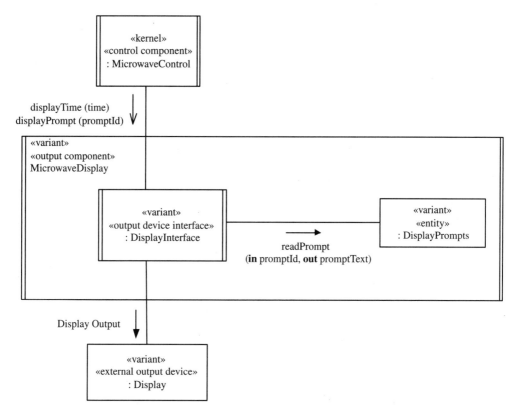

Figure 13.37 *Concurrent communication diagram for the* Microwave Display *component*

cannot be independently deployed, nor can any component that directly invokes the operations of a passive component (such as Microwave Oven Control and Oven Timer in Figure 13.36). In this situation, only the composite component (which contains the passive component and concurrent components that invoke operations of the passive component) can be deployed. Thus, in Figure 13.36, only the Microwave Control composite component can be deployed, as depicted in Figure 13.38.

13.8.4 Product Line Evolution: Optional and Variant Components

Consider the optional and variant components that need to be added as the product line evolves to address the microwave oven optional and alternative features. The optional components that need to be considered at this stage include

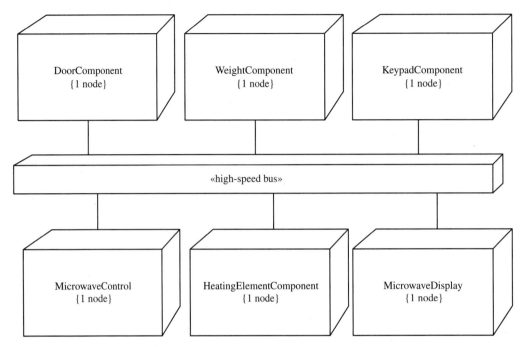

Figure 13.38 *Distributed kernel system configuration*

the three output components `Turntable Component`, `Beeper Component`, and `Lamp Component` (as shown in Figure 13.39). Furthermore, the revised version of the `Microwave Control` composite component could, depending on the features selected, contain the optional periodic component `TOD Timer` and passive `Recipes` entity component, in addition to `Microwave Oven Control`, `Oven Timer`, and `Oven Data` (see Figure 13.39). Depending on the features selected, variant components could replace default components—in particular, for `Heating Element Component`, `Weight Component`, `Display Interface`, or `Display Prompts`.

13.8.5 Product Line Evolution: Component Communication

The addition of the optional components does not change the architectural communication patterns used in the kernel system. Thus, Figure 13.40 depicts asynchronous communication from the input components to the control component and from the control component to the output components. `Microwave Control` communicates asynchronously with the `Lamp`, `Turntable`, and `Beeper` components, just as it does with the `Heating Element` and `Microwave Display` components.

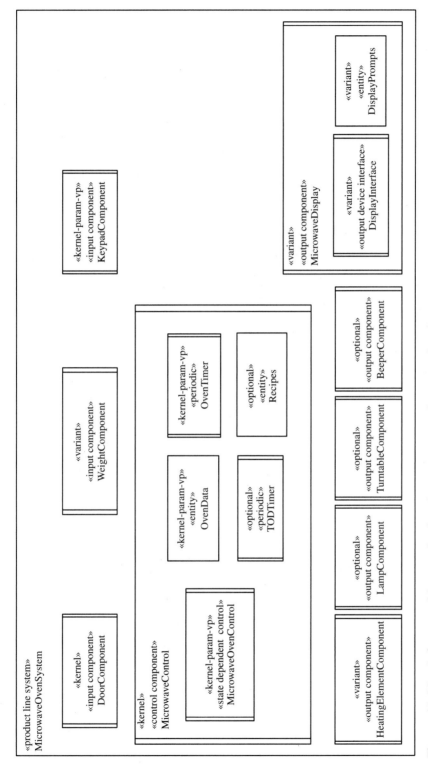

Figure 13.39 *Software architecture for the microwave oven software product line: component structuring*

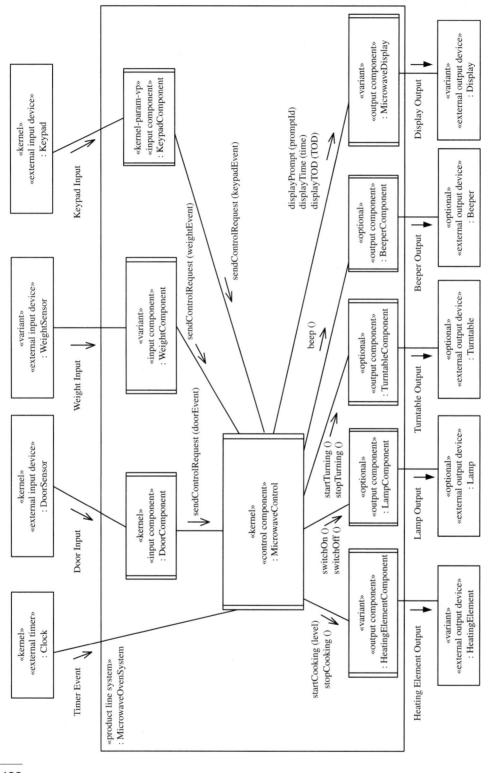

Figure 13.40 *Distributed software architecture for the microwave oven software product line: message interfaces*

The Synchronous Message Communication without Reply pattern is used, as earlier, inside the composite `Microwave Control` component. In particular, all communication with the passive entity objects is synchronous, representing operation calls. This version of the `Oven Data` entity object could, depending on the features selected, have all the optional variables in use. Consequently, `Oven Data` needs several additional operations, as shown in detail in Figure 13.41, for reading and updating the optional variables for weight, power level, recipe number, and time of day, as shown originally in Figure 13.32.

13.8.6   Product Line Architecture and Component Interfaces

Figure 13.42 depicts a UML composite structure diagram showing the overall microwave oven product line architecture, component interfaces, and connectors. All the components are concurrent and communicate with other components through ports. The overall architecture and connectivity among components is determined from the product line communication diagrams. Thus the composite structure of the component architecture depicted in Figure 13.42 is determined from the component communication design shown in Figure 13.40.

Because the three input components (`Door Component`, `Weight Component`, and `Keypad Component`) send messages to the `Microwave Control` component in Figure 13.40, each input component is designed to have an output port, referred to as a *required port*, which is joined by means of a connector to the control component's input port, referred to as a *provided port*, as shown in Figure 13.42. The name of the required port on each input component is `RMWControl`; by a PLUS convention, the first letter of the port name is R to emphasize that the component has a *required* port. The name of `Microwave Control Component`'s provided port is `PMWControl`; the first letter of the port name is P to emphasize that the component has a *provided* port. Connectors join the required ports of the three input components to the provided port of the control component. Because all the connectors are unidirectional, the direction in which messages are sent is explicitly shown on the composite structure diagram in Figure 13.42.

Each component port is defined in terms of its provided and/or required interfaces. Some producer components—in particular, the input components—do not provide a software interface, because they receive their inputs directly from the external hardware input devices. However, they require an interface provided by the control component in order to send messages to the control component. Figure 13.43 depicts the ports and required interfaces for the three input components of Figure 13.42: `Door Component`, `Weight Component`, and

(13.41a) Concurrent communication diagram for MicrowaveControl

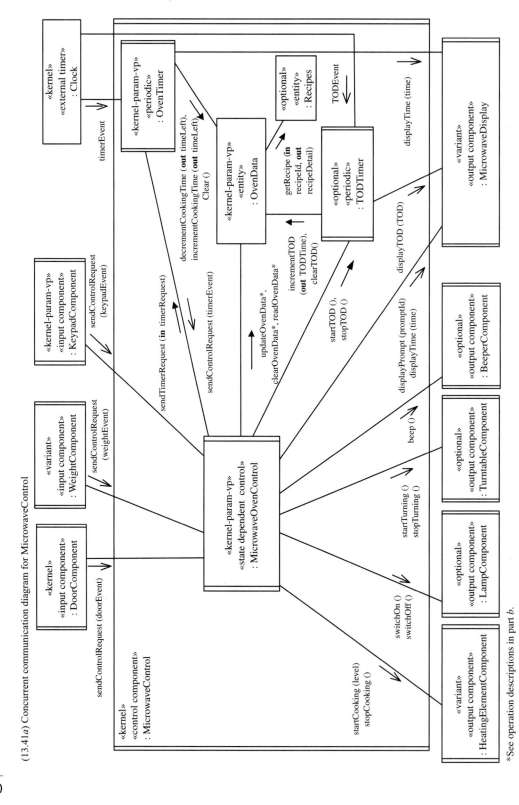

*See operation descriptions in part b.

430

(13.41b) Operation descriptions for OvenData

updateOvenData*   **clearOvenData***   **readOvenData***

setWeight (**in** weight)   clearCookingTime ()   readPower (**out** level)
setPower (**in** power)   clearRecipe ()
updateTOD (**in** time)   clearWeight ()
selectRecipe (**in** recipeId)   clearPower ()
updateCookingTime (**in** time)   clearTOD ()

Figure 13.41   *Concurrent communication diagram for the* Microwave Control *component*

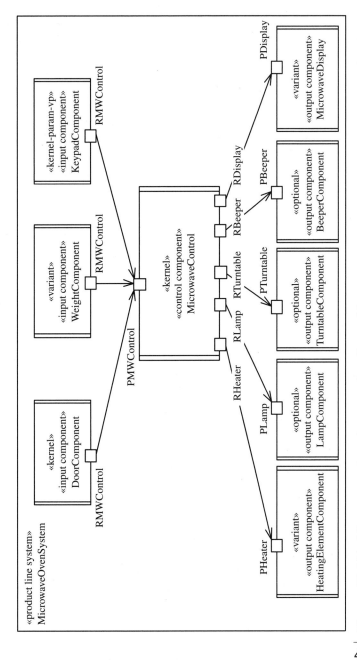

Figure 13.42   *Microwave oven software product line architecture*

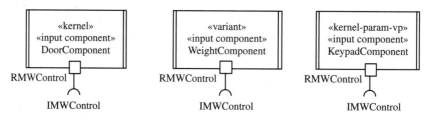

Figure 13.43 *Ports and required interfaces of input components*

`Keypad Component`. Each of the three input components has the same required interface—IMWControl—which is provided by the `Microwave Control` component.

The `Microwave Control` component has several required ports from which it sends messages to the provided ports of the five output components depicted in Figure 13.42 (`Heating Element Component`, `Lamp Component`, `Turntable Component`, `Beeper Component`, and `Microwave Display`).

The output components do not require a software interface, because their outputs go directly to external hardware output devices. However, they need to provide an interface to receive messages sent by the control component. Figure 13.44 depicts the ports and provided interfaces for all the default, variant, and optional output components of the product line. Figure 13.44 also shows the specifications of the interfaces in terms of the operations they provide. `Lamp Component`, `Turntable Component`, and `Beeper Component` are optional output components, each of which has a provided port—for example, `PLamp` for `Lamp Component`, which provides an interface (e.g., `ILamp`). However, each optional component is selected only for a given product line member if the appropriate feature is chosen, which in Figure 13.44 is depicted as a constraint on the interface—for example, {feature = Lamp} for the `ILamp` interface.

Consider next `Heating Element Component`, which has a provided port called `PHeater`, which in turn provides an interface called `IHeatingElement`. There are two variants of `Heating Element Component`: the default `One-level Heating Element Component` and the variant `Multi-level Heating Element Component`. To keep the interface simple, the two variants are designed to realize the same provided interface (`IHeatingElement`) and thus have the same provided port (`PHeater`). The interface specifies an operation called `start Cooking`, which has an input parameter: the heating level (`level`). For the one-level heater, the value of `level` would always be set to high. For the multi-level heater, the value of `level` could be set to high, medium, or low. The `level` parameter is in fact unnecessary for the one-level

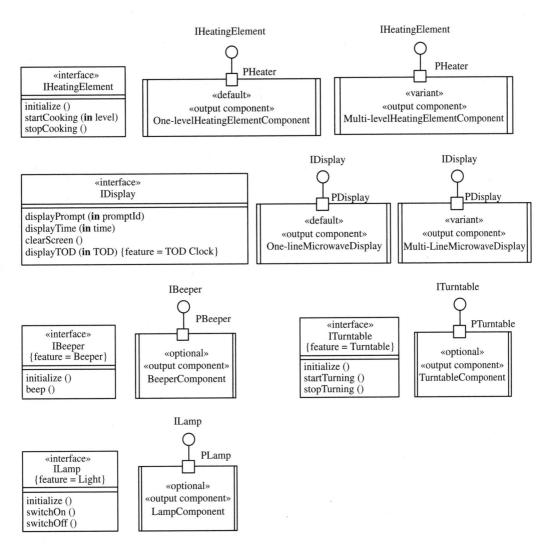

Figure 13.44 *Ports and provided interfaces of output components*

heater; however, providing the same interface for the two variants simplifies the design because it means that one variant can be substituted for the other without any change to the interface.

The `Microwave Display` component has a provided port called `PDisplay`, which in turn provides an interface called `IDisplay`. Figure 13.44 shows the specification of the interface. There are two variants of the `Microwave Display` component: the default `One-line Microwave Display` and the variant

Multi-line Microwave Display. As with the heating element components, the two variants realize the same provided interface. One of the operations provided by the IDisplay interface (display TOD) is implemented in full only by the multi-line display; it results in an exception in the one-line display. An alternative design would be for each component to have a different interface. However, two different interfaces would need two different provided ports for the two display variants and two different required ports for the Microwave Oven Control component and composite Microwave Control component to interface to the two alternative provided ports. This alternative is rejected because it results in a much more complicated design.

Some components, such as control components, need to provide interfaces for the input components to use and require interfaces that are provided by output components. The Microwave Control component has several ports—one provided port and five required ports—as shown in Figure 13.45. Each required port is used to interface to a different output component and is given the prefix *R*— for example, RLamp. The provided port, which is called PMWControl, provides the interface IMWControl, which is required by the input components. This interface is specified in Figure 13.45. It is kept simple by having only one operation (send Control Request), with a parameter for the type of request. As pointed out earlier, it is much simpler to make Microwave Control a parameterized component because the alternative is a very large number of variants.

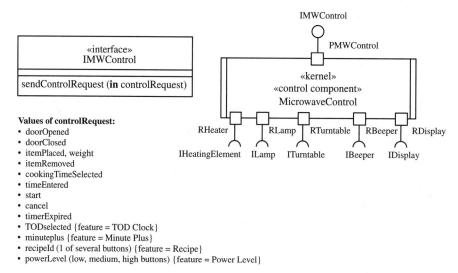

Figure 13.45 *Ports and interfaces of the* Microwave Control *component*

Having each control request as a separate operation would make the interface much more complicated, either through having several different interfaces or by having one interface with a large number of feature-dependent operations, many of which would not be needed in any given product line instance.

13.8.7 Design of Composite Components

The `Microwave Control` component is designed as a composite component that contains five simple part components; three of these are concurrent components (`Microwave Oven Control`, `Oven Timer`, and `TOD Timer`), and the other two are passive entity objects (`Oven Data` and `Recipes`). Figure 13.46 shows the decomposition of the `Microwave Control` component. The provided port of the composite `Microwave Control` component is connected directly to the provided port of the simple `Microwave Oven Control` component, and both ports are given the same name (`PMWControl`) because they provide the same interface. The connector joining the two ports is actually a delegation connector, meaning that the outer port provided by `Microwave Control` forwards each message it receives to the inner port provided by `Microwave Oven Control`. The required ports of `Microwave Oven Control` are also connected to the required ports of the composite `Microwave Control` component via delegation connectors.

The `Microwave Oven Control` component (see Figure 13.47), which conceptually executes the microwave oven statechart, is a parameterized component that receives asynchronous control request messages from several producer components. Rather than providing a large and variable number of operations, a simpler interface is to provide an asynchronous send `Control Request` operation, which has an input parameter (`control Request`) that holds the name and contents of the individual message. The component interface and different values that represent the individual messages that `control Request` can be assigned are shown in Figure 13.45.

The ports and interfaces of the periodic timer components are shown in Figure 13.48. There are two timer components: the kernel `Oven Timer` and the optional `TOD Timer`. `Oven Timer` has a required interface (`IMWControl`), which allows it to send control request messages to `Microwave Oven Control` in the same way as the input components do. `Oven Timer` has a provided interface (`IOvenTimer`) that allows it to receive timer messages from the `Microwave Oven Control` component; in particular, it provides a synchronous send `Timer Request` operation, which has an input parameter called `timer Request` that holds the name of the individual message—for example, start `Oven Timer`, cancel `Timer`, add `Minute`, start `Minute`.

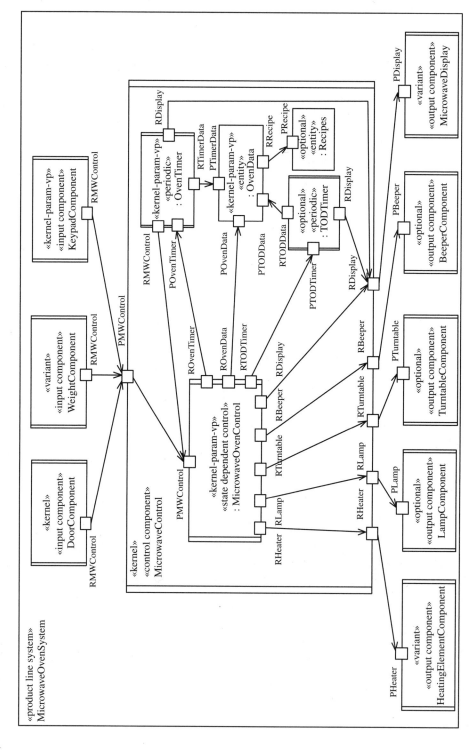

Figure 13.46 *Design of the* Microwave Control *composite component*

436

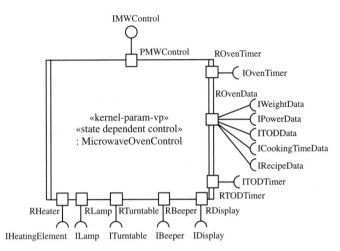

Figure 13.47 *Ports and interfaces of the* Microwave Oven Control *component*

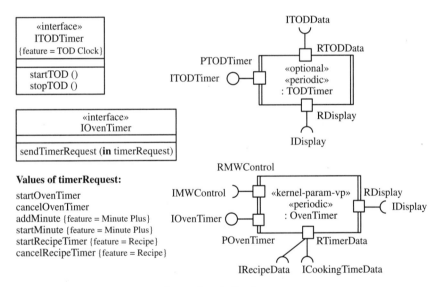

Figure 13.48 *Ports and interfaces of periodic timer components*

The ports and interfaces of the passive components are shown in Figure 13.49. Oven Data provides several interfaces because it supports several optional variables. Each variable, which relates to a particular feature, has an interface associated with it specifying the operations on that variable. For example, the

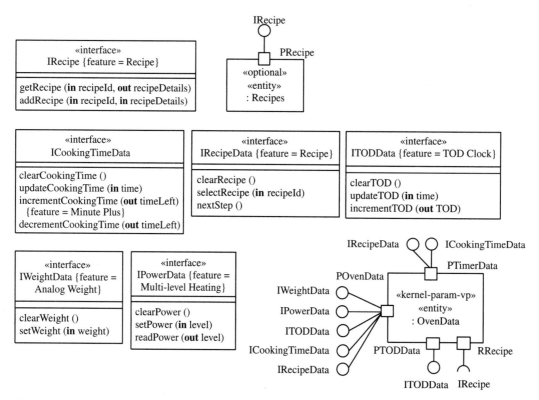

Figure 13.49   *Ports and interfaces of passive components*

IPowerData interface specifies operations for the Power Level feature, which are to clear, set, and read the power level. The ITODData interface specifies operations for the TOD Clock feature, which are to clear, update, and increment the time of day.

The Microwave Display component is also a composite component; it contains two simple part components, as shown in Figure 13.50: a concurrent component called Display Interface and a passive component called Display Prompts. The ports and interfaces of these components are depicted in Figure 13.51. Display Interface receives inputs at its port via a delegation connector from the container Microwave Display component. Given the prompt ID, Display Interface retrieves the appropriate message by invoking the read operation (Figure 13.51) provided by the IDisplayPrompt interface, which is realized by the passive Display Prompts component.

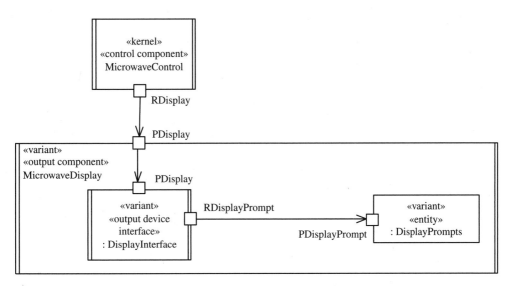

Figure 13.50   *Design of the* Microwave Display *composite component*

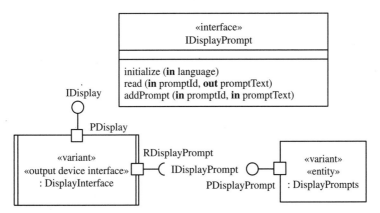

Figure 13.51   *Ports and interfaces of display components*

13.9   Software Application Engineering

To derive a given microwave oven application from the product line architecture and components, it is necessary to define the features selected for the specific oven. An example of deriving a microwave oven application from the microwave oven product line architecture is given in Chapter 12 (Section 12.5).

14

chapter

Electronic Commerce Software Product Line Case Study

The electronic commerce software product line case study is a highly distributed World Wide Web–based product line that handles business-to-business (B2B) as well as business-to-consumer (B2C) systems. Because there are two main systems—B2B and B2C—the *reverse evolutionary engineering* strategy is applied first to each type of system, from which the product line commonality is determined, followed by the product line variability. The solution uses software agents as intermediaries between user interface clients and servers. In addition, object brokers provide a standardized interface to several heterogeneous legacy databases.

The problem is described in Section 14.1. Section 14.2 describes the use case model for the electronic commerce product line, starting by modeling the use cases for B2B systems and B2C systems before synthesizing the two use case models into a product line use case model. Section 14.3 goes on to discuss the electronic commerce software product line feature model, in which common, optional, and alternative features are determined from the use case model. Section 14.4 describes the product line static model, which includes the product line context model that depicts the boundary between a product line member and the external environment. This section also describes the use of software agents and broker technology in this product line, before going on to describe static modeling of the entity classes—initially modeling entity classes in B2C and B2B systems, and then integrating them into a product line static model. Section 14.5 describes dynamic modeling, in which communication diagrams are initially developed for each of the kernel use cases. This process continues during software product line evolution, as described in Section 14.6, in which communication diagrams are developed for each of the optional and alternative use cases.

Section 14.7 discusses the feature/class dependency analysis, in which the classes that realize each feature are determined. Section 14.8 describes the design model for the electronic commerce software product line, which is designed as a layered architecture based on the Layers of Abstraction pattern combined with the Client/Agent/Server pattern. The design also develops a federated architecture linking the different business and customer organizations that operate in the e-commerce product line. Section 14.9 briefly describes software application engineering.

14.1 Problem Description

In electronic commerce B2B systems, there are customers and suppliers. Each customer has a contract with a supplier for purchases from that supplier, as well as one or more bank accounts through which payments to suppliers can be made. Each supplier provides a catalog of items, accepts customer orders, and maintains accounts with each customer for receiving payment.

A customer is able to browse through several World Wide Web–based catalogs provided by the suppliers and select items to purchase. The customer's order needs to be checked against the available contracts to determine if there is a valid customer contract with the supplier, which will be used for charging the purchase. Each contract has operation funds committed to it. It is necessary to determine that sufficient funds are available for the customer order. Assuming that the contract and funds are in place, a delivery order is created and sent to the catalog supplier. The supplier confirms the order and enters a planned shipping date. As time passes, the shipping order is monitored, and both supplier and customer are notified if there is a shipping delay. When the order is shipped, the customer is notified. The customer acknowledges when the shipment is received, and the delivery order is updated. After receipt of shipment, payment of the invoice is authorized. The invoice is first checked against the contract, available funds, and delivery order status, and then sent to Accounts Payable, which authorizes the payment of funds. Payment is made through electronic funds transfer from the customer bank to the supplier bank. The application uses several legacy databases, so object brokering and wrapper technologies are required.

Optionally, a supplier may create a purchase order (PO) requesting new inventory supplies from a wholesaler. The PO is sent directly to the wholesaler. When the PO is delivered to the supplier, the new supplies are entered into the supplier's inventory, and payment is made by electronic funds transfer from the supplier bank to the wholesaler bank.

In electronic commerce B2C systems, a customer requests to purchase one or more items from the supplier. The customer provides personal details, such as address and credit card information. This information is stored in a customer account. If the credit card is valid, then a delivery order is created and sent to the supplier. The supplier confirms the order and enters a planned shipping date. When the order is shipped, the customer is notified and the customer's credit card account is charged.

14.2 Use Case Modeling

Because there are two main systems—B2B and B2C—in the electronic commerce product line, a reverse engineering approach is applied first to each type of system, from which the product line commonality is determined, followed by the product line variability.

14.2.1 Business-to-Business Electronic Commerce Use Case Model

The use case model for B2B systems in the electronic commerce product line is depicted in Figure 14.1. There are three actors: Customer, Supplier, and Bank. The customer initiates four use cases: Browse Catalog, Create Requisition, Make Purchase Request, and Confirm Delivery. The supplier initiates three use cases: Process Delivery Order, Confirm Shipment, and Send Invoice. These are the main B2B use cases in the product line; other, less important use cases for querying the servers and monitoring progress have been omitted for brevity.

The B2B use cases are briefly described next. In the Browse Catalog use case, the customer browses the various World Wide Web catalogs, views various catalog items from a given supplier's catalog, and selects items from the catalog. In the Create Requisition use case, the customer makes a requisition request. The system has to find a customer contract with the catalog supplier for which there are sufficient operation funds. If a valid contract is found, the system authorizes the requisition and informs the customer. In Make Purchase Request, the customer asks the system to send a purchase request to the supplier.

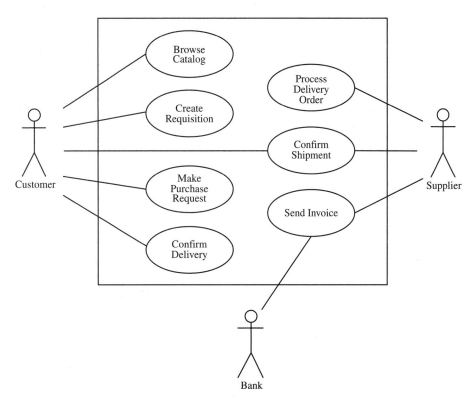

Figure 14.1   *B2B electronic commerce system: use cases*

Although an initial use case analysis might suggest that `Create Requisition` and `Make Purchase Request` should be combined into one use case (e.g., `Place Requisition`), the reason for splitting the two use cases is that `Create Requisition` applies only to B2B systems, while `Make Purchase Request` applies to all e-commerce systems.

In the `Process Delivery Order` use case, the supplier requests a delivery order, determines that the inventory is available to fulfill the order, and displays the order.

In the `Confirm Shipment` use case, the supplier prepares the shipment manually and then confirms the shipment.

In the `Confirm Delivery` use case, when the shipment arrives at the customer, the customer confirms the delivery. The operation funds are committed for payment.

In the `Send Invoice` use case, the supplier sends an invoice to the customer organization. After the customer confirms delivery, the invoice is approved by the customer organization's Accounts Payable department, and an electronic payment request is sent to the customer's bank.

14.2.2   Business-to-Consumer Electronic Commerce Use Case Model

The use case model for B2C systems in the electronic commerce product line is depicted in Figure 14.2. As in B2B systems, there are the three actors; this time, though, they are `Customer`, `Supplier`, and `Authorization Center`. The customer initiates three use cases: `Browse Catalog`, `Check Customer Account`, and `Make Purchase Request`. The supplier initiates three use cases: `Process Delivery Order`, `Confirm Shipment`, and `Bill Customer`.

Two of the B2C customer-initiated use cases—`Browse Catalog` and `Make Purchase Request`—are identical to B2B use cases; `Check Customer Account`,

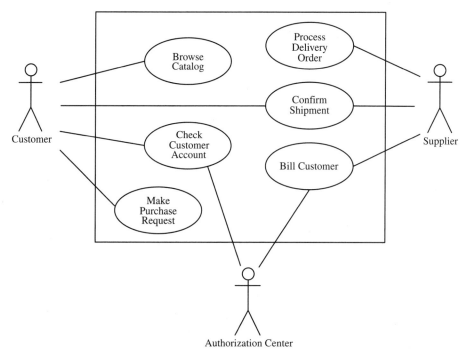

Figure 14.2   *B2C electronic commerce system: use cases*

however, is different from any of the B2B use cases. In the `Check Customer Account` use case, the customer enters personal details. The system creates a customer account if one does not already exist. The customer's credit card is checked for validity and sufficient credit to pay for the requested catalog items. If the credit card check shows that the credit card is valid and has sufficient credit, then the customer purchase is approved.

Two of the B2C supplier-initiated use cases—`Process Delivery Order` and `Confirm Shipment`—are identical to B2B use cases; `Bill Customer`, on the other hand, is different. In the `Bill Customer` use case, the system retrieves the customer's credit card details from the customer account and sends a payment request to the credit card authorization center.

14.2.3 Optional Purchase Order Use Cases

The supplier initiates two optional use cases that could be used in either B2B or B2C systems: `Prepare Purchase Order` and `Deliver Purchase Order` (see Figure 14.3). In the `Prepare Purchase Order` use case, the supplier checks inventory and requests creation of a purchase order for the inventory items that need to be replenished. In the `Deliver Purchase Order` use case, the system sends the purchase order to the wholesaler. When the delivery order arrives from the wholesaler, the supplier enters the information into the inventory database and approves electronic payment from the supplier bank to the wholesaler bank.

14.2.4 Use Case Model for the Electronic Commerce Software Product Line

In the reverse engineering approach, the use cases from the various use case models (see Figures 14.1–14.3) are integrated to produce the product line use case model. Two of the customer-initiated use cases (`Browse Catalog` and `Make Purchase Request`) are common to all electronic commerce systems and so become kernel use cases of the product line. Similarly, two of the supplier-initiated use cases (`Process Delivery Order` and `Confirm Shipment`) are common to all electronic commerce systems, so they become kernel use cases. On the other hand, two of the customer use cases (`Create Requisition` and `Confirm Delivery`) are used only in B2B systems, and a third use case (`Check Customer Account`) is used only in B2C systems. On the supplier side, one use case (`Send Invoice`) is used only in B2B systems, and another

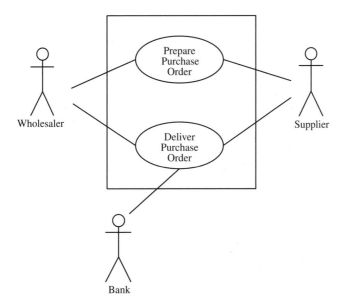

Figure 14.3   *Optional purchase order use cases*

use case (Bill Customer) is used only in B2C systems. Finally, the two purchase order use cases (Prepare Purchase Order and Deliver Purchase
Order) are optional and could be used in either B2B or B2C systems.

The use cases that can be used in only B2B or only B2C systems, but not
both, are categorized as *alternative* use cases. The optional purchase order use
cases, which have no such restriction, are categorized as *optional* use cases. The
use case model for the product line is shown in Figure 14.4.

14.3   Feature Modeling

In feature modeling, the requirements of the electronic commerce software
product line are viewed from a reuse perspective. The kernel use cases are
grouped into a common feature, called E-Commerce Kernel, and depicted as
a use case package consisting of the Browse Catalog, Make Purchase
Request, Process Delivery Order, and Confirm Shipment use cases.
There are also two alternative features—Business Customer and Home

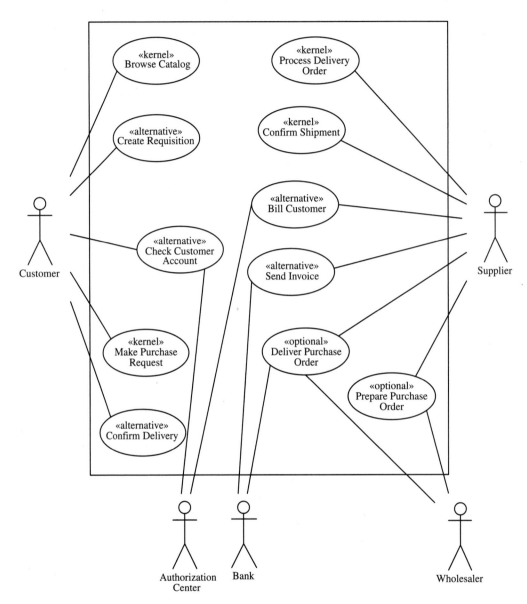

Figure 14.4 *Use cases of the electronic commerce software product line*

Customer—corresponding to the two major uses of this product line for B2B and B2C systems, respectively. The use cases that are used only in B2B systems (Create Requisition, Confirm Delivery, and Send Invoice) are combined into the alternative feature called Business Customer. The use cases that are used only in B2C systems (Check Customer Account and Bill Customer) are combined into the alternative feature called Home Customer. There is an exactly-one-of feature constraint between the alternative Business Customer and Home Customer features, meaning that one and only one of these features must be selected for a given electronic commerce system that is a member of the product line:

```
«exactly-one-of feature group» Customer {alternative = Business
Customer, Home Customer}
```

The optional purchase order use cases (Prepare Purchase Order and Deliver Purchase Order) are combined into an optional Purchase Order feature because they are always reused together.

The grouping of use cases into features is depicted with the UML package notation in Figure 14.5*a* and in tabular form in Table 14.1. The feature group is depicted in Table 14.2. Figure 14.5*b* depicts a feature dependency diagram showing the dependencies between the features by using the metamodeling and stereotype notation introduced in Chapter 5. Figure 14.5*b* shows an additional feature, Bank, which is factored out as a separate optional feature because it is needed by both the Business Customer alternative feature and Purchase Order optional feature, as explained in more detail in Section 14.7. The Business Customer and Purchase Order features are both explicit features that mutually include the Bank feature because it is an implicit feature that cannot be selected by itself. The exactly-one-of feature group Customer contains two mutually exclusive features: the Business Customer and Home Customer alternative features.

Many attributes need to be defined for any given member of the e-commerce product line. Several entity classes, as described in Section 14.4.4, have attributes that need to be populated when a member of the product family is derived from the product family architecture.

(a) Feature/use case dependencies

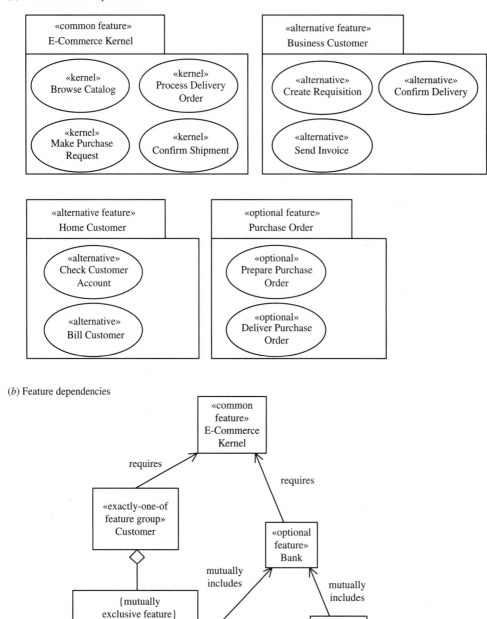

(b) Feature dependencies

Figure 14.5 *Feature model of the electronic commerce software product line*

Table 14.1 *Feature/use case dependencies of the electronic commerce software product line*

Feature Name	Feature Category	Use Case Name	Use Case Category
E-Commerce Kernel	common	Browse Catalog	kernel
		Make Purchase Request	kernel
		Process Delivery Order	kernel
		Confirm Shipment	kernel
Business Customer	alternative	Create Requisition	alternative
		Confirm Delivery	alternative
		Send Invoice	alternative
Home Customer	alternative	Check Customer Account	alternative
		Bill Customer	alternative
Purchase Order	optional	Prepare Purchase Order	optional
		Deliver Purchase Order	optional

Table 14.2 *Feature groups in the electronic commerce software product line*

Feature Group Name	Feature Group Category	Features in Feature Group	Feature Category
Customer	exactly-one-of	Business Customer	alternative
		Home Customer	alternative

14.4 Static Modeling

This section describes the static model, which consists of the product line context model and the entity class model. This section also discusses the use of brokering technology and agent technology in e-commerce product lines.

14.4.1 Software Product Line Context Modeling

The product line context model depicts three external user classes, depicted as actors: the kernel `Customer` and `Supplier` classes, and the optional `Wholesaler` external user. Furthermore, the `Customer` actor is specialized into two variant actors: `Business Customer` and `Home Customer`. There are two optional external system classes: `Authorization Center` and `Bank`. In this product line the context diagram (see Figure 14.6) is very similar to the use case diagram because the external classes correspond to the actors on the use case diagram.

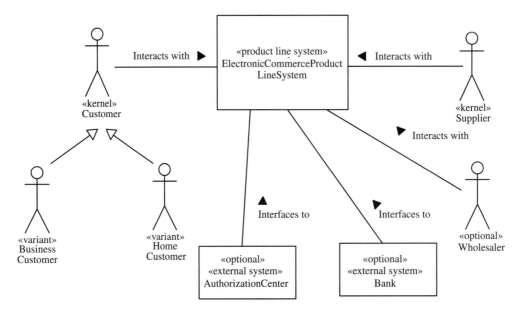

Figure 14.6   *Context class diagram of the electronic commerce software product line*

14.4.2   Agent Support for Electronic Commerce

This section outlines an approach that uses software agents in the electronic commerce product line. In this example there are client agents and server agents, where each agent defines the business rules for a particular aspect of the electronic commerce problem domain. In this application the client agents are user agents that act on behalf of users and assist users in performing their jobs. To do this, the client agents interact with server agents. The server agents receive requests from client agents. To satisfy a client agent request, a server agent typically interacts with server objects and with other agents.

The use of software agents is illustrated conceptually in Figure 14.7 for B2B e-commerce systems. In the electronic commerce problem, there are two types of client agents: Customer Agent and Supplier Agent. There is one instance of the Customer Agent for each customer and one instance of the Supplier Agent for each supplier. There are several server agents, with many instances of each. The server agents are

- Requisition Agent (one instance for each requisition)
- Delivery Order Agent (one instance for each delivery order)
- Invoice Agent (one instance for each invoice)

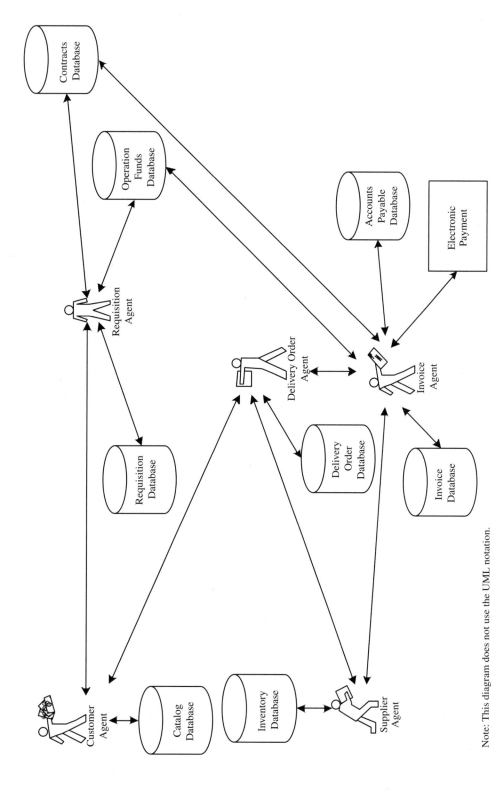

Note: This diagram does not use the UML notation.

Figure 14.7 *Agent-based B2B electronic commerce system: conceptual view*

453

- Billing Agent (one instance for each customer bill)
- Purchase Order Agent (one instance for each purchase order)

Customer Agent (see Figure 14.7) is a client agent that acts on behalf of the human customer. Customer Agent assists the customer who wishes to order one or more items from a catalog. It takes the customer's request and interacts with the server agents to further the processing of the customer's selection and to track the status. The customer may select several items from a catalog. When a customer completes catalog selection, Customer Agent acts on behalf of the customer and initiates certain actions. In particular, when the customer makes a catalog selection, Customer Agent sends a requisition request to a Requisition Agent.

Requisition Agent is a server agent that queries various databases and communicates with various agents to ensure the processing of a customer-initiated requisition. It queries the requisition database, contracts database, and operation funds database, as well as communicating with Customer Agent. It sends a contract query to the contracts database to determine if a contract is in place. It sends a funds query to the operation funds database to determine if the funds are in place. If the response to both queries is positive, Requisition Agent authorizes the requisition and sends the requisition status to Customer Agent. Customer Agent sends a purchase request to Delivery Order Agent.

Supplier Agent is a client agent that is instantiated to work with the supplier. It retrieves a delivery order from Delivery Order Agent and helps the supplier fulfill the order. Supplier Agent updates the inventory database, and the order status is sent to Delivery Order Agent and Customer Agent. The customer eventually acknowledges receipt of the goods, and the delivery order is updated to reflect the receipt date.

Supplier Agent sends the invoice to Invoice Agent at the customer organization. When notified by Delivery Order Agent that the goods have been received, Invoice Agent queries the contracts database and the operation funds database (see Figure 14.7). If both responses are positive, Invoice Agent authorizes payment and sends the invoice to the accounts payable database, which updates the account. Invoice Agent then sends the electronic payment request to the customer's bank.

Billing Agent is used in B2C applications to handle the validation and billing of the customer's electronic purchase by interacting with various agents and servers, as well as with the credit card authorization center, as shown in Figure 14.8. Purchase Order Agent (also shown in Figure 14.8) is an optional server agent that addresses the preparation and delivery of a purchase order by interacting with various agents and servers, as well as with the external wholesaler and the bank.

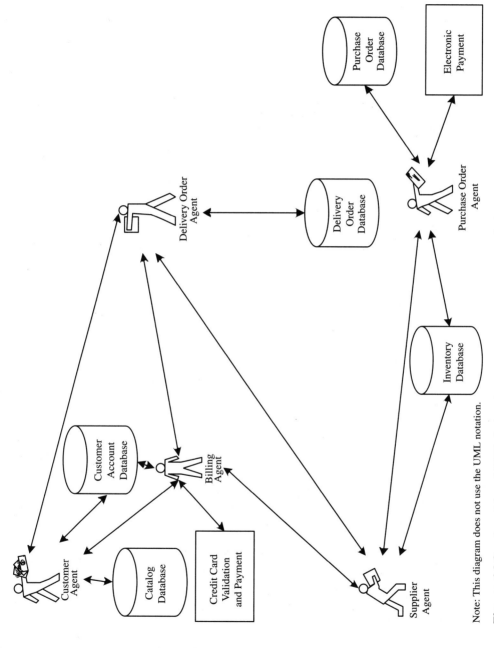

Note: This diagram does not use the UML notation.

Figure 14.8 *Agent-based B2C electronic commerce system: conceptual view*

455

14.4.3   Broker Support for Electronic Commerce

Several legacy databases are used in the electronic commerce software product line. Each of these is a stand-alone database residing on a mainframe. These databases need to be integrated into the electronic commerce application by means of a broker technology (see Chapters 2 and 10 for more information on brokers).

The legacy databases in the customer organizations are the contracts database, the operation funds database, the requisition database, the invoice database, and the accounts payable database. The legacy databases in the supplier organizations are the catalog database, the inventory database, and the delivery order database.

To integrate these databases into the electronic commerce application, the server objects that access them need to be database wrapper objects that encapsulate the details of how to read and update the individual databases. Thus, `Requisition Server`, `Contracts Server`, `Operation Funds Server`, `Accounts Payable Server`, `Invoice Server`, `Catalog Server`, `Delivery Order Server`, and `Inventory Server` are all database wrapper objects.

In addition, to maintain low coupling between clients, agents, and servers, a broker naming service is used to maintain the location of the specific services. Servers and agents register their services and locations with the object broker. When a service is required, a message is sent to the broker to determine the location of the service. An example is given in Figure 14.9 in which a client agent, `Customer Agent`, determines from the broker the location of a server agent, `Delivery Order Agent`. `Customer Agent` then communicates directly with `Delivery Order Agent`.

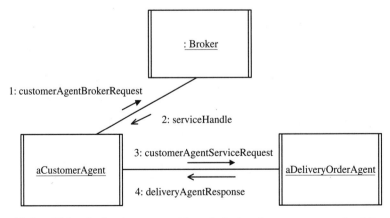

Figure 14.9   *Object broker in an agent-based electronic commerce product line*

14.4.4   Static Entity Class Modeling of the Problem Domain

A static model of the problem domain is developed and depicted on a class diagram (see Figure 14.10). Because this is a data-intensive application, the emphasis is on the entity classes, many of which represent the data stored in the legacy databases. The database wrapper objects will map between the conceptual objects and the actual databases. Because each customer and supplier organization is liable to have its own specific legacy database, many individual solutions to the wrapper problem are likely to exist. But if broker and wrapper technology is used, it is possible to have a systematic way of integrating the disparate legacy databases into a general solution.

Entity Classes

The electronic commerce software product line has two main groups of applications: B2C applications and B2B applications. The static entity class model for B2C applications is depicted in Figure 14.10, which shows the entity classes for all the important problem domain entities and the relationships among these classes. The classes include home customer classes (`Customer` and `Customer Account`), supplier classes (such as `Supplier`, `Inventory`, and `Catalog`), and classes that deal with the customer's order (such as `Delivery Order`, which is an aggregation of `Selected Item`).

The static entity class model for B2B applications is shown in Figure 14.11. These classes include business customer classes (such as `Requisition`, `Contract`, and `Operation Funds`), supplier classes (such as `Catalog` and `Inventory`), and classes that deal with the customer's order and payment (such as `Delivery Order`, `Payment`, and `Invoice`).

The integrated static entity class model for the product line is shown in Figure 14.12. In the product line static model, classes have a second stereotype to depict the reuse category of each class: either «kernel» or «optional». Classes such as `Customer` and `Catalog`, which exist in the static models of both B2C and B2B applications, become kernel classes in the product line static model. Classes that appear in only one of the static models, such as `Contract` (which appears only in the B2B static model) and `Customer Account` (which appears only in the B2C static model), become optional classes in the product line static model. Entity classes that might exist in either a B2B or a B2C application, such as `Purchase Order`, also become optional classes in the product line static model.

The attributes for the kernel and optional classes are shown in Figures 14.13 and 14.14, respectively. Many of the class attributes need to be defined at configuration or initialization time before a member of the product family can become

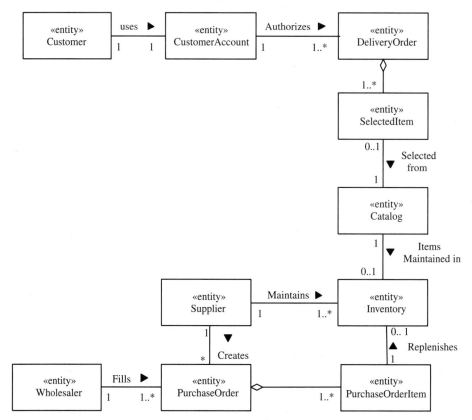

Figure 14.10 *Conceptual static model for e-commerce B2C entity classes*

operational. Included are attributes for the kernel classes, as well as for the optional and variant classes selected for the product line member. For a B2B system, these include attributes for the `Customer, Supplier, Contract, Operation Funds,` and `Bank Account` classes.

14.4.5   Object and Class Structuring

The entity classes determined in the previous section will all be incorporated into the server classes, which will provide the necessary legacy database wrapping as described in Section 14.4.3. User interface classes are needed to interact with the external users—in particular, `Customer Interface` and `Supplier Interface`. Furthermore, the software agents described in Section 14.4.2 are also needed.

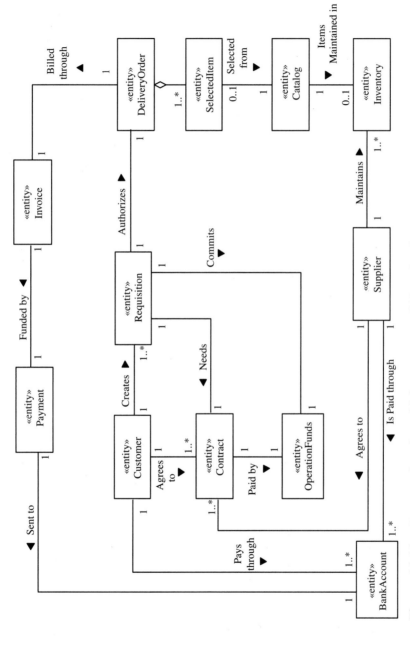

Figure 14.11 *Conceptual static model for e-commerce B2B entity classes*

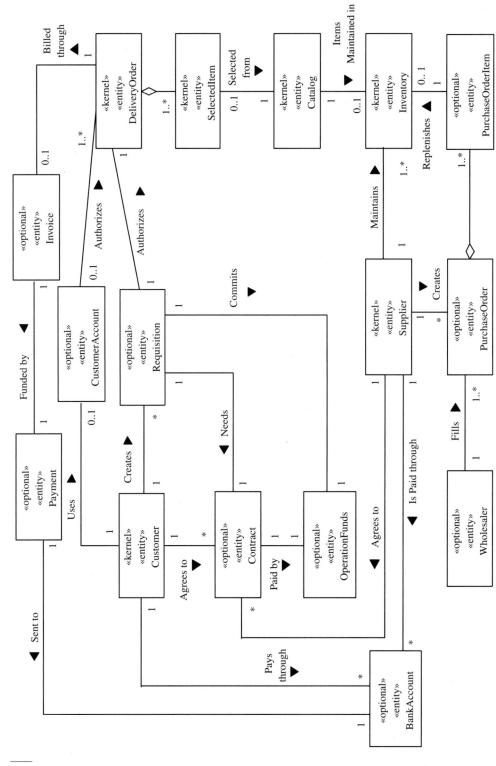

Figure 14.12 *Conceptual static model for e-commerce software product line entity classes*

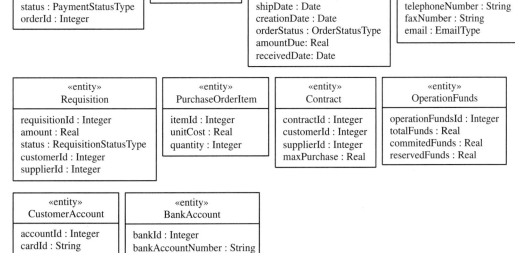

Figure 14.13 *Kernel entity classes for the e-commerce software product line*

«entity»
Payment

paymentId : String
amount : Real
date : Date
status : PaymentStatusType
orderId : Integer

«entity»
Invoice

invoiceId : Integer
amountDue : Real
invoiceDate : Date

«entity»
PurchaseOrder

orderId : Integer
supplierId : Integer
wholeSalerId : Integer
shipDate : Date
creationDate : Date
orderStatus : OrderStatusType
amountDue: Real
receivedDate: Date

«entity»
Wholesaler

wholesalerId : Integer
wholesalerName : String
address : String
telephoneNumber : String
faxNumber : String
email : EmailType

«entity»
Requisition

requisitionId : Integer
amount : Real
status : RequisitionStatusType
customerId : Integer
supplierId : Integer

«entity»
PurchaseOrderItem

itemId : Integer
unitCost : Real
quantity : Integer

«entity»
Contract

contractId : Integer
customerId : Integer
supplierId : Integer
maxPurchase : Real

«entity»
OperationFunds

operationFundsId : Integer
totalFunds : Real
commitedFunds : Real
reservedFunds : Real

«entity»
CustomerAccount

accountId : Integer
cardId : String
cardType : String
expirationDate: Date

«entity»
BankAccount

bankId : Integer
bankAccountNumber : String
accountType : String

Figure 14.14 *Optional entity classes for the e-commerce software product line*

14.5   Dynamic Modeling

For each use case, a communication diagram is developed depicting the objects that participate in the use case and the sequence of messages passed between them. With the kernel first approach, the communication diagrams for the four kernel use cases are developed first.

14.5.1   Dynamic Modeling for Browse Catalog

In the communication diagram for the Browse Catalog use case (Figure 14.15), Customer Interface interacts with Customer Agent, which in turn communicates with Catalog Server. The message descriptions are as follows:

A1: The customer makes a catalog request via Customer Interface.

A2: Customer Agent is instantiated to assist the customer. On the basis of the customer's request, Customer Agent selects one or more catalogs for the customer to browse.

A3: Customer Agent requests information from Catalog Server.

A4: Catalog Server sends catalog information to Customer Agent.

A5: Customer Agent forwards the information to Customer Interface.

A6: Customer Interface displays the catalog to the customer.

A7: The customer makes a catalog selection through Customer Interface.

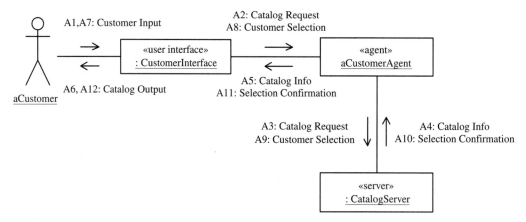

Figure 14.15   *Communication diagram for the* Browse Catalog *use case*

A8: `Customer Interface` passes the request on to `Customer Agent`.

A9: `Customer Agent` requests the catalog selection from `Catalog Server`.

A10: `Catalog Server` confirms the availability of the catalog items to `Customer Agent`.

A11: `Customer Agent` forwards the information to `Customer Interface`.

A12: `Customer Interface` displays the catalog confirmation to the customer.

14.5.2   Dynamic Modeling for Make Purchase Request

In the communication diagram for the `Make Purchase Request` use case (Figure 14.16), `Customer Agent` sends a purchase request to `Delivery Order Agent` and receives a confirmation. The message descriptions are as follows:

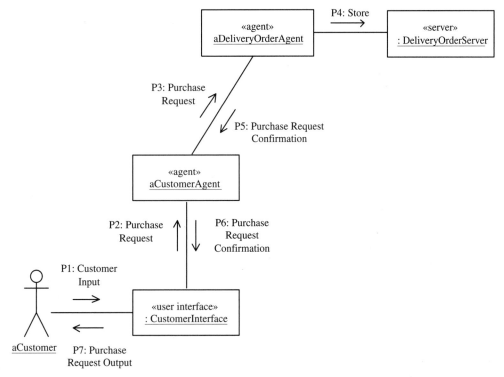

Figure 14.16   *Communication diagram for the* `Make Purchase Request` *use case*

P1: The customer makes a purchase request.

P2: `Customer Interface` sends the purchase request to `Customer Agent`.

P3: `Customer Agent` instantiates `Delivery Order Agent` and sends the purchase request to it.

P4: `Delivery Order Agent` creates a new delivery order and stores it with `Delivery Order Server`.

P5: `Delivery Order Agent` sends a purchase request confirmation with the order ID to `Customer Agent`.

P6: `Customer Agent` sends the purchase request confirmation to `Customer Interface`.

P7: `Customer Interface` displays the purchase request status to the customer.

14.5.3 Dynamic Modeling for Process Delivery Order

In the communication diagram for the next use case, `Process Delivery Order` (Figure 14.17), `Supplier Agent` queries `Delivery Order Agent` for a new delivery order, and `Delivery Order Agent` selects a delivery order. `Supplier Agent` checks the inventory and displays the order and inventory information to the supplier via the user interface. The message descriptions are as follows:

C1: The supplier requests a new delivery order.

C2: `Supplier Interface` forwards the request to `Supplier Agent`.

C3: `Supplier Agent` sends the order request to `Delivery Order Agent`.

C4, C5: `Delivery Order Agent` selects a delivery order by querying `Delivery Order Server`.

C6: `Delivery Order Agent` sends the delivery order to `Supplier Agent`.

C7, C8: `Supplier Agent` checks that the items are available in inventory.

C9: `Supplier Agent` sends the order status to `Supplier Interface`.

C10: `Supplier Interface` displays the delivery order and inventory information to the supplier.

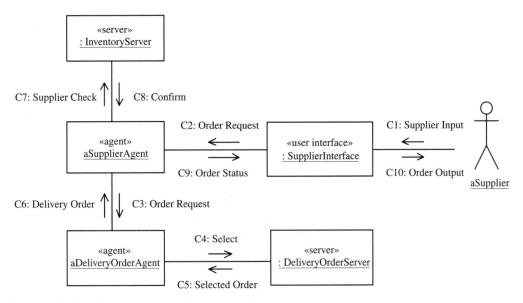

Figure 14.17 *Communication diagram for the* Process Delivery Order *use case*

14.5.4 Dynamic Modeling for Confirm Shipment

In the communication diagram for the Confirm Shipment use case (Figure 14.18), the supplier prepares the shipment manually. The supplier then confirms the shipment by entering the shipping information, including the shipping date. Supplier Agent updates the inventory, and the order status is sent to Delivery Order Agent and to Customer Agent, which displays the order status to the customer. The message descriptions are as follows:

S1: The supplier inputs the shipping information.

S2: Supplier Interface sends the confirm shipment request to Supplier Agent.

S3: Supplier Agent updates the inventory stored at Inventory Server.

S4: Supplier Agent sends the order status to Delivery Order Agent.

S5: Delivery Order Agent updates Delivery Order Server.

S6: Delivery Order Agent sends the order status to Customer Agent.

S7: Customer Agent forwards the order status to Customer Interface.

S8: Customer Interface displays the order status to the customer.

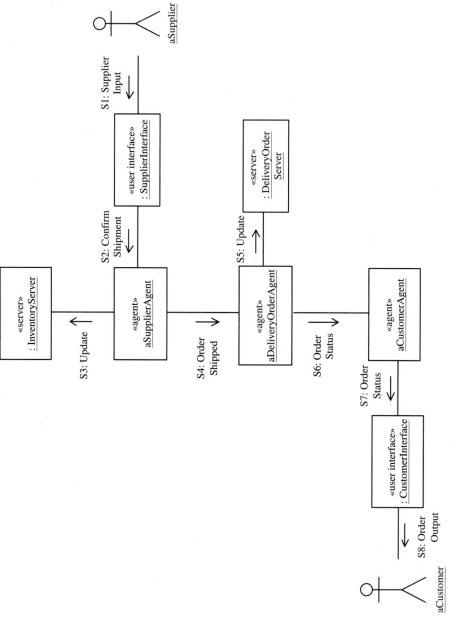

Figure 14.18 *Communication diagram for the* Confirm Shipment *use case*

14.6   Software Product Line Evolution

With the product line evolution approach, the communication diagrams are next developed for the optional and alternative use cases.

14.6.1   Dynamic Modeling for Create Requisition

In the communication diagram for the `Create Requisition` use case (Figure 14.19), `Requisition Agent` sends a contract query to `Contracts Server` to determine if a contract is in place. It also sends a funds query to `Operation Funds Server` to determine if the funds are in place. If the response to both queries

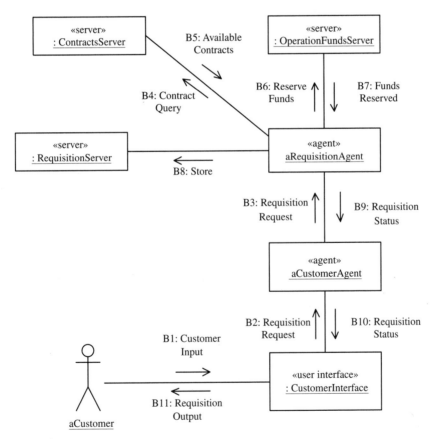

Figure 14.19   *Communication diagram for the* `Create Requisition` *use case*

is positive, `Requisition Agent` authorizes the requisition and sends the requisition status to `Customer Agent`. The message descriptions are as follows:

B1: The customer selects items from the catalog and requests the creation of a requisition.

B2: `Customer Interface` forwards the request to `Customer Agent`.

B3: `Customer Agent` instantiates `Requisition Agent`, passing to it the customer's requisition request.

B4: `Requisition Agent` sends a contract query to `Contracts Server`.

B5: `Contracts Server` returns the contracts available between the customer and the supplier.

B6: `Requisition Agent` sends a `Reserve Funds` request to `Operation Funds Server` to hold the funds from a given contract for this requisition.

B7: `Operation Funds Server` confirms that the funds have been reserved.

B8: `Requisition Agent` approves the requisition and sends it to be stored at `Requisition Server`.

B9: `Requisition Agent` sends the requisition status to `Customer Agent`.

B10: `Customer Agent` sends the requisition status to `Customer Interface`.

B11: `Customer Interface` sends the requisition status to the customer.

14.6.2 Dynamic Modeling for Confirm Delivery

In the communication diagram for the `Confirm Delivery` use case (Figure 14.20), when the shipment arrives at the customer, the customer acknowledges receipt of the goods, and the delivery order is updated to reflect the receipt date. `Requisition Agent` is also notified. The message descriptions are as follows:

R1: The customer acknowledges receipt of the shipment.

R2: `Customer Interface` sends the customer confirmation to `Customer Agent`.

R3: `Customer Agent` sends a `Shipment Received` message to `Delivery Order Agent`.

R4: `Delivery Order Agent` updates the status at `Delivery Order Server`.

R5: `Customer Agent` sends a `Shipment Received` message to `Requisition Agent`.

R6: `Requisition Agent` updates the status of the requisition stored at `Requisition Server`.

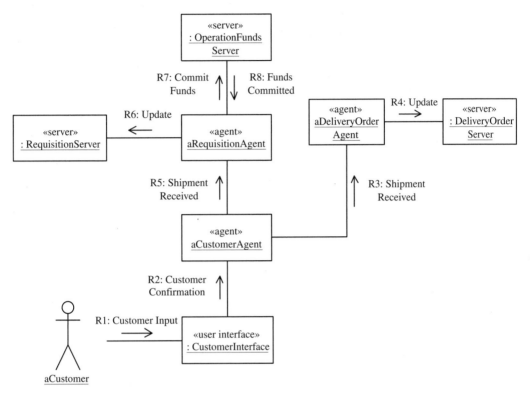

Figure 14.20 *Communication diagram for the* Confirm Delivery *use case*

R7, R8: Requisition Agent commits the funds for this requisition with Operation Funds Server.

14.6.3 Dynamic Modeling for Send Invoice

Because the supplier confirmed in the Confirm Shipment use case (see Figure 14.18) that the goods were sent to the customer, Supplier Agent sends the invoice automatically, as shown in the communication diagram for the Send Invoice use case (Figure 14.21). The arrival of the invoice at the customer organization causes the instantiation of Invoice Agent to follow through on the invoice. Invoice Agent subscribes to Delivery Order Agent to be notified when the goods have been received. When notified of the receipt of the goods, Invoice Agent queries Contracts Server and Operation Funds Server. If both responses are positive, Invoice Agent authorizes payment

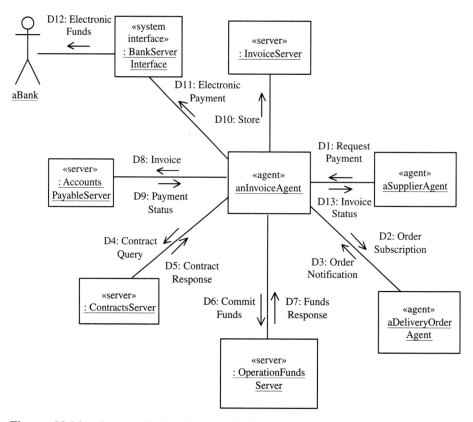

Figure 14.21 *Communication diagram for the* Send Invoice *use case*

and sends the invoice to Accounts Payable Server, which updates the account. Invoice Agent then sends the electronic payment to the customer's bank server and the invoice status to the supplier. The message descriptions are as follows:

D1: Supplier Agent sends the invoice information to Invoice Agent.

D2: Invoice Agent subscribes to Delivery Order Agent.

D3: Delivery Order Agent notifies Invoice Agent that the goods have been received.

D4: Invoice Agent sends a contract query to Contracts Server.

D5: Contracts Server confirms the contract.

D6: Invoice Agent sends a funds commitment request to Operation Funds Server.

D7: `Operation Funds Server` confirms that the funds are available and committed.

D8: `Invoice Agent` sends the invoice to `Accounts Payable Server`.

D9: `Accounts Payable Server` sends the payment status to `Invoice Agent`.

D10: `Invoice Agent` stores the invoice at `Invoice Server`.

D11: `Invoice Agent` sends the electronic payment to the customer's bank via `Bank Server Interface`.

D12: `Bank Server Interface` sends the electronic funds to the customer's bank for payment to the supplier.

D13: `Invoice Agent` sends the invoice status to `Supplier Agent`.

14.6.4 Dynamic Modeling for Prepare Purchase Order

In the communication diagram for the `Prepare Purchase Order` use case (Figure 14.22), the supplier requests a new purchase order to replenish low inventory. This interaction involves a new agent, `Purchase Order Agent`, as well as `Purchase Order Server` and an interface to the wholesaler, who has to fill the purchase order. The message descriptions are as follows:

K1: The supplier provides purchase order details.

K2: `Supplier Interface` sends the purchase order information to `Supplier Agent`.

K3: `Supplier Agent` sends the PO request to `Purchase Order Agent`.

K4: `Purchase Order Agent` checks the inventory via `Inventory Server`.

K5: `Inventory Server` responds with current inventory levels for the items of interest.

K6: `Purchase Order Agent` stores the purchase order with `Purchase Order Server`.

K7: `Purchase Order Agent` places the purchase order with `Wholesaler Interface`.

K8: `Wholesaler Interface` delivers the purchase order to the wholesaler.

K9, K10, K11: `Purchase Order Agent` confirms to `Supplier Agent` the sending of the purchase order, and `Supplier Agent` informs `Supplier Interface`, which in turn informs the supplier.

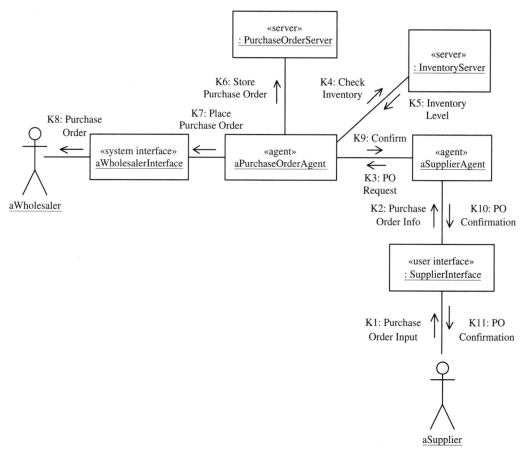

Figure 14.22 *Communication diagram for the* Prepare Purchase Order *use case*

14.6.5 Dynamic Modeling for Deliver Purchase Order

In the communication diagram for the Deliver Purchase Order use case (Figure 14.23), the supplier receives a new purchase order to replenish low inventory. Purchase Order Agent interacts with Purchase Order Server and Inventory Server, as well as with Bank Server Interface. The message descriptions are as follows:

> **H1**: The supplier receives a new purchase order and inputs the purchase order to Supplier Interface.

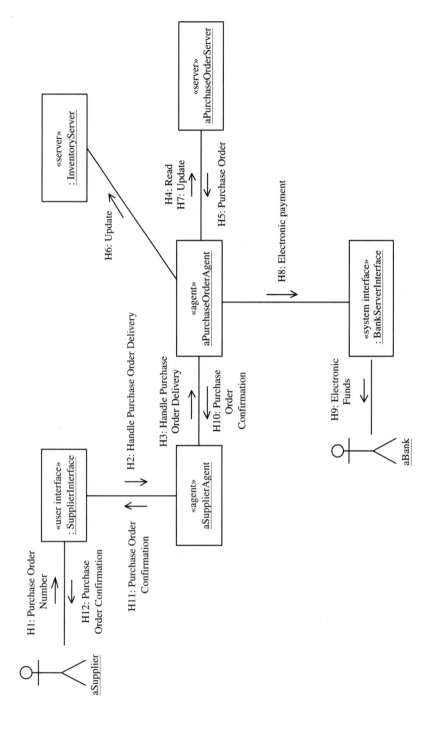

Figure 14.23 *Communication diagram for the* Deliver Purchase Order *use case*

H2: `Supplier Interface` sends a `Handle Purchase Order Delivery` request to `Supplier Agent`.

H3: `Supplier Agent` forwards this request with the PO number to `Purchase Order Agent`.

H4, H5: `Purchase Order Agent` requests the purchase order from `Purchase Order Server`.

H6: `Purchase Order Agent` sends an update message to `Inventory Server` to update the inventory with the new items received.

H7: `Purchase Order Agent` sends an update message to `Purchase Order Server` to record that the PO has been serviced.

H8, H9: `Purchase Order Agent` sends an electronic payment for the wholesaler to the bank via `Bank Server Interface`.

H10, H11, H12: `Purchase Order Agent` confirms delivery of the purchase order to `Supplier Agent`, which informs `Supplier Interface`, which in turn informs the supplier.

14.6.6   Dynamic Modeling for Check Customer Account

The communication diagram for the `Check Customer Account` use case (Figure 14.24) addresses the B2C case in which a customer provides the account information, which is checked by `Customer Agent` in conjunction with `Billing Agent`. The message descriptions are as follows:

F1: The customer provides account input to `Customer Interface`.

F2: `Customer Interface` sends the account request to `Customer Agent`.

F3, F4: `Customer Agent` sends the account request to `Customer Account Server` and receives the account information, including the customer's credit card details.

F5: `Customer Agent` sends the customer's credit card information to `Billing Agent`.

F6, F7: `Billing Agent` sends a credit card request to `Authorization Center Interface`, which forwards the request to the authorization center.

F8, F9: `Authorization Center` sends a credit card acknowledgment to `Billing Agent` via `Authorization Center Interface`.

F10, F11: `Billing Agent` forwards the credit card acknowledgment to `Customer Agent`, which sends an account confirmation to `Customer Account Server`.

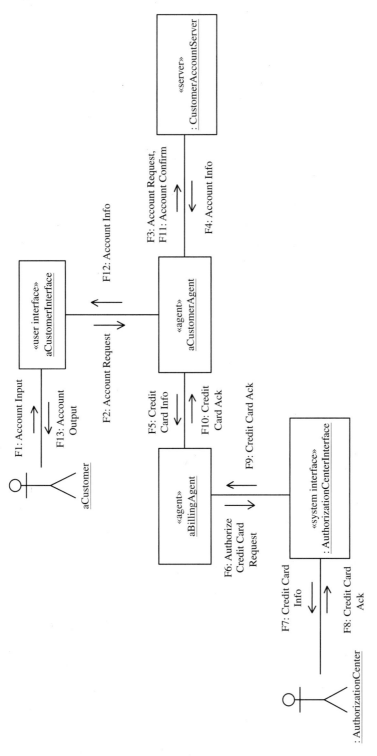

Figure 14.24 *Communication diagram for the* Check Customer Account *use case*

F12, F13: `Customer Agent` sends the account information to `Customer Interface`, which outputs it to the customer.

An alternative to this use case is that the customer does not have an account, in which case an account will be created.

14.6.7 Dynamic Modeling for Bill Customer

The communication diagram for the `Bill Customer` use case (Figure 14.25) addresses the B2C case in which a customer is billed for the purchase. This use case involves `Supplier Agent` and `Billing Agent`, as well as electronic billing. Because the supplier confirmed in the `Confirm Shipment` use case (see Figure 14.18) that the goods were sent to the customer, `Supplier Agent` sends the payment request automatically, as shown in Figure 14.25. The message descriptions are as follows:

B1: `Supplier Agent` sends the payment request for billing the customer to `Billing Agent`.

B2: `Billing Agent` subscribes to `Delivery Order Agent` to receive notification of order completion.

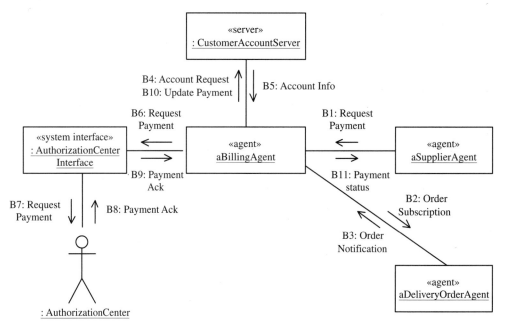

Figure 14.25 *Communication diagram for the* `Bill Customer` *use case*

B3: `Delivery Order Agent` notifies `Billing Agent` of order completion.

B4, B5: `Billing Agent` requests the customer's credit card information from `Customer Account Server` and receives the information.

B6: `Billing Agent` forwards the request to `Authorization Center Interface`.

B7: `Authorization Center Interface` sends the billing information to the external authorization center.

B8: The authorization center acknowledges that it has billed the customer and returns a billing reference number.

B9: `Authorization Center Interface` sends the billing reference number to `Billing Agent`.

B10: `Billing Agent` sends the billing reference number to `Customer Account Server`.

B11: `Billing Agent` sends the payment status to `Supplier Agent`.

14.7 Feature/Class Dependency Analysis

The feature/class dependencies of the electronic commerce software product line are shown in Table 14.3. There are kernel components, `Business Customer` components, `Home Customer` components, and optional `Purchase Order` and `Bank` components.

To identify the kernel components, it is necessary to analyze the communication diagrams that support the kernel use cases. Table 14.1 shows that the kernel use cases that support the common `E-Commerce Kernel` feature are `Browse Catalog`, `Make Purchase Request`, `Process Delivery Order`, and `Confirm Shipment`. Analyzing the communication diagram for `Browse Catalog` (Figure 14.15) indicates that the kernel objects are `Customer Interface`, `Customer Agent`, and `Catalog Server`. For `Make Purchase Request`, the communication diagram (Figure 14.16) shows that `Delivery Order Agent` and `Delivery Order Server` are also kernel objects. The communication diagram for `Process Delivery Order` (Figure 14.17) shows that `Supplier Interface`, `Supplier Agent`, and `Inventory Server` are additional kernel objects. The final communication diagram for a kernel use case is `Confirm Shipment` (Figure 14.18). However, the objects on this diagram have already been accounted for in the previous diagrams. Each of the identified kernel

Table 14.3 *Feature/class dependencies of the electronic commerce software product line*

Feature Name	Feature Category	Class Name	Class Category
E-Commerce Kernel	common	Customer Interface	kernel-abstract-vp
		Customer Agent	kernel-abstract-vp
		Supplier Interface	kernel-vp
		Supplier Agent	kernel-vp
		Catalog Server	kernel
		Delivery Order Agent	kernel
		Delivery Order Server	kernel
		Inventory Server	kernel
Business Customer	alternative	B2B Customer Interface	variant
		B2B Customer Agent	variant
		Requisition Agent	optional
		Requisition Server	optional
		Contracts Server	optional
		Operation Funds Server	optional
		Invoice Agent	optional
		Invoice Server	optional
		Accounts Payable Server	optional
Home Customer	alternative	B2C Customer Interface	variant
		B2C Customer Agent	variant
		Billing Agent	optional
		Customer Account Server	optional
		Authorization Center Interface	optional
Purchase Order	optional	Purchase Order Agent	optional
		Purchase Order Server	optional
		Wholesaler Interface	optional
		Purchase Order Supplier Interface	variant
		Purchase Order Supplier Agent	variant
Bank	optional	Bank Server Interface	optional

objects is an instance of a kernel class. The feature/class dependencies for the kernel e-commerce product line are shown in Table 14.3.

To determine the components in the `Business Customer` feature, it is necessary to analyze the communication diagrams for the alternative use cases that support this alternative feature—namely, `Create Requisition, Confirm`

Delivery, and Send Invoice, as shown in Table 14.1. Analysis of the Create Requisition communication diagram (Figure 14.19) identifies several objects: Customer Interface, Customer Agent, Requisition Agent, Requisition Server, Contracts Server, and Operation Funds Server. Because the first two objects behave differently in B2B systems, it is necessary to classify them further as B2B Customer Interface and B2B Customer Agent. From the Confirm Delivery communication diagram (Figure 14.20), no further objects are added because the only new objects compared to Create Requisition— namely, Delivery Order Agent and Delivery Order Server—have already been categorized as kernel objects. However, the final communication diagram for the alternative Send Invoice use case (Figure 14.21), adds several more objects: Invoice Agent, Invoice Server, and Accounts Payable Server. Supplier Agent has already been categorized as a kernel object.

At first glance, it would seem that Bank Server Interface should also be a class that supports the Business Customer feature. However, because this class is also needed in the Purchase Order feature, it is instead split off and allocated to its own feature, the Bank optional feature. Bank is an additional feature that is determined at design time and results when a class that is needed by two variable features is factored out. The feature/class dependencies for the alternative Business Customer feature are shown in Table 14.3.

To determine the components in the Home Customer feature, it is necessary to analyze the communication diagrams for the alternative use cases that support this alternative feature—namely, Check Customer Account and Bill Customer—as shown in Table 14.1. Analysis of the Check Customer Account communication diagram (Figure 14.24) determines that several objects support this feature: Customer Interface, Customer Agent, Billing Agent, Customer Account Server, and Authorization Center Interface. Because the first two objects behave differently in B2C systems, it is necessary to classify them further as B2C Customer Interface and B2C Customer Agent. From the Bill Customer communication diagram (Figure 14.25), no further objects are necessary. The feature/class dependencies for the alternative Home Customer feature are shown in Table 14.3.

To determine the components in the Purchase Order feature, it is necessary to analyze the communication diagrams for the optional use cases that support this optional feature—namely, Prepare Purchase Order and Deliver Purchase Order—as shown in Table 14.1. Analysis of the Prepare Purchase Order communication diagram (Figure 14.22) determines that five objects support this feature: Supplier Interface, Supplier Agent, Purchase Order Agent, Purchase Order Server, and Wholesaler Interface. Because the first two objects behave differently when handling purchase orders, it is necessary to classify them further as `Purchase Order Supplier Interface` and `Purchase Order Supplier Agent`. The only additional object, which comes from the `Deliver Purchase Order` communication diagram (Figure 14.23), is `Bank Server Interface`, which has already been allocated to the `Bank` feature. The feature/class dependencies for the optional `Purchase Order` feature are shown in Table 14.3.

14.8 Design Modeling

The electronic commerce software product line is designed as a layered architecture based on the Layers of Abstraction architecture pattern. In addition, this product line uses the Client/Agent/Server pattern. In particular, it uses a variation of the pattern that has two types of agents: a client agent and a server agent. Both the Layers of Abstraction and the Client/Agent/Server patterns are described in Chapter 10.

The kernel of the electronic commerce software product line is designed to consist of those components that are needed by all members of the product line. Because of the integration of the Client/Agent/Server pattern with the Layers of Abstraction pattern, the kernel of the product line actually encompasses four layers of the architecture. The B2C and B2B systems, which are two major members of the product line, are designed with optional and alternative components that complement and use the kernel components. Because this product line needs to be highly flexible and distributed, the decision is made to design a distributed component-based software architecture.

Because the electronic commerce software product line is an interorganizational product line involving multiple organizations, it is actually a federated system as well as being a distributed system. In particular, in the B2B versions of the product line, some components are business customer components while other components are supplier components. Because of the characteristics of this product line, it is useful to design higher-level abstractions than individual components, which are high-level aggregate subsystems that encompass multiple components. Thus, the Client/Agent/Server pattern is applied on a subsystem-by-subsystem basis.

There are six aggregate subsystems, as follows:

1. `Supplier Organization Subsystem` (one instance per supplier organization)

2. `Business Customer Organization Subsystem` (one instance per customer organization)

3. Home Customer Subsystem (one instance per home customer)

4. Purchase Order Subsystem (one instance per wholesaler)

5. Bank Subsystem (one instance per bank)

6. Authorization Subsystem (one instance per credit card company)

14.8.1   Static Modeling

Each subsystem can be depicted as a package that contains the components in that subsystem, depicted as classes. Each component is depicted with two stereotypes: the component stereotype (what kind of component it is, as specified by the component structuring criteria) and the product line stereotype (the reuse category, such as kernel, optional, or variant). The components in each subsystem are determined by analysis of the communication diagrams for those use cases that are required for B2C and B2B systems, respectively.

One additional consideration is that some of the objects behave differently in B2B systems than in B2C systems. In particular, this situation applies to the Customer Interface and Customer Agent classes. It is therefore necessary to design B2B and B2C variants of these classes. The kernel class is designed as a kernel abstract class, which captures the generalized properties of the class and provides an interface that is inherited by the subclasses. Each subclass then provides additional behavior specific to its needs. The generalization/specialization hierarchy for the Customer Interface and Customer Agent classes is shown in Figure 14.26.

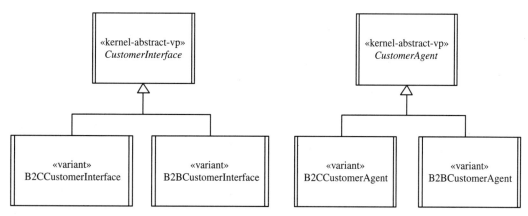

Figure 14.26   *Generalization/specialization hierarchies in the electronic commerce software product line*

14.8.2 Layered Software Architecture

The components are structured into the layered architecture such that each component is in a layer where it needs the services provided by components in the layers below but not the layers above. This layered architecture is based on the Flexible Layers of Abstraction pattern, which is a less restrictive variant of the Layers of Abstraction pattern in which a layer can use the services of any of the layers below it, not just the layer immediately below it. This architecture facilitates adaptation of the electronic commerce software product line architecture to derive individual application members of the product line. User interface components at the user interface layer communicate only with client agent components. Client agent components communicate with server agent components and server components. Server agent components communicate with server components. Applying the component structuring criteria, the following components, organized by subsystem and layer are determined:

Supplier Organization Subsystem

Supplier Organization Subsystem (see Figure 14.27) consists of the kernel supplier components, together with the optional Billing Agent and Customer Account Server components, which are used only in B2C systems:

Layer 1: Server components. There are three kernel server components (Catalog Server, Delivery Order Server, and Inventory Server) and one optional server component (Customer Account Server).

Layer 2: Server agent components. There are two server agents: the kernel Delivery Order Agent and the optional Billing Agent.

Layer 3: Client agent components. There is one kernel client agent: Supplier Agent.

Layer 4: User interface component. There is one kernel user interface component: Supplier Interface.

Home Customer Subsystem

Home Customer Subsystem (see Figure 14.28) consists of the variant B2C Customer Interface and B2C Customer Agent components:

Layer 1: Server components. There are no server components.

Layer 2: Server agent components. There are no server agent components.

Layer 3: Client agent components. There is one variant client agent: B2C Customer Agent.

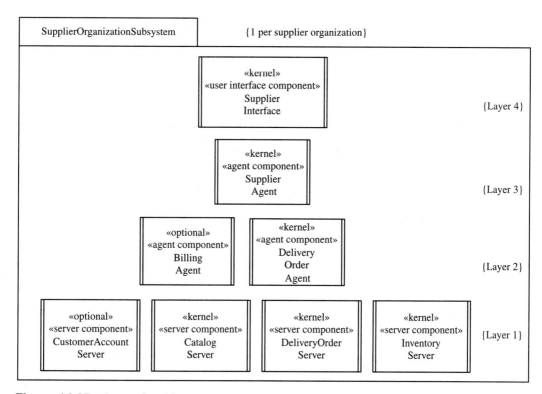

Figure 14.27   *Layered architecture:* Supplier Organization Subsystem

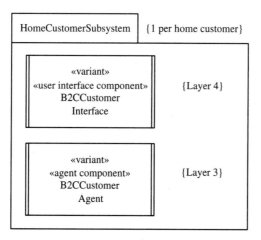

Figure 14.28   *Layered architecture:* Home Customer Subsystem

Layer 4: User interface component. There is one variant user interface component: B2C Customer Interface.

Business Customer Organization Subsystem

Business Customer Organization Subsystem (see Figure 14.29) consists of the variant B2B Customer Interface and B2B Customer Agent components, as well as several optional components that are used only in B2B systems:

Layer 1: Server components. There are several optional server components: Requisition Server, Contracts Server, Invoice Server, Operation Funds Server, and Accounts Payable Server.

Layer 2: Server agent components. There are two optional server agents: Requisition Agent and Invoice Agent.

Layer 3: Client agent components. There is one variant client agent: B2B Customer Agent.

Layer 4: User interface component. There is one variant user interface component: B2B Customer Interface.

Purchase Order Subsystem

Purchase Order Subsystem (see Figure 14.30) consists of optional components that exist at two layers and can be used with either B2B or B2C systems:

Layer 1: Server components. There is one optional server component (Purchase Order Server) and one optional system interface component (Wholesaler Interface).

Layer 2: Server agent components. There is one optional server agent: Purchase Order Agent.

Layer 3: Client agent components. There are no client agents.

Layer 4: User interface component. There is no user interface component.

Bank and Authorization Subsystems

Bank Subsystem and Authorization Subsystem (see Figure 14.30) have one server component each: the Bank Server Interface and Authorization Center Interface components, respectively.

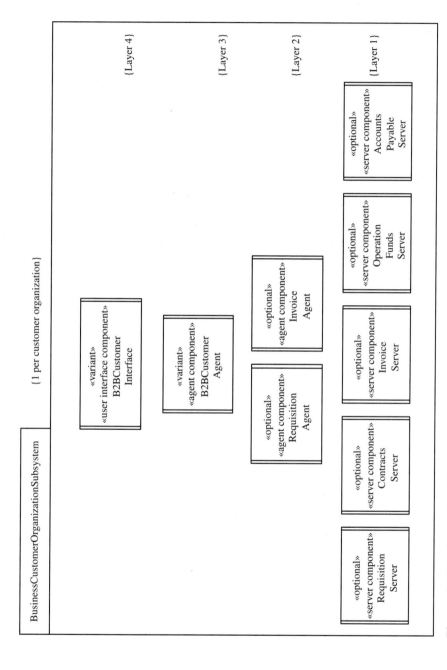

Figure 14.29 *Layered architecture*: Business Customer Organization Subsystem

485

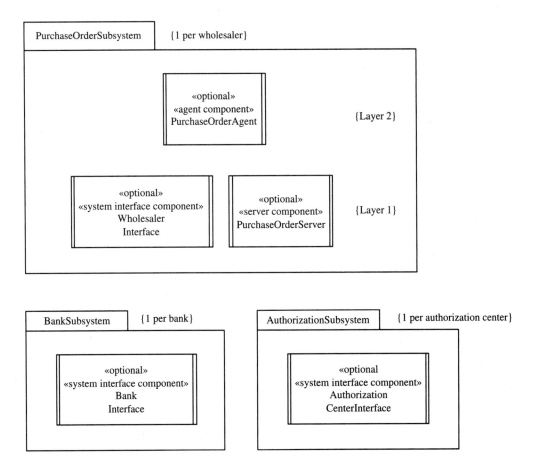

Figure 14.30 *Layered architecture:* Purchase Order, Bank, *and* Authorization Center *subsystems*

14.8.3 Architectural Communication Patterns

To handle the variety of communication between the components in the product line architecture, several communication patterns are applied:

- **Synchronous Message Communication with Reply.** This is the typical client/server pattern of communication and is used when the client needs information from the server and cannot proceed before receiving the response. This pattern is used between user interface clients and client agents. It is also used between server agents and various servers, which are primarily database wrappers.

- **Broker Handle**. Broker patterns are used during system initialization. Servers register their services and locations with the broker. The Broker Handle pattern allows clients to query the broker to determine the servers to which they should be connected.

- **Subscription/Notification (Multicast)**. `Invoice Agent` in B2B systems and `Billing Agent` in B2C systems both subscribe to `Delivery Order Agent` to be informed when a delivery order has been completed. `Customer Agent`, in both B2C and B2B systems, subscribes to `Delivery Order Agent` to be informed of the status of the delivery order as it is processed.

- **Asynchronous Message Communication**. This pattern is used for `Customer Agent` to asynchronously send `Customer Interface` the status of the delivery order after receiving it from `Delivery Order Agent`.

The concurrent communication diagrams for the B2C and B2B systems, shown in Figures 14.31 and 14.32, respectively, depict the concurrent components in the major applications that can be derived from the electronic commerce software product line architecture. They represent integrated generic communication diagrams determined from the individual communication diagrams supporting the use cases for B2C and B2B systems, respectively.

To keep the design simple, the Synchronous Message Communication with Reply pattern has been widely used in this case study. As described in Chapter 10, however, this approach has the disadvantage of suspending the client while it awaits a response from the server. An alternative design to avoid suspending the client is to use the Asynchronous Message Communication with Callback pattern. Examples of asynchronous communication are widely used in the microwave oven and factory automation product line case studies (Chapters 13 and 15, respectively).

14.8.4   Component-Based Software Architecture

The design of the components and component interfaces within the overall product line architecture is depicted in Figures 14.33 through 14.36. Each component has one or more ports, with provided interfaces, required interfaces, or both. In the four-layer architecture, each client user interface component has one required port, which supports a required interface. Each server has one provided port, which supports a provided interface. The agents have ports with both required and provided interfaces because they act as intermediaries between the clients and agents. Whereas clients and servers each have one port through which they can communicate, agents communicate through multiple ports because each one needs to communicate with several components.

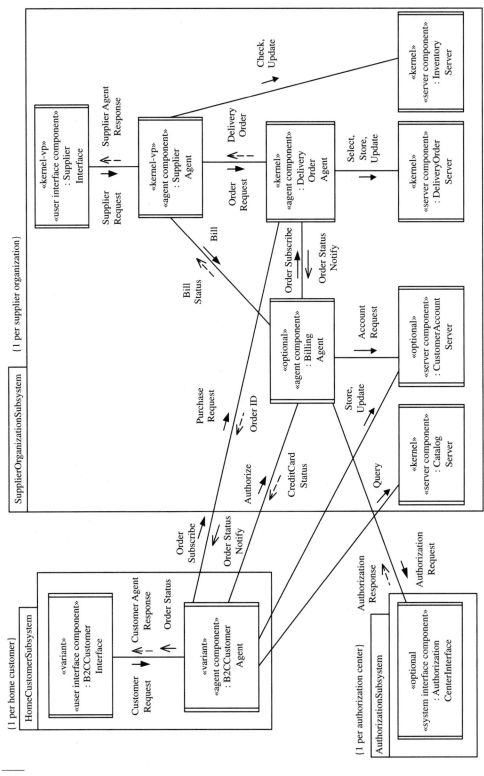

Figure 14.31 *Concurrent communication diagram for the B2C electronic commerce system*

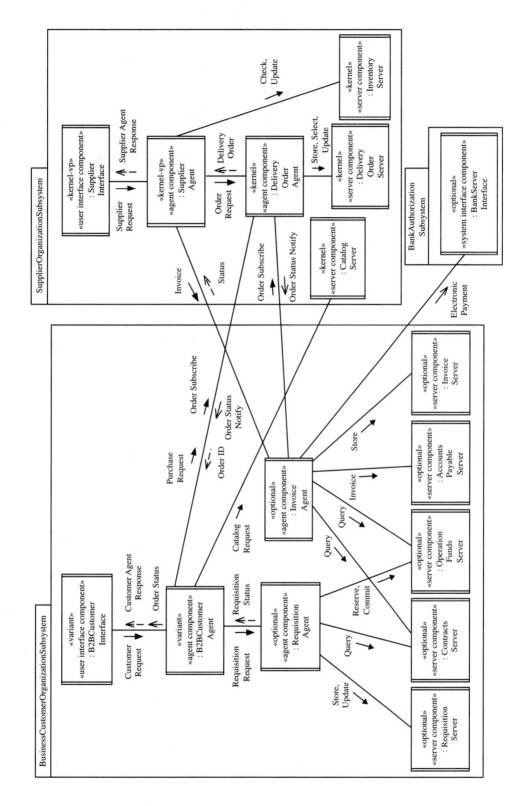

Figure 14.32 *Concurrent communication diagram for the B2B electronic commerce system*

The kernel components and ports are depicted in the kernel software architecture diagram in Figure 14.33. In `Customer Subsystem`, which consists of two kernel abstract classes, `Customer Interface` is a client and thus has only a required port. `Customer Agent` has both required and provided ports. Both of these components capture the commonality among all customers, home and business. In `Supplier Organization Subsystem`, the `Supplier Interface` and `Supplier Agent` components provide the same functionality in both B2B and B2C systems, and the three servers also provide common functionality. Both `Supplier Agent` and `Delivery Order Agent` also provide functionality accessed via ports, which are used by different B2B and B2C components.

Consider the software architecture for B2C systems. In `Home Customer Subsystem`, both `B2C Customer Interface` and `B2C Customer Agent` are variant components, which are specialized from the kernel components to provide additional B2C functionality, as shown in Figure 14.34. `B2C Customer Agent` also adds two required ports, which support required interfaces to two optional components in `Supplier Organization Subsystem` that operate only in B2C applications: `Billing Agent` and `Customer Account Server`. To bill for customer purchases from the supplier, `Supplier Agent` communicates through a connector that joins its `RPayment` required port to `Billing Agent`'s `PBillPayment` provided port. For the subscription/notification service, a bidirectional connector joins the `RSubscription` required port of the subscriber (`Billing Agent`) to the `PSubscription` provided port of `Delivery Order Agent`. The connector is bidirectional because `Billing Agent` sends a subscription message to `Delivery Order Agent`, which later responds with the notification. Customer payment is made by credit card, necessitating the optional `Authorization Center Interface` component.

In the software architecture for B2B systems (see Figure 14.35), `Business Customer Organization Subsystem` is much more complex than `Home Customer Subsystem`. In addition to variant `B2B Customer Interface` and `B2B Customer Agent` components, there are several optional agent and server components added to provide the B2B functionality. B2B customer billing is handled differently, with the optional `Invoice Agent` handling customer payment. For this purpose, a connector now joins `Supplier Agent`'s `RPayment` required port to `Invoice Agent`'s `PInvoicePayment` provided port. In B2B systems, it is `Invoice Agent` that subscribes to `Delivery Order Agent`'s subscription/notification service. Payment is made by electronic funds transfer via a request to the optional `Bank Interface` component.

If optional purchase order (PO) functionality is needed in either B2B or B2C systems, variant `PO Supplier Interface` and `PO Supplier Agent` components

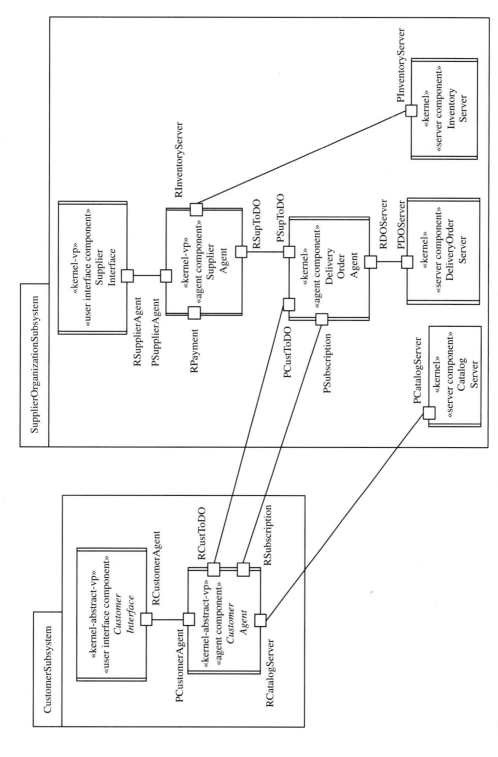

Figure 14.33 *Kernel software architecture of the economic commerce software product line*

491

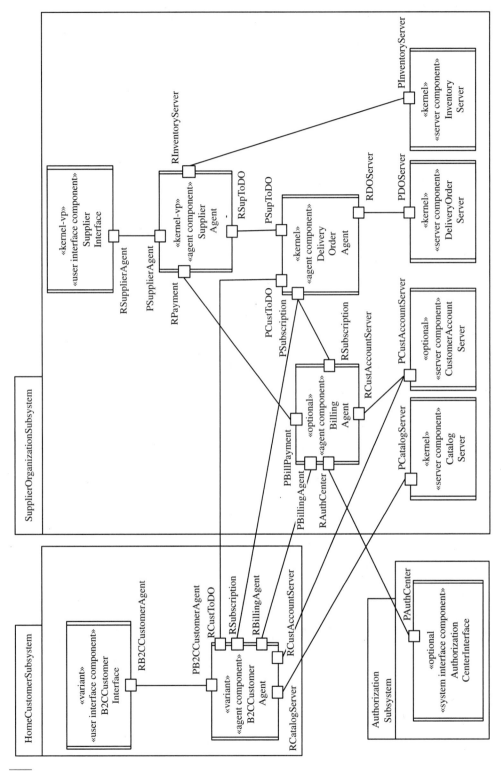

Figure 14.34 *Software architecture of the B2C system*

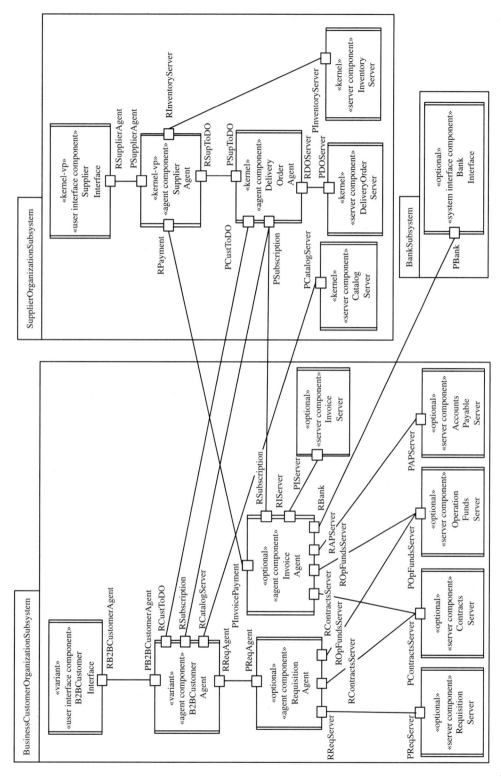

Figure 14.35 *Software architecture of the B2B system*

provide the additional PO functionality to initially make the order and then later install the delivered items. An optional `Purchase Order Subsystem` is also added, consisting of three optional components, as shown in Figure 14.36. Electronic payment is made by `Purchase Order Agent` via the optional `Bank Interface` component, which is also used in B2B applications.

14.8.5 Component Ports and Interfaces

The ports and interfaces for each component are described next. The component ports and interfaces for `Customer Agent` are depicted in Figure 14.37. A generalized interface is shown for `Customer Agent`, which is specialized to the interfaces for `B2C Customer Agent` and `B2B Customer Agent`, respectively. There is a corresponding `Customer Agent` component to realize each interface, with the ports and interfaces depicted on the customer agent component diagram. Each `Customer Agent` component has a bidirectional port to communicate with `Customer Interface`, thereby allowing for asynchronous responses from the agent. All other ports have required interfaces because `Customer Agent` is a client agent that initiates communication with server agents as well as with server components.

Billing Agent, which is an optional server agent, has five ports because it communicates with five components, as shown in Figure 14.38. It receives client requests from `Customer Agent` through the `PBillingAgent` port, which supports a provided interface called `IBillingAgent`. In its role as a client, `Billing Agent` has two required interfaces for communication with `Customer Account Server` and `Authorization Center Interface`. Its interaction with `Supplier Agent` and `Delivery Order Agent` has already been described.

Delivery Order Agent is a kernel server agent that operates in both B2B and B2C applications. However, it is designed to be versatile so that it can operate with different components, as shown in Figure 14.39. `Delivery Order Agent` has one provided interface to receive requests from `Supplier Agent` and another to receive requests from `Customer Agent`, either the B2B or B2C variant. It provides a subscription service via a bidirectional port to allow asynchronous responses to its subscribers. Finally, `Delivery Order Agent` has a required interface to allow it to be a client to `Delivery Order Server`.

Supplier Agent (see Figure 14.40) provides the same functionality for B2B systems and B2C systems. It receives supplier requests via the `PSupplierAgent` port, which supports a provided interface called `ISupplierAgent`. However, `PO Supplier Agent` can additionally provide optional functionality for purchase orders. This functionality is handled through a specialized provided

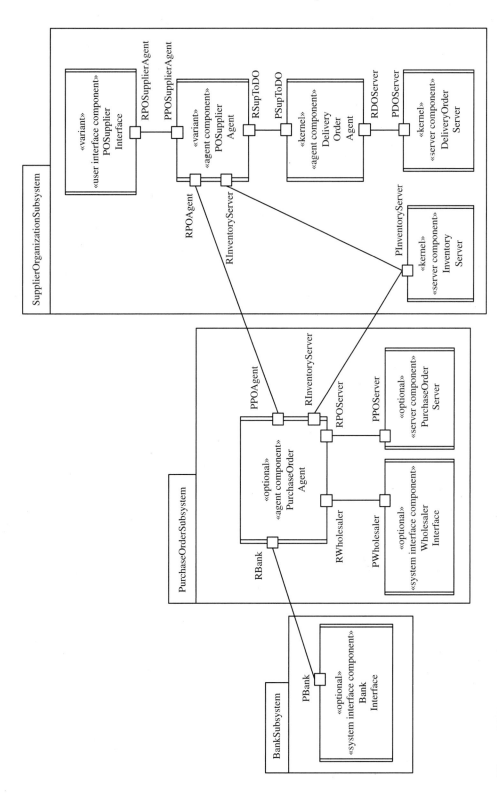

Figure 14.36   *Kernel architecture and optional purchase order components*

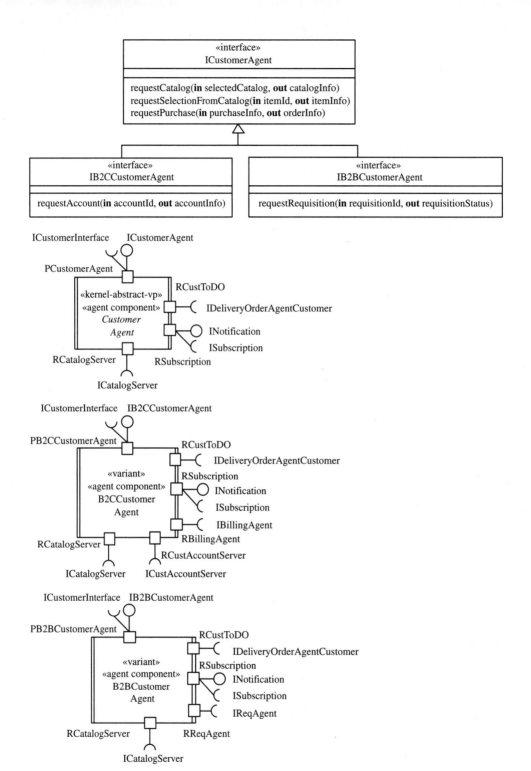

Figure 14.37 *Component ports and interfaces for* `Customer Agent`

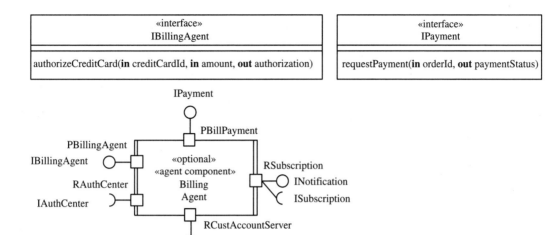

«interface» IBillingAgent	«interface» IPayment
authorizeCreditCard(**in** creditCardId, **in** amount, **out** authorization)	requestPayment(**in** orderId, **out** paymentStatus)

Figure 14.38   *Component ports and interfaces for* Billing Agent

«interface» IDeliveryOrderSupplier	«interface» ISubscription
orderRequest (**in** supplierId, **out** orderInfo) orderShipped (**in** orderId, **in** orderStatus)	orderSubscription (**in** orderId)

«interface» IDeliveryOrderAgentCustomer	«interface» INotification
purchaseRequest (**in** purchaseInfo, **out** orderId) shipmentReceived (**in** orderId)	orderNotify (**in** orderId, **in** orderStatus)

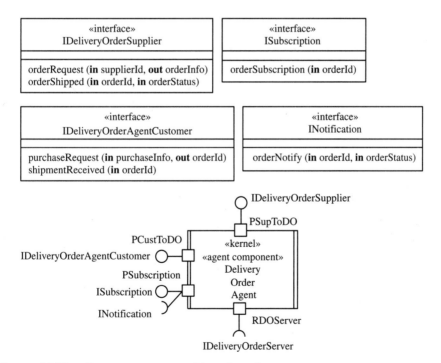

Figure 14.39   *Component ports and interfaces for* Delivery Order Agent

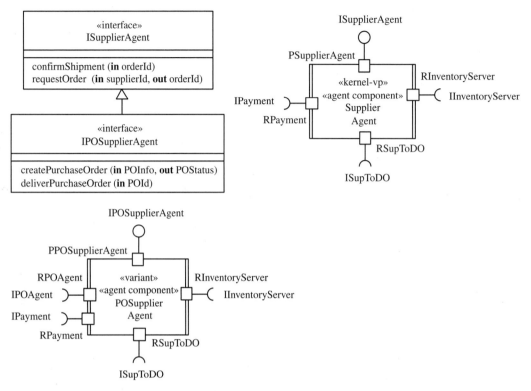

Figure 14.40   *Component ports and interfaces for* Supplier Agent

interface for PO requests called IPOSupplierAgent and a required interface (IPOAgent) to communicate with Purchase Order Agent. The component and port interfaces for the other optional agents (Requisition Agent, Purchase Order Agent, and Invoice Agent) are designed in a similar way, as depicted in Figure 14.41.

The component ports and interfaces for the server components—both kernel (Figure 14.42) and optional (Figure 14.43)—are all handled in the same way; each component has one port and provided interface through which the services are accessed. The clients of the server invoke the appropriate services synchronously.

Figure 14.44 shows the ports and interfaces for the user interface and system interface components. The required ports and required interfaces for the variant Customer Interface user interface components (see Figure 14.44),

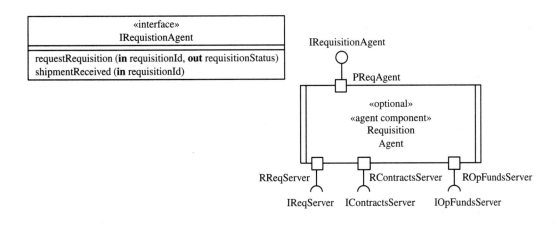

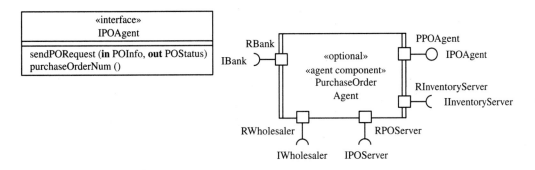

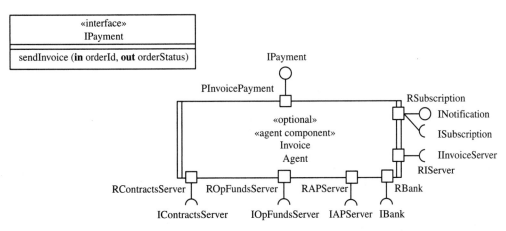

Figure 14.41   *Component ports and interfaces for other optional agents*

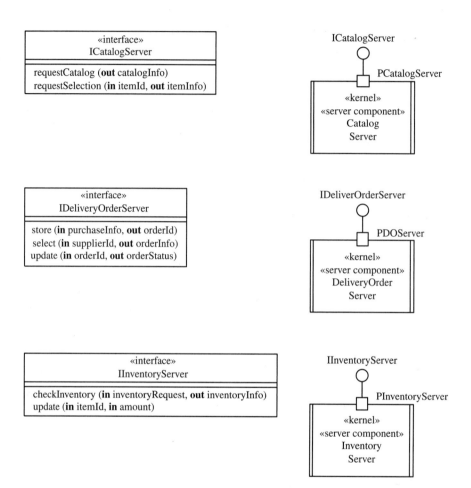

Figure 14.42 *Component ports and interfaces for kernel server components*

are specialized from a generalized `ICustomerAgent` interface into B2C and B2B versions (see Figure 14.37). The optional system interface components (`Bank Interface`, `Authorization Center Interface`, and `Wholesaler Interface`) each support one port with a provided interface.

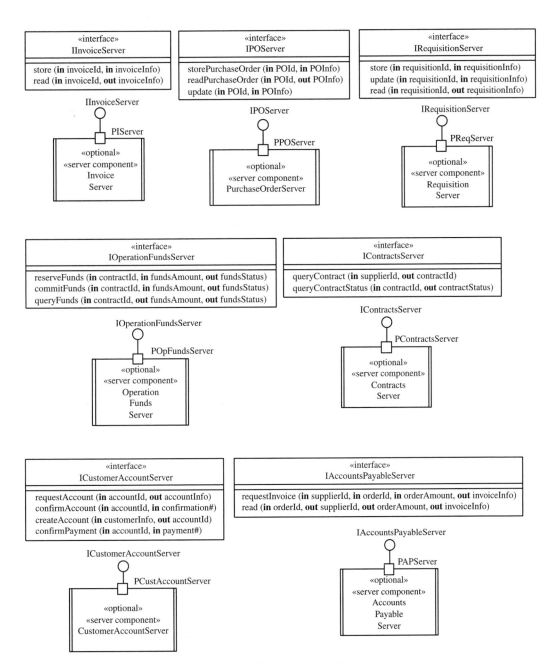

Figure 14.43 *Component ports and interfaces for optional server components*

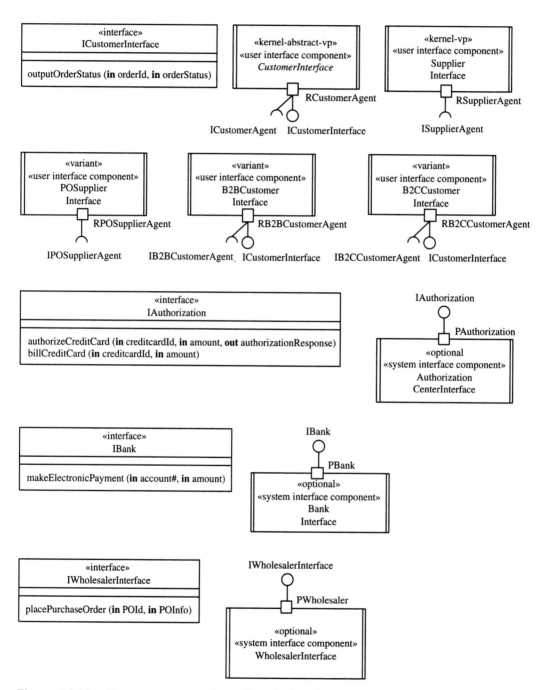

Figure 14.44   *Component ports and interfaces for interface components*

14.9   Software Application Engineering

Individual applications are derived from the software product line architecture and components by the selection of appropriate features, subject to the feature dependencies. In this case study, the main applications are either B2C systems or B2B systems—in either case with or without the purchase order option. The software architecture for a B2C system is depicted in Figures 14.31 and 14.34. The software architecture for a B2B system is depicted in Figures 14.32 and 14.35.

chapter

Factory Automation Software
Product Line Case Study

As another example of designing a software product line, this chapter describes a factory automation software product line. This is a highly distributed product line, with several clients and servers, a real-time control component, and examples of client/server communication, as well as peer-to-peer communication. Because this product line begins with existing factory automation systems that are candidates for modernization and inclusion in the product line, the *reverse evolutionary engineering* strategy is applied. This case study starts by analyzing the systems that are being considered for inclusion in the product line—namely, the factory monitoring, high-volume manufacturing, and flexible manufacturing systems. It then goes on to develop requirements, analysis, and design models for the integrated factory automation software product line.

The problem description is given in Section 15.1. Section 15.2 describes the use case model for the factory automation product line, which starts by modeling the use cases for factory monitoring, high-volume manufacturing, and flexible manufacturing systems in preparation for integration of the three use case models into a product line use case model. Section 15.3 goes on to describe the factory automation product line feature model, in which common, optional, and alternative features are determined from the use case model. Section 15.4 describes the product line static model, covering static modeling of both the product line context and entity classes. In both cases, static models for the factory monitoring, high-volume manufacturing, and flexible manufacturing systems are developed and then integrated into a product line static model. Section 15.5 describes dynamic modeling, starting with the kernel first approach in which communication diagrams are developed for each of the kernel use cases. Following this discussion, in Section 15.6 the product line evolution approach is used for dynamic modeling of the optional and alternative use cases. Section 15.7 describes the feature/class dependencies, explaining how they are determined from the dynamic model. Section 15.8 describes the design model for the factory automation software product line, which is designed as a layered architecture based on the Layers of Abstraction pattern combined with the client/server and control patterns. The design also takes an iterative approach in which the kernel software architecture is developed first, and then the optional and variant components are modeled. Section 15.9 describes software application engineering.

15.1 Problem Description

A factory automation system consists of several manufacturing workstations. The capabilities of factory automation systems vary widely. The factory automation product line encompasses high-volume manufacturing systems (which have high-volume production but low flexibility), flexible manufacturing systems (which have low-volume production but high flexibility), and factory monitoring systems.

15.1.1 Factory Monitoring Systems

Factory monitoring systems are relatively simple because part manufacturing is not carried out in these systems; instead, the status of the factory is monitored with a variety of sensors. These sensors are attached to factory robots, which send status information about the factory workstations to which they belong. In addition, they send factory alarms concerning undesirable situations in the factory that require human intervention. Factory operators view the status of the different workstations and view and update alarm conditions.

15.1.2 High-Volume Manufacturing Systems

In high-volume manufacturing plants, manufacturing workstations are physically laid out in a manufacturing line such as an assembly line (for an example, see Figure 15.1). Parts are moved between workstations on a conveyor belt. A part is processed at each workstation in sequence. Because workstations are programmable, variations on a given product can be handled. Typically, multiple parts of the same type are produced, followed by multiple parts of a different type.

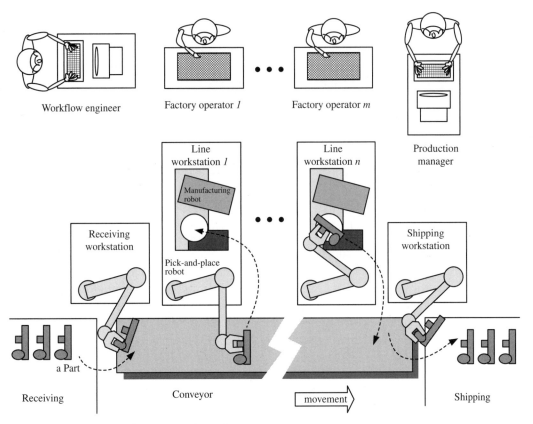

Figure 15.1 *High-volume manufacturing system*

Each manufacturing workstation has a manufacturing robot for operating on the product and a pick-and-place robot for picking parts off and placing parts on the conveyor. Each robot is equipped with sensors and actuators. Sensors are used for monitoring operating conditions (e.g., detecting part arrival), and actuators are used for switching automation equipment on and off (e.g., switching the conveyor on and off). The first workstation is the receiving workstation, and the last workstation is the shipping workstation. These workstations have only a pick-and-place robot. All other workstations are referred to as *line workstations*; they have a manufacturing robot in addition to the pick-and-place robot. Factory operators look at workstation status and alarms.

The manufacturing steps required to manufacture a given part in the factory, from raw material to finished product, are defined in a workflow plan. The

workflow plan defines the part type and the sequence of manufacturing operations. Each operation is carried out at a workstation. Workflow engineers create
workflow plans and their constituent operations.

The processing of new parts in the factory is initiated when a human production manager creates a work order. The work order defines the quantity of
parts required for a given part type.

15.1.3 Flexible Manufacturing Systems

In flexible manufacturing plants, a given part can be processed at any one of
several manufacturing workstations of the same type. A part is dynamically
allocated to a free workstation. Parts are moved between workstations on automated guided vehicles. Raw material, parts that have been partially processed,
and finished parts are stored in an automated storage and retrieval system.

A flexible manufacturing system is a computer-controlled system for the
automated manufacturing of parts in a factory. The flexible manufacturing system interfaces to robot controllers (abbreviated RC in Figure 15.2), an automated storage and retrieval system (ASRS), and an automated guided vehicle
(AGV). In addition, it interacts with several human users—namely, production
supervisors, human operators, and workflow engineers.

An example of the layout of the factory floor for a flexible manufacturing
system is shown in Figure 15.2. There are several manufacturing workstations,
most of which have the following components:

- A microcomputer-controlled factory manufacturing robot, which could be a
  numerically controlled machine tool or assembly robot.

- Two pickup/dropoff stands. One stand is used as an input stand (abbreviated IS in the figure), upon which an AGV can place a part. The second
  stand is used as an output stand (abbreviated OS), from which an AGV can
  remove a part.

- A microcomputer-controlled pick-and-place robot for picking up a part
  from the input stand and placing it in the work location before the start of a
  manufacturing or assembly operation. The robot also picks up the part after
  the operation has been completed and places it on the output stand.

An automated storage and retrieval system is similar to an automated warehouse and is used to store raw material, parts between operations (work in process), and finished parts (i.e., ready to be shipped). For storage, an automated
forklift truck takes a part from a pickup/dropoff stand (labeled S on Figure 15.2)
and stores it in a location in the ASRS. For retrieval, the truck removes the part

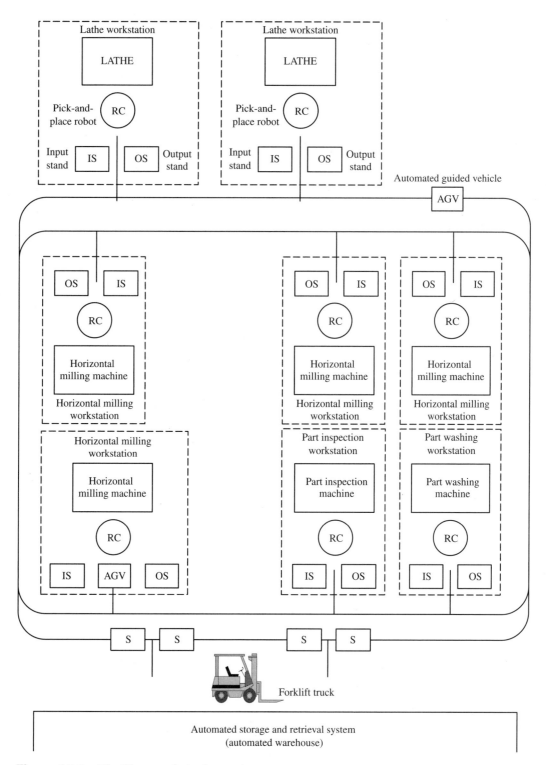

Figure 15.2 *Flexible manufacturing system*

from the ASRS and puts it on the stand. The ASRS has several stands, each of which may function as an input (IS) or output (OS) stand.

Parts are moved between workstations and to/from the ASRS via automated guided vehicles. An AGV picks up a part from a pickup/dropoff stand at the source workstation or ASRS, and delivers it to a stand at the destination workstation or at the ASRS.

The manufacturing steps required to manufacture a given part in the factory, from raw material to finished product, are defined in a workflow plan. The workflow plan defines the part type and the sequence of manufacturing operations. Each operation is carried out at a manufacturing workstation. The workflow plan is defined by a human workflow engineer.

The processing of new parts in the factory is initiated when a human production supervisor creates a work order. The work order defines the quantity of parts required for a given part type.

15.2   Use Case Modeling

This section describes the use case model for the factory automation software product line. With the reverse engineering approach, use cases are developed first for each of the major factory systems: factory monitoring systems, high-volume manufacturing systems, and flexible manufacturing systems. As the use cases are developed, it is useful to look for use cases that can be reused among these systems—in particular, to attempt to identify product line commonality, which can be described in kernel use cases.

15.2.1   Factory Monitoring Use Cases

Factory monitoring systems are the simplest of the three major kinds of factory systems. They have one human actor: `Factory Operator`. Four use cases involve `Factory Operator`, as either primary or secondary actor, as depicted in Figure 15.3 and described here:

1. **View Alarms**. The factory operator views outstanding alarms and acknowledges that the cause of an alarm is being addressed. The operator may also subscribe to receive notification of alarms of a given type.

2. **View Workstation Status**. The factory operator requests to view the current status of one or more factory workstations. Operator requests are made on demand. The operator may also subscribe to receive notification of changes in workstation status.

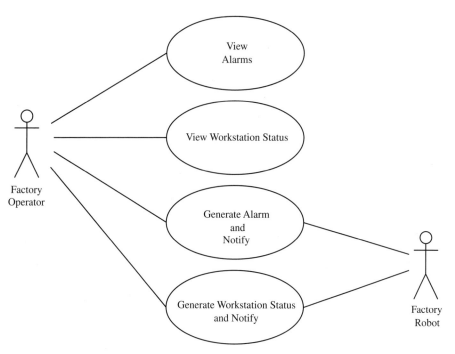

Figure 15.3 Factory Operator *use cases*

3. **Generate Workstation Status and Notify.** Workstation status is generated on an ongoing basis, for example, when processing of a part at a workstation starts or completes. Operators are notified of workstation status events to which they have subscribed. There is one variation point within the use case— Workstation Type—which can be a factory monitoring workstation, a high-volume manufacturing workstation, or a flexible manufacturing workstation.

4. **Generate Alarm and Notify.** If an alarm condition is detected during part processing, an alarm is generated. Operators are notified of alarms to which they have subscribed. There is one variation point within the use case—Workstation Type—which can be a factory monitoring workstation, a high-volume manufacturing workstation, or a flexible manufacturing workstation.

15.2.2 High-Volume Manufacturing System Use Cases

Next, the use cases for high-volume manufacturing systems are developed. The human actors are Production Manager, Factory Operator, and Workflow

Engineer. In addition, there are actors that correspond to external systems. These are the Manufacturing Robot and Pick & Place Robot actors. The use cases are described next and illustrated in Figures 15.3 through 15.5.

Factory Operator initiates or participates in four use cases, as described for factory monitoring systems in the previous section (see Figure 15.3). These use cases—View Alarms, View Workstation Status, Generate Alarm and Notify, and Generate Workstation Status and Notify—are also used in high-volume manufacturing systems.

Workflow Engineer defines several manufacturing operations and then creates a workflow plan to define a sequence of operations to manufacture a part. Two related use cases are developed for this purpose (see Figure 15.4). The workflow engineer uses the Create/Update Operation use case to create, update, and modify manufacturing operations. Create/Update Operation is a base use case that is executed once for each operation created. Workflow Engineer can then use the Create/Update Workflow Plan use case to create, update, and modify a workflow plan that defines the sequence of operations to manufacture a part. The Create/Update Workflow Plan use case extends the Create/Update Operation use case. Thus an optional alternative in the Create/Update Operation use case is to create a workflow plan.

Production Manager initiates the Create/Modify Work Order use case to create and modify work orders. Production Manager also initiates a complex use case called Manufacture High-Volume Part, which deals with processing parts in a high-volume factory (see Figure 15.5). The production manager releases a work order to be processed in the factory. Each part starts processing at the receiving workstation, where a raw part is loaded onto the

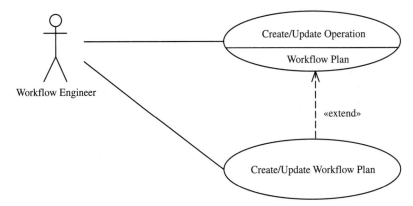

Figure 15.4 Workflow Engineer *use cases*

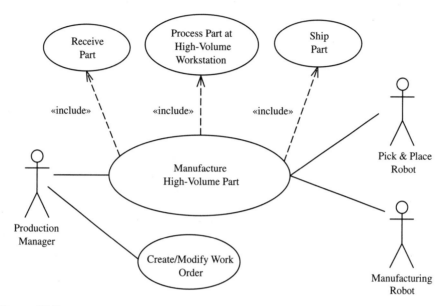

Figure 15.5   `Production Manager` *use cases in a high-volume manufacturing system*

conveyor belt. At the next workstation the part is picked off the conveyor belt by the pick-and-place robot, has a manufacturing operation performed on it by the manufacturing robot, and is then placed back on the conveyor belt by the pick-and-place robot and transported to the next workstation. This process continues until the finished part reaches the shipping workstation where it is picked off the conveyor in preparation for shipping to the customer. A *just-in-time* algorithm is used in the factory, meaning that a workstation receives a part only when it is ready to process a part, so parts do not pile up at each workstation.

From examination of the `Manufacture High-Volume Part` use case, it can be determined that the use case is made more general by being divided into the following three abstract use cases, which are included in the `Manufacture High-Volume Part` concrete use case:

1. **`Receive Part`**. The receiving workstation receives the request from the production manager to manufacture a new part and sends the part to the first line manufacturing workstation in the sequence.

2. **`Process Part at High-Volume Workstation`**. The line manufacturing workstation receives the part from the previous workstation (referred to as the *predecessor workstation*), performs the manufacturing operation on the part, and sends the part to the next line manufacturing workstation in the

sequence (referred to as the *successor workstation*). This use case is repeated several times.

3. **Ship Part**. The last line manufacturing workstation sends the finished part to the shipping workstation, which sends an acknowledgment of part completion to the production manager.

15.2.3 Flexible Manufacturing System Use Cases

Flexible manufacturing systems have several use cases in common with factory monitoring and high-volume manufacturing systems. They support the same four `Factory Operator` use cases described in Section 15.2.1 and illustrated in Figure 15.3. And like high-volume systems, flexible manufacturing systems need three additional use cases: `Create/Update Operation` and `Create/Update Workflow Plan` (for workflow planning), and `Create/Modify Work Order`, as described in Section 15.2.2. However, flexible manufacturing systems handle part processing quite differently from high-volume systems.

The `Flexibly Manufacture Part` use case addresses part processing in a flexible manufacturing system (see Figure 15.6). The raw material to make the part is initially stored in the ASRS. The part is then retrieved by an ASRS forklift truck and moved to the ASRS stand. Next, an AGV is sent to pick up the part and move it to the input stand of the first workstation. After delivery, the part is processed at the workstation and then placed on the workstation output stand. From there the part is picked up by an AGV and either moved to the next workstation or moved back to the ASRS for temporary storage. A finished part is moved back to the ASRS and then shipped.

It is possible to have a more limited flexible manufacturing system that uses the ASRS only for storing raw material prior to the start of part manufacturing and for storing finished parts after the completion of part manufacturing. This more limited form of part manufacturing is addressed by the `Flexibly Manufacture Part` use case. The more general use case, in which the ASRS is used for intermediate storage and retrieval during part manufacturing, consists of two extension use cases to the `Flexibly Manufacture Part` use case—`Store Part` and `Retrieve Part`—as shown in Figure 15.6.

The concrete `Flexibly Manufacture Part` use case can be divided into four abstract inclusion use cases as follows:

1. **Start Work Order**. The factory supervisor releases a work order to the factory floor. The first workstation for each part is determined from the workflow plan.

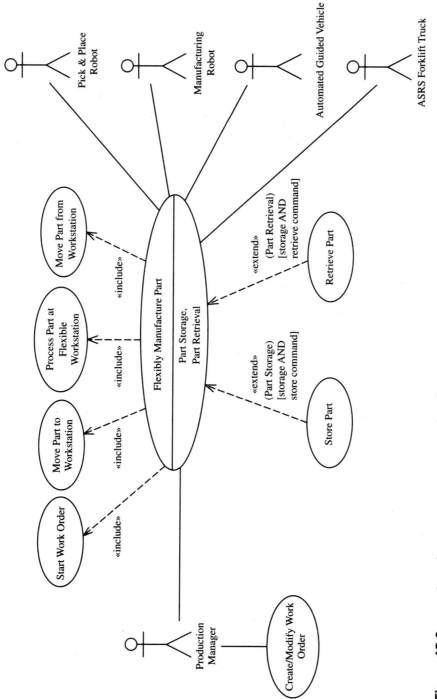

Figure 15.6 Production Manager *use cases in a flexible manufacturing system*

2. **Move Part to Workstation**. A workstation is allocated to a part. The part is moved from the ASRS to the workstation input stand.

3. **Move Part from Workstation**. The next workstation is determined for the part. If a workstation is available, an AGV moves the part to the next workstation's input stand. If a workstation is unavailable, the AGV moves the part to the ASRS.

4. **Process Part at Flexible Workstation**. The pick-and-place robot picks up the part from the workstation input stand and places it in the workplace (e.g., location, bench). The manufacturing robot operates on the part. When the operation is complete, the pick-and-place robot picks up the part and places it on the workstation output stand.

The `Store Part` extension use case extends `Flexibly Manufacture Part` at the extension point `Part Storage`, and the `Retrieve Part` extension use case extends `Flexibly Manufacture Part` at the extension point `Part Retrieval`, as shown in Figure 15.6.

As described in Section 4.8.2, there is a *product line condition* that must be true for the extension use case to be enabled. A product line member that provides the ASRS extensions for intermediate storage has the product line condition called [storage] set to true. In addition, for the extension use case to be executed, the *selection condition* must also be true during runtime execution. To invoke the `Store Part` extension use case at the extension point `Part Storage`, both the product line condition and the selection condition [store command] must be true; thus, [storage AND store command] must be true (see Figure 15.6). For the `Retrieve Part` extension use case to be invoked at the extension point `Part Retrieval`, both the product line condition and the selection condition [retrieve command] must be true; thus, [storage AND retrieve command] must be true.

15.3 Feature Modeling

Commonality/variability analysis of the factory automation software product line begins with analysis of the three use case models described in Section 15.2 in search of use cases that are common across the product line—that is, use cases that all members of the product line use. These common use cases are referred to as *kernel use cases*; they form the basis for determining the common features of the product line. After the kernel use cases have been determined, groups of use cases that are common to a subset of the members of the family are sought; these use cases form *optional use cases* or *optional features*.

Analysis of the factory automation software product line reveals that the following factory operator use cases are used by all factory automation systems, so they are categorized as kernel use cases (Figure 15.7): `View Alarms`, `View Workstation Status`, `Generate Alarm and Notify`, and `Generate Workstation Status and Notify`. Two of these use cases—`View Alarms` and `View Workstation Status`—are used directly by all factory systems. The other two use cases—`Generate Alarm and Notify` and `Generate Workstation Status and Notify`—are also used by all factory systems, but with one difference. The difference is that the workstations that generate the alarms and workstation status are different, although the way they behave in these use cases is identical. The nature of the alarms and workstation status varies in different factories. It is therefore necessary to provide the capability for different alarms and workstation status to be configured so that these two use cases can be reused. Because of this variability, a variation point called `Workstation Type`

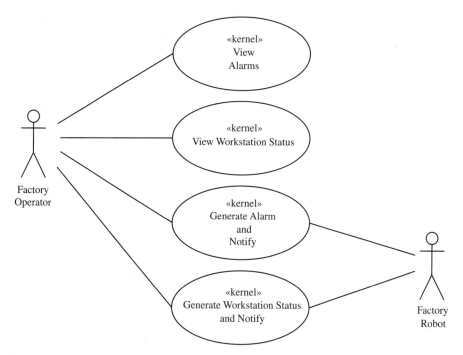

Figure 15.7   *Kernel use cases of the factory automation software product line*

needs to be introduced into each use case. The value of `Workstation Type` needs to be set during product line member derivation and remain unchanged for a given product line member.

These four use cases have the potential of being combined into one common feature. However, a factory could be totally automated, lacking any operator user interface, although still needing to store and retrieve workstation and alarm status, which could then be accessed remotely from a different system. To achieve this overall functionality, the preceding four use cases are mapped to two features: a common feature called `Factory Kernel` (which consists of the functionality of the four kernel use cases without the user interface) and an optional feature called `Factory Operations User` (which consists of the user interface functionality). With the feature notation described in Chapter 5, these features are depicted as follows:

```
«common feature» Factory Kernel
«optional feature» Factory Operations User {prerequisite = Factory
Kernel}
```

The `Create/Update Operation`, `Create/Update Workflow Plan`, and `Create/Modify Work Order` use cases are used by a subset of the family—namely, both high-volume and flexible manufacturing systems, but not factory monitoring systems. Hence they are categorized as optional use cases, as Figure 15.8 shows.

There are two approaches for handling workflow plans and operations because there must be some way of entering workflow plans into the system. It is possible for both to be present in any one system. For this reason, the `Create/Update Operation` and `Create/Update Workflow Plan` use cases are mapped to two features:

1. **Workflow Management**. Storing and updating workflow plans, either created locally by a workflow engineer or downloaded from an external system, imply the need for server functionality to manage, store, and update requests from different types of clients. The `Workflow Management` feature provides all the functionality of the use cases apart from the user interface:

   ```
   «optional feature» Workflow Management {prerequisite = Factory Kernel}
   ```

2. **Workflow Planning User**. Creation and modification of workflow plans imply the need for the client user interface to allow a workflow engineer to create and modify operations and workflow plans. The `Workflow Planning User` feature depends on the `Workflow Management` feature:

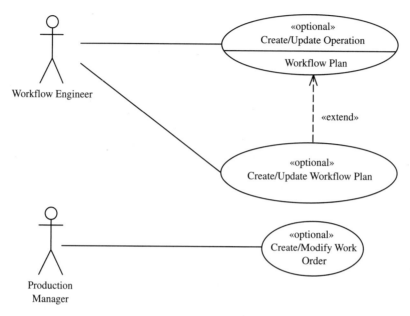

Figure 15.8 *Optional use cases of the factory automation software product line*

```
«optional feature» Workflow Planning User {prerequisite = Workflow
Management}
```

Work orders also could be downloaded from an external system. Consequently, the `Create/Modify Work Order` use case needs to be mapped to two optional features called `Work Order User` and `Work Order Management`, respectively—the former providing the user interface and the latter providing all the other functionality of the use case. The `Work Order User` feature depends on the `Work Order Management` feature:

```
«optional feature» Work Order Management {mutually includes = Workflow
Management}

«optional feature» Work Order User {prerequisite = Work Order
Management}
```

The `Manufacture High-Volume Part` use cases are specific to high-volume manufacturing systems. Consequently, the three abstract use cases and the one concrete use case are categorized as alternative use cases. Furthermore, they are considered as one alternative feature and depicted as one use case package called the `High-Volume Manufacturing` feature (see Figure 15.9):

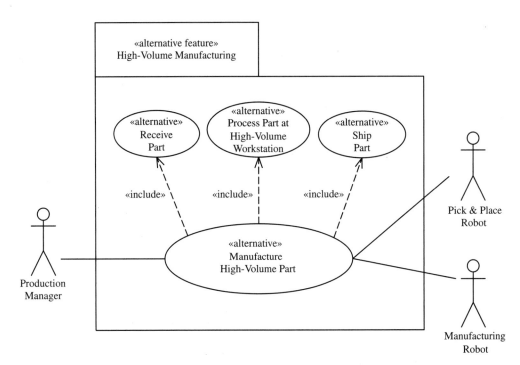

Figure 15.9 High-Volume Manufacturing *feature and use cases*

```
«alternative feature» High-Volume Manufacturing {mutually includes =
Work Order Management}
```

Because the Flexibly Manufacture Part use cases (see Section 15.2.3) are specific to flexible manufacturing systems, they are also categorized as alternative use cases and treated as one use case package representing an alternative feature. Within flexible manufacturing systems, there is a choice of whether or not to have parts stored in and retrieved from an automated storage and retrieval system during part processing. Hence the features are Flexible Manufacturing (encompassing the Flexibly Manufacture Part use case and its four abstract use cases) and Storage and Retrieval (see Figure 15.10), which consists of the Retrieve Part and Store Part extension use cases:

```
«alternative feature» Flexible Manufacturing {mutually includes = Work
Order Management}

«optional feature» Storage and Retrieval {prerequisite = Flexible
Manufacturing}
```

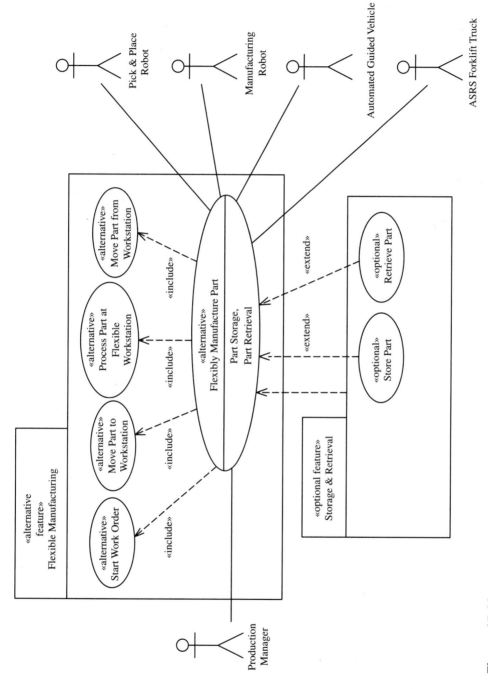

Figure 15.10 Flexible Manufacturing *feature and use cases*

In addition, an alternative `Factory Monitoring` feature captures the variability required by factory monitoring systems. This feature corresponds not to a use case but rather to a variation point called `Workstation Type` in the two use cases that deal with workstation status: `View Workstation Status` and `Generate Workstation Status and Notify`:

```
«alternative feature» Factory Monitoring {prerequisite = Factory
Kernel}
```

The feature/use case dependencies of the entire factory automation software product line are depicted in Table 15.1, which shows the features, feature categories, use cases that each feature depends on, and use case categories. Also depicted is a variation point that affects three features.

Table 15.1 *Feature/use case dependencies of the factory automation software product line*

Feature Name	Feature Category	Use Case Name	Use Case Category/ Variation Point (vp)	Variation Point
Factory Kernel	common	*All functionality except user interface*:		
		View Alarms	kernel	
		View Workstation Status	kernel	
		Generate Alarm and Notify	kernel	
		Generate Workstation Status and Notify	kernel	
Factory Operations User	optional	*User interface for*: View Alarms		
		View Workstation Status	kernel	
		Generate Alarm and Notify	kernel	
		Generate Workstation Status and Notify	kernel	
			kernel	
Factory Monitoring	alternative	Generate Alarm and Notify	vp	Workstation Type = Monitoring
		Generate Workstation Status and Notify	vp	
Workflow Management	optional	*All functionality except user interface*:		
		Create/Update Operation	optional	
		Create/Update Workflow Plan	optional	

Feature Name	Feature Category	Use Case Name	Use Case Category/ Variation Point (vp)	Variation Point
Workflow Planning User	optional	*User interface for*:		
		Create/Update Operation	optional	
		Create/Update Workflow Plan	optional	
Work Order Management	optional	*All functionality except user interface*:		
		Create/Modify Work Order	optional	
Work Order User	optional	*User interface for*:		
		Create/Modify Work Order	optional	
High-Volume Manufacturing	alternative	Manufacture High-Volume Part	alternative	
		Receive Part	alternative	
		Process Part at High-Volume Workstation	alternative	
		Ship Part	alternative	
		Generate Alarm and Notify	vp	Workstation Type = High-Volume
		Generate Workstation Status and Notify	vp	Workstation Type = High-Volume
Flexible Manufacturing	alternative	Flexibly Manufacture Part	alternative	
		Start Work Order	alternative	
		Move Part to Workstation	alternative	
		Process Part at Flexible Workstation	alternative	
		Move Part from Workstation	alternative	
		Generate Alarm and Notify	vp	Workstation Type = Flexible
		Generate Workstation Status and Notify	vp	Workstation Type = Flexible
Storage & Retrieval	optional	Store Part	optional	
		Retrieve Part	optional	

Once the features have been determined, they are organized into a feature dependency diagram (see Figure 15.11), which uses the static modeling notation. Each feature and feature group is depicted as a metaclass with the stereotype identifying the feature category or feature group category. The feature dependency diagram depicts the common feature as the root node. Apart from

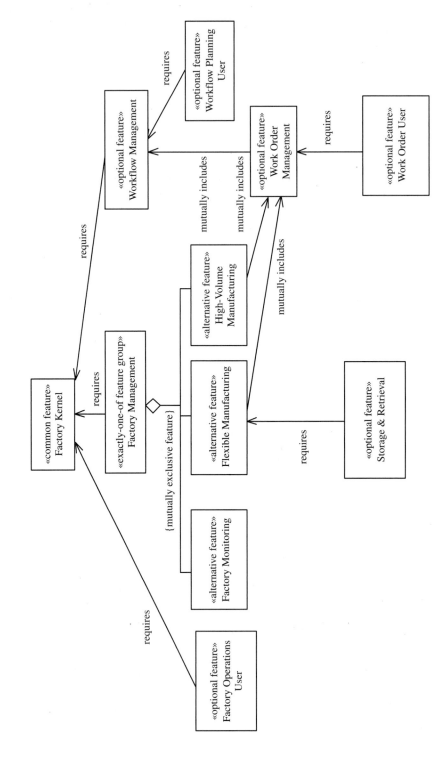

Figure 15.11 *Feature model of the factory automation software product line*

the common feature, all features are optional or alternative features. There is also one feature constraint in the form an exactly-one-of feature group: the Factory Management feature group, so called because a factory system must be one of the three alternatives—monitoring, high-volume manufacturing, or flexible manufacturing:

```
«exactly-one-of feature group» Factory Management {alternative =
Factory Monitoring, High-Volume Manufacturing, Flexible
Manufacturing}
```

Two optional features in Figure 15.11 (Workflow Management and Factory Operations User) and the Factory Management feature group depend directly on the Factory Kernel feature. Two alternative features (High-Volume Manufacturing and Flexible Manufacturing) depend mutually inclusively on the Work Order Management optional feature, which in turn depends mutually inclusively on the Workflow Management feature. The *mutually includes* dependency is used instead of the *requires* dependency so that the Workflow Management and Work Order Management optional features are prevented from being selected independently. They must be selected in conjunction with one of the alternative features (High-Volume Manufacturing or Flexible Manufacturing) to create a viable factory automation system. The remaining optional features—Workflow Planning User, Work Order User, and Storage & Retrieval—can be selected for a product line member if their prerequisite features are also selected.

In addition to the functional features that have been mentioned already, several configuration parameters need to be defined when a factory member system is deployed. These parameters include the following:

- Number of workstations, workstation IDs
- Number of operators, operator names, and operator IDs
- Workstation status ID and status text
- Alarm ID, alarm type, and alarm text
- At each workstation: IDs of robots and sensors

15.4 Static Modeling

The static model for the factory automation product line is developed with the reverse engineering strategy, whereby static models are developed first for the different kinds of factory automation systems—namely, factory monitoring systems, high-volume manufacturing systems, and flexible manufacturing systems. These three static models are then integrated into a static model for the entire factory automation product line.

15.4.1 Static Model for Factory Monitoring Systems

The static model for factory monitoring systems is quite simple, as shown in Figure 15.12. A factory consists of factory monitoring workstations, which generate alarms. Thus the `Factory` class is an aggregate class composed of the `Factory Monitoring Workstation` class.

Because a workstation can generate multiple alarms, there is a one-to-many relationship between the `Factory Monitoring Workstation` class and the `Alarm` class. Each `Factory Monitoring Workstation` also generates `Workstation Status` (a one-to-one association), which is viewed by the `Factory Operator`. Any operator can view the status of any workstation, which implies a many-to-many association.

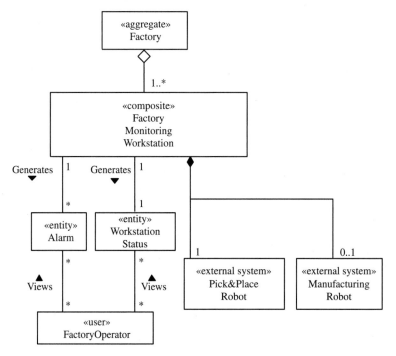

Figure 15.12 *Static model for a factory monitoring system*

15.4.2 Static Model for High-Volume Manufacturing Systems

The static model for the high-volume manufacturing system is shown in Figure 15.13. Because a factory consists of workstations, `Factory` is modeled as an aggregate class composed of `High-Volume Manufacturing Workstation` classes. There are three types of high-volume manufacturing workstations—receiving workstations, line workstations, and shipping workstations—so they are modeled as a generalization/specialization hierarchy; that is, the `High-Volume Manufacturing Workstation` class is specialized into three subclasses: `Receiving Workstation`, `Shipping Workstation`, and `Line Workstation`.

A workflow plan defines the steps for manufacturing a part of a given type; it contains several operations, where an operation defines a single manufacturing step carried out at a workstation. Consequently, there is a one-to-many association between the `Workflow Plan` class and the `Manufacturing Operation` class. Because several different operations are processed at a given factory workstation, there is also a one-to-many association between the `High-Volume Manufacturing Workstation` class and the `Manufacturing Operation` class. A work order defines the number of parts to be manufactured of a given part type. Thus the `Work Order` class has a one-to-many association with the `Part` class. Because a workflow plan defines how all parts of a given part type are manufactured, the `Workflow Plan` class also has a one-to-many association with the `Part` class.

15.4.3 Static Model for Flexible Manufacturing Systems

The static model for flexible manufacturing systems is more complicated, as shown in Figure 15.14. The factory is an aggregation of factory workstations, automated guided vehicles (AGVs), and an automated storage and retrieval system (ASRS). An ASRS consists of ASRS bins (where parts are stored), ASRS stands (where parts are placed after retrieval from an ASRS bin or prior to storage in an ASRS bin), and forklift trucks (which move parts from the stands to the bins for storage and vice versa for retrieval). The static model consists of an aggregate `Factory` class, which is composed of the `Flexible Manufacturing Workstation` class, the `Automated Guided Vehicle` class, and the `Automated Storage & Retrieval System (ASRS)` class. The `ASRS` class is also an aggregate class, composed of the `ASRS Bin`, `ASRS Stand`, and `Forklift Truck` classes. The `Workflow Plan`, `Manufacturing Operation`, `Work Order`, and `Part` classes are modeled in the same way as in the static model for the high-volume manufacturing system (see Figure 15.13).

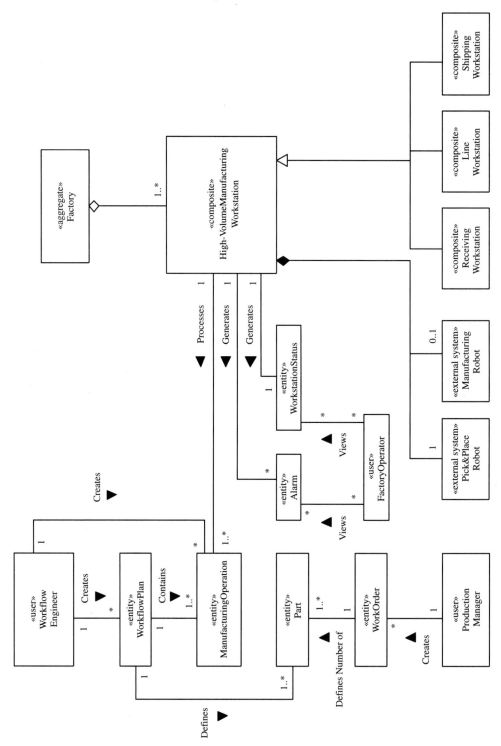

Figure 15.13 *Static model for a high-volume manufacturing system*

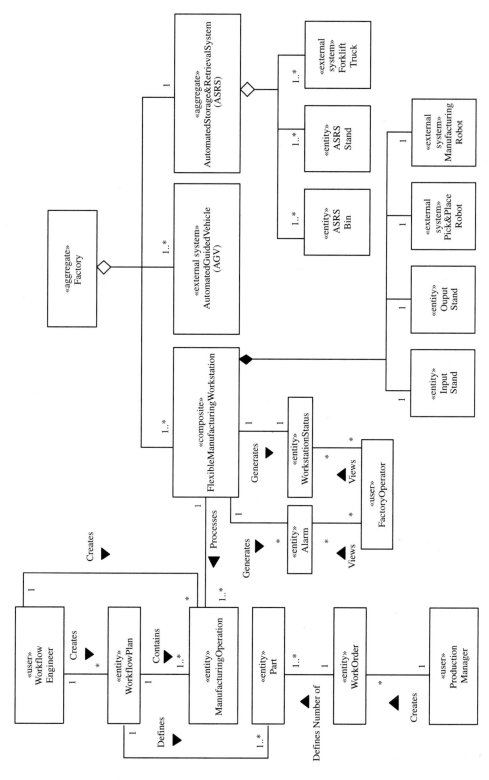

Figure 15.14 *Static model for a flexible manufacturing system*

15.4.4 Static Model for the Factory Automation Product Line

The way to develop the static model for the factory automation product line is to integrate the static models for the three different kinds of factory systems: factory monitoring systems, high-volume manufacturing systems, and flexible manufacturing systems. This kind of model integration is similar to view integration in logical database design, and for this reason the three different models are referred to as *views* in the following discussion. The integrated static model for the factory automation software product line is described in this section.

When the factory monitoring, high-volume manufacturing, and flexible manufacturing static models are integrated (see Figure 15.15), classes that are common to all three views become kernel classes. Classes that are in one view but not the others become optional classes. Classes that are different in each view are generalized so that the different classes become specialized subclasses of the superclass.

Some classes exist in one kind of system but not the others; for example, the AGV and ASRS classes exist only in flexible manufacturing systems. Some classes exist in more than one kind of system; for example, Workflow Plan and Manufacturing Operation exist in both flexible and high-volume manufacturing systems.

Classes that vary from one kind of system to another, such as Factory Workstation, are designed as subclasses of a generalized superclass. Thus a Factory Workstation superclass is introduced (which does not exist in any of the three views shown in Figures 15.12 through 15.14) and specialized to produce three subclass variants: Factory Monitoring Workstation, High-Volume Manufacturing Workstation, and Flexible Manufacturing Workstation. As in the static model for the high-volume manufacturing system, High-Volume Manufacturing Workstation is specialized into three subclasses: Receiving Workstation, Line Workstation, and Shipping Workstation.

Factory is an aggregate class composed of the Factory Workstation class, the optional Automated Guided Vehicle (AGV) class, and the optional Automated Storage and Retrieval System (ASRS) class. The first of these is used by all factory systems, albeit specialized as required. The latter two classes are used only in flexible manufacturing systems. As in the static model for the flexible manufacturing system, the ASRS class is an aggregate class composed of the ASRS Bin, ASRS Stand, and Forklift Truck classes.

The attributes of the classes in the static model are depicted in Figure 15.16. It is necessary to determine the attributes of the entity classes in particular before developing the communication diagrams because several of the objects in communication diagrams read or update the values of the entity class attributes.

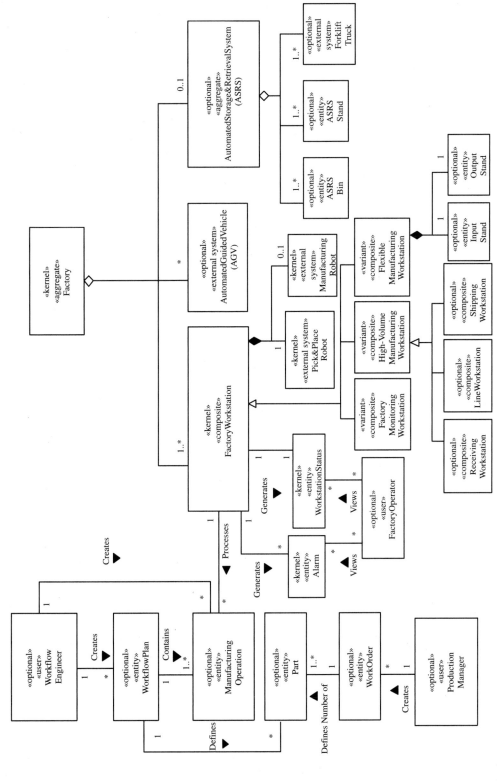

Figure 15.15 *Static model for the factory automation software product line*

531

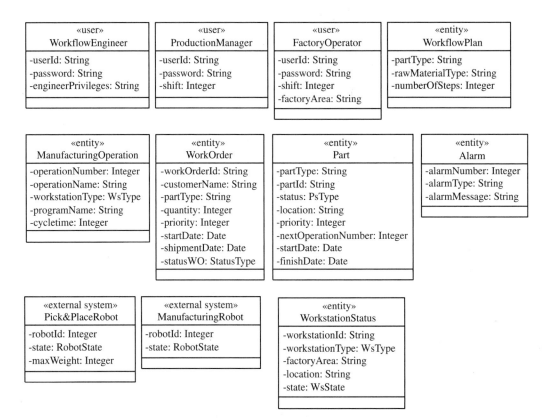

Figure 15.16 *Classes and attributes for the factory automation software product line*

15.4.5   Product Line Context Class Diagram

The product line context class diagram, which defines the boundary of a product line system, is determined in the reverse engineering approach by consideration of the context class diagrams of each of the major factory systems. For a factory monitoring system, the external classes consist of one external user (Factory Operator) and two external systems (Manufacturing Robot and Pick & Place Robot), as shown in Figure 15.17.

    For a high-volume manufacturing system (see Figure 15.18), the external classes consist of three external users (Production Manager, Workflow Engineer, and Factory Operator) and the same two external systems (Manufacturing Robot and Pick & Place Robot). A flexible manufacturing system has the same five external classes, as illustrated in Figure 15.19. In addition, there are

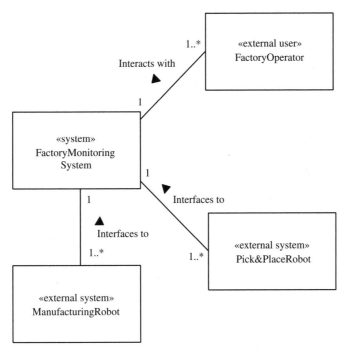

Figure 15.17 *Context class diagram for a factory monitoring system*

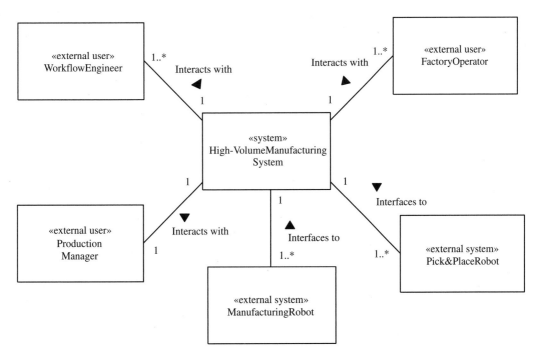

Figure 15.18 *Context class diagram for a high-volume manufacturing system*

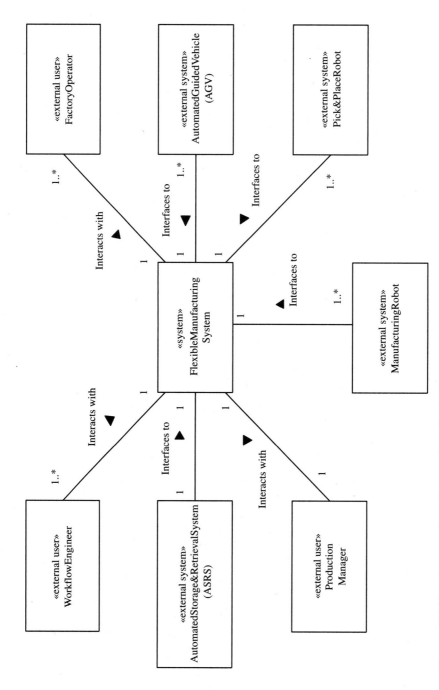

Figure 15.19 *Context class diagram for a flexible manufacturing system*

two further external systems: `Automated Guided Vehicle` (AGV) and `Automated Storage and Retrieval System` (ASRS).

The context class diagrams for each system are integrated to create the product line context class diagram, as shown in Figure 15.20. In this diagram the external classes that are required by all factory systems are kernel. Two of the external systems (`Manufacturing Robot` and `Pick & Place Robot`) and one external user (`Factory Operator`) fall into this category. However, because of an additional product line requirement that some factory systems should operate unmanned, the `Factory Operator` external user class is recategorized as optional. The remaining external classes are optional because they are needed in only some of factory automation systems, and individual members of the product line can be configured without them. The optional classes are the external systems `AGV` and `ASRS` (which are needed only in flexible manufacturing systems) and the two external users `Production Manager` and `Workflow Engineer` (which are needed by high-volume manufacturing systems and flexible manufacturing systems but not by factory monitoring systems).

15.5 Dynamic Modeling

In order to understand fully the relationship between the use cases, it is necessary to analyze how the objects in the factory automation product line participate in the use cases. The dynamic model for the product line is depicted on communication diagrams. Statecharts are also used for the dynamic modeling of state-dependent objects, as described in Chapter 8. Dynamic modeling is carried out first for the kernel of the product line, starting with the kernel use cases, and then (using product line evolution) for the optional and alternative use cases. Because object/class structuring and dynamic modeling are iterative activities, they are both described in this section.

15.5.1 Object Structuring

During dynamic modeling, the objects that participate in each use case are determined, and then the sequence of interactions among the objects is analyzed. The first step is to analyze how the factory automation product line is structured into objects.

Entity objects are long-living objects that store information. The entity objects for the factory automation product line are `Workflow Plan`, `Manufacturing Operation`, `Work Order`, and `Part`. There are also `Workstation Status`

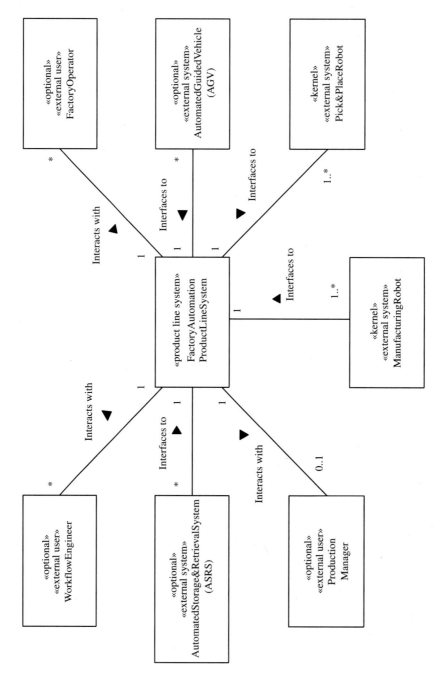

Figure 15.20 *Context class diagram for the factory automation software product line system*

and `Alarm` entity objects. The entity objects are depicted in the static model in Figure 15.15, and their attributes are given in Figure 15.16. The entity objects are all server objects that are accessed by various client objects. Hence, on communication diagrams the entity objects are depicted as server objects: `Workflow Plan Server`, `Manufacturing Operation Server`, `Work Order Server`, `Part Server`, `Workstation Status Server`, and `Alarm Server`.

For each of the human actors there needs to be a user interface object. These objects are `Workflow Engineer Interface`, `Production Manager Interface`, and `Factory Operator Interface`.

For the factory automation product line, which is distributed in nature, several control objects provide distributed control. Several instances of the `Workstation Controller` class exist—one instance for each manufacturing workstation. However, different variants of this class are used by the different members of the product line. For high-volume systems, there is one instance of `Receiving Workstation Controller`, one of `Shipping Workstation Controller`, and several of `Line Workstation Controller` (one for each workstation). For flexible systems, there is one instance of `Flexible Workstation Controller` for each workstation. For factory monitoring systems, there is one instance of `Monitoring Workstation Controller` for each workstation.

15.5.2 Communication Diagrams for Kernel Use Cases

After object structuring, dynamic modeling for product lines follows the *kernel first approach* as described in this section. First the communication diagrams for the kernel use cases—namely, the factory monitoring use cases—are determined. In analyzing the object communication for each use case, various architectural patterns are recognized for future reference during design,

Communication Diagrams for Client/Server Use Cases

Consider the `Factory Operator` use cases, which form the basis of the factory monitoring communication diagrams. Two of these communication diagrams involve the Client/Server pattern, in which a client—in this case a user interface client—interacts with a server. First consider the communication diagram for the `View Alarms` use case, depicted in Figure 15.21. The message sequence is as follows:

S1: The factory operator requests an alarm handling service—for example, to view alarms or to subscribe to receive alarm messages of a specific type.

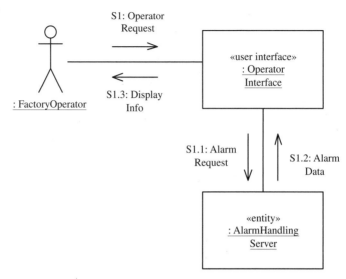

Figure 15.21 *Communication diagram for the* View Alarms *use case*

S1.1: Operator Interface sends the alarm request to Alarm Handling Server.

S1.2: Alarm Handling Server performs the request—for example, reads the list of current alarms or adds the name of this client to the subscription list—and sends a response to the Operator Interface object.

S1.3: Operator Interface displays the response—for example, alarm information—to the operator.

The communication diagram for the View Workstation Status use case also represents the Client/Server pattern and is very similar (Figure 15.22). The message sequence is as follows:

V1: The factory operator requests a workstation status service—for example, to view the current status of a workstation.

V1.1: Operator Interface sends a workstation status request to Workstation Status Server.

V1.2: Workstation Status Server responds—for example, with the requested workstation status data.

V1.3: Operator Interface displays the workstation status information to the operator.

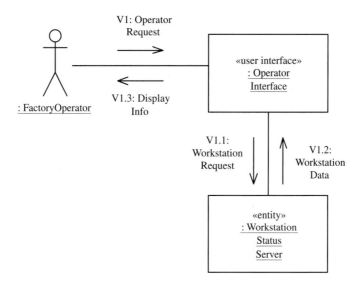

Figure 15.22 *Communication diagram for the* View Workstation Status *use case*

Communication Diagrams for Subscription/Notification Use Cases

The two other kernel use cases are Subscription/Notification patterns, in which a client is notified of new events previously subscribed to in a client/server use case. Consider the communication diagram for the Generate Alarm and Notify use case, shown in Figure 15.23. The message sequence is as follows:

M1: Workstation Controller receives workstation input from the external robot, indicating a problem condition.

M2: Workstation Controller sends an alarm to Alarm Handling Server.

M3: Alarm Handling Server sends a multicast message containing the alarm to all subscribers registered to receive messages of this type.

M4: Operator Interface receives the alarm notification and displays the information to the factory operator.

The communication diagram for the Generate Workstation Status and Notify use case is also a Subscription/Notification pattern and is shown in Figure 15.24. The message sequence is as follows:

N1: Workstation Controller receives workstation input from the external robot, indicating a change in workstation status—for example, part completed.

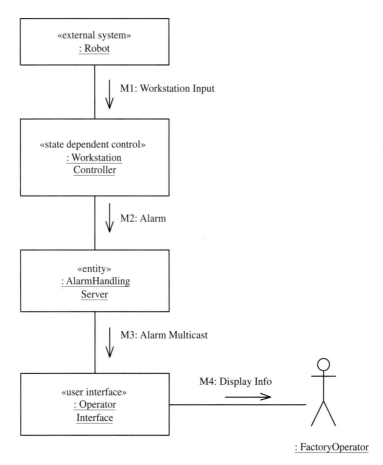

Figure 15.23 *Communication diagram for the* Generate Alarm and Notify *use case*

N2: Workstation Controller sends a workstation status message to Workstation Status Server.

N3: Workstation Status Server sends a multicast message containing the new workstation status to all subscribers registered to receive messages of this type.

N4: Operator Interface receives the workstation status message and displays the information to the factory operator.

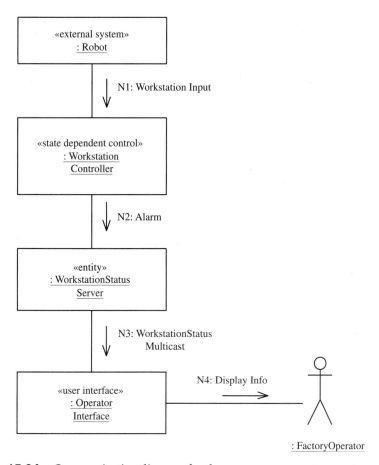

Figure 15.24 *Communication diagram for the* `Generate Workstation`
`Status` and `Notify` *use case*

15.6 Software Product Line Evolution

After the kernel first approach is applied to development of the kernel communication diagrams, the product line evolution approach is used to develop the
communication diagrams for the optional and alternative use cases. This
approach is used for both the high-volume and the flexible manufacturing use
cases.

15.6.1 Communication Diagrams for High-Volume Manufacturing Use Cases

With the product line evolution approach, the communication diagrams for the high-volume manufacturing use cases are determined next.

Consider first the interactions for the Factory Operator use cases. The first two communication diagrams—for View Alarms and View Workstation Status—are identical to the factory monitoring system diagrams for those use cases (see Figures 15.21 and 15.22). The other two communication diagrams—for Generate Alarm and Notify and Generate Workstation Status and Notify—are very similar to the factory monitoring system diagrams for those use cases (see Figures 15.23 and 15.24), with one subtle difference.

There are three different types of Workstation Controller objects: Monitoring Workstation Controller, (high-volume) Line Workstation Controller, and Flexible Workstation Controller. However, the way these three Workstation Controller variants operate in the Generate Alarm and Notify and Generate Workstation Status and Notify use cases is identical. Consequently, the generalized form of the Workstation Controller is used, rather than a specific subclass. (Workstation Controller is an abstract class that needs to be specialized as required for a given kind of factory before it can be instantiated.)

15.6.2 Communication Diagrams for Workflow and Work Order Use Cases

The workflow and work order use cases are those that involve workflow planning, as carried out by the workflow engineer, and work order management, as performed by the production manager.

Communication Diagrams for Workflow Planning Use Cases

Consider the workflow planning use cases initiated by Workflow Engineer. These use cases are used in both high-volume and flexible systems. A workflow engineer has to create manufacturing operations and then create a workflow plan that consists of a sequence of operations. Two use cases are used for this purpose (see Section 15.2.2 and Figure 15.8): Create/Update Operation and Create/Update Workflow Plan, where Create/Update Workflow Plan extends Create/Update Operation (see Figure 15.4). First consider the communication diagram for the Create/Update Operation use case (see Figure 15.25). The message sequence is as follows:

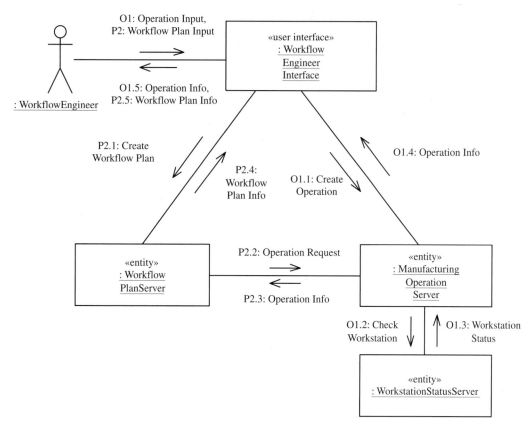

Figure 15.25   *Communication diagram for the* Create/Update Operation *and* Create/Update Workflow Plan *use cases*

O1: Workflow Engineer inputs information for creating an operation to Workflow Engineer Interface. This information includes the operation name, workstation type, and robot programs to be used.

O1.1: Workflow Engineer Interface sends a Create Operation request to Manufacturing Operation Server.

O1.2: Manufacturing Operation Server sends a Check Workstation message to Workstation Status Server, which maintains information about all the manufacturing workstations.

O1.3: Workstation Status Server responds with a Workstation Status message, allowing Manufacturing Operation Server to check whether the workstation type exists for the new operation.

O1.4: Manufacturing Operation Server sends the operation information to Workflow Engineer Interface.

O1.5: Workflow Engineer Interface object displays the operation information to Workflow Engineer. The engineer may iterate, creating more operations.

Now consider the Create/Update Workflow Plan use case (also shown in Figure 15.8), which extends Create/Update Operation because it creates the workflow plan from operations created in the Create/Update Operation use case. The message sequence for the communication diagram shown in Figure 15.25 is as follows (the sequence numbering starts with 2 because the sequence follows on from operation creation):

P2: Workflow Engineer inputs information for creating a workflow plan to Workflow Engineer Interface. This information includes the plan name and part type, raw material, and operation information for the first manufacturing operation.

P2.1: Workflow Engineer Interface sends a Create Workflow Plan request to Workflow Plan Server.

P2.2: Workflow Plan Server sends an Operation Request message to Manufacturing Operation Server.

P2.3: Manufacturing Operation Server responds with information about the requested operation.

P2.4: Workflow Plan Server sends the workflow plan information to Workflow Engineer Interface.

P2.5: Workflow Engineer Interface displays the workflow plan information to Workflow Engineer. The engineer adds other operations to the workflow plan.

Communication Diagrams for Work Order Management Use Cases

Next consider the communication diagram for the Create/Modify Work Order use case initiated by Production Manager, in which three entity objects—Work Order Server, Part Server, and Workflow Plan Server—are accessed (see Figure 15.26). The message sequence is as follows:

R1: Production Manager inputs production information to Production Manager Interface. This information includes the type of part to be manufactured.

R1.1: Production Manager Interface sends a Create request to Work Order Server.

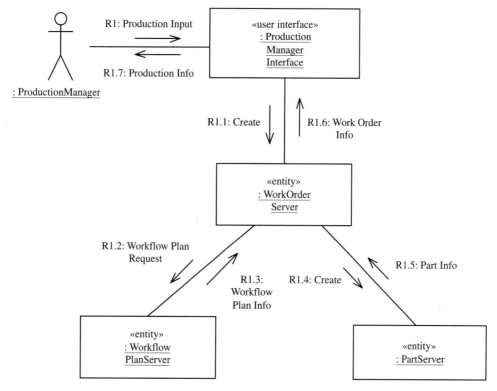

Figure 15.26 *Communication diagram for the* Create/Modify Work Order *use case*

R1.2: Work Order Server sends a Workflow Plan Request message to Workflow Plan Server, which retrieves workflow plan information for the specified part type.

R1.3: Workflow Plan Server returns the workflow plan information to Work Order Server.

R1.4: Work Order Server sends a Create request to Part Server for each part to be manufactured.

R1.5: Part Server acknowledges part creation.

R1.6: Work Order Server sends the work order information to Production Manager Interface.

R1.7: Production Manager Interface displays the production information to Production Manager.

15.6.3 Dynamic Modeling of High-Volume Manufacturing

The high-volume manufacturing use case is a complex use case initiated by the production manager and called `Manufacture High-Volume Part`, in which a part is manufactured in the high-volume factory from raw material to finished product. This use case requires three different types of workstation controllers: a `Receiving Workstation Controller` object, several `Line Workstation Controller` objects, and a `Shipping Workstation Controller` object. There is one instance of the `Line Workstation Controller` class for each manufacturing workstation, and the instances are connected in series. When the production manager releases a work order to the factory, a `Start Part` message identifying the part ID and number of parts required is sent to `Receiving Workstation Controller`. This step ensures that for each part to be manufactured, a piece of raw material of the appropriate type is obtained and loaded onto the conveyor. At the shipping workstation, the `Shipping Workstation Controller` object removes finished parts from the conveyor and places them in a shipping area.

In a just-in-time algorithm, a workstation requests a part only when it is ready to process a part, so parts do not pile up at a workstation. When a workstation completes a part, it waits for a message from its successor workstation requesting the part. When the message is received, the workstation controller sends a `Place` command to the `Pick & Place Robot` to place the part on the conveyor. Next, the workstation controller sends a `Part Coming` message to the successor workstation and a `Part Request` message to the predecessor workstation. The `Receiving Workstation Controller` object maintains a count of the remaining number of parts for a given work order. `Shipping Workstation Controller` controls the removal of each finished part from the conveyor in preparation for shipping, after which it sends a `Part Complete` message to `Production Manager Interface`.

The three abstract use cases for part manufacturing (shown in Figure 15.9) are as follows:

A. **Receive Part**. `Receiving Workstation Controller` sends the part to the first `Line Workstation Controller` object in the sequence.

B. **Process Part at High-Volume Workstation**. `Line Workstation Controller` n sends part to `Line Workstation Controller` n + 1. This use case is repeated several times.

C. **Ship Part**. The last `Line Workstation Controller` object sends the part to `Shipping Workstation Controller`.

A concrete use case for a part that has to visit n line workstations consists of one execution of the `Receive Part` use case (A), $w - 1$ (where w is the number of line workstation controllers) executions of the `Process Part at High-Volume Workstation` use case (B), and one execution of the `Ship Part` use case (C). The three part manufacturing abstract use cases are shown on communication diagrams (Figures 15.30 through 15.32), where events are labeled A, B, and C, corresponding to the three use cases described here.

In general, a workstation controller receives a part from a *predecessor* workstation controller (which could be a receiving or line workstation controller) and sends a part to a *successor* workstation controller (which could be a line or shipping workstation controller).

Because `Workstation Controller` is a state-dependent control object, it is defined by means of a statechart, which is described next, prior to the detailed description of the three communication diagrams.

15.6.4   Statechart for Line Workstation Controller

The statechart for `Line Workstation Controller` consists of two orthogonal statecharts: the `Part Processing` statechart and the `Part Requesting` statechart. The two orthogonal statecharts are depicted as superstates on a high-level statechart, with a dashed line separating them (see Figure 15.27). At any one time, a workstation controller is in one of the substates of the `High-Volume Part Processing` superstate (see Figure 15.28), reflecting the current situation in processing of the part at this workstation; and in one of the substates of the `Part Requesting` superstate (see Figure 15.29), reflecting whether or not a part has been requested by the successor workstation. This orthogonal statechart does not imply that there is any concurrency within a `Line Workstation Controller` object, but merely that it is simpler to model these relatively independent event occurrences in this way.

The `High-Volume Part Processing` superstate contains the following substates. The transitions between the substates are described in the context of the communication diagrams (Figures 15.30–15.32):

- **`Awaiting Part from Predecessor Workstation`**. This is the initial state, in which the workstation is idle, waiting for the arrival of a part.

- **`Part Arriving`**. This state is entered when the line workstation controller receives a `Part Coming` message from the predecessor workstation indicating that the next part is on the way.

- **`Robot Picking`**. The pick-and-place robot is picking the part off the conveyor belt and bringing it to the workstation. This state is entered when the part has arrived at the workstation.

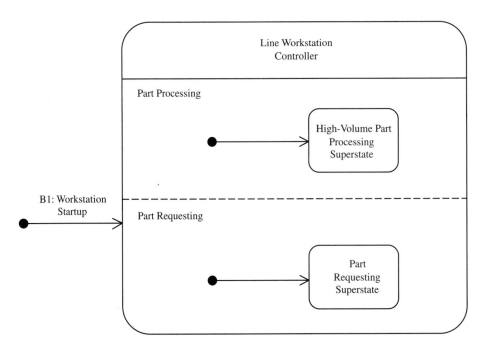

Figure 15.27 *Statechart for* Line Workstation Controller: *high-level statechart*

- **Operating on Part**. The manufacturing robot is operating on the part. This state is entered when the line workstation controller receives a message indicating that the part is ready at the workstation.

- **Robot Placing**. The pick-and-place robot is placing the part on the conveyor belt to send to the successor workstation. This state is entered when robot manufacturing at this workstation has been completed and a part request has been received from the successor workstation.

- **Awaiting Part Request from Successor Workstation**. This state is entered when robot manufacturing at this workstation has been completed but a part request has not been received from the successor workstation.

The Part Requesting superstate has the following substates:

- **Part Not Requested**. A part has not been requested by the successor workstation.

- **Part Has Been Requested**. A part has been requested by the successor workstation.

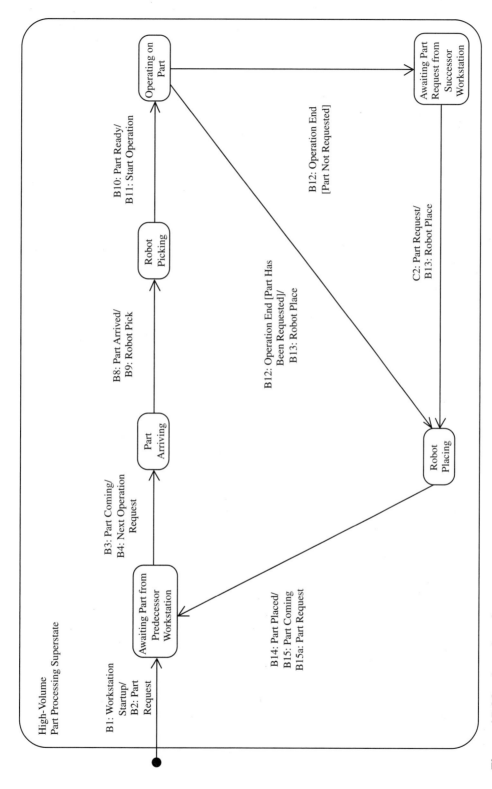

Figure 15.28 *Statechart for* Line Workstation Controller: *decomposition of the* High-Volume Part Processing *superstate*

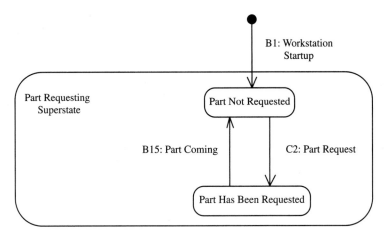

Figure 15.29 *Statechart for* Line Workstation Controller: *decomposition of the* Part Requesting *superstate*

These two substates are used as conditions to be checked in the Part Processing statechart for determining what state to enter when robot manufacturing has completed.

15.6.5 Communication Diagrams for Manufacture High-Volume Part Use Cases

The details of the three high-volume part manufacturing use cases are discussed in this section and illustrated in Figures 15.30 through 15.32. Each line and shipping workstation controller sends a Part Request message to its predecessor workstation at initialization. This message is represented by the B2 and C2 messages, which are also shown on the statechart in Figure 15.28. The production manager initiates the main event sequence by creating a work order (message A1). To make an abstract use case more reusable, an object in one use case–based communication diagram is allowed to send a message to an object in another use case–based communication diagram. Although the message numbers in the two use cases are usually different, the message numbers are said to be *equivalent*.

At system initialization, the message sequence is as follows:

B1, C1: When the internal Workstation Startup event occurs, Workstation Controller transitions to the Awaiting Part from Predecessor Workstation state, as shown in the statechart in Figure 15.28.

B2, C2: As a result of the state transition, the `Workstation Controller` object sends a `Part Request` message to the predecessor `Workstation Controller` object. `Part Request` is an output event on the `Part Processing` statechart that is propagated to the `Part Requesting` statechart of the predecessor, where it appears as an input event that causes a transition from the `Part Not Requested` state to the `Part Has Been Requested` state.

Communication Diagram for the Receive Part Use Case

In the communication diagram for the `Receive Part` abstract use case (Figure 15.30), the receiving workstation controller sends a part to the first line workstation controller. The message sequence is as follows:

A1: The actor, the human production manager, initiates processing of a work order, which necessitates the start of manufacturing each part in the work order.

A2: `Production Manager Interface` sends to `Receiving Workstation Controller` a `Start Part` message containing the part type and number of parts to be manufactured.

A3: `Receiving Workstation Controller` sends a command to `Pick & Place Robot` to place on the conveyor the raw material from which the part is to be manufactured.

A4: `Pick & Place Robot` places the material on the conveyor and notifies `Receiving Workstation Controller`.

A5 = B3: `Receiving Workstation Controller` sends a `Part Coming` message to `first Line Workstation Controller`. This message constitutes the end of the message communication (A5) for the `Receive Part` communication diagram and the next event in the event sequence (B3) of the `Process Part at High-Volume Workstation` communication diagram.

Communication Diagram for the Process Part at High-Volume Workstation Use Case

In the communication diagram for the `Process Part at High-Volume Workstation` use case (Figure 15.31), `Line Workstation Controller` n sends a part to `Line Workstation Controller` n + 1. The following event sequence is shown on both the `Process Part at High-Volume Workstation` communication diagram (Figure 15.31) and the statechart for `Line Workstation Controller` (Figure 15.28). The message sequence is as follows:

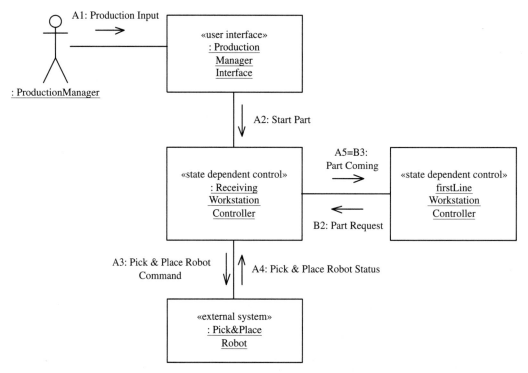

Figure 15.30 *Communication diagram for the* Receive Part *use case*

B1, B2: As explained at the start of this section.

B3: On receiving the Part Coming message from the predecessor workstation, Line Workstation Controller transitions into the Part Arriving state (see Figure 15.28).

B4: The action associated with the state transition is that Line Workstation Controller issues to Workflow Plan Server a Next Operation Request message containing the part type and current workflow step number (initially 1).

B5: Workflow Plan Server increments the workflow step number for this part's workflow plan, determines the operation ID for this workflow step, and issues an Operation Request message to Manufacturing Operation Server for the next operation in sequence.

B6: Manufacturing Operation Server retrieves the operation information and sends it back.

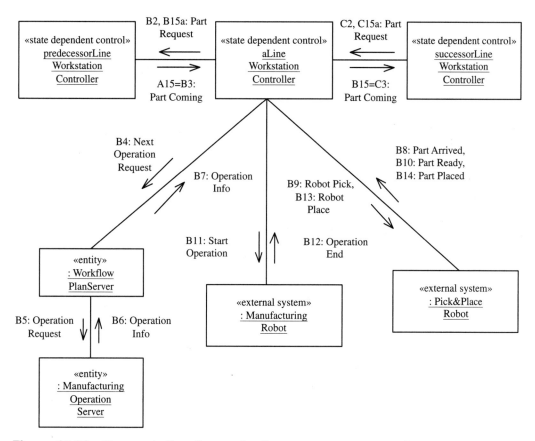

Figure 15.31 *Communication diagram for the* Process Part at High-Volume Workstation *use case*

B7: Workflow Plan Server sends the operation information to Line Workstation Controller.

B8: A sensor at Pick & Place Robot detects arrival of the part at the workstation and sends a Part Arrived message to Line Workstation Controller. As a result, Line Workstation Controller transitions to the Robot Picking state.

B9: As a result of the state transition, Line Workstation Controller sends a command to Pick & Place Robot to pick the part off the conveyor.

B10: Pick & Place Robot picks the part off the conveyor and places it in the workstation. On completion, Pick & Place Robot notifies Line

Workstation Controller. Line Workstation Controller transitions to the Operating on Part state.

B11: Line Workstation Controller sends the Start Operation command to Manufacturing Robot, which operates on the part.

B12: On completion of the manufacturing operation, Manufacturing Robot sends an Operation End status message to Line Workstation Controller. If a part has been requested (C2), Line Workstation Controller transitions to the Robot Placing state; if not, Line Workstation Controller transitions to Awaiting Part Request from Successor Workstation.

B13: As a result of the transition to Robot Placing state, Line Workstation Controller sends a command to Pick & Place Robot to place the part on the conveyor.

B14: On completion of its job, Pick & Place Robot sends a Part Placed message to Line Workstation Controller. Line Workstation Controller transitions to Awaiting Part from Predecessor Workstation. As a result of the transition, two concurrent actions take place: B15 and B15a.

B15 = C3: Line Workstation Controller sends a Part Coming message to the successor workstation. Part Coming is an output event on the Part Processing statechart that is propagated to the Part Requesting orthogonal statechart, where it appears as an input event that causes a transition from Part Has Been Requested to Part Not Requested.

B15a (parallel sequence): Line Workstation Controller sends a Part Request message to the predecessor workstation.

The communication diagram for the Ship Part abstract use case (Figure 15.32), in which last Line Workstation Controller sends a part to Shipping Workstation Controller, consists of the following message sequence (C1, C2, and C3 have been previously described):

C4: At Shipping Workstation Controller, a sensor detects part arrival and sends the Part Arrived message.

C5, C6: Pick & Place Robot picks the part off the conveyor and notifies Shipping Workstation Controller.

C7: Shipping Workstation Controller stores the part in the finished parts inventory and sends a Part Complete message to Production Manager Interface.

C8: Production Manager Interface displays the part completion information to the human production manager.

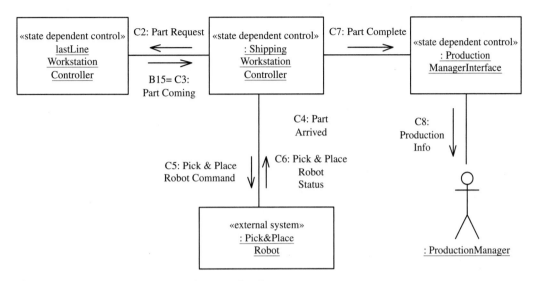

Figure 15.32 *Communication diagram for the* Ship Part *use case*

15.6.6   Dynamic Modeling of Flexible Manufacturing Use Cases

Now consider the communication diagrams for the flexible manufacturing use cases. In the Flexibly Manufacture Part use case, parts released to the factory floor are handled by Part Scheduler, which schedules parts to the various workstations on the basis of workstation availability and the workstation type required, as indicated by the next operation to be processed for that part. To move a part to the workstation, AGV Dispatcher is responsible for ensuring that the part is moved from its current location to the appropriate workstation. When the part has been delivered, Flexible Workstation Controller is informed that the part has arrived. Part Scheduler is informed of the completion of the operation so that it can schedule the part to the next workstation.

Flexible manufacturing systems use an automated storage and retrieval system (ASRS) to store raw material and finished parts. In some flexible manufacturing systems, parts in process are also temporarily stored in the ASRS as described by the Store Part and Retrieve Part extension use cases. In this situation, if all workstations are busy, Part Scheduler may decide to temporarily move the part to the ASRS. AGV Dispatcher is requested to move the part to the ASRS. When the part arrives at the ASRS, ASRS Handler is requested to place the part in storage.

To avoid having overly centralized part scheduling, part processing is divided as follows: Part Scheduler decides which workstation a part should move to next. `Part Agent` (one object for each part) acts on behalf of the part, making requests to the following objects:

- `Part Scheduler`, when a decision about the next workstation is required
- `AGV Dispatcher`, when a move to a workstation is required, which interfaces to an external AGV system
- `ASRS Handler`, if a move to the ASRS is required, which interfaces to an external ASRS
- `Flexible Workstation Controller`, to inform it of the part arriving and to receive part status information

This means that the part processing activity is divided between a decision maker (`Part Scheduler`) and an implementer of the scheduler's decisions for a given part (`Part Agent`). `Part Agent` executes a statechart that represents the part's progress through the factory. This design allows further decentralization, if deemed necessary, because it allows for a `Workcell Scheduler`, which schedules part processing for a given workcell (a *workcell* consists of all workstations of a given type). With this alternative design, there is no centralized `Part Scheduler`.

15.6.7 Statechart for Part Agent

A high-level statechart for the processing of a part in a flexible manufacturing system, which is executed by the `Part Agent` object, is shown in Figure 15.33 (more detail is provided later, in Figure 15.34). The states are described here. How the `Part Agent` object transitions between the different states is described in the scenarios in Section 15.6.8.

- **Part Initialization**. Raw material is found for the part from the ASRS, and the first operation for the part is retrieved.
- **Unfinished Part at ASRS**. The part is in the ASRS waiting to be dispatched to the next workstation.
- **Part Retrieval from ASRS**. The part is in the process of being removed from its bin by the forklift truck and placed on the ASRS stand. This superstate is decomposed into two substates, as shown in Figure 15.34:
  - **Part Retrieving**. The forklift truck is removing the part from the ASRS warehouse and taking it to the ASRS stand.
  - **Part at ASRS Stand**. The part has been placed on the ASRS stand by the forklift truck.

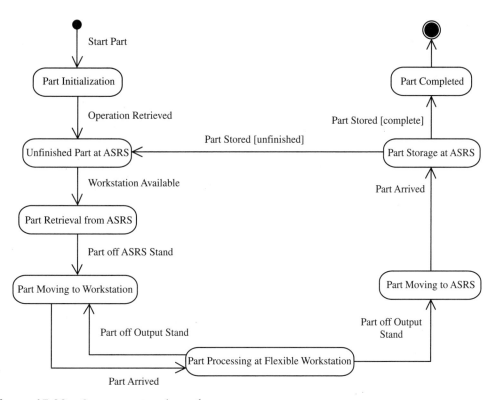

Figure 15.33   *Summary statechart of* `Part Agent`

- **Part Moving to Workstation**. The part is being moved to the next workstation by an AGV.

- **Part Processing at Flexible Workstation**. The part has arrived at the workstation input stand and is being processed at the workstation.

- **Part Moving to ASRS**. The part is being moved by an AGV from the workstation output stand to the ASRS stand for storage.

- **Part Storage at ASRS**. The part is being taken off the ASRS stand by the forklift truck to be stored in an ASRS bin. This superstate is decomposed into two substates, as shown in Figure 15.34:

  - **Part at ASRS Stand**. The part has been placed on the ASRS stand by the AGV.

  - **Part Storing**. The part is being taken to the ASRS by the forklift truck. The forklift truck is removing the part from the ASRS stand and taking it to the ASRS warehouse.

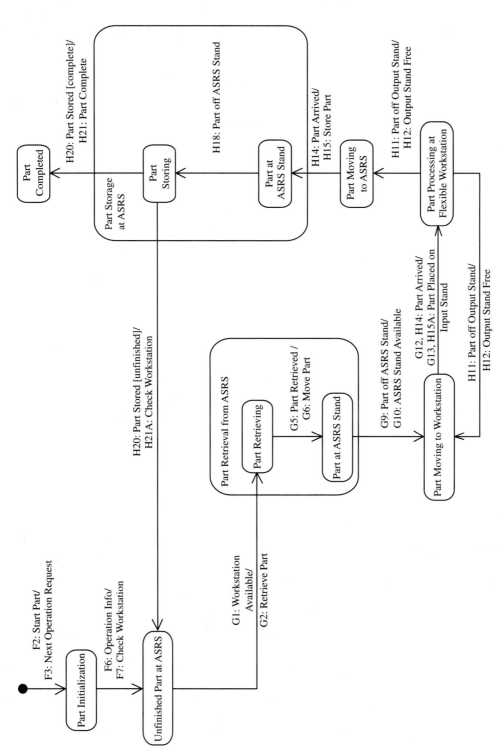

Figure 15.34 *More-detailed statechart of* Part Agent

- **Part Completed**. All operations on the part have been completed (or part processing failed), and the completed part has been stored in the ASRS.

A more detailed statechart for `Part Agent` is given in Figure 15.34, and the substates for the `Part Processing at Flexible Workstation` superstate are given in Figure 15.35. In each of these statecharts, both the events and the actions are shown.

The `Part Processing at Flexible Workstation` superstate is decomposed into the following states (see Figure 15.35):

- **Part on Workstation Input Stand**. The AGV has placed the part on the input stand.

- **Part Processing**. The part is being processed at the workstation.

- **Part on Workstation Output Stand**. The part is ready to be removed.

- **Checking Next Destination. Part Agent** is determining which workstation is next and whether that workstation is free.

- **Waiting for Next Workstation**. The part is on the output stand waiting for a workstation to become free (this state is entered only if the ASRS is unavailable for intermediate storage, as indicated by the feature condition [no storage]).

- **Part Waiting for AGV to Next Workstation**. The next workstation is free, and an AGV is coming to take the part to it.

- **Waiting for ASRS Stand**. The next workstation is not free, and the part is to be moved to the ASRS once a free stand has been located (this state is entered only if the ASRS is available for intermediate storage, as indicated by the feature condition [storage]).

- **Part Waiting for AGV to ASRS**. A free ASRS stand has been located, and an AGV is coming to take the part to the ASRS.

15.6.8 Communication Diagrams for Flexible Manufacturing Use Cases

The communication diagrams for the flexible manufacturing use cases are shown in Figures 15.36 through 15.38. Instead of having one large use case, the flexible manufacturing use cases are divided into the following abstract use cases:

- Start Work Order
- Move Part to Workstation
- Process Part at Flexible Workstation
- Move Part from Workstation

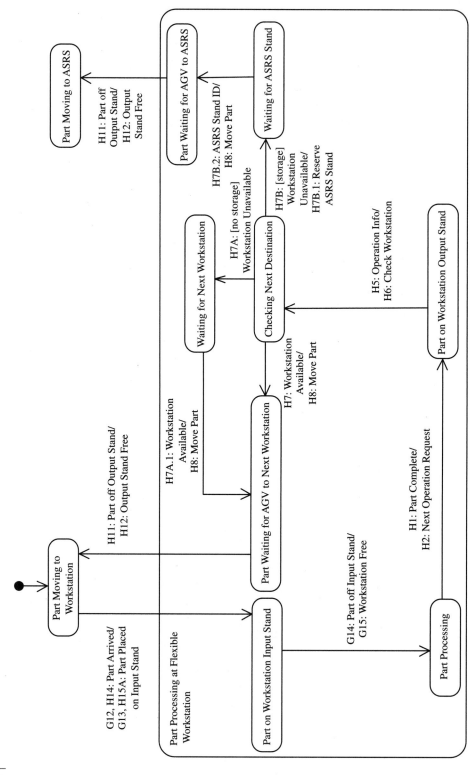

Figure 15.35 *Statechart of* Part Agent: *decomposition of* Part Processing at Flexible Workstation *superstate*

Because the use cases are state-dependent, events are shown on both communication diagrams and statecharts. The statecharts are for two particular state-dependent control objects that participate in these use cases: Part Agent and Flexible Workstation Controller. Thus, whenever an event is sent or received by one of these two objects, it is shown on both the communication diagram and the relevant statechart.

Communication Diagram for the Start Work Order Use Case

The communication diagram for the Start Work Order use case is described first. The production manager is the actor. The software objects participating in this use case are Production Manager Interface, Part Agent, Part Scheduler, Workflow Plan Server, and Manufacturing Operation Server. The communication diagram is shown in Figure 15.36. The message sequence is as follows:

F1: The human production manager creates a work order.

F2: Production Manager Interface instantiates Part Agent and sends a Start Part message to it.

F3: Part Agent sends a Next Operation Request message to Workflow Plan Server.

F4: Workflow Plan Server determines the next operation for this part and sends an Operation Request message to Manufacturing Operation Server.

F5: Manufacturing Operation Server responds with the operation information.

F6: Workflow Plan Server sends the operation information to Part Agent.

F7: Part Agent requests Part Scheduler to check if a workstation is available to process the part. If a workstation is available, the communication diagram for the Move Part to Workstation use case (see Figure 15.37) is initiated. Otherwise the request is added to the queue for workstations of this type.

Communication Diagram for the Move Part to Workstation Use Case

The communication diagram for the Move Part to Workstation use case is described next (see Figure 15.37). The software objects participating in this use case are Part Scheduler, Part Agent, ASRS Handler, AGV Dispatcher,

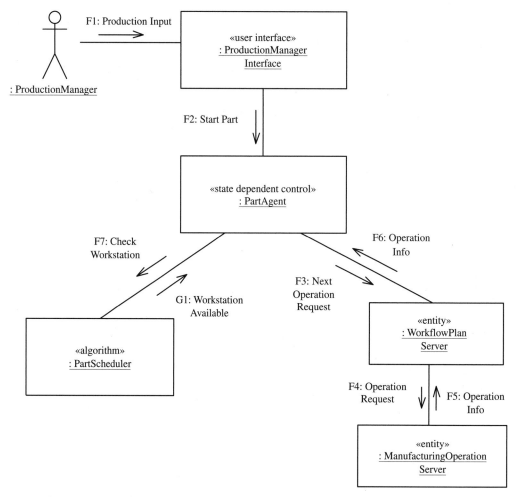

Figure 15.36 *Communication diagram for the* Start Work Order *use case*

and Flexible Workstation Controller. There are two external systems: ASRS Forklift Truck and AGV. The message sequence is as follows:

G1: Part Scheduler determines that a workstation is available for the part, either as a result of the F7 request (see Figure 15.36) or because a message arrives indicating that a workstation input stand has become free and this part is at the top of the queue. Part Scheduler reserves the workstation input stand for the part and sends a Workstation Available message to Part Agent.

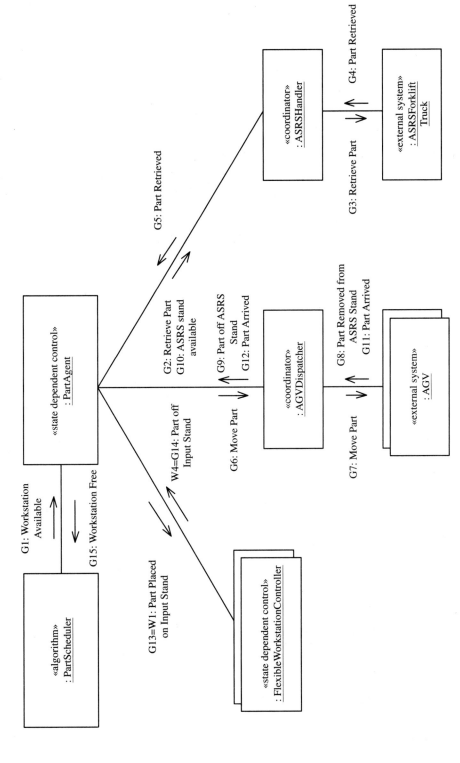

Figure 15.37 *Communication diagram for the* Move Part to Workstation *use case*

G2: Part Agent sends a Retrieve Part message to ASRS Handler.

G3: ASRS Handler selects a forklift truck and sends a Retrieve Part message to ASRS Forklift Truck to fetch the part from the ASRS bin and move it to the ASRS stand.

G4: ASRS Forklift Truck sends a message indicating that the part is on the ASRS stand.

G5: ASRS Handler sends a Part Retrieved message to Part Agent. (Part Scheduler does not need to know.)

G6: Part Agent sends a Move Part (ASRS stand to workstation x) message to AGV Dispatcher.

G7: AGV Dispatcher selects an AGV and sends AGV a Move Part (to workstation x input stand) message.

G8: AGV informs AGV Dispatcher that the part has been removed from the ASRS stand.

G9: AGV Dispatcher informs Part Agent that the ASRS stand is available.

G10: Part Agent informs ASRS Handler that the ASRS stand is available.

G11: AGV informs AGV Dispatcher that the part has arrived at the workstation input stand.

G12: AGV Dispatcher informs Part Agent that the part has arrived at the workstation input stand. (Part Scheduler does not need to know.)

G13 = W1: Part Agent sends a Part Placed on Input Stand message to Flexible Workstation Controller. (The *W* sequence is continued in the Flexible Workstation Controller interactions depicted in Figure 15.42 and described in Section 15.6.9.)

W4 = G14: Flexible Workstation Controller informs Part Agent that the workstation input stand is free.

G15: Part Agent informs Part Scheduler that the workstation input stand is free. Part Scheduler uses this information to schedule another part to this workstation (see step G1 at the start of this sequence).

Communication Diagram for the Move Part from Workstation Use Case

The communication diagram for the Move Part from Workstation use case is described next (see Figure 15.38). The software objects participating in this use case are Part Scheduler, Part Agent, Production Manager Interface, Workflow Plan Server, Manufacturing Operation Server, ASRS Handler, AGV Dispatcher, and Flexible Workstation Controller. As before, there are two external systems: `ASRS Forklift Truck` and `AGV`. The message sequence is as follows:

W10 = H1: `Flexible Workstation Controller` sends a `Part Complete` message to `Part Agent`.

H2–H5: `Part Agent` sends a `Next Operation Request` message to `Workflow Plan Server`. As in steps F3 through F6 (see Figure 15.36), `Workflow Plan Server` retrieves the manufacturing operation information, including the workstation type of the next workstation, from `Manufacturing Operation Server` and sends it to `Part Agent`.

H6: `Part Agent` requests `Part Scheduler` to to check whether a workstation of the required type is available.

H7: `Part Scheduler` reports to `Part Agent` that the required workstation is available, so the part will be moved by an AGV to the next workstation's input stand.

H7A: [no storage]. `Part Scheduler` reports to `Part Agent` that the required workstation is unavailable, so the part must wait on the output stand for a workstation to become available. (This variant branch is taken only if the ASRS is unavailable for intermediate storage, as indicated by the feature condition [no storage]).

H7A.1: `Part Scheduler` reports to `Part Agent` that the required workstation has become available, so the part can now be moved by an AGV to the next workstation's input stand.

H7B: [storage]. `Part Scheduler` reports to `Part Agent` that the required workstation is unavailable, so the part will be moved to the ASRS. (This variant branch is taken only if the ASRS is available for intermediate storage, as indicated by the feature condition [storage]).

H7B.1: `Part Agent` sends a `Reserve Stand` message to `ASRS Handler` to find an ASRS stand to which the part can be moved.

H7B.2: `ASRS Handler` responds with the ID of a vacant ASRS stand.

H8: `Part Agent` sends a `Move Part` message to `AGV Dispatcher` to move the part from the workstation output stand to a destination stand (either the next workstation input stand or an ASRS stand).

H9: `AGV Dispatcher` selects an AGV and instructs `AGV` to move the part to the destination stand.

H10: `AGV` informs `AGV Dispatcher` that the part has been removed from the workstation output stand.

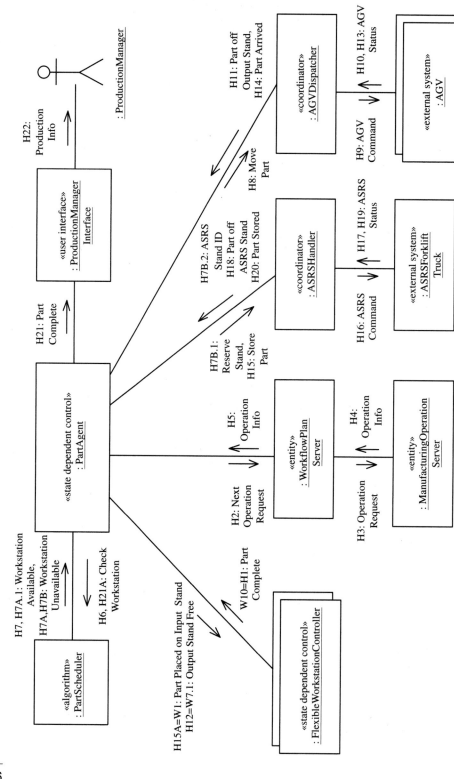

Figure 15.38 *Communication diagram for the* Move Part *from* Workstation *use case*

H11: AGV Dispatcher informs Part Agent that the workstation output stand is available.

H12 = W7.1: Part Agent notifies Flexible Workstation Controller that the workstation output stand is free.

H13: AGV informs AGV Dispatcher that the part has arrived at the destination stand.

H14: AGV Dispatcher informs Part Agent that the part has arrived at the destination stand.

H15A = W1: If the part destination stand is the workstation input stand, Part Agent informs Flexible Workstation Controller that the part is on the input stand. (This is the end of the sequence for this alternative branch; the *W* sequence is continued in the Flexible Workstation Controller interactions depicted in Figure 15.42 and described in Section 15.6.9).

H15: If the part destination stand is the ASRS stand, Part Agent sends a Store Part message to ASRS Handler.

H16: ASRS Handler instructs ASRS Forklift Truck to move the part from the ASRS stand and store it in an ASRS bin.

H17: ASRS Forklift Truck informs ASRS Handler that the part is off the ASRS stand.

H18: ASRS Handler informs Part Agent that the part is off the ASRS stand.

H19: ASRS Forklift Truck informs ASRS Handler that the part has been moved to an ASRS bin.

H20: ASRS Handler informs Part Agent that the part has been stored.

H21A: If this is not the last manufacturing operation of the workflow plan, then Part Agent requests Part Scheduler to check if the next workstation is available.

H21: If this is the last manufacturing operation of the workflow plan, then Part Agent informs Production Manager Interface that part processing is complete.

H22: Production Manager Interface informs the production manager that part processing is complete.

15.6.9 Dynamic Modeling for Flexible Workstation Control

This section discusses the dynamic modeling for flexible workstation control—first the statechart for the `Flexible Workstation Controller` class and then the communication diagram for the `Process Part at Flexible Workstation` use case.

Statechart for Flexible Workstation Controller

The `Flexible Workstation Controller` statechart (Figure 15.39) consists of three orthogonal statecharts (Figures 15.40 and 15.41), each of which is depicted as a superstate. The superstates are as follows:

1. **Input Stand Superstate.** This superstate consists of two substates: `Input Stand Available` and `Input Stand Occupied` (see Figure 15.41*a*).

2. **Output Stand Superstate.** This superstate consists of two substates: `Output Stand Available` and `Output Stand Occupied` (see Figure 15.41*b*).

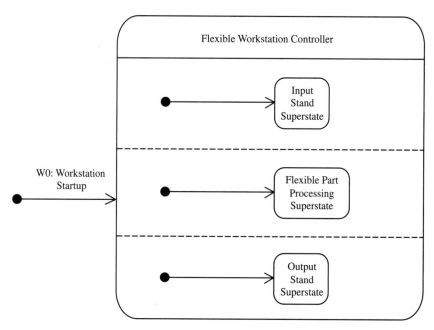

Figure 15.39 *Statechart of* `Flexible Workstation Controller`: *high-level statechart*

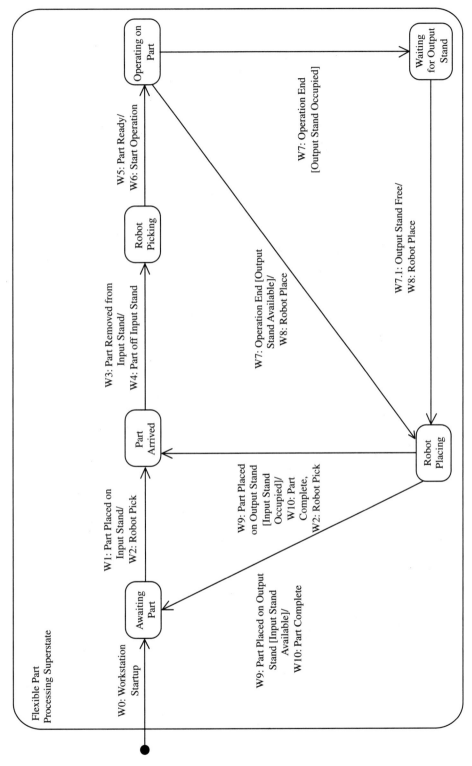

Figure 15.40 *Statechart of* Flexible Workstation Controller: *decomposition of the* Flexible Part Processing *superstate*

(a) Decomposition of the Input Stand superstate   (b) Decomposition of the Output Stand superstate

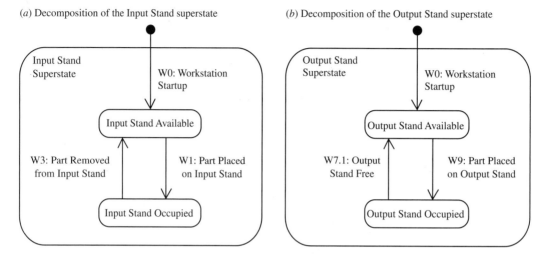

Figure 15.41 *Statechart of* Flexible Workstation Controller: *decomposition of the* Input Stand *and* Output Stand *superstates*

3. **Flexible Part Processing Superstate**. This superstate depicts the different states that a part goes through at a workstation. The Flexible Part Processing superstate contains the following substates (see Figure 15.40). The transitions between the substates are described in the context of the communication diagram (Figure 15.42):

   - **Awaiting Part**. This is the initial state, in which the workstation is idle, waiting for the arrival of a part.

   - **Part Arrived**. This state is entered when the workstation receives a message indicating that the next part has been placed on the input stand.

   - **Robot Picking. Flexible Workstation Controller** is in this state when pick-and-place robot is picking the part off the input stand and bringing it to the work location.

   - **Operating on Part. Flexible Workstation Controller** enters this state when it receives a message indicating that the part is ready at the workstation. The manufacturing robot is operating on the part.

   - **Robot Placing**. The pick-and-place robot is placing the part on the output stand. This state is entered when the robot operation has been completed and the output stand is available.

   - **Waiting for Output Stand**. This state is entered when robot manufacturing has been completed but the output stand is not available.

Communication Diagram for the Process Part at Flexible Workstation Use Case

The communication diagram for the `Process Part at Flexible Workstation` use case is shown in Figure 15.42. The software objects participating in this use case are `Flexible Workstation Controller`, `Part Agent`, and `Part Scheduler`. Two of these—`Part Agent` and `Flexible Workstation Controller`—are state-dependent control objects. There are also two external systems: `Pick & Place Robot` and `Manufacturing Robot`. The message sequence is as follows (see Figures 15.40 and 15.42):

G13 = W1: `Part Agent` informs `Flexible Workstation Controller` that the part is on the input stand.

W2: `Flexible Workstation Controller` requests `Pick & Place Robot` to move the part off the input stand.

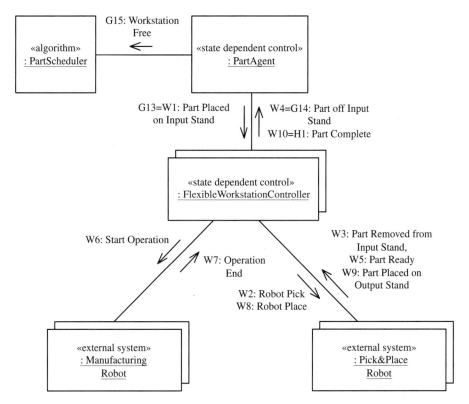

Figure 15.42 *Communication diagram for the* `Process Part at Flexible Workstation` *use case*

W3: `Pick & Place Robot` responds when it has moved the part off the input stand.

W4 = G14: `Flexible Workstation Controller` informs `Part Agent` that the workstation input stand is free.

W5: `Pick & Place Robot` sends a message to `Flexible Workstation Controller` when the part has been placed in the workstation and is ready for processing.

W6: `Flexible Workstation Controller` requests `Manufacturing Robot` to start the manufacturing operation.

W7: `Manufacturing Robot` informs `Flexible Workstation Controller` when the part manufacturing is complete. Depending on whether the output stand is free or not, the state transition is either to `Robot Placing` state or `Waiting for Output Stand` state.

H12 = W7.1: `Part Agent` notifies `Flexible Workstation Controller` that the workstation output stand is free (see Figure 15.38). The statechart transitions to `Robot Placing` state.

W8: `Flexible Workstation Controller` requests `Pick & Place Robot` to move the part to the workstation output stand.

W9: `Pick & Place Robot` informs `Flexible Workstation Controller` when the part is on the workstation output stand.

W10 = H1: `Flexible Workstation Controller` sends a `Part Complete` message to `Part Agent`. (`Part Scheduler` does not need to know.)

15.7   Feature/Class Dependency Analysis

A *feature* describes a requirement or characteristic that is provided by one or more members of the product line. During this step, feature/class dependencies are determined, describing the classes that support the feature and how they interact. The feature/class dependencies for the factory automation software product line are described in this section and summarized in Table 15.2.

15.7.1   Common Feature and Kernel Classes

The kernel of the product line consists of those classes that are required by every member of the product line. Thus the classes required to support the common features form the kernel of the product line. The kernel classes of the factory

Table 15.2   *Feature/class dependencies of the factory automation software product line*

Feature Name	Feature Category	Class Name	Class Category
Factory Kernel	common	Alarm Handling Server	kernel
		Workstation Status Server	kernel
		Workstation Controller	kernel-abstract-vp
Factory Operations User	optional	Operator Interface	optional
Factory Monitoring	alternative	Monitoring Workstation Controller	variant
Workflow Management	optional	Workflow Plan Server	optional
		Manufacturing Operation Server	optional
Workflow Planning User	optional	Workflow Engineer Interface	optional
Work Order Management	optional	Work Order Server	optional
		Part Server	optional
Work Order User	optional	Production Manager Interface	optional
High-Volume Manufacturing	alternative	Receiving Workstation Controller	variant
		Line Workstation Controller	variant
		Shipping Workstation Controller	variant
Flexible Manufacturing	alternative	Part Agent	optional
		Part Scheduler	optional
		Flexible Workstation Controller	variant
		AGV Dispatcher	optional
		ASRS Handler	optional
Storage & Retrieval	optional	Part Scheduler With Storage	variant

automation software product line are `Alarm Handling Server`, `Workstation Status Server`, and `Workstation Controller`. In order to accommodate all kinds of factory automation systems, `Workstation Controller` is designed as a generalized abstract workstation controller class, which needs to be specialized into a specific subclass before it can be instantiated. `Workstation Controller` is specialized to give the following subclasses: `Receiving Workstation Controller`, `Line Workstation Controller`, `Shipping Workstation Controller`, `Flexible Workstation Controller`, and `Monitoring Workstation Controller`, as shown in the generalization/specialization hierarchy in Figure 15.43. In addition to being abstract and a kernel class, `Workstation Controller` is a variation point, so product line variability can be introduced through specialization of this class.

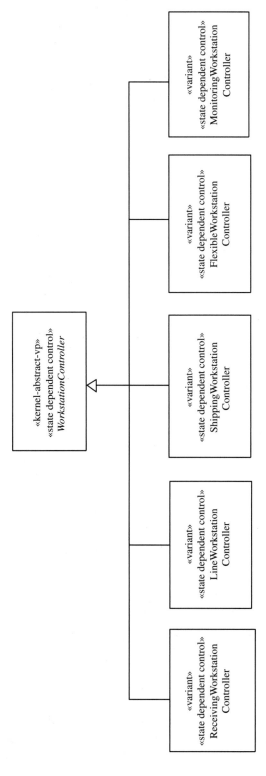

Figure 15.43 *Generalization/specialization hierarchy for* Workstation Controller

In order to determine the feature/class dependencies, it is necessary to determine the feature/object dependencies first. Thus it is necessary to analyze the dynamic model by considering the communication diagrams for each use case and the feature/use case dependencies. Start by considering the common feature, Factory Kernel, which relates to the four use cases involving the Factory Operator actor: View Alarms, View Workstation Status, Generate Alarm and Notify, and Generate Workstation Status and Notify (see Figure 15.7). The communication diagrams for these four use cases, created during dynamic modeling of the factory automation product line, are shown in Figures 15.21 through 15.24. The software objects that participate in these communication diagrams are Operator Interface, Alarm Handling Server, Workstation Status Server, and Workstation Controller. These four communication diagrams are integrated into a feature-based generic communication diagram as shown in Figure 15.44.

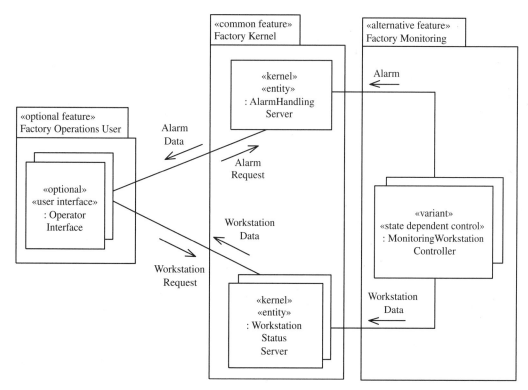

Figure 15.44 *Feature-based communication diagram for the* Factory Kernel *feature*

Because Workstation Controller is an abstract class, it does not have any instances; it is therefore necessary to depict an instance of one of its subclasses. For this exercise, the Monitoring Workstation Controller is chosen because it is the simplest to consider first. Usually the objects that participate in kernel use cases are all kernel objects supporting the Factory Kernel common feature. But because the product line needs to allow for factory systems that do not support a user interface (which is provided instead by an external system), it is necessary to categorize the Operator Interface object as an optional object, which supports a separate optional feature (Factory Operations User), as shown in Figure 15.44. Factory Kernel is supported by the two kernel objects: Alarm Handling Server and Workstation Status Server, which is a multi-instance object. Monitoring Workstation Controller is a variant object that supports the alternative feature Factory Monitoring.

The next step is to develop the feature/class dependencies, which follow directly from the feature-based communication diagram. The common Factory Kernel feature and the optional Factory Operations User feature are shown with the classes that support them in the feature-based class diagram in Figure 15.45, which is determined directly from Figure 15.44. The fact that the optional Factory Operations User feature depends on the common Factory Kernel feature is shown by the Is Client of association between the optional Operator Interface class and the kernel Alarm Handling Server and Workstation Status Server classes. Figure 15.45 also depicts the Factory Monitoring feature, which is an alternative feature because it is mutually exclusive with the High-Volume Manufacturing and Flexible Manufacturing features. The Factory Monitoring feature is supported by the variant Monitoring Workstation Controller class, which is a specialized subclass of the Workstation Controller kernel superclass, as shown in Figure 15.45. Thus a superclass can support one feature and be a kernel class while its variant subclasses support different features.

15.7.2 Optional Features and Classes

Next, consider the optional use cases initiated by Workflow Engineer—that is, Create/Update Operation and Create/Update Workflow Plan (see Figure 15.4). As described in Section 15.3, these use cases are organized into two features: Workflow Management and Workflow Planning User. The communication diagram for the two use cases is depicted in Figure 15.25, which shows four objects: Workflow Engineer Interface, Workflow Plan Server, Manufacturing Operation Server, and Workstation Status Server.

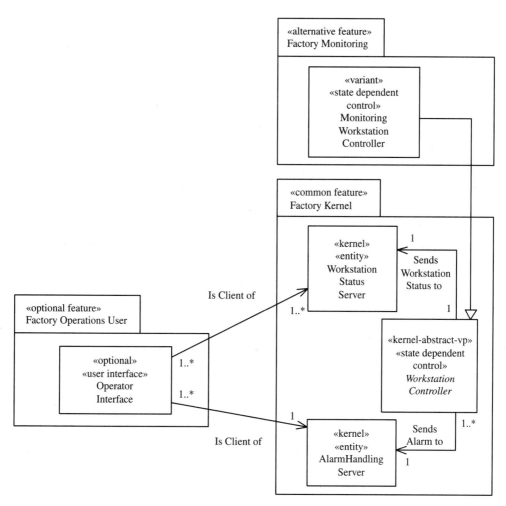

Figure 15.45 *Feature-based class diagram for the* Factory Kernel *feature*

Of these four objects, Workstation Status Server has already been catego-
rized as a kernel object. The other three objects are all categorized as optional
objects. Because of the need for factory systems without a user interface, however,
Workflow Engineer Interface is allocated to a different feature (Workflow
Planning User) than the remaining two server objects (Workflow Plan
Server and Manufacturing Operation Server), which are allocated to the
Workflow Management feature, as shown in the feature-based communication
diagram in Figure 15.46.

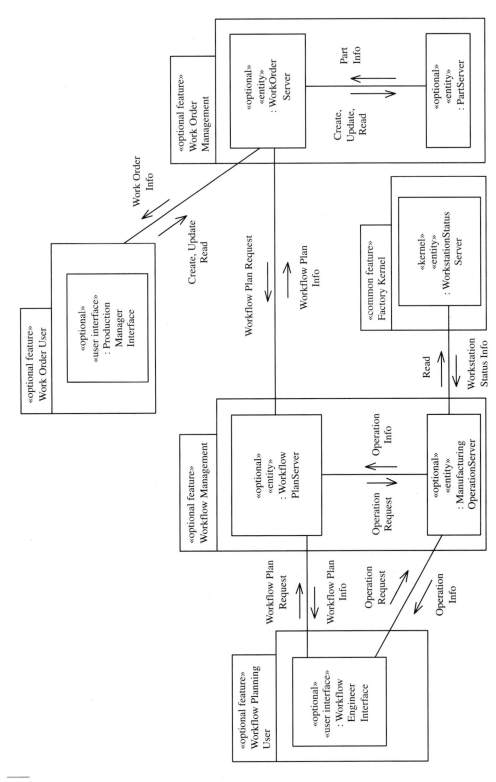

Figure 15.46 *Feature-based communication diagram for workflow and work order features*

Consider the optional use case initiated by `Production Manager: Create/ Modify Work Order`. This use case is supported by the communication diagram shown in Figure 15.26. Of the four objects depicted there, `Workflow Plan Server` has already been allocated to the `Workflow Management` feature. Following a similar approach to that taken for the `Workflow Engineer` features, `Work Order Server` and `Part Server` are categorized as optional objects that are allocated to the optional `Work Order Management` feature, and `Production Manager Interface` is categorized as an optional object allocated to the optional `Work Order User` feature. The feature-based class diagram for all these features (Figure 15.47) is determined directly from the feature-based communication diagram (Figure 15.46).

Consider how the workflow and work order features (those initiated by `Workflow Engineer` and `Production Manager`) are used in flexible and high-volume manufacturing systems. The `Workflow Planning User` and `Work Order User` features are optional because it is possible to have a system in which workflow plans and work orders are downloaded from an external system and are not created or modified on this system. Of the optional classes shown in Figure 15.47, the server classes (namely, `Workflow Plan Server` and `Manufacturing Operation Server`) are always required by flexible and high-volume manufacturing systems and therefore should be kept separate from the client class `Workflow Engineer Interface`, which is required only sometimes. Thus a `Workflow Management` feature that includes the `Workflow Plan Server` and `Manufacturing Operation Server` classes is defined. This optional class, called `Workflow Engineer Interface`, is kept separate and is placed in the `Workflow Planning User` feature.

15.7.3   Alternative High-Volume Manufacturing Features and Feature/Class Dependencies

Now consider the feature/class dependencies that apply to only one kind of factory system. Classes that have already been allocated to kernel and optional features in the previous sections are factored out. For feature/class dependencies determined from the `High-Volume Part Processing` communication diagrams, the classes `Production Manager Interface`, `Workflow Plan Server`, and `Manufacturing Operation Server` are factored out because they are already in the workflow and work order features. Similarly, for feature/class dependencies determined from the `Flexibly Manufacture Part` communication diagram, the same three classes are factored out.

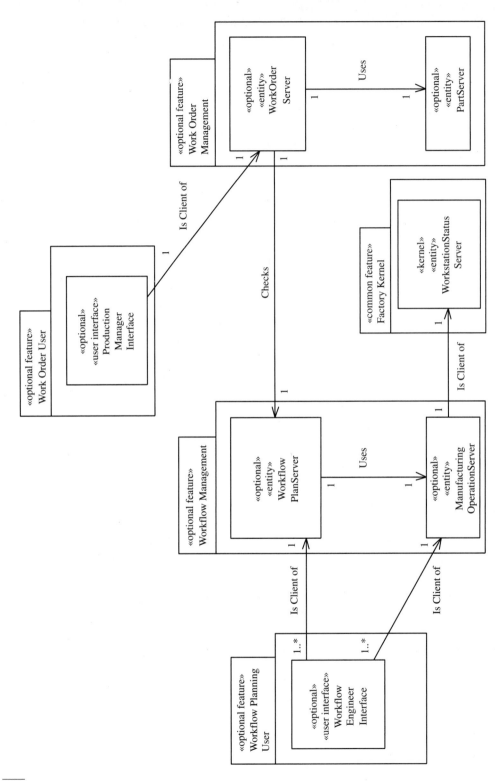

Figure 15.47 *Feature-based class diagram for workflow and work order features*

Consider the communication diagrams for the high-volume manufacturing use cases. There are four use cases, consisting of one concrete use case (Manufacture High-Volume Part) that includes three abstract use cases (Receive Part, Process Part at High-Volume Workstation, and Ship Part), which are are mapped to the alternative High-Volume Manufacturing feature, as shown in Figure 15.9. The abstract use cases contain all the functionality. The communication diagrams for these use cases are shown in Figures 15.30 through 15.32. The communication diagram for the Receive Part use case has the Production Manager Interface, Receiving Workstation Controller, and Line Workstation Controller objects (see Figure 15.30). The communication diagram for the Process Part at High-Volume Workstation use case has the Line Workstation Controller, Workflow Plan Server, and Manufacturing Operation Server objects (see Figure 15.31). The communication diagram for the Ship Part use case has the Line Workstation Controller, Shipping Workstation Controller, and Production Manager Interface objects (see Figure 15.32).

An integrated communication diagram would normally include all the objects from the three use case–based communication diagrams. In the feature-based communication diagram (Figure 15.48), however, the objects that appear in prerequisite communication diagrams are removed. In particular, the Workflow Plan Server, Manufacturing Operation Server, and Production Manager Interface objects are assigned to prerequisite communication diagrams and are thus removed from the feature-based communication diagram for the High-Volume Manufacturing feature. The remaining objects supporting this feature are Receiving Workstation Controller, Line Workstation Controller, and Shipping Workstation Controller.

The feature-based class diagram (Figure 15.49) is determined from the feature-based communication diagram in Figure 15.48. The class diagram also shows the abstract superclass Workstation Controller, from which the three subclasses Receiving Workstation Controller, Line Workstation Controller, and Shipping Workstation Controller are derived.

15.7.4 Alternative Flexible Manufacturing Features and Feature/ Class Dependencies

Now consider the flexible manufacturing use cases, which support the alternative Flexible Manufacturing feature, as shown in Figure 15.10. The Flexibly Manufacture Part use cases (Start Work Order, Move Part to Workstation, Process Part at Flexible Workstation, and Move Part from Workstation) are mapped to the Flexible Manufacturing feature.

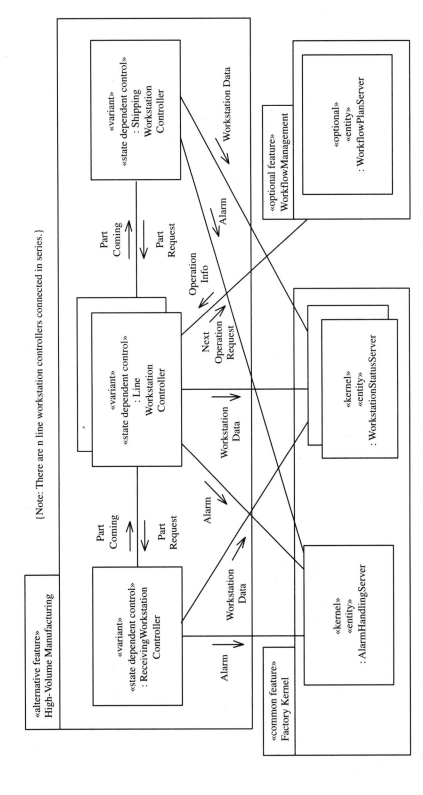

{Note: There are n line workstation controllers connected in series.}

Figure 15.48 *Feature-based communication diagram for the* High-Volume Manufacturing *feature*

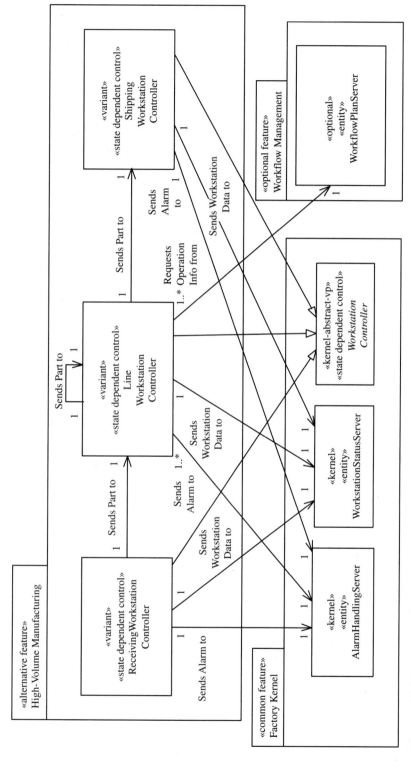

Figure 15.49 *Feature-based class diagram for the* High-Volume Manufacturing *feature*

The communication diagrams for the flexible manufacturing use cases are shown in Figures 15.36 through 15.38. The feature-based communication diagram is created by integration of the individual flexible manufacturing communication diagrams and then removal of the objects that have already been allocated to other kernel and optional features—following the approach used in the previous section for the High-Volume Manufacturing feature. The result is shown in Figure 15.50, where all the objects are categorized as optional except for Flexible Workstation Controller, which is a variant class because it is a subclass of Workstation Controller. Further analysis indicates that it is possible for a flexible manufacturing system either to support intermediate storage and retrieval, in which parts are temporarily stored in the ASRS, or not. This refinement leads to two features: Flexible Manufacturing and Storage & Retrieval.

The classes supporting the former feature are Part Scheduler, AGV Dispatcher, Flexible Workstation Controller, Part Agent, and ASRS Handler. The feature-based class diagram for this feature is shown in Figure 15.51.

The Store Part and Retrieve Part extension use cases are mapped to the Storage & Retrieval feature, which is supported by the specialized Part Scheduler With Storage class. The feature-based class diagram for this feature is shown in Figure 15.52.

Storage & Retrieval is an optional feature that requires Flexible Manufacturing as a prerequisite. However, it is also necessary to extend Part Scheduler (which now needs to schedule trips to and from the ASRS) and Part Agent (whose statechart needs to be extended to allow ASRS handling). This extension of functionality could be handled by specialization: having ASRS variants of Part Scheduler and Part Agent. Alternatively, it could be handled by parameterization, meaning that the ASRS functionality is built into the components from the start and then the feature conditions [storage] and [no storage] are used. If the feature condition were set to [no storage], Part Scheduler would never schedule a part to the ASRS; otherwise, if the feature condition were set to [storage], it would. If a part were never scheduled to the ASRS, those states in Part Agent would never be entered. The solution adopted is to use parameterization for Part Agent because the feature conditions [storage] and [no storage] (as depicted on the statechart in Figure 15.35) determine whether or not a part is moved to the ASRS when a workstation is unavailable. Specialization is used for Part Scheduler because the scheduling algorithm needs to be extended to handle intermediate scheduling to the ASRS.

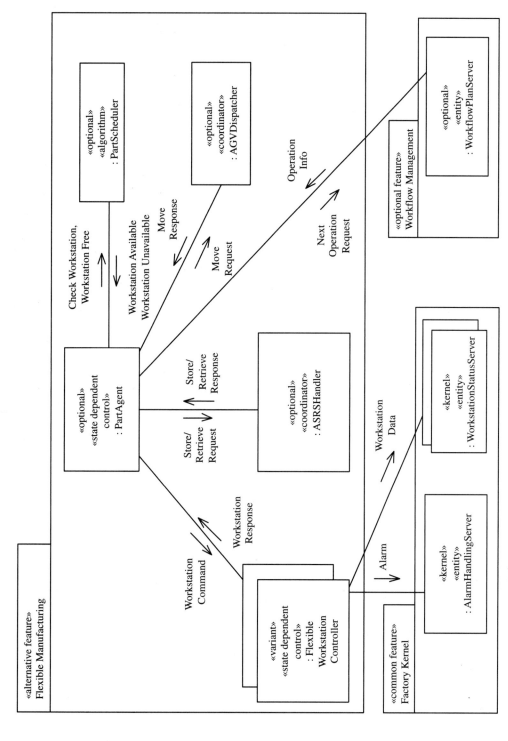

Figure 15.50 *Feature-based communication diagram for the* Flexible Manufacturing *feature*

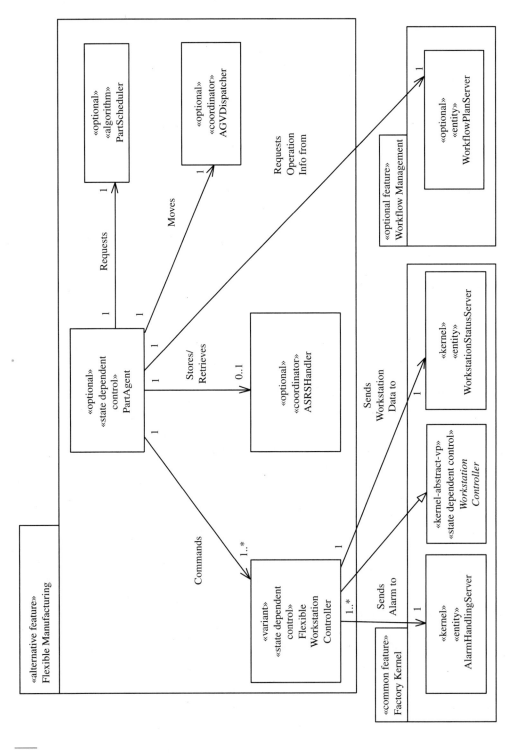

Figure 15.51 *Feature-based class diagram for the* Flexible Manufacturing *feature*

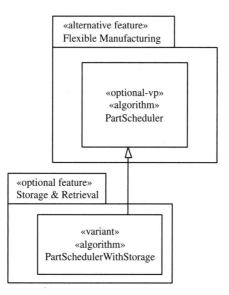

Figure 15.52 *Feature-based class diagram for the* Storage & Retrieval *feature*

15.7.5 Alternative Factory Monitoring Feature and Feature/Class Dependencies

Figure 15.45 shows the static model for the Factory Monitoring feature together with the Factory Kernel feature and the Factory Operations User feature. Grouped together, these three features form the Factory Monitoring System, which is one of the target systems of the factory automation product line. The Monitoring Workstation Controller class in the Factory Monitoring feature is a specialization of the Workstation Controller class in the Factory Kernel feature.

15.8 Design Modeling

The software architecture for the factory automation software product line is designed as a distributed component-based architecture that applies the software architectural patterns described in Chapter 10. The product line architecture is designed as a layered architecture based on the Layers of Abstraction architectural pattern. The kernel of the product line is designed as the lowest layer of the architecture.

15.8.1 Layered Component-Based Architecture

Applying the component structuring criteria, the following components are determined:

- **Server components**. The server components are `Alarm Handling Server`, `Workstation Status Server`, `Workflow Planning Server` (which is a composite component composed of the `Workflow Plan Server` and `Manufacturing Operation Server` classes), and `Production Management Server` (a composite component composed of the `Work Order Server` and `Part Server` classes).

- **User interface components**. The user interface components are `Operator Interface`, `Workflow Engineer Interface`, and `Production Manager Interface`.

- **Control components**. The control components are all the variant `Workstation Controller` components (as shown in Figure 15.43) and `Part Agent`. `Part Agent` is redesigned as a composite component that contains simple agents (one for each part).

- **Coordinator components**. The coordinator components are `Part Scheduler`, `AGV Dispatcher`, and `ASRS Handler`.

Each component is depicted with two stereotypes: the component stereotype (what kind of component it is, as specified by the component structuring criteria) and the product line stereotype (the reuse category—kernel, optional, or variant). The components are structured into the layered architecture such that each component is in a layer where it needs the service provided by components in the layers below but not the layers above. This layered architecture is based on the Flexible Layers of Abstraction pattern, which is a less restrictive variant of the Layers of Abstraction pattern in which a layer can use the services of any of the layers below it, not just the layer immediately below it. This layered architecture, depicted in Figure 15.53, facilitates adaptation of the factory automation software product line architecture to derive individual application members of the product line:

> **Layer 1: `Kernel Server Layer`**. This layer consists of the kernel server components: `Alarm Handling Server` and `Workstation Status Server`. This layer constitutes the kernel of the product line following the Kernel pattern.

> **Layer 2: `Workflow Server Layer`**. This layer consists of the optional `Workflow Planning Server` component. It requires the `Workstation Status Server` component from the `Kernel Server Layer`.

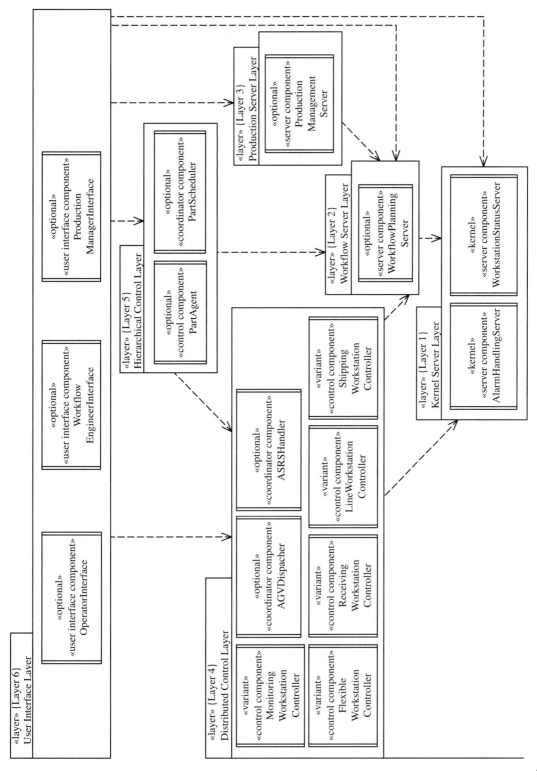

Figure 15.53 *Layered architecture of the factory automation software product line (Note: Layers are compressed due to page size.)*

Layer 3: `Production Server Layer`. This layer consists of the optional `Production Management Server` component. It requires the `Workflow Planning Server` component from the `Workflow Server Layer`.

Layer 4: `Distributed Control Layer`. This layer consists of the variant and optional control components that provide distributed control, including `AGV Dispatcher`, `ASRS Handler`, and the following `Workstation Controller` variants: `Monitoring Workstation Controller`, `Line Workstation Controller`, `Receiving Workstation Controller`, `Shipping Workstation Controller`, and `Flexible Workstation Controller`. All of the `Workstation Controller` components require `Alarm Handling Server` and `Workstation Status Server` from layer 1. `Line Workstation Controller` also requires `Workflow Planning Server` from layer 2.

Layer 5: `Hierarchical Control Layer`. This layer consists of the optional control and coordinator components that provide hierarchical control: `Part Agent` and `Part Scheduler`. `Part Agent` requires `Flexible Workstation Controller`, `AGV Dispatcher`, and `ASRS Handler` (all from the `Distributed Control Layer`); `Workflow Planning Server` (from the `Workflow Server Layer`), and `Part Scheduler` (from the same layer).

Layer 6: `User Interface Layer`. This layer consists of the optional user interface components: `Operator Interface`, `Workflow Engineer Interface`, and `Production Manager Interface`. `Operator Interface` requires `Alarm Handling Server` and `Workstation Status Server` from layer 1. `Workflow Engineer Interface` requires `Workflow Planning Server` from layer 2. `Production Manager Interface` requires `Production Management Server` (from layer 3), `Part Agent` (from layer 5), `Receiving Workstation Controller`, and `Shipping Workstation Controller` (both from layer 4).

If two layers do not depend on each other, such as layers 3 and 4 above, the choice of which layer should be higher is a design decision. In addition to the Layers of Abstraction and Kernel architectural patterns, several other architectural structure patterns are applied in the factory automation software product line architecture:

- **Client/Server pattern**. There are several client user interface/server and client control/server interactions in the architecture. In the Layers of Abstraction architecture, client components are designed to be at higher layers than the servers that they require. With the Flexible Layers of Abstraction architecture, a client can be at any of the higher levels. For example, `Operator Interface`, which is a client user interface component, is at layer 6, whereas the servers it uses (`Alarm Handling Server` and `Workstation Status Server`), are at layer 1.

- **Distributed Control pattern**. In high-volume manufacturing systems, control is distributed among several control components that are at the same layer of the architecture (layer 4). These are `Receiving Workstation Controller`, several instances of `Line Workstation Controller`, and `Shipping Workstation Controller`.

- **Hierarchical Control pattern**. In flexible manufacturing systems, there are two layers of control. At the lower layer (layer 4) are `AGV Dispatcher`, `ASRS Handler`, and multiple instances of `Flexible Workstation Controller`. At the higher layer (layer 5) are `Part Agent` and `Part Scheduler`. On the basis of manufacturing workstation availability, `Part Scheduler` determines which workstation a part should be moved to next or whether it should be moved to the ASRS for temporary storage. `Part Agent` then implements this decision by communicating with `AGV Dispatcher`, `ASRS Handler`, and the specific `Flexible Workstation Controller` components.

The major application systems that can be derived from the factory automation software product line architecture are shown in Figures 15.54 through 15.56. These are the static models for factory monitoring systems, high-volume manufacturing systems, and flexible manufacturing systems, respectively. The dependencies between the components are determined by the Layers of Abstraction architecture and are depicted in detail in the static models.

The class diagram for the factory monitoring system (Figure 15.54) is developed from the layered architecture of the product line in Figure 15.53, combined with consideration of the components needed by the relevant features in this system. The components and relationships are determined from the corresponding communication diagrams (Figures 15.21–15.24) and the feature/class diagram in Figure 15.45, which incorporates components from the `Factory Kernel`, `Factory Monitoring`, and `Factory Operations User` features. Four executable components and three layers are involved. Both `Monitoring Workstation Controller` and `Operator Interface` are clients of the kernel `Workstation Status Server` and `Alarm Handling Server` components.

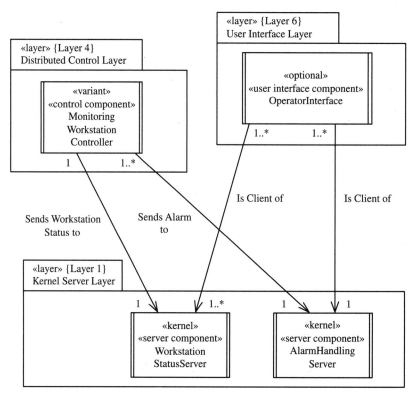

Figure 15.54 *Static model of a factory monitoring system*

The class diagram for the high-volume manufacturing system (Figure 15.55) has five layers and ten components. In addition to kernel components from Figure 15.45, this architecture incorporates components from the workflow and work order features of Figure 15.47 and the High-Volume Manufacturing feature of Figure 15.49. The Production Management Server component in Figure 15.55 is a composition of Work Order Server and Part Server from Figure 15.47, and the Workflow Planning Server component is a composition of Workflow Plan Server and Manufacturing Operation Server.

The class diagram for the flexible manufacturing system (Figure 15.56) has six layers and twelve components. In addition to kernel components from Figure 15.45, this architecture incorporates components from the workflow and work order features of 15.47 and the Flexible Manufacturing feature of Figure 15.51.

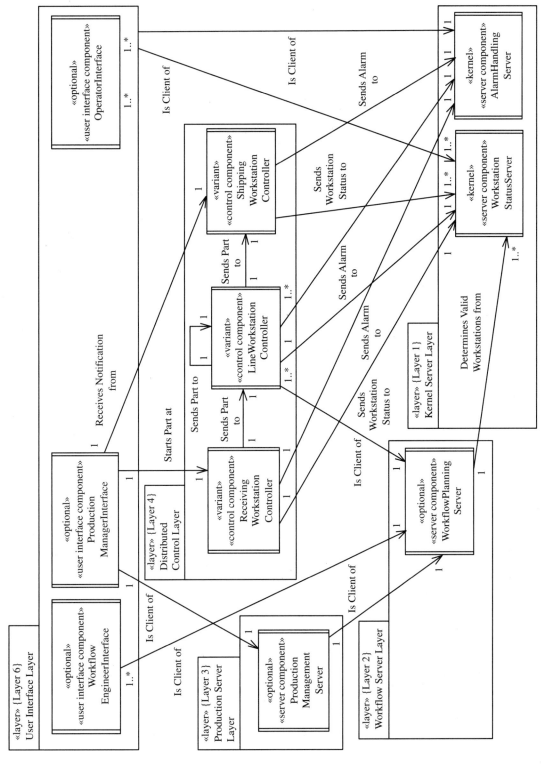

Figure 15.55 Static model of a high-volume manufacturing system. (Note: Layers are compressed due to page size.)

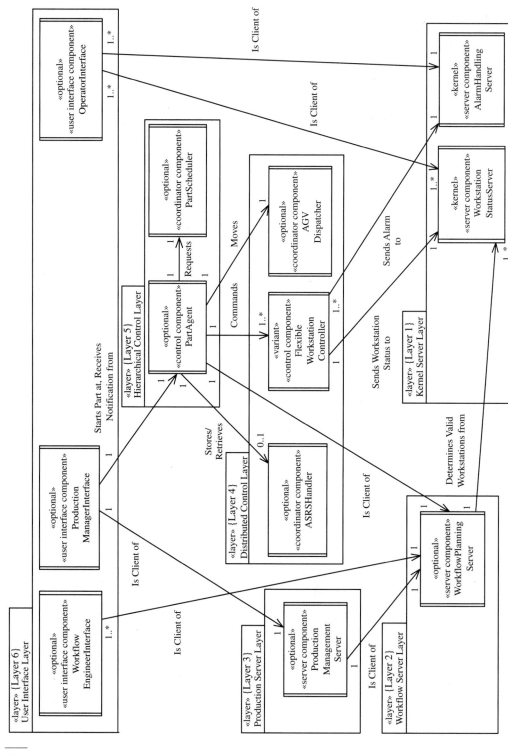

Figure 15.56 *Static model of a flexible manufacturing system. (Note: Layers are compressed due to page size.)*

15.8.2 Architectural Communication Patterns

The generic concurrent communication diagrams shown in Figures 15.57 through 15.59 depict the major application systems that can be derived from the factory automation software product line architecture. These diagrams are for factory monitoring, high-volume manufacturing, and flexible manufacturing systems, respectively. The diagrams depict the components structured according to the Layers of Abstraction architecture, but they omit the layer packages to make the communication between components clearer. The concurrent communication diagrams explicitly show the type of message communication—synchronous or asynchronous.

The components in the concurrent communication diagram for the factory monitoring system (Figure 15.57) are determined directly from the components in the class diagram in Figure 15.54. The communication between these components is determined from the communication diagrams in Figures 15.21 through 15.24 and the feature-based communication diagram of Figure 15.44, which show the messages passed between the components. Because of the client/server communication, the communication patterns used are Synchronous Message Communication with Reply and Subscription/Notification.

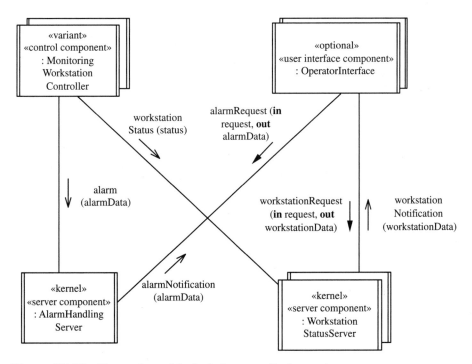

Figure 15.57 *Dynamic model of a factory monitoring system*

The concurrent communication diagram for the high-volume manufacturing system (Figure 15.58) is determined from the components in the class diagram in Figure 15.55 and the communication diagrams that support the high-volume manufacturing use cases (Figures 15.30–15.32), which show the messages passed between these components. This architecture adds asynchronous message communication between the distributed control components.

The communication diagram for the flexible manufacturing system (Figure 15.59) is determined from the components in the class diagram in Figure 15.56 and the communication diagrams that support the flexible manufacturing use cases (Figures 15.36–15.38), which show the messages passed between these components. This architecture also uses a combination of patterns, with asynchronous communication between the control and coordinator components.

To handle the variety of communication between the components in the software product line architecture, several communication patterns are applied, as depicted on the communication diagrams in Figures 15.57 through 15.59:

- **Asynchronous Message Communication**. The different `Workstation Controller` variants all send asynchronous messages to `Alarm Handling Server` and `Workstation Status Server` (as shown in all three figures: 15.57 through 15.59). The reason for asynchronous communication is that the `Workstation Controller` components need to post alarms and workstation status on a regular basis, they need to continue executing without delay, and they do not need a response.

- **Bidirectional Asynchronous Message Communication**. In high-volume manufacturing systems, each high-volume workstation controller communicates with its two neighbors, the predecessor workstation controller (`Receiving` or `Line`) and the successor workstation controller (`Line` or `Shipping`) via asynchronous messages (see Figure 15.58). A given `Workstation Controller` component sends an asynchronous `Part Request` message to its predecessor and then later receives an asynchronous `Part Coming` message from the predecessor. The messages are asynchronous to allow these two components to communicate with other components during the period when they are also communicating with each other.

- **Synchronous Message Communication with Reply**. This is the typical client/server pattern of communication and is used when the client needs information from the server and cannot proceed before receiving the response. This pattern is used between the user interface clients and servers. For example, it is used between `Workflow Engineer Interface` and `Workflow Planning Server`, as well as between `Production Manager Interface` and `Production Management Server` (see Figures 15.58 and 15.59).

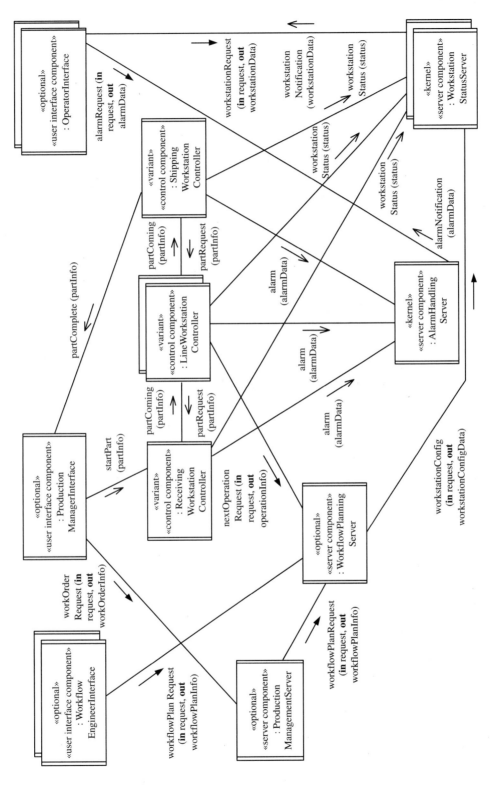

Figure 15.58 *Dynamic model of a high-volume manufacturing system*

597

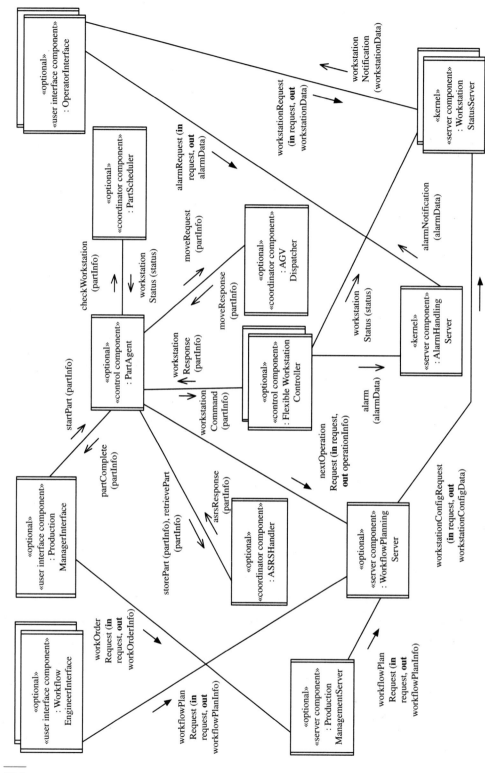

Figure 15.59 *Dynamic model of a flexible manufacturing system*

- **Broker Handle**. Broker patterns are used during system initialization. Servers register their services and locations with the broker. The Broker Handle pattern allows clients to query the broker to determine the servers to which they should be connected. Workstation controllers also use the Broker Handle pattern to determine the remote references of their neighbors.

- **Subscription/Notification (Multicast)**. `Operator Interface` has two patterns of communication with `Alarm Handling Server` and `Workstation Status Server` (see Figures 15.57, 15.58, and 15.59). The first is the regular client/server Synchronous Message Communication with Reply pattern, which is used to make alarm requests and receive responses. The second pattern is the Subscription/Notification pattern, in which `Operator Interface` subscribes to receive alarms of a certain type (e.g., high-priority alarms). When the workstation controller posts an alarm of that type to `Alarm Handling Server`, the server notifies all subscriber `Operator Interface` components of the new alarm. The same approach is used for communication with `Workstation Status Server`.

15.8.3 Software Architecture and Components

The software architecture of each of the main factory automation systems is depicted in Figures 15.60 through 15.62. All the concurrent components communicate through ports. The ports are provided ports that support provided interfaces, required ports that support required interfaces, or complex ports that support both provided and required interfaces. The interfaces are explicitly depicted in subsequent figures. By convention, the name of a port with a provided interface starts with the prefix P (e.g., `PAlarmServer`), and the name of a port with a required interface starts with the prefix R (e.g., `RAlarmServer`).

The software architecture of the factory monitoring system (Figure 15.60) depicts two server components that each support one provided port with a provided interface and one complex port with provided and required interfaces. The two client components each support one required port with a required interface and one complex port with provided and required interfaces. In this architecture, it is `Monitoring Workstation Controller` that sends alarm status and workstation status messages to `Alarm Handling Server` and `Workstation Status Server`, respectively.

In the software architecture of the high-volume manufacturing system (Figure 15.61), three different workstation controllers (`Receiving`, `Line`, and `Shipping`) send alarm status and workstation status messages to `Alarm Handling Server` and `Workstation Status Server`, respectively. The multiple instances

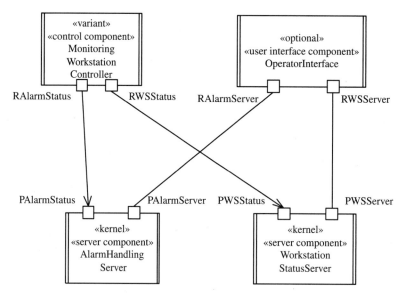

Figure 15.60   *Software architecture of a factory monitoring system*

of the `Workstation Controller` components are connected in series so that they can provide distributed control. For greatest flexibility, each `Line Workstation Controller` component has a required port to communicate with its predecessor and a provided port to communicate with its successor. The `Receiving Workstation Controller` component has only a provided port, and the `Shipping Workstation Controller` component has only a required port.

In the software architecture of the flexible manufacturing system (Figure 15.62), `Part Agent` and `Part Scheduler` together provide the hierarchical control, controlling the lower-level `Flexible Workstation Controller`, `AGV Dispatcher`, and `ASRS Handler` objects. The lower-level controllers have provided ports to receive the commands sent by `Part Agent` through its corresponding required ports.

The interfaces for the individual components are depicted in Figures 15.63 through 15.75. For each component port, the required and/or provided interface used by that port is depicted. In addition, the operations provided by each interface are specified. Consider an example of a server component with its ports, interfaces, and operations; consider also the clients that communicate with this server. The example is the `Alarm Handling Server` component, which has two ports: `PAlarmStatus` and `PAlarmServer` (as shown in Figure 15.63). The `PAlarmStatus` port consists of one provided interface called

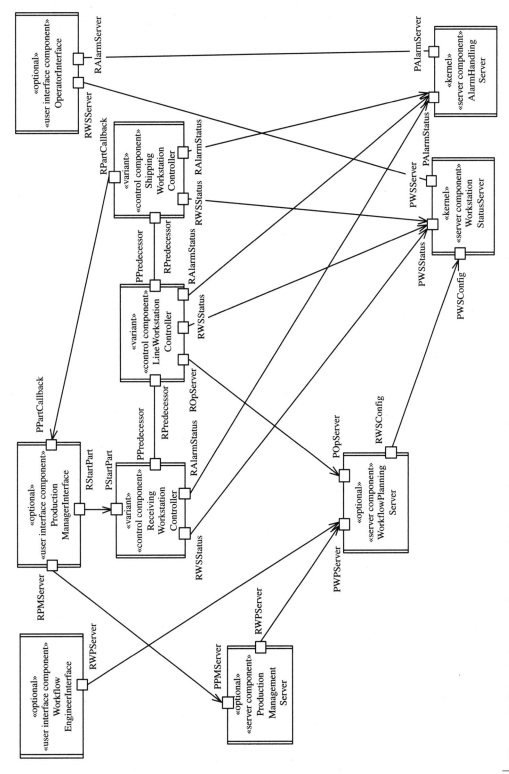

Figure 15.61 *Software architecture of a high-volume manufacturing system*

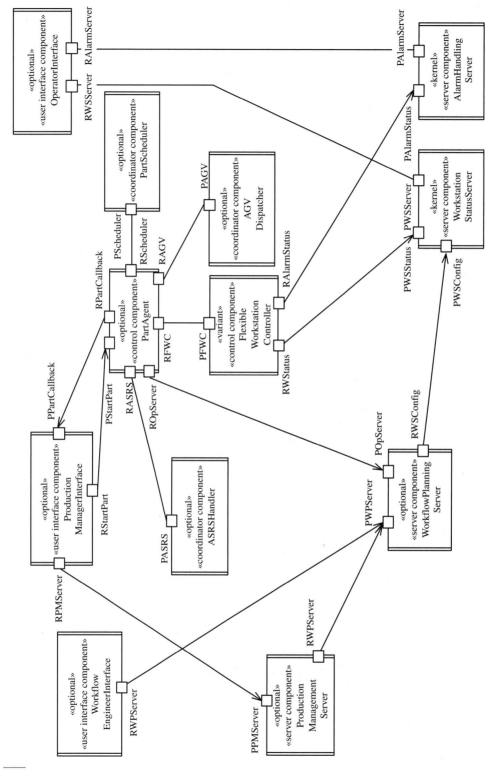

Figure 15.62 *Software architecture of a flexible manufacturing system*

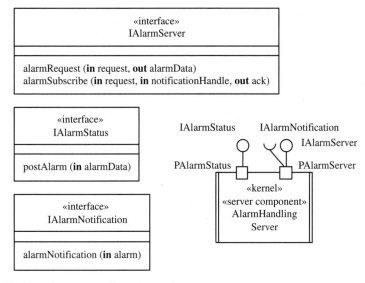

Figure 15.63 *Component interfaces of* Alarm Handling Server

IAlarmStatus, which provides one operation, called post Alarm. The PAlarmServer port has one provided interface (IAlarmServer) and one required interface (IAlarmNotification). The interfaces and operations are specified as follows:

- **Provided interface**: IAlarmServer
  Operations:
    - alarmRequest (**in** request, **out** alarmData)
    - alarmSubscribe (**in** request, **in** notificationHandle **out** ack)
- **Provided interface**: IAlarmStatus
  Operation: postAlarm (**in** alarmData)
- **Required interface**: IAlarmNotification
  Operation: alarmNotification (**in** alarm)

These interfaces are used as follows:

- The Operator Interface component (depicted in Figures 15.60 through 15.62) uses the IAlarmServer required interface (see Figure 15.75) via the RAlarmServer complex port to send alarm requests and subscriptions to Alarm Handling Server.

- The Workstation Controller components (depicted in Figures 15.60 through 15.62) use the IAlarmStatus required interface via the RAlarm-Status required port (e.g., see Figure 15.66) to post new alarms at Alarm Handling Server.

- The Alarm Handling Server component (depicted in Figures 15.60 through 15.62) sends alarm notifications to the Operator Interface component by using its IAlarmNotification required interface via the PAlarmServer complex port (see Figure 15.63).

In Figures 15.63 through 15.75, each component is depicted with both its ports and its provided and required interfaces. Each interface is explicitly depicted in terms of the operations it provides. Each operation specifies its name, input parameters, and output parameters.

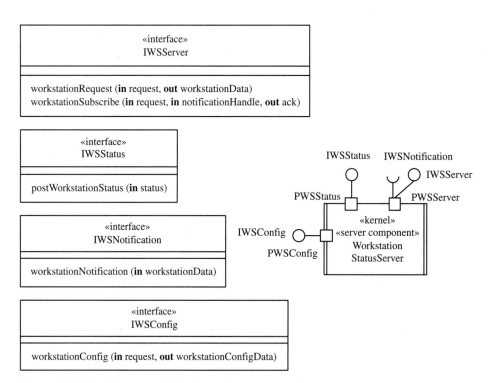

Figure 15.64 *Component interfaces of* Workstation Status Server

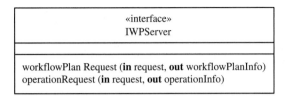

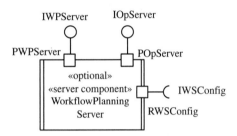

Figure 15.65 *Component interfaces of* Workflow Planning Server

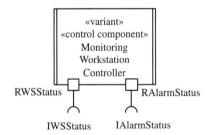

Figure 15.66 *Component interfaces of* Monitoring Workstation Controller

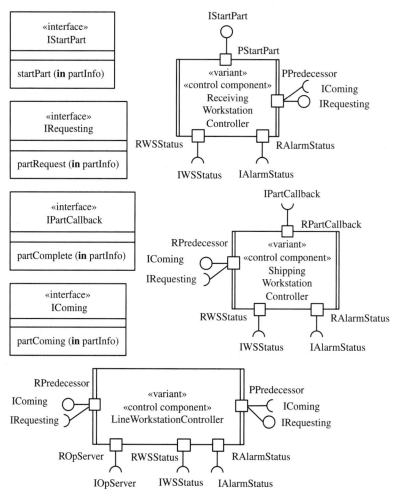

Figure 15.67 *Component interfaces of the* Receiving, Shipping, *and* Line *workstation controllers*

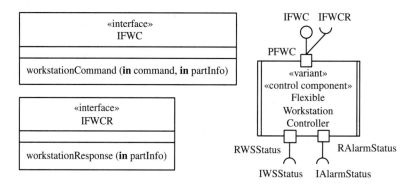

Figure 15.68 *Component interfaces of* Flexible Workstation Controller

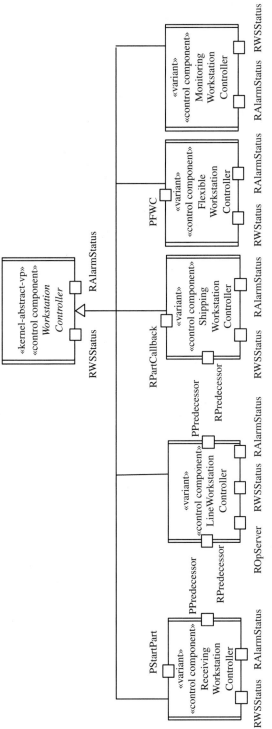

Figure 15.69 *Generalization/specialization hierarchy for* Workstation Controller

607

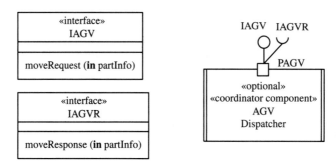

Figure 15.70   *Component interfaces of* AGVDispatcher

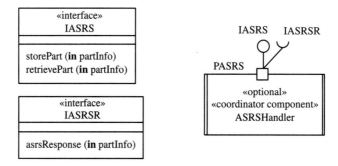

Figure 15.71   *Component interfaces of* ASRS Handler

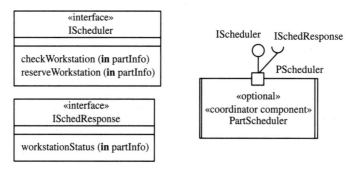

Figure 15.72   *Component interfaces of* Part Scheduler

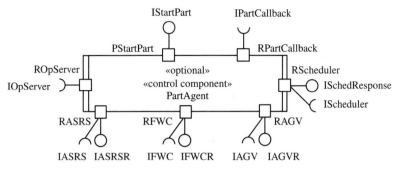

Figure 15.73 *Component interfaces of* Part Agent

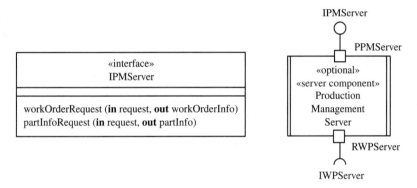

Figure 15.74 *Component interfaces of* Production Management Server

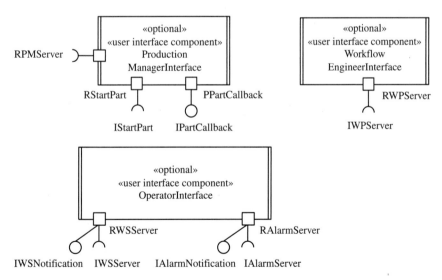

Figure 15.75 *Component interfaces of the user interface components*

15.9 Software Application Engineering

In order to derive a factory automation application from the factory automation software product line architecture and components, it is necessary to start with the feature model, which is depicted in Figure 15.11 and Table 15.1. There is also a feature group constraint in the form of an exactly-one-of feature group:

```
«exactly-one-of feature group» Factory Management {alternative =
Factory Monitoring, High-Volume Manufacturing, Flexible Manufacturing}
```

Software applications that can be derived from the factory automation product line architecture include high-volume manufacturing, flexible manufacturing, flexible manufacturing with storage, and factory monitoring applications, with possible smaller variations within each of these systems. These applications are derived from the product line architecture by selection of the High-Volume Manufacturing feature, the Flexible Manufacturing feature, the Storage & Retrieval feature, and the Factory Monitoring feature, respectively. The reason that each application can be derived by selection of only one feature is clear from Figure 15.11, which shows that, because of the feature dependencies, each of these four features depends on other features. Table 15.1 shows the feature/use case dependencies; Table 15.2 shows the feature/class dependencies.

To derive a factory system, it is necessary to choose among the High-Volume Manufacturing, Flexible Manufacturing, and Factory Monitoring features. One and only one of the corresponding features can be chosen. For this example, the High-Volume Manufacturing feature is selected. This feature mutually includes the Work Order Management implicit feature, which in turn mutually includes the Workflow Management implicit feature. An implicit feature cannot be selected on its own; it must be selected in conjunction with an explicit feature that requires it.

To derive a high-volume manufacturing system, the application engineer would need to select the High-Volume Manufacturing feature. This feature depends on the Work Order Management feature, which in turn depends on the Workflow Management feature. The common feature Factory Kernel is implicitly required by all optional features. Assume that the application engineer also selects the Factory Operations User, Workflow Planning User, and Work Order User features. The resulting high-volume manufacturing system would then have the following features:

- «common feature» Factory Kernel
- «optional feature» Factory Operations User {prerequisite = Factory Kernel}

- «optional feature» Workflow Management {prerequisite = Factory Kernel}
- «optional feature» Workflow Planning User {prerequisite = Workflow Management}
- «optional feature» Work Order Management {mutually includes = Workflow Management}
- «optional feature» Work Order User {prerequisite = Work Order Management}
- «alternative feature» High-Volume Manufacturing {mutually includes = Work Order Management}

Consider the feature/class dependencies shown in Table 15.2, tailored to contain only the features selected for the high-volume manufacturing application and the classes that support these features, as shown in Table 15.3.

The static model for the high-volume manufacturing system is depicted in Figure 15.55, the dynamic model is depicted in Figure 15.58, and the software architecture is depicted in Figure 15.61. The deployment diagram for the high-volume manufacturing system is depicted in Figure 15.76.

Table 15.3 *Feature/class dependencies of a high-volume manufacturing system*

Feature Name	Feature Category	Class Name	Class Category
Factory Kernel	common	Alarm Handling Server	kernel
		Workstation Status Server	kernel
		Workstation Controller	kernel-abstract-vp
Factory Operations User	optional	Operator Interface	optional
Workflow Management	optional	Workflow Plan Server	optional
		Manufacturing Operation Server	optional
Workflow Planning User	optional	Workflow Engineer Interface	optional
Work Order Management	optional	Work Order Server	optional
		Part Server	optional
Work Order User	optional	Production Manager Interface	optional
High-Volume Manufacturing	alternative	Receiving Workstation Controller	variant
		Line Workstation Controller	variant
		Shipping Workstation Controller	variant

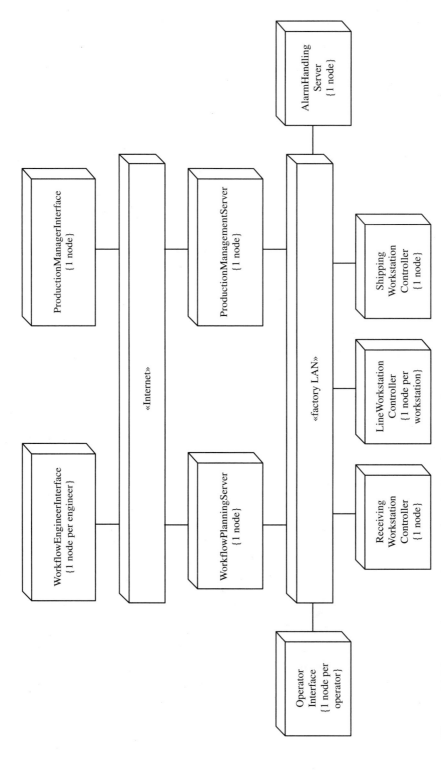

Figure 15.76 *Deployment diagram for a high-volume manufacturing system*

Overview of the UML Notation

The notation used for the PLUS method is the Unified Modeling Language (UML). This appendix provides a brief overview of the UML notation. The UML notation is described in more detail in introductory references—in particular *The Unified Modeling Language User Guide* (Booch et al. 2005) and *UML Distilled* (Fowler 2004)—and in *The Unified Modeling Language Reference Manual* (Rumbaugh et al. 2005). The UML notation has evolved since it was first adopted as a standard in 1997. A major revision to the standard was made in 2003, so the current version of the standard is UML 2.0. The previous versions of the standard are referred to as UML 1.x.

The UML notation has grown substantially over the years and it supports many diagrams. The approach taken in this book is the same as Fowler's (2004), which is to use only those parts of the UML notation that provide a distinct benefit. This appendix describes the main features of the UML notation that are particularly suited to the PLUS method. The purpose of this appendix is not to be a full exposition of UML, because several detailed books exist on this topic, but rather to provide a brief overview. The main features of each of the UML diagrams used in this book are briefly described, but lesser-used features are omitted. The differences between UML 2.0 notation and UML 1.x notation are also explained.

A.1 UML Diagrams

The UML notation supports the following diagrams for application development:

- **Use case diagram**, briefly described in Section A.2.
- **Class diagram**, briefly described in Section A.4.
- **Object diagram** (an instance version of the class diagram), which is not used by PLUS.
- **Communication diagram**, which in UML 1.x was called the *collaboration diagram*, briefly described in Section A.5.1.
- **Sequence diagram**, briefly described in Section A.5.2.
- **Statechart diagram**, briefly described in Section A.6.
- **Activity diagram**, which is not used by PLUS.
- **Component diagram**, which is not used by PLUS. The term *component* is used in this book to describe a distributed component, as used in component technology and described in Chapters 2, 10, and 11. The UML component diagram is more appropriate for modeling platform-specific details in a UML platform–specific model.
- **Composite structure diagram**, a new diagram introduced in UML 2.0 that is actually better suited for modeling distributed components in a UML platform–independent model. Because of its novelty, the composite structure diagram is described in the main text, in Chapter 11.
- **Deployment diagram**, briefly described in Section A.9.

How these UML diagrams are used by the PLUS method is described in Chapters 4 through 12 of this book.

A.2 Use Case Diagrams

An **actor** initiates a use case. A **use case** defines a sequence of interactions between the actor and the system. An actor is depicted as a stick figure on a use case diagram. The system is depicted as a box. A use case is depicted as an ellipse inside the box. Communication associations connect actors with the use cases in which they participate. Relationships among use cases are defined by means of *include* and *extend* relationships. The notation is depicted in Figure A.1.

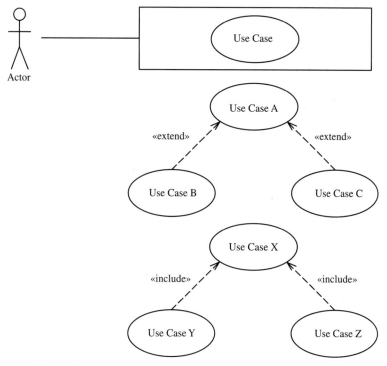

Figure A.1   *UML notation for a use case diagram*

A.3   Classes and Objects

Classes and objects are depicted as boxes in the UML notation, as shown in Figure A.2. The class box always holds the class name. Optionally, the attributes and operations of a class may also be depicted. When all three are depicted, the top compartment of the box holds the class name, the middle compartment holds the attributes, and the bottom compartment holds the operations.

To distinguish between a class (the type) and an object (an instance of the type), an object name is shown underlined. An object can be depicted in full with the object name separated by a colon from the class name—for example, anObject : Class. Optionally, the colon and class name may be omitted, leaving just the object name—for example, anObject. Another option is to omit the object name and depict just the class name after the colon, as in : Class. Classes and objects are depicted on various UML diagrams, as described in Section A.4.

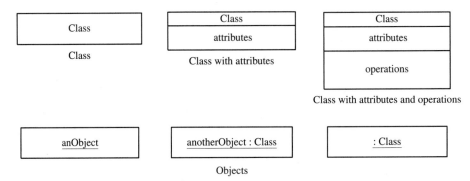

Figure A.2   *UML notation for objects and classes*

A.4   Class Diagrams

In a **class diagram**, classes are depicted as boxes, and the static (i.e., permanent) relationships between them are depicted as lines connecting the boxes. The following three main types of relationships between classes are supported: associations, whole/part relationships, and generalization/specialization relationships, as shown in Figure A.3. A fourth relationship, the dependency relationship, is often used to show how packages are related, as described in Section A.7.

A.4.1   Associations

An **association** is a static, structural relationship between two or more classes. An association between two classes, which is referred to as a *binary association*, is depicted as a line joining the two class boxes, such as the line connecting the ClassA box to the ClassB box in Figure A.3a. An association has a name and, optionally, a small black arrowhead to depict the direction in which the association name should be read. On each end of the association line joining the classes is the multiplicity of the association, which indicates how many instances of one class are related to an instance of the other class. Optionally, a stick arrow may also be used to depict the direction of navigability.

The **multiplicity** of an association specifies how many instances of one class may relate to a single instance of another class (Figure A.3a, right). The multiplicity of an association can be exactly one (1), optional (0..1), zero or more (*), one or more (1..*), or numerically specified (m..n), where *m* and *n* have numeric values.

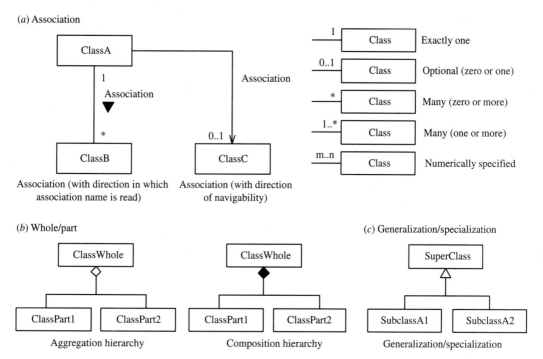

Figure A.3   *UML notation for relationships on a class diagram*

A.4.2   Aggregation and Composition Hierarchies

Aggregation and composition hierarchies are **whole/part** relationships. The composition relationship (shown by a black diamond) is a stronger form of whole/part relationship than the aggregation relationship (shown by a hollow diamond). The diamond touches the aggregate or composite (Class Whole) class box (see Figure A.3*b*).

A.4.3   Generalization/Specialization Hierarchy

A generalization/specialization hierarchy is an **inheritance** relationship. A generalization is depicted as an arrow joining the subclass (child) to the superclass (parent), with the arrowhead touching the superclass box (see Figure A.3*c*).

A.4.4   Visibility

Visibility refers to whether an element of the class is visible from outside the class, as depicted in Figure A.4. Depicting visibility is optional on a class diagram.

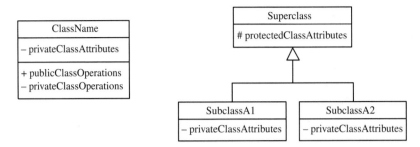

Figure A.4   *UML notation for visibility on a class diagram*

Public visibility, denoted with a + symbol, means that the element is visible from outside the class. **Private visibility**, denoted with a – symbol, means that the element is visible only from within the class that defines it and is thus hidden from other classes. **Protected visibility**, denoted with a # symbol, means that the element is visible from within the class that defines it and within all subclasses of the class.

A.5   Interaction Diagrams

UML has two kinds of interaction diagrams, which depict how objects interact: the communication diagram and the sequence diagram. Communication diagrams and sequence diagrams were semantically equivalent in UML 1.x, but in UML 2.0 this is true only of simple sequence diagrams; sequence diagrams that use new features introduced in UML 2.0 are no longer semantically equivalent to communication diagrams. The main features of these diagrams are described in Sections A.5.1 and A.5.2.

A.5.1   Communication Diagrams

A **communication diagram**, which was called a *collaboration diagram* in UML 1.x, shows how cooperating objects dynamically interact with each other by sending and receiving messages. The diagram depicts the structural organization of the objects that interact. Objects are shown as boxes, and lines joining boxes represent object interconnection. Labeled arrows adjacent to the arcs indicate the name and direction of message transmission between objects. The sequence of messages passed between the objects is numbered. The notation for

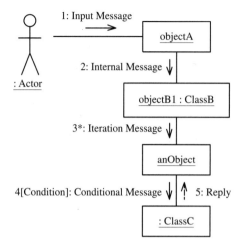

Figure A.5   *UML notation for a communication diagram*

communication diagrams is illustrated in Figure A.5. An optional iteration is indicated by an asterisk (*), which means that a message is sent more than once. An optional condition means that the message is sent only if the condition is true.

A.5.2   Sequence Diagrams

A different way of illustrating the interaction among objects is to show them on a sequence diagram, which depicts object interaction arranged in time sequence, as shown in Figure A.6. A **sequence diagram** is a two-dimensional diagram in which the objects participating in the interaction are depicted horizontally and the vertical dimension represents time. Starting at each object box is a vertical dashed line, referred to as a *lifeline*. Optionally, each lifeline has an activation bar, depicted as a double solid line, which shows when the object is executing.

UML 2.0 has substantially extended the notation for sequence diagrams. However, PLUS uses only the subset briefly described in this section, which is compatible with UML 1.x.

The actor is usually shown at the extreme left of the page. Labeled horizontal arrows represent messages. Only the source and destination of the arrow are relevant. The message is sent from the source object to the destination object. Time increases from the top of the page to the bottom. The spacing between messages is not relevant.

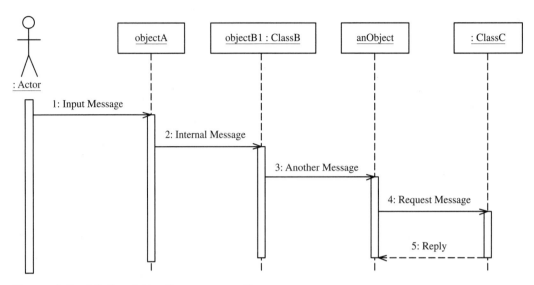

Figure A.6   *UML notation for a sequence diagram*

A.6   Statechart Diagrams

In the UML notation, a state transition diagram is referred to as a *statechart dia-gram*. In this book, the shorter term **statechart** is generally used. In the UML notation, states are represented by rounded boxes, and transitions are repre-sented by arcs that connect the rounded boxes, as shown in Figure A.7. The ini-tial state of the statechart is depicted by an arc originating from a small black circle. Optionally, a final state may be depicted by a small black circle inside a larger white circle, sometimes referred to as a *bull's-eye*. A statechart may be hierarchically decomposed such that a superstate is broken down into substates.

On the arc representing the state transition, the notation *Event [Condition]/ Action* is used. The **event** causes the state transition. The optional Boolean **con-dition** must be true, when the event occurs, for the transition to take place. The optional **action** is performed as a result of the transition. Optionally, a state may have any of the following:

- An **entry action**, performed when the state is entered
- An **activity**, performed for the duration of the state
- An **exit action**, performed on exit from the state

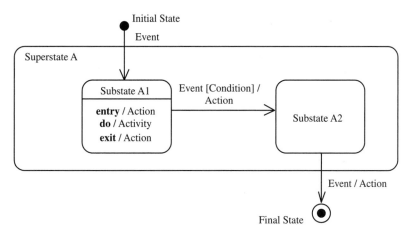

Figure A.7   *UML notation for a statechart: superstate with sequential substates*

Figure A.7 depicts a superstate (also known as composite state) A decomposed into sequential substates A1 and A2. In this case the statechart is in only one substate at a time; that is, first substate A1 is entered and then substate A2. Figure A.8 depicts a superstate B decomposed into concurrent substates BC and BD. In this case the statechart is in each of the concurrent substates, BC and BD, at the same time. Each concurrent substate is further decomposed into sequential substates. Thus, when the superstate B is initially entered, each of the substates B1 and B3 is also entered.

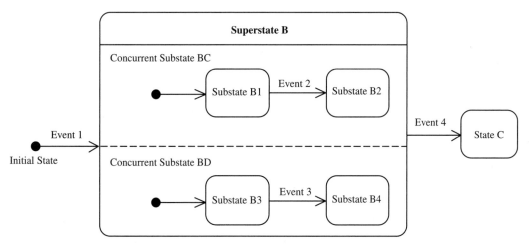

Figure A.8   *UML notation for a statechart: superstate with concurrent substates*

A.7   Packages

In UML, a **package** is a grouping of model elements—for example, to represent a system or subsystem. A package is depicted by a folder icon, a large rectangle with a small rectangle attached on one corner, as shown in Figure A.9. Packages may also be nested within other packages. Possible relationships between packages are dependency (shown in Figure A.9) and generalization/specialization relationships. Packages may be used to contain classes, objects, or use cases.

A.8   Concurrent Communication Diagrams

In the UML notation, an active object—which is also referred to as a *concurrent object*, *process*, *thread*, or *task*—is depicted by a rectangular box with two vertical parallel lines on the left- and right-hand sides. An **active object** has its own thread of control and executes concurrently with other objects. By contrast, a **passive object** has no thread of control. A passive object executes only when another object (active or passive) invokes one of its operations.

Active objects are depicted on **concurrent communication diagrams**, which depict the concurrency viewpoint of the system (Gomaa 2000, Douglass 2004). On a concurrent communication diagram, a UML 2.0 active object is depicted as a rectangular box with two vertical parallel lines on the left- and right-hand sides; a passive object is depicted as a regular rectangular box. The UML 1.x notation for active objects—rectangular boxes with thick black lines—is lno

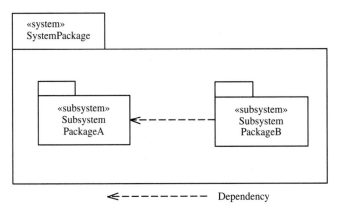

Figure A.9   *UML notation for packages*

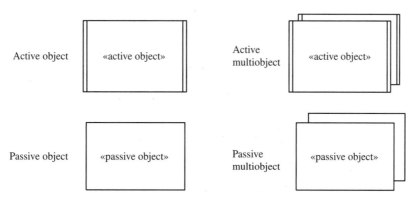

Figure A.10   *UML notation for active and passive objects*

onger used. An example is given in Figure A.10, which also shows the notation for multiobjects, used when more than one object is instantiated from the same class.

A.8.1   Message Communication on Concurrent Communication Diagrams

Message interfaces between tasks on concurrent communication diagrams are either **asynchronous** (loosely coupled) or **synchronous** (tightly coupled). With synchronous message communication, the producer sends a message to the consumer and then immediately waits for a response. For synchronous message communication, two possibilities exist: (1) synchronous message communication with reply and (2) synchronous message communication without reply.

The UML notation for message communication is summarized in Figure A.11. Figure A.12 depicts a concurrent communication diagram, a version of the communication diagram that shows active objects (concurrent objects, processes, tasks, or threads) and the various kinds of message communication between them. Note that from UML 1.4 onward, the UML notation for asynchronous communication has changed from an arrow with a half arrowhead to an arrow with a stick arrowhead. Note also that showing a simple message as an arrow with a stick arrowhead is a convention used in UML 1.3 and earlier. It is useful, however, to use simple messages during analysis modeling when no decision has yet been made about the type of message communication.

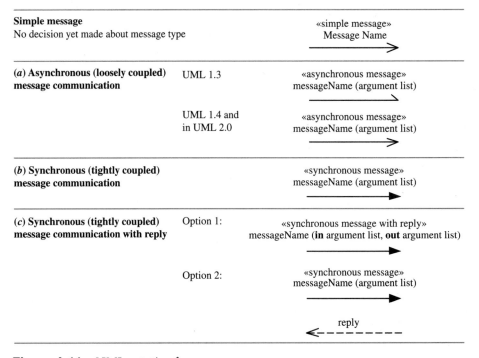

Figure A.11 *UML notation for messages*

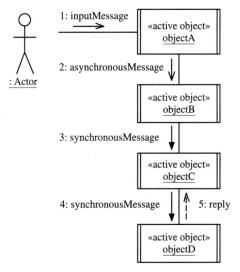

Figure A.12 *UML notation for a concurrent communication diagram*

A.9 Deployment Diagrams

A **deployment diagram** shows the physical configuration of the system in terms of physical nodes and physical connections between the nodes, such as network connections. A node is shown as a cube, and the connection is shown as an line joining the nodes. A deployment diagram is essentially a class diagram that focuses on the system's nodes (Booch et al. 2005).

In this book, a node usually represents a computer node, with a constraint (see Section A.10.3) describing how many instances of this node may exist. The physical connection has a stereotype (see Section A.10.1) to indicate the type of connection, such as «local area network» or «wide area network». Figure A.13 shows two examples of deployment diagrams: In the first example, nodes are connected via a wide area network (WAN); in the second, they are connected via a local area network (LAN). In the first example, the ATM Client node

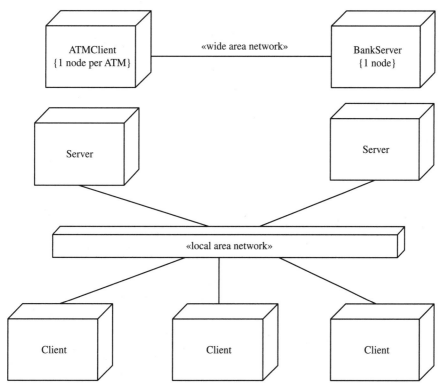

Figure A.13 *UML notation for a deployment diagram*

(which has one node for each ATM) is connected to a Bank Server that has one node. Optionally, the objects that reside at the node may be depicted in the node cube. In the second example, the network is shown as a node cube. This form of the notation is used when more than two computer nodes are connected by a network.

A.10   UML Extension Mechanisms

UML provides three mechanisms to allow the language to be extended (Booch et al. 2005; Rumbaugh et al. 2005). These are stereotypes, tagged values, and constraints.

A.10.1   Stereotypes

A **stereotype** defines a new building block that is derived from an existing UML modeling element but tailored to the modeler's problem (Booch et al. 2005). This book makes extensive use of stereotypes. Several standard stereotypes are defined in UML. In addition, a modeler may define new stereotypes. This appendix includes several examples of stereotypes, both standard and PLUS-specific. Stereotypes are indicated by guillemets (« »).

In Figure A.1, two specific kinds of dependency between use cases are depicted by the stereotype notation: «include» and «extend». Figure A.9 shows the stereotypes «system» and «subsystem» to distinguish between two different kinds of packages. Figure A.11 uses stereotypes to distinguish among different kinds of messages.

In UML 1.3, a UML modeling element could be depicted only with one stereotype. However, UML 1.4 onward extended the stereotype concept to allow a modeling element to be depicted by more than one stereotype. Therefore, different, possibly orthogonal, characteristics of a modeling element can now be depicted with different stereotypes. The PLUS method takes advantage of this additional functionality.

The UML stereotype notation allows a modeler to tailor a UML modeling element to a specific problem. In UML, stereotypes are enclosed in guillemets usually within the modeling element (e.g., class or object) as depicted in Figure A.14*a*. However, UML also allows stereotypes to be depicted as symbols. One of the most common such representations was introduced by Jacobson (1992) and is used in the Unified Software Development Process (USDP) (Jacobson et al.

(*a*) Standard UML notation for depicting stereotypes

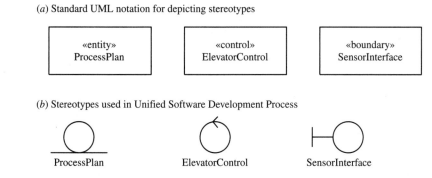

(*b*) Stereotypes used in Unified Software Development Process

Figure A.14   *Alternative notation for UML stereotypes*

1999). Stereotypes are used to represent «entity» classes, «boundary» classes (which are equivalent to «interface» classes in COMET), and «control» classes. Figure A.14*b* depicts the `Process Plan` «entity» class, the `Elevator Control` «control» class, and the `Sensor Interface» «boundary» class using the USDP's stereotype symbols.

A.10.2   Tagged Values

A **tagged value** extends the properties of a UML building block (Booch et al. 2005), thereby adding new information. A tagged value is enclosed in braces in the form {tag = value}. Commas separate additional tagged values. For example, a class may be depicted with the tagged values {version = 1.0, author = Gill}, as shown in Figure A.15.

A.10.3   Constraints

A **constraint** specifies a condition that must be true. In UML, a constraint is an extension of the semantics of a UML element to allow the addition of new rules

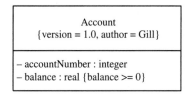

Figure A.15   *UML notation for tagged values and constraints*

or modifications to existing rules (Booch et al. 2005). For example, for the `Account` class depicted in Figure A.15, the constraint on the attribute `balance` is that the balance can never be negative, depicted as {balance >=0}. Optionally, UML provides the Object Constraint Language (Warmer and Kleppe 1999) for expressing constraints.

A.11   Conventions Used in This Book

For improved readability, the conventions used for depicting names of classes, objects, and so on in the figures are sometimes different from the conventions used for the same names in the text. In the figures, examples are shown in Times Roman font. In the body of the text, however, examples are shown in `Courier` font to distinguish them from the regular Times Roman font. Some specific additional conventions used in the book vary depending on the phase of the project. For example, the conventions for capitalization are different in the analysis model (which is less formal) than in the design model (which is more formal).

A.11.1   Requirements Modeling

In both figures and text, use cases are shown with initial uppercase and spaces in multiword names—for example, `Withdraw Funds`.

A.11.2   Analysis Modeling

The naming conventions for the analysis model are as follows.

Classes

Classes are shown with an uppercase initial letter. In the figures, there are no spaces in multiword names—for example, `CheckingAccount`. In the text, however, spacing is introduced to improve the readability—for example, `Checking Account`.

Attributes are shown with a lowercase initial letter—for example, `balance`. For multiword attributes, there are no spaces between the words in figures, but spaces are introduced in the text. The first word of the multiword name has an initial lowercase letter; subsequent words have an initial uppercase letter—for example, `accountNumber` in figures and `account Number` in text.

The type of the attribute has an initial uppercase letter—for example, `Boolean`, `Integer`, or `Real`.

Objects

Objects may be depicted in various ways. They are always underlined in the figures, but they are not underlined in the text. Furthermore, an object may be depicted as:

- **An individual named object**. In this case the first letter of the first word is lowercase, and subsequent words have an uppercase first letter. In figures, the objects appear as, for example, <u>aCheckingAccount</u> and <u>anotherCheckingAccount</u>. In the text, these objects appear as a `Checking Account` and another `Checking Account`. In situations where there is only one object instance, for conciseness the indefinite article may be omitted in the text; for example, the a may be omitted, leaving just the object name `Checking Account`.

- **An individual unnamed object**. Some objects are shown in the figures as class instances without a given object name—for example, <u>: CheckingAccount</u>. In the text, this object is referred to as `Checking Account`. For improved readability, the colon is removed, and a space is introduced between the individual words of a multiword name.

This means that, depending on how the object is depicted in a figure, it will appear in the text sometimes with a first word initial letter uppercase and sometimes with a first word initial letter lowercase.

Messages

In the analysis model, messages are always depicted as simple messages (see Figure A.11) because no decision has yet been made about the message type. Messages are depicted with an uppercase initial letter. Multiword messages are shown with spaces in both figures and text—for example, `Simple Message Name`.

Statecharts

In both figures and text, states, events, conditions, actions, and activities are all shown with initial letter uppercase and spaces in multiword names—for example, the state `Waiting for PIN`, the event `Cash Dispensed`, and the action `Dispense Cash`.

A.11.3   Design Modeling

The naming conventions for the design model are as follows.

Active and Passive Classes

The naming conventions for active classes (concurrent classes) and passive classes are the same as for classes in the analysis model (see Section A.11.2).

Active and Passive Objects

The naming conventions for active objects (concurrent objects) and passive objects are the same as for objects in the analysis model (see Section A.11.2).

Messages

In the design model, the first letter of the first word of the message is lowercase, and subsequent words have an uppercase first letter. In the figures, there is no space between words, as in `alarmMessage`. In the text, however, a space is introduced for improved readability, as in `alarm Message`.

Message parameters are shown with a lowercase initial letter—for example, `speed`. For multiword attributes, there are no spaces between the words in figures, but spaces are introduced in the text. The first word of the multiword name has a lowercase initial letter, and subsequent words have an uppercase initial letter—for example, `cumulativeDistance` in figures and `cumulative Distance` in the text.

A.12   Summary

This appendix briefly described the main features of the UML notation and the main characteristics of the UML diagrams used in this book.

For further reading on UML 2.0 notation at a tutorial level, Fowler (2004) provides an overview, and more detail can be found in Booch et al. 2005 and Eriksson et al. 2004. A comprehensive and detailed reference to UML is Rumbaugh et al. 2005.

Catalog of Software Architectural Patterns

A template for describing a pattern typically addresses the following topics:

- **Pattern name**.
- **Aliases**. Other names by which this pattern is known.
- **Context**. The situation that gives rise to this problem.
- **Problem**. Brief description of the problem.
- **Summary of solution**. Brief description of the solution.
- **Strengths of solution**.
- **Weaknesses of solution**.
- **Applicability**. When you can use the pattern.
- **Related patterns**.
- **Reference**. Where you can find more information about the pattern.

The architectural structure patterns, architectural communication patterns, and architectural transaction patterns are documented with this template in Sections B.1, B.2, and B.3, respectively.

B.1 Software Architectural Structure Patterns

This section describes the architectural structure patterns, which address the static structure of the architecture, in alphabetical order, using the standard template.

B.1.1 Broker Pattern

Pattern name	Broker.
Aliases	Object Broker, Object Request Broker.
Context	Software architectural design, distributed systems.
Problem	Distributed application in which multiple clients communicate with multiple servers. Clients do not know locations of servers.
Summary of solution	Use broker. Servers register their services with broker. Clients send service requests to broker. Broker acts as intermediary between client and server.
Strengths of solution	Location transparency: Servers may relocate easily. Clients do not need to know locations of servers.
Weaknesses of solution	Additional overhead because broker is involved in message communication. Broker can become a bottleneck if there is a heavy load at the broker. Client may keep outdated service handle instead of discarding.
Applicability	Distributed environments: client/server and distribution applications with multiple servers.
Related patterns	Broker Forwarding, Broker Handle.
Reference	Chapter 10, Section 10.2.4; Mowbray and Ruh 1997; Orfali et al. 1996.

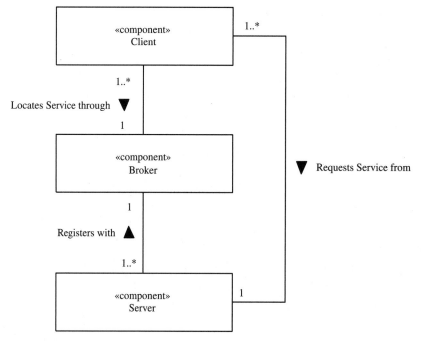

Figure B.1 *Broker pattern*

B.1.2 Centralized Control Pattern

Pattern name	Centralized Control.
Aliases	Centralized Controller, System Controller.
Context	Centralized application where overall control is needed.
Problem	Several actions and activities are state-dependent and need to be controlled and sequenced.
Summary of solution	There is one control component, which conceptually executes a statechart and provides the overall control and sequencing of the system or subsystem.
Strengths of solution	Encapsulates all state-dependent control in one component.
Weaknesses of solution	Could lead to overcentralized control, in which case decentralized control should be considered.
Applicability	Real-time control systems, state-dependent applications.
Related patterns	Distributed Control, Hierarchical Control.
Reference	Chapter 10, Section 10.2.6.

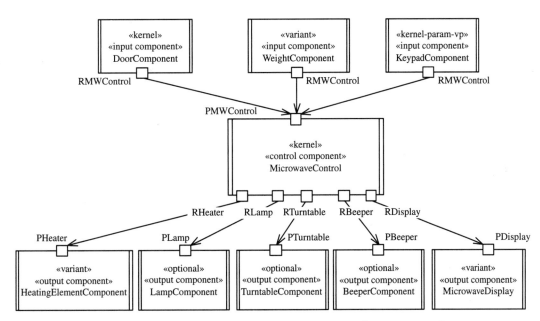

Figure B.2 *Centralized Control pattern: microwave oven control system example*

B.1.3   Client/Agent/Server Pattern

Pattern name	Client/Agent/Server.
Aliases	Distributed Agents, Multi-Agent.
Context	Distributed applications.
Problem	Client/server application in which negotiation between clients and servers is required.
Summary of solution	Agents negotiate with servers on behalf of their clients. Server might itself have an agent act on its behalf, in which case a client agent acts on behalf of the client and a server agent acts on behalf of the server.
Strengths of solution	Offloads negotiation details from clients and servers.
Weaknesses of solution	Negotiation may take longer by involving third party. Negotiation may be lengthy and inconclusive.
Applicability	Distributed environments: client/server and distribution applications with multiple servers.
Related patterns	Often used in conjunction with broker patterns (Broker Forwarding, Broker Handle, Discovery).
Reference	Chapter 10, Section 10.2.5.

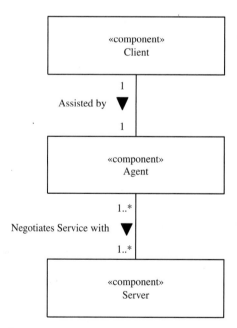

Figure B.3   *Client/Agent/Server pattern*

B.1.4   Client/Server Pattern

Pattern name	Client/Server.
Aliases	Multiple-Client/Single-Server
Context	Software architectural design, distributed systems.
Problem	Distributed application in which multiple clients require services from a single server.
Summary of solution	Server is a provider of services, and client requests services. Server provides services for multiple clients. Server responds to requests and does not initiate requests.
Strengths of solution	Good way for client to communicate with server when it needs a reply. Very common form of communication in client/server applications.
Weaknesses of solution	Client can be held up indefinitely if there is a heavy load at the server.
Applicability	Distributed processing: client/server and distribution applications with multiple servers.
Related patterns	Variations of this pattern include Multiple-Client/Multiple-Server and Multitier Client/Server.
Reference	Chapter 10, Section 10.2.3; Orfali et al. 1996.

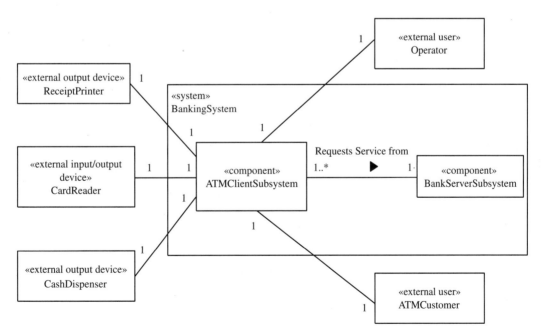

Figure B.4   *Client/Server pattern: banking system example*

B.1.5 Distributed Control Pattern

Pattern name	Distributed Control.
Aliases	Distributed Controller.
Context	Distributed application with real-time control requirement.
Problem	Distributed application with multiple locations where real-time localized control is needed at several locations.
Summary of solution	There are several control components, such that each component controls a given part of the system by conceptually executing a statechart. Control is distributed among the various control components; no single component has overall control.
Strengths of solution	Overcomes potential problem of overcentralized control.
Weaknesses of solution	Does not have an overall coordinator. If this is needed, consider using Hierarchical Control pattern.
Applicability	Distributed real-time control, distributed state-dependent applications.
Related patterns	Hierarchical Control, Centralized Control.
Reference	Chapter 10, Section 10.2.7.

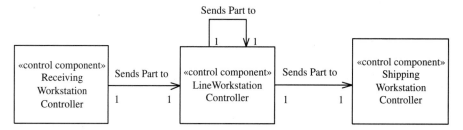

Figure B.5 *Distributed Control pattern: high-volume manufacturing system example*

B.1.6   Hierarchical Control Pattern

Pattern name	Hierarchical Control.
Aliases	Multilevel Control.
Context	Distributed application with real-time control requirement.
Problem	Distributed application with multiple locations where both real-time localized control and overall control are needed.
Summary of solution	There are several control components, each controlling a given part of a system by conceptually executing a statechart. There is also a coordinator component, which provides high-level control by deciding the next job for each control component and communicating that information directly to the control component.
Strengths of solution	Overcomes potential problem with Distributed Control pattern by providing high-level control and coordination.
Weaknesses of solution	Coordinator may become a bottleneck when the load is high.
Applicability	Distributed real-time control, distributed state-dependent applications.
Related patterns	Distributed Control, Centralized Control.
Reference	Chapter 10, Section 10.2.8.

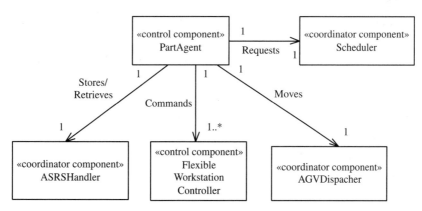

Figure B.6   *Hierarchical Control pattern: flexible manufacturing system example*

B.1.7 Kernel Pattern

Pattern name	Kernel.
Aliases	Microkernel.
Context	Software architectural design.
Problem	A small core of essential functionality that can be used by other components is needed.
Summary of solution	Kernel provides a well-defined interface consisting of operations (procedures or functions) that can be called by other parts of the software system.
Strengths of solution	Kernel can be designed to be highly efficient.
Weaknesses of solution	If care is not taken, kernel can become too large and bloated. Alternatively, essential functionality could be left out in error.
Applicability	Operating systems, software product lines.
Related patterns	Can be lowest layer of Layers of Abstraction architecture.
Reference	Chapter 10, Section 10.2.2; Bacon 1997; Buschmann et al. 1996.

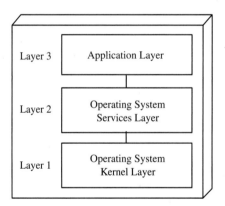

Figure B.7   *Kernel pattern: operating system kernel example*

B.1.8 Layers of Abstraction Pattern

Pattern name	Layers of Abstraction.
Aliases	Hierarchical Layers, Levels of Abstraction.
Context	Software architectural design.
Problem	A software architecture that encourages design for ease of extension and contraction is needed.
Summary of solution	Components at lower layers provide services for components at higher layers. Components may use only services provided by components at lower layers.
Strengths of solution	Promotes extension and contraction of software design.
Weaknesses of solution	Could lead to inefficiency if too many layers need to be traversed.
Applicability	Operating systems, communication protocols, software product lines.
Related patterns	Kernel can be lowest layer of Layers of Abstraction architecture. Variations of this pattern include Flexible Layers of Abstraction.
Reference	Chapter 10, Section 10.2.1; Hoffman and Weiss 2001; Parnas 1979.

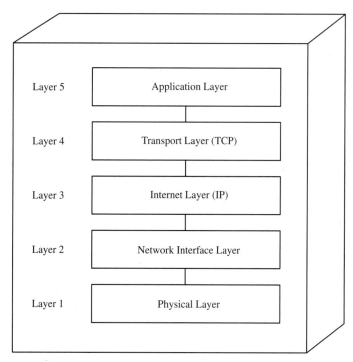

Figure B.8 *Layers of Abstraction pattern: TCP/IP example*

B.2   Software Architectural Communication Patterns

This section describes the architectural communication patterns, which address the dynamic communication among distributed components of the architecture, in alphabetical order, using the standard template.

B.2.1   Asynchronous Message Communication Pattern

Pattern name	Asynchronous Message Communication.
Aliases	Loosely Coupled Message Communication.
Context	Concurrent or distributed systems.
Problem	Concurrent or distributed application has concurrent components that need to communicate with each other. Producer does not need to wait for consumer. Producer does not need a reply.
Summary of solution	Use message queue between producer component and consumer component. Producer sends message to consumer and continues. Consumer receives message. Messages are queued FIFO if consumer is busy. Consumer is suspended if no message is available. Producer needs timeout notification if consumer node is down.
Strengths of solution	Consumer does not hold up producer.
Weaknesses of solution	If producer produces messages more quickly than consumer can process them, the message queue will eventually overflow.
Applicability	Centralized and distributed environments: real-time systems, client/server and distribution applications.
Related patterns	Asynchronous Message Communication with Callback.
Reference	Chapter 10, Section 10.3.1.

Figure B.9   *Asynchronous Message Communication pattern*

B.2.2   Asynchronous Message Communication with Callback Pattern

Pattern name	Asynchronous Message Communication with Callback.
Aliases	Loosely Coupled Communication with Callback.
Context	Concurrent or distributed systems.
Problem	Concurrent or distributed application in which concurrent components need to communicate with each other. Client does not need to wait for server but does need to receive a reply later.
Summary of solution	Use loosely coupled communication between client components and server component. Client sends service request to server, which includes client operation (callback) handle. Client does not wait for reply. After server services the client request, it uses the handle to call the client operation remotely (the callback).
Strengths of solution	Good way for client to communicate with server when it needs a reply but can continue executing and receive reply later.
Weaknesses of solution	Suitable only if the client does not need to send multiple requests before receiving the first reply.
Applicability	Distributed environments: client/server and distribution applications with multiple servers.
Related patterns	Consider Bidirectional Asynchronous Message Communication as alternative pattern.
Reference	Chapter 10, Section 10.3.4.

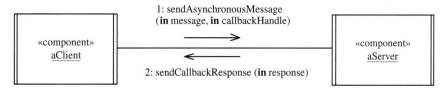

Figure B.10   *Asynchronous Message Communication with Callback pattern*

B.2.3   Bidirectional Asynchronous Message Communication Pattern

Pattern name	Bidirectional Asynchronous Message Communication.
Aliases	Bidirectional Loosely Coupled Message Communication.
Context	Concurrent or distributed systems.
Problem	Concurrent or distributed application in which concurrent components need to communicate with each other. Producer does not need to wait for consumer, although it does need to receive replies later. Producer can send several requests before receiving first reply.
Summary of solution	Use two message queues between producer component and consumer component: one for messages from producer to consumer, and one for messages from consumer to producer. Producer sends message to consumer on P→C queue and continues. Consumer receives message. Messages are queued if consumer is busy. Consumer sends replies on C→P queue.
Strengths of solution	Producer does not get held up by consumer. Producer receives replies later, when it needs them.
Weaknesses of solution	If producer produces messages more quickly than consumer can process them, the message (P→C) queue will eventually overflow. If producer does not service replies quickly enough, the reply (C→P) queue will overflow.
Applicability	Centralized and distributed environments: real-time systems, client/server and distribution applications.
Related patterns	Asynchronous Message Communication with Callback.
Reference	Chapter 10, Section 10.3.2.

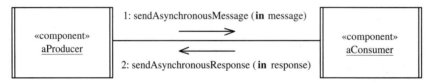

Figure B.11   *Bidirectional Asynchronous Message Communication pattern*

B.2.4   Broadcast Pattern

Pattern name	Broadcast.
Aliases	Broadcast Communication.
Context	Distributed systems.
Problem	Distributed application with multiple clients and servers. At times, servers need to send the same message to several clients.
Summary of solution	Crude form of group communication in which server sends a message to all clients, regardless of whether clients want the message or not. Client decides whether it wants to process the message or just discard the message.
Strengths of solution	Simple form of group communication.
Weaknesses of solution	Places an additional load on the client, because the client may not want the message.
Applicability	Distributed environments: client/server and distribution applications with multiple servers.
Related patterns	Similar to Subscription/Notification, except that it is not selective.
Reference	Chapter 10, Section 10.3.8.

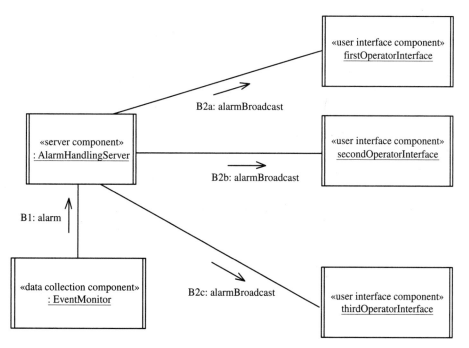

Figure B.12   *Broadcast pattern: alarm broadcast example*

B.2.5   Broker Forwarding Pattern

Pattern name	Broker Forwarding.
Aliases	White Pages Broker Forwarding, Broker with Forwarding Design.
Context	Distributed systems.
Problem	Distributed application in which multiple clients communicate with multiple servers. Clients do not know locations of servers.
Summary of solution	Use broker. Servers register their services with broker. Client sends service request to broker. Broker forwards request to server. Server services request and sends reply to broker. Broker forwards reply to client.
Strengths of solution	Location transparency: Servers may relocate easily. Clients do not need to know locations of servers.
Weaknesses of solution	Additional overhead because broker is involved in all message communication. Broker can become a bottleneck if there is a heavy load at the broker.
Applicability	Distributed environments: client/server and distribution applications with multiple servers.
Related patterns	Similar to Broker Handle; more secure, but performance is not as good.
Reference	Chapter 10, Section 10.3.6.

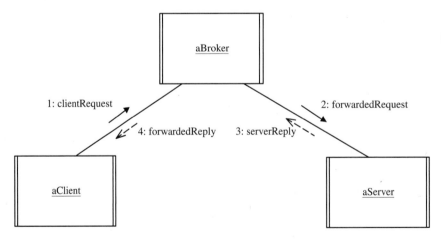

Figure B.13   *Broker Forwarding pattern*

B.2.6   Broker Handle Pattern

Pattern name	Broker Handle.
Aliases	White Pages Broker Handle, Broker with Handle-Driven Design.
Context	Distributed systems.
Problem	Distributed application in which multiple clients communicate with multiple servers. Clients do not know locations of servers.
Summary of solution	Use broker. Servers register their services with broker. Client sends service request to broker. Broker returns service handle to client. Client uses service handle to make request to server. Server services request and sends reply directly to client. Client can make multiple requests to server without broker involvement.
Strengths of solution	Location transparency: Servers may relocate easily. Clients do not need to know locations of servers.
Weaknesses of solution	Additional overhead because broker is involved in initial message communication. Broker can become a bottleneck if there is a heavy load at the broker. Client may keep outdated service handle instead of discarding.
Applicability	Distributed environments: client/server and distribution applications with multiple servers.
Related patterns	Similar to Broker Forwarding, but with better performance.
Reference	Chapter 10, Section 10.3.6.

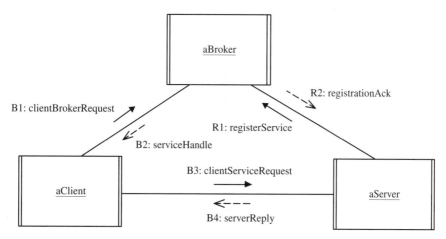

Figure B.14   *Broker Handle pattern*

B.2.7 Discovery Pattern

Pattern name	Discovery.
Aliases	Yellow Pages Broker, Broker Trader.
Context	Distributed systems.
Problem	Distributed application in which multiple clients communicate with multiple servers. Client knows the type of service required but not the specific server.
Summary of solution	Use broker's discovery service. Servers register their services with broker. Client sends discovery service request to broker. Broker returns names of all services that match discovery service request. Client selects a service and uses broker handle or forwarding service to communicate with server.
Strengths of solution	Location transparency: Servers may relocate easily. Clients do not need to know specific service, only the service type.
Weaknesses of solution	Additional overhead because broker is involved in initial message communication. Broker can become a bottleneck if there is a heavy load at the broker.
Applicability	Distributed environments: client/server and distribution applications with multiple servers.
Related patterns	Other broker patterns (Broker Forwarding, Broker Handle).
Reference	Chapter 10, Section 10.3.7.

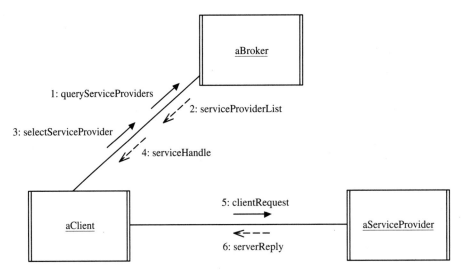

Figure B.15 *Discovery pattern*

B.2.8   Negotiation Pattern

Pattern name	Negotiation.
Aliases	Agent-Based Negotiation, Multi-Agent Negotiation.
Context	Distributed multi-agent systems.
Problem	Client needs to negotiate with multiple servers to find best available service.
Summary of solution	Client agent acts on behalf of client and makes a proposal to server agent, who acts on behalf of server. Server agent attempts to satisfy client's proposal, which might involve communication with other servers. Having determined the available options, server agent then offers client agent one or more options that come closest to matching the original client agent proposal. Client agent may then request one of the options, propose further options, or reject the offer. If server agent can satisfy client agent request, client agent accepts the request; otherwise, it rejects the request.
Strengths of solution	Provides negotiation service to complement other services.
Weaknesses of solution	Negotiation may be lengthy and inconclusive.
Applicability	Distributed environments: client/server and distribution applications with multiple servers.
Related patterns	Often used in conjunction with broker patterns (Broker Forwarding, Broker Handle, Discovery).
Reference	Chapter 10, Section 10.3.9.

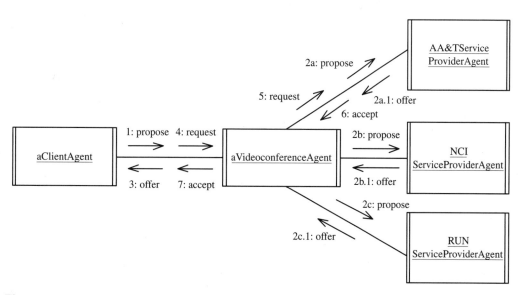

Figure B.16   *Negotiation pattern: videoconference example*

B.2.9 Subscription/Notification Pattern

Pattern name	Subscription/Notification.
Aliases	Multicast.
Context	Distributed systems.
Problem	Distributed application with multiple clients and servers. Clients want to receive messages of a given type.
Summary of solution	Selective form of group communication. Clients subscribe to receive messages of a given type. When server receives message of this type, it notifies all clients who have subscribed to it.
Strengths of solution	Selective form of group communication. Widely used on the Internet and in World Wide Web applications.
Weaknesses of solution	If client subscribes to too many servers, it may unexpectedly receive a large number of messages.
Applicability	Distributed environments: client/server and distribution applications with multiple servers.
Related patterns	Similar to Broadcast, except that it is more selective.
Reference	Chapter 10, Section 10.3.8.

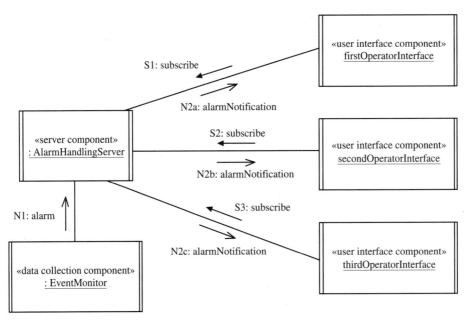

Figure B.17 *Subscription/Notification pattern: alarm notification example*

B.2.10   Synchronous Message Communication with Reply Pattern

Pattern name	Synchronous Message Communication with Reply.
Aliases	Tightly Coupled Message Communication with Reply.
Context	Concurrent or distributed systems.
Problem	Concurrent or distributed application in which multiple clients communicate with a single server. Client needs to wait for reply from server.
Summary of solution	Use tightly coupled communication between client components and server component. Client sends message to server and waits for reply. Use message queue at server because there are many clients. Server services message FIFO. Server sends reply to client. Client is activated when it receives reply from server.
Strengths of solution	Good way for client to communicate with server when it needs a reply. Very common form of communication in client/server applications.
Weaknesses of solution	Client can be held up indefinitely if there is a heavy load at the server.
Applicability	Distributed environments: client/server and distribution applications with multiple servers.
Related patterns	Asynchronous Message Communication with Callback.
Reference	Chapter 10, Section 10.3.3.

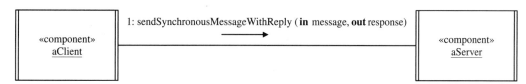

Figure B.18   *Synchronous Message Communication with Reply pattern*

B.2.11   Synchronous Message Communication without Reply Pattern

Pattern name	Synchronous Message Communication without Reply.
Aliases	Tightly Coupled Message Communication without Reply.
Context	Concurrent or distributed systems.
Problem	Concurrent or distributed application in which concurrent components need to communicate with each other. Producer needs to wait for consumer to accept message. Producer does not want to get ahead of consumer. There is no queue between producer and consumer.
Summary of solution	Use tightly coupled communication between producer and consumer. Producer sends message to consumer and waits for consumer to accept message. Consumer receives message. Consumer is suspended if no message is available. Consumer accepts message, thereby releasing producer.
Strengths of solution	Good way for producer to communicate with consumer when it wants confirmation that consumer received the message and producer does not want to get ahead of consumer.
Weaknesses of solution	Producer can be held up indefinitely if consumer is busy doing something else.
Applicability	Distributed environments: client/server and distribution applications with multiple servers.
Related patterns	Consider Synchronous Message Communication with Reply as alternative pattern.
Reference	Chapter 10, Section 10.3.5.

Figure B.19   *Synchronous Message Communication without Reply pattern*

B.3 Software Architectural Transaction Patterns

This section describes the architectural transaction patterns, which address the transaction management in client/server architectures, in alphabetical order, using the standard template.

B.3.1 Compound Transaction Pattern

Pattern name	Compound Transaction.
Aliases	
Context	Distributed systems.
Problem	Client has a transaction requirement that can be broken down into smaller, separate flat transactions.
Summary of solution	Break down compound transaction into smaller atomic transactions, where each atomic transaction can be performed separately and rolled back separately.
Strengths of solution	Provides effective support for transactions that can be broken into two or more atomic transactions. Effective if a rollback or change is required to only one of the transactions.
Weaknesses of solution	More work is required to make sure that the individual atomic transactions are consistent with each other. More coordination is required if the whole compound transaction needs to be rolled back or modified.
Applicability	Transaction processing applications, distributed databases.
Related patterns	Two-Phase Commit Protocol, Long-Living Transaction.
Reference	Chapter 10, Section 10.4.2.

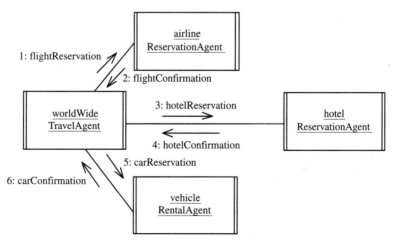

Figure B.20 *Compound Transaction pattern: airline/hotel/car reservation example*

B.3.2 Long-Living Transaction Pattern

Pattern name	Long-Living Transaction.
Aliases	
Context	Distributed systems.
Problem	Client has a long-living transaction requirement that has a human in the loop and that could take a long and possibly indefinite time to execute.
Summary of solution	Split a long-living transaction into two or more separate atomic transactions such that human decision making takes place between each successive pair of atomic transactions.
Strengths of solution	Provides effective support for long-living transactions that can be broken into two or more atomic transactions.
Weaknesses of solution	Situations may change because of long delay between successive atomic transactions that constitute the long-living transaction, resulting in an unsuccessful long-living transaction.
Applicability	Transaction processing applications, distributed databases.
Related patterns	Two-Phase Commit Protocol, Compound Transaction.
Reference	Chapter 10, Section 10.4.3.

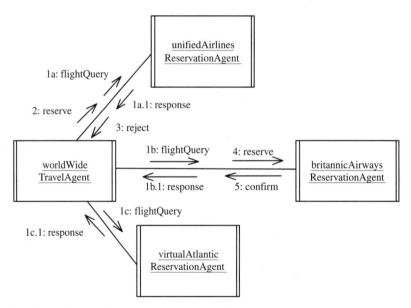

Figure B.21 *Long-Living Transaction pattern: airline reservation example*

B.3.3 Two-Phase Commit Protocol Pattern

Pattern name	Two-Phase Commit Protocol.
Aliases	Atomic Transaction.
Context	Distributed systems.
Problem	Clients generate transactions and send them to the server for processing. A transaction is atomic (i.e., indivisible). It consists of two or more operations that perform a single logical function, and it must be completed in its entirety or not at all.
Summary of solution	For atomic transactions, services are needed to begin, commit, or abort the transaction. The two-phase commit protocol is used to synchronize updates on different nodes in distributed applications. The result is that either the transaction is committed (in which case all updates succeed) or the transaction is aborted (in which case all updates fail).
Strengths of solution	Provides effective support for atomic transactions.
Weaknesses of solution	Effective only for short transactions; that is, there are no long delays between the two phases of the transaction.
Applicability	Transaction processing applications, distributed databases.
Related patterns	Compound Transaction, Long-Living Transaction.
Reference	Chapter 10, Section 10.4.1.

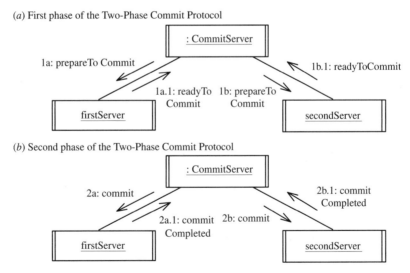

(*a*) First phase of the Two-Phase Commit Protocol

(*b*) Second phase of the Two-Phase Commit Protocol

Figure B.22 *Two-Phase Commit Protocol pattern*

Glossary

abstract class: A *class* that cannot be directly instantiated (Booch et al. 2005). Compare *concrete class*.

abstract data type: A data type that is defined by the *operations* that manipulate it and thus has its representation details hidden.

abstract interface specification: A specification that defines the external view of the *information hiding class*—that is, all the information required by the user of the *class*.

abstract operation: An *operation* that is declared in an *abstract class* but not implemented.

action: A computation that executes as a result of a *state transition*.

active object: See *concurrent object*.

activity: A computation that executes for the duration of a *state*.

actor: An outside user or related set of users who interact with the system (Rumbaugh et al. 2005).

aggregate class: A *class* that represents the whole in an *aggregation* relationship (Booch et al. 2005).

aggregate subsystem: A logical grouping of lower-level *subsystems* and/or *objects*.

aggregation: A *whole/part relationship*. Compare *composition*.

algorithm object: An object that encapsulates an algorithm used in the problem domain.

alternative feature: A *feature* that can be chosen in place of a different feature in the same *software product line*. Compare *common feature* and *optional feature*.

alternative use case: A *use case* that can be chosen in place of a different use case in the same *software product line*. Compare *kernel use case* and *optional use case*.

analysis modeling: A phase of the *PLUS* object-oriented software life cycle in which *static modeling* and *dynamic modeling* are performed. Compare *design modeling* and *requirements modeling*.

application deployment: A process for deciding which *component* instances are required, how component instances should be interconnected, and how the component instances should be allocated to physical *nodes* in a *distributed* environment.

application engineering: See *software application engineering*.

application logic object: An *object* that hides the details of the application logic separately from the data being manipulated.

architectural pattern: See *software architectural pattern*.

association: A relationship between two or more *classes*.

asynchronous component: A *component* that is activated on demand.

asynchronous I/O device: An input/output device that generates an interrupt when it has produced some input or when it has finished processing an output operation.

asynchronous message communication: A form of communication in which a *concurrent* producer component sends a message to a concurrent consumer component and does not wait for a response; a message queue could potentially build up between the concurrent components. Also referred to as *loosely coupled message communication*. Compare *synchronous message communication*.

at-least-one-of feature group: A *feature group* in which one or more *features* can be selected from the group, but at least one feature must be selected.

behavioral analysis: See *dynamic analysis*.

behavioral model: A model that describes the responses of the system to the inputs that the system receives from the external environment.

binary semaphore: A Boolean variable used to enforce *mutual exclusion*. Also referred to simply as *semaphore*.

black box specification: A specification that describes the externally visible characteristics of the system.

boundary object: See *interface object*.

broadcast communication: A form of group communication in which unsolicited messages are sent to all recipients.

broker: An intermediary in interactions between *clients* and *servers*. Also referred to as *object broker* or *object request broker*.

brokered communication: Message communication in a *distributed* object environment in which *clients* and *servers* interact via a *broker*.

business logic object: An *object* that encapsulates the business rules (business-specific application logic) for processing a *client* request.

callback: An *operation* handle sent by a *client* in an asynchronous request to a *server* and used by the server to respond to the client request.

CASE: See *Computer Aided Software Engineering*.

category: A specifically defined division in a system of classification.

class: An *object* type; hence, a template for objects. An implementation of an *abstract data type*.

class diagram: A *UML* diagram that depicts a static view of a system in terms of *classes* and the relationships between classes. Compare *interaction diagram*.

class interface specification: A specification that defines the externally visible view of a *class*, including the specification of the *operations* provided by the class.

class structuring criteria: See *object structuring criteria*.

client: A requester of services in a *client/server system*. Compare *server*.

client/server system: A system that consists of *clients* that request services and one or more *servers* that provide services.

collaboration diagram: *UML* 1.x name for *communication diagram*.

COM: See *Component Object Model*.

COMET: See *Concurrent Object Modeling and Architectural Design Method*.

commonality: The functionality that is common to all members of a *software product line*. Compare *variability*.

commonality/variability analysis: An approach for examining the functionality of a *software product line* to determine which functionality is common to all product line members and which is not.

common feature: A *feature* that must be provided by every member of the *software product line*. Compare *optional feature* and *alternative feature*.

Common Object Request Broker Architecture (CORBA): An open systems standard for *middleware* technology, developed by the Object Management

Group, that allows communication between *distributed* objects on heterogeneous platforms.

communication diagram: A *UML 2.0 interaction diagram* that depicts a dynamic view of a system in which *objects* interact by using messages. In *UML* 1.x, referred to as a *collaboration diagram*.

complex port: A *port* that supports both a *provided interface* and a *required interface*.

component: A *concurrent* self-contained *object* with a well-defined *interface*, capable of being used in different applications from that for which it was originally designed. Also referred to as *distributed component*.

component-based system: A system in which an infrastructure is provided that is specifically intended to accommodate preexisting *components*.

Component Object Model (COM): A Microsoft *component* technology that provides a framework for application interoperation in a Windows environment.

component structuring criteria: A set of heuristics for assisting a designer in structuring a system into *components*.

composite component: A *component* that contains nested components. Also referred to as *composite subsystem*. Compare *simple component*.

composite object: An *object* that contains nested objects.

composite state: A *state* on a *statechart* that is decomposed into two or more *substates*. Also referred to as a *superstate*.

composite structure diagram: A *UML 2.0* diagram that depicts the structure and interconnections of composite *classes*; often used to depict *components, ports,* and *connectors*.

composite subsystem: See *composite component*.

composition: A form of *whole/part relationship* that is stronger than an *aggregation*; the part *objects* are created, live, and die together with the composite (whole) object.

Computer Aided Software Engineering (CASE) tool: A software tool that supports a software engineering method or notation.

concrete class: A *class* that can be directly instantiated (Booch et al. 2005). Compare *abstract class*.

concurrent: Referring to a problem, process, system, or application in which many activities happen in parallel, where the order of incoming *events* is not usually predictable and is often overlapping. A concurrent system or application has many threads of control. Compare *sequential*.

concurrent collaboration diagram: See *concurrent communication diagram.*

concurrent communication diagram: A *communication diagram* that depicts a network of *concurrent* objects and their interactions in the form of *asynchronous* and *synchronous message communication.* In *UML* 1.x, referred to as a *concurrent collaboration diagram.*

concurrent object: An autonomous *object* that has its own thread of control. Also referred to as an *active object, process, task, thread, concurrent process,* or *concurrent task.*

Concurrent Object Modeling and Architectural Design Method (COMET): A software *design method* for *concurrent, distributed,* and *real-time* applications.

concurrent process: See *concurrent object.*

concurrent server: A *server* that services multiple *client* requests in parallel. Compare *sequential server.*

concurrent task: See *concurrent object.*

condition: The value of a Boolean variable that represents a particular aspect of the system that can be true or false over a finite interval of time.

connector: An *object* that encapsulates the interconnection protocol between two or more *components.*

consolidated collaboration diagram: See *integrated communication diagram.*

constraint: A *condition* that must be true.

control object: An *object* that provides overall coordination for a collection of objects.

coordinator object: An overall decision-making *object* that determines the overall sequencing for a collection of related objects and is not *state*-dependent.

CORBA: See *Common Object Request Broker Architecture.*

critical section: The section of a *concurrent object*'s internal logic that is *mutually exclusive.*

data abstraction: An approach for defining a data structure or data type by the set of *operations* that manipulate it, thus separating and hiding the representation details.

data abstraction class: A *class* that encapsulates a data structure or data type, thereby hiding the representation details; *operations* provided by the class manipulate the hidden data.

database wrapper class: A *class* that hides how to access data stored in a database.

data replication: Duplication of data in more than one location in a *distributed application* to speed up access to the data.

deadlock: A situation in which two or more *concurrent objects* are suspended indefinitely because each concurrent object is waiting for a resource acquired by another concurrent object.

default class: A *class* that is automatically selected from a group of *variant classes*, when no other class is explicitly chosen.

default feature: A *feature* out of a group of *alternative features* in the same *software product line* that is automatically chosen if no other feature is explicitly selected in its place.

delegation connector: A *connector* that joins the outer *port* of a *composite component* to the inner port of a *part component* such that messages arriving at the outer port are forwarded to the inner port.

deployment diagram: A *UML* diagram that shows the physical configuration of the system in terms of physical *nodes* and physical connections between the nodes, such as network connections.

design concept: A fundamental idea that can be applied to designing a system.

design method: A systematic approach for creating a design. The design method helps identify the design decisions to be made, the order in which to make them, and the criteria used in making them.

design modeling: A phase of the *PLUS* object-oriented software life cycle in which the *software architecture* of the system is designed. Compare *analysis modeling* and *requirements modeling*.

design notation: A graphical, symbolic, or textual means of describing a design.

design pattern: A description of a recurring design problem to be solved, a solution to the problem, and the context in which that solution works.

design strategy: An overall plan and direction for developing a design.

device interface object: An *information hiding object* that hides the characteristics of an I/O device and presents a virtual device *interface* to its users.

discrete data: Data that arrives at specific time intervals.

distributed: A system or application that is *concurrent* in nature and executes in an environment consisting of multiple *nodes*, which are in geographically different locations.

distributed application: An application that executes in a *distributed* environment.

distributed component: See *component*.

distributed kernel: The nucleus of an operating system that supports *distributed applications*.

distributed processing environment: A system configuration in which several geographically dispersed *nodes* are interconnected by means of a local area or wide area network.

distributed server: A *server* whose functionality is spread over several *nodes*.

domain analysis: Analysis of a *software product line*.

domain model: Model of a *software product line*.

domain modeling: Modeling of a *software product line*.

domain-specific pattern: A software pattern that is specific to a given *software product line*.

domain-specific software architecture: See *software product line architecture*.

dynamic analysis: A strategy to help determine how the *objects* that participate in a *use case* interact. Also referred to as *behavioral analysis*.

dynamic model: A view of a problem or system in which control and sequencing is considered, either within an *object* by means of a *finite state machine* or by consideration of the sequence of interaction among objects.

dynamic modeling: The process of developing the *dynamic model* of a system or *software product line*.

EJB: See *Enterprise JavaBeans*.

encapsulation: See *information hiding*.

Enterprise JavaBeans (EJB): A Java-based component technology.

entity class: A *class* whose instances are long-living *objects*, in many cases persistent, that encapsulate data.

entity object: A long-living *object*, in many cases persistent, that encapsulates data.

entry action: An *action* that is performed on entry into a *state*. Compare *exit action*.

ESPLEP: See *Evolutionary Software Product Line Engineering Process*.

event: (1) In *concurrent* processing, an external or internal stimulus used for synchronization purposes; it can be an external interrupt, a timer expiration, an internal signal, or an internal message. (2) On an *interaction diagram*, a stimulus that arrives at an *object* at a point in time. (3) On a *statechart*, the occurrence of a stimulus that can cause a *state transition* on a statechart.

event synchronization: Control of *concurrent object* activation by means of signals. Three types of event synchronization are possible: external interrupts, timer expiration, and internal signals from other concurrent objects.

event trace: A time-ordered description of each external input and the time at which it occurred.

Evolutionary Software Product Line Engineering Process (ESPLEP): An *iterative software development* process consisting of *software product line engineering* and *software application engineering*.

exactly-one-of feature group: A group of *features* from which one feature must always be selected for a given product line member. Also referred to as *one-and-only-one-of feature group*.

exit action: An *action* that is performed on exit from a *state*. Compare *entry action*.

Extensible Markup Language (XML): A technology that allows different systems to interoperate through exchange of data and text.

external class: A *class* that is outside the system and part of the external environment.

external event: An *event* from an external object, typically an interrupt from an external I/O device. Compare *internal event*.

explicit feature: A *feature* that can be selected individually for a given application member of the *software product line*. Compare *implicit feature*.

family of systems: See *software product line*.

feature: A functional requirement; a reusable product line requirement or characteristic. A requirement or characteristic that is provided by one or more members of the *software product line*.

feature-based impact analysis: A means of assessing the impact of a *feature* on the *software product line*, usually through *dynamic modeling*.

feature/class dependency: The relationship in which one or more *classes* support a *feature* of a *software product line* (i.e., realize the functionality defined by the feature).

feature/class dependency analysis: A means of assessing *features* and *classes* in order to determine *feature/class dependency*.

feature group: A group of *features* with a particular *constraint* on their usage in a *software product line* member.

feature modeling: The process of analyzing and specifying the *features* and *feature groups* of a *software product line*.

finite state machine: A conceptual machine with a finite number of *states* and *state transitions* that are caused by input *events*. The notation used to represent a finite state machine is a *state transition diagram, statechart,* or *state transition table.* Also referred to simply as *state machine.*

formal method: A software engineering method that uses a formal specification language—that is, a language with mathematically defined syntax and semantics.

forward evolutionary engineering: A *software product line engineering* strategy that focuses initially on analyzing the *kernel* of the *software product line* before proceeding with evolutionary development. Compare *reverse evolutionary engineering.*

generalization/specialization: A relationship in which common attributes and *operations* are abstracted into a superclass (generalized class) and are then inherited by subclasses (specialized classes).

idiom: A low-level pattern that describes an implementation solution specific to a given programming language.

implicit feature: A *feature* that is not allowed to be selected individually. Compare *explicit feature.*

incremental software development: See *iterative software development.*

information hiding: The concept of encapsulating software design decisions in *objects* in such a way that the object's *interface* reveals only what its users need to know. Also referred to as *encapsulation.*

information hiding class: A *class* that is structured according to the *information hiding* concept. The class hides an aspect of the system and is accessed by means of *operations.*

information hiding object: An instance of an *information hiding class.*

inheritance: A mechanism for sharing and reusing code between *classes.*

integrated communication diagram: A synthesis of several *communication diagrams* depicting all the *objects* and interactions shown on the individual diagrams. In *UML* 1.x, referred to as a *consolidated collaboration diagram.*

interaction diagram: A *UML* diagram that depicts a dynamic view of a system in terms of *objects* and the sequence of messages passed between them. *Communication diagrams* and *sequence diagrams* are the two main types of interaction diagrams. Compare *class diagram.*

interface: The external specification of a *class* or *component*; a collection of *operations* that are used to specify a service of a class or component (Booch et al. 2005).

interface object: An *object* that is part of the application and interfaces to the external environment. Also referred to as a *boundary object*.

internal event: A means of synchronization between two *concurrent objects*. Compare *external event*.

iterative software development: An incremental approach to developing software in stages. Also referred to as *incremental software development*.

JavaBeans: A Java-based *component* technology.

Jini: A connection technology used in embedded systems and network-based computing applications for interconnecting computers and devices.

kernel: The core of a *software product line* or operating system.

kernel class: A *class* that is required by all members of the *software product line*. Compare *optional class* and *variant class*.

kernel component: A *component* that is required by all members of the *software product line*. Compare *optional component* and *variant component*.

kernel first approach: A *dynamic modeling* approach to determine the *objects* that realize the *kernel use cases* and how they interact.

kernel object: An *object* that is required by all members of the *software product line*; an instance of a *kernel class*. Compare *optional object* and *variant object*.

kernel system: A minimal member of the *software product line* composed of the *kernel classes* and any required *default classes*.

kernel use case: A *use case* that is required by all members of the *software product line*. Compare *optional use case* and *alternative use case*.

loosely coupled message communication: See *asynchronous message communication*.

mathematical model: A mathematical representation of a system.

message buffer and response connector: A *connector* object that encapsulates the communication mechanism for *synchronous message communication with reply*.

message buffer connector: A *connector* object that encapsulates the communication mechanism for *synchronous message communication without reply*.

message dictionary: A collection of definitions of all aggregate messages depicted on *interaction diagrams* that consist of several individual messages.

message queue connector: A *connector* object that encapsulates the communication mechanism for *asynchronous message communication*.

message sequence description: A narrative description of the sequence of messages sent from source objects to destination objects, as depicted on a *com-*

munication diagram or *sequence diagram*, describing what happens when each message arrives at a destination object.

middleware: A layer of software that sits above the heterogeneous operating system to provide a uniform platform above which *distributed applications* can run (Bacon 1997).

monitor: A data *object* that encapsulates data and has operations that are executed *mutually exclusively*.

multicast communication: See *subscription/notification*.

multiple readers and writers: An algorithm that allows multiple readers to access a shared data repository concurrently; however, writers must have mutually exclusive access to update the data repository. Compare *mutual exclusion*.

mutual exclusion: An algorithm that allows only one concurrent object to have access to shared data at a time, which can be enforced by means of *binary semaphores* or through the use of *monitors*. Compare *multiple readers and writers*.

mutually exclusive feature group: A *feature group* from which no more than one *feature* can be selected for any given *software product line* member. Compare *mutually inclusive feature*.

mutually inclusive feature: A *feature* that must be used together with another feature. Compare *mutually exclusive feature group*.

negotiated communication: A communication approach used in multi-agent systems to allow software agents to negotiate with each other so that they can cooperatively make decisions.

node: In a *distributed* environment, a unit of deployment, usually consisting of one or more processors with shared memory.

object: An instance of a *class* that contains both hidden data and *operations* on that data.

object-based design: A software *design method* based on the concept of *information hiding*.

object broker: See *broker*.

object-oriented analysis: An analysis method that emphasizes identifying real-world objects in the problem domain and mapping them to software *objects*.

object-oriented design: A software *design method* based on the concept of *objects*, *classes*, and *inheritance*.

object request broker: See *broker*.

object structuring criteria: A set of heuristics for assisting a designer in structuring a system into *objects*. Also referred to as *class stucturing criteria*.

one-and-only-one-of feature group: See *exactly-one-of feature group*.

operation: A specification of a function performed by a *class*. An access procedure or function provided by a class.

optional class: A *class* that is required by some members of the *software product line*. Compare *kernel class* and *variant class*.

optional component: A *component* that is required by some members of the *software product line*. Compare *kernel component* and *variant component*.

optional feature: A *feature* that is required by some members of the *software product line*. Compare *common feature* and *alternative feature*.

optional object: An *object* that is required by some members of the *software product line*; an instance of an *optional class*. Compare *kernel object* and *variant object*.

optional use case: A *use case* that is required by some members of the *software product line*. Compare *kernel use case* and *alternative use case*.

package: A grouping of *UML* model elements.

parameterized feature: A *feature* that defines a *software product line* parameter whose value needs to be defined for a given product line member.

part component: A *component* within a *composite component*.

passive I/O device: A device that does not generate an interrupt on completion of an input or output *operation*. The input from a passive input device needs to be read either on a polled basis or on demand.

passive object: An *object* that has no thread of control; an object with *operations* that are invoked directly or indirectly by *concurrent objects*.

performance analysis: A quantitative analysis of a *real-time* software design conceptually executing on a given hardware configuration with a given external workload applied to it.

performance model: An abstraction of the real computer system behavior, developed for the purpose of gaining greater insight into the performance of the system, whether or not the system actually exists.

periodic object: A *concurrent object* that is activated periodically (i.e., at regular, equally spaced intervals of time) by a *timer event*.

PLUS: See *Product Line UML-Based Software Engineering*.

port: A connection point through which a *component* communicates with other components.

prerequisite feature: A *feature* that another feature depends on.

primary actor: An *actor* that initiates a *use case*. Compare *secondary actor*.

priority message queue: A queue in which each message has an associated priority. The consumer always accepts higher-priority messages before lower-priority messages.

process: See *concurrent object*.

product family: See *software product line*.

product family engineering: See *software product line engineering*.

product line: See *software product line*.

product line context class diagram: See *software product line context class diagram*.

product line engineering: See *software product line engineering*.

Product Line UML-Based Software Engineering (PLUS): A *design method* for *software product lines* that describes how to conduct *requirements modeling, analysis modeling*, and *design modeling* for software product lines in *UML*.

product line scoping: See *software product line scoping*.

product line system: See *software product line system*.

provided interface: A collection of *operations* that specify the services that a *component* must fulfill. Compare *required interface*.

provided port: A *port* that supports a *provided interface*. Compare *required port*.

pseudocode: A form of structured English used to describe the algorithmic details of an *object*.

queuing model: A mathematical representation of a computer system that analyzes contention for limited resources.

Rational Unified Process (RUP): See *Unified Software Development Process (USDP)*.

real-time: Referring to a problem, system, or application that is *concurrent* in nature and has timing *constraints* whereby incoming *events* must be processed within a given time frame.

remote method invocation (RMI): A *middleware* technology that allows *distributed* Java *objects* to communicate with each other.

required interface: The services that another *component* (or *object*) provides for a given component (or object) to operate properly in a particular environment. Compare *provided interface*.

required port: A *port* that supports a *required interface*. Compare *provided port*.

requirements modeling: A phase of the *PLUS* object-oriented software life cycle in which the functional requirements of the system are determined through the development of *use case models* and *feature models*. Compare *analysis modeling* and *design modeling*.

reuse category: A classification of a modeling element (*use case, feature, class,* etc.) in a *software product line* by its reuse properties, such as *kernel* or *optional*. Compare *role category*.

reuse stereotype: A *UML* notation for depicting the *reuse category* of a modeling element.

reverse evolutionary engineering: A product line engineering strategy that reverse-engineers the *software product line* functional requirements by analyzing existing systems and then integrating the individual *use case models* into a product line use case model, before proceeding with evolutionary development. Compare *forward evolutionary engineering*.

RMI: See *remote method invocation*.

role category: A classification of a modeling element (*class, object, component*) by the role it plays in an application, such as *control* or *entity*. Compare *reuse category*.

role stereotype: A *UML* notation for depicting the *role category* of a modeling element.

RUP: See *Rational Unified Process*.

scenario: A specific path through a *use case*.

secondary actor: An *actor* that participates in (but does not initiate) a *use case*. Compare *primary actor*.

semaphore: See *binary semaphore*.

sequence diagram: A *UML* 2.0 *interaction diagram* that depicts a dynamic view of a system in which the objects participating in the interaction are depicted horizontally, the vertical dimension represents time, and the sequence of message interactions is depicted from top to bottom.

sequential: Referring to a problem, process, system, or application in which activities happen in strict sequence; a sequential system or application has only one thread of control. Compare *concurrent*.

sequential server: A *server* that completes one *client* request before it starts servicing the next. Compare *concurrent server*.

server: A provider of services in a *client/server system*. Compare *client*.

simple component: A *component* that has no components within it. Compare *composite component*.

simulation model: An algorithmic representation of a system, reflecting system structure and behavior, that explicitly recognizes the passage of time, hence providing a means of analyzing the behavior of the system over time.

software application engineering: A process within *software product line engineering* in which the *software product line architecture* is adapted and tailored to derive a given software application, which is a member of the *software product line*. Also referred to as *application engineering*.

software architectural pattern: A recurring architecture used in a variety of software applications. Also referred to simply as *architectural pattern*.

software architectural communication pattern: A *software architectural pattern* that addresses the dynamic communication among *distributed components* of the *software architecture*.

software architectural structure pattern: A *software architectural pattern* that addresses the static structure of the *software architecture*.

software architecture: A high-level design that describes the overall structure of a system in terms of *components* and their interconnections, separately from the internal details of the individual components.

software decision class: A *class* that hides a software design decision that is considered likely to change.

software product family: See *software product line*.

software product family engineering: See *software product line engineering*.

software product line: A family of software systems that have some common functionality and some variable functionality; a set of software-intensive systems sharing a common, managed set of *features* that satisfy the specific needs of a particular market segment or mission and that are developed from a common set of core assets in a prescribed way (Clements and Northrop 2002). Also referred to as *family of systems, software product family, product family,* or *product line*.

software product line architecture: The architecture for a family of products, which describes the kernel, optional, and variable *components* in the *software product line*, and their interconnections. Also referred to as *domain-specific software architecture*.

software product line context class diagram: A *class diagram* that defines the hardware/software boundary of a member of the *software product line*. Also referred to as *product line context class diagram*.

software product line engineering: A process for analyzing the *commonality* and *variability* in a *software product line*, and developing a product line *use case* *model*, product line *analysis model*, *software product line architecture*, and reusable *components*. Also referred to as *software product family engineering*, *product family engineering*, or *product line engineering*.

software product line evolution approach: A *dynamic modeling* approach to determine the *objects* that realize the *optional* and *alternative use cases* and how they interact.

software product line scoping: An early *software product line* feasibility study to provide a preliminary estimate of the size of the product line, the degree of common functionality with respect to total product line functionality, the degree of variable functionality in the product line, and a preliminary identification of the potential members of the product line. Also referred to as *product line scoping*.

software product line system: A member of the *software product line*. Also referred to as *product line system*.

spiral model: A risk-driven software process model.

state: A recognizable situation that exists over an interval of time.

statechart: A *UML* hierarchical *state transition diagram* in which the *nodes* represent *states* and the arcs represent *state transitions*. Also referred to as *statechart diagram*.

statechart diagram: See *statechart*.

state-dependent control object: An *information hiding object* that hides the details of a *finite state machine*; that is, the object encapsulates a *statechart*, a *state transition diagram*, or the contents of a *state transition table*.

state machine: See *finite state machine*.

state transition: A change in *state* that is caused by an input *event*.

state transition diagram: A graphical representation of a *finite state machine* in which the *nodes* represent *states* and the arcs represent transitions between states.

state transition table: A tabular representation of a *finite state machine*.

static modeling: The process of developing a static, structural view of a problem, system, or *software product line*.

stereotype: A classification that defines a new building block that is derived from an existing *UML* modeling element but is tailored to the modeler's problem (Booch et al. 2005).

subscription/notification: A form of group communication in which subscribers receive *event* notifications. Also referred to as *multicast communication*.

substate: A *state* that is part of a *superstate*.

subsystem: A significant part of the whole system; a subsystem provides a subset of the overall system functionality.

subsystem communication diagram: A high-level *communication diagram* depicting the *subsystems* and their interactions.

superstate: A *composite state*.

synchronous message communication: A form of communication in which a producer *component* sends a message to a consumer component and then immediately waits for an acknowledgment. Also referred to as *tightly coupled message communication*. Compare *asynchronous message communication*.

synchronous message communication with reply: A form of communication in which a client (or producer) *component* sends a message to a server (or consumer) component and then waits for a reply. Also referred to as *tightly coupled message communication with reply*.

synchronous message communication without reply: A form of communication in which a producer *component* sends a message to a consumer component and then waits for acceptance of the message by the consumer. Also referred to as *tightly coupled message communication without reply*.

system context class diagram: A *class diagram* that depicts the relationships between the system (depicted as one *aggregate class*) and the *external classes* outside the system.

system context model: A model of a system or *software product line* boundary that is depicted on a *system context class diagram*.

system interface object: An *object* that hides the *interface* to an external system or *subsystem*.

task: See *concurrent object*.

task architecture: A description of the *concurrent objects* in a system or *subsystem* in terms of their *interfaces* and interconnections.

thread: See *concurrent object*.

tightly coupled message communication: See *synchronous message communication*.

tightly coupled message communication with reply: See *synchronous message communication with reply*.

tightly coupled message communication without reply: See *synchronous message communication without reply*.

timer event: A stimulus used for the periodic activation of a *concurrent object*.

timer object: A *control object* that is activated by an external timer.

timing diagram: A diagram that shows the time-ordered execution sequence of a group of *concurrent objects*.

transaction: A request from a *client* to a *server* consisting of two or more *operations* that must be completed in its entirety or not at all.

two-phase commit protocol: An algorithm used in *distributed applications* to synchronize updates to ensure that an atomic transaction is either committed or aborted.

UML: See *Unified Modeling Language.*

Unified Modeling Language (UML): A language for visualizing, specifying, constructing, and documenting the artifacts of a software-intensive system (Booch et al. 2005).

Unified Software Development Process (USDP): An iterative *use case*-driven software process that uses the *UML* notation. Also known as the *Rational Unified Process (RUP).*

USDP: See *Unified Software Development Process.*

use case: A description of a sequence of interactions between one or more *actors* and the system.

use case diagram: A *UML* diagram that shows a set of *use cases* and *actors* and their relationships (Booch et al. 2005).

use case model: A description of the functional requirements of the system or product line in terms of *actors* and *use cases.*

use case modeling: The process of developing the *use cases* of a system or *software product line.*

use case package: A group of related *use cases.*

user interface object: An *object* that hides the details of the *interface* to a human user.

variability: The functionality that is provided by some but not all members of the *software product line.* Compare *commonality.*

variant class: A *class* that is similar to but not identical to another class; a subclass that is similar to but not identical to another subclass of the same superclass. Compare *kernel class* and *optional class.*

variant component: A *component* that is similar to but not identical to another component. Compare *kernel component* and *optional component.*

variant object: An *object* that is similar to but not identical to another object; an instance of a *variant class*. Compare *kernel object* and *optional object*.

variation point: A location at which change can occur in a *software product line* artifact (e.g., in a *use case* or *class*).

visibility: The characteristic that defines whether an element of a *class* is visible from outside the class.

Web service: Business functionality provided by a service provider over the Internet to users of the World Wide Web.

white page brokering: A pattern of communication between a *client* and a *broker* in which the client knows the service required but not the location. Compare *yellow page brokering*.

whole/part relationship: A *composition* or *aggregation* relationship in which a whole class is composed of part classes.

wrapper component: A *distributed component* that handles the communication and management of *client* requests to legacy applications (Mowbray and Ruh 1997).

XML: See *Extensible Markup Language*.

yellow page brokering: A pattern of communication between a *client* and a *broker* in which the client knows the type of service required but not the specific service. Compare *white page brokering*.

zero-or-more-of feature group: A *feature group* consisting of *optional features*.

zero-or-one-of feature group: A *feature group* in which all *features* are *mutually exclusive*.

Bibliography

Alexander, C. 1979. *The Timeless Way of Building*. New York: Oxford University Press.

Arnold, K., B. O'Sullivan, R. W. Scheifler, J. Waldo, and A. Wollrath. 1999. *The Jini Specification*. Reading, MA: Addison-Wesley.

Atkinson, C., J. Bayer, O. Laitenberger, D. Muthig, C. Bunse, E. Kamsties, R. Laqua, B. Paech, J. Wust, and J. Zettel. 2002. *Component-Based Product Line Engineering with UML*. Boston: Addison-Wesley.

Awad, M., J. Kuusela, and J. Ziegler. 1996. *Object-Oriented Technology for RealTime Systems: A Practical Approach Using OMT and Fusion*. Upper Saddle River, NJ: Prentice Hall.

Bacon, J. 1997. *Concurrent Systems: An Integrated Approach to Operating Systems, Database, and Distributed Systems*, 2nd ed. Reading, MA: Addison-Wesley.

Bass, L., P. Clements, and R. Kazman. 2003. *Software Architecture in Practice*, 2nd ed. Boston: Addison-Wesley.

Bayer, J., O. Flege, P. Knauber, R. Laqua, D. Muthig, K. Schmid, T. Widen, and J. DeBaud. 1999. "PuLSE: A Methodology to Develop Software Product Lines." In *Proceedings of the Fifth Symposium on Software Reusability, SSR'99: Bridging the Gap between Research and Practice: May 21–23, 1999, Los Angeles, CA, USA*, pp. 122–131. New York: ACM Press.

Berners-Lee, T., R. Cailliau, A. Loutonen, H. F. Nielsen, and A. Secret. 1994. "The World-Wide Web." *Communications of the ACM* 37: 76–82.

Bjorkander, M., and C. Kobryn. 2003. "Architecting Systems with UML 2.0." *IEEE Software* 20(4): 57–61.

Blaha, J. M., and W. Premerlani. 1998. *Object-Oriented Modeling and Design for Database Applications*. Upper Saddle River, NJ: Prentice Hall.

Boehm, B. 1988. "A Spiral Model of Software Development and Enhancement." *IEEE Computer* 21(5): 61–72.

Boehm, B., and F. Belz. 1990. "Experiences with the Spiral Model as a Process Model Generator." In *Proceedings of the 5th International Software Process Workshop: "Experience with Software Process Models," Kennebunkport, Maine, USA, October 10–13, 1989*, D. E. Perry (ed.), pp. 43–45. Los Alamitos, CA: IEEE Computer Society Press.

Booch, G. 1994. *Object-Oriented Analysis and Design with Applications*, 2nd ed. Reading, MA: Addison-Wesley.

Booch, G., J. Rumbaugh, and I. Jacobson. 2005.* *The Unified Modeling Language User Guide*, 2nd ed. Boston: Addison-Wesley. (*In press, to be published Fall 2004.)

Bosch, J. 2000. *Design & Use of Software Architectures: Adopting and Evolving a Product-Line Approach*. Boston: Addison-Wesley.

Box, D. 1998. *Essential COM*. Reading, MA: Addison-Wesley.

Brooks, F. 1995. *The Mythical Man-Month: Essays on Software Engineering*, anniversary ed. Reading, MA: Addison-Wesley.

Brown, A. 2000. *Large-Scale, Component-Based Development*. Upper Saddle River, NJ: Prentice Hall PTR.

Budgen, D. 2003. *Software Design*, 2nd ed. Boston: Addison-Wesley.

Buhr, R. J. A., and R. S. Casselman. 1996. *Use Case Maps for Object-Oriented Systems*. Upper Saddle River, NJ: Prentice Hall.

Buschmann, F., R. Meunier, H. Rohnert, P. Sommerlad, and M. Stal. 1996. *Pattern-Oriented Software Architecture: A System of Patterns*. New York: Wiley.

Cheesman, J., and J. Daniels. 2001. *UML Components*. Boston: Addison-Wesley.

Clements, P., and Northrop, L. 2002. *Software Product Lines: Practices and Patterns*. Boston: Addison-Wesley.

Coad, P., and E. Yourdon. 1991. *Object-Oriented Analysis*. Upper Saddle River, NJ: Prentice Hall.

Coad, P., and E. Yourdon. 1992. *Object-Oriented Design*. Upper Saddle River, NJ: Prentice Hall.

Cohen, S., and L. Northrop. 1998. "Object-Oriented Technology and Domain Analysis." In *Fifth International Conference on Software Reuse: Proceedings:*

June 2–5, 1998, Victoria, British Columbia, Canada, P. Devanbu and J. Poulin (eds.), pp. 86–93. Los Alamitos, CA: IEEE Computer Society Press.

Coleman, D., P. Arnold, S. Bodoff, C. Dollin, H. Gilchrist, F. Hayes, and P. Jeremaes. 1993. *Object-Oriented Development: The Fusion Method*. Upper Saddle River, NJ: Prentice Hall.

Comer, D. E. 2004. *Computer Networks and Internets with Internet Applications*, 4th ed. Upper Saddle River, NJ: Pearson/Prentice Hall.

Coplien, J., D. Hoffman, and D. Weiss. 1998. "Commonality and Variability in Software Engineering." *IEEE Software* 15(6): 37–45.

Coulouris, G., J. Dollimore, and T. Kindberg. 2000. *Distributed Systems: Concepts and Design*, 3rd ed. Boston: Addison-Wesley.

Dahl, O., and C. A. R. Hoare. 1972. "Hierarchical Program Structures." In *Structured Programming*, O. Dahl, E. W. Dijkstra, and C. A. R. Hoare (eds.), pp. 175–220. London: Academic Press.

Davis, A. 1993. *Software Requirements: Objects, Functions, and States*, 2nd ed. Upper Saddle River, NJ: Prentice Hall.

Davis, A. 1995. *201 Principles of Software Development*. New York: McGraw Hill.

DeBaud, J. M., and K. Schmid. 1999. "A Systematic Approach to Derive the Scope of Software Product Lines." In *Proceedings of the IEEE International Conference on Software Engineering, Los Angeles, May, 1999*, pp. 34–43. Los Alamitos, CA: IEEE Computer Society Press.

Dijkstra, E. W. 1968. "The Structure of T.H.E Multiprogramming System." *Communications of the ACM* 11: 341–346.

Douglass, B. P. 1999. *Doing Hard Time: Developing Real-Time Systems with UML, Objects, Frameworks, and Patterns*. Reading, MA: Addison-Wesley.

Douglass, B. P. 2002. *Real-Time Design Patterns: Robust Scalable Architecture for Real-Time Systems*. Boston: Addison-Wesley.

Douglass, B. P. 2004. *Real Time UML: Advances in the UML for Real-Time Systems*, 3rd ed. Boston: Addison-Wesley.

Eeles, P., K. Houston, and W. Kozaczynski. 2002. *Building J2EE Applications with the Rational Unified Process*. Boston: Addison-Wesley.

Eriksson, H. E., M. Penker, B. Lyons, and D. Fado. 2004. *UML 2 Toolkit*. Indianapolis, IN: Wiley.

Fowler, M. 2002. *Patterns of Enterprise Application Architecture*. Boston: Addison-Wesley.

Fowler, M. 2004. *UML Distilled: Applying the Standard Object Modeling Language*, 3rd ed. Boston: Addison-Wesley.

Freeman, P. 1983a. "The Context of Design." In *Tutorial on Software Design Techniques*, 4th ed., P. Freeman and A. I. Wasserman (eds.), pp. 2–4. Silver Spring, MD: IEEE Computer Society Press.

Freeman, P. 1983b. "The Nature of Design." In *Tutorial on Software Design Techniques*, 4th ed., P. Freeman and A. I. Wasserman (eds.), pp. 46–53. Silver Spring, MD: IEEE Computer Society Press.

Freeman, P., and A. I. Wasserman (eds.). 1983. *Tutorial on Software Design Techniques*, 4th ed. Silver Spring, MD: IEEE Computer Society Press.

Gamma, E., R. Helm, R. Johnson, and J. Vlissides. 1995. *Design Patterns: Elements of Reusable Object-Oriented Software*. Reading, MA: Addison-Wesley.

Genesereth, M. R.., and S. P. Ketchpel. 1994. "Software Agents." *CACM* 37: 48–53.

Goldberg, A., and D. Robson. 1983. *Smalltalk-80: The Language and Its Implementation*. Reading, MA: Addison-Wesley.

Gomaa, H. 1984. "A Software Design Method for Real Time Systems." *Communications of the ACM* 27(9): 938–949.

Gomaa, H. 1986. "Software Development of Real Time Systems." *Communications of the ACM* 29(7): 657–668.

Gomaa, H. 1989a. "A Software Design Method for Distributed Real-Time Applications." *Journal of Systems and Software* 9: 81–94.

Gomaa, H. 1989b. "Structuring Criteria for Real Time System Design." In *Proceedings of the 11th International Conference on Software Engineering, May 15–18, 1989, Pittsburg, PA, USA*, pp. 290–301. Los Alamitos, CA: IEEE Computer Society Press.

Gomaa H. 1990. "The Impact of Prototyping on Software System Engineering." In *Systems and Software Requirements Engineering*, pp. 431–440. Los Alamitos, CA: IEEE Computer Society Press.

Gomaa, H. 1993. *Software Design Methods for Concurrent and Real-Time Systems*. Reading, MA: Addison-Wesley.

Gomaa, H. 1995. "Reusable Software Requirements and Architectures for Families of Systems." *Journal of Systems and Software* 28: 189–202.

Gomaa, H. 2001. "Use Cases for Distributed Real-Time Software Architectures." In *Engineering of Distributed Control Systems*, L. R. Welch and D. K. Hammer (eds.), pp. 1–18. Commack, NY: Nova Science.

Gomaa, H. 1999. "Inter-Agent Communication in Cooperative Information Agent-Based Systems." In *Cooperative Information Agents III: Third International Workshop, CIA'99, Uppsala, Sweden, July 31–August 2, 1999: Proceedings*, pp. 137–148. Berlin: Springer.

Gomaa, H. 2000. *Designing Concurrent, Distributed, and Real-Time Applications with UML.* Boston: Addison-Wesley.

Gomaa, H. 2002. "Concurrent Systems Design." In *Encyclopedia of Software Engineering*, 2nd ed., J. Marciniak (ed.), pp. 172–179. New York: Wiley.

Gomaa, H., and G. Farrukh. 1997. "Automated Configuration of Distributed Applications from Reusable Software Architectures." In *Proceedings of the IEEE International Conference on Automated Software Engineering, Lake Tahoe, November 1997*, pp. 193–200. Los Alamitos, CA: IEEE Computer Society Press.

Gomaa, H., and G. A. Farrukh. 1999. "Methods and Tools for the Automated Configuration of Distributed Applications from Reusable Software Architectures and Components." *IEEE Proceedings – Software* 146(6): 277–290.

Gomaa, H., and D. Menasce. 2001. "Performance Engineering of Component-Based Distributed Software Systems." In *Performance Engineering: State of the Art and Current Trends*, R. Dumke, C. Rautenstrauch, A. Schmietendorf, and A. Scholz (eds.), pp. 40–55. Berlin: Springer.

Gomaa, H., and E. O'Hara. 1998. "Dynamic Navigation in Multiple View Software Specifications and Designs." *Journal of Systems and Software* 41: 93–103.

Gomaa, H., and D. B. H. Scott. 1981. "Prototyping as a Tool in the Specification of User Requirements." In *Proceedings of the 5th International Conference on Software Engineering, San Diego, March 1981*, pp. 333–342. New York: ACM Press.

Gomaa, H., and M. E. Shin. 2002. "Multiple-View Meta-Modeling of Software Product Lines." In *Eighth International Conference on Engineering of Complex Computer Systems, December 02–04, 2002, Greenbelt, Maryland*, pp. 238–246. Los Alamitos, CA: IEEE Computer Society.

Gomaa, H., and D. Webber. 2004. "Modeling Adaptive and Evolvable Software Product Lines Using the Variation Point Model." In *Proceedings of the 37th Annual Hawaii International Conference on System Sciences, HICSS'04: January 05–08, 2004, Big Island, Hawaii, USA*, pp. 1–10. Los Alamitos, CA, IEEE Computer Society Press.

Gomaa, H., L. Kerschberg, V. Sugumaran, C. Bosch, I. Tavakoli, and L. O'Hara. 1996. "A Knowledge-Based Software Engineering Environment for Reusable Software Requirements and Architectures." *Journal of Automated Software Engineering* 3(3/4): 285–307.

Gomaa, H., D. Menasce, and L. Kerschberg. 1996. "A Software Architectural Design Method for Large-Scale Distributed Information Systems." *Journal of Distributed Systems Engineering* 3(3): 162–172.

Griss, M., J. Favaro, and M. d'Alessandro. 1998. "Integrating Feature Modeling with the RSEB." In *Fifth International Conference on Software Reuse: Proceedings: June 2–5, 1998, Victoria, British Columbia, Canada*, P. Devanbu and J. Poulin (eds.), pp. 1–10. Los Alamitos, CA: IEEE Computer Society Press.

Harel, D. 1987. "Statecharts: A Visual Formalism for Complex Systems." *Science of Computer Programming* 8: 231–274.

Harel, D. 1988. "On Visual Formalisms." *CACM* 31: 514–530.

Harel, D., and E. Gery. 1996. "Executable Object Modeling with Statecharts." In *Proceedings of the 18th International Conference on Software Engineering, Berlin, March 1996*, pp. 246–257. Los Alamitos, CA: IEEE Computer Society Press.

Harel, D., and M. Politi. 1998. *Modeling Reactive Systems with Statecharts: The Statemate Approach*. New York: McGraw-Hill.

Hayes-Roth, B. 1995. "A Domain-Specific Software Architecture for Adaptive Intelligent Systems." *IEEE Transactions on Software Engineering* 21: 288–301.

Hoffman, D., and D. Weiss (eds.). 2001. *Software Fundamentals: Collected Papers by David L. Parnas*. Boston: Addison-Wesley.

Hofmeister, C., R. Nord, and D. Soni. 2000. *Applied Software Architecture*. Boston: Addison-Wesley.

Jackson, M. 1983. *System Development*. Upper Saddle River, NJ: Prentice Hall.

Jacobson, I. 1992. *Object-Oriented Software Engineering: A Use Case Driven Approach*. Reading, MA: Addison-Wesley.

Jacobson, I., G. Booch, and J. Rumbaugh. 1999. *The Unified Software Development Process*. Reading, MA: Addison-Wesley.

Jacobson, I., M. Griss, and P. Jonsson. 1997. *Software Reuse: Architecture, Process and Organization for Business Success*. Reading, MA: Addison-Wesley.

Jazayeri, M., A. Ran, and P. van der Linden. 2000. *Software Architecture for Product Families: Principles and Practice*. Boston: Addison-Wesley.

Kang, K., S. Cohen, J. Hess, W. Novak, and A. Peterson. 1990. *Feature-Oriented Domain Analysis (FODA) Feasibility Study* (Technical Report No. CMU/SEI-90-TR-021). Pittsburgh, PA: Software Engineering Institute. Available online at http://www.sei.cmu.edu/publications/documents/90.reports/90.tr.021.html.

Keepence, B., and M. Mannion. 1999. "Using Patterns to Model Variability in Product Families." *IEEE Software* 16(4): 102–108.

Kobryn, C. 1999. "UML 2001: A Standardization Odyssey." *Communications of the ACM* 42(10): 29–37. New York: ACM Press.

Kramer, J., and J. Magee. 1985. "Dynamic Configuration for Distributed Systems." *IEEE Transactions on Software Engineering* 11(4): 424–436.

Kroll, P., and P. Kruchten. 2003. *The Rational Unified Process Made Easy: A Practitioner's Guide to the RUP*. Boston: Addison-Wesley.

Kruchten, P. 2003. *The Rational Unified Process: An Introduction*, 3rd ed. Boston: Addison-Wesley.

Larman, C. 2002. *Applying UML and Patterns*, 2nd ed. Boston: Prentice Hall.

Lea, D. 2000. *Concurrent Programming in Java: Design Principles and Patterns*, 2nd ed. Boston: Addison-Wesley.

Magee, J., and J. Kramer. 1999. *Concurrency: State Models & Java Programs*. Chichester, England: Wiley.

Magee, J., N. Dulay, and J. Kramer. 1994. "Regis: A Constructive Development Environment for Parallel and Distributed Programs." *Journal of Distributed Systems Engineering* 1(5): 304–312.

Magee, J., J. Kramer, and M. Sloman. 1989. "Constructing Distributed Systems in Conic." *IEEE Transactions on Software Engineering* 15(6): 663–675.

McComas, D., S. Leake, M. Stark, M. Morisio, G. Travassos, and M. White. 2000. "Addressing Variability in a Guidance, Navigation, and Control Flight Software Product Line." In *Software Product Lines: Experience and Research Directions: **Proceedings** of the First Software Product Lines Conference (SPLC1), August 28–31, 2000, Denver, Colorado*, P. Donohoe (ed.), pp. 1–11. Boston: Kluwer Academic.

Menascé, D. A., and H. Gomaa. 1998. "On a Language Based Method for Software Performance Engineering of Client/Server Systems." In *First International Workshop on Software Performance Engineering, Santa Fe, New Mexico, October 12-16, 1998*, pp. 63–69. New York: ACM Press.

Menascé, D. A., and H. Gomaa. 2000. "A Method for Design and Performance Modeling of Client/Server Systems." *IEEE Transactions on Software Engineering* 26: 1066–1085.

Menascé, D. A., H. Gomaa, and L. Kerschberg. 1995. "A Performance-Oriented Design Methodology for Large-Scale Distributed Data Intensive Information Systems." In *First IEEE International Conference on Engineering of Complex Computer Systems, Held Jointly with 5th CSESAW, 3rd IEEE RTAW and 20th IFAC/IFIP WRTP: Proceedings, Ft. Lauderdale, Florida, USA, November 6–10, 1995*, pp. 72–79. Los Alamitos, CA: IEEE Computer Society Press.

Meyer, B. 1989. "Reusability: The Case for Object-Oriented Design." In *Software Reusability,* Vol. 2: *Applications and Experience,* T. J. Biggerstaff and A. J. Perlis (eds.), pp. 1–33. New York: ACM Press.

Meyer, B. 1997. *Object-Oriented Software Construction,* 2nd ed. Upper Saddle River, NJ: Prentice Hall.

Mills, K., and H. Gomaa. 1996. "A Knowledge-Based Approach for Automating a Design Method for Concurrent and Real-Time Systems." In *Proceedings of the 8th International Conference on Software Engineering and Knowledge Engineering,* pp. 529–536. Skokie, IL: Knowledge Systems Institute.

Mills, K., and H. Gomaa. 2002. "Knowledge-Based Automation of a Design Method for Concurrent and Real-Time Systems." *IEEE Transactions on Software Engineering* 28(3): 228–255.

Morisio, M., G. H. Travassos, and M. E. Stark. 2000. "Extending UML to Support Domain Analysis." In *15th International Conference on Automated Software Engineering 2000,* pp. 321–324. Los Alamitos, CA: IEEE Computer Society Press.

Mowbray, T., and W. Ruh. 1997. *Inside CORBA: Distributed Object Standards and Applications.* Reading, MA: Addison-Wesley.

Orfali, R., and D. Harkey. 1998. *Client/Server Programming with Java and CORBA,* 2nd ed. New York: Wiley.

Orfali, R., D. Harkey, and J. Edwards. 1996. *Essential Distributed Objects Survival Guide.* New York: Wiley.

Orfali, R., D. Harkey, and J. Edwards. 1999. *Essential Client/Server Survival Guide,* 3rd ed. New York: Wiley.

Page-Jones, M. 2000. *Fundamentals of Object-Oriented Design in UML.* Boston: Addison-Wesley.

Parnas, D. 1972. "On the Criteria to Be Used in Decomposing a System into Modules." *Communications of the ACM* 15: 1053–1058.

Parnas, D. 1974. "On a 'Buzzword': Hierarchical Structure." In *Proceedings of IFIP Congress 74, Stockholm, Sweden,* pp. 336–339. Amsterdam: North Holland.

Parnas, D. 1979. "Designing Software for Ease of Extension and Contraction." *IEEE Transactions on Software Engineering* 5(2): 128–138.

Parnas, D., and D. Weiss. 1985. "Active Design Reviews: Principles and Practices." In *Proceedings, 8th International Conference on Software Engineering, August 28–30, 1985, London, UK,* pp. 132–136. Los Alamitos, CA: IEEE Computer Society Press.

Parnas, D., P. Clements, and D. Weiss. 1984. "The Modular Structure of Complex Systems." In *Proceedings, 7th International Conference on Software Engineering, March 26–29, 1984, Orlando, Florida*, pp. 408–419. Los Alamitos, CA: IEEE Computer Society Press.

Pettit, R., and H. Gomaa. 1996. "Integrating Petri Nets with Design Methods for Concurrent and Real-Time Systems." In *Proceedings of the IEEE Workshop on Real-Time Applications, October 21-25, 1996, Montreal, Canada*, pp. 168–172. Los Alamitos, CA: IEEE Computer Society Press .

Pitt, J., M. Anderton, and R. J. Cunningham. 1996. "Normalized Interactions between Autonomous Agents: A Case Study in Inter-Organizational Project Management." *Computer Supported Cooperative Work: The Journal of Collaborative Computing* 5: 201–222.

Pree, W., and E. Gamma. 1995. *Design Patterns for Object-Oriented Software Development*. Reading, MA: Addison-Wesley.

Pressman, R. 1996. *Software Engineering: A Practitioner's Approach*, 4th ed. New York: McGraw-Hill.

Prieto-Diaz, R. 1987. "Domain Analysis for Reusability." In *Compsac '87: Eleventh International Computer Software and Applications Conference Proceedings*, pp. 23–29. Los Alamitos, CA: IEEE Computer Society Press.

Prieto-Diaz, R., and P. Freeman. 1987. "Classifying Software for Reusability." *IEEE Software* 4(1): 6–16.

Pyster, A. 1990. "The Synthesis Process for Software Development." In *Systems and Software Requirements Engineering*, R. J. Thayer and M. Dorfman (eds.), pp. 528–538. Los Alamitos, CA: IEEE Computer Society Press.

Quatrani, T. 2003. *Visual Modeling with Rational Rose 2002 and UML*. Boston: Addison-Wesley.

Rosenberg, D., and K. Scott. 1999. *Use Case Driven Object Modeling with UML: A Practical Approach*. Reading, MA: Addison-Wesley.

Rumbaugh, J., M. Blaha, W. Premerlani, F. Eddy, and W. Lorenson. 1991. *Object-Oriented Modeling and Design*. Upper Saddle River, NJ: Prentice Hall.

Rumbaugh, J., G. Booch, and I. Jacobson. 2005.* *The Unified Modeling Language Reference Manual*, 2nd ed. Boston: Addison-Wesley. (*In press, to be published Summer 2004.)

Schmidt, D., M. Stal, H. Rohnert, and F. Buschmann. 2000. *Pattern-Oriented Software Architecture*, Vol. 2: *Patterns for Concurrent and Networked Objects*. Chichester, England: Wiley.

Schneider, G., and J. P. Winters. 2001. *Applying Use Cases: A Practical Guide*, 2nd ed. Boston: Addison-Wesley.

Selic, B. 1999. "Turning Clockwise: Using UML in the Real-Time Domain." *Communications of the ACM* 42(10): 46–54. New York: ACM Press.

Selic, B., G. Gullekson, and P. Ward. 1994. *Real-Time Object-Oriented Modeling*. New York: Wiley.

Shan, Y. P., and R. H. Earle. 1998. *Enterprise Computing with Objects*. Reading, MA: Addison-Wesley.

Shaw, M., and D. Garlan. 1996. *Software Architecture: Perspectives on an Emerging Discipline*. Upper Saddle River, NJ: Prentice Hall.

Shlaer, S., and S. Mellor. 1988. *Object-Oriented Systems Analysis*. Upper Saddle River, NJ: Prentice Hall.

Shlaer, S., and S. Mellor. 1992. *Object Lifecycles: Modeling the World in States*. Upper Saddle River, NJ: Prentice Hall.

Silberschatz, A., and P. Galvin. 1998. *Operating System Concepts*, 5th ed. Reading, MA: Addison-Wesley.

Silberschatz, A., H. F. Korth, and S. Sudarshan. 1999. *Database System Concepts*, 3rd ed. Boston: WCB/McGraw Hill.

Smith, C. U. 1990. *Performance Engineering of Software Systems*. Reading, MA: Addison-Wesley.

Sommerville, I. 2000. *Software Engineering*, 6th ed. Boston: Addison-Wesley.

Stevens, P., and R. Pooley. 2000. *Using UML: Software Engineering with Objects and Components*, updated ed. New York: Addison-Wesley.

Szyperski, C. 2003. *Component Software: Beyond Object-Oriented Programming*, 2nd ed. Boston: Addison-Wesley.

Tanenbaum, A. S. 2003. *Computer Networks*, 4th ed. Upper Saddle River, NJ: Prentice Hall.

Texel, P., and C. Williams. 1997. *Use Cases Combined with Booch/OMT/UML: Process and Products*. Upper Saddle River, NJ: Prentice Hall.

Vici, A. D., N. Argentieri, A. Mansour, M. d'Alessandro, and J. Favaro. 1998. "FODAcom: An Experience with Domain Modeling in the Italian Telecom Industry." In *Fifth International Conference on Software Reuse: Proceedings: June 2–5, 1998, Victoria, British Columbia, Canada*, P. Devanbu and J. Poulin (eds.), pp. 166–175. Los Alamitos, CA: IEEE Computer Society Press.

Warmer, J., and A. Kleppe. 1999. *The Object Constraint Language: Precise Modeling with UML*. Reading, MA: Addison-Wesley.

Webber, D., and H. Gomaa. 2002. "Modeling Variability with the Variation Point Model." In *Software Reuse: Methods, Techniques, and Tools, 7th International Conference, ICSR-7, Austin, TX, USA, April 15-19, 2002, Proceedings* (Lecture Notes in Computer Science, No. 2319), C. Gacek (ed.), pp. 109–122. Berlin: Springer.

Wegner, P. 1990. "Concepts and Paradigms of Object-Oriented Programming." *OOPS Messenger* 1(1): 7–87.

Weiss, D., and C. T. R. Lai. 1999. *Software Product-Line Engineering: A Family-Based Software Development Process*. Reading, MA: Addison-Wesley.

Wirfs-Brock, R., B. Wilkerson, and L. Wiener. 1990. *Designing Object-Oriented Software*. Upper Saddle River, NJ: Prentice Hall.

Index

informIT